Advanced Transact-SQL for SQL Server 2000

ITZIK BEN-GAN AND TOM MOREAU, PH.D.

Advanced Transact-SQL for SQL Server 2000
Copyright ©2000 by Itzik Ben-Gan and Tom Moreau

ISBN (pbk): 1-893115-82-8

Printed and bound in the United States of America 12345678910

Trademarked names may appear in this book. Rather than use a trademark symbol with every occurrence of a trademarked name, we use the names only in an editorial fashion and to the benefit of the trademark owner, with no intention of infringement of the trademark.

Editorial Directors: Dan Appleman, Gary Cornell, Karen Watterson

Editors: Andy Carroll, Kathryn Duggan

Projects Manager: Grace Wong

Page Composition and Skunk Relocation Services: Bookmakers

Artist: Karl Miyajima

Indexer: Valerie Perry

Cover: Karl Miyajima

Distributed to the book trade in the United States by Springer-Verlag New York, Inc.,175 Fifth Avenue, New York, NY, 10010

and outside the United States by Springer-Verlag GmbH & Co. KG, Tiergartenstr. 17, 69112 Heidelberg, Germany

In the United States, phone 1-800-SPRINGER; orders@springer-ny.com; http://www.springer-ny.com

Outside the United States, contact orders@springer.de; http://www.springer.de; fax +49 6221 345229

For information on translations, please contact Apress directly at 901 Grayson Street, Suite 204, Berkeley, CA, 94710

Phone: 510-549-5931; Fax: 510-549-5939; info@apress.com; http://www.apress.com

To Lilach

True Love, you think it happens every day?

To Sensei Yehuda and Kalen

"The person is aware of the endlessness of entering deeply into a certain way and never thinks of himself as having finished…" (Hagakure)

—Itzik Ben-Gan

To Diane

My compass, to help me to find my way;

My altimeter, to keep me from being too low;

My engine, to drive me;

My fuel to sustain me and

The wind beneath my wings.

—Tom Moreau

Contents at a Glance

Contents

SQL Puzzle Solutions 671

Foreword

I FEEL A GREAT HONOR in being asked by Itzik Ben-Gan and Tom Moreau to write the foreword to their magnificent work. I have been eagerly awaiting its appearance for many months, since long before I was asked to write this foreword, and to realize now that my words will also be a part of this book seems incredible to me.

I don't want to make this foreword too lopsided by talking specifically about the authors, since I know one of them much better than the other. So I won't talk about them for more than one paragraph. I know Itzik very well, from his participation in the private forum for SQL Server trainers (MCTs) and SQL Server MVPs, from the two weeks I spent in Israel teaching at his training center, and from countless e-mails we have sent back and forth asking each other for opinions and advice. I eagerly await anything at all written by Itzik, and I always learn something new when reading about any of his special SQL programming tricks. If there were anyone I would feel 100 percent confident in passing my baton to, if and when I retire, it would be Itzik. (I do buy lottery tickets, so it actually could happen any day now.) Tom Moreau I know from his writings, primarily in *SQL Server Professional*, and I have always had a great respect for his experience, expertise, and communication skills.

I'll spend a bit more time talking about the book. I am very grateful to Itzik and Tom for writing this book because it freed me from having to devote so much time to detailing T-SQL tips and tricks in my own book. When I wrote the earlier versions of my book, *Inside SQL Server,* there weren't any terrific T-SQL books available, so my book had several chapters just on Microsoft's dialect of the standard SQL language. I would much rather spend my time researching and writing about SQL Server internals, the query processor, and the storage engine, and when writing *Inside SQL Server 2000,* I knew that Tom and Itzik could do a far better and more complete job in their book than I could in a few chapters. I was therefore able to reduce my coverage of T-SQL and increase my coverage of engine internals. *Advanced Transact-SQL for SQL Server 2000* will definitely be first on the list of recommended readings in the SQL programming books section of my Web site.

Just browsing through the table of contents of *Advanced Transact-SQL for SQL Server 2000* assured me I was in for a treat. Tom and Itzik have a whole chapter on their own tips and tricks, and since they both contributed to this chapter, I knew it would be good. All of the great new programming features of SQL Server 2000 are covered in detail, including user-defined functions, distributed partitioned views, cascading referential actions with triggers, and indexed views. Query performance and tuning is stressed, which is an added bonus for a book that doesn't promote itself as a tuning book. Sure, almost anyone can come up with unusual ways to write a query, but not many can come up with the fast techniques that Tom and Itzik do, and fewer still can prove that their solution is optimal. Screenshots are not overused, but Itzik is a master when it comes to capturing the query plan output to demonstrate the points he is trying to make with regard to query performance.

In addition to the new SQL Server 2000 features, the "old" features are certainly not neglected. Don't expect any simple SELECT statements, however. This book truly lives up to its name as an advanced book. Chapter 1 is on JOINs, and in the first few pages they cover inner joins, outer joins, multitable joins, old-style joins, ANSI joins, and cross joins. Subqueries and derived tables, which are just about the most advanced topics covered in Microsoft's SQL Server programming class ("Implementing a Database Design with Microsoft SQL Server"), are covered in detail and with generous examples in Chapter 2. Stored procedures, triggers, and views have entire chapters devoted to each of these objects.

This book is a keeper, and I'm delighted that Itzik and Tom wrote it. I learned a lot in just the first few chapters, and there's no end to what you can get out of it.

Kalen Delaney
Author, *Inside SQL Server 2000,* Microsoft Press
Microsoft SQL Server MVP

About the Authors

Itzik Ben-Gan is a senior SQL Server instructor and consultant at Hi-Tech College in Israel. He has been working with databases and SQL in both AS/400 and PC environments since 1990, and in the last two years has been focusing mainly on SQL Server. Itzik is a columnist and a contributing editor for *SQL Server Magazine*. He holds the MCSE+I, MCSD, MCDBA, and MCT certifications and is also a Microsoft SQL Server MVP. Itzik is the manager of the Israeli SQL Server Users Group.

Dr. Tom Moreau has been programming since 1971, when he learned FORTRAN in the university. He progressed to C in 1989 and SQL in 1992. Tom has been using SQL Server since 1993. He began writing articles for *SQL Server Professional* in 1997 and is now a columnist with the journal. Tom has worked on a broad range of projects, including scientific data collection, transportation, banking, retail, and finance. He is an independent consultant and co-founder (with his wife Diane) of Brockman Moreau Consulting, Inc., which is based in Toronto, Canada. Tom holds the MCSE, MCDBA, and MCT certifications. When he is not playing with SQL Server, Tom enjoys flying and underwater photography.

Preface

THIS BOOK CAME ABOUT as a collaboration between two people born in different countries, during different eras in our history. Despite our dissimilar backgrounds and cultures, we have a common bond—our love of Microsoft SQL Server. We have each chosen to tell you in our own words how this book came about and about the many people who helped to shape it.

The Passing of Knowledge, by Itzik Ben-Gan

My wife, Lilach, has a great part in you now holding this book in your hands. I once swore to her that if I ever got the crazy idea of writing a book, she should do whatever was in her power to prevent me from doing so. I thought that it would be an endless thankless task, but I was wrong! Luckily, when I gently told Lilach that Karen Watterson from Apress had asked me to participate in writing this book, being sure she would hold me to my oath, she didn't try to prevent me from getting involved. Boy, am I glad she didn't...

The writing process was totally different from what I had expected. I found the research process invaluable. Delving deeper and deeper into smaller and smaller details is rewarding in a way that only someone who "has been there" can understand. Many times I continued writing until dawn broke, without even noticing. At times, the subject I was working on was so interesting that I couldn't keep seated from excitement. I would go out to the balcony, light a cigarette, and walk around to and fro under the light of the stars.

Lilach would stay alone in bed, waiting for me for a couple of hours until she fell asleep, only to find me near the computer in the morning. Well, Lilach, it's over now, and although I'm sorry it is over, I'm happy that now I will have a chance to spend more time with you. :-)

About two years ago I started to teach SQL Server and T-SQL. After more than eight years of involvement in various aspects of computing, I wasn't aware what sort of a sharp curve my life was about to take. Since than, I've been doing almost nothing but SQL. It has become my way of life. Through SQL and the Web, I've gotten to know many people who are now my colleagues, my friends, and my family. Among them, SQL Server MVPs Kalen Delaney, Trevor Dwyer, Fernando G. Guerrero, Roy Harvey, Gianluca Hotz, Umachandar Jayachandran, Tibor Karaszi, Bruce P. Margolin, Brian Moran, Neil Pike, Bob Pfeiff, Steve Robinson, Tony Rogerson, Wayne Snyder, Ron Talmage, and Andy Ball. This group of incredibly talented individuals share a passion for SQL Server and voluntarily help programmers and DBAs through the public newsgroups. I still need to pinch myself in order to believe that I'm really a part of this group and it is not some sort of fantastic dream.

This group of MVPs, and our Microsoft support buddies, Shawn Aebi and Steve Dybing, have made an invaluable contribution to this book. Many a time I took their advice, and the results are spread throughout the book.

For me, SQL Server is not merely a software product. Like the Silmarils in Tolkien's world, SQL Server has a certain spark in it that makes me feel as if the developers succeeded in somehow encapsulating their greatest visions and putting life into them. I'd like to express my gratitude to SQL Server Program Managers Hal Berenson, Euan Garden, David Campbell, Gert Drapers, Richard Waymire, and Lubor Kollar for aiding me in the course of my involvement with SQL Server, and for bringing SQL Server to light. My thanks extend to Iris Rothenberg and Tomer Ben-Moshe from Microsoft Israel.

The sharp curve in my life took place when I became a SQL Server MCT (Microsoft Certified Trainer). After eight years in the field, working with machines and with customers, I found the joy of teaching. I discovered how rewarding the receiving and passing on of knowledge can be. I found a warm and friendly group of MCTs from all around the world, among them Kalen Delaney, Fernando G. Guerrero, Tibor Karaszi, Morris Lewis, Chris Randall, Rob Vieira, and so many others. We share a private newsgroup where I feel more at home than in any other place. There we share our knowledge in incredibly illuminating discussions; we joke, we laugh, and we solve puzzles together. Microsoft Program Managers some-times join our discussions. Richard Waymire is always there, providing tremendous help, and whenever I see David Campbell's posts my heart fills with joy <sigh>... I wish he posted more (hint, hint ;-).

Two of the MCTs deserve special appreciation. Dejan Sarka, a very talented and knowledgeable trainer, became one of my dearest friends. We visited each other in our homelands, taught and spoke together, and he even had the misfortune of accompanying me to the airport in Slovenia where I threw up the fine wine that we finished together to celebrate our friendship (sorry about that Dejko.) One other very special MCT that I'd like to thank is Laura A. Robinson, a.k.a. delicate flower and saber-toothed tiger. Laura was one of the first MCTs to welcome me to the group. She's one of the sharpest, brightest, and funniest people I have ever known. Whenever I feel the need to read some really cool posts, I go and look her up. Laura, thanks for being you! In many ways, this book holds the spirit of this group of MCTs.

There are actually so many more MCTs I'd like to thank here, as I feel that they have a part in this book, but if I did, you would probably stop reading for the lengthy list. To make you realize what I'm talking about I'll tell you about my visit to Slovenia. Dejan and I formed a list of MCTs we know and care about. We named it the "Beer List" as we took it with us and journeyed in the countries surrounding Slovenia, having a drink for all our friends. I tell you, there were a lot of beers involved... <hiccup>. In fact, all of the pictures I have from my visit to Slovenia look quite similar. There's Dejan, there's me, and there are a couple of beers and the beer list.

Tom and I would also like to express a few specific acknowledgments to those who were generous enough to provide technical contributions to the book, mainly for the user-defined functions chapter. Eitan Farchi, Ph.D., from the IBM research laboratory in Haifa, Israel, provided mathematical proofs and algorithms. Pavel Yosifovich, a senior programming instructor at Hi-Tech College, Israel, provided the idea for the sound/image processing example. Gabriel Ben-Gan, mathematics teacher at Handesaim High School, Ramat-Aviv, Israel, (and co-creator of Itzik Ben-Gan ;-) provided help with the mathematical aspects of complex algebra and of other subjects covered in the book. Fernando G. Guerrero, a senior SQL Server instructor for the QA Group Ltd., U.K., and a SQL Server MVP, provided performance and other tips for the complex functions. Rick White, a fellow MCT, shared his knowledge on complex numbers. You will also find contributions from many other talented individuals in Chapter 17, Tips and Tricks.

One other project I'm most grateful for getting involved with is *SQL Server Magazine*. Whenever I go to teach at a customer's site, I take the magazine with me. On my breaks, I look for a quiet café or a shaded place where I can be alone and read it. I first look for Kalen's articles, but I like reading them all. Writing for the magazine is in many ways similar to writing this book. Whenever I get all excited about a certain new idea that has been cooking in my mind, I sit down and write about it and send it to the magazine. I have found a devoted group of people working for the magazine, among them Michele Crockett, Kathy Blomstrom, and Carol Martin. It is a pleasure working with you!

This book wouldn't have seen light had the group of devoted people at Apress not put in the long hours they did. I'd like to thank Gary Cornell, Kathi Duggan, Andy Carroll, Grace Wong, and all those who worked on the book "behind the scenes." To our editors—your edits have really been a pleasure to receive. And Grace, thanks for all of the hard work you've put into this book. I'd also like to thank Karen Watterson who started the whole thing when she suggested that Tom and I write the book. Karen thought that Tom and I would make a perfect match. I still find it hard to believe how natural our joined work has been. We both read through each other's work and really helped one another in making our visions come true on paper. From the early stages of writing, we both agreed that we shouldn't try to unify the spirit of the book. We both believe that you should get the writings of each of us from as close to the source as possible. We feel it's okay that the book has two spirits, as long as these are the true two spirits of its authors. The joined writing was a unique experience. Tom, it has been a pleasure!

I met Tom and Diane—Tom's wife—at a conference in Arizona only after we finished working on the book. We enjoyed each other's company as if we were old friends. Besides an incident in the bar where Tom told the bartender that I was his son, the fact that Tom wrote his first program in the year that I was born didn't seem to matter. In fact, when it comes to party energy, Tom has the strong side. Luckily, Diane was there to keep Tom from dancing on the tables... Thanks Diane for being there to support Tom in his writing process!

Hi-Tech College is the place where I spend most of my time and where I started to teach. I truly couldn't wish myself a better place to work in. I worked at several other places before, but those were all just jobs for me. Many people are in search of that one and only place that is probably waiting for them in their career.

Well, I have found this place. Instead of waiting for my workday to come to its end, I stay in my office until late at night when the technicians close the place, begging them for a couple of minutes more. Amit Haim, Shmuel Tal (Shmil), Yossi Lahmish, I can't thank you enough for allowing me to be a part of this college!

There are a couple of people who are thanked in every book's preface—Mom and Pup. Well in my case, they took an active part in it. Many hours I sat with my father working on the mathematical aspects of my writings, and he was always willing to help. Mom, Pup, your support means the world to me.

And now for the moment I've been waiting for since I started writing the book—the part where I get to thank Kalen. I remember the first time I saw her two years ago in a course in Seattle, at the start of my journey as an MCT. She came to our class and asked us riddles about SQL Server. Whoever answered one of those riddles got a SQL Server bag. One of those bags has been my companion ever since, and in it, my favorite technical book on earth—*Inside SQL Server*. I still remember how hypnotized I felt when she spoke, seeing the great knowledge and great love she holds for SQL Server. There was no way of mistaking it—she had that spark. Looking back, I feel like it was a magical moment that caught me and started the chain of events that led to this book. In many ways I feel that Kalen is responsible for the love I hold for SQL Server today. I can even remember the first post I sent to the MCT forum, which was answered by Kalen. Later on we started to work together on a few projects, parts of which you will see in this book. Today she's one of my dearest friends. I often take her advice, and I feel that her guidance is, and has been, too good to be true. Kalen, neither spoken nor written words will express what I hold for you in my heart. You are one of a kind.

There is another part in my life that is as important to me as SQL—Okinawan GoJu Ryu. Sensei Yehuda Pantanowitz is one of the most knowledgeable people I have ever met. He lives a modest life, but to me, he is one of the richest people in the world. I feel so fortunate that I've gotten to know him and to learn under his practice. One of my greatest joys during the week is our traditional gathering every Wednesday after practice, when we listen to his fascinating, enlightening stories, accompanied with a beer. Here are some words of wisdom from Sensei Yehuda Pantanowitz, which were passed to him, in turn, from a rabbi:

> *In Israel there's a river called the Jordan, and it fills two lakes. The one lake is known as the Kineret (Sea of Galilee), and further down there's another lake known as the Dead Sea. Around the Kineret, all is green and everything flourishes and grows. Fish swim in the waters of the Kineret. Around the Dead Sea there's a desert. Nothing grows. The lake is so salty that you can float on it without sinking. Nothing lives in the waters of the Dead Sea.*
>
> *Why?*

> *It's the same water that enters the lake of Kineret, and the same water that enters the Dead Sea... There's a small difference: the lake of Kineret has an entry from the Jordan River and an exit to the Jordan River. The Dead Sea only receives water from the Jordan River. There is no exit. So the water only evaporates, leaving the salt behind, and everything dies around it.*

> *What can we learn from this?*

> *That instructors must make their students feel that they are part of a river, and that this river is an ongoing flowing thing. This, in one way, might influence these students to convince other people to come and join and flow down this river together with us.*

> *The instructor must make his students understand that in order to make everything green around us, we must teach correctly and we must teach our students to teach correctly. That means an incoming of knowledge and an outgoing of knowledge, and that knowledge will then become like the lake of Kineret and not like the lake of the Dead Sea.*

This understanding extends to all learning experiences. This book is my way of fulfilling my Sensei's words. I hope that you will learn from it, and that after you do, you will pass that knowledge on.

I Can't Believe I'm Doing This..., by Tom Moreau

> *Never tell people how to do something, just tell them what to do and they will surprise you with their ingenuity.*
> —Gen. George S. Patton

> *The journey of a thousand miles begins with one single step.*
> —Lao-Tse

It's funny how things sometimes just work out.

Aviation safety investigators have a term they call the "Point of Inevitability." Beyond this point, an event will happen, despite efforts to change the outcome. However, any broken link in the chain leading up to this point prevents the event from occurring.

This book was no accident.

During my undergraduate career, I could not decide whether to be a physicist or a chemist. I also wanted to learn as much computer science as it would take to support my physics and chemistry habits. Like a typical Canadian, I compromised. I majored in physics and chemistry and took courses that used FORTRAN, which allowed me to put myself through school doing part-time programming. The FORTRAN also allowed me to analyze my laboratory work. Were it not for the job I took programming, I would not have been able to get my B.Sc.

It was during my undergraduate studies that I met Dr. Ralph Nicholls, my advanced calculus professor, who would ultimately become my Ph.D. thesis supervisor. One day while halfway through my graduate studies, my parents dropped by to the motorcycle safety course I was teaching on weekends to say that Dr. Nicholls had called. A water line on my experimental apparatus had worked itself loose and had flooded the lab. My work thus far had been one failure after another. I declared that I just wanted to quit. However, I didn't have the courage to face Dr. Nicholls. I also would not have any dividend for all the years I had spent. I decided to stick it out.

One thing that graduate school gave me was a degree of independence. Most of my work was centered on the laboratory, and much of that work involved waiting *ad infinitum* for experimental results. One of my former classmates had taken me up in his airplane and confirmed for me that which I already knew—I wanted to fly. Because of my lab schedule, I was able to take flying lessons and finally become a pilot.

My flying hobby kept me going to the airport frequently. One day, I attended a seminar and met Diane during the break. She was taking flying lessons and had not yet soloed. I offered to take her flying and she accepted. She was an independent consultant and specialized in IMS databases on mainframes. Diane would help me with my mainframe troubles when it came time to analyze the data that eventually sprang from my experiment. I would help her with her flying studies.

One day, Dr. Joyce Aspinall approached me with an offer to fill in for her while she was on sabbatical. She supervised the undergraduate physics and chemistry labs. She kept the students' marks on a Commodore PET that ran BASIC 4 and said that I could improve the software where I saw fit. I accepted the job. I rewrote the system with database advice from Diane and PET advice from a small, scientific software and research firm on campus. Good thing I met Diane.

I started my professional life as a scientist. I began to work for that same firm while I was finishing graduate school. The one condition was that I was to finish off my Ph.D. Good thing I didn't quit my thesis work. It was Diane who encouraged me to finish my degree.

The research was interesting but it soon became evident that I had software development skills that the firm wished to utilize, so I transferred from research to software development. I began doing BASIC and FORTRAN on a Commodore SuperPET. Good thing I had taken on that lab supervisor assignment.

Then, a defining moment occurred. IBM came out with what was called the Personal Computer—the PC. Our firm took on a contract to build software for a client. The catch was that the coding was to be done in C—on an IBM PC. Going from FORTRAN to C was a quantum jump. The first three months were arduous, since we were not sent on training and had to learn the language from a skinny little book. I wanted to quit learning C and go back to FORTRAN or BASIC, but it was too late to walk away.

The company later picked up another contract; this time on a UNIX box, where all programming was done in C. I guess it was okay that I didn't give up the C programming.

More than five years had elapsed since I joined the firm. Diane and I were now married, with the responsibilities that go with that. Assignments were starting to dry up, and the company wanted me to go back into research as well as to drum up business. I was also not getting any training. I had to take stock of my situation.

I looked around and finally landed a job at a railroad. I learned OS/2 and how to program Presentation Manager—its graphical user interface (GUI). Later, I was assigned to a project on a UNIX box with a Geographical Information System (GIS). I guess learning UNIX wasn't so bad after all. The data for the GIS was to come from DB2. I did not have much of an interest in GISs, but I did like databases, so I was sent on a course to learn DB2 and SQL.

Learning SQL was another turning point for me. I found that the harder the challenges that I faced, the more I could rise up to them. SQL was addictive. It still is.

My manager decided that he needed me to do COBOL programming on the mainframe—1960s technology. Again, it was time to take stock. I wanted more SQL, C, and OS/2, but less mainframe. I soon found a job at a Canadian subsidiary of a major U.S. investment bank. Their database was Microsoft SQL Server on OS/2, and it understood a dialect called Transact-SQL (T-SQL). Good thing I learned OS/2 and SQL.

I picked through the manual and was shortly put on on-call support for a production system. I was later sent to Sybase for a number of courses ramping up all the way to advanced administration. I learned about stored procs, triggers, DBCCs, backup and recovery, tuning, and more. It was like being given a new puppy. The more I played with SQL Server, the more fun it became. Just like a puppy, it grew and turned into a constant companion.

As I grew with SQL Server, I was able to work proactively and speed up the database while improving reliability. I was becoming more addicted.

It took more than just SQL Server for me to remain happy, however. A new manager was brought in, and the existing one was shoved aside. Impossible deadlines were imposed, and we were all forced to go back to UNIX and abandon the PC. This meant I had to say good-bye to Microsoft SQL Server. It was time to take stock again.

Diane had been a contractor since before I met her. She had learned what to do and what not to do. She also had confidence that I could carry myself as an independent contractor. With that, I secured a contract a block away from my now-former employer, and suddenly I was a consultant.

The assignment was specifically for Microsoft SQL Server—not Sybase SQL Server. It was also on Windows NT 3.51, something still new to me at the time. The manager of the DBA group was John Hui, 14 years my junior. He had high but reasonable expectations and gave me the freedom to seek my own solutions. Some problems required solutions for which I had no experience. These came in the form of Perl and Visual Basic (VB). The Perl language had its roots in C and UNIX, and VB was based on... well... BASIC. The faded memories of those once-used technologies were not so faded any more.

During this assignment, I started to get interested more in the Internet. I took out a trial subscription to *SQL Server Professional* (*SQL Pro*) after reading about it in the Usenet newsgroups. I looked forward to receiving each monthly issue and would circulate it to my colleagues.

On that same project, I met Scott Smith. He was a gifted DBA and loved to delve into anything with a Microsoft label. It was he who told me about Microsoft certification. I started reading what I could and concluded that I would like to take the SQL Server exams, but going the MCSD or MCSE route was for people far more capable than I. I studied whatever I could find, and after leaving the project, I took my SQL Server exams, just prior to landing my next assignment. Indeed, the certifications helped me get my new contract.

My knowledge of SQL Server was beginning to build. So, too, was my thirst for knowledge of Microsoft technologies. I had to write an operating system exam in order to get my Microsoft Certified Professional (MCP) designation at that time. It was only one more exam. After much study, I took the NT Workstation exam and collected my MCP. It was time to take stock again. At this point, I had written half of the required exams for the MCSE. Half way—I now had a new goal.

My work with SQL Server and monthly readings of *SQL Pro* got me itching to contribute but wondering what to write. Finally, I stumbled across a problem with left joins while using the ANSI-92 syntax. I proudly submitted the article and received an author style guide in return, with the implication that I had to rewrite the whole thing. I could have tossed it aside and given up on the idea, but there would have been no dividend for the work I had done. I overhauled the piece and soon saw my name in print.

The following year, I pushed forward with my studies toward the MCSE, which by now seemed like a carrot on a very long stick. I was also inspired to write another article, then another.

Meanwhile, Diane was working at a major Canadian bank. She was using the latest Microsoft technologies, including SQL Server. She needed a DBA—one she could trust. Soon, we were working together. In addition to database work, she needed someone to administer the LAN and do some VB programming. By now, I had but two exams left on my MCSE. The studies were directly related to the work that had to be done, and the timing of the two remaining exams meshed well with the work I was doing. Good thing Scott told me about certification. In the end, the application was delivered and described by the users as "too fast".

One day, I received an e-mail inviting me to speak at a conference. The sender had gotten my e-mail address from reading *SQL Pro*. I got part way through the e-mail and deleted it. A few months later, I got another one from the same source, and this time I read it completely. They wanted me to speak in Scottsdale, AZ. Having an affinity to very warm places, we decided to do it. I wrote Karen Watterson—my editor at *SQL Server Professional*—and she was happy for me. She said that she, too, would attend the conference and we could finally meet.

It was fun meeting Karen. It was like we had known her all our lives. The e-mails became even more frequent. I expressed an interest in writing a book, albeit on

Data Transformation Services (DTS). Careful, Tom. Karen remembers everything you say. She wrote to say she had someone looking for a co-author and sent me an outline. It wasn't my cup of tea, and I regretfully declined. Shortly after, she sent me one from Itzik. I recognized the name. The outline was for a book on Transact-SQL, not DTS, but the idea was intriguing. Why not? The show was on!

Meanwhile, one conference led to another. When we began to write this book, I had never met Itzik. I had never been to Israel, though he had visited Canada. I asked him to attend the conference to be held in the fall of 2000 and he agreed. Good thing I didn't delete that second invitation to speak. Good thing I didn't turn him down on writing the book.

I look back on the past 29 years and see it as links in a chain, with one link being added at a time. If any of those links had failed to join the chain, the remainder would have failed to exist. The Point of Inevitability would never have been crossed. If I had not learned to program, I would not have been able to afford an education. If I had not gone to graduate school, I would not have had the time to learn to fly. If I had not become a pilot, I would not have met Diane. If I had not met Diane, I would not have finished graduate school, been interested in databases, or SQL, or consulting. If I had not learned SQL and VB or gotten my MCSE, I would not have been able to help out Diane. If I had not used the Internet or developed my expertise in SQL, I would not have written articles for *SQL Pro* or met Karen. Had I not met Karen, I would not have gotten to work with and eventually meet Itzik, and that would be sad.

I am grateful to those who have contributed to the writing of this book. I am indebted to Karen, for bringing Itzik and me together. I would like to thank Gary Cornell and Grace Wong from Apress who managed things and brought us Kathi Duggan and Andy Carroll—our development and copy editors. Kathi and Andy, without you the text would have been a loosely coupled collection of thoughts. You did us proud. You have a wonderful gift. Thank you for sharing it with us.

Whenever I needed to get a straight answer from Microsoft, I got one—from Richard Waymire. Thanks, Richard, not just for your kind help but also for building one fine product—Microsoft SQL Server 2000. Joe Celko (SQL guru) and I have exchanged a number of interesting e-mails on aggregate queries, which inspired some of the code you will see in this book. Joe, I still owe you that beer. If we ever meet...

I also wish to thank my fellow readers and writers of *SQL Server Professional*. They have been an inspiration to me.

I was overjoyed to hear that Kalen Delaney—*the* Kalen Delaney—would be writing the foreword to this book. Kalen, I cannot begin to describe the honor that this brings to me. I have admired your work for quite some time. You are truly a master. Thank you for your kindness.

Of course, this book could not have happened without my new friend, Itzik. Itzik, I kept writing because I didn't want to let you down. Your dedication and ingenuity brought out the best in me. For two guys who never met each other until after our work was done, we certainly made a team. I feel I learned more from you than I was able to contribute. I hope that someday I can repay the debt. Thanks to Lilach, too, for letting you fulfill your dream. Since English is not Itzik's first language—SQL is—I'll sum up my thoughts in terms that he can understand. The following query would return no rows:

```
SELECT
  *
FROM
  Tom T
WHERE NOT EXISTS
(
  SELECT
    *
  FROM
    Itzik I
  WHERE
    T.Dream = I.Dream
)
```

Finally, I wish to thank the one person who has caused the last 19 years of my life to be the most meaningful. Diane, our life has had its ups and downs, but through it all, you have always been there for me. Your honesty, wit, courage, determination, wisdom, and of course, your love, are dear to me. I cannot bear to think of how life would have turned out if we had not met that day at the airport. Your patience while I constantly clacked the keys on this project can never truly be repaid.

Today, the technology with which I started my career is on display in the Smithsonian. It has been quite a ride.

Life is a journey. Wear comfortable shoes.

Introduction

MICROSOFT SQL SERVER 2000 is the most powerful database engine in existence today. It can be installed on anything from a basic Windows CE machine all the way up to the largest Windows 2000 Datacenter Server you can buy. The versatility of this product, coupled with its sheer ease of use and low cost, makes it the perfect choice as a database engine for virtually any application. If you have not been using SQL Server, you cannot afford not to any more!

Who Should Read This Book

This book is aimed at Information Technology professionals who are working with Microsoft SQL Server or who intend to use it as a development platform. Many books are written on the broad aspects of SQL Server or just on its administration. This book focuses on programming, with particular emphasis on the features of SQL Server 2000. However, references are made to releases 6.5 and 7.0 because we know there are still many installations of these releases in production today. These references will show you what's in and what's out, to get you up to speed on the new technology and enable you to upgrade your skills smoothly.

This book does not limit itself to single trivial examples. Rather, multiple cases are given of each feature in order to enforce your understanding. Not only are you provided with numerous examples, you are also shown real-world scenarios with real-world solutions, making this book a "must have" in your toolbox. Much of the code you will see is based upon cries for help posted in the Usenet newsgroup or from the readers of *SQL Server Professional* or *SQL Server Magazine*.

If you are a newbie or an old pro, this book is designed to develop you into a skilled, disciplined Transact-SQL programmer. If you are new to SQL Server, don't be intimidated by the title. SQL is easy to learn. Doing it well is why this book is essential reading. The basics are covered in Appendix A for you to review and to help you if you are new to SQL.

Our Feelings on Beta Software

Both of us are seasoned professionals who use Microsoft SQL Server extensively as well as read and write a great deal on this technology. As a fellow professional, we believe that you want high-quality literature to support you in your career. To that end, we do not believe that you should waste your time on books that are based upon beta software. Such software is always different from the end product.

Rather, we feel that that a relevant book is one that is based upon the Release To Manufacture (RTM) version—the "gold code". This is such a book.

We have scoured through the Books Online (BOL) and tested our code with the RTM version to ensure that it correlates with the version you will use in your professional life.

What You Will See

As mentioned in the Preface, this book came about because our friend, Karen Watterson, thought that we would make a good match. We come from two very different backgrounds and have both similar *and* different approaches and styles. The result is one book, two spirits.

Most chapters end with one or more puzzles. The puzzle approach was inspired by Joe Celko's books. They are there to challenge you and to allow you to put to use the skills you will develop through your readings.

There is much covered in this book:

Chapter 1, Joins in T-SQL: This chapter covers ANSI joins in all of their forms and compares them to the old-style syntax. You will also see how your data can be modified through the use of a join. Unequal joins and self-joins are also presented. Finally, performance considerations are presented.

Chapter 2, Subqueries and Derived Tables: Armed with your knowledge of joins, you will explore alternatives to joins in the form of subqueries. Performance comparisons are presented to show you cases where subqueries are superior to joins and vice-versa. Also, derived tables are explored as a tool to preclude the need for temporary tables.

Chapter 3, Populating Tables: While most of SQL centers on the SELECT statement, you also have the job of adding data to your tables. This chapter reveals how to use the INSERT statement in all its flavors, as well as BULK INSERT.

Chapter 4, Other Data Manipulation Issues: This chapter handles assorted SQL features that don't lend themselves to categorization. These include the CASE construct, pivot tables, TOP n, bitwise manipulation, leading zeroes, and date handling.

Chapter 5, Summarizing Data: Data can be summarized through the use of a GROUP BY clause. You can take this even further with the CUBE and ROLLUP Transact-SQL extensions. You will see these plus the non-relational COMPUTE BY clause in this chapter.

Chapter 6, Special Datatypes and Properties: SQL Server has a number of useful datatypes beyond the basic int, float, and char, and these are discussed here. Special emphasis is placed on the new datatypes introduced with SQL Server 2000.

Chapter 7, Writing Code in T-SQL: In preparation for writing stored procedures, triggers, and user-defined functions, you need to know how to write code in Transact-SQL. This chapter introduces the concept of variables, conditional processing, loops, error handling, and transactions.

Chapter 8, Views: Views allow you to encapsulate a SELECT statement into an object that looks and feels like a table. There are some restrictions, and they are covered here. Indexed Views, introduced with SQL Server 2000, are also covered in this chapter.

Chapter 9, Stored Procedures: One of the many powerful features of Microsoft SQL Server is the stored procedure. Here, you will see how to encapsulate your code inside a stored procedure with the goals of maintainability, performance, and security. Transactions are further explored beyond the preliminary discussion in Chapter 7.

Chapter 10, Triggers—the Hidden Stored Procedures: Extending your knowledge of stored procedures, you will discover the hidden stored procedure—the trigger. Although triggers have been with SQL Server since its inception, the latest features of triggers in SQL Server 2000, such as INSTEAD OF triggers and triggers on views, are fully explained here.

Chapter 11, User-Defined Functions: New to SQL Server 2000 are user-defined functions. These are provided to compensate for situations that cannot be covered by views or stored procedures alone. Such cases are parameterized views and embedding results in natural DML statements. This chapter unlocks the secrets behind this new feature.

Chapter 12, Working with Temporary Tables: Sometimes it is necessary to create temporary tables to handle business rules that do not lend themselves to single-pass solutions or to provide a means of storing a result set that will be used repeatedly. This chapter shows you how to use temporary tables and where they are most appropriate.

Chapter 13, Horizontally Partitioned Views: Your tables can grow and grow to the point where you may have to change your physical model. SQL Server 2000 is very scalable and allows you to distribute your data across multiple servers. Reconstituting the data into a single, logical table is done through horizontally partitioned views. This chapter builds on your knowledge of views and triggers to illustrate this concept.

Chapter 14, Implementing Cascading Operations: Although SQL Server 2000 now supports cascaded UPDATEs and DELETEs, you can still do your own cascaded operations through triggers.

Chapter 15, Server-Side Cursors—the SQL of *Last* Resort: Some problems are difficult to solve at set level. This chapter deals with cursors—the SQL of last resort. Alternatives to cursors are presented to help curb your dependency.

Chapter 16, Expanding Hierarchies: Hierarchies do not lend themselves readily to set-level queries. This chapter presents you with various methods to circumvent this limitation.

Chapter 17, Tips and Tricks: Here we summarize a number of very useful techniques we have discovered through our experiences and also from other T-SQL professionals who have kindly contributed some of their secrets.

CHAPTER 1
Joins in T-SQL

CONSIDER THE RATIONALE behind database normalization: How would you describe its essence?

Without covering the normal forms one by one, the main logic behind database normalization is to try to avoid data duplication. Avoiding duplicates means avoiding errors, so you don't need to modify repetitive information more than once. When you are done normalizing your database, you'll probably discover that your data is spread across more tables than when you started. Not only does this make your database less prone to errors, but in many cases it also makes data modifications more efficient. Of course, nothing comes without a cost. When you need to supply meaningful information from your database, you usually can't avoid querying more than one table. This is where *joins* come in handy. Joins are one of the mechanisms in SQL that enable you to relate data from more than one table and retrieve useful information.

This chapter covers the different types of joins—inner, cross, and outer—between two tables or more, and also self joins where you join a table to itself. The chapter also covers special join conditions where a non-equal sign is used. It explores both the functionality and performance aspects of each of these joins.

And Then There Were Two...

T-SQL supports two join syntaxes. In this chapter, the syntax that was supported prior to SQL Server 6.5 is referred to as the *old-style* syntax, and the new join syntax that was introduced with SQL Server 6.5 is referred to as the *SQL-92* syntax because it is ANSI SQL-92 compliant. Both syntaxes are still supported in SQL Server 2000, and you can still find programmers writing new code using the old-style syntax. It is more common, though, to find old-style code that was written a long time ago, and which no one bothered to migrate to SQL-92 syntax. As you go along and examine the different aspects of joins, you will also learn about the difference between the syntaxes, and hopefully, you will be convinced that it is better practice to migrate to the newer SQL-92 syntax. The advantages of using the SQL-92 syntax will be enumerated.

The Latex Manufacturing Company Example

In this chapter, you will be presented with many code samples, and most of them will be run against a Human Resources database of an imaginary latex manufacturing company. Other code samples in this chapter will be run against the Northwind sample database. Run the script shown in Listing 1-1 to create and populate the Human Resources database tables: Departments, Jobs, and Employees.

Listing 1-1: Schema Creation Script for the Human Resources Database

```
CREATE TABLE Departments
(
Deptno    int         NOT NULL
                      CONSTRAINT PK_dept_deptno PRIMARY KEY,
deptname varchar(15) NOT NULL
)

CREATE TABLE Jobs
(
jobid    int         NOT NULL
                      CONSTRAINT PK_jobs_jobid PRIMARY KEY,
jobdesc varchar(15) NOT NULL
)

CREATE TABLE Employees
(
empid    int         NOT NULL
                      CONSTRAINT PK_emps_empid PRIMARY KEY,
empname varchar(10) NOT NULL,
deptno   int         NULL
                      CONSTRAINT FK_emps_depts
                        REFERENCES Departments(deptno),
jobid    int         NOT NULL
                      CONSTRAINT FK_emps_jobs REFERENCES Jobs(jobid),
salary decimal(7,2) NOT NULL
)

INSERT INTO Departments VALUES(100, 'Engineering')
INSERT INTO Departments VALUES(200, 'Production')
INSERT INTO Departments VALUES(300, 'Sanitation')
INSERT INTO Departments VALUES(400, 'Management')
```

```
INSERT INTO Jobs VALUES(10, 'Engineer')
INSERT INTO Jobs VALUES(20, 'Worker')
INSERT INTO Jobs VALUES(30, 'Manager')
INSERT INTO Jobs VALUES(40, 'Cleaner')

INSERT INTO Employees VALUES(1, 'Leo', 400, 30, 10000.00)
INSERT INTO Employees VALUES(2, 'George', 200, 20, 1000.00)
INSERT INTO Employees VALUES(3, 'Chris', 100, 10, 2000.00)
INSERT INTO Employees VALUES(4, 'Rob', 400, 30, 3000.00)
INSERT INTO Employees VALUES(5, 'Laura', 400, 30, 3000.00)
INSERT INTO Employees VALUES(6, 'Jeffrey', NULL, 30, 5000.00)
```

Take a look at the Human Resources database schema shown in Figure 1-1 for a graphical view of the tables and the relationships between them.

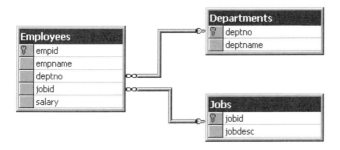

Figure 1-1: Human Resources database schema

Tables 1-1 through 1-3 delineate the contents of the Departments, Jobs, and Employees tables, respectively. As you read through this chapter, you may find it useful to refer back to these tables.

Table 1-1: Data from the Departments Table

deptno	deptname
100	Engineering
200	Production
300	Sanitation
400	Management

Table 1-2: Data from the Jobs Table

jobid	jobdesc
10	Engineer
20	Worker
30	Manager
40	Cleaner

Table 1-3: Data from the Employees Table

empid	empname	deptno	jobid	salary
1	Leo	400	30	10000.00
2	George	200	20	1000.00
3	Chris	100	10	2000.00
4	Rob	400	30	3000.00
5	Laura	400	30	3000.00
6	Jeffrey	NULL	30	5000.00

Inner Joins

Instead of jumping right in and writing your first inner-join query, first take a look at the different elements of an abbreviated form of the SELECT statement syntax, as shown in Listing 1-2.

Listing 1-2: Abbreviated Form of the SELECT Statement

```
SELECT
  <select_list>
FROM
  <table_source>
[WHERE
  <search_condition>]
```

Old-Style SQL-89 Join Syntax

In the old-style syntax, which in the case of inner joins is SQL-89 compliant,
`<table_source>` contains the list of tables separated by commas, and
`<search_condition>` contains both the join condition and the filter, as Listing 1-3
shows.

Listing 1-3: SQL-89 Join Syntax

```
SELECT
  <select_list>
FROM
  T1, T2
WHERE
  <join_condition> [AND <filter>]
```

Old-Style SQL-89 Two-Way Inner Joins

If you want to return employee and department information, you can write the
query shown in Listing 1-4.

Listing 1-4: Old-Style Two-Way Inner Join

```
SELECT
  empid,
  empname,
  salary,
  E.deptno,
  deptname
FROM
  Employees   AS E,
  Departments AS D
WHERE
  E.deptno = D.deptno
```

The output of this query is shown in Table 1-4.

Table 1-4: Output of an Old-Style Two-Way Inner Join

empid	empname	salary	deptno	deptname
1	Leo	10000.00	400	Management
2	George	1000.00	200	Production
3	Chris	2000.00	100	Engineering
4	Rob	3000.00	400	Management
5	Laura	3000.00	400	Management

Notice that in the query at the beginning of this section, the table qualifiers precede the column deptno. These qualifiers are used because the deptno column appears in both tables, and when you reference it, you need to specify from which of the tables it is taken. You could have used full table names, but in this case, short table qualifiers are used for coding convenience. Later in this chapter, you will see situations where table qualifiers are mandatory.

Also notice that in the output shown in Table 1-4, some of the information from the tables is missing. The name Jeffrey does not appear in the output, nor does the Sanitation department. The reason for this is that inner joins return only matching rows from both tables. Since this company doesn't care too much about sanitation, they have no employees in that department.

Jeffrey's disappearance is a bit more complicated. Jeffrey doesn't belong to any specific department, so he has NULL in the deptno column. You're probably asking yourself how that can be. Well, Leo, the company's owner, is Jeffrey's uncle. Before Jeffrey joined Leo's latex company, he used to work in the city hall's parks department and was Leo's pride and joy. However, he was just recently fired from his old job and joined Leo's company. After being the source of many troubles, and not contributing anything to the company, Leo decided to keep Jeffrey as a manager to justify his salary, but not assign him to any specific department.

Because there is no matching department for Jeffrey in the Departments table, his row is not returned. Even if you had a department with a NULL in the deptno column, you still wouldn't have gotten Jeffrey's details because NULLs are not equal to anything, not even to other NULLs.

SQL-92 Join Syntax

Before you go ahead and write the previous join query in the SQL-92 syntax, take a look at the general form of the SQL-92 syntax for joins, shown in Listing 1-5.

Listing 1-5: SQL-92 Join Syntax

```
SELECT
  <select_list>
FROM
    T1
  <join_type> JOIN
    T2 [ON <join_condition>]
  [<join_type> JOIN
    T3 [ON <join_condition>]
[WHERE
  <filter>]
```

SQL-92 Two-Way Inner Joins

Listing 1-6 is an abbreviated form of an SQL-92 inner join between two tables.

Listing 1-6: Abbreviated Form of an SQL-92 Two-Way Inner Join

```
SELECT
  <select_list>
FROM
    T1
  [INNER] JOIN
    T2 ON <join_condition>
[WHERE
  <filter>]
```

The keyword INNER is optional because it is the default join type. You can write a query like the previous one in SQL-92 syntax, as shown in Listing 1-7.

Listing 1-7: SQL-92 Two-Way Inner Join

```
SELECT
  empid,
  empname,
  salary,
  E.deptno,
  deptname
FROM
    Employees   AS E
  JOIN
    Departments AS D ON E.deptno = D.deptno
```

The output looks the same as the output from the old-style syntax. With inner joins, you will always get the same output in both syntaxes. ANSI defines a different logical order for the phases involved in processing the query for each syntax type, but because the output is the same in both cases, the query processor will probably come up with the same execution plan and process them the same way internally. With outer joins it's a totally different story, and in certain situations each of the syntaxes produces a different output. Outer joins and the way they are processed will be explained later in this chapter.

Old-Style SQL-89 Three-Way Inner Joins

If you want to add job information to the previous output, you can write the query shown in Listing 1-8 using the old-style syntax.

Listing 1-8: Old-Style Three-Way Inner Join

```
SELECT
  empid,
  empname,
  salary,
  E.deptno,
  deptname,
  E.jobid,
  jobdesc
FROM
  Employees   AS E,
  Departments AS D,
  Jobs        AS J
WHERE
    E.deptno = D.deptno
  AND
    E.jobid  = J.jobid
```

The output of this query is shown in Table 1-5.

Table 1-5: Output of an Old-Style Three-Way Inner Join

empid	empname	salary	deptno	deptname	jobid	jobdesc
1	Leo	10000.00	400	Management	30	Manager
2	George	1000.00	200	Production	20	Worker
3	Chris	2000.00	100	Engineering	10	Engineer
4	Rob	3000.00	400	Management	30	Manager
5	Laura	3000.00	400	Management	30	Manager

In the three-way inner join, a join condition was added to the WHERE clause based on the jobid column, which appears in both the Employees table and the Jobs table. The new join condition accommodates the Jobs table that was added to the previous two-way inner join.

SQL-92 Three-Way Inner Joins

Listing 1-9 shows the SQL-92 syntax for the previous three-way join query.

Listing 1-9: SQL-92 Three-Way Inner Join

```
SELECT
  empid,
  empname,
  salary,
  E.deptno,
  deptname,
  E.jobid,
  jobdesc
FROM
    Employees   AS E
  JOIN
    Departments AS D ON E.deptno = D.deptno
  JOIN
    Jobs        AS J ON E.jobid  = J.jobid
```

Adding a third table to an SQL-92 inner join requires adding another JOIN clause and another join condition in a separate ON clause.

Join Query Table Order

A common question that programmers ask regarding joining more than two tables is whether the order in which the tables appear in the query affects the internal order of the query processing and the performance of the query.

In the case of inner joins, it doesn't matter. You could rewrite the three-way SQL-92 join query so that you first join Employees to Jobs and then join it to Departments, but the output would be the same. The query processor is aware of that and will decide on the internal order in which it accesses the tables based on cost estimation, and it will come up with the same execution plan regardless of the order of the tables in the query.

With other types of joins, the order of the tables in the query might produce different results, and therefore might require a different execution plan. If you are testing the performance of the query and would like to see the effects of forcing a specific join order, you can add to the bottom of the query an OPTION clause that contains a FORCE ORDER hint, as shown in Listing 1-10.

Listing 1-10: Forcing the Order of Join Processing

```
SELECT
    empid,
    empname,
    salary,
    E.deptno,
    deptname,
    E.jobid,
    jobdesc
FROM
    Employees AS E
  JOIN
    Departments AS D ON E.deptno = D.deptno
  JOIN
    Jobs AS J ON E.jobid = J.jobid
OPTION(FORCE ORDER)
```

This hint has no effect on the number of rows returned or their content, and it has nothing to do with ANSI compatibility. It might affect the order of the returned rows, but this shouldn't bother you because unless you use the ORDER BY clause, no specific order of returned rows is guaranteed anyway.

Cross Joins

A cross join produces a Cartesian product of the tables involved. In other words, it matches all the rows from one table to each of the rows in the other table. If no filter is used, the number of rows in the result set is the number of rows in one table multiplied by the number of rows in the other. If you want to produce all possible combinations of jobs and departments, you can write the query shown in Listing 1-11 using the old-style syntax, which, in the case of cross joins, is also SQL-89 compliant.

Listing 1-11: Old-Style Cross Join Syntax

```
SELECT
  deptname,
  jobdesc
FROM
  Departments,
  Jobs
```

The output of this query is shown in Table 1-6.

Table 1-6: Output of an Old-Style Cross Join

deptname	jobdesc
Engineering	Engineer
Production	Engineer
Sanitation	Engineer
Management	Engineer
Engineering	Worker
Production	Worker
Sanitation	Worker
Management	Worker
Engineering	Manager
Production	Manager
Sanitation	Manager
Management	Manager
Engineering	Cleaner

Table 1-6: Output of an Old-Style Cross Join (Continued)

deptname	jobdesc
Production	Cleaner
Sanitation	Cleaner
Management	Cleaner

The SQL-92 syntax for this query is shown in Listing 1-12.

Listing 1-12: SQL-92 Cross Join Syntax

```
SELECT
   deptname,
   jobdesc
FROM
    Departments
  CROSS JOIN
    Jobs
```

Both syntaxes produce the same output and are processed the same way. However, there is more likelihood in the old-style syntax that a cross join was not the original programmer's intention, which brings us to the first advantage of the SQL-92 syntax.

Advantage 8   *Cross joins in the SQL-92 syntax should explicitly include the CROSS JOIN keywords, whereas in the old-style syntax, a cross join looks like an inner join where the join condition is simply not specified. This makes the old-style syntax prone to errors, because a programmer might forget to mention a join condition and instead of getting an error, get a cross join. This can be a really sneaky problem if you are joining two tables on two columns and specify only one column by mistake.*

Outer Joins

Outer joins enable you to define either one or both of the tables participating in the join as *preserved* tables. This means that besides returning matching rows from both tables, the rows from the preserved table that have no match in the other table are also returned, padded with NULLs instead of the values that were supposed to come from the other table. In the case of outer joins, the old-style syntax is not ANSI compliant. In fact, SQL-89 did not support outer joins, so other vendors also came up with their own syntax, which gives us another advantage of the SQL-92 syntax.

> **Advantage 9** *The old-style syntax for outer joins is not ANSI compliant and might not be supported in one of the next versions of SQL Server. The SQL-92 syntax is, of course, ANSI SQL-92 compliant.*

Old-Style Outer Joins

SQL Server's old-style syntax for outer joins looks very much like that for inner joins, with the addition of an asterisk on one of the sides of the equal sign in the join condition. The placement of the asterisk—on the left or right side of the equal sign—determines which of the tables is the preserved table. Listing 1-13 shows the old-style outer join syntax.

Listing 1-13: Old-Style Outer Join Syntax

```
SELECT
  <select_list>
FROM
  T1,
  T2
WHERE
  T1.key_col {*= | =*} T2.key_col [AND <filter>]
```

If the asterisk is on the left side of the equal sign, the table on the left side of the join condition is the preserved table. This is called a left outer join.

Old-Style Two-Way Left Outer Joins

Let's write a query in the old-style syntax that produces employee and department information, preserving all rows from the Employees table, even if there are no matching departments, as Listing 1-14 shows.

Listing 1-14: Old-Style Two-Way Left Outer Join

```
SELECT
  *
FROM
  Employees   AS E,
  Departments AS D
WHERE
  E.deptno *= D.deptno
```

The output of this query is shown in Table 1-7.

Table 1-7: Output of an Old-Style Two-Way Left Outer Join

empid	empname	deptno	jobid	salary	deptno	deptname
1	Leo	400	30	10000.00	400	Management
2	George	200	20	1000.00	200	Production
3	Chris	100	10	2000.00	100	Engineering
4	Rob	400	30	3000.00	400	Management
5	Laura	400	30	3000.00	400	Management
6	Jeffrey	NULL	30	5000.00	NULL	NULL

Notice that now Jeffrey appears in the output even though there is no match for his department in the Departments table because his row comes from the pre-served table. The Sanitation department, however, still doesn't appear in the output because its row is in the unpreserved table. Don't get confused with the NULLs in Jeffrey's details. The first NULL in the first deptno column in the output is the original NULL that appears in his row in the Employees table. The other two NULLs replace the values that were supposed to come from the Departments table, where there was no match to Jeffrey's row.

SQL-92 Two-Way Outer Joins

The SQL-92 syntax for an outer join between two tables is shown in Listing 1-15.

Listing 1-15: SQL-92 Two-Way Outer Join Syntax

```
SELECT
  <select_list>
FROM
    T1
  {LEFT | RIGHT | FULL} [OUTER] JOIN
    T2 ON <join_condition>
[WHERE
  <filter>]
```

Note that specifying the outer join type is mandatory, but specifying the keyword OUTER is optional.

SQL-92 Two-Way Left Outer Joins

You can write a query similar to the previous query in the SQL-92 syntax, as Listing 1-16 shows.

Listing 1-16: SQL-92 Two-Way Left Outer Join

```
SELECT
  *
FROM
    Employees   AS E
  LEFT OUTER JOIN
    Departments AS D ON E.deptno = D.deptno
```

The output looks the same as the output of Listing 1-14, but as mentioned earlier in the chapter, they are processed differently and *might* produce different results. Well, in this case they don't. But before delving into the differences, a few more issues need to be covered.

Old-Style Two-Way Right Outer Joins

If you want to preserve all rows from the Departments table, you can simply write a right outer join query. Listing 1-17 shows how to achieve this using the old-style syntax.

Listing 1-17: Old-Style Two-Way Right Outer Join

```
SELECT
  *
FROM
  Employees   AS E,
  Departments AS D
WHERE
  E.deptno =* D.deptno
```

The output of this query is shown in Table 1-8.

Table 1-8: Output of an Old-Style Two-Way Right Outer Join

empid	empname	deptno	jobid	salary	deptno	deptname
3	Chris	100	10	2000.00	100	Engineering
2	George	200	20	1000.00	200	Production
NULL	NULL	NULL	NULL	NULL	300	Sanitation
1	Leo	400	30	10000.00	400	Management
4	Rob	400	30	3000.00	400	Management
5	Laura	400	30	3000.00	400	Management

Jeffrey disappeared again because his row is now in the unpreserved table and it doesn't have a match in the Departments table. All of the output columns in the Sanitation department's row that were supposed to come from the Employees table were replaced with NULLs because no employee belongs to that department.

SQL-92 Two-Way Right Outer Joins

You can write the previous query in the SQL-92 syntax, as shown in Listing 1-18.

Listing 1-18: SQL-92 Two-Way Right Outer Join

```
SELECT
  *
FROM
   Employees   AS E
 RIGHT OUTER JOIN
   Departments AS D ON E.deptno = D.deptno
```

SQL-92 Two-Way Full Outer Joins

If you want to preserve all employees and all departments, you can write the query shown in Listing 1-19 using the SQL-92 syntax.

Listing 1-19: SQL-92 Two-Way Full Outer Join

```
SELECT
    *
FROM
    Employees   AS E
  FULL OUTER JOIN
    Departments AS D ON E.deptno = D.deptno
```

The output of this query is shown in Table 1-9.

Table 1-9: Output of an SQL-92 Two-Way Full Outer Join

empid	empname	deptno	jobid	salary	deptno	deptname
6	Jeffrey	NULL	30	5000.00	NULL	NULL
3	Chris	100	10	2000.00	100	Engineering
2	George	200	20	1000.00	200	Production
NULL	NULL	NULL	NULL	NULL	300	Sanitation
1	Leo	400	30	10000.00	400	Management
4	Rob	400	30	3000.00	400	Management
5	Laura	400	30	3000.00	400	Management

The output in this case consists of all of the following:

- All matching rows from both tables

- All rows from the Employees table with no matching department (in this case, Jeffrey's row), with NULLs replacing the values that were supposed to come from the Departments table

- All rows from the Departments table with no matching employee (in this case, the Sanitation department's row), with NULLs replacing the values that were supposed to come from the Employees table

Can you guess how to write this query in the old-style syntax? Well, in this case you are out of luck, which brings us to the third advantage of the SQL-92 syntax.

> **Advantage 10**   *The old-style syntax doesn't support full outer joins. The SQL-92 syntax does.*

SQL-92 Three-Way Outer Joins

Suppose you want to produce employee, department, and job information, preserving all employees and all jobs. This requires joining three tables. You can write the query shown in Listing 1-20 using the SQL-92 syntax.

Listing 1-20: SQL-92 Three-Way Outer Join, Example 1

```
SELECT
  *
FROM
    Employees   AS E
  LEFT OUTER JOIN
    Departments AS D ON E.deptno = D.deptno
  RIGHT OUTER JOIN
    Jobs        AS J ON E.jobid  = J.jobid
```

The output of this query is shown in Table 1-10.

Table 1-10: Output of an SQL-92 Three-Way Outer Join, Example 1

empid	empname	deptno	jobid	salary	deptno	deptname	jobid	jobdesc
3	Chris	100	10	2000.00	100	Engineering	10	Engineer
2	George	200	20	1000.00	200	Production	20	Worker
1	Leo	400	30	10000.00	400	Management	30	Manager
4	Rob	400	30	3000.00	400	Management	30	Manager
5	Laura	400	30	3000.00	400	Management	30	Manager
6	Jeffrey	NULL	30	5000.00	NULL	NULL	30	Manager
NULL	NULL	NULL	NULL	NULL	NULL	NULL	40	Cleaner

The output may look hard to explain at first, but if you logically separate the query to two steps, it will be easier.

Step 1. Let ED = Employees LEFT OUTER JOIN Departments.

The output of Step 1 is shown in Table 1-11.

Table 1-11: Output of Employees LEFT OUTER JOIN Departments

empid	empname	deptno	jobid	salary	deptno	deptname
1	Leo	400	30	10000.00	400	Management
2	George	200	20	1000.00	200	Production
3	Chris	100	10	2000.00	100	Engineering
4	Rob	400	30	3000.00	400	Management
5	Laura	400	30	3000.00	400	Management
6	Jeffrey	NULL	30	5000.00	NULL	NULL

Step 2. Perform ED RIGHT OUTER JOIN Jobs.

You should now get the desired output.

With left and right outer joins, the order in which the tables appear in the query determines the order of their processing. This, of course, makes sense, because their order affects the output. In the case of full outer joins, however, their order doesn't affect the output; hence, it doesn't determine their processing order.

The old-style syntax has very limited support for outer joins with more than two tables. For example, try to write the previous query in the old-style syntax. An illegal attempt is shown in Listing 1-21.

Listing 1-21: Illegal Old-Style Three-Way Outer Join, Example 1

```
SELECT
  *
FROM
  Employees   AS E,
  Departments AS D,
  Jobs        AS J
WHERE
    E.deptno *= D.deptno
  AND
    E.jobid  =* J.jobid
```

This query will produce an error, indicating that the query contains an outer join request that is not permitted.

If you want to supply employee, department, and job information for matching employees and departments, preserving all jobs, you can write the query in Listing 1-22 using the SQL-92 syntax.

Listing 1-22: SQL-92 Three-Way Outer Join, Example 2

```
SELECT
   *
FROM
   Employees   AS E
 JOIN
   Departments AS D ON E.deptno = D.deptno
 RIGHT OUTER JOIN
   Jobs        AS J ON E.jobid  = J.jobid
```

The output of this query is shown in Table 1-12.

Table 1-12: Output of an SQL-92 Three-Way Outer Join, Example 2

empid	empname	deptno	jobid	salary	deptno	deptname	jobid	jobdesc
3	Chris	100	10	2000.00	100	Engineering	10	Engineer
2	George	200	20	1000.00	200	Production	20	Worker
1	Leo	400	30	10000.00	400	Management	30	Manager
4	Rob	400	30	3000.00	400	Management	30	Manager
5	Laura	400	30	3000.00	400	Management	30	Manager
NULL	NULL	NULL	NULL	NULL	NULL	NULL	40	Cleaner

But you're out of luck again with the old-style syntax shown in Listing 1-23.

Listing 1-23: Illegal Old-Style Three-Way Outer Join, Example 2

```
SELECT
   *
FROM
  Employees AS E,
  Departments AS D,
  Jobs AS J
WHERE
    E.deptno = D.deptno
  AND
    E.jobid =* J.jobid
```

If you try to run this query, you will get an error indicating that the Employees table is an inner member of an outer-join clause, and that this is not allowed if the table also participates in a regular join clause. This brings us to the fourth advantage of the SQL-92 syntax.

Advantage 11   *Not all SQL-92 outer joins that join more than two tables can be written in the old-style syntax.*

The Catch

Now comes the catch—suppose you want to produce department and employee information, preserving all departments, and using the old style, as in Listing 1-24.

Listing 1-24: Old-Style Left Outer Join between Departments and Employees, Preserving All Departments

```
SELECT
  *
FROM
  Departments AS D,
  Employees   AS E
WHERE
  D.deptno *= E.deptno
```

The output of this query is shown in Table 1-13.

Table 1-13: Output of an Old-Style Left Outer Join between Departments and Employees

deptno	deptname	empid	empname	deptno	jobid	salary
100	Engineering	3	Chris	100	10	2000.00
200	Production	2	George	200	20	1000.00
300	Sanitation	NULL	NULL	NULL	NULL	NULL
400	Management	1	Leo	400	30	10000.00
400	Management	4	Rob	400	30	3000.00
400	Management	5	Laura	400	30	3000.00

So far, so good. Now suppose you want to filter this output and return only the departments that have no matching employees. Looks easy enough—you can add the filter `E.deptno IS NULL`, as in Listing 1-25.

Listing 1-25: Using the Old-Style Syntax to Look for Departments with No Employees

```
SELECT
  *
FROM
  Departments AS D,
  Employees   AS E
WHERE
    D.deptno *= E.deptno
  AND
    E.deptno IS NULL
```

The output shown in Table 1-14 is quite surprising.

Table 1-14: Wrong Output of an Old-Style Query Looking for Mismatches

deptno	deptname	empid	empname	deptno	jobid	salary
100	Engineering	NULL	NULL	NULL	NULL	NULL
200	Production	NULL	NULL	NULL	NULL	NULL
300	Sanitation	NULL	NULL	NULL	NULL	NULL
400	Management	NULL	NULL	NULL	NULL	NULL

To understand the reason for this result, take a look at the execution plan shown in Figure 1-2. (If you are unfamiliar with examining execution plans, see Appendix C, "Analyzing Query Performance.")

NOTE *The graphical execution plans have been slightly revised for readability.*

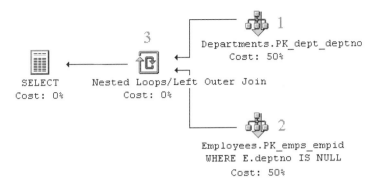

Figure 1-2: Execution plan for an outer join in the old-style syntax

Listing 1-26 shows the textual SHOWPLAN output for the same query.

Listing 1-26: Execution Plan for an Outer Join Using the Old-Style Syntax

```
3 |--Nested Loops(Left Outer Join, WHERE:([D].[deptno]=NULL))
   1 |--Clustered Index Scan(OBJECT:([testdb].[dbo].[Departments].[PK_dept_deptno]
         AS [D]))
   2 |--Clustered Index Scan(OBJECT:([testdb].[dbo].[Employees].[PK_emps_empid] AS
         [E]), WHERE:([E].[deptno]=NULL))
```

Notice that the filter WHERE:([E].[deptno]=NULL)), which means WHERE E.deptno IS NULL, is applied prior to the join operation. To understand what is going on here, examine this plan step by step.

Step 1. Let Input1 = all rows from Employees.

The output of Step 1 is shown in Table 1-15.

Table 1-15: Output of Step 1 in an Old-Style Query Looking for Mismatches

empid	empname	deptno	jobid	salary
1	Leo	400	30	10000.00
2	George	200	20	1000.00
3	Chris	100	10	2000.00
4	Rob	400	30	3000.00
5	Laura	400	30	3000.00
6	Jeffrey	NULL	30	5000.00

Step 2. Let Input2 = all rows from Departments WHERE deptno IS NULL.
    The output of Step 2 is shown in Table 1-16.

Table 1-16: Output of Step 2 in an Old-Style Query Looking for Mismatches

deptno	deptname
(Empty set)	

Step 3. Let Result = Input1 LEFT OUTER JOIN Input2.
    Since there are no rows in the second input, all the values that were supposed
to come from it are replaced with NULLs, as the output in Table 1-17 shows.

Table 1-17: Output of Step 3 in an Old-Style Query Looking for Mismatches

deptno	deptname	empid	empname	deptno	jobid	salary
100	Engineering	NULL	NULL	NULL	NULL	NULL
200	Production	NULL	NULL	NULL	NULL	NULL
300	Sanitation	NULL	NULL	NULL	NULL	NULL
400	Management	NULL	NULL	NULL	NULL	NULL

Controlling the Order of Join Processing

With the SQL-92 syntax, you can control the order of the query execution phases.
You can request that the filter be applied only after the join is performed, as shown
in Listing 1-27.

Listing 1-27: Using the SQL-92 Syntax to Look for Departments with No Employees

```
SELECT
  *
FROM
    Departments AS D
  LEFT OUTER JOIN
    Employees   AS E ON D.deptno = E.deptno
WHERE
  E.deptno IS NULL
```

The output of this query is shown in Table 1-18.

Table 1-18: Correct Output for an SQL-92 Query Looking for Mismatches

deptno	deptname	empid	empname	deptno	jobid	salary
300	Sanitation	NULL	NULL	NULL	NULL	NULL

The output looks like the desired output. Take a look the execution plan shown in Figure 1-3.

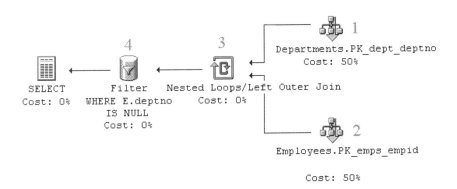

Figure 1-3: Execution plan for an outer join in the SQL-92 syntax

SHOWPLAN's textual output is shown in Listing 1-28.

Listing 1-28: Execution Plan for an Outer Join Using the SQL-92 Syntax

```
4 |--Filter(WHERE:([E].[deptno]=NULL))
   3 |--Nested Loops(Left Outer Join, WHERE:([D].[deptno]=[E].[deptno]))
      1 |--Clustered Index Scan(OBJECT:([testdb].[dbo].[Departments].
         [PK_dept_deptno] AS [D]))
      2 |--Clustered Index Scan(OBJECT:([testdb].[dbo].[Employees].[PK_emps_empid]
         AS [E]))
```

Let's examine this plan step by step.

Step 1. Let Input1 = all rows from Employees.

The output of Step 1 is shown in Table 1-19.

Table 1-19: Output of Step 1 in an SQL-92 Query Looking for Mismatches

empid	empname	deptno	jobid	salary
1	Leo	400	30	10000.00
2	George	200	20	1000.00
3	Chris	100	10	2000.00
4	Rob	400	30	3000.00
5	Laura	400	30	3000.00
6	Jeffrey	NULL	30	5000.00

Step 2. Let Input2 = all rows from Departments.
The output of Step 2 is shown in Table 1-20.

Table 1-20: Output of Step 2 in an SQL-92 Query Looking for Mismatches

deptno	deptname
100	Engineering
200	Production
300	Sanitation
400	Management

Step 3. Let Input3 = Input1 LEFT OUTER JOIN Input2.
The output of Step 3 is shown in Table 1-21.

Table 1-21: Output of Step 3 in an SQL-92 Query Looking for Mismatches

deptno	deptname	empid	empname	deptno	jobid	salary
100	Engineering	3	Chris	100	10	2000.00
200	Production	2	George	200	20	1000.00
300	Sanitation	NULL	NULL	NULL	NULL	NULL
400	Management	1	Leo	400	30	10000.00
400	Management	4	Rob	400	30	3000.00
400	Management	5	Laura	400	30	3000.00

Step 4. Let Result = filter Input3—WHERE empid IS NULL.
The output of Step 4 is shown in Table 1-22.

Table 1-22: Output of Step 4 in an SQL-92 Query Looking for Mismatches

deptno	deptname	empid	empname	deptno	jobid	salary
300	Sanitation	NULL	NULL	NULL	NULL	NULL

The nice thing about the SQL-92 syntax is that you can request a different order of execution by including the filter in the join condition, as shown in Listing 1-29.

Listing 1-29: Controlling the Order of Joining and Filtering Rows

```
SELECT
  *
FROM
   Departments AS D
  LEFT OUTER JOIN
   Employees   AS E ON  D.deptno = E.deptno
                    AND E.deptno IS NULL
```

The output of this query is shown in Table 1-23.

Table 1-23: Result of Moving the Filter to the Join Condition in an SQL-92 Query

deptno	deptname	empid	empname	deptno	jobid	salary
100	Engineering	NULL	NULL	NULL	NULL	NULL
200	Production	NULL	NULL	NULL	NULL	NULL
300	Sanitation	NULL	NULL	NULL	NULL	NULL
400	Management	NULL	NULL	NULL	NULL	NULL

Including the filter in the join condition is meaningless in this case, but you might find it useful in other situations. (The puzzle at the end of this chapter examines just such a situation.)

This brings us to the fifth advantage of the SQL-92 syntax.

> **Advantage 12** *With the SQL-92 syntax, you can control the order of the query execution, whereas with the old-style syntax you can't.*

Self and Non-Equal Joins

Most of the time when you write joins, the queries involve at least two different tables and the join condition is an equal sign where you look for exact matches between the rows in the participating tables. There are some situations, though, where you need to join a table to itself (*self-join*). There are also situations where the relationship between the rows in the participating tables is not based on exact matches; rather, it's based on another logical condition (*non-equal join*). This section describes how to deal with these situations.

The Dating Service Scenario

Consider the Candidates table in Listing 1-30, which holds candidate information for a dating service.

Listing 1-30: Schema Creation Script for the Candidates Table

```
CREATE TABLE Candidates
(
candname varchar(10) NOT NULL,
gender   char(1)    NOT NULL
                    CONSTRAINT CHK_gender
                       CHECK (gender IN('F', 'M'))
)

INSERT INTO Candidates VALUES('Neil'   , 'M')
INSERT INTO Candidates VALUES('Trevor' , 'M')
INSERT INTO Candidates VALUES('Terresa', 'F')
INSERT INTO Candidates VALUES('Mary'   , 'F')
```

The content of the Candidates table is shown in Table 1-24.

Table 1-24: Data from the Candidates Table

candname	gender
Neil	M
Trevor	M
Terresa	F
Mary	F

You need to match all possible couples, and for this example, the request is to match males with females. The list will be used to send each couple to a restaurant so they can get to know each other. After all possible couples have dated, each person decides who fits him or her the most, if at all, and if this matches the other's choice, then a match is made. But this is really not your problem—you only need to provide the initial list. First, there's no doubt you will need to use the table twice in your query so you can create couples. The problem is that there is no obvious join condition. The first idea that might come to mind is to start with the CROSS JOIN shown in Listing 1-31 and later filter all irrelevant matches.

Listing 1-31: Matching Couples Using a Cross Join; All Possible Couples

```
SELECT
  T1.candname,
  T2.candname
FROM
   Candidates AS T1
  CROSS JOIN
   Candidates AS T2
```

The output of this query is shown in Table 1-25.

Table 1-25: Output of Matching Couples Using a Cross Join; All Possible Couples

candname	candname
Neil	Neil
Trevor	Neil
Terresa	Neil
Mary	Neil
Neil	Trevor
Trevor	Trevor
Terresa	Trevor
Mary	Trevor
Neil	Terresa
Trevor	Terresa
Terresa	Terresa
Mary	Terresa
Neil	Mary
Trevor	Mary
Terresa	Mary
Mary	Mary

This is an example where you had to use table qualifiers; otherwise the column candname would have been ambiguous.

Now you have a lot of problems, but you can deal with them one at a time. First, you don't really want to send any one alone to the restaurant, so you write the query shown in Listing 1-32.

Listing 1-32: Matching Couples Using a Cross Join; Couples with Different Names

```
SELECT
  T1.candname,
  T2.candname
FROM
   Candidates AS T1
  CROSS JOIN
   Candidates AS T2
WHERE
  T1.candname <> T2.candname
```

The output of this query is shown in Table 1-26.

Table 1-26: Output of Matching Couples Using a Cross Join; Couples with Different Names

candname	candname
Trevor	Neil
Terresa	Neil
Mary	Neil
Neil	Trevor
Terresa	Trevor
Mary	Trevor
Neil	Terresa
Trevor	Terresa
Mary	Terresa
Neil	Mary
Trevor	Mary
Terresa	Mary

This did narrow the list, but you still have problems. Assuming that your task for this dating service is to match males with females, you need to eliminate couples with the same gender. You don't need an additional condition, because checking for unequal genders will also take care of the previous problem, so you write the query shown in Listing 1-33.

Listing 1-33: Matching Couples Using a Cross Join; Couples with Different Genders

```
SELECT
  T1.candname,
  T2.candname
FROM
   Candidates AS T1
  CROSS JOIN
   Candidates AS T2
WHERE
  T1.gender <> T2.gender
```

The output of this query is shown in Table 1-27.

Table 1-27: Output of Matching Couples Using a Cross Join; Couples with Different Genders

candname	candname
Terresa	Neil
Mary	Neil
Terresa	Trevor
Mary	Trevor
Neil	Terresa
Trevor	Terresa
Neil	Mary
Trevor	Mary

The only problem that you are left with is that you send each couple twice to the restaurant. Each couple has one row with a male in the first column and a female in the second column, and also a row with the reversed order. You can eliminate the duplicates by requesting only a specific gender in each column, as shown in Listing 1-34.

Listing 1-34: Matching Couples Using a Cross Join; Final Query

```
SELECT
  M.candname AS Guy,
  F.candname AS Girl
FROM
    Candidates AS M
  CROSS JOIN
    Candidates AS F
WHERE
    M.gender <> F.gender
  AND
    M.gender = 'M'
```

You can even use one condition that takes care of all problems, as shown in Listing 1-35.

Listing 1-35: Matching Couples Using a Cross Join; Using Minimalist Criteria

```
SELECT
  M.candname AS Guy,
  F.candname AS Girl
FROM
    Candidates AS M
  CROSS JOIN
    Candidates AS F
WHERE
  M.gender > F.gender
```

The output of this query is shown in Table 1-28.

Table 1-28: Output of Matching Couples Using a Cross Join; Final Query

guy	girl
Neil	Terresa
Neil	Mary
Trevor	Terresa
Trevor	Mary

In this output, no one dates himself or herself, the genders are different, and since the letter *M* sorts higher than the letter *F,* you made sure that only males would appear in the first column.

This is all well and good; however, some of you probably think that this problem deals with self-joins but has nothing to do with non-equal joins. Well, you can also look at the problem this way: "Generate a list of all possible combinations of couples and eliminate all couple suggestions that will make the dating service go into bankruptcy." Or you can look at it like this: "Show me a list of all males, and match them with all possible females." You already dealt with the former way of looking at the problem; to answer the latter, you can issue the query shown in Listing 1-36.

Listing 1-36: Matching Couples Using an Inner Join

```
SELECT
  M.candname AS Guy,
  F.candname AS Girl
FROM
    Candidates AS M
  JOIN
    Candidates AS F ON M.gender > F.gender
```

The output of this query is shown in Table 1-29.

Table 1-29: Output of Matching Couples Using an Inner Join

guy	girl
Neil	Terresa
Trevor	Terresa
Neil	Mary
Trevor	Mary

The Salary Levels Scenario

The following section presents another scenario that requires non-equal joins. In Leo's latex company, functionality and relations to the owner determine salary levels. Listing 1-37 shows the creation script of the Salarylevels table, which also exists in the company's Human Resources database.

Listing 1-37: Schema Creation Script for the Salarylevels Table

```
CREATE TABLE Salarylevels
(
lowbound  decimal(7,2) NOT NULL,
highbound decimal(7,2) NOT NULL,
sallevel  varchar(50)  NOT NULL
)

INSERT INTO Salarylevels
  VALUES(0.00, 1500.00, 'Doing most of the work')
INSERT INTO Salarylevels
  VALUES(1500.01, 2500.00, 'Planning the work')
INSERT INTO Salarylevels
  VALUES(2500.01, 4500.00, 'Tell subordinates what to do')
INSERT INTO Salarylevels
  VALUES(4500.01, 99999.99, 'Owners and their relatives')
```

Take a look at the content of the Salarylevels table, shown in Table 1-30.

Table 1-30: Data from the Salarylevels Table

lowbound	highbound	sallevel
.00	1500.00	Doing most of the work
1500.01	2500.00	Planning the work
2500.01	4500.00	Tell subordinates what to do
4500.01	99999.99	Owners and their relatives

Now, suppose you want to supply employee and salary-level information. The match between an employee and his or her salary level is based on the salary being between the lowbound and highbound values, so this is how you write your join condition, as shown in Listing 1-38.

Listing 1-38: Using the BETWEEN Predicate in the Join Condition

```
SELECT
  E.*,
  sallevel
FROM
  Employees   AS E
  JOIN
    Salarylevels AS SL ON E.salary BETWEEN lowbound AND highbound
```

The output of this query is shown in Table 1-31.

Table 1-31: Output of a Query Using the BETWEEN Predicate in the Join Condition

empid	empname	deptno	jobid	salary	sallevel
2	George	200	20	1000.00	Doing most of the work
3	Chris	100	10	2000.00	Planning the work
4	Rob	400	30	3000.00	Tell subordinates what to do
5	Laura	400	30	3000.00	Tell subordinates what to do
1	Leo	400	30	10000.00	Owners and their relatives
6	Jeffrey	NULL	30	5000.00	Owners and their relatives

More complex examples of non-equal joins are discussed in Chapter 16.

Using Joins to Modify Data

Sometimes you need to modify data but the criteria that define which rows need to be affected is based on data that doesn't exist in the modified table. Instead, the required data is in another table. One approach is to use subqueries, which are discussed in Chapter 2. Another approach is to use a syntax that originated from Sybase and uses joins in the DELETE and UPDATE statements.

You should be aware that the syntax discussed in this section is not ANSI compliant, and it may also seem a bit strange at first glance. However, once you feel comfortable with joins, you'll get used to it quickly, and you might find it very convenient.

Figure 1-4 shows the tables from the Northwind sample database that are used in this section's examples.

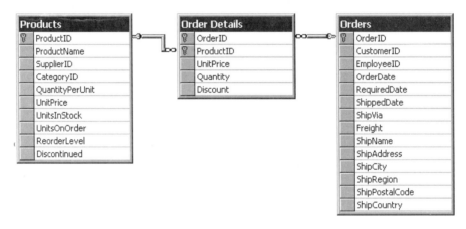

Figure 1-4: Schema of tables from the Northwind database

Using Joins to Delete Data

First, take a look at the abbreviated form of the DELETE statement syntax shown in Listing 1-39.

Listing 1-39: Syntax of DELETE with a Join

```
DELETE [FROM] <modified_table>
[FROM
    <modified_table>
  <join_type> JOIN
    <another_table> ON <join_condition>]
[WHERE
  <search_condition>]
```

Suppose you want to delete all rows from the Order Details table for orders made by the customer `'VINET'`. The problem is that the Order Details table doesn't hold customer information. This information exists in the Orders table. You can write the DELETE statement in Listing 1-40.

Listing 1-40: DELETE with a Join

```
DELETE FROM [Order Details]
FROM
    [Order Details] AS OD
  JOIN
    Orders          AS O ON OD.orderid = O.orderid
WHERE
  CustomerID = 'VINET'
```

Notice that there are two FROM clauses. This is the part of the syntax that might look a bit strange at the beginning. The first FROM clause is optional, and you might prefer not to use it if you find the query less confusing without it. Also, the Order Details table appears twice. The first occurrence (after the first FROM clause) specifies which table is modified, and the second occurrence (after the second FROM clause) is used for the join operation. This syntax doesn't allow you to specify more than one table after the first FROM clause. If it did, it wouldn't be possible to determine which table is modified. You can also use the table qualifier after the first DELETE clause to specify the table you are deleting from (for example, DELETE FROM OD).

Using Joins to Update Data

The UPDATE statement has a similar syntax to the DELETE statement, as shown in Listing 1-41.

Listing 1-41: Syntax of UPDATE with a Join

```
UPDATE <modified_table>
  SET col1 = <new_value>[,
  col2 = <new_value>]
[FROM
    <modified_table>
  <join_type> JOIN
    <another_table> ON <join_condition>]
[WHERE
  <search_condition>]
```

Suppose you want to add a 5 percent discount to items in the Order Details table whose parts are supplied by Exotic Liquids, SupplierID 1. The problem is that the SupplierID column appears in the Products table, and you want to update the Order Details table. You can write the UPDATE statement as shown in Listing 1-42.

Listing 1-42: UPDATE with a Join

```
UPDATE OD
  SET Discount = Discount + 0.05
FROM
    [Order Details] AS OD
  JOIN
    Products       AS P ON OD.productid = P.productid
WHERE
  SupplierID = 1
```

Note that you can use either the full table name or the table qualifier to specify the table you are modifying.

You are not limited to using inner joins to modify data. You can use outer joins as well. Chapters 14 and 16 deal with much more sophisticated updates and deletes using joins.

Performance Considerations

This section describes using hints to specify a certain join strategy and provides a few guidelines to help you achieve better performance with your join queries.

Completely Qualified Filter Criteria

SQL Server's optimizer is a very smart component, but sometimes it needs a little help. It might seem obvious to you that if A = B and B = C, then A = C, but it is not always obvious to the optimizer. Let's say that you want a list of orders and their details for order IDs from 11,000 upward. You could filter just the Orders table or just the Order Details table, which would be sufficient to get you the correct rows. However, if you apply the criteria to *both* tables, there is far less I/O. Listing 1-43 shows a query for an incompletely qualified filter criteria (run against the Northwind sample database).

Listing 1-43: A Query with an Incompletely Qualified Filter Criteria

```
SELECT
    *
FROM
    Orders          AS O
  JOIN
    [Order Details] AS OD ON OD.OrderID= O.OrderID
WHERE
    O.OrderID  >= 11000
```

Listing 1-44 shows the output of STATISTICS IO.

Listing 1-44: I/O Measures for a Query with an Incompletely Qualified Filter Criteria

```
Table 'Order Details'. Scan count 78, logical reads 158, physical reads 0, read-
ahead reads 0.
Table 'Orders'. Scan count 1, logical reads 3, physical reads 0, read-ahead reads 0.
```

Listing 1-45 shows the SHOWPLAN output.

Listing 1-45: SHOWPLAN Output for a Query with an Incompletely Qualified Filter Criteria

```
|--Nested Loops(Inner Join, OUTER REFERENCES:([O].[OrderID]))
    |--Clustered Index Seek(OBJECT:([Northwind].[dbo].[Orders].[PK_Orders] AS
        [O]), SEEK:([O].[OrderID] >= 11000) ORDERED FORWARD)
    |--Clustered Index Seek(OBJECT:([Northwind].[dbo].[Order
        Details].[PK_Order_Details] AS [OD]), SEEK:([OD].[OrderID]=[O].[OrderID])
        ORDERED FORWARD)
```

You can revise this query so that it uses a completely qualified filter criteria, as shown in Listing 1-46.

Listing 1-46: A Query with a Completely Qualified Filter Criteria

```
SELECT
    *
FROM
    Orders          AS O
  JOIN
    [Order Details] AS OD ON OD.OrderID = O.OrderID
```

```
WHERE
    O.OrderID  >= 11000
  AND
    OD.OrderID >= 11000
```

Listing 1-47 shows the output of STATISTICS IO for this new version of the query.

Listing 1-47: I/O Measures for a Query with a Completely Qualified Filter Criteria

```
Table 'Order Details'. Scan count 1, logical reads 3, physical reads 0, read-ahead
reads 0.
Table 'Orders'. Scan count 1, logical reads 3, physical reads 0, read-ahead reads 0.
```

Listing 1-48 shows the SHOWPLAN output.

Listing 1-48: SHOWPLAN Output for a Query with a Completely Qualified Filter Criteria

```
|--Merge Join(Inner Join, MERGE:([O].[OrderID])=([OD].[OrderID]),
   RESIDUAL:([O].[OrderID]=[OD].[OrderID]))
     |--Clustered Index Seek(OBJECT:([Northwind].[dbo].[Orders].[PK_Orders] AS
        [O]), SEEK:([O].[OrderID] >= 11000) ORDERED FORWARD)
     |--Clustered Index Seek(OBJECT:([Northwind].[dbo].[Order
        Details].[PK_Order_Details] AS [OD]), SEEK:([OD].[OrderID] >= 11000)
        ORDERED FORWARD)
```

Notice the significant difference in the number of logical reads required to satisfy the first query as opposed to the second one. Also, the first query plan uses a nested-loops join algorithm, and the second one uses the more efficient merge join algorithm.

Join Hints

SQL Server 6.5's query processor supports only one join algorithm, or strategy—the nested-loops join. As of SQL Server 7, three join strategies are available: nested loops, hash, and merge. If you are testing the performance of your query, and you would like to force a certain join algorithm, you can specify it by using a join hint, as shown in Listing 1-49.

Listing 1-49: Join Hints Syntax

```
SELECT
  <select_list>
```

```
FROM
    T1
  <join_type> <join_hint> JOIN
    T2
```

The `<join_hint>` clause stands for LOOP, MERGE, or HASH. Note that if you specify a join hint, specifying a join type becomes mandatory, and you cannot rely on the defaults as you did earlier in this chapter. An in-depth coverage of join algorithms is out of the scope of this book. See Appendix G for references to resources that cover the topic in depth.

Performance Guidelines

The following guidelines can help you achieve better performance for your join queries:

- Create indexes on frequently joined columns. Use the Index Tuning Wizard for recommendations.

- Create covering (composite) indexes on combinations of frequently fetched columns.

- Create indexes with care, especially covering indexes. Indexes improve the performance of SELECT queries but degrade the performance of modifications.

- Separate tables that participate in joins onto different disks by using filegroups to exploit parallel disk I/O.

References to additional information about joins, query performance, join internals, and indexes can be found in Appendix G.

SQL Puzzle 1-1: Joins

This first puzzle involves the human resources database presented in this chapter. Your task is to present department and employee information for the Sanitation and Management departments for employees earning more than $2,500.00. The required departments should be returned whether there are employees earning more than $2,500.00 belonging to them or not. The output should look like this:

deptno	deptname	empid	empname	deptno	jobid	salary
300	Sanitation	NULL	NULL	NULL	NULL	NULL
400	Management	1	Leo	400	30	10000.00
400	Management	4	Rob	400	30	3000.00
400	Management	5	Laura	400	30	3000.00

The answer to this puzzle can be found on pages 671–673.

CHAPTER 2

Subqueries and Derived Tables

SUBQUERIES ARE SPECIAL CASES of queries within queries. They eliminate the need to save data in temporary tables or variables so that it can be used in subsequent queries later in your code. They also provide you with an alternative to joins (described in Chapter 1) for obtaining the same result set. Indeed, many subqueries can be reduced to an equivalent join, as this chapter explains. The chapter also describes situations where a join won't do and you have to go with a subquery.

Derived tables are special subqueries that look and feel like tables. They were introduced in Microsoft SQL Server version 6.5. Without derived tables, you are often forced to use temporary tables, which can adversely affect your query's performance. This chapter will unlock the secrets behind derived tables and show you how to streamline your code. (Temporary tables are discussed in Chapter 12.)

Understanding Subqueries

Subqueries are the means by which you can do two or more SELECTs at the same time but return only one result set. They fall into two main categories: nested scalar subqueries and correlated subqueries. Although correlated subqueries are the most common, you'll start with nested subqueries in this section and then later build on your experience with them to create correlated subqueries.

Creating Nested Scalar Subqueries

Nested scalar subqueries are those subqueries that return a single row and column in their result set. Thus, they can be used just about anywhere that a scalar value can be used. This allows you flexibility in your code. You do not have to hard-code a value into your WHERE clause, which would limit the query to just that criterion. This type of subquery also enables you to avoid using a variable to save the result from one query just to feed it to another query.

Take a shot at a practical example using the Northwind database. Suppose you need to know all of the orders that were placed on the last day an order was recorded. Breaking this down into two parts, you first have to determine when the last order was placed, and then you have to compare the order date of each order to this date. The first of these queries is shown in Listing 2-1.

Listing 2-1: Finding the Date of the Last Order

```
SELECT
  MAX (OrderDate)
FROM
    Orders
```

You now have the date of the last order, so you can compare the order dates in the table to this value. For this to work, you need to put the first query in parentheses. The final query is presented in Listing 2-2.

Listing 2-2: Finding the Most-Recent Orders

```
SELECT
  *
FROM
    Orders
WHERE
    OrderDate =
(
  SELECT
    MAX (OrderDate)
  FROM
      Orders
)
```

Notice that the two queries are not correlated; there is no dependence inside the inner query on any column of the outer query.

The previous example showed a nested scalar subquery in the WHERE clause of your SELECT, but you can also have a meaningful nested scalar subquery in the SELECT list. For example, you can determine the difference between each product's price and the average price of all products. First you need to get the average price, and then you subtract this average price from each product's price. Check out the solution in Listing 2-3.

Listing 2-3: Finding the Difference between Price and Average Price

```
SELECT
  ProductID,
  UnitPrice -
  (
    SELECT
      AVG (UnitPrice)
    FROM
        Products
  ) AS Difference
FROM
    Products
```

Using the IN Predicate as a Subquery

Another example of a nested subquery is the IN predicate. *Predicates* are expressions that return TRUE, FALSE, or UNKNOWN. You have probably seen the IN predicate when you compared a column to a number of fixed values. Using IN is more elegant than using a bunch of OR predicates. In this scenario, you must know each of the values in the IN predicate, as well as the total number of values. What if you do not know ahead of time what the values will be or how many of them there will be? Here, you can do a SELECT of a single column and put this between parentheses. Next, use the IN predicate to use the list generated by the SELECT.

For example, suppose you've been asked to determine the number of transactions attributed to customers in the United Kingdom. First, you need a list of all Customer IDs from the U.K., and then you use the IN predicate and count the number of matches. The solution is presented in Listing 2-4:

Listing 2-4: Using the IN Predicate as a Subquery

```
SELECT
  COUNT (*)
FROM
    Orders
WHERE
    CustomerID IN
```

```
(
  SELECT
    CustomerID
  FROM
      Customers
  WHERE
      Country = 'UK'
)
```

Because you do not know ahead of time the customers that are based in the U.K., you cannot assemble a list of all UK customers and hard-code it into the IN predicate. That's why you need a subquery.

By the way, the query in Listing 2-4 can be "flattened" into an equivalent join, as shown in Listing 2-5:

Listing 2-5: The IN Predicate Flattened into a Join

```
SELECT
  COUNT (*)
FROM
    Orders     AS O
  JOIN
    Customers AS C ON C.CustomerID = O.CustomerID
WHERE
    C.Country = 'UK'
```

The queries in Listings 2-4 and 2-5 have exactly the same performance in SQL Server because the optimizer generates the same query plan for each.

The opposite of IN is NOT IN. Taking the example from Listing 2-4, if you wanted to know how many orders were placed by customers not based in the U.K., you would use the code in Listing 2-6.

Listing 2-6: Using the NOT IN Predicate as a Subquery

```
SELECT
  COUNT (*)
FROM
    Orders
WHERE
    CustomerID NOT IN
```

```
(
  SELECT
    CustomerID
  FROM
      Customers
  WHERE
      Country = 'UK'
)
```

Be careful using NOT IN when the inner query contains NULL values. Intuitively, you may think that you would get all of the rows that were not retrieved with the IN predicate, but in actuality, you will get *no* rows returned. The reason is subtle. First, the IN predicate can be written as a bunch of OR x = y clauses, while the NOT applies to the entire IN predicate, which can be massaged into AND x <> y clauses. Here's the rub—if *any* y is NULL, then the entire predicate is FALSE, because x <> NULL is FALSE.

> **TIP** *Be sure to filter out* NULLs *inside the inner query when using* NOT IN. *Take advantage of the* ISNULL() *and* COALESCE() *functions. (See the Books Online for further details on these common functions.)*

Using Correlated Subqueries

A *correlated subquery* is one where the "inner" SELECT is dependent upon a value from the "outer" SELECT. You've already seen a nested subquery, but there was nothing inside the inner query that linked it to the outer query. To turn this into a correlated subquery, you can add criteria to the WHERE clause of the inner query.

Using Correlated Subqueries in the WHERE Clause

The correlated subquery is best explained with an example. Suppose you want to know the orders that included more than three dozen of product 17 in the Northwind database. Your inner SELECT will go through the Order Details table looking for those instances of ProductID = 17, while the outer SELECT correlates the subquery to the Orders table through the OrderID. Listing 2-7 shows the code.

Listing 2-7: Example of a Correlated Subquery

```
SELECT
  O.*
FROM
    Orders AS O
WHERE
    36 <
(
  SELECT
    OD.Quantity
  FROM
      [Order Details] AS OD
  WHERE
      OD.ProductID = 17
    AND
      OD.OrderID   = O.OrderID  -- here is the correlation
)
```

The correlation is established by referring to columns from both the inner and the outer queries. In Listing 2-7, OrderID in the inner query is related to OrderID in the outer query.

The cost of the query in Listing 2-7 is 50.26 percent. This is slightly more than that of the equivalent join shown in Listing 2-8, which has a query cost of 49.74 percent. The *query cost* is basically the amount of resources used by the optimizer to process the query, be it memory, CPU, or I/O. (Performance comparisons are discussed later, in the "Comparing Performance" section of this chapter.)

Listing 2-8: Equivalent Join Query

```
SELECT
  O.*
FROM
    Orders          AS O
JOIN
    [Order Details] AS OD ON OD.OrderID = O.OrderID
WHERE
    OD.Quantity  > 36
AND
    OD.ProductID = 17
```

Using Correlated Subqueries in the SELECT Clause

So far, you've created a correlated subquery in the WHERE clause, but it can appear in the SELECT clause just as easily. To illustrate, you can use a correlated subquery to determine the product ID, price, and difference between the price and the average price for the same category, all in one query. The subquery would determine the average price for the same product, as in the outer query. Take a look at the code in Listing 2-9.

Listing 2-9: Correlated Subquery to Show Price Difference

```
SELECT
  P.ProductID,
  P.UnitPrice,
  P.UnitPrice -
(
  SELECT
    AVG (A.UnitPrice)
  FROM
      Products AS A
  WHERE
      A.CategoryID = P.CategoryID
  GROUP BY
    A.CategoryID
)  AS Difference
FROM
    Products AS P
```

Using Correlated Subqueries in the HAVING Predicate

Thought you were through with correlated subqueries? Stay tuned. You can also put them in the HAVING predicate of a GROUP BY clause. Think of the HAVING predicate as being the equivalent of a WHERE clause but only in GROUP BY situations. The mindset is the same.

In this example, you want to find orders in which the quantity ordered for a particular product exceeded by three times the average order for that product. Your first impulse might be to create a temporary table of average orders for each product and then join onto the Order Details table for the final result. However, this query can actually be done as a single SELECT with the subquery being in the HAVING predicate. Check out the solution in Listing 2-10.

Listing 2-10: Using a Correlated Subquery on the HAVING Predicate

```
SELECT
  OD1.ProductID,
  OD1.OrderID
FROM
    [Order Details] AS OD1
GROUP BY
  OD1.ProductID,
  OD1.OrderID
HAVING
  SUM (OD1.Quantity) > 3 *
(
  SELECT
    AVG (OD2.Quantity)
  FROM
      [Order Details] AS OD2
  WHERE
      OD2.ProductID = OD1.ProductID
)
```

You can also use a derived table to solve this type of problem, as you will see later in this chapter.

Using the EXISTS Predicate

The EXISTS predicate is a great feature of SQL. It is probably the most powerful version of a correlated subquery, yet it is under-used in the industry. It allows you to return a row if a given condition exists. You don't have to read a bunch of rows that satisfy the condition—one is all you need.

The following example will demonstrate the syntax. Suppose that for the Northwind database, a recall on product 64 has been declared. You want a list of customer contacts for customers who have ordered the product. You do not want repeated names if they ordered the product several times. The solution is presented in Listing 2-11.

Listing 2-11: Example of a Correlated Subquery Using an EXISTS Predicate

```
SELECT
    C.ContactName
FROM
    Customers AS C
WHERE EXISTS
(
  SELECT
    *
  FROM
     Orders          AS O
    JOIN
     [Order Details] AS OD ON OD.OrderID = O.OrderID
  WHERE
     OD.ProductID = 64
    AND
     O.CustomerID = C.CustomerID
)
```

> **NOTE** *In some other systems, it is recommended that you use a constant or an indexed column, instead of* * *inside the inner* SELECT. *In SQL Server, the optimizer is smart enough to create the correct plan regardless of what's in the* SELECT *list.*

When you use an EXISTS predicate, SQL Server has to do less work than if you used a COUNT(*) > 0 predicate. Once one row has been found to satisfy the EXISTS predicate, there is no need to search any further.

Now contrast this to the correlated subquery in Listing 2-12, where the COUNT(*) scalar aggregate is compared to 0.

Listing 2-12: Example of a Correlated Subquery Using COUNT(*)

```
SELECT
  C.ContactName
FROM
    Customers AS C
WHERE
    0 <
```

```
(
  SELECT
    COUNT (*)
  FROM
      Orders          AS O
    JOIN
      [Order Details] AS OD ON OD.OrderID = O.OrderID
  WHERE
      OD.ProductID = 64
    AND
      C.CustomerID = O.CustomerID
)
```

The relative query cost calculated by the Query Analyzer in SQL Server 2000 is 33.37 percent for the EXISTS version of the query in Listing 2-11 versus 66.63 percent for the COUNT(*) version in Listing 2-12. In SQL Server 7.0, it is 17.71 percent versus 82.29 percent, respectively. This shows that the EXISTS version of the query is less resource-intensive than the COUNT(*) version (although the difference is greater in release 7.0 than in release 2000).

Another thing to take into account is the size of the database. The Northwind database is not very large—the Customers, Orders, and Order Details tables have only 91, 830, and 2,155 rows, respectively. This is not typical of real-world databases, which can have millions of rows. Failure to use EXISTS instead of COUNT(*) > 0 for an industrial-strength database could take hours to process the query.

Using the NOT EXISTS Predicate

You can also use NOT EXISTS when you are interested in rows that do not match the query. For example, the code in Listing 2-13 can be used to produce a list of all customers who have never placed an order.

Listing 2-13: Correlated Subquery with NOT EXISTS Predicate

```
SELECT
  C.*
FROM
    Customers AS C
WHERE NOT EXISTS
```

```
(
  SELECT
     *
  FROM
      Orders AS O
  WHERE
      O.CustomerID = C.CustomerID
)
```

You can also solve this problem with a NOT IN predicate, as shown in Listing 2-14.

Listing 2-14: Equivalent Subquery with NOT IN

```
SELECT
   *
FROM
    Customers
WHERE
    CustomerID NOT IN
(
  SELECT
    CustomerID
  FROM
      Orders
)
```

Although the query cost reported by the Query Analyzer is the same (50.00 percent) for both the NOT EXISTS and NOT IN queries, the I/O statistics are doubled for the Orders table in the NOT IN version. The Profiler reports a tripling of the duration of the query, and the total reads go up by a factor of 15.

You can alter the NOT IN query in Listing 2-14 by changing the inner SELECT to a SELECT DISTINCT. In SQL Server 7.0, the relative query cost for the plain-vanilla SELECT is 54.23 percent versus 45.77 percent for SELECT DISTINCT. However, the optimizer in SQL Server 2000 calculates the same query plan and cost for both. Because there is no fundamental difference between the two queries, this shows that the optimizer in release 2000 has been enhanced.

From the Trenches

On one project, there was no referential integrity in the database. When attempts were made to apply foreign key constraints, error messages were raised about missing rows in the referenced table. The NOT EXISTS predicate was used to locate (and remove) the orphaned rows.

Handling Data Feeds

Those of you who do data feeds are often faced with the dilemma of having to update or insert depending on whether or not the keys in the destination table already exist. Using the NOT EXISTS predicate, you can insert only the new rows and not violate any referential integrity.

Here's a practical example. Suppose you have a feed of car license-plate numbers and the owner names. You want to update the owner if the car exists, and add the car and owner if it does not. You still have to do one UPDATE statement and one INSERT statement, but the INSERT adds only the new cars. See the solution in Listing 2-15.

Listing 2-15: INSERT Using Correlated Subquery with NOT EXISTS

```
-- Update the existing cars
UPDATE C
SET
  F.Owner
FROM
    Feed AS F
  JOIN
    Cars AS C ON C.License = C.License

-- Insert the new cars
INSERT Cars
SELECT
  License,
  Owner
FROM
    Feed AS F
```

```
WHERE NOT EXISTS
(
  SELECT
    *
  FROM
      Cars AS C
  WHERE
      C.License = F.License
)
```

Using Quantified Predicates

Quantified predicates use comparison operators to compare the outer query value to the inner query values. The comparison operators are =, <>, !=, >, >=, <, and <=. They fall into two categories: ANY (or SOME) and ALL.

Using the ANY or SOME Predicate

The ANY predicate returns TRUE if any value in the subquery satisfies the comparison operation, or FALSE if none of the values satisfies the condition or there are no rows inside the subquery. You can substitute the SOME keyword for the ANY keyword.

In this example, you'll use the pubs database to locate the authors who wrote the book with a title ID of BU1032. First, you need to determine the author IDs for the book from the titleauthor table and then compare these to the author IDs in the authors table. Listing 2-16 shows the solution.

Listing 2-16: Finding All Authors for a Book Using the ANY Predicate

```
SELECT
  *
FROM
    authors
WHERE
    au_id = ANY
(
  SELECT
    au_id
  FROM
      titleauthor
  WHERE
      title_id = 'BU1032'
)
```

Think of this type of subquery as a set of values to which you are comparing the value from the outer query to see if it is a member of the set.

The ANY predicate can be substituted for the equivalent IN predicate. In this case, you use = ANY, instead of IN. The same rules regarding the handling of NULLs apply. You can also flatten this into a join.

Using the ALL Predicate

The ALL predicate works much like the ANY predicate. It is more restrictive, how-ever, in that all of the values inside the subquery must satisfy the comparison condition. Remember, too, that you are not restricted to using equality here. You can get very useful results with inequality, as the following example shows.

In this example, you need to know which books in the pubs database are co-authored. In other words, when you count up the number of rows in the titleauthor table for a given book, the count must be greater than 1. Take a look at the solution in Listing 2-17.

Listing 2-17: Finding Co-authored Books Using the ALL Predicate

```
SELECT
  *
FROM
    titles AS T
WHERE
    1 < ALL
(
  SELECT
    COUNT (*)
  FROM
      titleauthor TA
  WHERE
      TA.title_id = T.title_id
)
```

Using ALL vs. Scalar Aggregates

One thing that becomes quite evident as you work with SQL is that there are many ways to obtain the same result set. This is a good thing! Were it not for this flexibility, you'd be stuck with whatever plan the optimizer happened to come up with, no matter how slow it might be.

Thus far in this chapter, you've seen how to convert correlated subqueries into equivalent joins. You've also seen how you can get better performance from an EXISTS predicate over the equivalent COUNT(*) > 0. This section will compare the use of the ALL quantified predicate with the equivalent MAX() and MIN() scalar aggregates.

Comparing ALL and MAX ()

You use MAX() when you want to find the highest value of something. You can use ALL to do the same thing.

In this example, Northwind has been alerted that there's a problem with the latest shipments and you need to find all orders that were shipped on the most recent shipping date. This involves a nested scalar subquery that finds the last shipping date, and this will be the inner part of the query. The outer part of the query then compares shipping dates of all orders to the result of the inner query. This comparison can be done using a MAX() scalar aggregate, as shown in Listing 2-18.

Listing 2-18: Finding the Most Recently Shipped Orders Using MAX()

```
SELECT
  *
FROM
    Orders
WHERE
    ShippedDate =
(
  SELECT
    MAX (ShippedDate)
  FROM
      Orders
)
```

Now rewrite the query using the ALL predicate. The code changes only slightly, as shown in the solution in Listing 2-19.

Listing 2-19: Finding the Most Recently Shipped Orders Using ALL

```
SELECT
  *
FROM
    Orders
WHERE
    ShippedDate >= ALL
```

```
(
  SELECT
    ShippedDate
  FROM
    Orders
)
```

In both Listings 2-18 and 2-19, the aim is to pick the value of ShippedDate in the outer query so that it is the highest value of ShippedDate in the inner query. Both of the solutions will have the same the result set—or will they? If you run these two queries, you will find that the one in Listing 2-18 returns three rows but the one in Listing 2-19 returns *no* rows. What is going on here?

The ShippedDate column in the Orders table allows NULLs. In Listing 2-18, the MAX() aggregate function discards all NULLs and returns the most recent non-NULL ShippedDate. The outer query then compares the ShippedDate column to this date.

In Listing 2-19, the ALL predicate compares all values of ShippedDate in the outer query to all of the values of ShippedDate in the inner query. Unfortunately, ALL literally means "all." In other words, *all* values of ShippedDate in the outer query must be greater than or equal to *all* values of ShippedDate in the inner query. If there is at least one NULL in the ShippedDate column, then the ALL predicate is FALSE, because any comparison with a NULL is FALSE.

All is not lost (pun intended). You can still use the ALL predicate to get the rows you want. You just have to filter out any NULLs inside the inner query. This is done in Listing 2-20.

Listing 2-20: Finding the Most Recently Shipped Orders Using ALL with NULL Handling

```
SELECT
  *
FROM
  Orders
WHERE
  ShippedDate >= ALL
(
  SELECT
    ShippedDate
  FROM
    Orders
  WHERE
    ShippedDate IS NOT NULL
)
```

Comparing ALL and MIN()

Just as you can use ALL to find the maximum value of something, you can also use it to find the minimum. In this case, the MAX() changes to MIN(), and the >= sign changes to <=. Continuing with the shipping problem in the previous section, this time you need the orders from the earliest shipping day. Check out the solution in Listing 2-21.

Listing 2-21: Finding the Earliest Shipped Orders Using MIN()

```
SELECT
  *
FROM
    Orders
WHERE
    ShippedDate =
(
  SELECT
    MIN (ShippedDate)
  FROM
      Orders
)
```

Now, recast the query using the ALL predicate, as shown in Listing 2-22. (Note the sign reversal.)

Listing 2-22: Finding the Most Recently Shipped Orders Using ALL

```
SELECT
  *
FROM
    Orders
WHERE
    ShippedDate <= ALL
(
  SELECT
    ShippedDate
  FROM
      Orders
)
```

Once again, you do not get any rows returned with the ALL predicate because of the presence of NULLs. In other words, the same rules apply here as they do when you use ALL and MAX(). Both the MAX() and MIN() functions discard NULLs; the ALL predicate does not. Add the WHERE clause from Listing 2-20 to the query in Listing 2-22 and you get the correct result set.

In both the MIN() vs. <= ALL and the MAX() vs. >= ALL scenarios, although the rows returned are identical in each of the two cases (assuming there are no NULLs in the subquery), the performance can differ. You'll learn more about this in the "Comparing Performance" section of this chapter.

Calculating Running Totals

At times, it's nice to have a running total when you are retrieving rows. For example, you may want to look at a sum of sales to date from a particular customer for all of his or her orders. This will require a correlated subquery in the SELECT list, as shown in Listing 2-23. Here, the CustomerID has been set to 'BOTTM'.

Listing 2-23: Calculating Running Totals

```
SELECT
  CONVERT (char (11), O1.OrderDate)  AS OrderDate,
  SUM (OD1.UnitPrice * OD1.Quantity) AS Sales,
(
  SELECT
    SUM (OD2.UnitPrice * OD2.Quantity) AS Sale
  FROM
      Orders          AS O2
    JOIN
      [Order Details] AS OD2 ON OD2.OrderID = O2.OrderID
  WHERE
      O2.CustomerID = 'BOTTM'
  AND
      O2.OrderDate  <= O1.OrderDate
)  AS 'Sales to Date'
FROM
    Orders          AS O1
  JOIN
    [Order Details] AS OD1 ON OD1.OrderID = O1.OrderID
WHERE
    O1.CustomerID = 'BOTTM'
GROUP BY
  O1.OrderDate
```

The results of this query are presented in Table 2-1.

Table 2-1: Sales to Date with Running Totals

OrderDate	Sales	Sales to Date
Dec 20 1996	1832.8000	1832.8000
Jan 10 1997	2010.5000	3843.3000
Jan 30 1997	2523.0000	6366.3000
Apr 1 1997	896.0000	7262.3000
Nov 14 1997	3118.0000	10380.3000
Mar 2 1998	1930.0000	12310.3000
Mar 12 1998	1139.1000	13449.4000
Mar 13 1998	4422.0000	17871.4000
Mar 25 1998	717.5000	18588.9000
Mar 27 1998	1014.0000	19602.9000
Apr 16 1998	1170.3000	20773.2000
Apr 23 1998	1309.5000	22082.7000
Apr 24 1998	525.0000	22607.7000

The inner query takes the same sum as the outer query. However, it does not use grouping, and it sums all orders with an order date greater than or equal to the order date of the outer query. Be careful with this type of query—if you run it against tables with many rows, you will get a lot of I/O, which can have a performance impact. Even if you use your own join hints, this can still be a problem.

> **NOTE** *Just because you can do something in SQL doesn't mean that you should do it. A running total can easily be calculated by front-end or middle-tier software. Put the "client" back into "client/server"—let the client program handle running totals, grand totals, sorts, and the like, and relieve the server of this burden.*

Creating Derived Tables

Just about anything that looks like a table can be used as a table. So what is a table? A *table* is a collection of zero or more rows and one or more columns, with all columns having unique names. A table also has a name or an alias. Anything meeting such a definition can be used where a table is required (including *views*, which are discussed in Chapter 8).

Now what happens if you perform a SELECT where all of the returned columns have names? This, too, looks like a table and can thus be used in place of a table in such things as joins, updates, and the like. How this is done is quite simple, although it is under-used in many sites. All you need to do is place parentheses around the SELECT, and everything inside the parentheses is treated as a single table.

Derived tables are SELECT statements in the FROM clause of a query, and they are referred to with an alias. Derived tables came about with the ANSI-92 SQL standard and were implemented in Microsoft SQL Server with the release of version 6.5.

You already saw one form of a derived table when you worked with scalar sub-queries earlier in this chapter. In that case, the table had only one row and one column. You also saw another form of a derived table with the IN, ANY, and ALL predicates. In those examples, the table had one column and any number of rows. Now you're ready for the next level—tables with multiple rows and multiple columns.

Using a SELECT with a GROUP BY as a Derived Table

One of the best applications of a derived table is one that uses a GROUP BY clause. An example using the Northwind database will show you what we mean.

Suppose you want a list of products with their prices, together with the average price for the category of product. You must break down the query into two parts: first get the average price for each product category, and then present the product list with the averages by joining the product table onto the derived table.

The list of average prices is retrieved with the code presented in Listing 2-24.

Listing 2-24: Determining Average Price by Category

```
SELECT
  CategoryID,
  AVG (UnitPrice) AS AvgPrice
FROM
    Products
GROUP BY
  CategoryID
```

This meets all but one of the criteria for a table. You have columns, and all have unique names. The table itself still needs a name or an alias. The alias will be placed after the right parenthesis when you actually use it as a derived table.

Now, join the Products table onto this derived table as shown in Listing 2-25, and you get the desired result.

Listing 2-25: Example of SELECT with GROUP BY as a Derived Table

```
SELECT
  P.ProductID,
  P.UnitPrice,
  P.AvgPrice
FROM
    Products AS P
  JOIN
  (
    SELECT
      CategoryID,
      AVG (UnitPrice) AS AvgPrice
    FROM
        Products
    GROUP BY
      CategoryID
  )          AS A ON A.CategoryID = P.CategoryID
```

As stated earlier, you can get the same result set in SQL using many different methods. The query depicted in Listing 2-25 can also be done using a correlated subquery, as shown in Listing 2-26.

Listing 2-26: Equivalent Correlated Subquery

```
SELECT
  P.ProductID,
  P.UnitPrice,
  (
    SELECT
      AVG (UnitPrice)
    FROM
        Products AS A
    WHERE
        A.CategoryID = A.CategoryID
    GROUP BY
      A.CategoryID
  ) AS AvgPrice
FROM
    Products AS p
```

> **TIP** *When you join a derived table to another table, make the names of any aliased key columns within the derived table the same as those for the table to which you are joining. This can prevent a lot of confusion.*

Finding Duplicate Rows in a Table

Often, you will need to determine the duplicate rows in a table. More specifically, you will want the rows where the primary key has been duplicated. (Assume for now that a PRIMARY KEY constraint has not been applied to the table to prevent this.) Not only do you want a list of the duplicate keys but also the entire rows themselves.

You can find the duplicate keys by using a derived table to find the duplicate keys, and then join the original table to it to get the final result set. The code for this is in Listing 2-27.

Listing 2-27: Finding Duplicate Rows in a Table

```
SELECT
  T.*
FROM
   MyTable AS T
 JOIN
 (
    SELECT
      keycol1,
      keycol2
    FROM
       MyTable
    GROUP BY
      keycol1,
      keycol2
    HAVING
      COUNT (*) > 1
 )        AS D ON  D.keycol1 = T.keycol1
              AND D.keycol2 = T.keycol2
```

This example uses two columns for the key, but you can adapt it to your particular situation. The derived table gives you keys only where the count is greater than 1 (in other words, where there are duplicates). This derived table is then joined to the same table on which you did the count in order to get the actual rows.

Updating Rows with a GROUP BY Clause

You know that you can join onto a table to make an update. However, you cannot make an update with a GROUP BY clause, right? Yes you can—with a derived table.

For example, say you're a greedy merchant and you want to hike the price of your top five selling products by 20 percent. Without a derived table, you would write a SELECT to populate a temporary table with the five top-selling products. You would then join this table to the Products table to update the price.

However, by casting the TOP n query in the form of a derived table, you can avoid the temporary table altogether and solve the problem in a single statement. Take a look at the solution in Listing 2-28.

> **CAUTION** *Do not try this in your sample Northwind database unless you do it inside a transaction with a* ROLLBACK. *Otherwise, the changes will be permanent.*

Listing 2-28: Update with a GROUP BY

```
UPDATE P
SET
  P.UnitPrice = P.UnitPrice * 1.2
FROM
    Products AS p
  JOIN
  (
    SELECT TOP 5
      ProductID,
      SUM (Quantity) AS Quantity
    FROM
        [Order Details]
    GROUP BY
      ProductID
    ORDER BY
      Quantity DESC
  )          AS S ON S.ProductID = P.ProductID
```

This query uses a SELECT TOP n statement as the derived table. The SELECT TOP n statement is discussed in Chapter 4.

Using Unions in Derived Tables

Before leaving this topic, have a look at the role of unions in derived tables. The classic example of a union in a derived table comes in the case of *horizontal partitioning*. This is where you have a huge table and decide to distribute the rows in a number of tables for performance reasons. A row does not appear in more than one table. For example, you may have sales information dating back a number of years, so you might put each year's information into a separate Sales table. Your most frequent queries go to the current year but might span the current and the previous year. Occasionally, you may go back further in history.

To reconstitute the original logical table, you would use a UNION clause or, more specifically, UNION ALL. The difference between these is that UNION removes duplicate rows while UNION ALL does not. If you have partitioned your data as discussed in the previous paragraph, there are no duplicate rows and UNION ALL will work fine. The UNION clause has more overhead associated with it because it has to create a work table to eliminate the duplicates.

As an example, say you have broken the Sales table into two physical tables: CurrentSales and PastSales. CurrentSales has the current calendar year, while the PastSales table has the previous six calendar years. Your fiscal year ends on October 31. Assuming that the calendar year is the year 2000 and that an index exists on Sale-Date in both tables, you would use the code shown in Listing 2-28 to get sales broken down by ProductID for the current fiscal year.

Listing 2-28: Using a UNION ALL Clause in a Derived Table

```
SELECT
  ProductID,
  SUM (Amount) AS Sales
FROM
(
  SELECT
    SaleDate,
    ProductID,
    Amount
  FROM
      CurrentSales
  UNION ALL
  SELECT
    SaleDate,
    ProductID,
    Amount
  FROM
      PastSales
) AS S
WHERE
    SaleDate >= '19991101'
  AND
    SaleDate <= '20001031'
GROUP BY
  ProductID
```

In SQL Server 6.x, a table scan would have occurred on both tables, and then the WHERE clause would have been applied to that result set. The performance was appalling. Alert programmers would realize this and move the WHERE clause, adding it to *both* SELECTs inside the derived table query. With release 7.0, the optimizer was enhanced so that the one WHERE clause would be applied to each of the tables to take advantage of the index. (The situation also applied to views—6.5 was bad when applying a WHERE clause to a view, whereas 7.0 had the smarts to figure things out on its own.)

From the Trenches

A large, monthly report application was previously written for SQL Server 4.21a in Visual Basic and Transact-SQL, and it used to take *two days* to execute. After the conversion to SQL Server 6.5, the rebuilt query took 20 minutes—all in Transact-SQL—thanks to UNION ALL and derived tables.

Creating Histograms

Derived tables can be very useful in situations where statistical data are needed. One such scenario requires a histogram. A *histogram* depicts the distribution of counts of values. You can generate the data required for this by using a derived table.

As an example, suppose you want a histogram of the number of orders placed by a customer (using the Northwind database). Again, you break down the problem into parts, one of which is creating the derived table. First, the derived table contains the number of orders per customer. The important number for the histogram is not the customer ID but the count.

Once you have the counts, you need a "count of counts," which you can generate with another GROUP BY clause. The final code is presented in Listing 2-29.

Listing 2-29: Generating Data for a Histogram

```
SELECT
  Cnt,
  COUNT (*) AS Frequency
FROM
(
  SELECT
    CustomerID,
    COUNT (*) AS Cnt
```

```
FROM
    Orders
GROUP BY
    CustomerID
) AS X
GROUP BY
    Cnt
```

If you want a quasi-graphical representation of the histogram, just change COUNT(*) to REPLICATE('*', COUNT(*)) and see what happens—an instant bar chart!

Comparing Performance

As stated previously, one of the first things that becomes evident when you play around with SQL is that there are many ways of doing the same thing. This is both good and bad. The good part is that you have flexibility; the bad part is that you have to be aware of all of the ways to cast a query, as well as of how things work.

Say, for example, that you want to look at the last row in the Products table, (the one with the highest product ID). Breaking this down, you need to find the highest product ID value and then use it to retrieve the row corresponding to that value. You have essentially two ways of doing this, each with a nested scalar subquery. First, let the subquery find MAX(ProductID), as shown in Listing 2-30.

Listing 2-30: Finding the Last Row in Products Using MAX()

```
SELECT
    *
FROM
    Products
WHERE
    ProductID =
(
  SELECT
    MAX (ProductID)
  FROM
      Products
)
```

This gives a scan count of 1 and a logical read count of 2. Not bad. (In SQL Server 7.0, the numbers were doubled.) Now see what happens when you rewrite the query using the equivalent ALL predicate, as shown in Listing 2-31.

Listing 2-31: Finding the Last Row in Products Using ALL

```
SELECT
  *
FROM
    Products
WHERE
    ProductID >= ALL
(
  SELECT
    ProductID
  FROM
      Products
)
```

This gives you a scan count of 78 and 156 logical reads! The Query Analyzer reports a relative query cost of 11.25 percent in the MAX() query (Listing 2-30) versus 88.75 percent in the ALL query (Listing 2-31).

In the first case, the optimizer had to find the maximum product ID, which it did quickly by traversing the index. It then compared the product ID in the outer query against this one value. This, too, went quickly, because it used a clustered index scan, yielding only one row.

In the second case, the optimizer had to go through the entire Products table to find all of the product IDs. Having this information, it then compared each product ID value in the outer query with all of the values in the inner query to satisfy the ALL condition. Both of these caused clustered index scans.

You can also get performance differences when you use ALL on a correlated subquery. As an example, say you need the first order row for each customer. (Assume "first" means the lowest order ID.) You approach things the same way as in the previous scenario, by using the MIN() function. The code would be as shown in Listing 2-32.

Listing 2-32: Finding the First Order for Each Customer Using MIN()

```
SELECT
  O1.*
FROM
    Orders AS O1
WHERE
    O1.OrderID =
```

```
(
  SELECT
    MIN (O2.OrderID)
  FROM
      Orders AS O2
  WHERE
      O2.CustomerID = O1.CustomerID
)
```

This gives a scan count of 90 and logical reads of 250. It looks like a bit of I/O has occurred, but it is still acceptable. You can change the query slightly to use the ALL predicate, as shown in Listing 2-33.

Listing 2-33: Finding the First Order for Each Customer Using the ALL Predicate

```
SELECT
  O1.*
FROM
    Orders AS O1
WHERE
    O1.OrderID <= ALL
(
  SELECT
    O2.OrderID
  FROM
      Orders AS O2
  WHERE
      O2.CustomerID = O1.CustomerID
)
```

The I/O statistics are given in Table 2-2. Although the numbers are down for the Orders table, the worktable that was created behind the scenes showed a considerable amount of I/O. Another bad score for the ALL predicate.

> **NOTE** *In SQL Server 7.0, the relative query cost was 92.59 percent and 7.41 percent for MAX() and ALL, respectively, but the scan count and logical I/Os were both higher for the ALL version. This is because I/O cost for the worktable in version 7.0 was not included in the I/O statistics output.*

Table 2-2: I/O Statistics for ALL

Table	Scan Count	Logical Reads
Orders	2	25
Worktable	1,007	1,927

You're not finished with this scenario yet. The next thing you need to do is recast the previous query as a derived table, as shown in Listing 2-34.

Listing 2-34: Finding First Orders Using a Derived Table

```
SELECT
  O.*
FROM
    Orders AS O
JOIN
(
  SELECT
    MIN (OrderID) AS OrderID
  FROM
      Orders
  GROUP BY
    CustomerID
)        AS X ON  X.OrderID = O.OrderID
```

The I/O statistics and query plan are the same as in the MIN() example in Listing 2-31. You will often find that the MIN() (or MAX()) subquery produces similar I/O statistics to the equivalent derived table.

The final scenario is a little different and involves aggregation. This time, you want to sum up the quantity of items for each customer's most recent order. ("Most recent" means the latest in time.) You will need to find the last order date for each customer and then sum the quantity for all orders placed by that customer on that date. Using the MAX() version, your correlated subquery should look like the one in Listing 2-35.

Listing 2-35: Finding the Total Quantity for Each Customer's
Most Recent Order Using MAX()

```
SELECT
  O1.CustomerID,
  SUM (OD.Quantity) AS Quantity
FROM
    Orders        AS O1
```

```
JOIN
    [Order Details] AS OD ON OD.OrderID = O1.OrderID
WHERE
    O1.OrderDate =
(
  SELECT
    MAX (O2.OrderDate)
  FROM
      Orders AS O2
  WHERE
      O2.CustomerID = O1.CustomerID
)
GROUP BY
  O1.CustomerID
```

The I/O statistics are displayed in Table 2-3.

Table 2-3: I/O Statistics for MAX()

Table	Scans	Logical Reads
Orders	2	8
Order Details	90	182

NOTE *In SQL Server 7.0, the numbers were higher.*

Now, take a look at the ALL predicate version in Listing 2-36.

Listing 2-36: Finding the Total Quantity for Each Customer's Most Recent Order Using the ALL Predicate

```
SELECT
  O1.CustomerID,
  SUM (OD.Quantity) AS Quantity
FROM
    Orders        AS O1
  JOIN
    [Order Details] AS OD ON OD.OrderID = O1.OrderID
WHERE
    O1.OrderDate >= ALL
```

```
(
  SELECT
    O2.OrderDate
  FROM
      Orders AS O2
  WHERE
      O2.CustomerID = O1.CustomerID
)
GROUP BY
  O1.CustomerID
```

The I/O statistics are displayed in Table 2-4.

Table 2-4: I/O Statistics for ALL

Table	Scans	Logical Reads
Orders	2	42
Order Details	90	182

This time, the Orders table was busier.

This query can also be recast as a derived table. Take a look at Listing 2-37.

Listing 2-37: Finding the Total Quantity for Each Customer's Most Recent Order Using a Derived Table

```
SELECT
  O1.CustomerID,
  SUM (OD.Quantity) AS Quantity
FROM
    Orders         AS O1
  JOIN
    [Order Details] AS OD ON OD.OrderID = O1.OrderID
  JOIN
   (
    SELECT
      CustomerID,
      MAX (OrderDate) AS OrderDate
    FROM
        Orders
    GROUP BY
      CustomerID
   )            AS O2 ON O2.CustomerID = O1.CustomerID
                    AND O2.OrderDate  = O1.OrderDate
GROUP BY
  O1.CustomerID
```

The I/O statistics for this derived table query are identical to those for the MAX() query in Listing 2-35. The relative query costs as calculated by the Query Analyzer are 26.89 percent, 46.22 percent, and 26.89 percent for MAX(), ALL, and the derived table, respectively.

The whole point of this exercise is to experiment. It also stresses the importance of volume testing. The Orders table has only 830 rows and Order Details has 2,155 rows—but this could get quite ugly with millions of rows. The volume and distribution of data, coupled with the indexing on each table, will determine which strategy gives the best performance. If you are already getting satisfactory performance with your style of query and a production-sized volume of data, then you can probably stop there. If not, it's time to explore other options.

SQL Puzzle 2-1: Bank Interest

Now that you know all about correlated subqueries and derived tables, you can put that knowledge to work in a practical example. This scenario is a banking application that calculates daily interest for a given month.

Sounds simple, doesn't it? We'll throw a wrench into the works by saying that the rate can change throughout the month. Well, maybe you can handle that. Okay, we'll throw the other wrench in—you have a stepped interest rate structure where the rate depends on the daily balance. Arrgh!

Oh, come on, it's not that bad! We'll give you a few balances and interest rates, so you have some real numbers against which you can verify the results. First, the bank balances:

AccountID	Date	Balance
1	1May99	$1,000
1	2May99	$6,000
1	3May99	$4,000
1	4May99	$1,000
1	5May99	$3,000
2	1May99	$4,000
2	2May99	$4,000
2	3May99	$4,000
2	4May99	$5,000
2	5May99	$5,000

Here are the interest rates:

Date	Step	Rate
1May99	$0	4.00
1May99	$5,000	4.50
1May99	$9,000	5.00
3May99	$0	4.00
3May99	$2,000	4.25
3May99	$6,000	4.50

SQL Puzzle 2-2: Managing Orders and Their Payments

You are provided with these tables: Orders, OrderDetails, and OrderPayments. Each order in the Orders table can have one or more order parts in the OrderDetails table and zero or more payments in the OrderPayments table. Your task is to write a query that produces order information along with the sum of its order parts and order payments. The following script creates the tables involved:

```
CREATE TABLE Orders
(
  orderid int      NOT NULL
                   CONSTRAINT PK_orders_orderid PRIMARY KEY,
  custid  int      NOT NULL,
  odate   datetime NOT NULL
)

CREATE TABLE OrderDetails
(
  orderid int NOT NULL
              CONSTRAINT FK_odetails_orders REFERENCES Orders,
  partno  int NOT NULL,
  qty     int NOT NULL,
  CONSTRAINT PK_odetails_orderid_partno PRIMARY KEY(orderid, partno)
)
```

```
CREATE TABLE OrderPayments
(
  orderid    int NOT NULL
                CONSTRAINT FK_opayments_orders REFERENCES Orders,
  paymentno int NOT NULL,
  value     int NOT NULL,
  CONSTRAINT PK_opayments_orderid_paymentno PRIMARY KEY(orderid, paymentno)
)
```

The schema is presented in Figure 2-1.

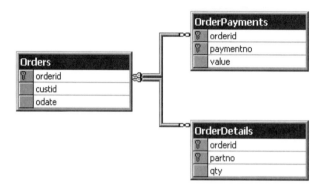

Figure 2-1: Schema of the Orders, OrderDetails, and OrderPayments tables

The data are populated as follows:

```
INSERT INTO Orders VALUES(1, 1001, '20010118')
INSERT INTO Orders VALUES(2, 1002, '20010212')

INSERT INTO OrderDetails VALUES(1, 101, 5)
INSERT INTO OrderDetails VALUES(1, 102, 10)
INSERT INTO OrderDetails VALUES(2, 101, 8)
INSERT INTO OrderDetails VALUES(2, 102, 2)

INSERT INTO OrderPayments VALUES(1, 1, 75)
INSERT INTO OrderPayments VALUES(1, 2, 75)
INSERT INTO OrderPayments VALUES(2, 1, 50)
INSERT INTO OrderPayments VALUES(2, 2, 50)
```

The Orders table will look like this:

orderid	custid	odate
1	1001	2001-01-18 00:00:00.000
2	1002	2001-02-12 00:00:00.000

The OrderDetails table will look like this:

orderid	partno	qty
1	101	5
1	102	10
2	101	8
2	102	2

The OrderPayments table will look like this:

orderid	paymentno	value
1	1	75
1	2	75
2	1	50
2	2	50

The expected output is shown in the following table:

orderid	custid	odate	sum_of_qty	sum_of_value
1	1001	2001-01-18 00:00:00.000	15	150
2	1002	2001-02-12 00:00:00.000	10	100

SQL Puzzle 2-3: Finding Unread Messages

In this scenario, you have users and messages, as well as an associative object—MessagesRead—that tracks which messages have been read by which user. Your task is to provide the list of users that did not read messages and the messages they did not read. The following script creates the Users, Messages, and MessagesRead tables:

```
CREATE TABLE Users
(
  userid   int        NOT NULL PRIMARY KEY,
  username varchar(25) NOT NULL
)

CREATE TABLE Messages
(
  msgid int           NOT NULL PRIMARY KEY,
  msg   varchar(100) NOT NULL
)

CREATE TABLE MessagesRead
(
  msgid  int NOT NULL REFERENCES Messages(msgid),
  userid int NOT NULL REFERENCES Users(userid)
)

INSERT INTO Users VALUES(1, 'Bruce')
INSERT INTO Users VALUES(2, 'Darren')
INSERT INTO Users VALUES(3, 'Umachandar')

INSERT INTO Messages
  VALUES(1, 'Someone called and said that you made her heart double-click')
INSERT INTO Messages
  VALUES(2, 'Your Floppy disk experienced a crash')
INSERT INTO Messages
  VALUES(3, 'Someone sprayed instant glue on all keyboards. Don''t touuuccchhh')

INSERT INTO MessagesRead VALUES(1, 1)
INSERT INTO MessagesRead VALUES(1, 2)
INSERT INTO MessagesRead VALUES(2, 2)
INSERT INTO MessagesRead VALUES(2, 3)
INSERT INTO MessagesRead VALUES(3, 3)
INSERT INTO MessagesRead VALUES(3, 1)
```

The Users table will look like this:

userid	username
1	Bruce
2	Darren
3	Umachandar

The Messages table will look like this:

msgid	msg
1	Someone called and said that you made her heart double-click
2	Your Floppy disk experienced a crash
3	Someone sprayed instant glue on all keyboards. Don't touuuccchhh

The MessagesRead table will look like this:

msgid	userid
1	1
1	2
2	2
2	3
3	3
3	1

The answers to these puzzles can be found on pages 673–681.

Populating Tables

ONCE YOU HAVE CREATED the tables in your database, you need to fill them with data. There are several ways to do this. First, you can use a Transact-SQL INSERT statement, which comes in many flavors. Second, you can use the BULK INSERT statement, introduced in version 7.0. Third, you can use the tried-and-true bulk copy utility (bcp), the progenitor of the BULK INSERT statement. (This one has been around since the Sybase days and is not part of Transact-SQL.) Finally, you can use Data Transformation Services (DTS), also introduced in version 7.0. DTS offers a broad range of ways to load a table.

This chapter deals with the mechanics of the Transact-SQL statements that you can use to populate your tables, as well as including a brief discussion of the bcp program. It also gives you solutions to practical problems. (DTS is beyond the scope of this book.)

Using the INSERT Statement

The most basic way of loading data into a table in Transact-SQL is the INSERT statement. The INSERT statement typically can be broken down into INSERT VALUES, INSERT SELECT, and INSERT EXEC. Take a moment to study the syntax in Listing 3-1.

Listing 3-1: Syntax for the INSERT Statement

```
INSERT [INTO]
 {
  table_name WITH ( <table_hint_limited> [...n])
  | view_name
  | rowset_function_limited
 }

 { [(column_list)]
  { VALUES ( { DEFAULT
      | NULL
      | expression
      }[,...n]
    )
```

```
 | derived_table
 | execute_statement
 }
}
| DEFAULT VALUES

<table_hint_limited> ::=
 { INDEX(index_val [,...n])
  | FASTFIRSTROW
  | HOLDLOCK
  | PAGLOCK
  | READCOMMITTED
  | REPEATABLEREAD
  | ROWLOCK
  | SERIALIZABLE
  | TABLOCK
  | TABLOCKX
  | UPDLOCK
 }
```

Clearly there is a lot there. However, there are parts that are common to all versions of the INSERT statement. First, you have to identify the table or view into which you will be inserting the data. If you are going directly into a table, you can also use table hints that may help or hinder the insertion. The table hints in Listing 3-1 are the same table hints you can use in a SELECT statement, except that READPAST, NOLOCK, and READUNCOMMITTED are not permitted. (Both READUNCOMMITTED and NOLOCK have the same meaning—locks are not created.) Typically, you would hardly ever use such table hints, but they do give you flexibility if you need it for those oddball cases that crop up on occasion.

Next in the syntax in Listing 3-1 comes the column list, separated by commas and surrounded with parentheses. List all of the columns that will be stated in the VALUES or SELECT clause. In the syntax diagram, the term derived_table is used, which is just a SELECT statement in this context. (Derived tables are explained in Chapter 2.)

If you use an EXEC statement, the columns you list will correspond to those returned by the SELECT inside the EXEC. (The EXEC statement is covered in detail in Chapter 9.) The column list can be omitted in some cases, such as when you use DEFAULT VALUES (discussed shortly in the "Using the INSERT DEFAULT VALUES Statement" section in this chapter). The column list can also be omitted when you have an exact match in the number, type, and position of the columns listed in the VALUES, SELECT, or EXEC portion of the INSERT statement.

Even though you are allowed to omit a column list, you should always have a column list, because tables and views sometimes get rebuilt and data originally intended for one column could end up in another. It is better to have your code fail during testing than to have it pump garbage into your production table.

There are some instances where you should not list a particular column inside your column list, nor should you provide data for it. One such case is the IDENTITY column, for which SQL Server will generate the value. (You can override this, however. This is explained further in Chapter 6.)

Another such case where you cannot specify a column inside your column list is the rowversion (or timestamp) column. Like the IDENTITY column, a rowversion is generated by SQL Server. Unlike the IDENTITY column, however, the rowversion column cannot be overridden. The rowversion column has nothing to do with time and is used in optimistic locking as a way of row versioning. (Optimistic locking is discussed in Chapter 15, and the rowversion datatype is covered in Chapter 6.)

Finally, no matter which version of the INSERT statement you use, if any row violates a constraint, the entire INSERT fails and is rolled back—not just the row that caused the violation. The only exception is where you have a unique index with the IGNORE_DUP_KEY option. In this case, those rows that violate the uniqueness requirement are ignored and are not inserted into the table, whereas those that do not violate uniqueness are inserted.

This covers the common parts of the INSERT statement. Now take a look at the INSERT DEFAULT VALUES version of the INSERT statement.

Using the INSERT DEFAULT VALUES Statement

The INSERT DEFAULT VALUES statement tells SQL Server to insert defaults for every column in the table. Typically, you do not specify a column list. The DEFAULT VALUES statement is handy when you want to generate some sample data quickly. Take a look at the example in Listing 3-2.

Listing 3-2: Example of an INSERT DEFAULT VALUES Statement

```
CREATE TABLE MyTable
(
  ID          int         NOT NULL
                          IDENTITY (1, 1),
  EntryDate   datetime    NOT NULL
                          DEFAULT (GETDATE ()),
  Description varchar (20) NULL
)
GO

INSERT MyTable DEFAULT VALUES
```

The code presents a table followed by an INSERT. Both of the NOT NULL columns have a default—ID will use a value generated by the IDENTITY property, while EntryDate can be populated by the declared default, GETDATE(). (The IDENTITY property is discussed in Chapter 6.) The Description column is NULLable, so it does not need a default—it will automatically be set to NULL if no value is specifically given.

Using the INSERT VALUES Statement

In its most basic form, the INSERT statement inserts a single row with values listed in the VALUES clause. For online transaction processing (OLTP) environments, this is how you will get data into your database. After your column list, you add the VALUES keyword, followed by the list of corresponding values, separated by commas and bounded by parentheses in the same manner as the column list. An example is presented in Listing 3-3. (Assume the ID column is not an IDENTITY column.)

Listing 3-3: Example of INSERT VALUES

```
INSERT Mytable
(
  ID,
  EntryDate,
  Description
)
VALUES
(
  43217,
  '2000/05/09',
  'Boeing 747'
)
```

The position in the column list of the INSERT clause corresponds to the position in the VALUES clause. For example, ID is assigned the value 43217 in Listing 3-3. Note also that you don't have to have hard-coded constants in the VALUES lists; you can use variables and functions, such as GETDATE(). (Variables are explained in detail in Chapter 7.) If the table gets rebuilt, and the columns of the table occur in a different order, the statement in Listing 3-3 will continue to work.

If you write this statement without a column list, the order will correspond to the physical order in the table itself. The same INSERT, without the column list, is shown in Listing 3-4.

Listing 3-4: Example of INSERT VALUES without a Column List

```
INSERT Mytable
VALUES
(
  43217,
  '2000/05/09',
  'Boeing 747'
)
```

In this case, if the table gets rebuilt with the columns in a different order, you will have type mismatches, and the statement will fail.

If you are an aficionado of ANSI-92 SQL, you may be aware of the option for inserting a number of rows with a single INSERT VALUES statement, as shown in Listing 3-5.

Listing 3-5: Inserting Multiple Rows with a Single INSERT VALUES Statement

```
INSERT MyTable
VALUES
(
  (43217, '2000/05/31', 'Boeing 747'),
  (90210, '1941/12/07', 'Curtiss P-40'),
  (41268, '1970/01/24', 'Concorde')
)
```

Unfortunately, this style of the INSERT VALUES statement is not yet supported in SQL Server.

Using the INSERT SELECT Statement

Using INSERT VALUES can get to be very time-consuming. It is also wasteful if the data are already stored in tables elsewhere, and all you have to do is form a query to get the data you want. The INSERT SELECT statement has been around since the early days of SQL and is presented in this section. The INSERT EXEC statement, however, is specific to Microsoft SQL Server, and you'll see that later in this chapter.

With the INSERT SELECT statement, instead of the VALUES keyword and a list of explicit values, you now have a SELECT statement. Although you can use a SELECT *, don't! You can end up with the same type mismatch problems as you can if you don't include a column list in your INSERT clause. An example of the safest way to do an INSERT SELECT statement is presented in Listing 3-6.

Listing 3-6: Example of an INSERT SELECT Statement

```
INSERT MyTable
(
  ID,
  EntryDate,
  Description
)
SELECT
  ID,
  GETDATE (),
  Description
FROM
  HisTable
WHERE
  ID BETWEEN 4500 AND 5000
GO
```

This example also shows that you do not necessarily have to use all of the columns in the source table. You can use a function, a constant, or a local variable in any column position. Indeed, some developers don't use the INSERT VALUES statement when inserting a single row; they use the INSERT SELECT and simply specify constants and omit the FROM clause. The SELECT can be as simple or as complicated as you want.

Leveraging Defaults

You have already seen how to insert a row into a table where every column uses its default value. Most of the time, you will want to specify values for some of the columns explicitly and let SQL Server handle defaults for those not supplied. For this to happen, the table must have defaults assigned to those columns (either through DEFAULT constraints or by binding to a default) or the columns must be NULLable. If either or both of those conditions exist, you can simply omit those columns from the column list as well as from the INSERT list. Alternatively, you can include those columns in the INSERT list and use the keyword DEFAULT as a placeholder in the VALUES list. As an example, check out the code in Listing 3-7.

Listing 3-7: Inserting Data into a Table with Defaults

```
CREATE TABLE MyTable
(
  RowNum   int      NOT NULL
                    PRIMARY KEY,
  Txt      char (5) NOT NULL
                    DEFAULT 'abc',
  TheDate datetime NOT NULL
                    DEFAULT getdate()
)
GO

INSERT MyTable (RowNum) VALUES (1)
INSERT MyTable (RowNum, Txt) VALUES (3, 'xyz')
INSERT MyTable (RowNum, Txt, TheDate) VALUES (5, 'ghi', '20001001')
INSERT MyTable (RowNum, Txt, TheDate) VALUES (7, DEFAULT, '20001101')
GO

INSERT MyTable
(
  RowNum
)
SELECT
  RowNum * 2
FROM
  MyTable
GO
```

In all cases in this example, you have to specify a value for RowNum, because there is no default. The first INSERT used implied defaults for Txt and TheDate by omitting any reference to those columns. The second INSERT uses a default only for TheDate, again by not referencing this column. The third INSERT uses no defaults because all columns are specified in the INSERT list and values for each column are supplied in the VALUES list. The fourth INSERT shows how to use the DEFAULT keyword for the INSERT VALUES statement. The final INSERT is an example of an INSERT SELECT that also uses implied defaults in the same manner as the INSERT VALUES statement.

Using the INSERT EXEC Statement

The INSERT EXEC statement is used to populate a table with the results of an EXEC statement. SQL developers often found the need to insert rows into a table from the execution of a stored procedure but did not have that capability until release 6.5.

Indeed, there was no way to receive rows from a remote SQL Server unless you did it by executing a remote stored procedure. The stored procedure does all the data massaging behind the scenes and then does a SELECT statement as its grand finale. It is this SELECT that provides you with the rows you will insert into the target table.

The downside is that you have to inspect the code of the stored procedure to determine which columns you will receive and the datatypes of those columns. As an example, if you want to capture the results of the system stored procedure sp_who into a local table, use the statement depicted in Listing 3-8.

Listing 3-8: Example of an INSERT EXEC Statement

```
CREATE TABLE MyTable
(
   spid      smallint,
   ecid      smallint,
   status    nchar (30),
   loginame nchar (128),
   hostname nchar (128),
   blk       char (5),
   dbname    nchar (128),
   cmd       nchar (16)
)
GO

INSERT MyTable
(
   spid,
   ecid,
   status,
   loginame,
   hostname,
   blk,
   dbname,
   cmd
)
EXEC sp_who
```

Using Remote Stored Procedures

A remote stored procedure is very similar to a local stored procedure, except that in a remote stored procedure you must specify the server on which you wish the procedure to be executed. Prior to release 7.0, there was no way to do a cross-server join. Transact-SQL developers faked this by using INSERT EXEC with a remote stored procedure to populate a local temporary table and then subsequently joining onto that. (Temporary tables are discussed in Chapter 12.) Nevertheless, it is still a way of populating a table based on a remote query.

Now recast the previous query, making it execute on the server Toronto. The solution is in Listing 3-9.

Listing 3-9: Example of an INSERT EXEC Statement on a Remote Server

```
INSERT MyTable
(
  spid,
  ecid,
  status,
  loginame,
  hostname,
  blk,
  dbname,
  cmd
)
EXEC Toronto.master..sp_who
```

The stored procedure is executed on the remote server and uses its resources. The procedure then sends its rows back to the local server where they are stored in the table stated in the INSERT.

> **NOTE** *You set up remote servers with the* sp_addlinkedserver *system stored procedure.*

Using Cross-Server and Cross-Database INSERTs

You are not limited to inserting into a table in your current database or even on your current server. Using the fully qualified name of the object in the INSERT statement, you are free to insert the rows anywhere you like, provided you have sufficient permissions. For example, if you are in the Northwind database of your local server, and you need to add rows in the NW2 database on the Hadera server, you can use the code in Listing 3-10.

Listing 3-10: Example of a Remote INSERT

```
INSERT Hadera.NW2.dbo.Orders
SELECT
  *
FROM
  Orders
```

Here, a SELECT * has been used, and the column list has been omitted for brevity.

Using the SELECT INTO Statement

The SELECT INTO statement is a SQL Server twist on creating a table and loading it all at the same time. The most common use of this feature is to create temporary tables, but you can also create permanent ones, with some restrictions. (You'll look at temporary tables in detail in Chapter 12.) The SELECT INTO statement is just like a regular SELECT statement, with the addition of an INTO clause where you put the name of the new table to be created. Because you are creating a table, you must have CREATE TABLE permission, either explicitly or through role membership. However, if you are creating a temporary table, you do not need such permission.

Up to and including release 7.0, the destination database had to turn on the option select into/bulk copy, which was done using sp_dboption. Without this, you could not execute the SELECT INTO statement in your database. (You didn't need to worry about this for temporary tables.) In SQL Server 2000, this requirement is now gone.

One consequence of the select into/bulk copy option in releases prior to SQL Server 2000 is that it allows the database to carry out unlogged operations as well as bulk loads. Unlogged operations are typically faster than logged ones, because there is little or no involvement in the transaction log. The downside is that you need to back up the entire database after any of these unlogged operations has occurred because you cannot make a transaction log backup after an unlogged operation until you do a full backup. Finally, unlogged operations such as SELECT INTO are mutually exclusive with backup operations—if one of these is running and the other one is started, the second one fails. All of these restrictions have been eliminated in SQL Server 2000.

> **NOTE** *The recovery model of the database determines the amount of logging. Both the simple- and bulk-logged recovery models permit certain unlogged transactions to occur. The recovery model is a feature new to SQL Server 2000.*

Before you go any further, take a look at the partial syntax diagram in Listing 3-11.

Listing 3-11: Partial Syntax for the SELECT INTO Statement

```
SELECT
  <column _list>
INTO
  <destination_table>
FROM
  <table_list>
WHERE
  <filter_conditions>
```

It looks pretty much like a regular SELECT, except for the INTO clause, doesn't it? Be sure to give any computed columns a unique name, because every column in a table must have a unique name. One restriction is that the SELECT must yield a relational result set. This means that you cannot use the COMPUTE clause. (The COMPUTE clause is discussed in Chapter 5.)

> **NOTE**   SELECT INTO *had its own set of locking issues before release 7.0. Locks on system tables, such as sysobjects, sysindexes, and syscolumns stayed in effect for the duration of the execution of the* SELECT INTO *statement. If there were many rows, you could be blocking other users who were attempting to do the same thing. The problem got more pronounced in tempdb, because all temporary objects are created there.*

SELECT INTO can be used to create a table, even if you don't immediately need any rows. Sure, you can do this using the standard CREATE TABLE statement, but you can also use SELECT INTO with a WHERE clause that has a false criterion. A sample is presented in Listing 3-12.

Listing 3-12: Using SELECT INTO to Create an Empty Table

```
SELECT
  OrderID,
  ProductID,
  Quantity
```

```
INTO
  OrderDetails
FROM
  [Order Details]
WHERE
  1 = 0
```

This statement executes quickly, and the result is that you have created a table with the same column names and datatypes as specified in the SELECT, but you have no data. This technique is often used to copy a table layout into another table. This would be a legitimate use of SELECT *, because you are copying all columns to make an identical copy. NULLability is also copied. Bear in mind that you do not copy constraints or indexes into the new table. You will have to build these afterward.

What if you are building a table that has a column you want to populate in the future, but you have no data now? For example, say you have an inventory of items and you want a NULLable DateSold column? You want to put a datetime in there, and it has to be NULL until the item is sold. In that case, you can use the CONVERT() function to convert NULL into the datatype that you want. You just have to ensure that you give the new column a name. The sample code in Listing 3-13 shows you how.

Listing 3-13: Creating a NULLable Column Using SELECT INTO

```
SELECT
  ItemID,
  ItemType,
  CAST (NULL AS datetime) AS DateSold
INTO
  NewInventory
FROM
  Inventory
WHERE
  ItemID >= 11000
```

Obviously, if you want your column to be NOT NULL, then you will have to convert an appropriate default value other than NULL.

The SELECT INTO statement can be a handy tool when used wisely, but if (for some reason) you are still using version 6.5, avoid using this statement to load a table in an online environment. You can use SELECT INTO to create an empty table or during conversions or migrations. Be aware of backup issues, because a SELECT INTO is not logged in versions of SQL Server prior to version 2000.

The Bulk Copy Program—bcp

While this is a book on advanced Transact-SQL, this chapter is about getting data into tables. The next section deals with BULK INSERT, a Transact-SQL statement introduced in version 7.0. The BULK INSERT statement is the child of the bulk copy program (bcp).

bcp is a command line program that takes a flat file and loads the rows directly into a table or view. Alternatively, you can use it to extract rows from a table, view, or ad hoc query and copy them into a file. The ad hoc query feature did not exist until release 7.0. You need INSERT permission on a table to load it and SELECT permission to extract to a file. You also need to set the database option select into/ bulk copy in order to allow bcp to load tables in your database in releases of SQL Server prior to version 2000.

Using the BULK INSERT Statement

The BULK INSERT statement was introduced with SQL Server 7.0. It is essentially a Transact-SQL version of the bulk copy program (bcp) but on steroids—the performance has been optimized over that of bcp, making it easier for you to load tables in your database without having to switch back and forth between SQL and bcp. Only the sa login or those logins who are members of the sysadmin or bulkadmin fixed server roles can execute this statement. (The bulkadmin role was added in SQL Server 2000.)

Unlike bcp, BULK INSERT can only load rows into a table, not extract them to a file. The syntax in Listing 3-14 shows many of the BULK INSERT attributes.

Listing 3-14: Syntax for the BULK INSERT Statement

```
BULK INSERT [['database_name'.]['owner'].]{'table_name' FROM data_file}
[WITH
(
[ BATCHSIZE [= batch_size]]
[[,] CHECK_CONSTRAINTS]
[[,] CODEPAGE [= 'ACP' | 'OEM' | 'RAW' | 'code_page']]
[[,] DATAFILETYPE [=
{'char' | 'native'| 'widechar' | 'widenative'}]]
[[,] FIELDTERMINATOR [= 'field_terminator']]
[[,] FIRSTROW [= first_row]]
[[,] FIRETRIGGERS]
[[,] FORMATFILE [= 'format_file_path']]
[[,] KEEPIDENTITY]
[[,] KEEPNULLS]
```

```
[[,] KILOBYTES_PER_BATCH [= kilobytes_per_batch]]
[[,] LASTROW [= last_row]]
[[,] MAXERRORS [= max_errors]]
[[,] ORDER ({column [ASC | DESC]} [,...n])]
[[,] ROWS_PER_BATCH [= rows_per_batch]]
[[,] ROWTERMINATOR [= 'row_terminator']]
[[,] TABLOCK]
)
]
```

The file to which the statement refers is in the context of the server on which the statement is executed. In other words, if the statement uses the D: drive, BULK INSERT will refer to the D: drive of the server, *not* the D: drive of your workstation. That confuses many people. Also, if you are using files that are on other servers, use the full UNC name of the file, not a drive letter. The file name is limited to between 1 and 255 characters.

You do not need to use most of the options that are in Listing 3-14. All you need are those items listed before the WITH keyword: the table or view name (qualified, if necessary) and the file name. All of the BULK INSERT options and their equivalent bcp options are discussed in the following sections.

BATCHSIZE

This option determines the number of rows in a batch. Each batch is committed as a single transaction. By default, the entire file is treated in a single batch. This is equivalent to the -b option in bcp.

CHECK_CONSTRAINTS

Normally, constraints are not checked during a BULK INSERT, except PRIMARY KEY and UNIQUE constraints. This option enables you to turn on constraint checking during the load, at the cost of decreased speed. This is equivalent to the -h"CHECK_CONSTRAINTS" option in bcp.

CODEPAGE

This option specifies the code page of the data in the input file and is relevant only if you have character data—char, varchar, or text—where the character values are less than 32 or greater than 127. This is equivalent to the -C option in bcp. There are three general code page options (ACP, OEM, and RAW) and one specific code page option, which are described in the following sections.

ACP

This option converts char, varchar, or text columns from the ANSI/Microsoft code page, ISO 1252, to the SQL Server code page.

OEM

This is the default. Here, char, varchar, or text columns are converted from the system OEM page to the SQL Server code page.

RAW

This is the fastest option because no conversion takes place.

Specific Page Number

In this case, you simply provide a code page number, such as 850.

DATAFILETYPE

SQL Server is not limited to plain text files. You can specify four different data file types (char, native, widechar, and widenative), as described in the following sections.

Char

This is the default. Here, the data are in plain text. The field terminator is a tab (\t), while the row terminator is a linefeed (\n). This option enables you to take plain text files from any source. You are not using any Unicode characters in this case. This is equivalent to the -c option in bcp.

Native

This type allows you to import data files that were previously extracted from SQL Server. They are in binary form and take up less disk space than the equivalent plain text file. SQL Server does not have to do any fancy conversion, and this option is quite fast. You are not using any Unicode characters in this case. Native format is the fastest of the four DATAFILETYPE options. This is equivalent to the -n option in bcp.

Widechar

This is the same as the char option discussed previously, except that you are using Unicode characters. (Unicode is discussed in Chapter 6.) Because you are using Unicode, however, this option is used for SQL Server to SQL Server transfers. This is equivalent to the -w option in bcp.

Widenative

This is the same as the native option discussed previously, except that you are using Unicode characters for all character and text columns. This is equivalent to the -N option in bcp.

FIELDTERMINATOR

This option allows you to determine the field terminator to be used for char and widechar data files. By default, it is the tab character (\t). This is equivalent to the -t option in bcp.

FIRETRIGGERS

By default, insert triggers are not fired during a bulk insert operation. The FIRETRIGGERS option overrides this behavior. This is equivalent to the -h"FIRE_TRIGGERS" option in bcp.

FIRSTROW

This specifies the first row from the file to insert. The default is 1. In the event that a BULK INSERT or bcp fails, you can pick up where you left off by specifying this parameter. This is equivalent to -F in bcp.

FORMATFILE

If a format file is being used, it must be specified with the FORMATFILE option. You must provide the full path name of the file, and this file must contain the responses from a previous usage of bcp. This is equivalent to -f in bcp.

KEEPIDENTITY

This option can be ignored if you do not have an IDENTITY column in your table. If you do have an IDENTITY column, this option enables you to override the values SQL Server would normally generate for you and use the ones actually contained in the file. If the input file does not have a column for the IDENTITY, you will need a format file to tell SQL Server to skip the IDENTITY column in the load. This is equivalent to -E in bcp.

KEEPNULLS

This option is used when you have NULLs in the file and you want to retain them instead of letting SQL Server provide default values. These defaults come from DEFAULT constraints or from binding a column or datatype to a user-defined default object. This is equivalent to -k in bcp.

KILOBYTES_PER_BATCH

This specifies the approximate number of kilobytes in a single batch. This is unknown by default. This is equivalent to -h "KILOBYTES_PER_BATCH" in bcp.

LAST_ROW

This specifies the last row from the file to insert. The default is 0, which means "go to end of file." This is equivalent to -L in bcp.

MAXERRORS

This specifies the maximum number of errors you can tolerate before the statement will fail. The default is 10. This is equivalent to -m in bcp.

ORDER

This determines the sort order of the input file. Performance is improved if the data are sorted on the same columns as the clustered index. The option is ignored if there is no clustered index or the data are not in the correct order. By default, BULK INSERT assumes the data are unsorted. This is equivalent to -h"ORDER (...)" in bcp.

ROWS_PER_BATCH

In the event that BATCHSIZE is not specified, then all of the rows are processed in a single transaction. In this case, the server uses ROWS_PER_BATCH to optimize the bulk load. This is equivalent to -h"ROWS_PER_BATCH" in bcp.

ROWTERMINATOR

This option enables you to determine the row terminator to be used for char and widechar data files. By default, it is the newline character (\r). This is equivalent to the -r option in bcp.

TABLOCK

BULK INSERT is already very fast, potentially loading thousands of rows per second. You can accelerate this even more by lowering the amount of locking with the TABLOCK option. This overrides the table option table lock on bulk load. Even though this is referred to as a table lock, it's actually a Bulk Update (BU) lock—you can do parallel loads into the same table (using BULK INSERT, bcp, or a combination), provided the table has no indexes. This is equivalent to the -h"TABLOCK" hint in bcp.

As an example of using BULK INSERT, consider a tab-delimited file containing aircraft types. You could load your AircraftTypes table as shown in Listing 3-15.

Listing 3-15: Using BULK INSERT to Load a Table

```
CREATE TABLE AircraftTypes
(
  TypeID          int            NOT NULL
                                 PRIMARY KEY,
  ManufacturerID int            NOT NULL
                                 REFERENCES Manufacturer (ManufacturerID),
  TypeName        char (20)      NOT NULL,
  GrossWeight     numeric (10,1) NOT NULL
)
GO

BULK INSERT AircraftTypes
 FROM 'C:\Temp\AircraftTypes.txt'
 WITH
  (CHECK_CONSTRAINTS)
GO
```

The default field delimiter is the tab character, so you do not have to specify the FIELDTERMINATOR option. This example uses the CHECK_CONSTRAINTS option to ensure that the FOREIGN KEY constraint is fired for each row.

Loading Data

Thus far, you have seen the tactical level of adding rows to tables. It's time to apply this knowledge strategically. If you have been involved in upgrades to systems or conversions from one system to another, then you are familiar with the issues involved in moving legacy data to the new database. Often, the reason for building a new system is that the old one was poorly designed. Sometimes, you just want to populate a database with representative data to try out a few ideas. This section will build upon some of the ideas you have seen earlier in this chapter, as well as in Chapter 1.

Normalizing Data

Very often, the source of bad designs is denormalization. For example, your legacy system could have repeating groups, which violates First Normal Form. Your assignment, should you choose to accept it, is to normalize the legacy data as it is added into the new system. To do this, you need to identify a candidate key and split off each member of the repeating group as an individual row in a table. The remainder of the original row will now occupy a row in its own table.

As a practical example, consider the table depicted in Listing 3-16.

Listing 3-16: Denormalized Legacy Table

```
CREATE TABLE Legacy
(
  CustomerID    int           NOT NULL
                              PRIMARY KEY,
  CustomerName varchar (30) NOT NULL,
  HomePhone     char (10)    NULL,
  WorkPhone     char (10)    NULL,
  CellPhone     char (10)    NULL,
  FaxPhone      char (10)    NULL
)
```

The Legacy table has four phone numbers, constituting a repeating group. This can be normalized into two tables: one for the basic customer information and one for telephone information. This is done in Listing 3-17.

Listing 3-17: Normalized Tables

```
CREATE TABLE Customers
(
 CustomerID  int           NOT NULL
                           PRIMARY KEY,
 CustomerName varchar (30) NOT NULL,
)
GO

CREATE TABLE Phones
(
  CustomerID int        NOT NULL
                        REFERENCES Customers (CustomerID),
  Type       char (1)   NOT NULL
                        CHECK (Type IN ('H', 'W', 'C', 'F')),
  Phone      char (10)  NOT NULL,
                        PRIMARY KEY (CustomerID, Type)
)
```

You add the Type column to distinguish between the different phones for each customer. The primary key is now CustomerID and Type. Notice that the Phone column is now NOT NULL, instead of NULL. This is because a row will not be added unless there is actually data for that CustomerID and Type.

This looks great, but how do you populate the new tables? Because of referential integrity, you need to add rows to the Customers table before adding rows to the Phones table. This will require a single INSERT SELECT from the Legacy table into the Customers table, as shown in Listing 3-18.

Listing 3-18: Populating the Customers Table

```
INSERT Customers
(
  CustomerID,
  CustomerName
)
SELECT
  CustomerID,
  CustomerName
FROM
  Legacy
```

You are now ready to populate the Phones table. Because the Legacy table is denormalized, you have to make one pass for each of the phone numbers in the original Legacy table. You only want those phone numbers that are NOT NULL. The solution is presented in Listing 3-19.

Listing 3-19: Populating the Phones Table

```
INSERT Phones
(
  CustomerID,
  Type,
  Phone
)
SELECT
  CustomerID,
  'H',
  HomePhone
FROM
  Legacy
WHERE
  HomePhone IS NOT NULL
GO

INSERT Phones
(
  CustomerID,
  Type,
  Phone
)
SELECT
  CustomerID,
  'W',
  WorkPhone
FROM
  Legacy
WHERE
  WorkPhone IS NOT NULL
GO

INSERT Phones
(
  CustomerID,
  Type,
  Phone
)
```

```
SELECT
  CustomerID,
  'C',
  CellPhone
FROM
  Legacy
WHERE
  CellPhone IS NOT NULL
GO

INSERT Phones
(
  CustomerID,
  Type,
  Phone
)
SELECT
  CustomerID,
  'F',
  FaxPhone
FROM
  Legacy
WHERE
  FaxPhone IS NOT NULL
GO
```

Before leaving this problem, you should know that a single SELECT can populate the Phones table, but it is done in a sneaky way. The INSERT SELECT will work for any SELECT that produces a relational result set. This also includes SELECT statements that have UNION or UNION ALL clauses. The four INSERT SELECT statements in Listing 3-19 can now be merged into a single INSERT that does a SELECT with UNION ALL, as shown in Listing 3-20.

Listing 3-20: Populating the Phones Table with a UNION ALL

```
INSERT Phones
(
  CustomerID,
  Type,
  Phone
)
```

```
SELECT
  CustomerID,
  'H',
  HomePhone
FROM
  Legacy
WHERE
  HomePhone IS NOT NULL
UNION ALL
SELECT
  CustomerID,
  'W',
  WorkPhone
FROM
  Legacy
WHERE
  WorkPhone IS NOT NULL
UNION ALL
SELECT
  CustomerID,
  'C',
  CellPhone
FROM
  Legacy
WHERE
  CellPhone IS NOT NULL
UNION ALL
SELECT
  CustomerID,
  'F',
  FaxPhone
FROM
  Legacy
WHERE
  FaxPhone IS NOT NULL
GO
```

This monster is treated as a single INSERT statement with all the baggage that goes with it. Locks are kept for the duration of the entire INSERT. You may even run out of memory or transaction log space if you are dealing with billions of rows. You would normally be doing this during a conversion when your users are not connected to the system, so there really is no need to use the UNION ALL. Breaking this down into separate INSERT statements will reduce the overhead required to service the query.

Generating Test Data

You can generate data to populate your tables by using CROSS JOINs. This entails building and populating subtables and then cross joining these tables to insert the rows into the destination table.

As an example, say you want to populate a Products table. Each product will have a ProductID as its primary key, and the attributes will be ItemSize, Color, Price, and Description. To produce rows that will give you all possible combinations of size, color, price, and description, you first need to create and populate a table for each of these attributes. This is demonstrated in Listing 3-21.

Listing 3-21: The Product Attribute Tables

```
CREATE TABLE Colors
(
  Color char (10) NOT NULL
                  PRIMARY KEY
)
GO


INSERT Colors VALUES ('Black')
INSERT Colors VALUES ('White')
INSERT Colors VALUES ('Green')
INSERT Colors VALUES ('Red')
GO


CREATE TABLE Descriptions
(
  Description char (25) NOT NULL
                        PRIMARY KEY
)
GO


INSERT Descriptions VALUES ('Widget')
INSERT Descriptions VALUES ('Dohickey')
INSERT Descriptions VALUES ('Whatchamacallit')
INSERT Descriptions VALUES ('Doflingy')
INSERT Descriptions VALUES ('Gizmo')
GO
```

```
CREATE TABLE Prices
(
  Price money NOT NULL
             PRIMARY KEY
)
GO


INSERT Prices VALUES (2.50)
INSERT Prices VALUES (3.50)
INSERT Prices VALUES (4.50)
INSERT Prices VALUES (5.50)
INSERT Prices VALUES (6.50)
INSERT Prices VALUES (7.50)
GO


CREATE TABLE ItemSizes
(
  ItemSize char (20) NOT NULL
                     PRIMARY KEY
)
GO


INSERT ItemSizes VALUES ('Small')
INSERT ItemSizes VALUES ('Medium')
INSERT ItemSizes VALUES ('Large')
GO
```

Now you can put it all together. Once you create your Products table, just CROSS JOIN the tables shown in Listing 3-21 through an INSERT and you're done. Check out the code in Listing 3-22.

Listing 3-22: Populating the Products Table with a CROSS JOIN

```
CREATE TABLE Products
(
  ProductID   int       NOT NULL
                        IDENTITY (1, 1)
                        PRIMARY KEY,
  Color       char (10) NOT NULL,
  Description char (25) NOT NULL,
  Price       money     NOT NULL,
  ItemSize    char (20) NOT NULL
)
GO
```

```
INSERT Products
(
  Color,
  Description,
  Price,
  ItemSize
)
SELECT
  C.Color,
  D.Description,
  P.Price,
  S.ItemSize
FROM
    Colors        C
  CROSS JOIN
    Descriptions D
  CROSS JOIN
    Prices        P
  CROSS JOIN
    ItemSizes    S
GO
```

In this example, IDENTITY() automatically generates a number for the ProductID column (although it has other purposes, as described in Chapter 6). Now your Products table is populated, and you can drop the individual attribute tables.

Beyond just inserting data into tables, you can determine the distribution of the data. A good tool to use to control this is the *modulo* (%) operator. This gives you the remainder of an integer division. For example, 10 % 3 gives you 1, because 10 divided by 3 is 3, with a remainder of 1. One interesting side effect of this is that the numbers you get as a result of A % B range from 0 to $(B-1)$. Therefore, (A % B) + 1 gives you a number between 1 and B.

You can leverage this feature of the modulo operator when you are trying to calculate the quantity of a product for a row in an order details table. This way, you can control the range of values for the quantity. For example, suppose you need to have the quantity range from 1 to 10. The solution is presented in Listing 3-23. (You can assume that the Products and Orders tables already exist.)

Listing 3-23: Using the Modulo Operator and a CROSS JOIN to Populate a Table

```
CREATE TABLE OrderDetails
(
  OrderID   int NOT NULL,
  ProductID int NOT NULL,
  Quantity  int NOT NULL
)
GO

INSERT OrderDetails
(
  OrderID,
  ProductID,
  Quantity
)
SELECT
  O.OrderID,
  P.ProductID,
  (O.OrderID * P.ProductID) % 10 + 1
FROM
    Orders  O
  CROSS JOIN
    Products P
```

That was a great way to get a range of quantities. However, this also requires that every order has every product, which is not very realistic. It would be better to vary the actual products ordered. In a viable business, you have far more orders than you have products. Therefore, the maximum OrderID is greater than the maximum ProductID. Consequently, if you take (OrderID % MAX(ProductID)) + 1, then you can get a number between 1 and the maximum ProductID. This gives you a starting point for the ProductID in a given order.

The next job is to find an upper limit on ProductID. Clearly, this number must be greater than or equal to the lower limit you just calculated. Also, you want to vary the number of different products within an order. Here, you can use the same trick as you did to calculate the quantity. In this case, you can just use (OrderID % 10) + 1 to get a value between 1 and 10. All you have to do is add this to the lower limit.

You're probably asking yourself, "Why all this talk about lower and upper limits? I'm using a CROSS JOIN." Well, not any more. The upper and lower limits are for the ProductID for each OrderID. This then gives you JOIN criteria to limit the products in each order. Check out the final solution in Listing 3-24.

Listing 3-24: Using the Modulo Operator and a JOIN to Populate a Table

```
DECLARE
  @ProductCount int

SELECT
  @ProductCount = MAX (ProductID)
FROM
    Products

INSERT OrderDetails
(
  OrderID,
  ProductID,
  Quantity
)
SELECT
  O.OrderID,
  P.ProductID,
  (O.OrderID * P.ProductID) % 10 + 1
FROM
    Orders  O
  JOIN
    Products P ON  P.ProductID BETWEEN ((O.OrderID % @ProductCount) + 1)
              AND ((O.OrderID % @ProductCount) + 2
                  + O.OrderID % 10)
```

Although variables are discussed in detail in Chapter 6, you can see that a variable—@ProductCount—is being used to store the maximum ProductID in the Products table. It is then used as the divisor in the modulo calculations as part of the JOIN criteria. The result is that each order has between 1 and 10 different products. Also, the specific products ordered vary from order to order.

SQL Puzzle 3-1: Populating the Customers Table

You've seen how to fill an order details table based upon OrderID and ProductID, while at the same time calculating the Quantity column as well as the number of rows for each order. This was done using the modulo operator (%). This time, you need to create the Customers table and generate data to fill it. The Customers table is as follows:

```
CREATE TABLE Customers
(
  CustomerID int       NOT NULL
                       IDENTITY (1, 1)
                       PRIMARY KEY,
  FirstName  char (25) NOT NULL,
  LastName   char (30) NOT NULL,
  Number     int       NOT NULL,
  Street     char (50) NOT NULL,
  City       char (30) NOT NULL,
  Province   char (2)  NOT NULL
)
GO
```

You want enough variability in the addresses so that your customers do not all live at the same address. Therefore, you will need to come up with a different building number for every customer located on the same street.

The answer to this puzzle can be found on pages 681–684.

CHAPTER 4

Other Data
Manipulation Issues

THIS CHAPTER UNVEILS some of the greatest features of SQL. A few of these are the result of SQL Server's support for the ANSI-92 SQL standard. Others are specific to SQL Server. After reading this chapter, you will be able to take advantage of the CASE expression to build pivot tables in a single SELECT; roll your own sort order or do updates without the need for temporary tables; use TOP n queries; master logical operations and bitwise manipulation; and handle dates in any way, shape, or form.

Taking advantage of these tools can speed up your queries, minimize the code you have to create, and decrease your development cycle. They can also make the difference between your query executing safely or raising an error and halting in its tracks. In many cases, you can eliminate the need for temporary tables altogether.

Leveraging CASE Expressions

The CASE expression allows for conditional processing with a query. It is the secret behind generating pivot tables, which are discussed in the "Creating Pivot Tables" section of this chapter. The CASE expression is part of the ANSI-92 standard and was implemented by SQL Server in release 6.0. It allows you to have several different values based upon various conditions. It frees you from having to create temporary tables and perform multiple passes for each set of conditions. It can be used in SELECT, INSERT, UPDATE, or DELETE statements. It can also be used inside function calls, aggregates, and the like. There are two different syntaxes for the CASE statement—*simple* and *searched*.

Using the Simple CASE Expression

In the simple CASE expression, you can test one particular expression and compare it against a series of different expressions or values, as shown in Listing 4-1.

Listing 4-1: Syntax for the Simple CASE Expression

```
SELECT
  CASE <expression>
    WHEN <expression1a> THEN <expression1b>
    WHEN <expression2a> THEN <expression2b>
    ...
    ELSE ValueN
  END
FROM
    Table1
```

> **NOTE** *If you do not have an* ELSE *clause, and you have no "hits" in your* WHEN *clauses, the result returned will be* NULL. *If you are doing this as an* INSERT ... SELECT *into a table that does not allow* NULLs, *the transaction will be rolled back. It is usually a good idea to have an* ELSE *clause.*

As you saw in earlier chapters, NULL is not equal to anything, including NULL. When you use a simple CASE statement, you will not get a "hit" if either the expression immediately following the CASE keyword is NULL or the one you are comparing it to in the WHEN expression is NULL.

Have a go at some example code that uses the Northwind database. Suppose Tokyo Traders (supplier ID 4) calls you and says that due to their manufacturing costs going up, they have to increase the price of the units they ship to you. These increases depend upon the category of the merchandise being shipped. The hikes will be 10 percent, 20 percent, and 25 percent for categories 6, 7, and 8, respectively. You need a report of the old and new prices, based upon the same percentage increase in each category. Using the CASE statement, it can be done in a single SELECT without having to create a temporary table. See the solution in Listing 4-2.

Listing 4-2: Example of a Simple CASE Expression

```
SELECT
  ProductID,
  ProductName,
  CategoryID,
  UnitPrice AS 'Old Price',
  UnitPrice *
```

```
    CASE CategoryID
      WHEN 6 THEN 1.10
      WHEN 7 THEN 1.20
      WHEN 8 THEN 1.25
      ELSE       1.00
    END     AS 'New Price'
FROM
    Products
WHERE
    SupplierID = 4
```

Because only those products that fall into categories 6, 7, and 8 are going to be increased in price, you need an ELSE clause to handle those products that do not fall into those categories.

Using the Searched CASE Expression

You've just seen the simple CASE expression. The other form of the CASE statement—the searched CASE expression—has a Boolean expression for each WHEN clause. Check out the syntax in Listing 4-3.

Listing 4-3: Syntax for the Searched CASE Expression

```
SELECT
  CASE
    WHEN <expression1a> THEN <expression1b>
    WHEN <expression2a> THEN <expression2b>
    ...
    ELSE ValueN
  END
FROM
    Table1
```

The behavior of the CASE expression in SQL is similar to the Select statement in Visual Basic. If a comparison is TRUE, the THEN expression is returned and the test goes no further. If it's FALSE, it continues down the chain of WHENs until it gets a hit or it finds the ELSE clause.

As an example, say you want to get a report of the number of orders placed by each customer, together with a star rating based upon the number of orders. This is easily done with a searched CASE expression, and the code in Listing 4-4 shows how to do it.

Listing 4-4: Example of a Searched CASE Expression

```
SELECT
  CustomerID,
  COUNT (*) AS 'Orders',
  CASE
    WHEN COUNT (*) BETWEEN  1 AND 10 THEN '*'
    WHEN COUNT (*) BETWEEN 11 AND 20 THEN '**'
    WHEN COUNT (*) BETWEEN 21 AND 30 THEN '***'
    ELSE '****'
  END       AS 'Rating'
FROM
    Orders
GROUP BY
  CustomerID
```

Note that there is an ELSE clause in the CASE statement so that you do not get any NULL values.

There is nothing stopping you from having nested CASE statements—in fact, they can make code quite readable. But before you do this, be sure to read the following tip.

> **TIP** *Code the template for your* CASE *expression first and then fill in the rest of your code. In other words, write out the* CASE *and* END *keywords first, insert some* WHEN/THENs *and always finish up with the* ELSE. *Now, put in the expressions. You will find that you avoid unbalanced* CASE/ENDs *this way—especially if you have nested* CASEs. *In SQL Server 2000, you can create a template for laying out your* CASE *statements.*

Determining Your Own Sort Order

The more you work with SQL, the more you find how much power it has. If you make the assumption that you *can* do something in SQL, then you're probably right. You just have to find out how.

Picking your own sort order is just one of the cool things you can do with the CASE expression. To pick a sort order, place the CASE expression inside the ORDER BY clause.

As an example, take a situation where you want to sort your customers based on the North American Free Trade Agreement (NAFTA). NAFTA includes the nations of Canada, USA, and Mexico, from north to south. Suppose you want to see customers from these countries in that order first, and the remaining countries of the world in alphabetical order. You also want to sort by region within country. Sounds impossible, right?

You can use char(1), char(2), and char(3) for Canada, USA, and Mexico, respectively, and use the actual country names for the rest of the countries to determine the sort order. Listing 4-5 shows the code.

Listing 4-5: Using a CASE Expression in an ORDER BY Clause

```
SELECT
  *
FROM
   Customers
ORDER BY
  CASE Country
    WHEN 'Canada' THEN char (1)
    WHEN 'USA'    THEN char (2)
    WHEN 'Mexico' THEN char (3)
    ELSE Country
  END,
  Region
```

This code takes advantage of the fact that char(1) through char(3) will be sorted ahead of the alphabetical characters.

However, the preceding code can produce unpredictable outcomes if you pick non-default sort orders and code pages when you install SQL Server. The code in Listing 4-6 lets you essentially sort on your own NAFTA region before you sort on country.

Listing 4-6: Using a CASE Expression in an ORDER BY Clause (Alternative)

```
SELECT
  *
FROM
  Customers
ORDER BY
  CASE Country
    WHEN 'Canada' THEN 1
    WHEN 'USA'    THEN 2
    WHEN 'Mexico' THEN 3
    ELSE             4
  END,    -- Dummy NAFTA Region
  Country,
  Region
```

Even though you don't display the dummy region, it is used in the ORDER BY clause to control the sort.

Creating Updates with the CASE Expression

The CASE expression is not limited to only SELECT statements. It can be used in all data modification statements. Returning to the price-hike example presented in Listing 4-2, suppose you are now told to put the price increase into effect immediately. The UPDATE statement is implemented in Listing 4-7.

Listing 4-7: UPDATE Using a CASE Expression

```
UPDATE Products
SET
  UnitPrice = UnitPrice *
    CASE CategoryID
      WHEN 6 THEN 1.10
      WHEN 7 THEN 1.20
      WHEN 8 THEN 1.25
      ELSE        1.00
    END
WHERE
    SupplierID = 4
```

Creating Pivot Tables

Now that you are an expert in the use of the CASE expression, we will show you how to make it sing. Quite often, developers are asked to create *pivot tables*, otherwise known as *cross-tabs*. (Many cries for help in the Usenet newsgroups concern pivot tables.) These are tables where the columns are based on rows and vice-versa, and where there is a column or group of columns that is used as a key. The remaining columns represent a value of an input column or columns.

Without the CASE expression, the coding is quite ugly and involves temporary tables with multiple passes. In an OLTP environment, the speed penalty can be unacceptable.

As mentioned previously, you can use the CASE statement inside any function—including aggregate functions, such as SUM(), COUNT(), AVG(), and so on. You can leverage this power to create pivot tables in single SELECT statements with no temporary tables.

Using the Northwind database, you can get a cross-tab of unit sales (quantities) of meat and seafood sold, broken down by customer. The meat category is 6 and the seafood category is 8. Take a look at the solution in Listing 4-8.

Listing 4-8: Example of a Pivot Table Query

```
SELECT
  O.CustomerID,
  SUM (CASE WHEN P.CategoryID = 6
            THEN OD.Quantity
            ELSE 0 END)  AS MeatUnits,
  SUM (CASE WHEN P.CategoryID = 8
            THEN OD.Quantity
            ELSE 0 END)  AS SeafoodUnits
FROM
    Orders        AS O
  JOIN
    [Order Details] AS OD ON OD.OrderID  = O.OrderID
  JOIN
    Products      AS P  ON P.ProductID = OD.ProductID
WHERE
    P.CategoryID   IN (6, 8)  -- Meat, Seafood
GROUP BY
  O.CustomerID
ORDER BY
  O.CustomerID
```

Note that in each sum there is a CASE expression. The CASE expression tests the category of the product and then adds the quantity to the sum if it is TRUE, or adds 0 if it is not. In other words, only if the product belongs to the appropriate category will it be included in the sum.

The calculations are significant. Summing only the quantity gives the number of units sold, as you just saw in Listing 4-8. Summing quantity × price gives total sales, as the fragment shown in Listing 4-9 demonstrates.

Listing 4-9: Finding the Total Sales

```
SUM (CASE WHEN P.CategoryID = 6
          THEN OD.Quantity * P.UnitPrice
          ELSE 0 END)  AS MeatSales
```

Summing the number 1 gives the number of individual Order Detail items, as shown in the code fragment in Listing 4-10.

Listing 4-10: Finding the Number of Items

```
SUM (CASE WHEN P.CategoryID = 6
        THEN 1
        ELSE 0 END)  AS MeatItems
```

If you want the number of *orders* where meat was ordered—regardless of the number of individual meat *items* in the order—you can use the CASE expression inside a COUNT(DISTINCT). Listing 4-11 shows the individual column from the SELECT list.

Listing 4-11: Finding the Distinct Meat Orders

```
COUNT (DISTINCT
      CASE WHEN P.CategoryID = 6
          THEN O.OrderID
          ELSE NULL END)  AS MeatOrders
```

So, how does this work? The COUNT(DISTINCT) function throws away NULLs. The CASE expression tests CategoryID and produces OrderID if it is to be included or NULL if it is not. Because of the possibility of multiple meat items in the query, the DISTINCT keyword then reduces the count to the number of orders.

From the Trenches

A banking application required many daily cross-tab reports. One such report originally used ten stored procedures and took quite some time execute. However, a new program was able to replace the original code for that report with a single SELECT that executed in under one second.

Creating TOP Queries

The TOP clause addition to the SELECT statement was introduced with SQL Server 7.0. It enables you to limit the number of rows in the result set. TOP is a non-ANSI-compliant extension to T-SQL, as it doesn't conform to the relational model. It is, however, an answer to many practical problems that programmers often face.

Using the TOP n Option

The TOP n option enables you to specify the number of rows by which you want to limit your result set. To control the order of the rows that will be returned, you must specify the ORDER BY clause, because the optimizer builds a plan that is cost-based. Otherwise, the optimizer might consider a few different access paths, each of which might result in a different order of the rows in the output, and it would use the one with the lowest cost.

Listing 4-12 shows a query that uses the TOP n option to return only six rows from the sales table in the pubs sample database. The results are shown in Table 4-1.

Listing 4-12: TOP n Query

```
SELECT TOP 6
  *
FROM
  sales
```

Table 4-1: TOP 6 Query Result

stor_id	ord_num	ord_date	qty	payterms	title_id
6380	6871	1994-09-14	5	Net 60	BU1032
6380	722a	1994-09-13	3	Net 60	PS2091
7066	A2976	1993-05-24	50	Net 30	PC8888
7066	QA7442.3	1994-09-13	75	ON invoice	PS2091
7067	D4482	1994-09-14	10	Net 60	PS2091
7067	P2121	1992-06-15	40	Net 30	TC3218

Notice that there is no specific order to the rows in the output. If you use the ORDER BY clause, your output becomes meaningful. The values of the columns in the ORDER BY clause determine which rows will be returned. Using an ascending order means, "Bring me the first *n* rows with the lowest values." Using a descending order means, "Bring me the first *n* rows with the highest values." For example, if you want to return the first six rows with the highest quantities, you can write the query in Listing 4-13 to obtain the results shown in Table 4-2.

Listing 4-13: TOP n Query with ORDER BY

```
SELECT TOP 6
  *
FROM
  sales
ORDER BY
  qty DESC
```

Table 4-2: Result of TOP 6 Query with ORDER BY

stor_id	ord_num	ord_date	qty	payterms	title_id
7066	QA7442.3	1994-09-13	75	ON invoice	PS2091
7066	A2976	1993-05-24	50	Net 30	PC8888
7067	P2121	1992-06-15	40	Net 30	TC3218
7896	X999	1993-02-21	35	ON invoice	BU2075
8042	QA879.1	1993-05-22	30	Net 30	PC1035
7131	N914014	1994-09-14	25	Net 30	MC3021

Using the WITH TIES Option

Take another look at Listing 4-13. Can you really guarantee that the output includes the six rows with the highest quantities and that you will always get the same output, assuming that the data in the table doesn't change?

Suppose this query was requested by the WOCAQ (We Only Care About Quantities) organization, and they gave a large bonus to the authors of the six top-selling titles. A week after the bonuses were already delivered to the authors of the titles in your list, WOCAQ's headquarters receives four angry calls. Can you guess who called and which books caused the problem? (Hint: Start by looking at the whole sales table.)

Obviously, the problem had to do with the fact that there were titles that were sold in the same quantity as the last one in your list—25. To find out which titles are missing from the list, you need to request to return all the rows that have the same quantities as the last row in the result, even though this means that you get more than six rows in the output.

The WITH TIES option does exactly what you need. It is relevant only if you have an ORDER BY clause in your query. The rows that follow the last row in the original result are compared with the last row in the result, and if they have the same values in the columns that participate in the ORDER BY clause, they are returned. As soon as there is no match, no more rows are returned. Listing 4-14 shows how to use the WITH TIES option.

Listing 4-14: TOP n WITH TIES Query

```
SELECT TOP 6 WITH TIES
  *
FROM
  sales
ORDER BY
  qty DESC
```

Table 4-3 shows the results of this query.

Table 4-3: TOP 6 WITH TIES Query Result

stor_id	ord_num	ord_date	qty	payterms	title_id
7066	QA7442.3	1994-09-13	75	ON invoice	PS2091
7066	A2976	1993-05-24	50	Net 30	PC8888
7067	P2121	1992-06-15	40	Net 30	TC3218
7896	X999	1993-02-21	35	ON invoice	BU2075
8042	QA879.1	1993-05-22	30	Net 30	PC1035
8042	P723	1993-03-11	25	Net 30	BU1111
7131	N914014	1994-09-14	25	Net 30	MC3021
7131	P3087a	1993-05-29	25	Net 60	PS2106
7131	P3087a	1993-05-29	25	Net 60	PS7777

Comparing the result in Table 4-3 to the previous one in Table 4-2, you now see that the title IDs BU1111, PS2106, and PS7777 have been added. You can now run the query shown in Listing 4-15 to determine the titles and authors' names.

Listing 4-15: Authors Who Did Not Get a Bonus

```
SELECT
  au_lname,
  au_fname,
  S.title_id,
  title
FROM
    sales      AS S
  JOIN
    titleauthor AS TA ON S.title_id  = TA.title_id
  JOIN
    authors    AS A  ON TA.au_id     = A.au_id
  JOIN
    titles     AS T  ON TA.title_id = T.title_id
WHERE
  S.title_id IN ('BU1111', 'PS2106', 'PS7777')
```

Table 4-4 shows the results of this query.

Table 4-4: Authors Who Did Not Get a Bonus

au_lname	au_fname	S.title_id	title
O'Leary	Michael	BU1111	Cooking with Computers: Surreptitious Balance Sheets
MacFeather	Stearns	BU1111	Cooking with Computers: Surreptitious Balance Sheets
Ringer	Albert	PS2106	Life without Fear
Locksley	Charlene	PS7777	Emotional Security: A New Algorithm

Using the TOP n PERCENT Option

The TOP n PERCENT option is very similar to the TOP n option except that it returns a percentage of rows from the total number of rows in the table, rounded up, instead of returning a fixed number of rows. For example, if you run TOP 10 PERCENT on the sales table, you get three rows in the output. Ten percent of the total of 21 rows is 2.1, rounded up to 3, as the query in Listing 4-16 shows.

Listing 4-16: TOP 10 PERCENT Query

```
SELECT TOP 10 PERCENT
   *
FROM
   sales
ORDER BY
   qty DESC
```

Table 4-5 shows the results of this query.

Table 4-5: TOP 10 PERCENT Query Result

stor_id	ord_num	ord_date	qty	payterms	title_id
7066	QA7442.3	1994-09-13	75	ON invoice	PS2091
7066	A2976	1993-05-24	50	Net 30	PC8888
7067	P2121	1992-06-15	40	Net 30	TC3218

Using the SET ROWCOUNT Option

The SET ROWCOUNT option is a *session* option, as opposed to TOP, which is a *query* option. SET ROWCOUNT determines the number of rows affected by a statement, after which SQL Server stops processing the statement, be it a SELECT statement or any other statement (such as an INSERT inside a trigger). This option was available prior to SQL Server 7.0. You can turn it on as shown in Listing 4-17.

Listing 4-17: Syntax for SET ROWCOUNT

```
SET ROWCOUNT n
```

If *n* is greater than 0, then the number of rows returned is limited to a maximum of *n*. It remains in effect until you set it to another value. If you set it to 0, as shown in Listing 4-18, then the row limit is removed.

Listing 4-18: Resetting ROWCOUNT

```
SET ROWCOUNT 0
```

For example, the script shown in Listing 4-19 returns a similar output to the query in Listing 4-13 from in the TOP n section. Table 4-6 has the results.

Listing 4-19: Using the SET ROWCOUNT Option

```
SET ROWCOUNT 6

SELECT
  *
FROM
  sales
ORDER BY
  qty DESC

SET ROWCOUNT 0
```

Table 4-6: Result of Using the SET ROWCOUNT Option

stor_id	ord_num	ord_date	qty	payterms	title_id
7066	QA7442.3	1994-09-13	75	ON invoice	PS2091
7066	A2976	1993-05-24	50	Net 30	PC8888
7067	P2121	1992-06-15	40	Net 30	TC3218
7896	X999	1993-02-21	35	ON invoice	BU2075
8042	QA879.1	1993-05-22	30	Net 30	PC1035
8042	P723	1993-03-11	25	Net 30	BU1111

Note that the Books Online of SQL Server 7.0 with SP2 incorrectly specifies the following difference between TOP n with an ORDER BY and using SET ROWCOUNT and a query with an ORDER BY:

> "The SET ROWCOUNT limit applies to building the rows in the result set before an ORDER BY is evaluated. Even if ORDER BY is specified, the SELECT statement is terminated when n rows have been selected. n rows are selected, then ordered and returned to the client."

However, from the last example and from other tests, it is apparent that the ORDER BY is applied first. The Books Online of SQL Server 2000 corrects this mistake.

Using Logical Expressions and Bitwise Operations

Logical and bitwise operators do not have a lot in common. The main similarity between them is probably their names (the AND logical operator and the AND (&) bitwise operator, for example). But still, we decided to discuss them in the same chapter. (How many times have you given more attention to a person—or even started to talk with someone—for no other reason than that he or she has the same name as yours?)

Using Logical Expressions

Logical expressions are expressions that use a combination of comparison operators (=, >, <, >=, <=, <>, !=, !>, !<) and/or logical operators (AND, NOT, OR, IS NULL, IS NOT NULL, ALL, ANY, SOME, IN, BETWEEN, EXISTS, LIKE) and result in TRUE, FALSE, or UNKNOWN. A single expression is usually referred to as a *simple expression*, and a combination of simple expressions using one of the logical operators—AND or OR—is usually referred to as a *complex expression*. Some of these logical operators, or predicates, are discussed in other chapters, mainly in Chapter 2. This section will focus on the others.

Logical expressions can be used in a WHERE clause, HAVING clause, join condition, IF statements, WHILE statements, and CASE expressions. T-SQL does not allow you to store the result of a logical expression in a column or a variable, as some 3GLs (third generation languages), such as C/C++, allow. For example, the code shown in Listing 4-20 is not legal in T-SQL.

Listing 4-20: Illegal Use of Expression

```
SELECT
  col1,
  col2,
  (col1 = col2) AS equale
FROM
  T1
```

You can, however, use an expression, be it simple or complex, in a SELECT statement, as Listing 4-21 shows.

Listing 4-21: Use Logical Expressions in a SELECT Statement

```
SELECT
  <select_column_list>
FROM
    T1
  JOIN
    T2 ON <logical_expression>
WHERE
  <logical_expression>
GROUP BY
  <group_by_column_list>
HAVING
  <logical_expression>
ORDER BY
  <order_by_column_list>
```

Listing 4-22 shows how to use expressions in an IF statement. (IF statements are covered in Chapter 7.)

Listing 4-22: Use of a Logical Expression in an IF Statement

```
IF <logical_expression>
  <statement or statement_block>
```

Listing 4-23 shows how to use expressions in a WHILE statement. (The WHILE statement is covered in Chapter 7.)

Listing 4-23: Use of a Logical Expression in a WHILE Statement

```
WHILE <logical_expression>
  <statement or statement_block>
```

Listing 4-24 shows how to use expressions in a CASE expression. (The CASE expression was covered earlier in this chapter.)

Listing 4-24: Use of Logical Expressions in a CASE Query

```
CASE
  WHEN <logical_expression1> THEN value1
  WHEN <logical_expression2> THEN value2
  ...
  ELSE valuen
END
```

The next few sections will cover the logical operators AND, OR, NOT, IS NULL, and IS NOT NULL, which are not discussed in other chapters in any more detail. If you've programmed in any development environment, you're probably familiar with the functionality of the basic logical operators: AND, OR, and NOT. However, SQL in general, and T-SQL specifically, has its own issues concerning logical operators, such as three-valued-logic, short circuits, and handling NULLs.

"And Then There Were THREE..."

In some development environments other than T-SQL, the result of a logical expression can be either TRUE or FALSE. T-SQL uses NULLs to express an unknown or an irrelevant value. When there is an unknown value as one of the arguments in a logical expression using the AND or NOT operators, the result is also unknown.

When there is an unknown value as one of the arguments in a logical expression using the OR operator, the result is unknown only if the *second* argument is FALSE or unknown. If one of the arguments is TRUE, the result is always TRUE. The participating unknown value can be either an explicit NULL, as in Listing 4-25, or it can be a result of a logical expression, as in Listing 4-26.

Listing 4-25: Using an Expression with an Explicit Unknown Value

```
IF 1 = NULL
  PRINT 'TRUE'
ELSE
  PRINT 'FALSE or UNKNOWN'
```

Listing 4-26: Using an Expression with an Unknown Value Returned from One of the Participating Simple Logical Expressions

```
IF (1 = 1) AND (1 > NULL)
  PRINT 'TRUE'
ELSE
  PRINT 'FALSE or UNKNOWN'
```

When you use logical expressions in a WHERE clause, HAVING clause, join condition, IF statement, WHILE statement, or CASE expression, only logical expressions that return TRUE qualify to be processed, executed, or to return values (where relevant). Logical expressions that return either FALSE or UNKNOWN do not. For this reason, it is very important to be aware of the possible return values, based on the arguments in the logical expression. Think of the table of arguments and return values as a truth table. Now prepare to explore the truth tables for the operators AND, OR, and NOT.

"AND Then There Were Three…"

Table 4-7 shows the truth table for complex logical expressions using the AND operator.

Table 4-7: AND Truth Table

AND	true	false	unknown
True	True	False	Unknown
False	False	False	False
Unknown	Unknown	False	Unknown

Only when you AND a TRUE with a TRUE do you get a TRUE as a result.

"(To Be) OR (Not to Be)"

Table 4-8 shows the truth table for complex logical expressions using the OR operator.

Table 4-8: OR Truth Table

OR	true	false	unknown
True	True	True	True
False	True	False	Unknown
Unknown	True	Unknown	Unknown

As long as at least one of the two values is TRUE, you get TRUE as the result.

"NOT (to Be)"

Table 4-9 shows the truth table for simple logical expressions using the NOT operator.

Table 4-9: NOT Truth Table

	NOT
True	False
False	True
Unknown	Unknown

Is It Nothing or Is It Something?

NULLs have been the source of many troubles, but on the other hand, they solve many others. For example, say a certain employee's salary is not yet entered in the database because she's a new hire and her contract is not yet finalized. Would it be wise to enter a 0 in her salary column? Probably not. Storing a 0 as her salary would render inaccurate queries if you calculate the average salary of each department. This is one example where the use of NULLs is advisable.

Suppose that you want to query the Personnel table for all of the employees that have missing values in the salary column. A common mistake for beginners in the SQL world is to issue the query presented in Listing 4-27.

Listing 4-27: The Wrong Way to Look for NULLs

```
SELECT
  *
FROM
  Personnel
WHERE
  salary = NULL
```

However, a NULL is not equal to another NULL, as ANSI defines it, because both sides hold unknown or irrelevant values, and one unknown value most likely is not equal to another unknown value. So, it is safer to say that the result is UNKNOWN than to say that it is either TRUE or FALSE. For this reason, Query Analyzer sets a session option that causes any equality expression with a NULL value to return UNKNOWN. In fact, any simple logical expression having at least one NULL as an argument results in an unknown value. This is the way the ANSI SQL-92 standard defines it. You can change this behavior, but note that it is not advisable. To control whether a comparison between two NULLs returns UNKNOWN as ANSI defines it, or TRUE, you can use the following options:

- Server wide: Set the user_options server configuration option by using the sp_configure system stored procedure (see sp_configure in the Books Online for details).

- Database wide: Set the ANSI nulls database option using the ALTER DATABASE command.

- Session wide: Set the ANSI_NULLS session option to either ON or OFF using the SET statement.

These options enable you to control the way two NULLs compare using the equal sign, but it's important to note that if you decide to use the non-ANSI behavior with NULL comparisons, you are asking for trouble. You'd be better off leaving your system with the ANSI behavior, and using the IS NULL or IS NOT NULL operators instead of using regular comparison operators when dealing with NULLs. The latter two operators are "safe" in the sense that they are not affected by your current session's configuration regarding comparisons with NULLs. For example, you can rewrite the previous query (Listing 4-27) as shown in Listing 4-28.

Listing 4-28: The Right Way to Look for NULLs

```
SELECT
  *
FROM
  Personnel
WHERE
  salary IS NULL
```

If you want to return all employees that do not have NULLs in the salary column, simply change it to the query shown in Listing 4-29.

Listing 4-29: The Right Way to Look for Non-NULLs

```
SELECT
  *
FROM
  Personnel
WHERE
  salary IS NOT NULL
```

Table 4-10 shows the truth table for IS NULL and IS NOT NULL.

Table 4-10: Truth Table for IS NULL and IS NOT NULL

IS NULL	Evaluates to	IS NOT NULL	Evaluates to
known-value	False	known-value	True
NULL	True	NULL	False

Short Circuit

Some 3GLs, such as the C language, have a very nice feature referred to as *short circuit*, which aborts any further processing of a logical expression as soon as its result can be determined. This can be better explained with an example. Consider the complex expression shown in Listing 4-30.

Listing 4-30: Short Circuit Using the AND Operator

```
(1 = 0) AND (1 = 1)
```

The expression is evaluated from left to right. In systems where short circuit is supported, the second simple expression (1 = 1) is not evaluated at all, as the first one (1 = 0) is FALSE and there is no way that the whole expression would evaluate to TRUE. This, of course, improves performance, but it also has other implications.

Consider the complex expression shown in Listing 4-31.

Listing 4-31: Short Circuit and Divide by Zero Using the AND Operator

```
IF (0 <> 0) AND (1/0 > 0)
  PRINT 'Greater Than 0'
```

In a system that supports short circuits, the second simple expression (1/0 > 0) is not evaluated at all if the first one is FALSE, as in this example. This way, no runtime error, such as "divide by zero" is returned.

The same applies to using the OR operator, as presented in Listing 4-32.

Listing 4-32: Short Circuit and Divide by Zero Using the OR Operator

```
IF (1 > 0) OR (1/0 > 0)
  PRINT 'Greater Than 0'
```

Here, you can tell from the first simple expression (1 > 0) that the whole expression evaluates to TRUE, so there's no need to continue processing it.

Now try a more practical example. Consider the T1 table created and populated by the script shown in Listing 4-33.

Listing 4-33: Schema Creation Script for the T1 Table

```
CREATE TABLE T1(
col1 int NOT NULL,
col2 int NOT NULL)

INSERT INTO T1 VALUES(1, 1)
INSERT INTO T1 VALUES(1, 0)
INSERT INTO T1 VALUES(-1, 1)
```

Suppose you want to return all the rows from T1 where the result of col1 / col2 is greater than 0 (zero). The query shown in Listing 4-34 results in a "divide by zero" error.

Listing 4-34: All Rows From T1, Where col1 / col2 is Greater than Zero—First Try

```
SELECT
  *
FROM
  T1
WHERE
    (col1 / col2 > 0)
```

If you rewrite the query as shown in Listing 4-35, it runs successfully, returning one row.

> **NOTE** *When you test the following queries you might get different results. This point will be explained shortly.*

Listing 4-35: All Rows from T1, Where col1 / col2 is Greater than Zero—Second Try

```
SELECT
  *
FROM
  T1
WHERE
    (col2 <> 0)
  AND
    (col1 / col2 > 0)
```

Listing 4-36 has the SHOWPLAN output.

Listing 4-36: Showplan Output for All Rows From T1, Where col1 / col2 is Greater than Zero—Second Try

```
|--Table Scan(OBJECT:([testdb].[dbo].[T1]),
            WHERE:([T1].[col2]<>0 AND [T1].[col1]/[T1].[col2]>0))
```

If you rewrite the query as you see in Listing 4-37, flipping the simple expressions, it might still run successfully, returning one row.

Listing 4-37: All Rows from T1, Where col1 / col2 is Greater than Zero—Third Try

```
SELECT
  *
FROM
  T1
WHERE
    (col1 / col2 > 0)
  AND
    (col2 <> 0)
```

Listing 4-38 has the SHOWPLAN output.

Listing 4-38: Showplan Output for All Rows From T1, Where col1 / col2 is Greater than Zero—Third Try

```
|--Table Scan(OBJECT:([testdb].[dbo].[T1]),
            WHERE:([T1].[col2]<>0 AND [T1].[col1]/[T1].[col2]>0))
```

If you examine the execution plan of both queries, you will see that the optimizer used the same complex expression for both of them, regardless of how you specified it. This query would have failed if short circuit were not supported in SQL Server. There are two issues to consider, though. First, SQL Server will short circuit an expression if the expression evaluates to either TRUE or FALSE. Second—and here's the catch—you can't tell the optimizer to use the expression that you wrote as is. It might revise your expression in the plan that it builds. You've seen that it revised the logical expression in the first example—it flipped the order of the simple expressions—and the result was that a query that should have failed didn't. You have no guarantee that it won't do the opposite. This certainly puts a damper on any plans you have to count on this feature.

If you want to guarantee a certain order of processing in your expression, you can do so using a CASE expression. Check out Listing 4-39.

Listing 4-39: All Rows from T1, Where col1 / col2 is Greater than Zero—Fourth Try

```
SELECT
  *
FROM
  T1
WHERE
  CASE
    WHEN col2 = 0        THEN 0
    WHEN col1 / col2 > 0 THEN 1
    ELSE 0
  END = 1
```

No confusion here. :-)

Using Bitwise Operations

Bitwise operations perform a bit-wise operation. And now for something completely serious: *bitwise operations* perform operations on bits. If you're familiar with electronics, these are the very same logical gates: binary AND (&), OR (|), and XOR (^), and the unary NOT(~). *Binary bitwise operators* (&, |, ^) operate on two bits and return a result bit according to the truth table defined for them. *Unary operators*—or, in our case, *operator*—operate on one bit and return a result bit according to the truth table defined for them.

SQL Server supplies the datatype bit, in which you can store a single bit. You can use it to represent "flag" values such as TRUE/FALSE, yes/no, etc. However, if you have lots of values of this nature to store, you can end up with a lot of columns in your table, and a lot of parameters in your stored procedures or user-defined functions that manipulate them. (Stored procedures and user-defined functions are covered in Chapters 9 and 11, respectively.) Furthermore, SQL Server 7 didn't allow you to create an index on a bit column, and this was one of the reasons to store flags in integer columns instead of storing them in bit columns. SQL Server 2000 allows you to create indexes on bit columns.

For the reasons mentioned, you might prefer to store several flag values in a single binary or integer column. In fact, SQL Server itself stores a lot of flag values in various columns in system tables. For example, the status column in the *sysindexes* system table is an integer column that stores information about the index characteristics in several bits (bit 2 on = unique index, bit 4 on = clustered index, etc.). To manipulate such values, you can use bitwise operators.

Bitwise Operators' Validity

Before continuing, you should be aware that the bitwise operators don't accept all combinations of argument datatypes. Tables 4-11 and 4-12 list the datatype combinations accepted by the bitwise operations.

Table 4-11: Bitwise AND (&), OR (|), XOR (^) Validity Table

&/|/^	int	binary	bit	NULL
int	valid	valid	valid	NULL
binary	valid	error	valid	error
bit	valid	valid	valid	NULL
NULL	NULL	error	NULL	NULL

int stands for any of the following integer datatypes: `tinyint`, `smallint`, `int`, and `bigint`

Table 4-12: Bitwise NOT (~) Validity Table

Datatype	~
int	valid
binary	error
bit	valid
NULL	NULL

int stands for any of the following integer datatypes: `tinyint`, `smallint`, `int`, and `bigint`)

Notice that as surprising as it might seem, the binary bitwise operators (&, |, and ^) do not allow both arguments to be of a `binary` datatype, and the unary bitwise operator (~) does not allow its single argument to be of a `binary` datatype. To overcome this problem, you need to cast an argument to a datatype that will result in one of the valid combinations of arguments in the two validity tables.

Before delving into the meaning of the bitwise operators, consider the following example. Suppose that you want to perform a bitwise AND (&) between two binary values. (Note that the binary values in the following query are represented in hex base; four binary bits are represented by one hex digit; a pair of hex digits make a byte.) Listing 4-40 demonstrates an illegal bitwise operation.

Listing 4-40: Illegal Bitwise Operation

```
SELECT
    0x00000001
  &
    0x00000001
```

Consulting the validity tables, you can see that a bitwise AND (&) cannot be performed between two `binary` datatypes. It can, however, be performed between a `binary` datatype and an `int` datatype, so you can cast one of the arguments to an `int` datatype, as you can see in Listing 4-41.

Listing 4-41: Legal Bitwise Operation

```
SELECT
    CAST(0x00000001 AS int)
  &
    0x00000001
```

This might be a limitation in some situations. For example, you can't perform a bitwise operation between two binaries, where one of them is larger than eight bytes (which is the largest integer to which it can be cast), without truncating some of its data. This problem is tackled in Chapter 11, where you will see user-defined functions.

> **NOTE** *You might find it surprising that there's no support for bitwise operations between two binary values; rather, one of them has to be of an integer datatype. The reason for this is probably that the designers included support for bitwise operations to manipulate strings of bits stored in integer columns instead of in many bit columns. As soon as support for bitwise operations was added to the product, programmers wanted to use it for other purposes...of course!*

Bit Values According to Their Position

Integer numbers are stored as a series of bits (1s or 0s). An `int` datatype, for example, consumes 4 bytes, which is equivalent to 32 bits. One of the bits is used as the *sign bit* to indicate whether the value in it is negative or positive, and all of the other bits represent a value, which is $2^{(\text{bit\_number}-1)}$. The actual integer value that is stored in an `int` column or variable is the sum of all of the values represented by the 31 value bits, with the sign indicated by the sign bit.

When you just want to store numbers that represent quantities, you don't have much use for this knowledge. However, it will be important to know when you manipulate a series of flags stored in a single column or variable. To make your life easier, you can consult Table 4-13 when you need to manipulate a certain bit in an int datatype.

Table 4-13: Bit Values According to Their Position

Bit Number	Bit Value
1	1
2	2
3	4
4	8
5	16
6	32
7	64
8	128
9	256
10	512
11	1,024
12	2,048
13	4,096
14	8,192
15	16,384
16	32,768
17	65,536
18	131,072
19	262,144
20	524,288
21	1,048,576
22	2,097,152
23	4,194,304
24	8,388,608

Table 4-13: Bit Values According to Their Position (Continued)

Bit Number	Bit Value
25	16,777,216
26	33,554,432
27	67,108,864
28	134,217,728
29	268,435,456
30	536,870,912
31	1,073,741,824

Bitwise AND (&)

The bitwise AND (&) operator is commonly used in T-SQL. It returns 1 only when both of its arguments are 1, and 0 in all other cases. (This is on a bit-by-bit basis.) It is often used to verify whether a certain flag bit "hiding" in an integer or a binary column is 1 or 0 (turned on or off). This is known as *bit masking*. Table 4-14 shows the truth table for the bitwise AND (&) operator.

Table 4-14: Bitwise AND (&) Truth Table

&	0	1
0	0	0
1	0	1

To understand how the bitwise AND (&) operator helps you find out if a certain bit is turned on, consider the string of bits "10101010". To find out if the first bit (from the right) is turned on, you AND it with the number 1, which represents the first bit, as Listing 4-42 demonstrates.

Listing 4-42: Finding Out if the First Bit Is Turned On, Behind the Scenes

```
  10101010 -- 170
&
  00000001 -- 1
  --------
  00000000 -- 0
```

Notice that the result is different from 1, so you don't have a match. To find out if the second bit is turned on, you AND it with the number 2, which represents the second bit, as Listing 4-43 shows:

Listing 4-43: Finding Out if the Second Bit Is Turned On, Behind the Scenes

```
  10101010 -- 170
&
  00000010 -- 2
  --------
  00000010 -- 2
```

The same query is presented in T-SQL in Listing 4-44.

Listing 4-44: Finding Out if the Second Bit is Turned On, Using T-SQL

```
SELECT
  170 & 2
```

The result is 2, meaning that you have a match. You could continue ANDing with 4 for the third bit, 8 for the fourth, and so on.

Next, you'll embed a bitwise AND operation in a query. For example, suppose you want to provide the properties of the indexes stored in the *sysindexes* table. You need to decipher the status column of each index according to the following bit values:

- 2 (bit 2) = Unique index

- 16 (bit 5) = Clustered index

- 2048 (bit 12) = Index used to enforce PRIMARY KEY constraint

- 4096 (bit 13) = Index used to enforce UNIQUE constraint

You can now issue the query shown in Listing 4-45.

Listing 4-45: Retrieving Index Properties by Using the Bitwise AND (&) Operator

```
SELECT
  object_name([id]) AS table_name,
  [indid] AS index_id,
  [name] as index_name,
  status,
  CASE
    WHEN status & 2 = 2 THEN 'Yes'
    ELSE 'No'
  END AS is_unique,
  CASE
    WHEN status & 16 = 16 THEN 'Yes'
    ELSE 'No'
  END AS is_clustered,
  CASE
    WHEN status & 2048 = 2048 THEN 'Yes'
    ELSE 'No'
  END AS is_PK_CNS,
  CASE
    WHEN status & 4096 = 4096 THEN 'Yes'
    ELSE 'No'
  END AS is_UNQ_CNS
FROM
  sysindexes
WHERE
  indid BETWEEN 1 AND 254 -- clustered and nonclustered indexes
ORDER BY
  table_name,
  index_id
```

> **NOTE** *The system tables can change from release to release.*

Bitwise OR (|)

The bitwise OR operator returns 1 if either of its arguments is 1. This, too, is on a bit-by-bit basis. It returns 0 only if both arguments are 0. Take a look at its truth table, shown in Table 4-15.

Table 4-15: Bitwise OR (|) Truth Table

|	0	1
0	0	1
1	1	1

The bitwise OR (|) operator is mainly used to form a string of flag bits to be stored in a variable or column. For example, suppose you want to create a bit string with bits 1, 2, 3, and 4 turned on. You can achieve that by ORing values that the bits represent—1, 2, 4, and 8 respectively—as you can see in Listing 4-46.

Listing 4-46: Combining Multiple Flags Using the Bitwise OR Operator, Behind the Scenes

```
  00000001 -- 1
|
  00000010 -- 2
|
  00000100 -- 4
|
  00001000 -- 8
  --------
  00001111 -- 1+2+4+8 = 15
```

You can also do this in T-SQL, as shown in Listing 4-47.

Listing 4-47: Combining Multiple Flags Using the Bitwise OR Operator, in T-SQL

```
SELECT
  1 | 2 | 4 | 8
```

Bitwise Exclusive Or (^)

The bitwise XOR (^) operator is probably less commonly used in T-SQL than the other bitwise operators. It returns 1 if the arguments are different—1 ^ 0 or 0 ^ 1.

Again, this is done on a bit-by-bit basis. It returns 0 if both of its arguments are the same—0 ^ 0 or 1 ^ 1. Table 4-16 shows the bitwise XOR truth table.

Table 4-16: Bitwise XOR (^) Truth Table

^	0	1
0	0	1
1	1	0

There are two common uses for the bitwise XOR (^) operator in computing environments in general (not necessarily in T-SQL): simple encryption using a key and storing parity information. Both uses rely on the fact that the result of a bitwise XOR operation is reversible, as opposed to the result of a bitwise AND or a bitwise OR operation.

For example, if A ^ B = C, you can always deduce that A ^ C = B and also B ^ C = A. This is also true for multiple bitwise XOR operations—if A ^ B ^ C = D, you can always deduce that A ^ B ^ D = C, and so on.

With bitwise AND and bitwise OR, you can't regenerate an argument if you only have the result and the other argument. For example, if A & B = C, you can neither deduce that A & C = B, nor that B & C = A.

Consider the two integer arguments 3 and 5 and the result of the bitwise operations between them. Table 4-17 shows the arguments as integer values and also the bit representation of the last byte of the integers.

Table 4-17: Table of Arguments for Bitwise Operations

Argument	Integer	Binary (last byte)
arg1	3	00000011
arg2	5	00000101

Table 4-18 shows the result of the bitwise operations AND (&), OR (|), and XOR (^) between the two arguments.

Table 4-18: Result = arg1 (value 3) <bitwise operator> arg2 (value 5)

Argument	Integer	Binary (last byte)
AND (&)	1	00000001
OR (|)	7	00000111
XOR (^)	6	00000110

Now, suppose you "lost" arg2 (value 5) and you want to reconstruct it from the existing arg1 (value 3) and the result shown in Table 4-18. Only a bitwise XOR operation between the available argument and the result will render the missing argument. Take a look at Table 4-19.

Table 4-19: arg1 (value 3) < bitwise operator> Result

Argument	Integer	Binary (last byte)
AND (&)	1	00000001
OR (|)	7	00000111
XOR (^)	5	00000101

The same applies to trying to reconstruct arg1 (value 3) from the result and the available arg2 (value 5), as Table 4-20 shows.

Table 4-20: arg2 (value 5) < bitwise operator> Result

Argument	Integer	Binary (last byte)
AND (&)	1	00000001
OR (|)	7	00000111
XOR (^)	3	00000011

With this background, the uses of the bitwise XOR can now be discussed.

Encrypting Using Bitwise XOR

One of the most basic ways to *encrypt* data is by XORing it with an encryption key. Suppose you have a piece of data that you want to encrypt—for this discussion, call it *A*. You generate an encryption key—call it *B*. At this point, you and your client store this key in a safe place. You encrypt your data by XORing it with the encryption key—A ^ B = C. You deliver *C* to your client, who in turn performs the same operation between the piece of data they received (*C*) and the encryption key (*B*). The result is the original source data—*A*.

Using this encryption method is simple, but you should be aware that it is useless if two of the arguments are available to an unauthorized third party. If you have access to the source data (*A*) and the encrypted data (*C*), you can always calculate the encryption key (*B*) by XORing *A* and *C*.

Suppose you do not expose the encryption key but you do supply the function f(), where f(A) = C, which accepts an argument and returns its encrypted form by

XORing it with the encryption key. Those who have access to the function can always deduce the encryption key by supplying it their own source data (*A*)—
`f(A) = C, A ^ C = B.`

So, if you have any plans to encrypt your data by XORing it with an encryption key, make sure that the key is stored in a safe place and that only authorized applications can use the encryption function.

Storing Parity Information Using Bitwise XOR

You can use the bitwise XOR operator to store "safety check" information along with your data and later use it to see if your data was corrupted. You can also use *parity information* to regenerate corrupted data.

To understand how parity information is used as a safety check, suppose you have a few pieces of data—*A*, *B*, *C*, and *D*—and you want to deliver them from point 1 to point 2. You generate the parity information—call it *E*—by performing a bitwise XOR operation between all the pieces of data you want to deliver—`A ^ B ^ C ^ D = E`. You deliver the parity information along with the data to the target application.

The target application, in turn, performs the same bitwise XOR operation on the data pieces it receives. If the result is equal to the parity information it received (*E*), it is some assurance that the data was not corrupted. This is not 100 percent reliable, as data corruption might have occurred in more than one piece of data, resulting in the same parity. However, if the parity information calculated from the received data is different than the parity information delivered along with the data, the target application can be sure that data corruption occurred and can request that the data be resubmitted from the source application.

To understand how parity information can be used to reconstruct corrupt data, consider the previous example, using *A*, *B*, *C*, and *D* as the pieces of data and *E* as the parity information. If one of the pieces of data was corrupted—let's say *B*—and you know which piece of data it was, you can always construct it from the available pieces of data and the parity—`A ^ C ^ D ^ E = B`.

Bitwise NOT (~)

The bitwise NOT operator simply flips bits, turning 1 to 0 and 0 to 1. Table 4-21 shows the truth table for bitwise NOT (~).

Table 4-21: Bitwise NOT (~) Truth Table

Value	~
0	1
1	0

Operator Precedence

Expressions can get quite complex as you add more and more criteria. You can fairly quickly get to a point where it's hard to decipher your own code. Consider the query shown in Listing 4-48.

Listing 4-48: Use of a Complex Expression in the WHERE Clause—First Try

```
SELECT
  *
FROM
  Orders
WHERE
    CustomerID IN ('VINET', 'TOMSP', 'HANAR')
  AND
    EmployeeID = 3
  OR
    EmployeeID = 4
  AND
    ShipVia = 3
```

First of all, it is essential to know the system's operator precedence to figure out the order in which an expression will be evaluated. Operators with higher precedence are evaluated first, and operators with the same precedence are simply evaluated from left to right. Table 4-22 shows the operator precedence.

Table 4-22: Operator Precedence

Precedence	Operator(s)
1	() (parentheses)
2	+ (Positive), – (Negative), ~ (Bitwise NOT)
3	* (Multiply), / (Divide), % (Modulo)
4	+ (Add), (+ Concatenate), – (Subtract)
5	=, >, <, >=, <=, <>, !=, !>, !< (Comparison operators)
6	^ (Bitwise XOR), & (Bitwise AND), | (Bitwise OR)
7	NOT
8	AND
9	ALL, ANY, BETWEEN, IN, LIKE, OR, SOME
10	= (Assignment)

You can indent the complex logical expression in a way that will represent its order of evaluation, as Listing 4-49 demonstrates.

Listing 4-49: Use of a Complex Expression in the WHERE Clause—Second Try

```
SELECT
  *
FROM
  Orders
WHERE
      CustomerID IN ('VINET', 'TOMSP', 'HANAR')
    AND
      EmployeeID = 3
  OR
      EmployeeID = 4
    AND
      ShipVia = 3
```

Now the query is readable! The query returns orders that were made by employee 3 for customers VINET, TOMSP, HANAR and also will return orders that were made by employee 4 and were shipped by shipper 3. Is this what you really wanted to return? Maybe your intention was to return orders that were made by employees 3 or 4 for customers VINET, TOMSP, HANAR, which were shipped by shipper 3.

The bottom line is that you should use parentheses, as they have the highest precedence, and indent your expressions properly to avoid confusion. An unambiguous version of a query that returns orders that were made by employees 3 or 4 for customers VINET, TOMSP, HANAR, which were shipped by shipper 3, is presented in Listing 4-50.

Listing 4-50: Use of a Complex Expression in the WHERE Clause—Third Try

```
SELECT
  *
FROM
  Orders
WHERE
    (
      CustomerID IN ('VINET', 'TOMSP', 'HANAR')
    AND
      (
        EmployeeID = 3
```

```
   OR
       EmployeeID = 4
     )
   )
 AND
   ShipVia = 3
```

Displaying Leading Zeroes

You will often have a need for leading zeroes when you present numerical data. Your first impulse may be to do some row-by-row processing, fiddling with individual bytes. However, there's a Transact-SQL solution that makes this unnecessary.

In such a case, you use the STR() and REPLACE() functions. The STR() function, as the name implies, takes a number and converts it to a string. You can control the number of digits in the result, together with the number of digits after the decimal. Add 1 to the total number of digits to get the final length of the string—this accounts for the decimal place. The final result is padded with leading blanks where needed. The syntax is presented in Listing 4-51.

Listing 4-51: Syntax for the STR() Function

```
STR (float_expression[, length[, decimal]])
```

The REPLACE() function picks up where the STR() function left off. This function inspects a character string and replaces a given character sequence with another given character sequence. You can use this to convert the leading blanks to leading zeroes. See the syntax in Listing 4-52.

Listing 4-52: Syntax for the REPLACE() Function

```
REPLACE ('string_expression1', 'string_expression2', 'string_expression3')
```

The REPLACE() function searches string_expression1 for occurrences of string_expression2 and replaces each with string_expression3.

Now, all that is left is to put them together. The code in Listing 4-53 returns the number 25 with two decimal places and three leading zeroes (00025.00).

Listing 4-53: Sample Code for Numerics with Leading Zeroes

```
SELECT

  REPLACE (STR (25, 8, 2), ' ', '0') AS TwentyFive
```

In the next section, you'll see where this technique can prove quite useful for handling dates.

Handling Dates

Date manipulation is heavily used in the business world, and SQL Server has a rich set of functions to handle just about anything you throw at it. Whether you wish to increment or decrement, compare to a value, convert to a different datatype, or do other data manipulation, SQL Server can support it all. This section describes how to do these tasks, as well as some of the traps you may encounter. Many of the topics discussed here are the result of pleas for help found on the Usenet newsgroups.

When you work with dates, you are actually working with `datetime` or `smalldatetime` datatypes. As the names imply, they hold both date *and* time information. In fact, there is no such thing as a date-only or time-only datatype. If you feed a `datetime` or `smalldatetime` only a date, it will assume the time to be midnight.

> **NOTE**   *The* `datetime` *datatype maintains the time down to 3.33 milliseconds and uses eight bytes. Its values range from 1 Jan 1753 to 31 Dec 9999 23:59:59.999. The* `smalldatetime` *datatype maintains time down to the minute and uses four bytes. Its values range from 1 Jan 1900 to 6 Jun 2079 23:59.*

Using DATEPART() and YEAR(), MONTH(), and DAY()

Very often, you will need to pick dates apart, searching for the year, month, or day. All of these tasks can be handled by the DATEPART() function. You feed it the part that you want, together with the date you are examining. Check out the syntax in Listing 4-54.

Listing 4-54: Syntax for the DATEPART() Function

```
DATEPART (datepart, date)
```

Table 4-23 lists the `datepart` parameter values used by the DATEPART() function. You can use either the full `datepart` name or the equivalent abbreviation. You will find that the dateparts listed will appear in the DATEADD(), DATEPART(), and DATEDIFF() functions.

Table 4-23: Dateparts and Abbreviations

Datepart	Abbreviation
year	yy, yyyy
quarter	qq, q
month	mm, m
dayofyear	dy, y
day	dd, d
week	wk, ww
weekday	dw
hour	hh
minute	mi, n
second	ss, s
millisecond	ms

Although you can extract any portion of the date using the DATEPART() function, there are some functions that do the equivalent and their names are more intuitive. For example, if you wish to extract the year portion of the date, use the YEAR() function. The same goes for the MONTH() and DAY() functions. (These functions were introduced in version 7.0) The statements in Listing 4-55 are equivalent:

Listing 4-55: Examples of DATEPART(), YEAR(), MONTH(), and DAY() Functions

```
SELECT
  DATEPART (yy, getdate ()),
  DATEPART (mm, getdate ()),
  DATEPART (dd, getdate ())

SELECT
  YEAR (getdate ()),
  MONTH (getdate ()),
  DAY (getdate ())
```

Using the DATENAME() Function

Just as you can extract date parts from a date, you can also get the equivalent name of the part where appropriate. For example, you can get the month name or day of the week using the DATENAME() function. The name is a character string in the language of the current connection. This is handy if you have users who have different language settings. The name returned will be in the appropriate language, and you can avoid specialized code for each language.

It's time to put some of your knowledge into action. Suppose you need a report from the Northwind database of the number of orders broken down by year and month. You want the name of the month in the result set, not the month number. However, you want it sorted on year and month number, not year and month name. The solution is in Listing 4-56.

Listing 4-56: Finding Orders Broken Down by Year and Month

```
SELECT
   YEAR (OrderDate)          AS 'Year',
   MONTH (OrderDate)         AS 'Month',
   DATENAME (mm, OrderDate) AS 'Month Name',
   COUNT (*)                 AS 'Count'
FROM
   Orders
GROUP BY
   YEAR (OrderDate),
   MONTH (OrderDate),
   DATENAME (mm, OrderDate)
ORDER BY
   YEAR (OrderDate),
   MONTH (OrderDate)
```

Using the DATEADD() Function

Both incrementing and decrementing dates is done through the DATEADD() function. Take a moment to review the syntax in Listing 4-57.

Listing 4-57: DATEADD() Function Syntax

```
DATEADD (datepart, number, date)
```

You will recognize the datepart parameter—it's the same parameter that's used in other date functions. The date parameter is self-explanatory. The number parameter is the number of dateparts you wish to add to the date parameter. In other words, if you want to add five days to the current date, use the following (see Listing 4-58):

Listing 4-58: Using the DATEADD() Function

```
SELECT
  DATEADD (dd, 5, GETDATE ())
```

If you wish to subtract from a date, just give the function a negative number parameter.

The addition operator has been enhanced as of release 7.0. Now, you can add days to a given date using the + sign, instead of using the DATEADD() function. You are not restricted to integer days, either. If you wish to add 1.5 days (36 hours), you can. For an example, look at Listing 4-59.

Listing 4-59: Adding to a Date Using the Addition Operator

```
SELECT
  GETDATE () + 1.5
```

Using the DATEDIFF() Function

The DATEDIFF() function enables you to find how many days, months, years, quarters, hours, minutes, seconds, or milliseconds there are between two different dates. Take a moment to review the syntax in Listing 4-60.

Listing 4-60: DATEDIFF() Function Syntax

```
DATEDIFF (datepart, startdate, enddate)
```

This function gives you the difference between startdate and enddate in units of datepart.

Avoiding WHERE Clause Traps in Date Manipulation

If you are using your datetime and smalldatetime columns to store only date information without including time, you can skip this section. However, if you are like most SQL developers, you will have to include time information as well. This can lead to some unexpected result sets when you are searching a range of dates. Often, people will use the BETWEEN predicate, specifying two dates, expecting that all values that occurred on the final day will be included. However, if time information is included in those values, *none* of them will be in the result set.

For example, say you are storing point-of-sale data. Each transaction has a date and time, stored in a datetime column. You want to find all transactions that occurred between two dates, *inclusive*—in this case, you want to determine the transactions for the month of July 2000. The WHERE clause may look like the one shown in Listing 4-61.

Listing 4-61: WHERE Clause for a Date Range Search

```
WHERE
    SalesDateTime BETWEEN '1Jul2000' and '31Jul2000'
```

At first glance, this code looks fine. However, you get only the transactions for July 1–30. Don't forget that there is a time component to datetime fields and that '31Jul2000' has a time component of midnight. This means that anything after midnight that day will be lost.

The task can be accomplished by recasting the WHERE clause. The correct solution is shown in Listing 4-62.

Listing 4-62: Correct WHERE Clause for a Date Search

```
WHERE
    SalesDateTime >= '1Jul2000'
AND SalesDateTime <  '1Aug2000'
```

> **TIP** *Naming conventions are important. If your* datetime *column contains only date information, make sure the word Date appears in the column name, (as in OrderDate). If it contains both date and time information, then put DateTime in the column name (for example, SalesDateTime). This way, you have a built-in reminder of what the column contains.*

Using the CONVERT() Function

The CONVERT() function is used to change the datatype of an expression. Take a moment to review the syntax in Listing 4-63 and the supporting styles in Table 4-24.

> **NOTE** *You have probably seen* CONVERT() *used for something other than dates; however, for the purposes of this chapter, just concentrate on its use in the context of date handling.*

Listing 4-63: CONVERT() Function Syntax

```
CONVERT (data_type[(length)], expression [, style])
```

Table 4-24: CONVERT() Function Styles

Without Century	With Century	Standard	Input/Output*
-	0 or 100 (**)	Default	mon dd yyyy hh:miAM (or PM)
1	101	USA	mm/dd/yy
2	102	ANSI	yy.mm.dd
3	103	British/French	dd/mm/yy
4	104	German	dd.mm.yy
5	105	Italian	dd-mm-yy
6	106	-	dd mon yy
7	107	-	mon dd, yy
8	108	-	hh:mm:ss
-	9 or 109 (**)	Default + milliseconds	mon dd yyyy hh:mi:ss:mmmAM (or PM)
10	110	USA	mm-dd-yy
11	111	JAPAN	yy/mm/dd
12	112	ISO	yymmdd
-	13 or 113 (**)	Europe default + milliseconds	dd mon yyyy hh:mm:ss:mmm(24h)
14	114	-	hh:mi:ss:mmm(24h)
-	20 or 120 (**)	ODBC canonical	yyyy-mm-dd hh:mi:ss(24h)
-	21 or 121 (**)	ODBC canonical (with milliseconds)	yyyy-mm-dd hh:mi:ss.mmm(24h)
-	126 (***)	ISO8601	yyyy-mm-ddThh:mi:ss.mmm (no spaces)
-	130 (**)	Kuwaiti	dd mon yyyy hh:mi:ss.mmmAM
-	131 (**)	Kuwaiti	dd/mm/yyyy hh:mi:ss.mmmAM

* Input when converting to datetime, and output when converting to character data.

** The values (*styles* 0 or 100, 9 or 109, 13 or 113, 20 or 120, 21 or 121, and 130 or 131) always return the century (yyyy).

*** Designed for XML use.

The datatype to which you will convert your date will usually be a char of some length. This length controls how much of the string is relevant to you. The style is also very important. It controls what goes where inside the result string. You can control whether or not you get the date, time, or both, as well as the number of digits in the year.

The style that is most useful for date calculation is style 112—ISO with a 4-digit year. It converts the date into YYYYMMDD format. This is great when you have users with different languages using your stored procedures. (Stored procedures are discussed in Chapter 9.) There are no delimiters with style 112, and stripping out parts of the string is straightforward.

Thus far, the discussion of the CONVERT() function has focused on its role in date manipulation scenarios. However, it can also be used to convert back and forth between other datatypes, such as from int to float. Alternatively, you can use the CAST() function to do this. However, you cannot convert to a user-defined datatype.

Finding the First Day of the Month

The CONVERT() function makes it easy to find the first day of the month. By converting your date to a char(6) with style 112, you have the four-character year and two-character month as YYYYMM. Now, all you have to do is add '01' to the end of the string to get the first day of the month. An example is shown in Listing 4-64.

Listing 4-64: Calculating the First Day of the Month

```
SELECT
  CONVERT (char (6), OrderDate, 112) + '01'
FROM
    Orders
```

Finding the Last Day of the Month

Finding the last day of the month is less of a SQL Server problem than it is one of defining the month end. The month end can be thought of as the day before the first day of the next month. The first step is to find the first day of the current month. Next, you add one month to that to get the first day of the next month. Finally, you subtract one day, and you now have the last day of the current month. This works all of the time, including leap years.

You can get the first day of the month by using the CONVERT() function and shaving off the day of the month, forcing it to be the first by concatenating '01' to the end, as discussed in the previous section. The rest involves the DATEADD() function. To get the month end of the order date, you use the method shown in Listing 4-65.

Listing 4-65: Calculating the Month End

```
SELECT
  DATEADD (dd, -1,
    DATEADD (mm, 1,
      CONVERT (char (6), OrderDate, 112) + '01'))
FROM
    Orders
```

Adding Months to a Date

Here again, the issue is not related to SQL Server. If you add a number of months to the end of a month, the results are predictable but surprising. Adding one month to December 31 yields January 31. Adding one month to that yields February 28 or 29, depending on whether or not it is a leap year. Thus far, adding one month to the end of a month yields another month end. Here comes the stickler. Add one month again and you have March 28 or 29, not March 31. At this point, you have added three months—one at a time—to December 31 and got March 28 or 29. Now, add three months in one shot to December 31 and you will get March 31.

Look at the last few days in March and add one month to each. If you add one month to March 28 or 29, you will get April 28 or April 29, respectively. If you add one month to either March 30 or 31, you will get April 30 in *both* cases. If the date forms all or part of the primary key, then incrementing the date by an integer number of months can give you primary key violations.

From the Trenches

For Y2K testing, a banking-application development team wanted to increment the date data in the database. A copy of the production server data was used as the test data, and the year 2000 was still over two years away. When the data were incremented by about 20 months, the update failed due to primary key violations. The solution was to increment by a fixed number of days, using 30 days for every month.

Finding the Month Name Based on the Month Number

SQL Server does not have a function to give you a month name based on just the month number. However, a simple trick will get you what you want. Just keep in mind that month 2 is always February, regardless of the year in which it occurs. It also remains February throughout the entire month of February!

What does this mean to the programmer? Simple—you can make up any old date, as long as it has the right month. Then take the DATEPART() of that date, and you get the month name.

Assuming that @Month contains the month number, the code in Listing 4-66 will give you the month name.

Listing 4-66: Calculating Month Name from Month Number

```
SELECT
  DATENAME (mm, '2000' + REPLACE (STR (@Month, 2, 2), ' ', '0') + '01')
```

Here, you used 2000 for the year and 1 for the day of the month. The name of the month is returned in the same language as the current setting for your connection.

Handling Language-Independent Date Input

Date handling can serve up some surprises when you change the language setting. For example, the date 01/10/2000 can be interpreted as October 1, 2000 or January 10, 2000, depending on where you live. More specifically, it depends on your language setting. If your application serves many users with varying languages, then you have to accommodate this variance.

Don't assume that 2000/10/01 will always be interpreted as October 1, 2000. If your language setting is French, you will find it interprets this date as January 10, 2000. There is a way around this, however.

Although the YYYY/MM/DD format described in the previous paragraph is not consistent across languages, the YYYYMMDD format is. The drawback is that you must specify all digits, including leading zeroes. This can be managed by using the REPLACE() and STR() functions discussed in the section "Displaying Leading Zeroes." Some sample code is presented in Listing 4-67.

Listing 4-67: Generating a Date in YYYYMMDD Format

```
SELECT
  STR (2000, 4) + STR (10, 2) + REPLACE (STR (1, 2), ' ', '0') AS 'Date'
```

This generates the string '20001001'. Now that you can create the proper date string on the fly, the string can then be used when passing a datetime parameter to a stored procedure, and you will have the correctly interpreted date, regardless of the language setting.

> **NOTE** *You can also use the* SET DATEFORMAT *statement to tell SQL Server explicitly how you are feeding it dates. Unfortunately, you would have to set this for every time a user connects or inside each stored procedure. This can leave you exposed if you are not careful.*

Using the GETUTCDATE() Function

With the release of SQL Server 2000, Microsoft introduced another date-related function: GETUTCDATE(). This function returns to you the current Coordinated Universal Time (UTC), formerly known as Greenwich Mean Time (GMT). This is the time at 0° longitude, based upon standard time. It uses the local time plus the regional setting of the server to determine the UTC time. This syntax is the same as for GETDATE(), as you can see in Listing 4-68.

Listing 4-68: Sample Code for the GETUTCDATE() Function.

```
SELECT
  GETUTCDATE()
```

SQL Puzzle 4-1: Euro 2000 Theme (posted by Colin Rippey)

You are given the following data for participating teams and results of matches in the Euro 2000 soccer contest.

First the code that creates the Teams table:

```
CREATE TABLE Teams
(
  teamid   int        NOT NULL PRIMARY KEY,
  country varchar(25) NOT NULL
)

INSERT INTO Teams VALUES(1, 'England')
INSERT INTO Teams VALUES(2, 'Germany')
INSERT INTO Teams VALUES(3, 'Portugal')
INSERT INTO Teams VALUES(4, 'Romania')

SELECT * FROM Teams
```

The Teams table should be as follows:

teamid	country
1	England
2	Germany
3	Portugal
4	Romania

Now the code that produces the Results table:

```
CREATE TABLE Results
(
  matchid    int NOT NULL PRIMARY KEY,
  team1      int NOT NULL REFERENCES Teams(teamid),
  team2      int NOT NULL REFERENCES Teams(teamid),
  team1goals int NOT NULL,
  team2goals int NOT NULL
)

INSERT INTO Results VALUES(1, 2, 4, 1, 1)
INSERT INTO Results VALUES(2, 1, 3, 2, 3)

SELECT * FROM Results
```

The Results table looks like this:

matched	team1	team2	team1goals	team2goals
1	2	4	1	1
2	1	3	2	3

Your task is to produce the following summary table:

Country	P	W	D	L	F	A	Points
Portugal	1	1	0	0	3	2	3
Romania	1	0	1	0	1	1	1

Country	P	W	D	L	F	A	Points
Germany	1	0	1	0	1	1	1
England	1	0	0	1	2	3	0

The column names in the summary table represent the following computations:

P: Total matches

W: Matches won

D: Matches with a draw

L: Matches lost

F: Goals in opponent's net

A: Goals in team's own net

P: Points (Win: 3, Draw: 1, Lose: 0)

The answer to this puzzle can be found on pages 684–687.

CHAPTER 5
Summarizing Data

GROUP BY QUERIES GIVE YOU a lot of power when you want to summarize your data. The problem is that sometimes you want to see different levels of aggregation in the same output. T-SQL has a few extensions, such as CUBE, ROLLUP, and COMPUTE, which enable you to get such views of your data. The extensions discussed in this chapter are not ANSI compliant, but the ANSI committee is considering adding the CUBE and ROLLUP extensions to the standard. This chapter requires previous knowledge of GROUP BY queries. If you are not familiar with those, take a look at Appendix A, "DML Basics" before you continue.

Refining Your GROUP BY Queries

GROUP BY queries calculate aggregations only for the requested level of aggregation, which is the level specified in the GROUP BY clause. For example, you can run the query shown in Listing 5-1 against the Orders table in the Northwind sample database to get the total number of orders made by each customer each year.

Listing 5-1: Total Number of Orders by Customer and Year

```
SELECT
  CustomerID,
  YEAR(OrderDate) AS Order_Year,
  COUNT(*)        AS Order_Count
FROM
  Orders
WHERE
  CustomerID LIKE 'A%'
GROUP BY
  CustomerID,
  YEAR(OrderDate)
```

The output of this query is shown in Table 5-1.

Table 5-1: Total Number of Orders by Customer and Year

CustomerID	Order_Year	Order_Count
ANATR	1996	1
ANTON	1996	1
AROUT	1996	2
ALFKI	1997	3
ANATR	1997	2
ANTON	1997	5
AROUT	1997	7
ALFKI	1998	3
ANATR	1998	1
ANTON	1998	1
AROUT	1998	4

Notice that a filter is used to limit the result to only customers starting with the letter *A*. This filter is used so you can see a small number of rows and to keep the examples simple, but you can omit this filter if you want to work on the whole set of orders.

If you want to supply the total number of orders for each customer, you would either calculate it manually or write a new GROUP BY query. The same thing applies to calculating the total number of orders for each year or the grand total number of orders. No big deal—what are three additional queries? But suppose your original query included employee information as well, as shown in Listing 5-2.

Listing 5-2: Total Number of Orders by Customer, Employee, and Year

```
SELECT
  CustomerID,
  EmployeeID,
  YEAR(OrderDate) AS Order_Year,
  COUNT(*)        AS Order_Count
FROM
  Orders
WHERE
  CustomerID LIKE 'A%'
```

```
GROUP BY
  CustomerID,
  EmployeeID,
  YEAR(OrderDate)
```

The output of this query is shown in Table 5-2.

Table 5-2: Total Number of Orders by Customer, Employee, and Year

CustomerID	EmployeeID	Order_Year	Order_Count
ALFKI	1	1998	2
ALFKI	3	1998	1
ALFKI	4	1997	2
ALFKI	6	1997	1
ANATR	3	1997	2
ANATR	4	1998	1
ANATR	7	1996	1
ANTON	1	1997	1
ANTON	3	1996	1
ANTON	3	1997	1
ANTON	3	1998	1
ANTON	4	1997	1
ANTON	7	1997	2
AROUT	1	1997	3
AROUT	3	1997	2
AROUT	4	1997	2
AROUT	4	1998	2
AROUT	6	1996	1
AROUT	8	1996	1
AROUT	9	1998	2

Now that you are grouping by three columns instead of two, you have a lot more requests that require a new query:

1. Show me the total number of orders for each customer made by each employee.

2. Show me the total number of orders for each customer, each year.

3. Show me the total number of orders for each customer.

4. Show me the total number of orders for each employee, each year.

5. Show me the total number of orders for each employee.

6. Show me the total number of orders for each year.

7. Show me the grand total number of orders.

You can calculate the number of additional possible requests that require a new query. Think of each request as asking for a different variation on the details (such as about specific employees) and summaries (such as about all employees) from the columns in the GROUP BY clause. These variations are shown in Table 5-3.

Table 5-3: Variations of Detail and Summary of the Columns in the GROUP BY *Clause*

No.	CustomerID	EmployeeID	Order_Year
1.	detail	detail	summary
2.	detail	summary	detail
3.	detail	summary	summary
4.	summary	detail	detail
5.	summary	detail	summary
6.	summary	summary	detail
7.	summary	summary	summary

In each request, each column's information can be either detailed or summarized. You can use a binary representation for this in the table, where detail is 0 and summary is 1, as shown in Table 5-4.

Table 5-4: Variations of Detail and Summary of the Columns in the GROUP BY *Clause Represented by 1s and 0s*

No.	CustomerID	EmployeeID	Order_Year
1.	0	0	1
2.	0	1	0
3.	0	1	1
4.	1	0	0
5.	1	0	1
6.	1	1	0
7.	1	1	1

Now it's easy to calculate the number of possible requests: `2^(num_cols) - 1`.

CUBE

Let's assume you are convinced that you'd rather not write so many queries, if you had an alternative. Well, your alternative is called CUBE. Let's add the CUBE option to the original query, as shown in Listing 5-3.

Listing 5-3: Basic CUBE Query

```
SELECT
  CustomerID,
  YEAR(OrderDate) AS Order_Year,
  COUNT(*)        AS Order_Count
FROM
  Orders
WHERE
  CustomerID LIKE 'A%'
GROUP BY
  CustomerID,
  YEAR(OrderDate)
WITH CUBE
```

The output of this query is shown in Table 5-5.

Table 5-5: Result of a Basic CUBE Query

CustomerID	Order_Year	Order_Count
ALFKI	1997	3
ALFKI	1998	3
ALFKI	NULL	6
ANATR	1996	1
ANATR	1997	2
ANATR	1998	1
ANATR	NULL	4
ANTON	1996	1
ANTON	1997	5
ANTON	1998	1
ANTON	NULL	7
AROUT	1996	2
AROUT	1997	7
AROUT	1998	4
AROUT	NULL	13
NULL	NULL	30
NULL	1996	4
NULL	1997	17
NULL	1998	9

This output contains the original eleven rows from the GROUP BY output and also all eight possible detail and summary combinations answering all three additional possible requests in this case. Notice that NULLs are used to represent summarized column information.

The potential number of rows in the output is the product of all possible distinct values in each column, including the NULL. In our example, there are four different customers and three different years, so the potential number of rows is $(4 + 1) \times (3 + 1) = 20$. In practice, not all possible value combinations exist in the database, so you might get fewer rows than the potential number. In our example, the customer ALFKI didn't place any orders in 1996, so the number of rows in our output is 19.

As If There Aren't Enough Problems with NULLs...

Let's go back to the fact that NULLs were chosen to represent the summaries. This was no doubt a difficult choice, but measured against the other options the planners of this extension had, using NULLs can be considered the best of all awkward alternatives. If only character-based columns were used to represent grouped data, a character string such as <ALL> or <SUMMARY> might have been a better choice, but because you can also group data by numeric columns, any option would have been awkward.

How does this affect you? Look again at the output of the last query, and see if you can tell, without knowing how the base data in the Orders table looks, whether a NULL in the result was generated by the CUBE operation. If the NULL was generated by the CUBE operation, this means it represents a super aggregate. If it wasn't, this means that it is a NULL that represents a group of NULLs that might exist in the base table. Considering the problematic nature of NULLs, you now have another layer of complexity to face.

GROUPING() Comes to the Rescue

Okay, now that you know a NULL in our result might mean different things, you're really in trouble, right? This is where the GROUPING() function comes to rescue. (You didn't really believe that you would be left with no options to solve this, did you?)

You use the GROUPING() function with an expression that might contain NULLs that are in doubt as a parameter. Its return value is only relevant when the value is NULL. It returns 1 when the NULL represents a super aggregate and 0 when the NULL represents a group of NULLs in the base table. Let's add it to the previous query, as in Listing 5-4.

Listing 5-4: CUBE Query and the GROUPING() function

```
SELECT
  CustomerID,
  GROUPING(CustomerID)      AS Grp_Cust,
  YEAR(OrderDate)           AS Order_Year,
  GROUPING(YEAR(OrderDate)) AS Grp_Year,
  COUNT(*) as Order_Count
FROM
  Orders
```

```
WHERE
  CustomerID LIKE 'A%'
GROUP BY
  CustomerID,
  YEAR(OrderDate)
WITH CUBE
```

The output of this query is shown in Table 5-6.

Table 5-6: Result of a CUBE Query with the GROUPING() Function

CustomerID	Grp_Cust	Order_Year	Grp_Year	Order_Count
ALFKI	0	1997	0	3
ALFKI	0	1998	0	3
ALFKI	0	NULL	1	6
ANATR	0	1996	0	1
ANATR	0	1997	0	2
ANATR	0	1998	0	1
ANATR	0	NULL	1	4
ANTON	0	1996	0	1
ANTON	0	1997	0	5
ANTON	0	1998	0	1
ANTON	0	NULL	1	7
AROUT	0	1996	0	2
AROUT	0	1997	0	7
AROUT	0	1998	0	4
AROUT	0	NULL	1	13
NULL	1	NULL	1	30
NULL	1	1996	0	4
NULL	1	1997	0	17
NULL	1	1998	0	9

For each NULL that is in doubt, you can now determine whether it is a super aggregate by looking for a 1 to the right on the return value of the GROUPING() function. As you can see in Table 5-6, none of the NULLs is in doubt—all represent super aggregates.

So, you have a solution. But you've probably already started imagining the long hours you are going to sit with users, teaching them how to "read" this information, and anticipating that neither of you is going to appreciate this much. But you're not done yet…

Providing a "Cleaner" Solution

First, try wrapping the previous query with a view, as shown in Listing 5-5. (Views are discussed in detail in Chapter 8, but for now, think of a view as a named SELECT statement.)

Listing 5-5: Creating the Vbase_cube View to Hide the CUBE Query Complexity

```
CREATE VIEW Vbase_cube
AS

SELECT
  CustomerID,
  GROUPING(CustomerID)       AS Grp_Cust,
  YEAR(OrderDate)            AS Order_Year,
  GROUPING(YEAR(OrderDate)) AS Grp_Year,
  COUNT(*) as Order_Count
FROM
  Orders
WHERE
  CustomerID LIKE 'A%'
GROUP BY
  CustomerID,
  YEAR(OrderDate)
WITH CUBE
GO
```

Now that you've created the view, the query shown in Listing 5-6 returns the same result as the previous query in Listing 5-4, but it is much simpler.

Listing 5-6: Selecting All Rows from the Vbase_cube View

```
SELECT
  *
FROM
  Vbase_cube
```

Merging the Output of the GROUPING() Function and the Source Column

Now you need a way somehow to merge the customer column with its GROUPING() information, and to do the same with the year information. You need to replace NULLs with more meaningful information.

Dealing with the CustomerID column is easier. First, you want to leave the original CustomerID as is if it isn't NULL, and if it is NULL, you want to replace it with your own meaningful value. The function ISNULL() fits like a glove, as Listing 5-7 shows.

Listing 5-7: Replacing NULLs with Your Own Value

```
ISNULL(CustomerID, <your_own_value>)
```

Now you need to decide what to return if the CustomerID is NULL. In other words, you need to ask a question similar to the one Fezzik the giant asked Vizzini in *The Princess Bride* when he told him to do it his own way—"What is my own way?" In this case, the question is "What is <your_own_value>?" Well, it depends— you want to return one value if the NULL is a super aggregate, and another value if it isn't. You, as the programmer or the DBA, should know your database and figure out values that *won't* be used as the CustomerID and *will* represent their meaning in an appropriate way.

Using the values 'ALL' and 'UNKNOWN' as an example, you can use a CASE statement to check the Grp_Cust column and decide which of the values to return, as in Listing 5-8.

Listing 5-8: Expanding Your Own Value

```
<your_own_value> :=
CASE Grp_Cust
  WHEN 1 THEN 'ALL'
  ELSE 'UNKNOWN'
END
```

Now merge the functions, as shown in Listing 5-9.

Listing 5-9: Replacing NULLs with Your Own Value, Expanded

```
ISNULL(CustomerID,
  CASE Grp_Cust
    WHEN 1 THEN 'ALL'
    ELSE 'UNKNOWN'
  END)
```

You're almost done. The CustomerID column is defined as char(5). If you have NULLs in the base data, you should return the value 'UNKNOWN', but the ISNULL() function casts the value of its second parameter to the datatype of the first parameter. In this case, the implication of this behavior is that only the first five characters of the 'UNKNOWN' string will be returned, as Listing 5-10 shows.

Listing 5-10: UNKNOWN is Truncated to UNKNO

```
ISNULL(NULL /* which is char(5) */, 'UNKNOWN') = 'UNKNO'
```

This problem can also be handled easily. Just cast the CustomerID column to a larger datatype, as shown in Listing 5-11.

Listing 5-11: Avoiding Truncation of UNKNOWN in the CustomerID Column

```
ISNULL(CAST(CustomerID AS varchar(7)),
  CASE Grp_Cust
    WHEN 1 THEN 'ALL'
    ELSE 'UNKNOWN'
  END)
```

This trick will also take care of a problem with the Order_Year column—you can't mix character and numeric data in the same column. The solution is shown in Listing 5-12.

Listing 5-12: Handling Mixed Datatypes in the Order_Year Column

```
ISNULL(CAST(Order_Year AS varchar(7)),
  CASE Grp_Year
    WHEN 1 THEN 'ALL'
    ELSE 'UNKNOWN'
  END)
```

Take a look at the full query in Listing 5-13.

Listing 5-13: Replacing NULLs with ALL and UNKNOWN

```
SELECT
  ISNULL(CAST(CustomerID AS varchar(7)),
    CASE Grp_Cust
      WHEN 1 THEN 'ALL'
      ELSE 'UNKNOWN'
    END) AS Customer,
  ISNULL(CAST(Order_Year AS varchar(7)),
    CASE Grp_Year
      WHEN 1 THEN 'ALL'
      ELSE 'UNKNOWN'
    END) AS Order_Year,
  Order_Count
FROM
  Vbase_cube
```

The output of this query is shown in Table 5-7.

Table 5-7: Result of Replacing NULLs with ALL and UNKNOWN

Customer	Order_Year	Order_Count
ALFKI	1997	3
ALFKI	1998	3
ALFKI	ALL	6
ANATR	1996	1
ANATR	1997	2
ANATR	1998	1
ANATR	ALL	4
ANTON	1996	1
ANTON	1997	5
ANTON	1998	1
ANTON	ALL	7
AROUT	1996	2
AROUT	1997	7
AROUT	1998	4

Table 5-7: Result of Replacing NULLs with ALL and UNKNOWN (Continued)

Customer	Order_Year	Order_Count
AROUT	ALL	13
ALL	ALL	30
ALL	1996	4
ALL	1997	17
ALL	1998	9

There are no NULLs in the CustomerID or the OrderDate column in the Orders table, so all NULLs in our query were replaced with "ALL".

Putting It All Together

You can make things even simpler by wrapping the previous query in a view as well, as Listing 5-14 shows.

Listing 5-14: Creating the Vcube View on Top of the Vbase_cube View to Hide the Query Complexity

```
CREATE VIEW Vcube
AS

SELECT
  ISNULL(CAST(CustomerID AS varchar(7)),
    CASE Grp_Cust
      WHEN 1 THEN 'ALL'
      ELSE 'UNKNOWN'
    END) AS Customer,
  ISNULL(CAST(Order_Year AS varchar(7)),
    CASE Grp_Year
      WHEN 1 THEN 'ALL'
      ELSE 'UNKNOWN'
    END) AS Order_Year,
  Order_Count
FROM
  Vbase_cube
GO
```

It should now be easy to generate queries that answer questions in all levels of aggregation. For example, the query shown in Listing 5-15 answers the question, "How many orders did all customers make in all years?"

Listing 5-15: Querying the Vcube View, Example 1

```
SELECT
   *
FROM
   Vcube
WHERE
   Customer   = 'ALL'
  AND
   Order_Year = 'ALL'
```

The output of this query is shown in Table 5-8.

Table 5-8: Orders Made by All Customers in All Years

Customer	Order_Year	Order_Count
ALL	ALL	30

The query shown in Listing 5-16 answers, "How many orders did customer 'ALFKI' make?"

Listing 5-16: Querying the Vcube View, Example 2

```
SELECT
   *
FROM
   Vcube
WHERE
   Customer   = 'ALFKI'
  AND
   Order_Year = 'ALL'
```

The output of this query is shown in Table 5-9.

Table 5-9: Orders Made by Customer ALFKI in All Years

Customer	Order_Year	Order_Count
ALFKI	ALL	6

And last but not least, the query in Listing 5-17 answers, "How many orders were made in the year 1998?"

Listing 5-17: Querying the Vcube View, Example 3

```
SELECT
  *
FROM
    Vcube
WHERE
    Customer   = 'ALL'
  AND
    Order_Year = '1998'
```

The output of this query is shown in Table 5-10.

Table 5-10: Orders Made by All Customers in 199

Customer	Order_Year	Order_Count
ALL	1998	9

ROLLUP

In terms of the output, you can consider ROLLUP to be a private case of CUBE. Take another look at how CUBE works by reviewing the query in Listing 5-18.

Listing 5-18: CUBE Returns All Possible Levels of Super Aggregation

```
SELECT
  CustomerID,
  EmployeeID,
  YEAR(OrderDate) AS Order_Year,
  COUNT(*)        AS Order_Count
FROM
  Orders
WHERE
  CustomerID LIKE 'A%'
GROUP BY
  CustomerID,
  EmployeeID,
  YEAR(OrderDate)
WITH CUBE
```

The possible levels of super aggregation for this CUBE query are shown in Table 5-11.

Table 5-11: Table of Possible Levels of Super Aggregation for a CUBE Query

No.	CustomerID	EmployeeID	Order_Year
1.	detail	detail	summary
2.	detail	summary	detail
3.	detail	summary	summary
4.	summary	detail	detail
5.	summary	detail	summary
6.	summary	summary	detail
7.	summary	summary	summary

Possible Levels of Super Aggregation Using ROLLUP

ROLLUP doesn't calculate super aggregates for combinations where the detail appears to the right of the summary. If you remove all those cases, you're left with the levels of super aggregation shown in Table 5-12.

Table 5-12: Table of Possible Levels of Super Aggregation for a ROLLUP Query

No.	CustomerID	EmployeeID	Order_Year
1.	detail	detail	summary
2.	detail	summary	summary
3.	summary	summary	summary

In fact, the number of combinations is the number of columns you're grouping by. Consider the query shown in Listing 5-19.

Listing 5-19: ROLLUP Returns Super Aggregation Only in One Direction

```
SELECT
  CustomerID,
  EmployeeID,
  YEAR(OrderDate) AS Order_Year,
  COUNT(*)        AS Order_Count
```

```
FROM
  Orders
WHERE
  CustomerID LIKE 'A%'
GROUP BY
  CustomerID,
  EmployeeID,
  YEAR(OrderDate)
WITH ROLLUP
```

The output of this query is shown in Table 5-13.

Table 5-13: ROLLUP Returns Super Aggregation Only in One Direction

CustomerID	EmployeeID	Order_Year	Order_Count
ALFKI	1	1998	2
ALFKI	1	NULL	2
ALFKI	3	1998	1
ALFKI	3	NULL	1
ALFKI	4	1997	2
ALFKI	4	NULL	2
ALFKI	6	1997	1
ALFKI	6	NULL	1
ALFKI	NULL	NULL	6
ANATR	3	1997	2
ANATR	3	NULL	2
ANATR	4	1998	1
ANATR	4	NULL	1
ANATR	7	1996	1
ANATR	7	NULL	1
ANATR	NULL	NULL	4
ANTON	1	1997	1
ANTON	1	NULL	1
ANTON	3	1996	1
ANTON	3	1997	1

Table 5-13: ROLLUP Returns Super Aggregation Only in One Direction (Continued)

CustomerID	EmployeeID	Order_Year	Order_Count
ANTON	3	1998	1
ANTON	3	NULL	3
ANTON	4	1997	1
ANTON	4	NULL	1
ANTON	7	1997	2
ANTON	7	NULL	2
ANTON	NULL	NULL	7
AROUT	1	1997	3
AROUT	1	NULL	3
AROUT	3	1997	2
AROUT	3	NULL	2
AROUT	4	1997	2
AROUT	4	1998	2
AROUT	4	NULL	4
AROUT	6	1996	1
AROUT	6	NULL	1
AROUT	8	1996	1
AROUT	8	NULL	1
AROUT	9	1998	2
AROUT	9	NULL	2
AROUT	NULL	NULL	13
NULL	NULL	NULL	30

Notice that ROLLUP adds a super aggregate for each unique combination of values from left to right, but not from right to left.

Calculating the Number of Potential Rows of a ROLLUP Query

To help calculate the number of potential rows in the previous result (keep in mind that not all possible combinations exist in the base table), you can use the following pseudo-variables:

```
Let X1 = the number of unique values in the first column
Let X2 = the number of unique values in the second column
...
Let Xn = the number of unique values in the nth column
```

To see how these variables work, perform each calculation step by step, keeping the output of the previous query in mind. To start with, examine the second combination of possible levels of super aggregation, as shown in Table 5-14.

Table 5-14: Levels of Super Aggregation, EmployeeID and Order_Year Summarized

No.	CustomerID	EmployeeID	Order_Year
2.	detail	summary	summary

There is a potential supper aggregate row for each unique value in the first column, which in the example is the total for each customer. Therefore, there are X1 super aggregate rows.

Additionally, there is a potential super aggregate row for each unique combination of values in the first and the second columns, which in the example is the total for each combination of customer and year, as Table 5-15 shows. Therefore, there are X1 × X2 super aggregate rows.

Table 5-15: Levels of Super Aggregation, EmployeeID Summarized

No.	CustomerID	EmployeeID	Order_Year
1.	detail	detail	summary

Although the detailed level of base aggregation was not included in the table of possible levels of super aggregation, it can be referred to as "All Detailed," as in Table 5-16.

Table 5-16: Levels of Super Aggregation, All Detailed

No.	CustomerID	EmployeeID	Order_Year
0.	detail	detail	detail

This one is easy. The number of rows is the product of the unique values in each column: $X1 \times X2 \times \ldots \times Xn$. Additionally, there is one super aggregate for the grand total, as shown in Table 5-17.

Table 5-17: Grand Total Super Aggregation

No.	CustomerID	EmployeeID	Order_Year
0.	summary	summary	summary

You can now write a general formula for the total number of potential rows in the result:

```
X1 + X1 × X2  + ... + X1 × X2 × ... × Xn + 1
```

Should I CUBE or ROLLUP?

Putting performance issues to the side for now, when would you choose CUBE and when would you choose ROLLUP? You've already seen a useful scenario for CUBE, but suppose you want to get the order count by year and month? You can do this with ROLLUP, as Listing 5-20 shows.

Listing 5-20: Using ROLLUP to Get the Order Count by Year and Month

```
SELECT
  YEAR(OrderDate)  AS Oyear,
  MONTH(OrderDate) AS Omonth,
  COUNT(*)         AS Order_Count
FROM
  Orders
GROUP BY
  YEAR(OrderDate),
  MONTH(OrderDate)
WITH ROLLUP
```

The output of this query is shown in Table 5-18.

Table 5-18: Result of Using ROLLUP to Get the Order Count by Year and Month

Oyear	Omonth	Order_Count
1996	7	22
1996	8	25
1996	9	23
1996	10	26
1996	11	25
1996	12	31
1996	NULL	152
1997	1	33
1997	2	29
1997	3	30
1997	4	31
1997	5	32
1997	6	30
1997	7	33
1997	8	33
1997	9	37
1997	10	38
1997	11	34
1997	12	48
1997	NULL	408
1998	1	55
1998	2	54
1998	3	73
1998	4	74
1998	5	14
1998	NULL	270
NULL	NULL	830

Usually you would want to see the total number of orders for each year across all months, but you don't always need the total number of orders for each month across all years. So, why not simply ignore the irrelevant values and always use CUBE? You still get all the information you need. Well, in terms of performance, this is a whole different story...

To CUBE or Not to CUBE

This section examines the execution plans of three queries: a simple GROUP BY query, a ROLLUP query, and a CUBE query.

Starting Simple

Start with a simple GROUP BY query, as in Listing 5-21.

Listing 5-21: Comparing Performance, Query 1—Simple GROUP BY Query

```
SELECT
  CustomerID,
  EmployeeID,
  ShipVia,
  COUNT(*) AS Order_Count
FROM
  Orders
GROUP BY
  CustomerID,
  EmployeeID,
  ShipVia
```

The graphical execution plan for the simple GROUP BY query is shown in Figure 5-1.

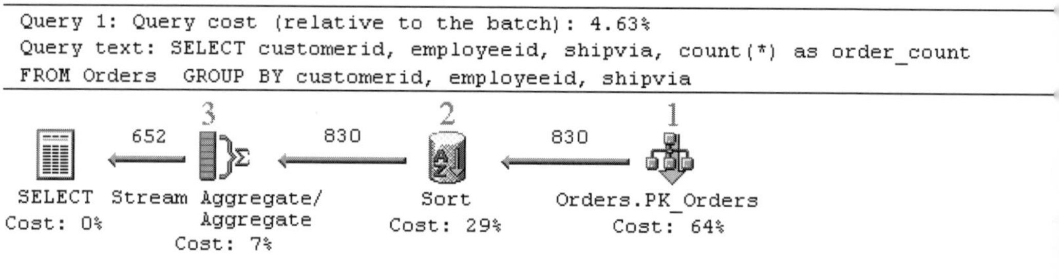

Figure 5-1: Execution plan for a GROUP BY query

The SHOWPLAN textual output for this simple GROUP BY query is shown in Listing 5-22.

Listing 5-22: SHOWPLAN's Output for Query 1—GROUP BY Query

```
3 |--Stream Aggregate(GROUP BY:([Orders].[CustomerID], [Orders].[EmployeeID],
     [Orders].[ShipVia]) DEFINE:([Expr1002]=COUNT(*)))
  2 |--Sort(ORDER BY:([Orders].[CustomerID] ASC, [Orders].[EmployeeID] ASC,
       [Orders].[ShipVia] ASC))
    1 |--Clustered Index Scan(OBJECT:([Northwind].[dbo].[Orders].[PK_Orders]))
```

The first execution plan is pretty straightforward:

1. Fetch all rows from the Orders table.

2. Sort the rows by CustomerID, EmployeeID, and ShipVia.

3. Calculate the aggregates.

Notice that the cost of this query is 4.63 percent of the whole batch, which includes the base GROUP BY query, the GROUP BY query with the ROLLUP option, and the GROUP BY query with the CUBE option.

Trying ROLLUP

The next query, shown in Listing 5-23, uses the ROLLUP option.

Listing 5-23: Comparing Performance, Query 2—ROLLUP Query

```
SELECT
 CustomerID,
  EmployeeID,
  ShipVia,
  COUNT(*) AS Order_Count
FROM
  Orders
GROUP BY
  CustomerID,
  EmployeeID,
  ShipVia
WITH ROLLUP
```

The graphical execution plan for this ROLLUP query is shown in Figure 5-2.

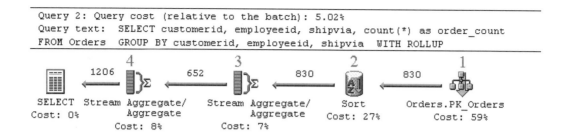

```
Query 2: Query cost (relative to the batch): 5.02%
Query text:  SELECT customerid, employeeid, shipvia, count(*) as order_count
FROM Orders  GROUP BY customerid, employeeid, shipvia  WITH ROLLUP
```

Figure 5-2: Execution plan for a ROLLUP query

The SHOWPLAN textual output for this ROLLUP query is shown in Listing 5-24.

Listing 5-24: SHOWPLAN's Output for Query 2—ROLLUP Query

```
4 |--Stream Aggregate(GROUP BY:([Orders].[CustomerID], [Orders].[EmployeeID],
       [Orders].[ShipVia]) DEFINE:([Expr1002]=SUM([Expr1003])))
  3 |--Stream Aggregate(GROUP BY:([Orders].[CustomerID], [Orders].[EmployeeID],
         [Orders].[ShipVia]) DEFINE:([Expr1003]=COUNT(*)))
    2 |--Sort(ORDER BY:([Orders].[CustomerID] ASC, [Orders].[EmployeeID] ASC,
           [Orders].[ShipVia] ASC))
      1 |--Clustered Index Scan(OBJECT:([Northwind].[dbo].[Orders].[PK_Orders]))
```

This second execution plan performs the same three steps as the first (simple GROUP BY) execution plan, and adds a step:

4. Calculate the super aggregates, based on the base aggregates calculated in the previous step.

The fourth step is simple to perform because the previous step was performed on an ordered set, which fits the order that is needed to calculate the super aggregates in a ROLLUP operation. Think of the ordered result of the base GROUP BY operation. It produces an output, which is ordered by CustomerID, EmployeeID, and ShipVia. The ROLLUP operation works from the right-most column to the left:

1. Return every base aggregate row.

2. Every time the ShipVia column changes its value, return the CustomerID, EmployeeID, and NULL combination.

3. Every time the CustomerID column changes its value, return the CustomerID, NULL, and NULL combination.

4. Return the NULL, NULL, and NULL grand total combination.

Notice that the cost of this query is 5.02 percent of the whole batch, which is slightly higher than the cost of the previous (simple GROUP BY) query but is still relatively small. The cause of the extra cost is the additional fourth step, which calculates the super aggregates. The additional cost was very little because the GROUP BY operation produced a sorted result in the same order as is required by the ROLLUP operation.

Trying CUBE

The last query in this performance comparison, shown in Listing 5-25, uses the CUBE option.

Listing 5-25: Comparing Performance, Query 3—CUBE Query

```
SELECT
    CustomerID,
    EmployeeID,
    ShipVia,
    COUNT(*) as Order_Count
FROM
    Orders
GROUP BY
    CustomerID,
    EmployeeID,
    ShipVia
WITH CUBE
```

The graphical execution plan for this cube query is shown in Figure 5-3.
The SHOWPLAN textual output for this CUBE query is shown in Listing 5-26.

```
Query 3: Query cost (relative to the batch): 90.35%
Query text:  SELECT customerid, employeeid, shipvia, count(*) as order_count
FROM Orders  GROUP BY customerid, employeeid, shipvia  WITH CUBE
```

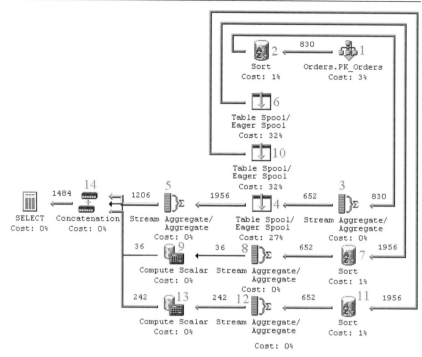

Figure 5-3: Execution plan for a CUBE query

Listing 5-26: SHOWPLAN's Output for Query 3—CUBE Query

```
14 |--Concatenation
     5 |--Stream Aggregate(GROUP BY:([Orders].[CustomerID], [Orders].[EmployeeID],
         [Orders].[ShipVia]) DEFINE:([Expr1002]=SUM([Expr1003])))
       |   4 |--Table Spool
       |       3 |--Stream Aggregate(GROUP BY:([Orders].[CustomerID],
       |               [Orders].[EmployeeID], [Orders].[ShipVia])
       |               DEFINE:([Expr1003]=COUNT(*)))
       |           2 |--Sort(ORDER BY:([Orders].[CustomerID] ASC,
       |                   [Orders].[EmployeeID] ASC, [Orders].[ShipVia] ASC))
       |               1 |--Clustered Index
       |                   Scan(OBJECT:([Northwind].[dbo].[Orders].[PK_Orders]))
     9 |--Compute Scalar(DEFINE:([Expr1004]=NULL))
       |   8 |--Stream Aggregate(GROUP BY:([Orders].[EmployeeID],
       |           [Orders].[ShipVia]) DEFINE:([Expr1002]=SUM([Expr1003])))
       |       7 |--Sort(ORDER BY:([Orders].[EmployeeID] ASC, [Orders].[ShipVia] ASC))
       |           6 |--Table Spool
```

```
13 |--Compute Scalar(DEFINE:([Expr1005]=NULL))
      12 |--Stream Aggregate(GROUP BY:([Orders].[ShipVia], [Orders].
         [CustomerID]) DEFINE:([Expr1002]=SUM([Expr1003])))
         11 |--Sort(ORDER BY:([Orders].[ShipVia] ASC, [Orders].[CustomerID]
            ASC))
            10 |--Table Spool
```

The execution plan for the CUBE operation looks far scarier than the previous ones. Also, its relative cost to the whole batch is quite considerable—90.35 percent—about 20 times more than the previous queries! Obviously, this requires a thorough explanation.

The execution plan shows three processes with similar activities: Steps 1–5, Steps 6–9, and Steps 10–13. Each process produces output rows for different levels of aggregation, which are concatenated in Step 14. The reason for the three separate processes is that for certain levels of CUBE aggregation, a different order of the base aggregation is required, as opposed to a ROLLUP operation. The remainder of this section examines each process and its steps in detail.

Process 1:

1. Scan the clustered index to get all required rows from the Orders table.

2. Sort the rows by CustomerID, EmployeeID, and ShipVia.

3. Calculate the base aggregates.

4. Store the base aggregates from the previous step in a temporary table, to be used in future steps.

5. Calculate the possible super aggregates based on the current order of the base aggregates, as shown in Table 5-19.

Table 5-19: Possible Levels of Aggregation Based on the Column Order— CustomerID, EmployeeID, and ShipVia

CustomerID	EmployeeID	ShipVia
detail	detail	summary
detail	summary	summary
summary	summary	summary

Process 2:

6. Get the base aggregation from the temporary table created in Step 4.

7. Sort the rows by EmployeeID and ShipVia.

8. Calculate the possible super aggregates based on the current order of the base aggregates, as shown in Table 5-20.

9. Store NULL in a variable for later use.

Table 5-20: Possible Levels of Aggregation Based on the Column Order— EmployeeID and ShipVia

CustomerID	EmployeeID	ShipVia
summary	detail	detail
summary	detail	summary

Process 3:

10. Get the base aggregation from the temporary table created in Step 4.

11. Sort the rows by ShipVia and CustomerID.

12. Calculate the possible super aggregates based on the current order of the base aggregates, as shown in Table 5-21.

13. Store NULL in a variable for later use.

Table 5-21: Possible Levels of Aggregation Based on the Column Order— ShipVia and CustomerID

CustomerID	EmployeeID	ShipVia
detail	summary	detail
summary	summary	detail

Process 4:

14. Concatenate the output of the three processes.

Notice that Steps 4, 6, and 10, which populate and scan the temporary table, make up 91 percent of the total query cost. Neither the first (simple GROUP BY) query nor the second (ROLLUP) query involved such steps. These performance tests were run on SQL Server 7.0. Running the same performance tests on SQL Server 2000 shows different ratios between the costs of the queries (Query 1: 22.89 percent, Query 2: 24.85 percent, Query 3: 52.26 percent), but as you can see, the general picture remains the same.

So what should you glean from this comparison? That you should use ROLLUP instead of CUBE whenever possible, because CUBE incurs a considerably larger cost.

COMPUTE

The COMPUTE extension enables you to generate aggregates, which appear in the output along with the base detailed rows. COMPUTE can aggregate values from the input as a whole, or on defined breakpoints.

> **NOTE** *The* COMPUTE *extension is still supported in T-SQL for backward compatibility, but it may not be supported in future releases. Therefore, it is only covered briefly in this chapter to give you a basic understanding of its functionality and the alternatives.*

Using the COMPUTE Option

To aggregate values from the whole input, you add the COMPUTE clause to the end of the query using the syntax shown in Listing 5-27.

Listing 5-27: COMPUTE Syntax

```
COMPUTE
  <aggregate_function>(expression)
```

For example, if you want to produce a list of orders and the grand total of their freight, you can use the query shown in Listing 5-28 (note that the filter is used only to limit the number of rows in the output).

Listing 5-28: Using COMPUTE in a Query

```
SELECT
  CustomerID,
  EmployeeID,
  OrderID, Freight
FROM
  Orders
WHERE
  CustomerID LIKE 'A%'
COMPUTE
  SUM(Freight)
```

The output of this query is shown in Table 5-22.

Table 5-22: Result of a COMPUTE Query

CustomerID	EmployeeID	OrderID	Freight
ANATR	7	10308	1.6100
AROUT	6	10355	41.9500
ANTON	3	10365	22.0000
AROUT	8	10383	34.2400
AROUT	1	10453	25.3600
ANTON	7	10507	47.4500
ANTON	4	10535	15.6400
AROUT	1	10558	72.9700
ANTON	7	10573	84.8400
ANATR	3	10625	43.9000
ALFKI	6	10643	29.4600
ANTON	1	10677	4.0300
ANTON	3	10682	36.1300
ALFKI	4	10692	61.0200
ALFKI	4	10702	23.9400
AROUT	4	10707	21.7400
AROUT	4	10741	10.9600
AROUT	1	10743	23.7200

Table 5-22: Result of a COMPUTE Query (Continued)

CustomerID	EmployeeID	OrderID	Freight
ANATR	3	10759	11.9900
AROUT	3	10768	146.3200
AROUT	3	10793	4.5200
ALFKI	1	10835	69.5300
ANTON	3	10856	58.4300
AROUT	4	10864	3.0400
AROUT	4	10920	29.6100
ANATR	4	10926	39.9200
ALFKI	1	10952	40.4200
AROUT	9	10953	23.7200
ALFKI	3	11011	1.2100
AROUT	9	11016	33.8000
			sum
			1063.4700

Using the COMPUTE BY Option

To aggregate values on defined breakpoints, you use the COMPUTE BY syntax shown in Listing 5-29.

Listing 5-29: COMPUTE BY Syntax

```
COMPUTE
   <aggregate_function>(expression) BY expression[,...n]
```

All expressions defining the breakpoints must appear in the ORDER BY clause; otherwise the aggregates will have no meaning.

You can combine several COMPUTE and COMPUTE BY clauses. For example, if you want to add breakpoints to the previous output with the sum of the Freight value for each customer, you can write the query shown in Listing 5-30.

Listing 5-30: Using COMPUTE BY in a Query

```
SELECT
  CustomerID,
  EmployeeID,
  OrderID,
  Freight
FROM
  Orders
WHERE
  CustomerID LIKE 'A%'
ORDER BY
  CustomerID
COMPUTE
  SUM(Freight) BY CustomerID
COMPUTE
  SUM(Freight)
```

The output of this query is shown in Table 5-23.

Table 5-23: Result of a COMPUTE BY Query

CustomerID	EmployeeID	OrderID	Freight
ALFKI	6	10643	29.4600
ALFKI	4	10692	61.0200
ALFKI	4	10702	23.9400
ALFKI	1	10835	69.5300
ALFKI	1	10952	40.4200
ALFKI	3	11011	1.2100
			sum
			225.5800
ANATR	7	10308	1.6100
ANATR	3	10625	43.9000
ANATR	3	10759	11.9900
ANATR	4	10926	39.9200
			sum
			97.4200

Table 5-23: Result of a COMPUTE BY Query (Continued)

CustomerID	EmployeeID	OrderID	Freight
ANTON	3	10365	22.0000
ANTON	7	10507	47.4500
ANTON	4	10535	15.6400
ANTON	7	10573	84.8400
ANTON	1	10677	4.0300
ANTON	3	10682	36.1300
ANTON	3	10856	58.4300
			sum
			268.5200
AROUT	6	10355	41.9500
AROUT	8	10383	34.2400
AROUT	1	10453	25.3600
AROUT	1	10558	72.9700
AROUT	4	10707	21.7400
AROUT	4	10741	10.9600
AROUT	1	10743	23.7200
AROUT	3	10768	146.3200
AROUT	3	10793	4.5200
AROUT	4	10864	3.0400
AROUT	4	10920	29.6100
AROUT	9	10953	23.7200
AROUT	9	11016	33.8000
			sum
			471.9500
			sum
			1063.4700

You can continue adding breakpoints in a finer grain. For example, to add a breakpoint for each combination of customer and employee, you can write the query shown in Listing 5-31.

Listing 5-31: Using COMPUTE BY with a Finer Grain

```
SELECT
  CustomerID,
  EmployeeID,
  OrderID, Freight
FROM
  Orders
WHERE
  CustomerID LIKE 'A%'
ORDER BY
  CustomerID,
  EmployeeID
COMPUTE
  SUM(Freight) BY CustomerID,
                  EmployeeID
COMPUTE
  SUM(Freight) BY CustomerID
COMPUTE
  SUM(Freight)
```

COMPUTE Considerations

The results of COMPUTE queries are very inflexible. Consider the following issues:

- There are totally different types of rows in the same output—it is far from being relational. You can't use it in the following operations: JOIN, SELECT INTO, INSERT SELECT, etc. In fact, you can't do anything with the result other than examine or print it.

- You can't control the qualifier of the aggregate, nor its position.

- From the viewpoint of the client application, you can retrieve the result of a COMPUTE BY query using ActiveX Data Objects (ADO), but you will get them as multiple record sets just as you would with stored procedures that have multiple SELECT statements. You can use the NextRecordset method of the Recordset object to move from one Recordset to the next once you've finished processing the previous one.

Alternatives for using COMPUTE are the ROLLUP extension and Microsoft SQL Server Analysis Services. If you have code written with COMPUTE, you should consider revising it.

SQL Puzzle 5-1: Management Levels

The following script creates the Mgrlevels table in the Northwind database:

```
CREATE TABLE Mgrlevels(
MinCusts int NOT NULL,
MaxCusts int NULL,
MgrLvl int NOT NULL)

INSERT INTO Mgrlevels VALUES(1, 3, 1)
INSERT INTO Mgrlevels VALUES(4, 10, 2)
INSERT INTO Mgrlevels VALUES(11, 15, 3)
INSERT INTO Mgrlevels VALUES(16, NULL, 4)
```

Figure 5-4 shows a graphical view of the Customers and Mgrlevels tables.

Figure 5-4: Schema for the Customers and Mgrlevels tables

Suppose each country, region, and city has a manager, and there's also a general manager for the whole world. Your task is to assign each area's manager the correct management level based on the number of customers in his or her responsibility. You need to calculate the number of customers in each area from the Customers table and find the matching management level in the Mgrlevels table, based on the minimum and maximum range of numbers of customers for each level.

The country and city columns are relevant for all customers, but the region column is not always relevant. For example, it represents the state for U.S. customers, but it is NULL for U.K. customers. Notice that management level 4 only has a minimum because it is the highest level of management.

The answer to this puzzle can be found on pages 687–689.

Special Datatypes
and Properties

SQL SERVER PROVIDES YOU with more than just the basic numeric and character datatypes. Some have been around for years; others are recent developments. This chapter examines those datatypes beyond the basic int, char, and float.

Unicode datatypes enable you to handle international characters that ASCII cannot. Thus, inserting Japanese Kanji characters, for example, is no problem at all. The rowversion datatype enables you to leverage optimistic locking. The text, ntext, and image datatypes handle Binary Large Objects (BLOBs) up to 2GB in size. The bigint datatype enables you to handle very large integers. The uniqueidentifier and its related function NEWID() enable you to manage globally unique identifiers (GUIDs) in your databases.

The sql_variant is a handy datatype that can enable you to put data with differing base datatypes into the same column or variable. This can get you past some of your weirdest business rules. The table datatype has some similarities to temporary tables but enables you to use user-defined functions (UDFs) to return result sets. Finally, the IDENTITY properties of tables and all of the related functions will help you to simplify your designs.

Using Unicode Datatypes

Unicode datatypes were introduced in SQL Server version 7.0. The Unicode datatypes are nchar, nvarchar, and ntext. They are Unicode (two-byte) versions of the corresponding char, varchar, and text datatypes. Consequently, they take up double the space of their single-byte siblings. When you specify the length for the nchar and nvarchar datatypes, you use the number of characters—not the number of bytes—just as you do for char and varchar.

Unicode uses the UNICODE UCS-2 character set. The ANSI-92 SQL synonyms for nchar are *national char* and *national character*, while for nvarchar, they are *national char varying* and *national character varying*. The word "national" comes in because many languages—particularly Japanese and Chinese—have alphabets that cannot be represented by the standard ASCII character set.

The maximum number of characters for nchar and nvarchar is 4,000. The SET option ANSI_PADDING OFF does not apply to nchar and nvarchar datatypes. Unicode constants are designated with a leading *N*, as in N'This is a Unicode string'.

Two functions help to support Unicode datatypes—NCHAR() and UNICODE(). The NCHAR() function takes a positive integer between 0 and 65,535 and returns a datatype of nchar(1) with the corresponding Unicode character. The syntax is straightforward and is presented in Listing 6-1.

Listing 6-1: Syntax for NCHAR()

```
NCHAR ( integer_expression )
```

For example, if you wanted the Unicode character corresponding to 252, you would use the code in Listing 6-2.

Listing 6-2: Using NCHAR()

```
SELECT
 NCHAR (252)
```

This returns the character *ü*.

The sister function of NCHAR()—UNICODE()—does the opposite. You give it a string, and it gives you the corresponding number of the Unicode first character in the string. Check out the syntax in Listing 6-3.

Listing 6-3: Syntax for UNICODE ()

```
UNICODE ( 'ncharacter_expression' )
```

For example, to find the Unicode value for 'ß', use the code in Listing 6-4.

Listing 6-4: Using UNICODE()

```
SELECT
 UNICODE ('ß')
```

This returns the number 223.

Unicode datatypes are especially handy in SQL Server 7.0 where you have a global character set for the whole server but you need to store different languages in your database.

Using the rowversion Datatype

The rowversion datatype is new to SQL Server 2000 and takes the place of the timestamp datatype from previous releases of SQL Server. It is an 8-byte binary datatype. There can be only one rowversion datatype per table, and the value changes with every INSERT and UPDATE statement. Because an UPDATE will change the value of the rowversion column, this datatype, though unique in value throughout the database, is a poor candidate for a primary key. This can be demonstrated with a small example—consider the table created in Listing 6-5 and shown in Table 6-1.

> **NOTE** *The* timestamp *datatype is still available for backward compatibility, but you should migrate to save yourself trouble in the future.*

Listing 6-5: Using a Table with a rowversion Column

```
CREATE TABLE MyTable
(
  DataValue int       NOT NULL,
  RowVer    rowversion NOT NULL
)
GO

INSERT MyTable (DataValue) VALUES (1)
INSERT MyTable (DataValue) VALUES (2)
INSERT MyTable (DataValue) VALUES (3)
INSERT MyTable (DataValue) VALUES (4)
GO
```

Table 6-1: Sample Table with rowversion Column

DataValue	RowVer
1	0x0000000000000205
2	0x0000000000000206
3	0x0000000000000207
4	0x0000000000000208

Now update one row, as shown in Listing 6-6. The resulting table is shown in Table 6-2.

Listing 6-6: Updating a Row in a Table with a rowversion Column

```
UPDATE MyTable
SET
  DataValue = 10
WHERE
  DataValue = 3
GO

SELECT
  *
FROM
  MyTable
GO
```

Table 6-2: Sample Table after Single-Row Update

DataValue	RowVer
1	0x0000000000000205
2	0x0000000000000206
10	0x000000000000020A
4	0x0000000000000208

The code in Listing 6-6 updates a single row, but you'll find that not only has the DataValue column changed, the RowVer column is also updated. Also, the value of RowVer for the changed row is now the highest in the table, as seen in the Table 6-2.

As the name implies, this datatype acts as a version number for a row when optimistic locking is used. This technique is used in cursors where it is possible that an outside process could change the values in a row between the time when your process reads the row and when it updates the row. Optimistic locking is typically used in high transaction volume environments where updates of a row by two different processes at approximately the same time are not very likely—but not impossible—to occur. The approach taken is not to lock the row in question but to read it and release the lock. When you then go to update the row you might find out that it has been changed.

When a row has been changed between the time you read it and the time you go to update it, you will get a 16934 error, "Optimistic concurrency check failed. The row was modified outside of this cursor." Your code will have to handle this either by reading the new values and presenting them to the user or by discarding the changes done by the background process and overwriting. In either case, you still need to fetch the row to overwrite. (You'll see a whole lot more about cursors and optimistic locking in Chapter 15.)

The only comparison operators allowed with rowversion datatypes are equality and inequality: =, <>, <, >, <=, and >=. Typically, you will never do a direct compare. Rather, you will let SQL Server raise an error if there has been a change in the row.

Using the text, ntext, and image Datatypes

The text and image datatypes have been around since the Sybase days, and ntext was introduced in version 7.0. These datatypes handle large pieces of data up to 2GB in size. The text and ntext datatypes handle character information, whereas image handles binary information. The image datatype is useful for storing bitmaps. Whenever you think of BLOBs, think of text, ntext, and image.

> **NOTE** *Since version 7.0, you can store character datatypes up to 8,000 bytes in length. In version 6.x, you were limited to 255 bytes.*

There are some restrictions in the use of these datatypes. For example, you may not refer to them directly in WHERE clauses. However, they can be used as parameters in functions that return other datatypes inside WHERE clauses, such as ISNULL(), SUBSTRING(), PATINDEX(), and the IS NULL, IS NOT NULL, and LIKE expressions. You also may not use them as variables, but you may use them as parameters for a stored procedure. (Stored procedures are discussed in Chapter 9.)

Using Text in Row

Text in row is a new feature of SQL Server 2000. This allows you to store the text, ntext, or image data on the same page as the rest of the row data instead of on a separate page. This can speed retrievals as well as updates of these columns, which makes your queries just about as fast as those involving varchar, nvarchar, or binary columns. The text in row feature applies only to small- or medium-sized character or binary strings.

You turn on this option by using sp_tableoption, as shown in Listing 6-7.

Listing 6-7: Turning on 'text in row'

```
sp_tableoption
 'MyTable',
 'text in row',
 'ON'
```

You turn on `text in row` for the entire table, not a specific column. The syntax shown in Listing 6-7 simply turns on the feature and automatically sets the number of bytes that can be stored for all `text`, `ntext`, and `image` datatypes to 256. This number strikes a good balance—it allows sufficient space for small strings and root text pointers to be stored, but it is not so large as to reduce the number of rows per page to the point where performance is affected.

You can, however, set the limit between 24 and 7,000 manually by specifying a number (in quotes), instead of `ON`. For example, to set the limit to 1,000, use the code in Listing 6-8.

Listing 6-8: Setting a 'text in row' Limit

```
sp_tableoption
 'MyTable',
 'text in row',
 '1000'
```

In general, do not set the limit below 72, but be careful about setting it too high. If you do not frequently need the BLOB data as often as the other row data, then you are making the row length larger and reducing the number of rows per page.

Finally, you can turn off this feature by setting the option to `OFF` or 0 as presented in Listing 6-9.

Listing 6-9: Turning Off 'text in row'

```
sp_tableoption
 'MyTable',
 'text in row',
 'OFF'
```

Just because `text in row` has been enabled for a table does not necessarily mean that a particular piece of BLOB data will be saved within the row. The following conditions must also exist:

- The size of the data must be less than or equal to the limit set by `sp_dboption`.

- There must be space available in the row.

If `text in row` has been enabled and the above conditions do not exist, pointers will be stored in the row instead. Here, too, there must be enough space to hold the pointers.

To illustrate how this threshold is used, create a simple table of two columns—one with an `int` column and one with `text`. Next, set the `text in row` limit to 1,000. Finally, add one row and then run `sp_spaceused` to see how much space was dedicated to data. The code is shown in Listing 6-10.

Listing 6-10: Sample Table Containing Text

```
CREATE TABLE MyTextTable
(
 id int NOT NULL PRIMARY KEY,
 txt text NULL
)
GO

EXEC sp_tableoption 'MyTextTable', 'text in row', '1000'
GO

INSERT MyTextTable
 VALUES (1, NULL)

UPDATE MyTextTable
SET
 txt = REPLICATE ('x', 1000)
```

If at this point you run `sp_spaceused`, you will see 8KB (one page) dedicated to data. Change the parameter in `REPLICATE()` from 1,000 to 1,001 and re-run. Suddenly, the size jumps to 24KB (three pages). Now, the text data are no longer stored in a row but in separate pages.

Try this again but exclude the call to `sp_dboption`. You will see three pages dedicated to the table. This is true even if you set the text data to `'x'`. Thus, `text in row` is proven to use less space when the strings are small.

Using the `sp_invalidate_textptr` Stored Procedure

You can have a maximum of 1,024 active, valid in-row text pointers per database per transaction. If you need to exceed this number, then you have to free up some or all of the active text pointers by using `sp_invalidate_textptr`. The syntax is simple, as you can see in Listing 6-11.

Listing 6-11: Syntax for sp_invalidate_textptr

```
sp_invalidate_textptr [ [ @TextPtrValue = ] textptr_value ]
```

If you invoke this stored procedure with no parameters or with a NULL parameter, then it will invalidate all active pointers in the transaction.

Using Text Pointers and the TEXTPTR() and TEXTVALID() Functions

When BLOBs get large—as their name implies—then using regular SELECT and UPDATE statements just won't cut it. At this point, you have to manipulate such data on a block-by-block basis. (Even though you can use database APIs from a front-end or middle-tier client program to do this kind of work, here you'll see how to do it with Transact-SQL functions instead.)

In a moment, you'll find out how to use the three basic statements for handling BLOBs, READTEXT, WRITETEXT, and UPDATETEXT, regardless of whether or not the BLOBs are text or image. Each one of these requires a pointer to the text, ntext, or image column to which you are referring. You do this by using the TEXTPTR() function. Check out the syntax in Listing 6-12.

Listing 6-12: Syntax for the TEXTPTR() Function

```
TEXTPTR ( column )
```

This returns a varbinary(16) and provides you with the text pointer of the BLOB. To put this in context, you typically do a single-row SELECT and use TEXTPTR() to pick up the pointer. Next, you use the appropriate function to manipulate the BLOB data. You'll soon see it in use when each function is discussed.

A complimentary function to TEXTPTR() is TEXTVALID(). This function tests the pointer you have to make sure it is a valid text pointer. Check out the syntax in Listing 6-13.

Listing 6-13: Syntax for TEXTVALID() Function

```
TEXTVALID ( 'table.column' , text_ptr )
```

Notice how the table name must be included. This function returns an int—1 if it is valid and 0 if it is not.

Using the READTEXT Statement

The READTEXT statement is the means by which you pick up BLOB data from a column. First, you use TEXTPTR() to pick up the pointer. Next, you use READTEXT to retrieve the portion of the BLOB you want to receive. Check out the syntax in Listing 6-14.

Listing 6-14: Syntax for the READTEXT Statement

```
READTEXT { table.column text_ptr offset size } [ HOLDLOCK ]
```

Note that you have to specify the table name as well as the column. This is because you are not using a SELECT, which would specify the table name. The text_ptr parameter is the one you picked up from the TEXTPTR() function. The offset determines how many bytes from the beginning to start the retrieval, and size determines the number of bytes to retrieve. If size is 0, up to 4KB are read. A 0 offset means to start at the beginning. (There are no commas between the parameters.) The HOLDLOCK keyword acts as it does in a SELECT—it maintains locks on the BLOB until the transaction is completed. The READTEXT statement returns only one BLOB, or a portion thereof, from one row.

To demonstrate this, you'll use the pubs database. The pub_info table has two BLOBs—one text and one image. Suppose you want to pick up the 47-character piece of the pr_info column that starts at byte position 224 for publisher 9999. Take a look at the code in Listing 6-15.

Listing 6-15: Sample Code for READTEXT

```
DECLARE
 @ptr varbinary (16)

SELECT
 @ptr = TEXTPTR (pr_info)
FROM
  pub_info
WHERE
  pub_id = 9999

READTEXT pub_info.pr_info @ptr 223 47
```

You should get back the following: "Lucerne publishing is located in Paris, France."

When you deal with text in row, you need to pick up the text pointer and do the READTEXT within a transaction. This is because the pointer that you get is valid only inside a transaction. Thus, if you run TEXTVALID() on a pointer both inside a transaction and immediately following the COMMIT, it will return 0 after the COMMIT, even though you are testing the same pointer value.

The READTEXT statement cannot be used on BLOB columns in a view.

Using the WRITETEXT Statement

You use the WRITETEXT statement when you want to overwrite BLOB data. It has the same look and feel as the READTEXT statement. Here again, you pick up the pointer using TEXTPTR(). Next, you use WRITETEXT to write the entire BLOB to the row. The syntax is in Listing 6-16.

Listing 6-16: Syntax for WRITETEXT Statement

```
WRITETEXT { table.column text_ptr }
 [ WITH LOG ] { data }
```

The column and pointer arguments are the same as in READTEXT. The data parameter contains the data you want to write. The WITH LOG option has meaning only for SQL Server releases prior to release 2000.

The WRITETEXT statement cannot be used on BLOB columns in a view.

Logging of WRITETEXT and UPDATETEXT

Prior to SQL Server 2000, the WRITETEXT and UPDATETEXT statements were not logged by default. Consequently, you could not back up the log after these statements and instead had to back up the entire database. This could leave you exposed. The WITH LOG option told SQL Server to log the operation anyway. This caused the log to grow quickly, but the transaction was logged, so you could back up the log. SQL Server 2000 handles logging differently, based on how you have set the recovery model. The WITH LOG option is ignored, but it allows backward compatibility.

Suppose you want to overwrite the pr_info column in the previous example with new information. You pick up the text pointer and then use WRITETEXT to do the write. The code is presented in Listing 6-17.

Listing 6-17: Sample Code for WRITETEXT

```
DECLARE
 @ptr varbinary (16)

SELECT
 @ptr = TEXTPTR (pr_info)
```

```
FROM
  pub_info
WHERE
  pub_id = 9999

WRITETEXT pub_info.pr_info @ptr 'This is the new information.'
```

> **NOTE** *You must have* UPDATE *permission on the table in order to use the* WRITETEXT *statement.*

Using the UPDATETEXT Statement

You use the UPDATETEXT statement when you want to update just part of your BLOB data. It is much the same as WRITETEXT with some extra parameters. Take a look at the syntax in Listing 6-18.

Listing 6-18: Syntax for UPDATETEXT

```
UPDATETEXT { table_name.dest_column_name dest_text_ptr }
 { NULL | insert_offset }
 { NULL | delete_length }
 [ WITH LOG ]
 [ inserted_data
  | { table_name.src_column_name src_text_ptr } ]
```

The table_name.dest_column_name parameter is the column that you want to update. The dest_text_ptr parameter is the text pointer for that column, which you picked up with the TEXTPTR() function. The insert_offset parameter contains the number of bytes from the beginning of the column to where the update should start. If this parameter is NULL, the data will be appended to the existing data. The delete_length parameter contains the number of bytes from the offset position to delete prior to writing the new data. If this parameter is NULL, then all data from the offset position to the end of the existing column will be deleted.

The WITH LOG option is ignored in SQL Server 2000 but is kept for backward compatibility.

The inserted_data parameter is the new data. However, you can take the data from an existing table and column by using the table_name.src_column_name and src_text_ptr parameters. These designate the source column and its text pointer, respectively. This is much like an UPDATE statement where you are joining to another table to pick up its data.

Let's return to the `insert_offset` and `delete_length` parameters. If you want to insert new data, specify a value for `insert_offset` and 0 for `delete_length`. If you want to delete data and not replace it, then specify a non-NULL `insert_offset` and a non-zero `delete_length`. Do not specify `inserted_data`. Finally, if you want to replace existing data, specify a non-NULL `insert_offset`, a non-zero `delete_length`, and the new data.

You can use UPDATETEXT to add more data to a `text`, `ntext`, or `image` column. For example, using the Northwind database, you can insert the string `'Venerable '` before the phrase `'World Wide Web'` in the HomePage column for supplier ID 6 in the Suppliers table. The code to do this is in Listing 6-19.

> **CAUTION** *For this and the following examples, execute the code inside a transaction with a* ROLLBACK *so that you will not permanently change the data.*

Listing 6-19: Using UPDATETEXT to Insert Data

```
DECLARE
 @ptr varbinary (16)

SELECT
 @ptr = TEXTPTR (HomePage)
FROM
  Suppliers
WHERE
  SupplierID = 6

UPDATETEXT Suppliers.HomePage @ptr 17 0 'Venerable '
```

The `insert_offset` of 17 positions puts you at the beginning of the word `'World'`. The `delete_length` of 0 means that no characters are to be deleted. Then, the string `'Venerable '` is inserted.

You can use UPDATETEXT to change part of a `text`, `ntext`, or `image` column in a table. For example, suppose you want to change the phrase `'World Wide Web'` to `'World Wide Wait'` in the HomePage column for supplier ID 6. The code to do this is shown in Listing 6-20.

Listing 6-20: Using UPDATETEXT to Update Data

```
DECLARE
 @ptr varbinary (16)

SELECT
 @ptr = TEXTPTR (HomePage)
FROM
  Suppliers
WHERE
  SupplierID = 6

UPDATETEXT Suppliers.HomePage @ptr 28 3 'Wait'
```

The `insert_offset` of 28 positions puts you at the beginning of the word `'Web'`. The `delete_length` of 3 will delete the three characters corresponding to the word `'Web'`. Then, the word `'Wait'` is inserted.

Using the Northwind database, you can see how to remove part of the Home-Page information for supplier ID 6, as shown in Listing 6-21.

Listing 6-21: Using UPDATETEXT to Delete Data

```
DECLARE
 @ptr varbinary (16)

SELECT
 @ptr = TEXTPTR (HomePage)
FROM
  Suppliers
WHERE
  SupplierID = 6

UPDATETEXT Suppliers.HomePage @ptr 17 11
```

This code removes the string `'World Wide '` from the HomePage column for the supplier ID 6. Since no `inserted_data` was specified, the existing data were simply deleted.

As for the `WRITETEXT` statement, you need `UPDATE` permission on a table in order to use the `UPDATE` statement.

Using SET TEXTSIZE

You can adjust the maximum size of text and ntext data returned with a SELECT statement by using SET TEXTSIZE. The syntax is straightforward, as shown in Listing 6-22.

Listing 6-22: Syntax for SET TEXTSIZE

```
SET TEXTSIZE { number | @number_var }
```

You can SET TEXTSIZE up to 2GB, specified in bytes. Setting it to 0 resets the value to the default of 4KB. To find out what the current setting is, use SELECT @@TEXTSIZE.

Using the bigint Datatype

One element of scalability that is often ignored is the size of the datatypes that the relational database management system (RDBMS) supports. The bigint datatype is new to SQL Server 2000. It is a 64-bit (8-byte) integer and can store numbers from -2^{63} through $2^{63}-1$. If your data exceed the space normally provided by the 4-byte int, then bigint is your lifeboat. For most applications, you can probably get away with using int. Bear in mind that if you choose to use bigint instead of int, you are doubling the amount of space your data column will require. This can make your indexes grow quite large if keys are based upon this datatype. Make sure, during your capacity planning analysis, that you really need this datatype.

Because SQL Server 2000 is so scalable, you can end up with a considerable number of rows in a table. If the number of rows to be counted exceeds $2^{31}-1$, then using the COUNT() function won't work for you. Here, you need the BIG_COUNT() function, which has the same look, feel, and functionality as its smaller brother COUNT(), but it returns the count as a bigint instead of an int.

Using the uniqueidentifier Datatype

The uniqueidentifier datatype was introduced in version 7.0. It is a 16-byte hexadecimal value that is a GUID. This is very useful when you have a large enterprise with data distributed across multiple databases and perhaps even multiple servers. Its use is very evident in merge replication. The uniqueidentifier datatype is populated with the NEWID() function, although you can feed it your own value—if you dare. This generates a number that is unique in the world. In Windows NT 4.0, the NEWID() function takes the MAC address of the server's network card and combines it with a unique number from the CPU clock. The algorithm is different in Windows 2000 and the MAC address is not exposed.

The best way to use this datatype is to make it a primary key in a table and add a default constraint that uses NEWID(). Make sure that none of your INSERTs specify the primary key, and you're there!

Listing 6-23 shows you the syntax for creating a sample table and some INSERTs, and Table 6-3 shows the resulting contents of this table.

Listing 6-23: Sample Table Using the uniqueidentifier and NEWID() Function

```
CREATE TABLE MyTable
(
 PK_ID      uniqueidentifier NOT NULL
                             PRIMARY KEY
                             DEFAULT (NEWID ()),
 CustomerName char (30)      NOT NULL
)
GO

INSERT MyTable (Name) VALUES ('Fred')
INSERT MyTable (Name) VALUES ('Wilma')
```

Table 6-3: Contents of the Sample Table with uniqueidentifier

PK_ID	Name
9079CCAA-5B45-11D4-B37C-00D05906331F	Fred
9079CCAB-5B45-11D4-B37C-00D05906331F	Wilma

In both of the rows in Table 6-3, the default generates the value for the uniqueidentifier. If you need to know the value of the key generated by NEWID(), and you do not have an alternative key, then you will have to save the value generated by NEWID() into a variable and include the variable in the INSERT statement, thus avoiding the default constraint.

A uniqueidentifier is 16 bytes compared with 4 bytes for an integer, so the index based on it is going to be considerably larger than that for the int. The NEWID() function generates values randomly, so serializing the values is not possible. They are not user-friendly; trying to type them into a dialog box would be a nightmare. Nevertheless, this datatype can be very useful when uniqueness within your enterprise is essential.

Using the sql_variant Datatype

The sql_variant datatype is new to SQL Server 2000. It can contain most other SQL datatypes, with some exceptions, as described later in this section. It may be used in variables, parameters, column names, and user-defined function return values. Think of it as a Variant in Visual Basic and you get the idea.

Since a table column can be sql_variant, you can have many rows of several different base datatypes in the same table column. However, the base types that cannot be stored in an sql_variant are text, ntext, image, timestamp, and sql_variant. A sql_variant also may not be used in a LIKE predicate, CONTAINSTABLE, or FREETEXTTABLE.

Behind the scenes, SQL Server stores the metadata information as well as the data itself for every sql_variant column. Consequently, you should expect the sql_variant to use up more space than the equivalent base datatype. Nevertheless, it gives you some options for those weird business rules that cannot be handled any other way.

In order to use an sql_variant in calculations such as addition or subtraction, you must first cast the sql_variant to an appropriate base type. You may assign it a NULL, but there will be no equivalent base type associated with the NULL.

Comparisons of sql_variants are handled based upon the hierarchy shown in Table 6-4. Essentially, when you compare two sql_variants of *different* datatype families, the value whose *datatype family* is higher in the hierarchy is considered to contain the higher value of the two sql_variants, *regardless of the actual value stored in each of the two* sql_variants. However, when the two sql_variants being compared are of the *same* datatype family, then the datatype of the one that is lower in the hierarchy is implicitly converted into the higher of the two. When you compare two sql_variants with the base types char, varchar, nchar, or nvarchar, the evaluation is calculated based on LCID (locale ID), LCID version, comparison flags, and sort ID. They are compared as integer values in the order listed.

Table 6-4: sql_variant Hierarchy

Data Type	Datatype Family
sql_variant	sql_variant
datetime	datetime
smalldatetime	datetime
float	approximate number
real	approximate number
decimal	exact number
money	exact number

Table 6-4: sql_variant Hierarchy (Continued)

Data Type	Datatype Family
smallmoney	exact number
bigint	exact number
int	exact number
smallint	exact number
tinyint	exact number
bit	exact number
nvarchar	Unicode
nchar	Unicode
varchar	Unicode
char	Unicode
varbinary	binary
binary	binary
uniqueidentifier	uniqueidentifier

Be careful with comparisons of different base types—you can get results opposite to what you might expect. For example, say you have two sql_variant values: A = '234' (char) and B = 123 (int). Intuitively, you may think that A > B. However, in the hierarchy, char is lower than int, and they are of different datatype families. Thus, when these two values are compared as sql_variants, A < B. However, when you compare them by casting them in their base datatypes, then A > B.

Okay, so you can accept that comparisons between char and int can produce less-than-intuitive results. Guess what happens when you use float and int base datatypes? For example, make A = 20000 (int) and B = 20 (float). If you compare these as sql_variants, then A < B! This is because float is a member of the Approximate Number family, which is higher than int's Exact Number data family. If you cast each of these as their base datatypes, then you get A > B, as expected.

When you assign an sql_variant to a non-sql_variant, you must use CAST() or CONVERT() explicitly before making the assignment. There is no implicit conversion.

The sql_variant can be used in indexes as well as unique, primary, and foreign keys. You are restricted to the length of the key columns not exceeding 900 bytes. They may not be used to support the IDENTITY property, nor can they be used in computed columns.

If you want to change the datatype of a column in a table to sql_variant, use the ALTER TABLE statement. You may not convert text, ntext, image, timestamp, or sql_variant to sql_variant. The existing values are converted into sql_variant using the original base datatype.

You cannot use ALTER TABLE to change an existing sql_variant column to a base datatype, even if all of the rows in that column are the same base datatype. This is because there are no implicit conversions from sql_variant to any other datatype. However, you can add a column with the correct datatype, populate it from the original column, drop the original column, and rename the new column. Keep in mind that the column order is now different.

You cannot use a COLLATE clause on an sql_variant column.

The sql_variant datatype gives you a great deal of power, but with power comes responsibility. Make sure you cast your sql_variant variables and columns to their base datatypes wherever possible and avoid those unpleasant surprises. The next section shows you how to keep track.

Using the SQL_VARIANT_PROPERTY() Function

Because just about anything can be stored in an sql_variant, you need a way of extracting the metadata that is also stored with it. The SQL_VARIANT_PROPERTY() function enables you to obtain various properties about an sql_variant, be it a variable, column, or any expression evaluating to an sql_variant. Take a look at the syntax in Listing 6-24.

Listing 6-24: Syntax for the SQL_VARIANT_PROPERTY() Function

```
SQL_VARIANT_PROPERTY (expression, property)
```

The expression parameter is the sql_variant you are testing. The property parameter is a varchar(128) that can take on the following values:

```
'BaseType'
'Precision'
'Scale'
'TotalBytes'
'Collation'
'MaxLength'
```

Ironically, the SQL_VARIANT_PROPERTY() function itself returns an sql_variant. This is because the results returned can be in either character form or integer form. The following sections describe the possible sql_variant return value information produced by SQL_VARIANT_PROPERTY() for each value of property.

BaseType

The `'BaseType'` property gives you the base datatype of the `sql_variant`. In this case, the return value is a `sysname`. The returned result can take on the following values:

```
'char'
'int'
'money'
'nchar'
'ntext'
'numeric'
'nvarchar'
'real'
'smalldatetime'
'smallint'
'smallmoney'
'text'
'timestamp'
'tinyint'
'uniqueidentifier'
'varbinary'
'varchar'
```

In the case of an invalid input, `NULL` is returned.

Precision

`'Precision'` gives you the number of digits of the numeric base datatype, as depicted in Table 6-5.

Table 6-5: Precision of Base Datatypes

Datatype	Number of Digits
datetime	23
smalldatetime	16
float	53
real	24
decimal (p,s) and numeric (p,s)	p
money	19

Table 6-5: Precision of Base Datatypes (Continued)

Datatype	Number of Digits
smallmoney	10
int	10
smallint	5
tinyint	3
bit	1

For the decimal and numeric types, the *p* and *s* refer to precision and scale, respectively. All other types return 0. The return value is an int. In the case of an invalid input, NULL is returned.

Scale

Related to 'precision' is 'scale', which is the number of digits after the decimal point. Here, too, an int is returned. The scales for base datatypes are depicted in Table 6-6.

Table 6-6: Scale of Base Datatypes

Datatype	Scale
decimal (p,s) and numeric (p,s)	s
money and smallmoney	4
datetime	3

All other datatypes return 0, while an invalid input returns NULL.

TotalBytes

The 'TotalBytes' property gives you the total number of bytes needed to hold not only the data of the given sql_variant but also the metadata. The value returned is an int, or NULL if there is invalid input. You would typically not need this in your programming. However, when you are doing physical design and are looking at indexing, this property can come in handy. For example, if the maximum size that an sql_variant column requires is more than 900 bytes, then index creation on that column will fail. Using OBJECTPROPERTY() with the 'TotalBytes' property to test an sql_variant's size before you attempt to create an index will enable you to determine whether you can create the index.

Collation

The 'Collation' property enables you to determine the collation of the particular sql_variant being tested. It applies only to character-based datatypes—char, nchar, varchar, and nvarchar. The value is returned as a sysname; invalid input returns NULL.

MaxLength

The 'MaxLength' property—unlike 'TotalBytes'—*is* relevant to the programmer. It gives the maximum datatype length in bytes. Bear in mind, however, that nchar and nvarchar take up exactly twice the number of bytes as the equivalent char and varchar. For example, a char(4) will have a 'MaxLength' value of 4, while an nchar(4) will have a 'MaxLength' value of 8. The value is returned as an int; invalid input returns NULL.

Using the table Datatype

The table datatype is also new to SQL Server 2000. You use it instead of a temporary table. (You'll see more about temporary tables in Chapter 12.) It can have many, but not all, of the features of a regular table; for example, PRIMARY KEY, UNIQUE, and CHECK constraints are all allowed with the table datatype. However, you cannot have FOREIGN KEY constraints. These constraints must be part of the table declaration statement; they may not be added later. Also, you may not create an index on the table after the table has been created.

The table datatype is used as a local variable and cannot be used as a stored procedure parameter. However, a user-defined function (UDF) may return a table variable. (User-defined functions are discussed in Chapter 11.)

The declaration of a table variable is like a combination of the regular CREATE TABLE and DECLARE statements. An example is shown in Listing 6-25.

Listing 6-25: Sample DECLARE Statement for a table Variable

```
DECLARE
@MyTable table
   (
     ItemID    int        PRIMARY KEY,
     Descr     char (20)  NOT NULL,
     Quantity  smallint   NOT NULL
                          CHECK (quantity < 20)
   )
```

One odd restriction on this datatype is that you cannot declare a table variable in conjunction with any other variable; it requires its own, separate DECLARE statement. You can use table variables and UDFs that return a table variable in certain SELECT and INSERT statements and where tables are supported in UPDATE, DELETE, and DECLARE CURSOR statements to manipulate data in the table. However, table variables and UDFs that return a table variable cannot be used in any other Transact-SQL statements. For example, you cannot do a SELECT INTO with a table variable.

As an example, to populate the table variable previously shown in Listing 6-25, you can use the INSERT statements in Listing 6-26.

Listing 6-26: Sample INSERT into a table Variable

```
INSERT @MyTable VALUES (1, 'Widget', 15)
INSERT @MyTable VALUES (2, 'Gizmo', 10)
INSERT @MyTable VALUES (3, 'Thingy', 12)
```

You can retrieve the values in the table by using a SELECT, as presented in Listing 6-27.

Listing 6-27: Sample SELECT from a table Variable

```
SELECT
  *
FROM
  @MyTable
```

> **NOTE** *You cannot use table variables as a means of passing tables between stored procedures. In this case, you will have to create a temporary table in one procedure and then work on it with another procedure. Stored procedures and temporary tables are discussed in Chapters 9 and 12, respectively.*

Using the IDENTITY Property and the IDENTITY() Function

The IDENTITY property enables you to assign an auto-number to a numeric column. Values for a column with an IDENTITY property are generated automatically when new rows are inserted into the table according to the seed and increment values supplied when the property was assigned to the column.

Using the IDENTITY Property

You can assign the IDENTITY property to one—and only one—numeric column in a table. The IDENTITY column must be of datatype int, bigint, smallint, tinyint, decimal, or numeric with a scale of 0, and it must be constrained to be non-NULLable.

Creating and Querying Tables with IDENTITY Columns

The syntax for creating a table with an IDENTITY column is shown in Listing 6-28.

Listing 6-28: Syntax for Creating a Table with an IDENTITY *Column*

```
CREATE TABLE <table_name>
(
 <col_name> <datatype> NOT NULL IDENTITY[(seed, increment)],
...other columns...
)
```

The seed argument is the value that will be assigned to the first row's IDENTITY column, and the increment argument determines the value that will be added (or subtracted in case it is negative) from the previously inserted IDENTITY value to generate the new value for the next inserted row. Notice, in the syntax just presented, that supplying the seed and increment values is optional—the defaults are (1, 1).

Now create a table called Identable. Assign the IDENTITY property to the column key_col and insert a few rows. The script is presented in Listing 6-29.

Listing 6-29: Schema Creation Script for the Identable Table

```
CREATE TABLE Identable
(
 key_col int    NOT NULL IDENTITY (1,1),
 abc      char(1) NOT NULL
)

INSERT INTO Identable VALUES ('a')
INSERT INTO Identable VALUES ('b')
INSERT INTO Identable VALUES ('c')
```

Notice that because the IDENTITY values are generated automatically, you need to "think" that the IDENTITY column does not exist when you insert new rows.

Now, look at the rows in Identable. The query is in Listing 6-30, and the rows are shown in Table 6-7.

Listing 6-30: Retrieving the Initial Identable's Content

```
SELECT
 *
FROM
 Identable
ORDER BY
 key_col
```

Table 6-7: The Initial Identable's Content

key_col	abc
1	a
2	b
3	c

There can be only one IDENTITY column in a table, so you can use the IDENTITYCOL keyword in your queries instead of using the actual column name. Listing 6-31 shows you the revised query.

Listing 6-31: Using the IDENTITYCOL Keyword

```
SELECT
 IDENTITYCOL,
 abc
FROM
 Identable
```

If you delete a row from the table and then insert another row, its IDENTITY column's value is not reused. The code in Listing 6-32 shows you how to prove this. The results are in Table 6-8.

Listing 6-32: Deleting and Inserting Rows from Identable

```
DELETE FROM Identable
WHERE
 key_col = 2

INSERT INTO Identable VALUES ('d')

SELECT
 *
```

```
FROM
 Identable
ORDER BY
 key_col
```

Table 6-8: Content of Identable after Deletion and Insertion of Rows

key_col	abc
1	a
3	c
4	d

Notice that the IDENTITY value 2 was not reused for the row that was deleted. Moreover, if you insert a new row inside an explicit transaction, the identity value for the new inserted row will not be reused even if you roll back the transaction. See Listing 6-33 and Table 6-9.

Listing 6-33: Inserting a Row into Identable and Rolling Back the Transaction

```
BEGIN TRAN
 INSERT INTO Identable VALUES ('e')
ROLLBACK TRAN

INSERT INTO Identable VALUES ('f')

SELECT
 *
FROM
 Identable
ORDER BY
 key_col
```

Table 6-9: Content of Identable after Rolling Back a Transaction that Inserted a Row

key_col	abc
1	a
3	c
4	d
6	f

Notice that the IDENTITY value 5 was not reused for the row that was inserted inside the transaction, .

If you want to find out the seed and increment values for a certain table, you can use the IDENT_INCR() and IDENT_SEED() functions shown in Listing 6-34, supplying the table name as an argument.

Listing 6-34: Retrieving the Seed and Increment Values

```
SELECT
 IDENT_SEED ('Identable') AS seed,
 IDENT_INCR ('Identable') AS increment
```

Using the IDENTITY_INSERT Session Option

If you want to supply your own explicit values for the IDENTITY column in an INSERT statement, you have to turn the session option IDENTITY_INSERT to ON for your table; otherwise your INSERT will be rejected. You can't update an IDENTITY column, whether IDENTITY_INSERT is turned on or not. For example, if you want to add a new row with the value 2 in the column key_col, you can use the code in Listing 6-35.

Listing 6-35: Using the IDENTITY_INSERT Option

```
SET IDENTITY_INSERT Identable ON

INSERT INTO Identable (key_col, abc) VALUES(2, 'g')

SELECT
 *
FROM
 Identable
ORDER BY
 key_col
GO

SET IDENTITY_INSERT Identable OFF
```

As Table 6-10 shows, you were able to specify an explicit value for the IDENTITY column.

Table 6-10: Result of Using the IDENTITY_INSERT Option

key_col	abc
1	a
2	g
3	c
4	d
6	f

There are a few issues you should be aware of when using the IDENTITY_INSERT option:

- This option affects only the session in which it was set; it does not have any effect on the other sessions.

- You can turn IDENTITY_INSERT on for only one table in your session. If you already turned it on for one table and try to turn it on for another, you will get an error message. You have to turn it off for the current table before you can turn it on for another.

- If you turned IDENTITY_INSERT on for a certain table, and you inserted a value that is higher than the current IDENTITY value for the table, the new value will become the current IDENTITY value for the table. If you turn off IDENTITY_INSERT, the next IDENTITY value that will be inserted will be the current IDENTITY value *plus* the increment defined with the property.

- When IDENTITY_INSERT is turned on, you can specify explicit values for the IDENTITY column in your INSERT statements; however, you must explicitly supply the column list as well.

- The IDENTITY property itself does not enforce uniqueness. If you do not have a PRIMARY KEY or UNIQUE constraint, or a unique index defined on the IDENTITY column, you can insert duplicate values when the IDENTITY_INSERT option is turned on for the table.

What Did I Just Insert?

Suppose you just inserted the row depicted in Listing 6-36.

Listing 6-36: Inserting a New Row into Identable

```
INSERT INTO Identable VALUES ('g')
```

Now suppose you need to know the IDENTITY value of the new row because you want to use it to insert child rows into another table that references this table. How do you find that out? In SQL Server 7.0, you had only one option—retrieving the value of the @@IDENTITY function—but it didn't return the correct value in all situations. To solve the problematic situations, SQL Server 2000 introduced two new functions: SCOPE_IDENTITY() and IDENT_CURRENT(). The following sections discuss the functionality and uses of the system functions @@IDENTITY, SCOPE_IDENTITY(), and IDENT_CURRENT(), and the differences between them.

Understanding the @@IDENTITY Function

The @@IDENTITY function returns the last IDENTITY value inserted by the current session into any table that has an IDENTITY column. @@IDENTITY is affected both by an explicit INSERT statement issued in the current scope, as well as by an implicit INSERT statement issued in an inner scope, such as by a trigger.

At this point, you're probably saying, "Hold your horses!" But if you look at this one step at a time, it should all make sense.

Currently, you don't have an INSERT trigger on your table. (Triggers are covered in Chapter 10, but for now, think of a *trigger* as a stored procedure or code attached to a modification action on a table.) @@IDENTITY holds the last IDENTITY value you inserted in your session. If you've been running all of the scripts thus far, the code in Listing 6-37 will return the value 7.

Listing 6-37: Retrieving the @@IDENTITY Value

```
SELECT
  @@IDENTITY
```

If you need this value for later use, you'd be better off saving it in a local variable as shown in Listing 6-38. Otherwise, the next INSERT statement that you issue against a table—any table—with an IDENTITY column, will change it. Therefore, it will be lost.

Listing 6-38: Saving the @@IDENTITY Value in a Variable

```
DECLARE @mylastident AS int
SET @mylastident = @@IDENTITY
PRINT @mylastident
```

Now, suppose you had a trigger on your table that inserts a row into another table that has an IDENTITY column. When you add a new row to your table, the trigger is fired and adds a new row to the other table, and the @@IDENTITY value is changed to the IDENTITY value generated by the INSERT statement issued by the trigger. @@IDENTITY doesn't hold the IDENTITY value of the row that you explicitly inserted.

There are ways to overcome this. For example, you can create a temporary table before you issue your INSERT, have the trigger insert the @@IDENTITY value into your temporary table before it issues its INSERT, and then retrieve the value from the temporary table after your INSERT and not by using the faulty value in @@IDENTITY. This is costly in terms of performance, and no doubt a "dirty" solution, but with SQL Server 7.0 you don't have any cleaner ways to overcome this issue, outside of having no triggers. The good news is that SQL Server 2000 has solved this problem, as you will see in the next section.

Using the SCOPE_IDENTITY() Function

The SCOPE_IDENTITY() function returns the last IDENTITY value inserted by your session into any table that has an IDENTITY column, but only in the current scope. A *scope* is a batch, a stored procedure, a trigger, or a function.

Note that this solves the problem you saw in the previous section, as a trigger has a different scope from the INSERT statement that caused it to fire. Hence, an INSERT statement issued by a trigger will not affect the return value of SCOPE_IDENTITY() for the session that issued an INSERT that caused it to fire.

If you add another row from the same scope to a table with an IDENTITY column, the current value of SCOPE_IDENTITY() will be changed, so make sure you store it in a local variable right after your INSERT statement so it won't be lost. Check out the code in Listing 6-39.

Listing 6-39: Saving the SCOPE_IDENTITY() Value in a Variable

```
DECLARE @mylastident AS int
SET @mylastident = SCOPE_IDENTITY ()
PRINT @mylastident
```

> **NOTE** *See Chapter 10 for more discussion on the* SCOPE_IDENTITY() *function.*

Using the IDENT_CURRENT() Function

Both @@IDENTITY and SCOPE_IDENTITY() return an IDENTITY value that was inserted by the current session. What if you want to know the last inserted IDENTITY value for a certain table, no matter which session generated it? One option that you might be thinking of is the query in Listing 6-40.

Listing 6-40: Retrieving the Maximum Value of key_col from Identable

```
SELECT
 MAX (key_col) AS max_key_col
FROM
 Identable
```

What if, for example, you had turned IDENTITY_INSERT on and inserted a value that was lower than the maximum IDENTITY column's value? This is where the IDENT_CURRENT() function comes in handy. This function returns the last IDENTITY value inserted into a given table (with the table name supplied to the IDENT_CURRENT() function as an argument), from any session or scope. Listing 6-41 shows you how to use the IDENT_CURRENT() function to find the last IDENTITY value inserted to Identable.

Listing 6-41: Retrieving the IDENT_CURRENT() Value

```
SELECT
 IDENT_CURRENT ('Identable')
```

Using DBCC CHECKIDENT

There have been situations where the IDENTITY value of a table became corrupted. The occurrence of these situations lessened as SQL Server advanced in its versions, but they might still occur. If you suspect a corruption of your IDENTITY value, you can issue the statement in Listing 6-42, which returns both the current IDENTITY value of your table and the value it should be.

Listing 6-42: Syntax for Retrieving the Current IDENTITY Value of a Table and the Correct Value

```
DBCC CHECKIDENT ('table_name', NORESEED)
```

Run this statement against Identable (see Listing 6-43) and look at the output.

Listing 6-43: Retrieving the Current IDENTITY Value of the Table Identable and Its Correct Value

```
DBCC CHECKIDENT ('Identable', NORESEED)

Checking identity information: current identity value '7',
current column value '7'.
DBCC execution completed. If DBCC printed error messages,
contact your system administrator.
```

If you want to fix the current IDENTITY value to hold the maximum current value in the IDENTITY column, you can issue the statement in Listing 6-44.

Listing 6-44: Reseeding the IDENTITY Value

```
DBCC CHECKIDENT ('table_name', RESEED)
```

Regardless of whether your table's current IDENTITY value is corrupted or not, you can change it to hold an explicit value of your choice, using the statement in Listing 6-45.

Listing 6-45: Syntax for Reseeding the IDENTITY Value with a New Explicit Value

```
DBCC CHECKIDENT ('table_name', RESEED, new_reseed_value)
```

For example, if you want to reseed Identable with the value 50, you can use the statement in Listing 6-46.

Listing 6-46: Reseeding the IDENTITY Value of Identable with a New Explicit Value

```
DBCC CHECKIDENT ('Identable', RESEED, 50)
```

Note that the new_reseed_value changes the current IDENTITY value for the table. Hence, the next inserted value will be new_reseed_value + increment. For example, if you insert a new row to your table as shown in Listing 6-47, the value 51 will be inserted into the key_col column and not 50. See the results in Table 6-11.

Listing 6-47: Inserting a New Row into Identable

```
INSERT INTO Identable VALUES('h')

SELECT
 *
FROM
 Identable
ORDER BY
 key_col
```

Table 6-11: Result of Inserting a New Row to Identable after Reseeding the Current IDENTITY Value

key_col	abc
1	a
2	g
3	c
4	d
6	f
7	g
51	h

Using the IDENTITY() Function

The IDENTITY() function is used in a SELECT INTO statement to generate a result column with automatically generated values, in the same way that the IDENTITY property generates them when you use it in a table. Look at the syntax of a SELECT INTO statement using the IDENTITY() function in Listing 6-48.

Listing 6-48: Syntax for Using the IDENTITY() Function

```
SELECT
 IDENTITY(<data_type> [, <seed>, <increment>]) AS column_name,
 <other_columns>
INTO
 <new_table_name>
FROM
 <table_name>
WHERE
 <search_criteria>
```

This will be better explained with an example. Suppose you want to provide an ordered output of the values in the abc column in the table Identable, with an additional column in the result that holds the number 1 for the first returned row and is incremented by 1 for each row that follows. You can issue the query depicted in Listing 6-49. The results are shown in Table 6-12.

Listing 6-49: Query that Returns Result Row Numbers, Starting with 1 and Incremented by 1

```
SELECT
 (SELECT
   COUNT (*)
  FROM
   Identable AS T2
  WHERE
   T2.abc <= T1.abc) AS rownum,
 abc
FROM
 Identable AS T1
ORDER BY
 abc
```

Table 6-12: Result Row Numbers, Starting with 1 and Incremented by 1

rownum	abc
1	a
2	c
3	d
4	f
6	g
6	g
7	h

There are two problems with this query. First, it is a "killer" in terms of performance, and second, in order to provide the correct result, it depends on the fact that the abc column is unique. If abc isn't unique, as in this case, you get the same values in rownum for rows with the same value in abc. In this example, the character *g* appears twice in the abc column, so you get the same value, 6, in the rownum column for both. You might be even thinking of a third problem—What if you don't want each following row to be incremented by one?—but this can easily be solved.

For example, suppose you want to start with 1 and increment by 3. The solution is in Listing 6-50 and the results are shown in Table 6-13.

Listing 6-50: Query that Returns Result Row Numbers, Starting with 1 and Incrementing by 3

```
SELECT
  1 +
  3 *
  (SELECT
    count(*)
   FROM
    Identable AS T2
   WHERE
    T2.abc < T1.abc) AS rownum,
  abc
FROM
 Identable AS T1
ORDER BY
 abc
```

Table 6-13: Result Row Numbers, Starting with 1 and Incrementing by 3

rownum	abc
1	a
4	c
7	d
10	f
13	g
13	g
19	h

Still, the first two problems remain. This is where the IDENTITY() function comes in handy. First, you use it in a SELECT INTO statement to create a temporary table that has the additional rownum column. Temporary tables are covered in detail in Chapter 12, but for now, just note that the names of temporary tables begin with #. Listing 6-51 shows an example.

Listing 6-51: Storing the Results in a Temporary Table Using the IDENTITY() Function

```
SELECT
 IDENTITY (int , 1, 1) AS rownum,
 abc
INTO
 #temp
FROM
 Identable
ORDER BY
 abc
```

Now you can issue your query against the #temp table, as shown in Listing 6-52.

Listing 6-52: Retrieving the Results of Using the IDENTITY() Function from the Temporary Table

```
SELECT
 *
FROM
 #temp
ORDER BY
 Abc
```

The output of this query is shown in Table 6-14.

Table 6-14: Results of Using the IDENTITY() Function

rownum	abc
1	a
2	c
3	d
4	f
5	g
6	g
7	h

Chapter 17 has further discussion of the IDENTITY() function.

SQL Puzzle 6-1: Customers with and without Sales

You want to get a list of total sales for all of your French and Spanish customers in the Northwind database. However, for those customers who have not placed an order, you want to see the word 'None' in the TotalSales column of the result set.

The answer to this puzzle can be found on pages 689–690.

CHAPTER 7
Writing Code in Transact-SQL

TRANSACT-SQL GOES FURTHER than your plain vanilla SQL. You have a broad range of features available to you beyond what you have seen in the previous chapters. Transact-SQL is not limited to data retrieval; it can be programmed in the classical sense. It is not as rich as C++ or Visual Basic, but it can handle most of what you throw at it. In Chapter 9, you will be introduced to stored procedures, which act like subroutines that can be called from front-end clients or from other SQL code. What you learn in this chapter will be used heavily inside stored procedures.

This chapter assumes that you have had some programming experience. Programming is generally based on the same set of skills, and what you do in one language can often be done in another—you just have to learn how.

Working with Variables

In Chapter 6, you learned about datatypes. Every variable that you use must be declared, together with its datatype, in a DECLARE statement. You can declare more than one variable at a time in a single DECLARE as long as you separate the variables with commas. This relieves you of a few keystrokes. Ideally, you should have one variable per line so that you can comment each. Take a look at the syntax in Listing 7-1.

Listing 7-1: Syntax for the DECLARE Statement

```
DECLARE
 {@local_variable [AS] data_type}
[,...n]
```

Note that variables begin with an "at sign" (@), and the name must conform to the rules for identifiers. The AS keyword is optional. You cannot declare constants like you can in VB. Instead, you have to declare them as variables and then assign them their constant values. It is up to you to ensure they remain constant. The scope of the variable is local to the batch, so when a batch completes, the variables evaporate. If the variable is declared inside a stored procedure, it is local to that stored procedure. It can, however, be passed as a parameter to another stored procedure.

> **TIP** *Do not use variable names beginning with @@. This can cause confusion with system functions.*

A sample declaration is depicted in Listing 7-2.

Listing 7-2: Example of the DECLARE Statement

```
DECLARE
 @OrderID    int,
 @CustomerID int,
 @ShipDate   datetime
```

It's good practice to adopt a naming convention that is consistent across your enterprise, whether you are naming table columns or variables. Variable names should be the same as corresponding column names, where applicable, but this is not always possible. For example, you may be picking out the first and last ship date of a product from the Orders and Order Details tables. You are referencing the ShipDate column in both cases, so you would have to go with @FirstShipDate and @LastShipDate or something similar.

Assigning Values with SET and SELECT

Once you have declared your variables, you then have to assign values to them. Prior to SQL Server version 7.0, the only way to do this was to use a SELECT statement. From release 7.0 onward, you can also use the SET command. The syntax for variable assignment is straightforward, as shown in Listing 7-3.

Listing 7-3: Syntax for Variable Assignment with the SELECT Statement

```
SELECT {@local_variable = expression } [,...n]
```

The expression can be any valid SQL Server expression. As an example, you can save the CustomerID value for a particular OrderID in the Orders table of the Northwind database as shown in Listing 7-4.

Listing 7-4: Using SELECT to Assign a Variable

```
DECLARE
  @Customerid AS char(5)

SELECT
  @CustomerID = CustomerID
FROM
  Orders
WHERE
  OrderID = 10248

PRINT @CustomerID
```

Needless to say, you are expecting only one row when you assign a value to a scalar variable. What happens when multiple rows are returned? The variable is updated repeatedly until the last row is returned. Only the value from the last row is stored in the local variable.

You can take advantage of repeated concatenation when more than one row is returned. This is shown in Listing 7-5.

Listing 7-5: Using Aggregate Concatenation

```
DECLARE
  @OrderIDs AS varchar (8000)
SET
  @OrderIDs = ''
SELECT
  @OrderIDs = @OrderIDs + CAST (OrderID AS varchar) + ';'
FROM
  Orders
WHERE
  CustomerID = 'VINET'

PRINT @OrderIDs
```

After declaration, the @OrderIDs variable is initialized to an empty string. Then, each row in the result set causes the @OrderIDs variable to be updated, concatenating itself with the current OrderID and a semicolon. Finally, the result is printed: 10248;10274;10295;10737;10739;.

The syntax for the SET command is quite simple, as you can see in Listing 7-6.

Listing 7-6: Syntax for Variable Assignment with the SET Statement

```
SET
  @local_variable = expression
```

The big difference between SET and SELECT is that SELECT can assign multiple variables at one time, whereas the SET statement can assign only one.

> **CAUTION** *It is very important to initialize your variables; otherwise, they are NULL by default. Also, be careful when using variables where no rows are returned by the query that is used to assign a value to a variable. In this case, your variable retains the value it had prior to the assignment statement.*

Consider the code in Listing 7-7. The variable @CustomerID is initialized to 0. Next, the variable is updated through a SELECT with a WHERE clause that guarantees no rows, since there is no OrderID of 1. The value shown by the final SELECT statement will have the original value of 0.

Listing 7-7: Example of a Variable Not Updated Due to No Rows Being Returned

```
DECLARE
  @CustomerID int

SELECT
  @CustomerID = 0

SELECT
  @CustomerID = CustomerID
  FROM
    Orders
  WHERE
    OrderID = 1

SELECT
  @CustomerID
```

If you assign a variable through a subquery, and no rows are found in the subquery to satisfy the selection criteria, your variable will be set to NULL. This is different from the behavior you saw in Listing 7-7 when no rows were found in a regular SELECT.

Here's an example. Suppose you want the CustomerID for the case where OrderID = 1. The code in Listing 7-8 will set CustomerID to NULL, because there is no such OrderID. Examine the code in Listings 7-7 and 7-8 carefully. You will see that they do essentially the same work, but the outcome is quite different.

Listing 7-8: Assignment with a Subquery

```
DECLARE
  @CustomerID int

SELECT
  @CustomerID = 0

SELECT
  @CustomerID =
  (
    SELECT
      CustomerID
    FROM
      Orders
    WHERE
      OrderID = 1
  )

SELECT
  @CustomerID
```

SQL Server 7.0 brought with it more ANSI-92 compliance. This comes into play with regard to variables when you are concatenating strings and one of the values is NULL. The ANSI-92 standard says that NULL plus anything is NULL. In releases prior to 7.0, this was not the case. Rather, a string plus NULL gave you the original string.

You can turn off this feature by putting your database into 6.5-compatibility mode until all of your code has migrated to ANSI-92 compliance. The downside is that you cannot avail yourself of any of the new features in versions 7.0 or 2000. You can, however, use SET options to turn off CONCAT_NULL_YIELDS_NULL. This stays in effect only for the session or stored procedure from which it is invoked. You can go one better and set it for the whole database by using ALTER DATABASE SET CONCAT_NULL_YIELDS_NULL or by using sp_dboption with the 'concat null yields null' parameter.

Similarly, the string ' ' (single quote–single quote) is not the same as ' ' (single quote–blank–single quote) as it was in pre-7.0 versions. You have to be mindful of this when you are migrating legacy code from 6.x systems. There is no SET option to turn this off—you will have to go into 6.5 compatibility mode.

Control of Flow

In many programming situations, you are faced with controlling the logical flow of the program. This breaks down into two basic categories—conditional processing and loops. You carry out conditional processing through the use of the IF ELSE construct. You perform loops with a WHILE.

The IF ELSE Construct

If you have written even the simplest of programs in other languages, you have come across conditional processing. This is a situation where you test for a condition. If it is true, you take one course of action; if it is false, you take another course. In Transact-SQL, this is implemented with an IF ELSE construct, as in most other languages. The test condition must evaluate to TRUE, FALSE, or UNKNOWN. Take a moment to study the syntax in Listing 7-9.

Listing 7-9: Syntax for the IF ELSE Statement

```
IF Boolean_expression
  {sql_statement | statement_block}
[ELSE
  {sql_statement | statement_block}]
```

The Boolean expression can test for equality or inequality. It can even use the EXISTS predicate or a nested subquery. (Subqueries are discussed in Chapter 2.) Generally, anything you would see in the WHERE clause of a SELECT can be used as the Boolean expression in an IF statement. Indeed, each predicate in a WHERE clause is effectively an IF statement on its own. The ELSE clause is optional. If the Boolean expression evaluates to TRUE, the first statement or block is executed; otherwise, the second statement or block is carried out, if it exists.

The SQL statement that gets executed is any valid, single Transact-SQL statement. The statement block is a collection of statements, carried out in sequence. The statements in a block are delineated with the BEGIN and END keywords. The BEGIN and END keywords are not necessary if you have only one statement to execute. Just as in other languages, you can nest IF ELSE statements as deep as you like.

An example of a simple IF ELSE is shown in Listing 7-10.

Listing 7-10: Example of a Simple IF ELSE

```
IF @@ERROR <> 0 OR @@ROWCOUNT = 0
  RAISERROR ('Houston, we have a problem.', 16, 1)
ELSE
BEGIN
  PRINT 'Success'

  UPDATE Orders
  SET
    ShipDate = GETDATE ()
  WHERE
    OrderID = @OrderID
END
```

This example executes a RAISERROR if the Boolean expression is TRUE and a statement block—PRINT followed by UPDATE—if the Boolean is FALSE. (The RAISERROR statement and @@ERROR function are covered later in this chapter, in the "Raising Errors" and "Trapping Errors" sections, respectively.)

One odd feature of the IF ELSE construct comes into play when you use the CREATE TABLE and SELECT INTO statements in the IF or ELSE areas of the IF ELSE block. If you create the same *temporary* table in each of the IF and ELSE blocks, you will get an error. This is because the optimizer believes the object already exists, even though there is no way that both the IF and ELSE blocks will be executed. See the sample code in Listing 7-11.

Listing 7-11: Illegal Table Creation with IF ELSE Construct

```
IF 1 = 1
  CREATE TABLE #MyTable
  (
    i int NOT NULL
  )
ELSE
  CREATE TABLE #MyTable
  (
    i int      NOT NULL,
    a char (5) NOT NULL
  )
GO
```

Now rerun the script in Listing 7-11, but remove the # signs from the table names, thus making them permanent. This time, no errors are generated. It appears that SQL Server has a double standard when it deals with temporary versus permanent tables inside `IF ELSE` constructs.

The WHILE Construct

The other control-of-flow construct is the `WHILE` loop. You use this to do repetitive work. Typically, you would initialize a counter variable prior to entering the loop and then increment the counter somewhere inside the loop. Most often, you will need the `BEGIN` and `END` keywords, because you typically have one statement to increment the counter and at least one other statement to do the real work. The syntax is shown in Listing 7-12.

Listing 7-12: Syntax of the WHILE Loop

```
WHILE Boolean_expression
  {sql_statement | statement_block}
  [BREAK]
  {sql_statement | statement_block}
  [CONTINUE]
```

Some explanation is in order here. The `BREAK` and `CONTINUE` keywords must occur *inside* the scope of the `WHILE`. This means that you will have the `WHILE` keyword, together with the Boolean expression, followed by a statement block, delineated by the `BEGIN` and `END` keywords.

The `BREAK` statement enables you to exit the `WHILE` loop immediately. If you have a nested `WHILE` loop, this will exit the *innermost* loop. On the other hand, the `CONTINUE` statement enables you to skip the remaining statements in the loop and go directly to the Boolean expression. If you have done any C programming, these keywords and their behavior will be familiar.

The `WHILE` construct is best explained through an example. To practice your SQL, add 100 rows with default values to a table. Check out the script in Listing 7-13.

Listing 7-13: Sample Code for a WHILE Loop

```
DECLARE
  @Count int

SET
  @Count = 1
```

```
WHILE @Count <= 100
BEGIN
  INSERT MyTable VALUES (@Count)

  IF @@ERROR <> 0
    BREAK

  SET
    @Count = @Count + 1
END
```

This script declares a counter and initializes it to 1. It then loops through 100 iterations and performs an INSERT. It tests to see if the INSERT was successful: if the
INSERT fails, it exits the loop; otherwise, it increments the counter and continues.

> **CAUTION**   *Be careful when you use the* CONTINUE *statement. It will skip back to
> the Boolean statement, and if it skips over the code that increments your
> counter, it may place you into an infinite loop.*

It is possible to have a WHILE loop that executes only one statement, instead of a
block, yet is still able to exit gracefully. This is a case where all you are doing is executing a stored procedure until you get a favorable return code. (You will learn more
about stored procedures in Chapter 9.) Take a look at the example in Listing 7-14.

Listing 7-14: A WHILE Loop with a Single Statement Using an EXEC

```
SET
  @rc = 1

WHILE @rc <> 0
  EXEC @rc = sp_MyProc
```

Make sure you initialize the return code variable—@rc—before you start the loop.
It is also possible not to use return codes or counters and use a single SQL
statement for the iterative work—you can make the Boolean a subquery with an
appropriate test. Use the Northwind database, and suppose you are greedy and
want to raise the price of your products by 5 percent increments until the average
price of your products is $20 or more. The Boolean can test the average price and
compare it to $20. The SQL statement will do the incrementing. The code is pre-
sented in Listing 7-15.

Listing 7-15: Using a Subquery with a Single-Statement WHILE Loop

```
WHILE (SELECT AVG (UnitPrice) FROM Products) < $20
  UPDATE Products
  SET
    UnitPrice = UnitPrice * 1.05
```

Not bad, eh? You will see the WHILE construct used extensively when you look at cursors in Chapter 15.

Handling Errors

Much of what you do, when you build software, centers around error handling. SQL Server enables you to detect errors as well as notify calling software that an error has occurred. When SQL Server detects an error, it sets the value of @@ERROR to a non-zero value. Your code can test the value of @@ERROR and take appropriate action.

Managing Error Messages

SQL Server maintains a table of all errors in *sysmessages*. There is only one copy of this table, and it is kept in the master database. Each row is keyed on (error, dlevel, msglangid). The error column is the message number, dlevel is used internally, and msglangid is the system message group ID. The msglangid essentially refers to the language of the error message. This way, you can have the same error number across all languages.

Using sp_addmessage

You add user-defined error messages with the sp_addmessage system stored procedure. Check out the syntax in Listing 7-16.

Listing 7-16: Syntax for the sp_addmessage System Stored Procedure

```
sp_addmessage [ @msgnum = ] msg_id ,
 [ @severity = ] severity ,
 [ @msgtext = ] 'msg'
 [ , [ @lang = ] 'language' ]
 [ , [ @with_log = ] 'with_log' ]
 [ , [ @replace = ] 'replace' ]
```

The parameters are defined as follows:

- The @msgnum parameter is an int that specifies the number of the message.
  User-defined message numbers start at 50001. The combination of @msgnum
  and @lang must be unique.

- The @severity parameter is a smallint that specifies the severity of the error
  in the range 1 through 25; only members of the sysadmin role can add severity levels greater than 18.

- The @msgtext parameter is an nvarchar(255) that contains the text of the
  error message.

- The @lang parameter is a sysname that specifies the language of the message.
  If this parameter is missing, the language used is that of the current session.

- The @with_log parameter is a varchar(5) and is either 'TRUE' if the error is
  always written to the Windows NT/2000 application log or 'FALSE'—the
  default—if it is not, although you can optionally write to the log at the time
  you raise the error. You must be a member of the sysadmin fixed server role
  to use this option.

- The @replace parameter is a varchar(7) that can have the value 'REPLACE'.
  If specified, you are telling SQL Server to replace an existing error message
  with the new text and severity level. You must specify this option if the message already exists.

Only members of the sysadmin and serveradmin fixed server roles are permitted
to use this system stored procedure.

As an example, say you want to create an error message with a severity level of
16 to warn the user that a customer does not exist. The code in Listing 7-17 shows
you how this is done.

Listing 7-17: Using sp_addmessage

```
sp_addmessage
  60000,
  16,
  'Customer does not exist.'
```

Later in this chapter, in the "Raising Errors" section, you will see how to create
messages that can use parameter substitution.

Using `sp_altermessage`

The `sp_altermessage` system stored procedure is used to alter the state of an error message—specifically, its ability to write to the Windows NT/2000 application log. The syntax is shown in Listing 7-18.

Listing 7-18: Syntax for the sp_altermessage System Stored Procedure

```
sp_altermessage [ @message_id = ] message_number ,
  [ @parameter = ] 'write_to_log' ,
  [ @parameter_value = ] 'value'
```

The `@message_id` parameter is the same as that for `sp_addmessage`. You set `@parameter`—a sysname—to `'WITH_LOG'`. The `@parameter_value` is a `varchar(5)` and can be either `'TRUE'` or `'FALSE'`; no defaults are permitted. As an example, change the message created in Listing 7-15 to write to the log. The code is presented in Listing 7-19.

Listing 7-19: Using sp_altermessage

```
sp_altermessage
  60000,
  'WITH_LOG',
  'true'
```

Using `sp_dropmessage`

If you want to remove an error message, you use the `sp_dropmessage` system stored procedure. The syntax is shown in Listing 7-20.

Listing 7-20: Syntax for the sp_dropmessage System Stored Procedure

```
sp_dropmessage [ @msgnum = ] message_number
  [ , [ @lang = ] 'language' ]
```

The parameters specified here correspond to those for `sp_addmessage`. If you specify `'all'` for `@lang`, then all language versions of the message will be dropped.

For example, to drop the message you added in Listing 7-17, use the code in Listing 7-21.

Listing 7-21: Using sp_dropmessage

```
sp_dropmessage
  60000
```

Raising Errors

SQL Server can raise errors when it detects specific error conditions, such as a deadlock. Typically, the error messages are not very user-friendly, particularly for an end user. However, you do have the option of raising your own errors. You can do this in two ways, both of which involve the RAISERROR statement. The syntax is presented in Listing 7-22.

Listing 7-22: Syntax for the RAISERROR Statement

```
RAISERROR ( { msg_id | msg_str } { , severity , state }
  [ , argument [ ,...n ] ] )
  [ WITH option [ ,...n ] ]
```

You can have your error messages take parameters, and to do this, you will need to insert placeholders into the message text. If you have done any C programming, these placeholders will look familiar. They are derived from the printf() function in that language. The format of a placeholder in a message string is shown in Listing 7-23.

Listing 7-23: Placeholder Format

```
% [[flag] [width] [precision] [{h | l}]] type
```

The percent sign (%) indicates the beginning of the placeholder. The flag determines the spacing and justification of the item inside the message. See Table 7-1 for descriptions of values for the flag parameter.

Table 7-1: Spacing and Justification

Code	Prefix or Justification	Description
– (minus)	Left-justified	Left-justify the result within the given field width.
+ (plus)	+ (plus) or – (minus) prefix	Preface the output value with a + or – sign if the output value is of signed type.
0 (zero)	Zero padding	If the width is prefaced with 0, zeros are added until the minimum width is reached. When 0 and – appear, 0 is ignored. When 0 is specified with an integer format (i, u, x, X, o, d), 0 is ignored.

Table 7-1: Spacing and Justification (Continued)

Code	Prefix or Justification	Description
# (number)	0x prefix for a hexadecimal type of x or X	When used with the o, x, or X format, the # flag prefaces any nonzero value with 0, 0x, or 0X, respectively. When d, i, or u are prefaced by the # flag, the flag is ignored.
' ' (blank)	Space padding	Prefaces the output value with blank spaces if the value is signed and positive. This is ignored when included with the + flag.

The width is an integer that determines the minimum width. If you use * instead of a number, then the precision will determine the width. The precision determines the maximum number of characters or the minimum number of digits for an integer. The h or l is used with the types d, i, o, x, X, or u, and creates short int (h) or long int (l) values. The types are described in Table 7-2.

Table 7-2: RAISERROR Type Codes

Character Type	Represents
d or I	Signed integer
o	Unsigned octal
p	Pointer
s	String
u	Unsigned integer
x or X	Unsigned hexadecimal

Note that float, double- and single-character types are not supported.

The severity is the same as in sp_addmessage. The state represents information about the invocation state of the error and can range from 1 to 127. This can represent anything you want, such as the line of code within a procedure, an application-defined severity, and so on.

The argument is the value to be inserted into the message string. You can have zero or more substitution parameters, but the number cannot exceed 20. The substitution parameters can be tinyint, smallint, int, char, varchar, binary, or varbinary. Options can take on the values in Table 7-3.

Table 7-3: RAISERROR Options

Value	Description
LOG	Logs the error in the SQL Server error log and the application log. Errors logged in the SQL Server error log are currently limited to a maximum of 440 bytes.
NOWAIT	Sends messages immediately to the client.
SETERROR	Sets @@ERROR value to *msg_id* or 50000, regardless of the severity level.

The simplest way to use the RAISERROR statement is with an error number. As an example, raise the user-defined error of 60000. This is done in Listing 7-24.

Listing 7-24: Using RAISERROR with an Error Number

```
RAISERROR (60000, 16, 1)
```

The output is shown in Listing 7-25.

Listing 7-25: Output from RAISERROR

```
Server: Msg 60000, Level 16, State 1, Line 1
Customer does not exist.
```

Alternatively, you can use RAISERROR without an error number, supplying the message text, severity, state, and optional parameters. In this case, you get a message number of 50000. This is convenient because you do not have to go to the trouble of adding messages to *sysmessages*. Your application-level error handling will have to trap only message 50000. Any front-end code will have to parse the message text.

Another reason for avoiding the use of stored messages is the potential for conflict with other applications. For example, if you are a software vendor and want to add messages to support your application, then you could conflict with the same error numbers on your customers' servers. A way to get around this with SQL Server 2000 is to create a separate instance of SQL Server for your application.

As an example of using RAISERROR without specifying a message number, suppose you want to raise an error with the message test, "Houston, we have a problem." This is done in Listing 7-26.

Listing 7-26: Using RAISERROR without an Error Number

```
RAISERROR ('Houston, we have a problem.', 16, 1)
```

The output is shown in Listing 7-27.

Listing 7-27: Output from RAISERROR

```
Server: Msg 50000, Level 16, State 1, Line 1
Houston, we have a problem.
```

This example is the simplest form of using RAISERROR without supplying an error number. You can take this one step further by using parameter substitution. For example, you can raise an error that includes the CustomerID, as shown in Listing 7-28.

Listing 7-28: Using RAISERROR

```
RAISERROR ('Unable to find Customer ID %09d', 16, 1, @CustomerID)
```

The CustomerID in the error message will have leading zeroes and will have a width of at least nine digits. If you want to make this into a permanent message with its own error number, you can use sp_addmessage with the same message text as in Listing 7-28. This is done in Listing 7-29.

Listing 7-29: Using sp_addmessage to Add an Error with Parameter Substitution

```
sp_addmessage
  60001,
  16,
  'Unable to find Customer ID %09d'
```

Now, if you want to raise error number 60001 for CustomerID 23, you use the code in Listing 7-30.

Listing 7-30: Raising a Numbered Message with Parameter Substitution

```
RAISERROR (60001, 16, 1, 23)
```

If you want to log the error in the error log, you can add the WITH LOG option, as shown in Listing 7-31.

Listing 7-31: Raising an Error with Logging

```
RAISERROR (60001, 16, 1, 23) WITH LOG
```

Finally, you can use the WITH SETERROR option so that @@ERROR will be set to the value of msg_id, regardless of the severity level. Check out the sample code in Listing 7-32.

Listing 7-32: Using RAISERROR with the SETERROR Option

```
RAISERROR (60001, 1, 2)
SELECT @@ERROR
GO

RAISERROR (60001, 1, 2) WITH SETERROR
SELECT @@ERROR
```

The first RAISERROR will set @@ERROR to 0, while the second one will set it to 60001.

Trapping Errors

It's nice to know that you have an error. Now what are you going to do about it? Once an error has been raised—either by SQL Server or by your code—you can use @@ERROR to determine the value of the error. For example, you could determine whether you should delete from the Orders table after you check @@ERROR for a DELETE on the Order Details table, as shown in Listing 7-33.

Listing 7-33: Using @@ERROR

```
DELETE [Order Details]
WHERE
  OrderID = @OrderID

IF @@ERROR = 0
  DELETE Orders
  WHERE
    OrderID = @OrderID
```

The error value is reset after each individual Transact-SQL statement. This means that if the first statement has an error and the second statement is OK, the value for @@ERROR after the second statement will be 0. Therefore, if you want to use the value of @@ERROR later in your code, you should save it immediately after a Transact-SQL statement. Check out the sample code in Listing 7-34. This technique is developed further in Chapter 17.

Listing 7-34: Saving the Value of @@ERROR

```
DECLARE
  @Error int

DELETE [Order Details]
WHERE
  OrderID = @OrderID

SET
  @Error = @@ERROR

IF @Error = 0
  DELETE Orders
  WHERE
    OrderID = @OrderID
ELSE
  RAISERROR (
    'Unable to delete Order ID %d because of error number %d.',
    @OrderID,
    @Error, 16, 1)
```

Just as in any other programming language, you should test each Transact-SQL statement, particularly where it involves altering data. Make your error messages user-friendly. If you are raising an error inside a stored procedure or trigger, then include the name of the procedure or trigger in the RAISERROR statement. (Stored procedures and triggers are covered in Chapters 9 and 10, respectively.)

Processing Batches

A *batch* is a group of statements sent to SQL Server to be executed at one time, though not necessarily as a single transaction. (Transactions are discussed in more detail in the "Using Transactions" section, later in this chapter.) Each batch is parsed and compiled as a unit. If the compile is successful, the batch is then executed in the sequence as laid out in the batch's SQL code. If the compile is unsuccessful, the batch will not execute and an error will be raised. Several batches can be executed in sequence on the same connection by separating each batch with the batch separator. This is usually a GO statement.

In most cases, if a statement within the batch fails, then the remainder of the batch is halted. For example, if a syntax error is found, the batch is not executed. Some runtime errors, such as primary key violations, stop only the current statement and do execute the remaining statements in the batch. The statements executed before the failed statement are unaffected. This raises an important issue. If a statement within the transaction fails, but the batch completes up to and including the COMMIT, your changes to the database will take effect, even though the data may be inconsistent because of the error. You must test for errors after each statement to ensure that your modifications have all taken place correctly before you commit your work.

The following statements must not be combined with any other statements within a batch:

```
CREATE DEFAULT

CREATE PROCEDURE

CREATE RULE

CREATE TRIGGER

CREATE VIEW
```

Also, you cannot alter a table and then refer to the altered or added columns within the same batch.

Commenting Code

Adding comments to your code is as important as the code itself. Some of the examples and puzzles you see in this book can get complicated, and without supporting documentation, the aim of the code can be quite confusing. In some IT shops, specifications are things that are talked about and even wished for, but rarely seen, so the developer cannot turn to them when he or she tries to debug or enhance someone else's scripts. Comments are the last line of defense against complete confusion.

Begin by writing the comments *first*, before writing the actual executable parts of your script. This focuses you on *what* it is that you wish to write. Then, start adding the code, which tells SQL Server *how* you want it done. If you later change a script because requirements have changed, be sure to change the comments as well. Otherwise, a developer will come along and see that the comments don't match the code and may change the code to match the comments. The ideal script will have a header block that states what the script is supposed to do.

Add inline comments to your SQL statements, particularly if you are using hard-coded constants, because often the constant has no self-evident meaning. Inline comments should also be added to variable declarations, stored procedure parameter lists, WHERE clause predicates, and so on.

Coding Styles

Coding styles are as personal and various as speaking styles. Still, if code is written sloppily or has no structure or white space, it can be difficult to maintain. You have seen one coding style used in this book. It came about as a compromise between the two authors, each of whom has his own way of writing. In the following sections, we present some styles to get you thinking about your own code and how you would like to write yours. Each section begins with an explanation of why the author codes the way he does, followed by a sample query written in his own style. The goal here is *readability*, which translates to *maintainability*.

From the Trenches

In one project, the previous developers wrote triggers that were 500-lines long. There was no structure to the code, and everything was packed together. It was impossible to read. When the code needed to be debugged, it had to be restructured first before troubleshooting began.

Tom's Style

I like to code as quickly as my fingers will allow. This translates to minimizing the number of keystrokes I have to type. For this reason, I like to use lowercase for all table aliases, functions, and keywords. I do, however, code column names exactly as they appear in the tables. Also, I use tabs—not spaces—so that my code lines up easily and correctly. My tab setting is eight spaces.

I left-justify SELECT, FROM, JOIN, WHERE, AND, GROUP BY, and ORDER BY keywords. All column names are specified in the SELECT list, separated by leading commas. I find the leading-commas approach a little easier to edit and to read; if I have to add another column name, I don't have to go to the end of the last line to add a comma. All table names are lined up, as are the ON keywords. If I'm using LEFT JOIN, I tab all of the table names so that they line up. I do not use the INNER or OUTER keywords unless I'm using join hints.

I indent subqueries and derived tables by one tab. I use a tab between the AND keyword and the predicate that follows. I do not use the AS keyword, either for column or table aliases. I alias table names on all joins to one or two characters and use the same alias, where possible, for each table throughout the entire database. Wherever I need column aliases, I use the <alias> = <expression> form, although I also use the <expression> <alias> form.

For CASE statements, I indent the WHEN/THENs and align the CASE and END keywords. I separate a function name and the left parenthesis with a space. I use the double-dash form of comments, and I use inline comments anywhere a hard-coded value is used. I insert a tab before the equal sign (=) and add a space after it.

Now, for the query. See Listing 7-35.

Listing 7-35: Tom's Coding Style

```
select
        o.CustomerID
,       Products        = sum (od.Quantity)
,       Sales           = sum (od.Quantity * od.Price)
from
        Orders          o
join    [Order Details] od      on      od.OrderID      = o.OrderID
join    Products        p       on      p.ProductID     = od.ProductID
where
        p.CategoryID    = 8  -- seafood
group by
        o.CustomerID
order by
        o.CustomerID
```

Itzik's Style

I prefer to use a different case for different elements in the query, provided that I'm not in a rush. If I'm supposed to be on my way out of the house and my wife is standing by the door with a frying pan ("I'm waiting…") and I'm in the middle of an answer in the newsgroups, then I'll settle for all my code being in lowercase. Otherwise, I'll have all the keywords and system functions in UPPERCASE, table names Capitalized, and column names all lowercase. In the latter case (pun intended), if there's a chance that the query will be run in a case-sensitive environment, I will use the existing table columns' case.

I use the AS keyword with variable declarations and column and table aliases. I use short table aliases, preferably single letters. If single letters are not adequate, as in a query referencing the tables Salutations and Shrubberies, I'll use short descriptive aliases, such as SL and SB, respectively. In queries referencing the same table more than once, I'll simply enumerate the aliases, as in S1, S2, and so on.

As for the general form of the query, it depends on its length. If it is very short, such as a simple SELECT * query, I'll write it all in one line, as in Listing 7-36.

Listing 7-36: Itzik's Short Coding Style

```
SELECT * FROM T1
```

If it's a bit longer, but the elements following the various clauses are short enough to fit in one line in a readable form, I'll have each clause on a separate line, with its elements appearing in the same line. See Listing 7-37.

Listing 7-37: Itzik's Short-But-Not-Too-Short Coding Style

```
SELECT col1, col2, col3
FROM T1
WHERE col1 > 10
ORDER BY col1
```

If the elements following a certain clause won't fit in the clause's line in a readable form, I'll have each element appear in its own line beneath the clause itself, indented with two spaces. This brings me to my variation of Tom's query, shown in Listing 7-38.

Listing 7-38: Itzik's Long Coding Style

```
SELECT
 O.customerid,
 SUM(OD.quantity) AS total_qty,
 SUM(OD.quantity * OD.price) AS total_volume
FROM
 Orders AS O JOIN [Order Details] AS OD
  ON OD.orderid = O.orderid
 JOIN Products AS P
  ON P.productid = OD.ProductID
WHERE P.categoryid = 8
GROUP BY O.customerid
ORDER BY O.customerid
```

Having said all this, I'd like to point out that if I look at my query and it doesn't "feel" right, I'll make adjustments in indentation and aligning so it's more readable.

Other Styles

Clearly, there is no one right way to code, except that your style should be consistent. There are wrong ways to code, though. Tightly packed code will be difficult to troubleshoot, as will code that has no comments. Some coding styles right-justify the keywords of the SELECT statement. Some right-align the commas. Some put all of the columns on one line, while others write one per line. Some write the keywords in all uppercase or all lowercase, and others use mixed case.

The point is that whatever style you choose, make it *readable* and *consistent*.

Using Transactions

If databases were always read-only, there would be no need for transactions. There would also be no data! Even single INSERT, UPDATE, and DELETE statements are implicit transactions. This section goes beyond the implicit transaction and deals with those cases where you are doing "simultaneous" changes to two or more tables. In a single batch, you can't really do anything simultaneously. You issue one data modification statement followed by another. However, you need to have all of the statements within the transaction work as a unit so that they all complete or, if there's a failure, they will all roll back to the way they were prior to the transaction.

The classic example of a transaction is the transfer of funds from one bank account to another. Suppose you want to decrement one account and increment another one. If this is not done "atomically"—as a single unit of work—then you could lose money if the system were to crash in the middle of the transaction.

To begin a transaction, issue the BEGIN TRANSACTION (or BEGIN TRAN) statement. This tells SQL Server that all the following changes to the database occur as a unit of work. Have a look at the syntax in Listing 7-39.

Listing 7-39: Syntax for BEGIN TRANSACTION

```
BEGIN TRAN [ SACTION ] [ transaction_name | @tran_name_variable
  [ WITH MARK [ 'description' ] ] ]
```

You can elect to name your transaction, but it is not necessary unless you are using the WITH MARK option. This feature—new to SQL Server 2000—allows the DBA to restore the transaction log up to the marked transaction, either exclusively or inclusively. (Restoring transaction logs is beyond the scope of this text.) You can optionally add a description to the mark. Bear in mind that using the WITH MARK option adds overhead to the log.

Now that your transaction is under way, you come to the point where you want the work to be either committed to the database or completely undone due to an error condition. If you decide that all is well, you can issue the COMMIT TRAN or COMMIT WORK statement. The syntax is given in Listing 7-40.

Listing 7-40: Syntax for COMMIT TRAN and COMMIT WORK

```
COMMIT [ TRAN [ SACTION ] [ transaction_name | @tran_name_variable ] ]

COMMIT [ WORK ]
```

As you can see, you can simply get away with the keyword COMMIT. The basic difference between COMMIT and COMMIT WORK is that COMMIT WORK is the ANSI-92 standard and does not provide for a transaction name. The transaction name in the COMMIT TRAN statement is ignored anyway, but it does give you the opportunity to make your code more self-documenting. The name must conform to the rules for identifiers, but only the first 32 characters are used. (What happens behind the scenes will be discussed in a moment.)

If your error checking determines that you need to undo all of your work, you can issue a ROLLBACK TRAN or ROLLBACK WORK statement. This is your way of telling SQL Server that none of the changes you made are to go into the database. Check out the syntax in Listing 7-41.

Listing 7-41: Syntax for ROLLBACK TRAN and ROLLBACK WORK

```
ROLLBACK [ TRAN [ SACTION ]
 [ transaction_name | @tran_name_variable
 | savepoint_name | @savepoint_variable ] ]

ROLLBACK [ WORK ]
```

The rules for ROLLBACK are the same as those for COMMIT. This syntax also introduces savepoints, which will be described shortly.

Here's an example of how to use a transaction, using the pubs database. Suppose you need to change the royalty percentage between two authors of the same book. Listing 7-42 shows how you do it inside a transaction.

Listing 7-42: Changing the Royalty Percentage inside a Transaction

```
BEGIN TRAN

UPDATE titleauthor
SET
  royaltyper = 60
WHERE
  au_id    = '213-46-8915'
  AND
  title_id = 'BU1032'
```

```
UPDATE titleauthor
SET
  royaltyper = 40
WHERE
    au_id    = '409-56-7008'
  AND
    title_id = 'BU1032'
```

```
COMMIT TRAN
```

There is no error checking in this example, for the sake of brevity. However, you do need to handle errors. (By the way, this query can actually be done with a single UPDATE statement, using a CASE expression. Do you know how?)

Obviously, you don't want to do work that is not necessary when an error condition is raised, but the issue goes deeper than that. During a transaction, exclusive locks are held until the transaction is committed or rolled back. The longer it takes for a transaction to complete, the longer the locks are in place and the greater the likelihood is of your transaction locking out another user process. The shorter a transaction is, the better.

Another way of cutting down locking is to restrict the transaction to work that must be atomic. For example, if a customer calls and wants to change her address as well as place an order, the two pieces are not related and therefore this work should not be done in a single transaction. Instead, the two pieces can—and should— be done separately.

> **TIP** *When you are doing ad hoc updates, always write* BEGIN TRAN *and* ROLLBACK TRAN *into your Query Analyzer first, before you write anything else. Then, put your code between these two statements. You can try out your code and see if it produces the results you expect. If it does, then change the* ROLLBACK *to a* COMMIT.

Using Implicit Transactions

If you're not in the mood to write a BEGIN TRAN every time you want to set up a transaction, you can use SET IMPLICIT_TRANSACTIONS ON. With this option turned on, your data modifications are considered part of a transaction until you explicitly issue a COMMIT.

Once issued, the SET IMPLICIT_TRANSACTIONS ON statement stays in effect until you issue the SET IMPLICIT_TRANSACTIONS OFF statement.

Understanding Deadlocks

Deadlocks are situations where two processes each have a lock on a resource and want each other's resource. They don't want to give up their own resource until the other one relinquishes the one it has. Eventually, SQL Server intervenes and kills one of the processes, sending it a 1205 error with a user-hostile message to the effect that it has been chosen as the "deadlock victim." In the example in Listing 7-42, a deadlock could occur if another process ran the same transaction but went for the authors in reverse order.

The way to avoid—but not completely prevent—this situation is to access your resources in exactly the same order across all transactions. Start by setting corporate standards. For example, you could access tables in alphabetical order or parent-child order, but be consistent. Bear in mind that the longer you hold locks, the greater the risk you have of deadlocking. In a database with update activity, you cannot completely prevent deadlocks; you can simply reduce their likelihood.

If you want to determine the longest-running transaction in a database, you can use the DBCC OPENTRAN statement. This is discussed in detail in Appendix C.

Understanding Nested Transactions and @@TRANCOUNT

You can optionally nest transactions—you can have a transaction within a transaction up to 32 levels deep. You can keep track of the nesting level with the global variable @@TRANCOUNT. It is incremented by 1 for every BEGIN TRAN and decremented by 1 for every COMMIT TRAN. The transaction is never truly committed until the transaction that takes @@TRANCOUNT to 0 from 1 is committed. Simply put, the transaction is not committed until the "outermost" transaction is committed.

The effect of ROLLBACK on @@TRANCOUNT is different. The ROLLBACK statement always rolls the entire transaction back to the beginning of the outermost transaction, regardless of how deep you are nested; it also sets @@TRANCOUNT to 0. Your code has to take this into consideration. If you issue a COMMIT or ROLLBACK and there is no outstanding transaction, then the statement will cause an error.

> **NOTE** *Nested transactions and the effect of* COMMIT TRAN *and* ROLLBACK TRAN *confuse many people. Be sure you understand these concepts fully before you build your code. These concepts are fair game on a technical interview.*

Leveraging Savepoints

The *savepoint* is a way of beginning a transaction without really beginning a transaction, and it has meaning only inside a nested transaction. It is invoked with the SAVE TRAN statement. Check out the syntax in Listing 7-43.

Listing 7-43: Syntax for the SAVE TRANSACTION Statement

```
SAVE TRAN [ SACTION ] { savepoint_name | @savepoint_variable }
```

Notice how the savepoint name must be given, unlike the BEGIN TRAN statement. Unlike BEGIN TRAN, the SAVE TRAN statement does not increment @@TRANCOUNT. Things get interesting when you then issue a ROLLBACK statement. If you provide ROLLBACK TRAN with the name of the savepoint, then the work that was done after the SAVE TRAN statement will be rolled back but the work done prior to that statement is unaffected. This lets you pick and choose what stays and what goes.

Savepoints do not have to have unique names within a session. In other words, you can issue two SAVE TRAN statements with the same name. What happens is that SQL Server remembers the *last* savepoint. If you choose to do a ROLLBACK and use the savepoint name, the work will be rolled back to the last savepoint. This is a way of making the savepoint act like a high-water mark. When you are satisfied that a portion of your work is okay, you can update the savepoint. The drawback to this approach is that it makes debugging more difficult.

SQL Puzzle 7-1: Eliminating an Explicit Transaction

Re-do the query in Listing 7-42 so that the same work gets done in a single transaction but without using an explicit transaction.

The answer to this puzzle can be found on pages 690–691.

Views

VIEWS ARE STORED, named `SELECT` statements; they are not a copy of your data. They have the look and feel of a table. You can, with certain limitations, issue all DML statements against a view, but actually, when you issue a query against a view, it is internally merged with the underlying `SELECT` statement and then issued against the base table or tables. This chapter covers issues you need to be aware of when creating, retrieving, and modifying data through views and indexed views.

View Limitations and Requirements

Before you start creating and using views, you need to know about a few requirements and limitations of views.

Not every valid ad hoc `SELECT` statement is valid inside a view. The following sections describe a few requirements for a `SELECT` to be valid inside a view.

Each Column Must Have a Name and the Name Must Be Unique

This requirement makes sense. If your applications and users were to treat your view as if it were a table, how would they refer to a column with no name or distinguish between columns that have the same name?

Take the ad hoc query shown in Listing 8-1, for example. It looks for authors and the titles that they wrote, preserving all authors (including those authors who did not write books). Run this query in your Query Analyzer while you are connected to the pubs sample database.

Listing 8-1: Authors and the Titles They Wrote

```
SELECT
  A.au_id,
  au_fname + ', ' + LEFT(au_fname, 1),
  TA.au_id,
  TA.title_id
FROM
    Authors     AS A
  LEFT OUTER    JOIN
    Titleauthor AS TA ON A.au_id = TA.au_id
```

The output in Table 8-1 shows that two columns have the name au_id, and one column has no name.

Table 8-1: Output of a Query that Does Not Supply a Qualifier to an Expression

au_id	(No column name)	au_id	title_id
409-56-7008	Abraham, A	409-56-7008	BU1032
648-92-1872	Reginald, R	648-92-1872	TC4203
238-95-7766	Cheryl, C	238-95-7766	PC1035
722-51-5454	Michel, M	722-51-5454	MC3021
712-45-1867	Innes, I	712-45-1867	MC2222
427-17-2319	Ann, A	427-17-2319	PC8888
213-46-8915	Marjorie, M	213-46-8915	BU1032
213-46-8915	Marjorie, M	213-46-8915	BU2075
527-72-3246	Morningstar, M	NULL	NULL
472-27-2349	Burt, B	472-27-2349	TC7777
846-92-7186	Sheryl, S	846-92-7186	PC8888
756-30-7391	Livia, L	756-30-7391	PS1372
486-29-1786	Charlene, C	486-29-1786	PC9999
486-29-1786	Charlene, C	486-29-1786	PS7777
724-80-9391	Stearns, S	724-80-9391	BU1111
724-80-9391	Stearns, S	724-80-9391	PS1372
893-72-1158	Heather, H	NULL	NULL
267-41-2394	Michael, M	267-41-2394	BU1111
267-41-2394	Michael, M	267-41-2394	TC7777
807-91-6654	Sylvia, S	807-91-6654	TC3218
998-72-3567	Albert, A	998-72-3567	PS2091
998-72-3567	Albert, A	998-72-3567	PS2106
899-46-2035	Anne, A	899-46-2035	MC3021
899-46-2035	Anne, A	899-46-2035	PS2091
341-22-1782	Meander, M	NULL	NULL

Table 8-1: Output of a Query that Does Not Supply a Qualifier to an Expression (Continued)

au_id	(No column name)	au_id	title_id
274-80-9391	Dean, D	274-80-9391	BU7832
724-08-9931	Dirk, D	NULL	NULL
172-32-1176	Johnson, J	172-32-1176	PS3333
672-71-3249	Akiko, A	672-71-3249	TC7777

Now suppose you were allowed to create a view called VAllauthors with this SELECT statement. How would you query it? Maybe something like the query shown in Listing 8-2?

Listing 8-2: Requesting Duplicate Column Names and Unnamed Columns from an Imaginary View

```
SELECT
  [this column, you know, the one that has no name],
  [au_id...wait, wait, the second one, not the first one!]
FROM
  VAllauthors
```

If this were a legal request, the parser would probably also appreciate a DUDE clause as a finale. Lucky for you, SELECT statements that fail the requirements mentioned previously are not legal in a view. To handle this, you need to give each of your result columns a unique name.

You have two options. The first option is to give all columns that have no names and columns with duplicate names a qualifier in the SELECT statement, as shown in Listing 8-3.

Listing 8-3: Supplying Different Names and Qualifiers to Illegal Columns in the View

```
CREATE VIEW VAllauthors
AS
SELECT
  A.au_id                         AS au_id_A,
  au_fname + ', ' + LEFT(au_fname, 1) AS au_name,
  TA.au_id                        AS au_id_TA,
  TA.title_id
```

```
FROM
    Authors AS A
  LEFT OUTER JOIN
    Titleauthor AS TA ON A.au_id = TA.au_id
GO
```

The other option is to give each result column a name in the header of the CREATE VIEW statement, as in Listing 8-4.

Listing 8-4: Supplying Column Names in the Header of the View

```
CREATE VIEW VAllauthors(au_id_a, au_name, au_id_ta, title_id)
AS
SELECT
  A.au_id                            AS au_id_A,
  au_fname + ', ' + LEFT(au_fname, 1) AS au_name,
  TA.au_id                           AS au_id_TA,
  TA.title_id
FROM
    Authors     AS A
  LEFT OUTER    JOIN
    Titleauthor AS TA ON A.au_id = TA.au_id
GO
```

Cannot Use SELECT INTO in a View

Using SELECT INTO is not allowed in a view because it is a combined data definition language (DDL) and data manipulation language (DML) statement, which results in the creation of a new table. You can, however, issue a SELECT INTO statement where the view is used in the FROM clause.

In other words, you can't use a SELECT INTO statement inside a view, but you can use a view in a SELECT INTO statement.

Cannot Use the ORDER BY Clause in a View

Some people find this limitation quite surprising. Why not allow the ORDER BY clause in a view? What if you want to issue a SELECT * against a view and get your results ordered? Actually, T-SQL's implementation of this restriction follows the ANSI standard, which in turn follows the rules of the relational model. A view is supposed to return a rowset that looks like a table, and a table doesn't have any specific order to its rows.

Suppose you want to produce an ordered phone list of all of the authors. Keeping the limitations in mind, you can create a view that selects only the relevant columns and issue a query against the view that orders the result, as shown in Listing 8-5.

Listing 8-5: The Authors Phone List View

```
CREATE VIEW VAuPhoneList
AS
SELECT
  au_fname,
  au_lname,
  phone
FROM
  Authors
GO
SELECT
  *
FROM
  VAuPhoneList
ORDER BY
  au_fname,
  au_lname
```

Now try to alter the view so it will use the ORDER BY clause, as shown in Listing 8-6.

Listing 8-6: Trying to Use the ORDER BY Clause in a View

```
ALTER VIEW VAuPhoneList
AS
SELECT
  au_fname,
  au_lname,
  phone
FROM
  Authors
ORDER BY
  au_fname,
  au_lname
GO
```

This gives you the following error:

```
Server: Msg 1033, Level 15, State 1, Procedure VAuPhoneList, Line 13
An ORDER BY clause is invalid in views, inline functions, derived tables, and
subqueries unless TOP is also specified.
```

Pay close attention to the error. It says that an ORDER BY clause is invalid in a view *unless* TOP is also specified. TOP queries are not ANSI compliant, and the order of rows in a TOP query is mandatory if your output is to make some sense. If T-SQL is to allow TOP queries in a view, it has to allow using the ORDER BY clause in such queries.

So, if you wanted the list of the first five authors ordered by name, you could alter the view, as in Listing 8-7.

Listing 8-7: Using the ORDER BY Clause in a View with a TOP Statement

```
ALTER VIEW VAuPhoneList
AS
SELECT TOP 5
  au_fname,
  au_lname,
  phone
FROM
  Authors
ORDER BY
  au_fname,
  au_lname
GO
```

Wait a minute; TOP queries also support specifying a percentage of rows rather than specifying a fixed number! Nothing prevents you from using the form of the TOP query shown in Listing 8-8.

Listing 8-8: Using the ORDER BY Clause in a View with TOP 100 PERCENT

```
ALTER VIEW VAuPhoneList
AS
SELECT TOP 100 PERCENT
  au_fname,
  au_lname,
  phone
FROM
  Authors
ORDER BY
  au_fname,
  au_lname
GO
```

Although this might seem like a nice trick, look what happens when you try to produce the same phone list, only now order the rows by last name first. Issue the query shown in Listing 8-9 against the view.

Listing 8-9: Redundant Sorting

```
SELECT
  *
FROM
  VAuPhoneList
ORDER BY
  au_lname,
  au_fname
```

Take a look at the execution plan shown in Figure 8-1.

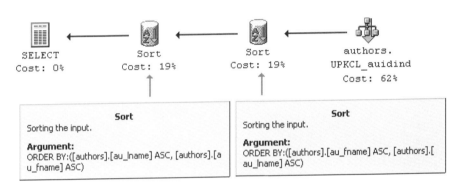

Figure 8-1: Execution plan of SELECT FROM a view with a TOP query

Notice that two sort operations were performed here, one of which is redundant. The first one is the result of the ORDER BY in the view, and the second is the result of the ORDER BY against the view.

Hiding the Complexity of the Underlying Query

Some queries might become very complex, making them unreadable. Others are simply used repeatedly as derived tables. Wrapping those queries with a view makes your code more readable and easier to maintain. Also, developing a solution in a modular fashion, where you solve each step at a time and wrap it with a view, is usually less prone to error. Recall the GROUP BY queries with the CUBE option you saw in Chapter 5? You first produced a query that adds the GROUPING() function so you could distinguish NULLs that stand for super aggregates from NULLs that originated in the base table. Later you wrapped it with a view (run in the Northwind sample database), as shown in Listing 8-10.

Listing 8-10: Hiding the Complexity of the Underlying Query, Step 1

```
CREATE VIEW Vbase_cube
AS
SELECT
  CustomerID,
  GROUPING(CustomerID)      AS Grp_Cust,
  YEAR(OrderDate)           AS Order_Year,
  GROUPING(YEAR(OrderDate)) AS Grp_Year,
  COUNT(*) as Order_Count
FROM
  Orders
WHERE
  CustomerID LIKE 'A%'
GROUP BY
  CustomerID,
  YEAR(OrderDate)
WITH CUBE
GO
```

Later, you "cleaned" the output of this view by merging the information in the base columns and the output of the GROUPING() function, so that NULLs in the base columns would be replaced with either ALL or UNKNOWN where relevant. Again, you wrapped the query with a view, as shown in Listing 8-11.

Listing 8-11: Hiding the Complexity of the Underlying Query, Step 2

```
CREATE VIEW Vcube
AS
SELECT
  ISNULL(CAST(CustomerID AS varchar(7)),
  CASE Grp_Cust
    WHEN 1 THEN 'ALL'
    ELSE 'UNKNOWN'
  END) AS customer,
  ISNULL(CAST(Order_Year AS varchar(7)),
  CASE Grp_Year
    WHEN 1 THEN 'ALL'
    ELSE 'UNKNOWN'
  END) AS Order_Year,
  Order_Count
FROM
  Vbase_cube
GO
```

And eventually, your applications and users were able to issue simple and intuitive queries against this view, as shown in Listing 8-12.

Listing 8-12: Retrieving Data through a View with a Complex Query

```
SELECT
  *
FROM
  Vcube
WHERE
    customer = 'ALL'
  AND
    Order_Year = 'ALL'
```

Using Views as a Security Mechanism

Although SQL Server enables you to manage table permissions at the column level (permissions on a vertical portion of a table), it doesn't supply row-level permissions (permissions on a horizontal portion of your table). Also, you sometimes may want to allow certain users to see the result of a certain query, be it a JOIN, UNION, GROUP BY, or a query that simply filters a certain horizontal portion of a table. This is where views come in handy.

You can grant permissions to users and groups on a view, allowing them DML access as long as they issue their queries against the view, but not allowing them access to the underlying tables. These users can be granted relevant permissions on the view (not on the underlying objects) as long as the following conditions are met:

- The owner of the view and the owner of the underlying objects are one and the same. This is an *unbroken ownership chain*.

- If the view references objects in another database, the login issuing the query against the view needs to be allowed access to that database.

Failing the first condition requires granting the user explicit permissions on all of the objects that are not owned by the owner of the view. For example, suppose you have a view called dbo.V1 that references two tables, dbo.T1 and dbo.T2, as shown in Figure 8-2.

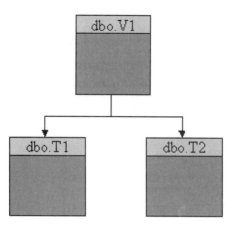

Figure 8-2: Unbroken ownership chain

Because you have an unbroken ownership chain, granting user1 SELECT permissions on the view, as shown in Listing 8-13, is sufficient for him or her to successfully retrieve data from the view.

Listing 8-13: Granting SELECT Permission on a View

```
GRANT SELECT ON dbo.V1 TO user1
```

But suppose, for example, that Tony owned the table T1, as Figure 8-3 shows.

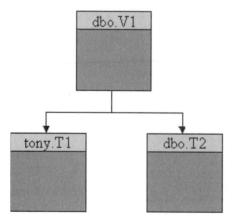

Figure 8-3: Broken ownership chain

In this case, user1 would have to be granted explicit SELECT permissions on tony.T1, as shown in Listing 8-14, in order to successfully retrieve data from the view.

Listing 8-14: Granting SELECT Permission on a Table

```
GRANT SELECT ON tony.T1 TO user1
```

Altering a View

The ALTER VIEW statement enables you to change the view's content or one of its options (ENCRYPTION, SCHEMABINDING, CHECK OPTION). Take a look at the syntax for altering a view, shown in Listing 8-15.

Listing 8-15: ALTER VIEW Syntax

```
ALTER VIEW view_name [(column [,...n])]
[WITH ENCRYPTION | SCHEMABINDING]
AS
  select_statement
[WITH CHECK OPTION]
```

Notice that the SELECT statement is not optional, even if you only want to change one of the options and keep the current SELECT statement. So, why not simply drop the view using the DROP VIEW statement and re-create it? Besides the chance that someone will try to access the view in between the time you issue the DROP VIEW and the CREATE VIEW statements, if you drop the view, all permissions on the view will be lost. With ALTER VIEW, permissions are retained.

Note that the view's column-level permissions are maintained by the column IDs, which are maintained in the *syscolumns* system table. If a user has permissions to a certain column in the view, say col1, which is the first column in the view, and you alter the view so that col2 is now the first column in the view, the user will have permissions on col2.

To demonstrate this, create an SQL Server login called user1, and map it to a user called user1 in the pubs database. From the Query Analyzer, make sure you are connected to the pubs database while logged on as dbo. This connection will be referred to as "connection 1." Run the script shown in Listing 8-16 to create a view on the Authors table and to grant permissions to user1 only on the au_id column in the view.

Listing 8-16: Granting Permission on a Column in a View

```
CREATE VIEW VAunames
AS
SELECT
  au_id,
  au_lname,
  au_fname
FROM
  Authors
GO
GRANT SELECT ON VAunames(au_id) TO user1
GO
```

Now log on as user1 from another connection, which will be referred to as "connection 2." First try to select all columns from the view to make sure you are not allowed to, and then try to select only the au_id column to make sure you are allowed to, as shown in Listing 8-17 .

Listing 8-17: Testing Permissions Granted on a View

```
-- Should get error 230 (permissions denied) on columns au_fname and au_lname
SELECT
  *
FROM
  VAunames

-- Should get a valid output
SELECT
  au_id
FROM
  VAunames
```

Now go back to "connection 1" and alter the view with the code shown in Listing 8-18. Note that the column au_fname is now the first column in the view.

Listing 8-18: Altering a View with Previously Granted Permissions

```
ALTER VIEW VAunames
AS
SELECT
  au_fname,
  au_id,
  au_lname
FROM
  Authors
GO
```

From "connection 2", try to select the au_fname column, as shown in Listing 8-19.

Listing 8-19: Column Permissions in a View Preserved by Column Name

```
SELECT
  au_fname
FROM
  Vaunames
```

The query returns the authors' first names. This is because permissions were retained by column IDs in the view.

Encrypting the View Definition

The WITH ENCRYPTION option is available with the CREATE <object> or the ALTER <object> statements. It enables you to encrypt the definition of views, stored procedures, triggers, and user-defined functions. Definitions of objects are kept in the *syscomments* system table.

The WITH ENCRYPTION option enables developers to hide their code even from members of the *sysadmin* server role, without losing functionality. SQL Server uses an internal cryptographic algorithm, and it can, of course, decrypt the object's code internally when it needs to compile it. Before you encrypt your object, make sure you save the CREATE <object> or ALTER <object> statement as a script file in a secured folder—otherwise you will not be able to restore it.

You have a few options for retrieving an unencrypted object's definition from the *syscomments* system table. One option is to use the sp_helptext system stored procedure. Give it a try on the VAunames view you created in the previous section, as shown in Listing 8-20.

Listing 8-20: Using sp_helptext to View an Object's Definition

```
EXEC sp_helptext VAunames
```

Another option is to double-click the object's name in Enterprise Manager. And the third and final option is to query the *syscomments* system table directly, as shown in Listing 8-21. This is the least recommended way because there is no guarantee that the *syscomments* system table will have the same structure as SQL Server advances in versions.

Listing 8-21: Retrieving an Object's Definition from syscomments

```
SELECT
  [text]
FROM
  syscomments
WHERE
  [id] = OBJECT_ID('dbo.VAunames')
```

If you want your object's code to be unavailable, don't even consider deleting the object's row from *syscomments*, because SQL Server uses it every time it needs to compile the object. Instead, you can use the WITH ENCRYPTION option in the CREATE <object> or ALTER <object> statement to encrypt it, as shown in Listing 8-22.

Listing 8-22: Encrypting an Object's Definition

```
ALTER VIEW VAunames
WITH ENCRYPTION
AS
SELECT
  au_id,
  au_lname,
  au_fname
FROM
  Authors
GO
```

Now you can try any of the three methods discussed in this section to retrieve the object's definition, and you will see that it is no longer available.

Using the SCHEMABINDING Option

The SCHEMABINDING option was introduced with SQL Server 2000. This option prevents changes to the schema of the objects referenced by the view, including tables and other views. An attempt to alter or drop one of the objects referenced by the view will fail.

When you are using this option, all objects referenced by the view must use the two-part object name, in the form of owner.object, as in dbo.T1. An example of using the SCHEMABINDING option is shown later in this chapter in the "Indexed Views in SQL Server 2000" section.

Using Views to Modify Data

When you update a view, keep in mind that the view is a stored SELECT statement and not a copy of the data. When you issue a modification against the view, SQL Server needs to translate it internally to a modification against the underlying table(s). This explains some of the limitations for modifying data through views, and why sometimes, when you issue a modification against a view and then query it to see the result, you might get totally different results than you expect. To understand this, you can run a few examples against the Warriors and Weapons tables.

The script that creates and populates the Warriors and Weapons tables is shown in Listing 8-23.

Listing 8-23: Schema and Data of the Warriors and Weapons Tables

```
IF db_id('testdb') IS NULL
  CREATE DATABASE testdb
GO
USE testdb
GO
CREATE TABLE Weapons(
weaponid int       NOT NULL PRIMARY KEY,
weapon  varchar(25) NOT NULL)
CREATE TABLE Warriors(
warriorid int      NOT NULL PRIMARY KEY,
fname   varchar(15) NOT NULL,
lname   varchar(15) NOT NULL,
weaponid int        NOT NULL REFERENCES Weapons(weaponid))
GO
SET NOCOUNT ON
GO
INSERT INTO Weapons VALUES(100, 'Mangoes in syrup')
INSERT INTO Weapons VALUES(200, 'Passion fruit')
INSERT INTO Weapons VALUES(300, 'Black cherries')
INSERT INTO Weapons VALUES(400, 'Banana')
INSERT INTO Weapons VALUES(500, 'Pointed stick')
INSERT INTO Warriors VALUES(1,  'Andy'     , 'Ball'       , 100)
INSERT INTO Warriors VALUES(2,  'Bob'      , 'Pfeiff'     , 100)
INSERT INTO Warriors VALUES(3,  'Bruce'    , 'P. Margolin', 100)
INSERT INTO Warriors VALUES(4,  'Brian'    , 'Moran'      , 200)
INSERT INTO Warriors VALUES(5,  'Darren'   , 'Green'      , 200)
INSERT INTO Warriors VALUES(6,  'Gianluca' , 'Hotz'       , 200)
INSERT INTO Warriors VALUES(7,  'Kalen'    , 'Delaney'    , 300)
INSERT INTO Warriors VALUES(8,  'Neil'     , 'Pike'       , 300)
INSERT INTO Warriors VALUES(9,  'Ron'      , 'Talmage'    , 300)
```

```
INSERT INTO Warriors VALUES(10, 'Roy'        , 'Harvey'       , 400)
INSERT INTO Warriors VALUES(11, 'Steve'      , 'Robinson'     , 400)
INSERT INTO Warriors VALUES(12, 'Tibor'      , 'Karaszi'      , 400)
INSERT INTO Warriors VALUES(13, 'Tony'       , 'Reogerson'    , 500)
INSERT INTO Warriors VALUES(14, 'Trevor'     , 'Dwyer'        , 500)
INSERT INTO Warriors VALUES(15, 'Umachandar', 'Jayachandran', 500)
INSERT INTO Warriors VALUES(16, 'Wayne'      , 'Snyder'       , 500)
INSERT INTO Warriors VALUES(17, 'Fernando'   , 'G. Guerrero' , 500)
GO
SET NOCOUNT OFF
GO
```

Using the CHECK Option

Consider the VCherryWarriors view shown in Listing 8-24, which filters the warriors that fight with black cherries.

Listing 8-24: Creating the VCherryWarriors View

```
CREATE VIEW VCherryWarriors
AS
SELECT
  *
FROM
  Warriors
WHERE
  Weaponid = 300
GO
SELECT
  *
FROM
  VCherryWarriors
```

If you select all rows from the VCherryWarriors view, you should get the output shown in Table 8-2.

Table 8-2: Initial Cherry Warriors

warriorid	fname	lname	weaponid
7	Kalen	Delaney	300
8	Neil	Pike	300
9	Ron	Talmage	300

Suppose Ron doesn't want to fight with black cherries any more. Instead, he wants to fight with a pointed stick! You issue the UPDATE shown in Listing 8-25 against the view.

Listing 8-25: Modifying a Row in the View so It Doesn't Qualify for the Filter Criteria

```
UPDATE VCherryWarriors
  SET weaponid = 500
WHERE
  warriorid = 9
```

The update was successful, but Ron disappeared from your view because his row in the Warriors table doesn't match the view's filter criteria anymore.

Now try to add Itzik with his favorite weapon—mangoes in syrup—through the view, as shown in Listing 8-26.

Listing 8-26: Inserting a Row that Doesn't Qualify for the Filter Criteria in the View

```
INSERT INTO VCherryWarriors VALUES(18, 'Itzik', 'Ben-Gan', 100)
```

Your insert is successful even though Itzik's weapon doesn't match the view's filter criteria.

Selecting all rows from your view, as in Listing 8-27, shows that neither Ron's nor Itzik's rows are returned.

Listing 8-27: Retrieving Cherry Warriors after Modifications

```
SELECT
  *
FROM
  VCherryWarriors
```

The output of this query is shown in Table 8-3.

Table 8-3: Cherry Warriors after Modifications

warriorid	fname	lname	weaponid
7	Kalen	Delaney	300
8	Neil	Pike	300

If you want to prevent updates and inserts that don't fit the view's filter criteria—in this case, changing a warrior's weapon to one other than black cherries or adding a warrior with a weapon other than black cherries—you need to add the CHECK OPTION to the view definition, as in Listing 8-28.

Listing 8-28: Using the CHECK OPTION

```
ALTER VIEW VCherryWarriors
AS
SELECT
  *
FROM
  Warriors
WHERE
  weaponid = 300
WITH CHECK OPTION
GO
```

Now try to update or insert a row that doesn't fit the view's filter criteria, and you'll see that the modification will be rejected.

Limitations to Modifying Data through Views

In order for your view to be updateable, the SELECT statement inside it has certain restrictions. It should not include aggregate functions: TOP, GROUP BY, DISTINCT, or UNION (unless the view is a partitioned view, as described in Chapter 13). Also, INSERT, UPDATE, and DELETE statements issued against the view have certain restrictions, as described in the following sections.

INSERT Restrictions

An INSERT statement must supply values for all of the affected base table's columns unless the column meets one or more of the following qualifications:

- Allows NULLs

- Has a default value

- Has an IDENTITY property

- Is of datatype rowversion (timestamp)

Note that if a view does not include all of the columns from a table it references, and the columns that are not included don't meet at least one of the qualifications just mentioned, you will never be able to add rows to that table through the view. For example, consider the VWarriorNames view shown in Listing 8-29.

Listing 8-29: Creating the VWarriorNames View

```
CREATE VIEW VWarriorNames
AS
SELECT
  fname,
  lname
FROM
  Warriors
GO
```

Notice that there is no way you can specify values for warriorid and weaponid, which are non-NULLable, have no default value, do not have the IDENTITY property, and are not of the rowversion datatype. Thus, you cannot issue an INSERT against this view.

UPDATE Restrictions

An UPDATE statement cannot modify a column that is a result of an expression. For example, you cannot modify the warriorname column in the view shown in Listing 8-30.

Listing 8-30: Creating the VWarriorsWithFullNames View

```
CREATE VIEW VWarriorsWithFullNames
AS
SELECT
  warriorid,
  fname + ' ' + lname AS warriorname,
  weaponid
FROM
  Warriors
GO
```

Modifying a View that References More than One Table

UPDATE and INSERT statements can modify only one table at a time if the SELECT statement in the view references more than one table. To demonstrate this, create the VWarriorsWeapons view as shown in Listing 8-31.

Listing 8-31: Creating the VWarriorsWeapons View

```
CREATE VIEW VWarriorsWeapons
AS
SELECT
  warriorid,
  fname,
  lname,
  WP.weaponid,
  weapon
FROM
   Warriors AS WR
  JOIN
   Weapons  AS WP ON WR.weaponid = WP.weaponid
GO
```

Now query VWarriorsWeapons as shown in Listing 8-32.

Listing 8-32: Querying the VWarriorsWeapons View

```
SELECT
  *
FROM
  VWarriorsWeapons
```

The output of this query is shown in Table 8-4.

Table 8-4: Initial Warriors and Their Weapons

warriorid	fname	lname	weaponid	weapon
1	Andy	Ball	100	Mangoes in syrup
2	Bob	Pfeiff	100	Mangoes in syrup
3	Bruce	P. Margolin	100	Mangoes in syrup
4	Brian	Moran	200	Passion fruit
5	Darren	Green	200	Passion fruit

Table 8-4: Initial Warriors and Their Weapons (Continued)

warriorid	fname	lname	weaponid	weapon
6	Gianluca	Hotz	200	Passion fruit
7	Kalen	Delaney	300	Black cherries
8	Neil	Pike	300	Black cherries
9	Ron	Talmage	500	Pointed stick
10	Roy	Harvey	400	Banana
11	Steve	Robinson	400	Banana
12	Tibor	Karaszi	400	Banana
13	Tony	Reogerson	500	Pointed stick
14	Trevor	Dwyer	500	Pointed stick
15	Umachandar	Jayachandran	500	Pointed stick
16	Wayne	Snyder	500	Pointed stick
17	Fernando	G. Guerrero	500	Pointed stick
18	Itzik	Ben-Gan	100	Mangoes in syrup

Unsatisfied with his weapon's name, Itzik wants you to change it to "The Mangoes in syrup", and while he's already applying for a weapon name change, he asks you to change his last name to "BG". You try to do this with the UPDATE statement shown in Listing 8-33.

Listing 8-33: Trying to Modify Columns from Different Tables through a View

```
UPDATE VWarriorsWeapons
  SET lname = 'BG',
      weapon = 'The Mangoes in syrup'
WHERE
  warriorid = 18
```

The UPDATE statement fails because you're trying to affect two tables at the same time. You get the error shown in Listing 8-34.

Listing 8-34: Error Returned when Modification against a View Affects Multiple Base Tables

```
Server: Msg 4405, Level 16, State 2, Line 1
View or function 'VWarriorsWeapons' is not updatable because the modification
affects multiple base tables referenced.
```

No problem, right? You can try to issue two separate UPDATEs. Try the modification shown in Listing 8-35.

Listing 8-35: Modifying One Column at a Time through a View, Step 1

```
UPDATE VWarriorsWeapons
  SET lname = 'BG'
WHERE
  warriorid = 18
SELECT
  *
FROM
  VWarriorsWeapons
```

So far, so good. Itzik's last name has changed. Now you issue the second UPDATE shown in Listing 8-36.

Listing 8-36: Modifying One Column at a Time through a View, Step 2

```
UPDATE VWarriorsWeapons
  SET weapon = 'The Mangoes in syrup'
WHERE
  warriorid = 18
SELECT
  *
FROM
  VWarriorsWeapons
```

And you get the output shown in Table 8-5.

Table 8-5: Warriors and Their Weapons after Changing a Weapon Name through the View

warriorid	fname	lname	weaponid	weapon
1	Andy	Ball	100	The Mangoes in syrup
2	Bob	Pfeiff	100	The Mangoes in syrup
3	Bruce	P. Margolin	100	The Mangoes in syrup
4	Brian	Moran	200	Passion fruit
5	Darren	Green	200	Passion fruit
6	Gianluca	Hotz	200	Passion fruit
7	Kalen	Delaney	300	Black cherries

Table 8-5: Warriors and Their Weapons after Changing a Weapon Name through the View (Continued)

warriorid	fname	lname	weaponid	weapon
8	Neil	Pike	300	Black cherries
9	Ron	Talmage	500	Pointed stick
10	Roy	Harvey	400	Banana
11	Steve	Robinson	400	Banana
12	Tibor	Karaszi	400	Banana
13	Tony	Reogerson	500	Pointed stick
14	Trevor	Dwyer	500	Pointed stick
15	Umachandar	Jayachandran	500	Pointed stick
16	Wayne	Snyder	500	Pointed stick
17	Fernando	G. Guerrero	500	Pointed stick
18	Itzik	BG	100	The Mangoes in syrup

Ouch! Itzik's weapon's name changed like you wanted it to, but the weapon names also changed for Andy Ball, Bob Pfeiff, and Bruce P. Margolin. Again, you need to remember that the underlying base tables are affected. In this case, the Weapons table has only one row with the weapon "Mangoes in syrup", and this row was changed. This row is repeated for each relevant warrior in the view because it's on the one side of the one-to-many relationship between Weapons and Warriors.

> **NOTE**   *In many cases, you can overcome the limitations mentioned in the previous sections by using* INSTEAD OF *triggers.* INSTEAD OF *triggers are discussed in Chapter 10.*

DELETE Restrictions

A DELETE statement is valid against a view only if the SELECT statement inside it references one and only one table.

Updating Views through SQL Server Enterprise Manager

You can perform modifications through your views graphically using the visual tools in SQL Server Enterprise Manager. Simply right-click the view you want to modify, choose Open View from the pop-up menu that appears, and then select Return All Rows.

You can sometimes perform a successful modification through your view graphically, even though the modification isn't supposed to be allowed. For example, suppose Neil decides to change his weapon to a "Pointed stick". Now remember that you placed a CHECK OPTION in your VCherryWarriors view, and such a change should not be allowed through the view. However, you can open it graphically and modify Neil's row that way, as Figure 8-4 shows.

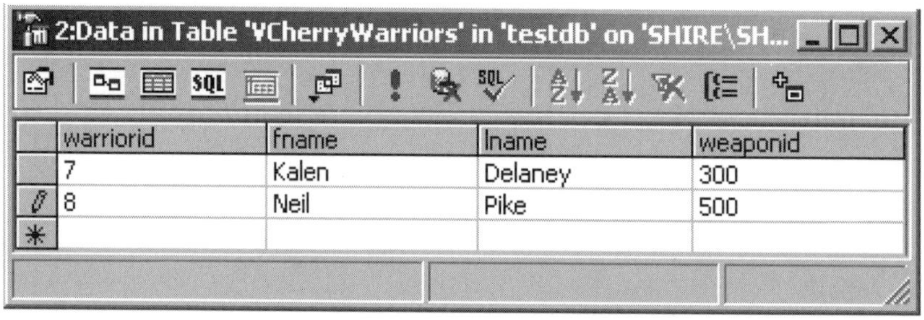

Figure 8-4: Updating the VCherryWarriors view graphically

The update is successful!

> **NOTE** *To refresh the result on the screen, click the Run (!) icon.*

Tracing the activity that was performed behind the scenes with Profiler reveals that Enterprise Manager did not issue a modification against the view, but rather against the base table, Warriors, as shown in Listing 8-37.

Listing 8-37: Profiler's Output of Updating the VCherryWarriors View Graphically

```
exec sp_executesql N'UPDATE "testdb".."Warriors" SET "weaponid"=@P1
WHERE "warriorid"=@P2 AND "fname"=@P3 AND "lname"=@P4 AND "weaponid"=@P5', N'@P1
int,@P2 int,@P3 varchar(15),@P4 varchar(15),@P5 int', 500, 8, 'Neil', 'Pike', 300
```

Similarly, modifying two columns from two different tables is possible through Enterprise Manager. For example, you can open VWarriorsWeapons graphically and modify Itzik's last name and weapon name back to their original values, as shown in Figure 8-5.

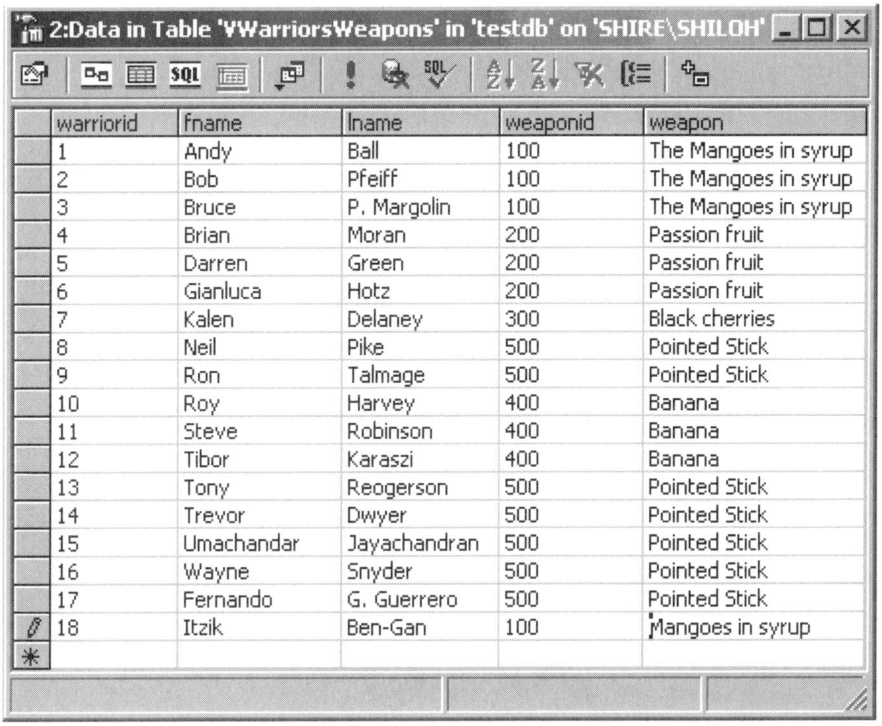

2:Data in Table 'VWarriorsWeapons' in 'testdb' on 'SHIRE\SHILOH'

warriorid	fname	lname	weaponid	weapon
1	Andy	Ball	100	The Mangoes in syrup
2	Bob	Pfeiff	100	The Mangoes in syrup
3	Bruce	P. Margolin	100	The Mangoes in syrup
4	Brian	Moran	200	Passion fruit
5	Darren	Green	200	Passion fruit
6	Gianluca	Hotz	200	Passion fruit
7	Kalen	Delaney	300	Black cherries
8	Neil	Pike	500	Pointed Stick
9	Ron	Talmage	500	Pointed Stick
10	Roy	Harvey	400	Banana
11	Steve	Robinson	400	Banana
12	Tibor	Karaszi	400	Banana
13	Tony	Reogerson	500	Pointed Stick
14	Trevor	Dwyer	500	Pointed Stick
15	Umachandar	Jayachandran	500	Pointed Stick
16	Wayne	Snyder	500	Pointed Stick
17	Fernando	G. Guerrero	500	Pointed Stick
18	Itzik	Ben-Gan	100	Mangoes in syrup

Figure 8-5: Updating the VWarriorsWeapons view graphically

Again, successful! Profiler's trace shows that the UPDATE was not issued against the view, but rather two separate UPDATEs were issued, each to a different base table, as shown in Listing 8-38.

Listing 8-38: Profiler's Output of Updating the VWarriorsWeapons View Graphically

```
exec sp_executesql N'UPDATE "testdb".."Weapons" SET "weapon"=@P1 WHERE
"weaponid"=@P2 AND "weapon"=@P3', N'@P1 varchar(25),@P2 int,@P3 varchar(25)',
'Mangoes in syrup', 100, 'The Mangoes in syrup'
exec sp_executesql N'UPDATE "testdb".."Warriors" SET "lname"=@P1 WHERE "warriorid"=@P2
AND "fname"=@P3 AND "lname"=@P4', N'@P1 varchar(15),@P2 int,@P3 varchar(15),
@P4 varchar(15)', 'Ben-Gan', 17, 'Itzik', 'BG'
```

Indexed Views in SQL Server 2000

As you've seen earlier in this chapter, a view can be used as a security mechanism or as a way to hide the complexity of the underlying query, but it does not provide any performance benefit because it is no more than a named SELECT statement. If you wrap a very intensive query with a view (such as a query with computations, aggregations, or joins), each query issued against the view is merged with the inner query in the view and is issued internally against the underlying tables.

Indexed views, introduced with SQL Server 2000, on the other hand, *materialize* the view's output, storing it on disk. Materializing a view can improve the performance of SELECT queries dramatically because there is no need to process the view's inner query. However, they degrade the performance of modifications to the underlying tables, because SQL Server modifies the indexed views each time you modify the underlying tables, in order to keep the indexed view in sync with the underlying data in the base tables. (This concept also applies to regular indexes that you place on a table—they improve the performance of SELECT queries and usually have a negative effect on modifications.)

Tuning without Indexed Views

To demonstrate the performance improvements involved with the use of indexed views, first examine a sample query and the options you have to improve its performance without using indexed views. Consider the following Departments and Employees tables. Fill the Departments table with four different departments and the Employees table with 100,000 employees, as shown in Listing 8-39.

Listing 8-39: Schema and Data for the Employees and Departments Tables

```
CREATE TABLE Departments(
deptno   int         NOT NULL
                     CONSTRAINT PK_Departments_deptno PRIMARY KEY,
deptname varchar(25) NOT NULL)
GO
CREATE TABLE Employees(
empid int         NOT NULL
                  CONSTRAINT PK_Employees_empid PRIMARY KEY,
fname varchar(25) NOT NULL,
lname varchar(25) NOT NULL,
deptno int        NOT NULL
                  CONSTRAINT FK_Employees_Departments
                    FOREIGN KEY
                    REFERENCES Departments(deptno),
```

```
salary money      NOT NULL)
GO
SET NOCOUNT ON
INSERT INTO Departments VALUES(100, 'HR')
INSERT INTO Departments VALUES(200, 'Marketing')
INSERT INTO Departments VALUES(300, 'Production')
INSERT INTO Departments VALUES(400, 'Finance')
DECLARE @i AS int
SET @i = 1
WHILE @i <= 100000
BEGIN
  INSERT INTO Employees(empid, fname, lname, deptno, salary)
    VALUES(@i,
           'fname' + cast(@i AS varchar(6)),
           'lname' + cast(@i AS varchar(6)),
           100 * ((@i - 1) % 4 + 1), -- 4 different departments
           1000.00 + 50 * ((@i - 1) % 50 + 1)) -- 50 different salaries
  SET @i = @i + 1
END
GO
```

Next, issue the query shown in Listing 8-40, which calculates the number of employees and the total salary for each department.

Listing 8-40: Calculating the Number of Employees and the Total Salary for Each Department

```
SET STATISTICS IO ON
SELECT
  E.deptno,
  deptname,
  COUNT(*)      AS num_employees,
  SUM(salary)   AS total_salary
FROM
    dbo.Employees AS E
  JOIN
    dbo.Departments AS D ON E.deptno = D.deptno
GROUP BY
  E.deptno,
  deptname
```

Only four rows are returned because you have only four different departments, as Table 8-6 shows.

Table 8-6: Number of Employees and the Total Salary for Each Department

deptno	deptname	num_employees	total_salary
300	Production	25000	56250000.0000
100	HR	25000	56250000.0000
200	Marketing	25000	57500000.0000
400	Finance	25000	57500000.0000

Take a look at the execution plan shown in Figure 8-6.

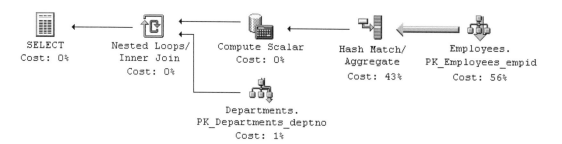

Figure 8-6: Execution plan for an aggregate query with no covering index or indexed view

A full clustered index scan is performed on the PK_Employees_empid index, followed by a hash match aggregate that calculates the aggregations for each deptno, followed by a nested loop join with the Departments table to retrieve the deptname column. Currently there is a clustered index on the empid column in the Employees table, as well as a clustered index on the deptno column in the Departments table. You don't have an index on the Employees table that will allow the optimizer to avoid a full clustered index scan on it. The I/O cost of this query is quite large because all of the clustered index pages (the data pages in the large Employees table) are scanned, as shown in Listing 8-41.

Listing 8-41: I/O Statistics for an Aggregate Query with No Covering Index or Indexed View

```
Table 'Departments'. Scan count 4, logical reads 8, physical reads 0, read-ahead
reads 0.
Table 'Employees'. Scan count 1, logical reads 632, physical reads 0, read-ahead
reads 0.
```

You can try to improve performance by creating a covering index on the deptno and salary columns. This way, all of the data that is needed from the Employees table will be located in the covering index. Each index row is much smaller than the full data row, so many more index rows fit in one 8KB page than full data rows; and the covering index consumes much less disk space than all of the data pages. The result is less I/O.

To illustrate this, create the covering index, as shown in Listing 8-42, and reissue the previous query.

Listing 8-42: Creating a Covering Index on the deptno and salary Columns of the Employees Table

```
CREATE NONCLUSTERED INDEX idx_nci_deptno_salary ON Employees(deptno, salary)
```

The execution plan of your query, which was run after adding the covering index, is shown in Figure 8-7.

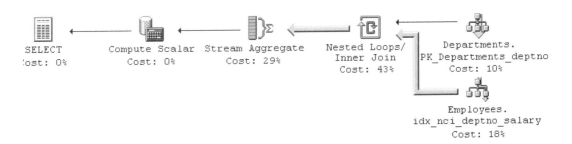

Figure 8-7: Execution plan for an aggregate query using a covering index

The optimizer decides, based on pure query-cost estimation, to perform the join between Departments and Employees first, and then to calculate the aggregations. Notice that instead of scanning the whole clustered index on the Employees table, four ordered index seeks are performed on the covering index you placed on deptno, salary—one for each department. The I/O cost, 242 logical reads in the Employees table, as shown in Listing 8-43, is a bit more than a third of the I/O cost without the covering index.

Listing 8-43: I/O Statistics for an Aggregate Query Using a Covering Index

```
Table 'Employees'. Scan count 4, logical reads 242, physical reads 0, read-ahead
reads 0.
Table 'Departments'. Scan count 1, logical reads 2, physical reads 0, read-ahead
reads 0.
```

Tuning with Indexed Views

You gained a considerable performance improvement by using the covering index, but is this the best you can do? Not if you use an *indexed view.* Creating an indexed view can be as simple as creating a view and placing indexes on it, but there are a few limitations and considerations you need to be aware of, as not every view can be indexed.

Indexed View Limitations and Considerations

You need to make sure that the view will always return the same results based on the same underlying data in the base tables. To do this, you first need to ensure that the environment variables have the appropriate settings, as follows:

- ANSI_NULLS should be ON

- ANSI_PADDING should be ON

- ANSI_WARNINGS should be ON

- ARITHABORT should be ON

- CONCAT_NULL_YIELDS_NULL should be ON

- QUOTED_IDENTIFIERS should be ON

- NUMERIC_ROUNDABORT should be OFF

To check your current session's settings you can use DBCC USEROPTIONS.

Also, in order to make sure that the view will always return the same results based on the same underlying data in the base tables, all of the functions used in the view must be deterministic. *Deterministic* functions, by definition, return the same value given the same input. For example, ISNULL() is a deterministic function, but GETDATE() isn't. (For a complete list of deterministic and non-deterministic functions, see the Books Online topic, "Deterministic and Nondeterministic Functions.")

In order to make sure that no changes will be made to the underlying referenced objects, your view needs to be schema-bound. You can use the SCHEMABINDING option in the CREATE VIEW statement to guarantee this, as explained earlier in the chapter.

There are also a few limitations that the SELECT statement inside the view has to meet in order for your view to be indexable:

- The column names in the column list must be explicitly specified. You cannot use the asterisk (* or table.*).

- A column can be referenced only once by its name alone. All other references must be a parameter to a function or part of a complex expression.

- You cannot use derived tables, rowset functions, UNION, subqueries, outer or self joins, TOP, ORDER BY, DISTINCT, CONTAINS, FREETEXT, COMPUTE, or COMPUTE BY.

- You cannot use the following aggregate functions: AVG, MAX, MIN, STDEV, STDEVP, VAR, VARP, or COUNT(*). However, the use of COUNT_BIG(*) is allowed.

- If you use GROUP BY, you must include COUNT_BIG(*).

Before you go on and create an index on a view, you can use the OBJECTPROPERTY() function to determine if it is indexable, as shown in Listing 8-44.

Listing 8-44: Using the OBJECTPROPERTY Function to Check Whether a View is Indexable

```
SELECT OBJECTPROPERTY(OBJECT_ID('view_name'), 'IsIndexable')
```

Creating and Using Indexed Views

Now that you are aware of the limitations involved in creating an indexed view, go ahead and create the VDeptSalaries view shown in Listing 8-45.

Listing 8-45: Creating a View for Indexing

```
CREATE VIEW VDeptSalaries WITH SCHEMABINDING
AS
SELECT
  E.deptno,
  deptname,
  COUNT_BIG(*) AS num_employees,
  SUM(salary)  AS total_salary
```

```
FROM
    dbo.Employees   AS E
  JOIN
    dbo.Departments AS D ON E.deptno = D.deptno
GROUP BY
  E.deptno,
  deptname
GO
```

Next, create an index on the view. First you need to create a unique clustered index, thus materializing the view, and then you can create nonclustered indexes as well. Create a unique clustered index on deptno, as shown in Listing 8-46.

Listing 8-46: Creating an Index on a View

```
CREATE UNIQUE CLUSTERED INDEX idx_ci_deptno ON VDeptSalaries(deptno)
```

Now you can issue the query shown in Listing 8-47 against your view, which returns the same results as the query you're trying to tune.

Listing 8-47: Querying an Indexed View

```
SELECT
  *
FROM
  VDeptSalaries
```

Take a look at the execution plan shown in Figure 8-8.

Figure 8-8: Execution plan for a query against a view using the index on the view

Looks simple? Well, it is! And the I/O cost is dramatically improved, as shown in Listing 8-48.

Listing 8-48: I/O Statistics for a Query Against a View Using the Index on the View

```
Table 'VDeptSalaries'. Scan count 1, logical reads 2, physical reads 0, read-ahead
reads 0.
```

More amazingly, issuing the original query against the base table also uses the index on the view, resulting in the same improved I/O cost, of course. The optimizer is smart enough to know that you have an indexed view that can satisfy the query. Try it.

You're not done yet. Issue the query shown in Listing 8-49, which calculates the average salary for each department.

Listing 8-49: Querying Base Tables with an Indexed View Defined

```
SELECT
  E.deptno,
  deptname,
  AVG(salary)      AS avg_salary
FROM
    dbo.Employees AS E
  JOIN
    dbo.Departments AS D ON E.deptno = D.deptno
GROUP BY
  E.deptno,
  deptname
```

Take a look at the execution plan shown in Figure 8-9.

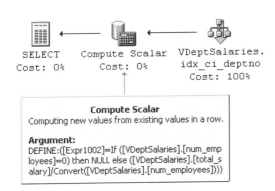

Figure 8-9: Execution plan for a query against the base table using the index on the view

Notice that, again, the index on the view was used, even though it doesn't include the AVG() function that the query requested. But it does include the COUNT_BIG(*) and the SUM(salary) aggregate functions, and the compute scalar operation calculates the average by dividing the sum of the salary by the number of rows. This, of course, results in the same improved I/O cost, as shown in Listing 8-50.

Listing 8-50: I/O Statistics for a Query Against the Base Table Using the Index on the View

```
Table 'VDeptSalaries'. Scan count 1, logical reads 2, physical reads 0, read-ahead
reads 0.
```

Using the Index Tuning Wizard to Recommend Indexed Views

The *Index Tuning Wizard* (ITW) is a tool that gives recommendations for creating indexes based on a given workload of queries saved as a script file or as a Profiler trace file or table. In SQL Server 2000 it can also recommend creating indexes on views and even creating the views themselves. To demonstrate this, first drop the existing VDeptSalaries view and the covering index you placed on the Employees table so you can start from scratch, as shown in Listing 8-51.

Listing 8-51: Starting from Scratch—Dropping the Existing Indexed View and Covering Index

```
DROP VIEW VDeptSalaries
GO
DROP INDEX Employees.idx_nci_deptno_salary
GO
```

Save the query shown in Listing 8-52, which you want to tune, in a script file called `workload.sql`.

Listing 8-52: Saving the Workload to Be Tuned by the ITW in a Script File

```
USE testdb
GO
SELECT
  E.deptno,
  deptname,
  COUNT(*)      AS num_employees,
  SUM(salary)   AS total_salary
FROM
    dbo.Employees AS E
  JOIN
    dbo.Departments AS D ON E.deptno = D.deptno
GROUP BY
  E.deptno,
  deptname
GO
```

Now load the Index Tuning wizard by choosing Wizards, under the Management category, from SQL Server Enterprise Manager's Tools Menu. In the "Select Server and Database" screen make sure of the following:

- You chose the correct database.

- The "Keep All Existing Indexes" option is unchecked.

- The "Thorough" analysis and "Add Indexed Views" options are checked as shown in Figure 8-10.

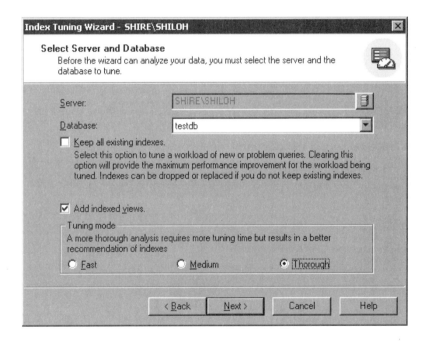

Figure 8-10: ITW—Select Server and Database

In the "Specify Workload" screen, point to the workload file you just saved, as shown in Figure 8-11.

In the "Select Tables to Tune" screen, make sure you select both the Employees and the Departments tables, as shown in Figure 8-12.

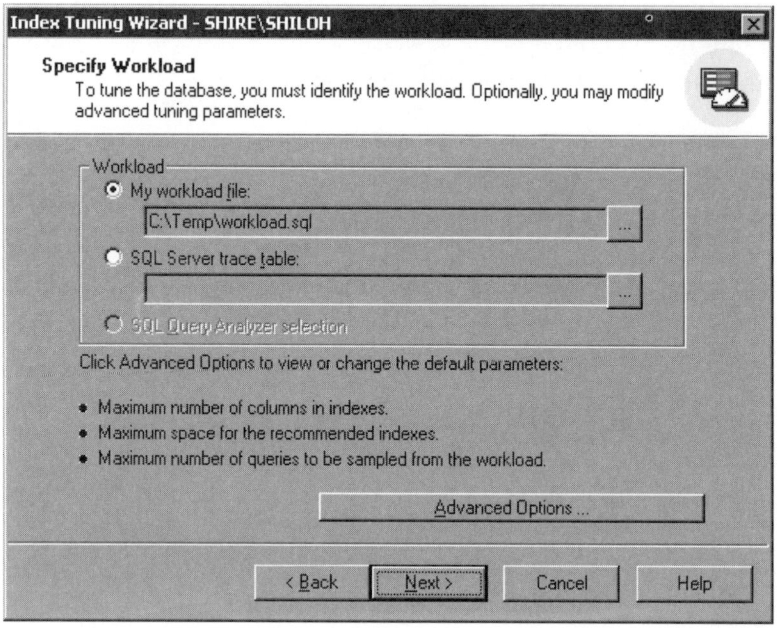

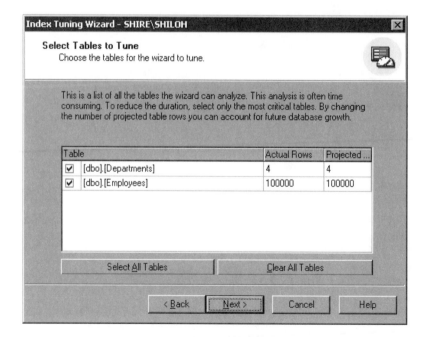

Figure 8-11: ITW—Specify Workload screen

Figure 8-12: ITW—Select Tables to Tune screen

After confirming your selection, the Index Tuning Wizard starts to analyze the workload and considers indexed views as well as regular indexes, all the while providing you with a progress bar to view, as shown in Figure 8-13.

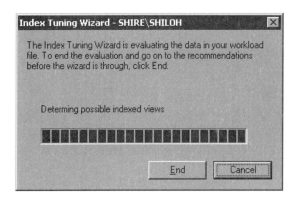

Figure 8-13: ITW—evaluating indexes

When the Index Tuning Wizard finishes the evaluation process, it displays its recommendations, as shown in Figure 8-14.

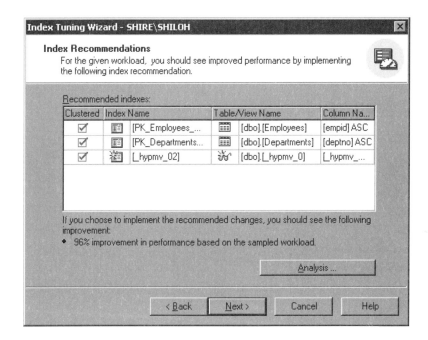

Figure 8-14: ITW—Index Recommendations screen

Notice that it recommends the already existing clustered indexes on Employees and Departments, but also a new indexed view. To see the exact recommendations, in the "Schedule Index Update Job" screen (which appears after you click the Next button), choose to save the ITW's recommendations to a script file called indexes.sql as shown in Figure 8-15.

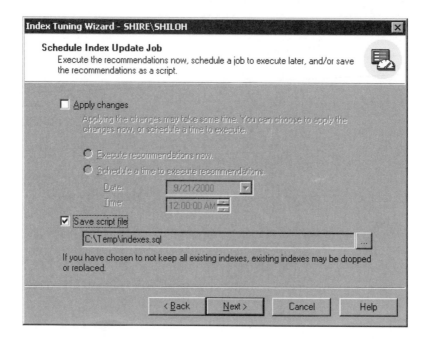

Figure 8-15: ITW—Schedule Index Update Job screen

Click Next, Finish, and OK, and then open the script file indexes.sql in your Query Analyzer. The script file content is shown in Listing 8-53.

Listing 8-53: Script File with the ITW's Recommendations

```
/* Created by: Index Tuning Wizard */
/* Date: 9/20/2000 */
/* Time: 6:35:30 PM */
/* Server Name: SHIRE\SHILOH */
/* Database Name: testdb */
/* Workload File Name: C:\Temp\workload.sql */


USE [testdb]
go
```

```
SET QUOTED_IDENTIFIER ON
SET ARITHABORT ON
SET CONCAT_NULL_YIELDS_NULL ON
SET ANSI_NULLS ON
SET ANSI_PADDING ON
SET ANSI_WARNINGS ON
SET NUMERIC_ROUNDABORT OFF
go

DECLARE @bErrors as bit

go
CREATE VIEW [dbo].[_hypmv_0] WITH SCHEMABINDING
AS

SELECT
   [dbo].[employees].[deptno] as _hypmv_0_col_1,
   [dbo].[departments].[deptname] as _hypmv_0_col_2,
   COUNT_BIG(*) as _hypmv_0_col_3,
   SUM([testdb].[dbo].[Employees].[salary]) as _hypmv_0_col_4
FROM
   [dbo].[employees],
   [dbo].[departments]
WHERE
   ( [dbo].[departments].[deptno] = [dbo].[employees].[deptno] )
GROUP BY
   [dbo].[employees].[deptno],
   [dbo].[departments].[deptname]
go

DECLARE @bErrors as bit

BEGIN TRANSACTION
SET @bErrors = 0

CREATE UNIQUE CLUSTERED INDEX [_hypmv_02] ON [dbo].[_hypmv_0] ([_hypmv_0_col_1] ASC
)
IF( @@error <> 0 ) SET @bErrors = 1

IF( @bErrors = 0 )
  COMMIT TRANSACTION
ELSE
  ROLLBACK TRANSACTION
```

```
/* Statistics to support recommendations */

CREATE STATISTICS [hind_2009058193_4A_5A] ON [dbo].[employees] ([deptno], [salary])
```

Notice that the ITW recommends the same view and the same index that you created earlier in the chapter.

SQL Puzzle 8-1: Updateable Ordered View (by Zoltan Kovacs)

In this chapter you saw a trick to create an ordered view using the TOP 100 PERCENT option. The problem with this solution is that views using the TOP option are not updateable. Your task is to create an updateable ordered view! Note that your solution should work on SQL Server 7.0 as well.

You can work on the following T1 table:

```
CREATE TABLE T1
(
  key_col  int NOT NULL PRIMARY KEY,
  data_col int NOT NULL
)
GO

... your code goes here ...
```

Once your view is created, you should be able to add rows to it as follows:

```
INSERT INTO V1 VALUES(1, 4)
INSERT INTO V1 VALUES(2, 1)
INSERT INTO V1 VALUES(3, 3)
INSERT INTO V1 VALUES(4, 2)
```

When you SELECT all rows from the view, like this:
```
SELECT * FROM V1
```

you should get a result sorted by data_col, like this:

key_col	data_col
2	1
4	2
3	3
1	4

The answer to this puzzle can be found on page 691.

Stored Procedures

STORED PROCEDURES AND TRIGGERS are yet another powerful feature of SQL Server. Indeed, they have been around from the early Sybase days. (You'll see triggers in Chapter 10.) Stored procedures allow you to keep code inside the database, which allows you to make a change that takes effect immediately, regardless of the number of client machines you have. It also permits you to divide the work between SQL developers working on server code and, say, Visual Basic developers working on client code. This way, you can hire the appropriate resources and put them where they will do the most good. Because the procedure is often already cached in RAM, you can get speed improvements. Finally, you reduce network traffic substantially when all you send across the wire is a single line of code instead of hundreds.

From the Trenches

The speed of a batch application that loaded customer information was increased by 33 times simply by changing it from embedded SQL to stored procedures. The client was shocked.

From a code management perspective, consider the troubleshooting nightmare if you are using a tool such as the SQL Server Profiler to track down some errant code. Without stored procedures, all you get is the raw SQL, and it will take quite some time to figure out where in the front end or middle tier this occurs. However, if all you have in the calling software is the stored procedure call, it will be very easy to track down the pieces of code that call it. For the same reason, you should avoid rapid application development (RAD) tools that generate SQL.

So, what is a stored procedure? It's a saved batch of precompiled SQL code that gets executed as a unit (not necessarily as a transaction). It can take input and output parameters, just like a subroutine in Visual Basic or C. You can do just about anything inside a stored procedure, although there are some restrictions, as you'll see later. It can be up to 128MB in size. Pretty hefty, eh?

First, you'll see how to create one.

The CREATE PROCEDURE Statement

The procedure begins with the CREATE PROCEDURE statement. This statement must be the first in a batch. Take a moment to study the syntax in Listing 9-1; there's a lot to see.

Listing 9-1: Syntax for the CREATE PROCEDURE Statement

```
CREATE PROC[EDURE] [owner_name.]procedure_name [;number]
    [
        {@parameter data_type} [VARYING] [= default] [OUTPUT]
    ]
    [,...n]
[WITH
    {
        RECOMPILE
        | ENCRYPTION
        | RECOMPILE, ENCRYPTION
    }
]
[FOR REPLICATION]
AS
    sql_statement [...n]
```

The statement is broken down into a number of clauses. The CREATE PROCEDURE clause is where you name the procedure. It is also abbreviated CREATE PROC (and "proc" is a common abbreviation of "procedure"). The name must be unique to the database and not exceed 128 characters in length. It must also follow the rules for identifiers.

> **NOTE**   *The rules for identifiers are covered in the Books Online.*

You can optionally specify the owner name, as well. However, like all other SQL Server objects, it's best that the dbo be the owner. Adopt a naming convention that is consistent, descriptive, and does not cause confusion with system stored procedures. You'll learn about system stored procedures later in the chapter.

You can optionally add a number to the end of the procedure name, separated by a semicolon. This allows you to have a number of procedures of the same name that you can drop in a single DROP PROCEDURE statement. Although this is a feature, it can lead to confusion because you have a number of procedures all with the same name. As said previously, the name should be descriptive and reflect what the procedure does for you.

The next clause contains the parameters, if any. You need to specify each parameter with its datatype, a default (if any), and indicate whether it is an output parameter. Use the same naming convention for your parameters as you do for the columns in the tables to which they refer. Commas are used to separate each parameter declaration. It's good practice to put each parameter declaration on a separate line, preferably with a comment on each. Although it is not mandatory, you should put the parameter list inside parentheses to separate them from the rest of your code. You are limited to a maximum of 1,024 parameters, although you can imagine how difficult something that size would be to maintain. The figure 1,024 may look familiar to you; it is the maximum number of columns allowed in a table or view. This should cover you for creating stored procedures that replace base DML statements, such as INSERT, UPDATE, DELETE, and SELECT.

Listing 9-2 shows an example of a CREATE PROC statement with a parameter list. This is only the header of the procedure, and this format will be used in a number of examples that follow.

Listing 9-2: Example of a CREATE PROC Header with Parameters

```
CREATE PROC usp_DisplayCustomers
(
  @Country  AS nvarchar (15),
  @Region      nvarchar (15)
)
```

> **TIP** *Just as you would test the input parameters of a subroutine in any other language, you should do the same in Transact-SQL stored procedures. These are not tested in the parameter list; rather, they are tested inside the procedure itself.*

Use a consistent, unambiguous naming convention for your stored procedures. Avoid the "sp_" prefix to prevent confusion between your procedures and system stored procedures. System stored procedures are discussed later in this chapter.

The code in Listing 9-2 shows two different ways of declaring the parameters for the stored procedure. The first, for @Country, uses the optional AS keyword, while the second, for @Region, does not. This is similar to the DECLARE statement, which is covered in Chapter 7. Use whichever syntax you prefer—just be consistent.

Now that you've seen the parameters, take a look back to the rest of the CREATE PROCEDURE statement in Listing 9-1. Next comes the VARYING keyword, which is covered in detail in Chapter 15, which discusses cursors.

Then come the output parameters, which are very useful for communicating information back to the calling program, whether it be an ad hoc script, another stored procedure, or a client using ADO. All you have to do is add the OUTPUT keyword to the parameter declaration. The syntax is positional—the OUTPUT keyword must appear after the datatype and default, if any.

An example will make this clear. Suppose you need a stored procedure that returns the customer's last order date, based upon the input CustomerID. The declaration is shown in Listing 9-3.

Listing 9-3: Example of a CREATE PROC with Output Parameters

```
CREATE PROC usp_LastOrderDate
(
  @CustomerID  nchar (5),
  @OrderDate   datetime    OUTPUT
)
```

You'll see how to retrieve output variables in the "Retrieving an Output Parameter" section, later in the chapter.

The examples you have seen thus far require that all parameters be specified when you call the procedure; none are optional. SQL Server allows you to make some or all of the arguments optional. To do this, you must specify a default value for each optional parameter. The default must be a constant or NULL. You may not use a function, such as GETDATE().

Suppose you want the order details for a customer's order, and if the OrderID is specified, you will use it; otherwise you will take the most recent order. The CREATE PROC statement is shown in Listing 9-4.

Listing 9-4: Example of a CREATE PROC with Default Parameter

```
CREATE PROC usp_GetOrderDetails
(
  @CustomerID  nchar (5),
  @OrderID     int        = NULL
)
```

In this case, the @OrderID parameter is set to NULL unless you specify it explicitly when you call the procedure.

The WITH clause has two possible options. First, you can specify RECOMPILE, which tells the optimizer to recompile the procedure every time it is invoked. You would do this if the data distribution for the given parameters would vary substantially every time the procedure is used, meaning that one execution plan would not be efficient for all invocations, and that the optimizer should look at each on a case-by-case basis. There is a small cost for doing this on each and every occasion, but the payback is that the optimizer is using the right plan every time. If you find that the execution time of a procedure varies, based on the given parameters, then it is best to use the WITH RECOMPILE option. However, if the distribution of data is consistent across calls, then do not use the WITH RECOMPILE option because the plan will not remain in memory to be used by the next call. Listing 9-5 shows the WITH RECOMPILE option added to the code from Listing 9-4.

Listing 9-5: CREATE PROC Using WITH RECOMPILE

```
CREATE PROC usp_GetOrderDetails
(
  @CustomerID  nchar (5),
  @OrderID     int        = NULL
)
WITH RECOMPILE
```

The consequences of the WITH RECOMPILE option are more fully explained later in this chapter, in the "Using WITH RECOMPILE" section.

The second possible WITH option is ENCRYPTION. When you create a procedure, the code that comprises the procedure gets stored in *syscomments*. If you wish to conceal that code, you can use the WITH ENCRYPTION option. Generally, it is not a good idea to use this option unless you are a vendor selling a packaged database solution and do not want to reveal your intellectual property. In most cases, you are likely to be writing procedures for your own use.

If a stored procedure has been created without the ENCRYPTION option, you can use sp_helptext or Enterprise Manager to inspect the code to see if it is consistent with what you have in version control. Later in this chapter, in the "Useful System Stored Procedures" section, we will look at sp_helptext, a system stored procedure that is used to read the *syscomments* table to get the source code for a procedure.

The final part of the CREATE PROCEDURE statement is the optional FOR REPLICATION clause. This indicates that the procedure is used by the replication process and cannot be invoked directly on the subscribing server. Keep in mind that FOR REPLICATION and WITH RECOMPILE are mutually exclusive. A complete treatment of replication is beyond the scope of this book.

After you have built the CREATE PROC statement, the mandatory AS keyword is added to designate where the code for the procedure begins. SQL Server will assume that all code following AS is part of the stored procedure until it sees the GO statement.

You can forego the GO if you are running the CREATE PROC as a single batch inside the Query Analyzer.

> **TIP** *Always put a GO statement at the end of every stored procedure definition. This will allow you to concatenate all of your scripts into a single build script without a problem. Also, put a PRINT statement just ahead of the CREATE PROC statement indicating the procedure being built, and another one right after the GO. This will allow you to determine where you are in the build as it is executing, but it will also help you if you have to troubleshoot why your build script failed.*

> **NOTE** *One common myth is that you need a BEGIN and an END statement to designate the start and finish of the code inside your procedure. These are completely unnecessary.*

It's time for another example. Suppose you want the most recent order information for a given customer. You must specify the CustomerID in this example; the complete stored procedure is presented in Listing 9-6.

Listing 9-6: Stored Procedure to Retrieve a Customer's Most Recent Order

```
CREATE PROC usp_GetRecentOrder
(
  @CustomerID  nchar (5)
)
AS
SELECT TOP 1
  *
FROM
  Orders
WHERE
    CustomerID = @CustomerID
ORDER BY
  OrderDate DESC
GO
```

In this example, a SELECT * statement has been used for brevity. In practice, you should avoid this, since the table could be altered, and you would then get unexpected results. Always state the SELECT list explicitly.

The ALTER PROCEDURE Statement

Before the introduction of SQL Server version 7.0, the only way to update a stored procedure was to drop and re-create it. This caused problems from two standpoints. First, during the period between the DROP PROC and the CREATE PROC statements, the procedure did not exist, and any front-end software that used the procedure would fail. The second problem was that of security—when you drop a procedure, all of the permissions granted to it are dropped as well. This meant that the procedure would not be available to the general public until you finished granting permissions again. If you had an intricate permission system, this could take some time.

The ALTER PROCEDURE statement allows you to change the code of a stored procedure without actually dropping it. Users cannot access the stored procedure while it is being altered, which only makes sense. All previously granted permissions remain intact.

The syntax of the ALTER PROC statement is identical to that of the CREATE PROC statement. Just like the CREATE PROC statement, the ALTER PROC statement must also be the first in a batch.

The DROP PROCEDURE Statement

If you want to get rid of the stored procedure, you use the DROP PROCEDURE statement as you would DROP TABLE or DROP VIEW. The rules for referencing owners are also the same. However, you cannot specify a database name in the identifier. You must be using the database from which you wish to drop a procedure. For example, to drop the spMyProc stored procedure, use the code in Listing 9-7.

Listing 9-7: Using the DROP PROCEDURE Statement

```
DROP PROCEDURE spMyProc
```

Calling a Stored Procedure

Once you have created a stored procedure, you have to be able to invoke it. To do so, you use the EXECUTE statement, which can be abbreviated EXEC. Take a moment to review the syntax in Listing 9-8.

Listing 9-8: Syntax for the EXEC Statement

```
[[EXEC[UTE]]
{
  [@return_status =]
  {procedure_name [;number ] | @procedure_name_var
}
  [[@parameter =]{value | @variable [OUTPUT] | [DEFAULT]]
  [,...n ]
[WITH RECOMPILE]
```

To execute a stored procedure, simply type the EXEC keyword, followed by the procedure name, followed by the parameters, if any. Commas must separate the parameters. For example, to execute the procedure usp_GetOrderDetails created in Listing 9-5, use the code in Listing 9-9.

Listing 9-9: Executing a Stored Procedure

```
EXEC usp_GetOrderDetails
  'BOTTM',
  10410
```

> **NOTE** *You are not limited to specifying constants in the argument list. It is common to use variables. You cannot, however, use a function call as an argument.*

This is the most common calling syntax. The parameters are specified in the same order as they appear in the CREATE PROC statement. Alternatively, you can specify the parameters by name, in which case they can appear in any order. Listing 9-10 shows the same stored procedure call specifying the parameters by name in reverse order from how they appear in the CREATE PROC statement.

Listing 9-10: Alternative Calling Syntax for a Stored Procedure

```
EXEC usp_GetOrderDetails
  @OrderID    = 10410,
  @CustomerID = 'BOTTM'
```

One advantage to this style of syntax comes where you are using default values. If you have parameters that you want set to their defaults, then you will have to name the parameters which do not have defaults and optionally those whose defaults you wish to override. Alternatively, you can use the DEFAULT keyword as a placeholder for those parameters that you wish set to their default values. There is no way of setting placeholders. Take the following example. You have a procedure where the first parameter has a default but the remaining two are not optional. You can specify those parameters as demonstrated in Listing 9-11.

Listing 9-11: Calling a Stored Procedure With Defaults

```
EXEC usp_DefaultProc
  @Parm2 = 909,
  @Parm3 = 50
```

Looks like any other named parameter call, doesn't it? That's because it is! Listing 9-12 shows you how to call the same stored procedure, using the DEFAULT keyword.

Listing 9-12: Calling a Stored Procedure With Defaults

```
EXEC usp_DefaultProc
  DEFAULT
  909,
  50
```

> **TIP** *If you have a stored procedure with default parameters, place those parameters at the end of the* CREATE PROC *statement. Of those, place the ones most likely to be overridden ahead of those least likely. This way, you will probably be able to use both calling syntaxes.*

You do not need the EXEC keyword if the stored procedure call is the first statement in a batch. Consider the code in Listing 9-13.

Listing 9-13: A SELECT Followed by an EXEC

```
SELECT
  *
FROM
  Customers

EXEC sp_help
```

The EXEC is necessary because the call to sp_help is not the first in the batch. Now, remove the EXEC keyword, as shown in Listing 9-14.

Listing 9-14: A SELECT Followed by a Stored Procedure Call without an EXEC

```
SELECT
  *
FROM
  Customers

sp_help
```

The code now executes, or does it? You get the results of the SELECT, but the call to sp_help disappears. To make this problem easier to see, some white space is removed in Listing 9-15.

Listing 9-15: A SELECT Followed by a Stored Procedure Call without an EXEC, Reformatted

```
SELECT
  *
FROM
  Customers sp_help
```

Now, the Customers table is aliased to sp_help, which explains why the SELECT ran but the stored procedure call evaporated. This is why either the EXEC keyword is required or you have to run it as the first statement in a batch; you need to resolve the ambiguity.

Referencing a Stored Procedure

A stored procedure is just another database object. You reference it the same way that you would any other object. This means that if a user other than the dbo owns the procedure, you must prepend the owner name to the procedure name, separated by a period (for example, Tom.usp_GetOrder).

It gets more complicated in the case where a user and the dbo have each created a stored procedure with the same name. If the user does not specify the owner prefix, SQL Server looks to see if there is a procedure of that name owned by that user. If one exists, that user's own procedure will be used; otherwise, the one owned by the dbo is used. If the user wishes to use the dbo's procedure, then the dbo prefix must be used.

Calling a stored procedure in another database is easy. Simply prepend the database name to the owner name, separated by a period (for example, `OtherDB.Itzik.usp_GetOrder`). The remaining rules mentioned in the previous paragraph are then applied.

You can invoke a stored procedure on a linked server. (Prior to version 7.0, you would have used remote servers.) In this case, you must prepend the server name to the database name, separated by a period, just as for owners and databases (for example, `OtherBox.OtherDB.Tom.usp_GetOrder`).

Calling a Stored Procedure with an Output Parameter

You have already seen how to create a stored procedure that has output parameters. Now, you have to call the stored procedure. To do this, you first need to declare variables in the calling code and then pass them into the `EXEC` statement. Each output parameter must also have the `OUTPUT` (or `OUT`) keyword appearing after it in the argument list.

For example, suppose you wish to call a procedure that gives you the OrderID of the last order for a given CustomerID and then present it to the user. First, you must `DECLARE` a variable into which the output parameter will be passed. Next, you `EXEC` the stored procedure with that variable, designated with the `OUTPUT` keyword. Finally, you manipulate the variable any way you like—after the call. The code is shown in Listing 9-16.

Listing 9-16: Calling a Stored Procedure with an Output Parameter

```
DECLARE
  @OrderID  int

EXEC usp_GetLastOrderID
  'BOTTM',
  @OrderID  OUTPUT

SELECT
  @OrderID
```

Using WITH RECOMPILE

You saw earlier how to use the `WITH RECOMPILE` option when creating a stored procedure. The downside of this is that it always recompiles the stored procedure. You can alternatively omit the `WITH RECOMPILE` option in the `CREATE PROC` statement and then specify `WITH RECOMPILE` when you call the procedure. This way, you can determine for yourself whether the parameters will cause a deviation from the average usage. The keywords are placed after the parameter list, as shown in Listing 9-17.

Listing 9-17: Using the WITH RECOMPILE Option with a Stored Procedure Call

```
EXEC usp_GetCustomerList
  'Canada',
  'Ontario'
WITH RECOMPILE
```

The query plan for such a call is removed from memory after the call.

To understand the need for recompilation, consider the query in Listing 9-18.

Listing 9-18: Query Resulting in Clustered Index Scan

```
SELECT
  *
FROM
  Orders
WHERE
  OrderDate >= '1996-07-04 00:00:00.000'
```

This query results in a clustered index scan, because all orders were placed on or before July 4, 1996. The query plan for this query is given in Figure 9-1.

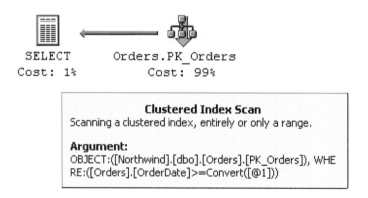

Figure 9-1: Query plan for Listing 9-18

The statistics I/O output shows a scan count of 1 and 21 logical reads. Now change the date constant to May 6, 1998. See Listing 9-19.

Listing 9-19: Query Resulting in Nonclustered Index Seek

```
SELECT
  *
FROM
  Orders
WHERE
  OrderDate >= '1998-05-06 00:00:00.000'
```

This gives a nonclustered index seek on OrderDate, since only four rows meet the WHERE clause criterion. The query plan for this query is shown in Figure 9-2.

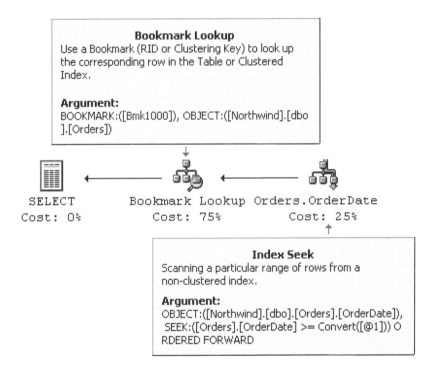

Figure 9-2: Query plan for Listing 9-19

The statistics I/O output shows a scan count of 1 but only 10 logical reads this time. Thus, the optimizer has chosen a different course of action, based upon the search argument. Both of the preceding queries were run as ad hoc SQL. Thus, they were compiled and optimized for each invocation, which resulted in different plans each time.

The queries in Listings 9-18 and 9-19 can be consolidated into a single stored procedure that feeds the required OrderDate criterion in the form of a parameter. This is presented in Listing 9-20.

Listing 9-20: Stored Procedure to Retrieve Orders Based Upon Order Date

```
CREATE PROC usp_GetOrders
(
  @OrderDate AS datetime
)
AS

SELECT
  *
FROM
  Orders
WHERE
  OrderDate >= @OrderDate
GO
```

Now that you have a procedure, it's time to do some testing. For the tests to be meaningful, ensure that no one else is connected to SQL Server. Also, you'll need to start by purging the memory of existing plans. This you do with the script in Listing 9-21.

Listing 9-21: Clearing Out Memory

```
DBCC FREEPROCCACHE
DBCC DROPCLEANBUFFERS
GO
```

The DBCC FREEPROCCACHE command removes all elements from procedure cache so that any new query will require recompilation instead of being reused from cache. You need to be a member of the sysadmin or serveradmin fixed server role to run this command.

The DBCC DROPCLEANBUFFERS command removes clean buffers from the buffer pool. It allows you to test queries with a cold buffer cache without stopping and starting SQL Server. You must be a member of the sysadmin fixed server role to run this command.

Now, you're ready to go. First, run the procedure with the same date (May 6, 1998) as you did in Listing 9-19. This is done in Listing 9-22.

Listing 9-22: Using the usp_GetOrders Stored Procedure for May 6, 1998

```
EXEC usp_GetOrders
  '1998-05-06 00:00:00.000'
```

As expected, you get the same query plan as you did for the equivalent ad hoc SQL you ran in Listing 9-19 (see Figure 9-2). You also got the same I/O statistics.

Now, here comes the interesting part. Run the procedure again, but this time use the date of July 4, 1996. See Listing 9-23.

Listing 9-23: Using the usp_GetOrders Stored Procedure for July 4, 1996

```
EXEC usp_GetOrders
  '1996-07-04 00:00:00.000'
```

Intuitively, you would expect the same plan involving a clustered index scan as you had for the equivalent ad hoc SQL you ran in Listing 9-18. However, you got the same plan as for the previous invocation of the procedure. To make matters worse, the I/O statistics give a scan count of 1 but the logical reads shot up to 1,664. What happened?

The optimizer saw that there was a plan for this same stored procedure already in cache. It involved a nonclustered index seek, since that is what it used the first time the procedure was executed. Now, any invocation of that procedure is going to use that plan, whether or not it is appropriate for the parameter given to it. The 1,664 logical reads came about because the optimizer had to touch the index and then the table itself for each and every row retrieved.

Now, alter the procedure to use the same SELECT statement, but this time use the WITH RECOMPILE option. See the script in Listing 9-24.

Listing 9-24: ALTER PROC Statement Using WITH RECOMPILE

```
ALTER PROC usp_GetOrders
(
  @OrderDate AS datetime
)
WITH RECOMPILE
AS

SELECT
  *
FROM
  Orders
WHERE
  OrderDate >= @OrderDate
GO
```

Before you continue with the tests, be sure to purge the cache as you did in Listing 9-21.

If you rerun the query for May 6, 1998 (Listing 9-22), you get the same plan as shown in Figure 9-2. Thus far, there is no change in behavior. Now run it again for July 4, 1996. This time, you get the same plan (see Figure 9-1) and I/O statistics as you did for the equivalent ad hoc SQL.

The lesson to be learned here is that if the parameter(s) you feed a stored procedure will result in a vastly different number of rows than the average run, it is best to use the WITH RECOMPILE option. Similarly, you can create the procedure using the WITH RECOMPILE option if most calls result in significantly different numbers of rows retrieved.

Using Return Codes and the RETURN Statement

Good programming practice dictates that you should have a return code for every procedure call. This is a way of determining whether the call was successful or not. If not, it can convey what the problem was and let the calling program determine what the appropriate course of action should be. SQL Server reserves the values –1 through –99, although only the values of –1 through –14 have been defined. A return value of 0 indicates success. The reserved return values are presented in Table 9-1.

Table 9-1: Reserved Stored Procedure Return Codes

Return Code Value	Description
0	Success
-1	Object missing
-2	Datatype error
-3	Process chosen as deadlock victim
-4	Permission error
-5	Syntax error
-6	Miscellaneous user error
-7	Resource error, e.g., out of space
-8	Non-fatal internal problem
-9	System limit reached
-10	Fatal internal consistency
-11	Fatal internal consistency

Table 9-1: Reserved Stored Procedure Return Codes (Continued)

Return Code Value	Description
-12	Table or index is corrupt
-13	Database is corrupt
-14	Hardware error

You can have your own set of return codes, provided that they are integers. All other datatypes must be sent back to the calling program via the output parameter mechanism discussed earlier.

> **TIP**   *Use a consistent set of return codes across all of your stored procedures. For example, if you use a return code of 100 to mean no record was found, it should be 100 across all of your stored procedures. You could then call a standard routine to handle your errors.*

So how do you return the return code's value to the calling routine? Simple, just use the RETURN statement. For example, to return the number 5, use the code in Listing 9-25.

Listing 9-25: Using the RETURN Statement

```
RETURN 5
```

Here again, you are not limited to using a constant. All you need is an expression that evaluates to an integer. The RETURN statement does not have to appear in the procedure at all, nor is it restricted to being the last statement—you can use it to bail out early. The RETURN statement not only allows you to communicate a *value* back to the calling program, it is the means by which you return *control* back to the calling program. (Of course, control is returned to the calling program after execution of the last line of code.)

So now you know how to send the value back to the caller, but how does the caller capture it? Revisit the EXEC statement. The partial syntax is shown in Listing 9-26.

Listing 9-26: Partial Syntax for EXEC with a Return Code

```
EXEC @ReturnCode = ProcName
... parameter list ...
PRINT @ReturnCode
```

This code captures the return code in @ReturnCode and then prints the result. You should test the value of the return code to ensure it is what you expected.

Leveraging Dynamic Execution with the EXEC () Statement

Sometimes you do not know what SQL you need to run inside a stored procedure until execution time. Instead of conjuring up different pieces of code inside the procedure or even coding a bunch of procedures, you can use the EXEC() statement and build the SQL statement you want to execute on the fly. This feature has been around since version 6.x and has proven itself very useful in many situations. Check out the syntax in Listing 9-27.

Listing 9-27: Syntax for EXEC () Statement

```
EXEC [ UTE ] ( { @string_variable | [ N ] 'tsql_string' } [ + ...n ] )
```

As an example, recall the SELECT TOP n statement you learned about in Chapter 4. Unfortunately, the *n* must be hard-coded; there is no way of feeding it a variable for *n*. You can skate around this by building a string and using EXEC() to execute the statement. Suppose you want the last five orders, sorted by OrderID. The code is shown in Listing 9-28.

Listing 9-28: Using EXEC () to Execute a Dynamic TOP n Query

```
DECLARE
  @ExecStr varchar (2000),
  @N       int

SELECT
  @N = 5

SELECT
  @ExecStr = 'SELECT TOP ' + STR (@N, 2) + ' * '
           + 'FROM Orders ORDER BY OrderID DESC'

EXEC (@ExecStr)
```

> **NOTE** *You cannot use EXEC() directly on code that evaluates to a string when that code contains a function, as shown in Listing 9-28. You need to create the string first and then use it as a parameter for the EXEC() call.*

Now, all you have to do is change the value in `@N` and you can control the number of rows. For this demonstration, a `DECLARE` statement is used for `@N`, and `@N` is set inside the batch. In real life, of course, `@N` would actually be a parameter of a stored procedure. This is where the `EXEC()` function earns its keep. Now, your stored procedures can change their behavior dynamically, according to your parameters.

The `EXEC()` statement is a one-shot thing. Any variables created inside the `EXEC()` last only for that one invocation. The `EXEC()` cannot reference variables from the calling batch, and the database context, if changed inside the `EXEC()`, reverts back to the context of the calling statement. For example, the database context after the piece of code in Listing 9-29 is Northwind, not pubs.

Listing 9-29: Example of Dynamic Database Context with EXEC()

```
USE Northwind
EXEC ('USE pubs SELECT * FROM authors')
```

Since `EXEC()` is completely dynamic, there is no way to check security or whether the objects it references even exist until execution of the SQL string. If the `EXEC()` is within a stored procedure, the permissions are checked against the user who invokes the stored procedure, not against the owner of the procedure. This point is explained further in Appendix D.

Finally, there is the issue of compilation. The query plan from an `EXEC()` is not reused as the plans of regular stored procedures are. Rather, statements inside the `EXEC()` are not compiled until the `EXEC()` command is executed. The next section will show you an alternative approach that can take advantage of cached query plans.

Leveraging Dynamic Execution with `sp_executesql`

While `EXEC()` was a handy tool for SQL Server 6.5 developers and DBAs, SQL Server 7.0 introduced an enhanced means of running dynamic SQL. In SQL Server 7.0 and 2000, if a plan is found in cache that will satisfy the query but differs only in the parameters of the query, then, instead of creating a new plan, the optimizer will likely use the existing plan. To take advantage of this feature, Microsoft created the extended stored procedure `sp_executesql`. Take a look at the syntax in Listing 9-30.

Listing 9-30: Syntax for sp_executesql

```
sp_executesql [@stmt =] stmt
[
    {, [@params =] N'@parameter_name  data_type [,...n]' }
    {, [@param1 =] 'value1' [,...n] }
]
```

The first parameter, @stmt, contains the basic statement you want to have executed. It must be a Unicode string (nchar, nvarchar, or ntext)—a regular character string will not do. You may not use a complex Unicode expression, such as a concatenation, but you can build the Unicode string and put it into a variable. If you specify a parameter in the @params parameter, then it must appear in the @stmt parameter. The @stmt parameter can even be a batch of statements; you are not limited to just one.

The second parameter, @params, contains the list of parameters to be used by the statement. This is a list of all of the parameters much like in a DECLARE statement but without the DECLARE keyword. It, too, must be a Unicode string. The final pieces of the sp_executesql statement are designated in the syntax diagram by @param1.

If a parameter is defined in the @params parameter, then that parameter must be present in the call to sp_executesql. You can include your parameters in your code in one of two ways. You can assign values to your own parameter names as stated in your declaration inside @params, or you can pass them in the same order as they were declared and omit the parameter names. Changing only the parameter values makes the cached execution plan "reusable."

Let's look at a simple example. Suppose you want to get all of the information for an employee, based upon his or her EmployeeID. First, you need to create the SELECT statement. Next, you need to create the parameter declaration. Finally, you need to set the parameter. Check out the code in Listing 9-31.

Listing 9-31: Using sp_executesql to Find Employee Information

```
DECLARE
    @ExecStr nvarchar (4000)

SET
    @ExecStr = N'SELECT * FROM '
            + N'Northwind.dbo.Employees '
            + N'WHERE EmployeeID = @EmployeeId'

sp_executesql
    @stmt       = @ExecStr,
    @params     = N'@EmployeeId int',
    @EmployeeId = 1
```

Once you have run this stored procedure, you can execute it again, changing only the value of @EmployeeID. SQL Server will see that this execution differs only by the parameter in cache and may reuse the existing plan.

The optimizer's plan-matching algorithms require fully qualified object names to take advantage of plan reuse. In other words, use Northwind.dbo.Employees, not just Employees.

The previous example was simple and not like what you would see in the real world. One useful application of sp_executesql is in cases where you are inserting into a horizontally partitioned view. (Horizontally partitioned views divide up the rows of a table among multiple tables, and they are discussed in detail in Chapter 13.) You have to determine which table the data should be inserted into, based upon the partitioning criteria.

For example, you could partition an order table based on the year in which a customer's order was placed. Your naming convention would then include the year in the table name. The code in Listing 9-32 gives an example for the year 2000.

Listing 9-32: Sample Order Table

```
CREATE TABLE Orders2000
(
  OrderID     int      NOT NULL PRIMARY KEY,
  OrderDate   datetime NOT NULL,
  CustomerID  int      NOT NULL,
  Total       money    NOT NULL
)
```

You build one table for each of the years in which you are maintaining data. Next, you have to build the @stmt string. This is done in Listing 9-33.

Listing 9-33: Building the @stmt String

```
SET
  @stmt = N'INSERT MyDB.dbo.Orders' + STR (YEAR (@OrderDate), 4)
        + N' (OrderID, OrderDate, CustomerID, Total)'
        + N' VALUES (@OrderID, @OrderDate, @CustomerID, @Total)'
```

This statement assumes that you are using stored procedure parameters to supply the values for @OrderID, @OrderDate, @CustomerID, and @Total. The INSERT statement dynamically generates the table name.

You can build the @params string as shown in Listing 9-34:

Listing 9-34: Building the @params String

```
SET
  @params = N'@OrderID int, '
          + N'@OrderDate datetime, '
          + N'@CustomerID int, '
          + N'@Total money'
```

The call to sp_executesql is displayed in Listing 9-35.

Listing 9-35: Executing sp_executesql

```
EXEC sp_executesql
  @stmt,
  @params     = @params,
  @OrderID    = @OrderID,
  @OrderDate  = @OrderDate,
  @CustomerID = @CustomerID,
  @Total      = @Total
```

Behind the scenes, as you execute the code, you will place into cache one copy of the generated INSERT statement for each order year—that is, one for each table. Subsequent executions of the sp_executesql stored procedure for a particular year will use the cached copy.

This approach is elegant from the standpoint that you can keep your INSERT code down to a minimum and eliminate conditional processing. Also, if you now add another table for subsequent years, you do not have to modify your code.

SET Statements

SET statements are fairly common in Transact-SQL. These turn on and off various options in your procedure. If you issue these in a session, they remain in effect until you change them or you disconnect from SQL Server. However, if you issue the SET statement inside a stored procedure call, it overrides the session value and stays in effect only for the duration of the call. This way, you can tune a procedure to your specific needs, regardless of the settings already in effect.

Place your SET statement at the beginning of the body of your stored procedure code.

We won't present you with all of them here. Rather, you'll see the ones that you are most likely to use inside a stored procedure.

NOCOUNT

This option is one that you will use frequently. Failure to use this one means that you get those nagging messages about how many rows were affected, as shown in Listing 9-36.

Listing 9-36: Example of Rows Affected

```
(91 row(s) affected)
```

These messages can get annoying, particularly if your procedure has many statements. To turn off the reporting of rows affected, use the code in Listing 9-37.

Listing 9-37: Turning off Rows Affected

```
SET NOCOUNT ON
```

ANSI_DEFAULTS

As new versions of SQL Server are released, the product incorporates more ANSI SQL features. SQL Server is not 100 percent ANSI-92 compliant. Indeed, it introduces proprietary SQL extensions with just about every release. Nevertheless, expect to have to upgrade your code to comply with ANSI standards over time. You can turn off the default ANSI behavior with the ANSI_DEFAULTS option, as shown in Listing 9-38.

Listing 9-38: Turning off ANSI Defaults

```
SET ANSI_DEFAULTS OFF
```

Turning on and off ANSI defaults affects all ANSI behavior, and you can fine-tune this. The following individual ANSI settings can be turned on and off in a similar manner:

- ANSI_NULLS

- ANSI_NULL_DFLT_ON

- ANSI_PADDING

- CURSOR_CLOSE_ON_COMMIT

- IMPLICIT_TRANSACTIONS

- QUOTED_IDENTIFIER

You can get the details on each one of these in the Books Online.

> **CAUTION** *It is better not to turn off ANSI behavior. Rather, you should tailor your code to conform to the ANSI standards now, because you may be forced to do it in the future when you upgrade or add a service pack.*

TRANSACTION ISOLATION LEVEL

From a performance and tuning viewpoint, it is best to limit the amount of locking that your query generates. This reduces the effect you have on other users who are concurrently connected to your database. Using the TRANSACTION ISOLATION LEVEL option can do this for you. The syntax is shown in Listing 9-39.

Listing 9-39: Syntax for SET TRANSACTION ISOLATION LEVEL

```
SET TRANSACTION ISOLATION LEVEL
  { READ COMMITTED
    | READ UNCOMMITTED
    | REPEATABLE READ
    | SERIALIZABLE
}
```

The default is READ COMMITTED, which disallows "dirty reads." Dirty reads allow you to read rows that are in the process of being altered in a transaction. READ UNCOMMITTED allows nonrepeatable reads.

Between the time that you run a SELECT and you later in the session run the same SELECT, it is possible for another process to update rows that would be picked up by the second SELECT. These are referred to as *phantom rows*. Because the second read (SELECT) is not the same as the first read, it earns its name—*nonrepeatable*. The code in Listing 9-40 demonstrates the possibility of nonrepeatable reads. Pay close attention to the inline comments.

Listing 9-40: Script which Allows Nonrepeatable Reads

```
SET TRANSACTION ISOLATION LEVEL READ COMMITTED  -- nonrepeatable reads
                                                -- are now possible
-- initial SELECT
SELECT
  *
```

```
FROM
  Orders
WHERE
  CustomerID = 'VINET'

-- another process now updates an order for
-- Customer ID = 'VINET'

-- this SELECT does not return exactly the same data as
-- the previous SELECT
SELECT
  *
FROM
  Orders
WHERE
  CustomerID = 'VINET'
```

The READ UNCOMMITTED option allows dirty reads—this is the same as using the NOLOCK or READUNCOMMITTED table hint. It does not create locks nor does it honor any locks. The data you read while it is in effect may be in the process of being changed. This permits the greatest degree of concurrency but at the cost of potentially inaccurate data.

The REPEATABLE READ option is like the READ COMMITTED but it additionally disallows phantom rows. Shared locks remain in place for the duration of the transaction. In this case, outside processes that need to change your data will wait until you commit or roll back your transaction. Note, however, that the outside process can still insert rows that will be picked up by your second SELECT. This takes you to the next option, SERIALIZABLE.

The SERIALIZABLE option is the most restrictive. It behaves like the REPEATABLE READ option but additionally prevents other processes from inserting rows between your first and second SELECTs. If the INSERT will make no difference to your two SELECTs, it is allowed; otherwise, it is not. This is best illustrated by an example.

Suppose you are interested only in the order information for OrderID 11000, and someone inserts a new order—in that case, no one is affected. However, if your SELECT has no WHERE clause, all rows are to be retrieved and therefore the two SELECTs will differ. Consequently, the INSERT will wait until your transaction is complete.

Listing 9-41 shows you how to set the transaction isolation level to SERIALIZABLE.

Listing 9-41: Setting the Transaction Isolation Level

```
SET TRANSACTION ISOLATION LEVEL SERIALIZABLE
```

LOCK_TIMEOUT

Setting LOCK_TIMEOUT is a way of dealing with concurrency issues. This option allows you to specify the maximum number of milliseconds you are willing to have a query wait for a lock to be released. The default is –1, which means to wait indefinitely. Setting the value to 0 means the query should return as soon as a lock is encountered. This allows you to return control back to the calling program instead of waiting potentially forever. The code in Listing 9-42 shows you how to set the lock timeout to one minute.

Listing 9-42: Setting the LOCK_TIMEOUT to One Minute

```
SET LOCK_TIMEOUT 60000
```

QUERY_GOVERNOR_COST_LIMIT

Along the lines of LOCK_TIMEOUT, the QUERY_GOVERNOR_COST_LIMIT option allows you to set the maximum time, in seconds, that a query is allowed to run. This gives you a way of throttling certain known nasty queries that should be run at off-hours. If you know that a particular procedure can take a long time to run in certain circumstances, you can set a time limit so that control can be returned to the calling program, which can then decide how to proceed. To set the limit to one minute, use the code in Listing 9-43.

Listing 9-43: Setting the QUERY_GOVERNOR_COST_LIMIT to One Minute

```
SET QUERY_GOVERNOR_COST_LIMIT 60
```

System Stored Procedures

Thus far, you have seen stored procedures that you build yourself. Typically, these are used for handling application data manipulation. *System stored procedures* are those stored procedures that ship with SQL Server. We'll first show you some of the most useful ones and then show you what is involved in building your own.

Useful System Stored Procedures

A number of system stored procedures can help keep your stored procedures running at optimum speed. Some have existed as far back as the Sybase days. Since there are so many system stored procedures, we will present only those that are relevant to stored procedures.

Using sp_helptext

The sp_helptext system stored procedure gives you a source listing of another procedure, provided that it was not created with the WITH ENCRYPTION option. This system stored procedure is useful when trying to determine whether the version of your procedure in production matches what you have under version control. Just provide sp_helptext with the name of the procedure you wish to examine, as shown in Listing 9-44. You must be in the same database as the procedure in question.

Listing 9-44: Example of sp_helptext

```
EXEC sp_helptext
  usp_GetOrderDetails
```

Just as you can run sp_helptext against a stored procedure to determine its code, you can run it for a view, trigger, or function. As mentioned previously, you can also use Enterprise Manager to reveal the contents of views, procedures, functions, and triggers.

> **TIP**   *Looking at the contents of system stored procedures is a great way to learn.*

Using sp_help

Related to sp_helptext is sp_help. If you use this against a table, you get the structure of the table, including all columns, constraints, and indexes. Running this against a stored procedure gives you information on the expected parameters of the procedure. The syntax is the same as that of sp_helptext.

Using sp_updatestats

Before SQL Server 7.0, it was important to update index statistics, because the distribution of data could change over time. Failure to do this meant that the optimizer had out-of-date information to generate an efficient query plan. The statistics could potentially suggest to the optimizer that a table scan would be efficient when an index seek would be more appropriate. As of version 7.0, statistics can be kept up-to-date, obviating the need for such administration. However, this automatic update can be turned off.

By using `sp_updatestats`, you can update the index statistics on every table in your database. This has the effect of executing UPDATE STATISTICS iteratively across all tables. Where this becomes relevant to stored procedures is discussed next.

Using `sp_recompile`

If you create an index, the index statistics for the new index are updated automatically. Nevertheless, you can update statistics manually, as just discussed, and your stored procedure needs a way of picking up those new statistics. If it is not made aware of the statistics, the cached copy of the procedure may just go ahead with what it already knows and generate a table scan when that strategy is no longer appropriate. Enter `sp_recompile`.

The `sp_recompile` system stored procedure can mark a table, view, trigger, or stored procedure such that when the stored procedure or trigger is next used or when stored procedures or triggers that reference the table or view are next used, their query plans will be recompiled. This will cause them to use the most recent statistics.

SQL Server does recompile stored procedures and triggers when it deems it appropriate. However, it is good practice to run `sp_recompile` after you have done a large amount of insert, delete, or update activity.

An example of the syntax for `sp_recompile` is shown in Listing 9-45.

Listing 9-45: Example of Using sp_recompile

```
EXEC sp_recompile
   Customers
```

Using `sp_procoption`

Sometimes, you want a stored procedure to run when SQL Server starts up. This feature appeared in version 6.x in the form of `sp_makestartup`. However, this was changed to `sp_procoption` with the introduction of version 7.0. Take a moment to review the syntax in Listing 9-46.

Listing 9-46: Syntax for sp_procoption

```
sp_procoption
    [[@ProcName =] 'procedure']
    [,[@OptionName =] 'option']
    [,[@OptionValue =] 'value']
```

First, you give `sp_procoption` the name of the procedure you want to run, followed by `'startup'`, followed by `'TRUE'` or `'FALSE'` to turn on or off the feature, respectively. Alternatively, you may use `'on'` or `'off'`, instead of `'TRUE'` or `'FALSE'`, respectively.

In version 7.0, if you give `sp_procoption` no parameters, it will list all of the available options for `sp_procoption`. Currently, the only option is `'startup'`. In version 2000, all parameters must be specified. Also in version 2000, you can find out if a particular procedure is to be executed on startup by using the `OBJECTPROPERTY()` function to test for the `ExecIsStartup` property.

Creating System Stored Procedures

SQL Server ships with hundreds of system stored procedures. Most are documented, but many are not. These stored procedures cover just about anything you may encounter. However, there are many DBAs who just can't resist rolling their own system stored procedures. These fall into two main categories—those that modify data and those that simply retrieve it. Typically, system stored procedures access the database or system catalogs.

System stored procedures are stored in the master database and are prefixed with "sp_". You use them without having to prepend the database name to the procedure, so you would, for example, use `sp_who`, not `master..sp_who`.

If you are intending to access database catalogs, such as *sysobjects*, you will want the procedure to access the object in your current database, not the one in master. You will also want it to work in every database. If you create it in master and prefix it with "sp_", SQL Server is smart enough to figure out that you want the current database. However, you can run it in the context of another database just by prefixing it with the database name, just as you would a procedure inside that database. For example, if you were in tempdb and ran `Northwind..sp_help`, you would get a list of objects in the Northwind database.

The "sp_" prefix can lure you into making system stored procedures that have the same name as that of an existing or future system stored procedure written by Microsoft. Ed Barlow, New York–based Sybase guru, came up with a useful suggestion. He prefixes his system stored procedures with "sp__" ("sp" and *two* underscores). This way, you'll never have a clash with the existing or future system stored procedures, and the procedure names will sort before the regular system stored procedures, thus grouping together all of your hand-rolled masterpieces.

As always, Microsoft reserves the right to change system tables at any time. This means that your handy-dandy system stored procedures may break down with the installation of the latest service pack. However, what will likely not change (or will change infrequently) are the ANSI views of the system tables. Try to make your homegrown system stored procedures use these views wherever possible.

Finally, if your system stored procedure is going to modify a system table, you must configure SQL Server to allow updates before you create your procedure and then remember to disallow updates when you are finished. This is demonstrated in Listing 9-47.

Listing 9-47: Creating a System Stored Procedure that Modifies a System Table

```
sp_configure 'allow', 1
GO
RECONFIGURE WITH OVERRIDE
GO
CREATE PROC sp__MySystemProc AS ...
GO
sp_configure 'allow', 0
GO
RECONFIGURE WITH OVERRIDE
GO
```

Server settings such as `'allow updates'` and some `SET` options are determined at `CREATE PROC` time and not at run time. The stored procedure will be able to modify system tables even though, at run time, you have not turned on this option.

> **CAUTION** *Always remember to reconfigure SQL Server to disallow updates immediately after you create your system stored procedure. Leaving this option on will allow you to do some serious damage to the system tables.*

Don't forget to grant `EXEC` permissions on your system stored procedures if you want users that don't belong to the sysadmin role to be able to use them. Security is discussed later in this chapter, in the "Security and Stored Procedures" section.

Creating Temporary Stored Procedures

Just as you can create a temporary table, you can also create a temporary stored procedure. (Temporary tables are covered in Chapter 12.) The naming rules are the same for any other identifier. However, since you are dealing with a temporary object, you need to prefix it with "#" for a local temporary procedure and "##" for a global temporary procedure.

The local object lasts as long as the session that created it does, unless you delete it first. It is accessible only to the session that created it. The global temporary object is shared among all sessions and also lasts as long as the session that created it does. However, if the session that created it disconnects and other sessions still use it, it will be deleted only when the last session that uses it releases it.

> **NOTE** *Clients can communicate with SQL Server via an ODBC connection. This enables a client program to send SQL to SQL Server. When you create an ODBC connection, you can configure a number of options. One of these is to allow the ODBC connection to generate temporary stored procedures on its own. If your application is already using stored procedures (as it should), you can turn this off.*

From the Trenches

A banking application used temporary stored procedures as a workaround with a reporting tool. The tool could use stored procedures, but none with parameters. A global temporary stored procedure was created on the fly as a wrapper to a procedure call that used the actual parameters. The reporting tool then accessed the temporary procedure.

In most situations, you can avoid creating temporary stored procedures and use sp_executesql instead.

Nesting Stored Procedures

You can easily nest your stored procedures, which means you can have procedures calling procedures. Simply put an EXEC statement inside your calling stored procedure, and you are under way. However, there is one issue you should note.

A stored procedure cannot be nested more than 32 levels deep. You can test how far down you are by checking the value of the @@NESTLEVEL function. It is incremented for each EXEC and decremented for each RETURN. If you reach that magical 32, your code is probably too complex, and you should look at simplifying it!

Recursion

Speaking of complexity, have a look at recursion. Recursion is the phenomenon of a procedure calling itself. There are not that many cases where you will need to do this, but it can save your bacon in those odd circumstances where nothing else will do.

One such case would be to traverse your way up a tree. A classic example is determining the reporting structure above a given employee. (Hierarchies are discussed in detail in Chapter 16.) In other words, who is the employee's boss, who is that boss's boss, and so on. For this scenario, you will use the Northwind database. The code in Listing 9-48 shows you how to do it.

Listing 9-48: Example of Recursion Using a Stored Procedure

```
CREATE PROC usp_FindBoss
(
  @EmployeeID  int
)
AS
DECLARE
  @ReportsTo  int

SELECT
  @ReportsTo  = ReportsTo
FROM
    Employees
WHERE
    EmployeeId = @EmployeeID

IF @ReportsTo IS NOT NULL AND @@NESTLEVEL <= 32
BEGIN
  SELECT
    @EmployeeID AS Employee,
    @ReportsTo  AS Manager

  EXEC usp_FindBoss
    @ReportsTo
END
GO
```

When you create this stored procedure, you will get a warning message to the effect that SQL Server was unable to add a row to *sysdepends* for the missing object, usp_FindBoss. This is because, at create time, the procedure that usp_FindBoss called, namely usp_FindBoss, did not already exist.

The SELECT picks out the EmployeeID of the person's boss and stores it in @ReportsTo. This is then SELECTed with @EmployeeID and is fed to the procedure as the input parameter. Notice how you checked @@NESTLEVEL to see if it was okay to go any deeper. You also checked to see whether you had reached the limit of the reporting tree by testing whether @ReportsTo was NULL.

If you run this stored procedure for EmployeeID 7, you get the results in Listing 9-49.

Listing 9-49: Results of Executing sup_FindBoss for EmployeeID 7

```
Employee    Manager
----------- -----------
        7           5


Employee    Manager
----------- -----------
        5           2
```

Security and Stored Procedures

Not only can stored procedures make your life easier from a developer's perspective, but they can also do this from a DBA's point of view. Any industrial-strength database has to control who can do what inside it. Typically, you do not want just anyone deleting or updating rows without proper authority. Also, you may have privileged information that only certain users are allowed to see. Finally, you may not want underqualified users throwing ad hoc SQL at the database, causing table scans, deadlocks, etcetera, while others are trying to do their work. This is where stored procedures solve many security issues.

Fixed database roles are roles that pertain just to a particular database. You cannot alter these roles, but you can control who can be a member of the role. The public role is a role that includes all database users. The db_datareader and db_datawriter roles permit members of those roles to read (INSERT) or write (INSERT, UPDATE, or DELETE) data in all tables in the database, respectively. Conversely, the db_denydatareader and db_denydatawriter roles permit *no* members of those roles to read (INSERT) or write (INSERT, UPDATE, or DELETE) data in all tables in the database, respectively. You cannot add the public role to the db_datareader, db_datawriter, db_denydatareader, or db_denydatawriter fixed database roles.

First, look at who is allowed to create a stored procedure. Since the sysadmin has unlimited authority on the server, obviously this fixed server role is permitted. So, too, are members of the db_owner fixed database role, since they have unlimited authority within the database itself. Sometimes, this authority is too broad if all a person needs is the authority to create a stored procedure. The db_ddladmin fixed database role allows a member to create objects within the database. This, too, could be too broad, since this role can also create tables, views, defaults, etcetera, and maybe you don't wish them to go that far. In that case, you can explicitly grant them CREATE PROC permission.

Once a user has permission to create a stored procedure, you then have to grant EXEC permission to users or roles. Otherwise, only the user who created the stored procedure and any members of the sysadmin or db_owner roles could use it. Here, you will need to use the GRANT EXEC statement. Take a look at the example in Listing 9-50.

Listing 9-50: Example of GRANT EXEC Statement

```
GRANT EXEC on usp_FindBoss to
  Itzik,
  Tom
```

> **TIP** *Avoid granting* EXEC *permission to individual users—it makes adminis-tration a nightmare. Put them into user-defined database roles and grant the roles* EXEC *permission. This makes things easier when people are added to and removed from jobs within your enterprise.*

Don't forget that you can grant EXEC permission to users *or* to roles.

> **TIP** *In your build script, create your user-defined roles first. Then create the procedures. Inside each procedure script, add the* GRANT EXEC *statements. This keeps the permission with the procedure, and all that is left to do is to add data-base users to the roles.*

Things get more complicated when you call a stored procedure that will call stored procedures in databases other than the current database *if* the owner is dif-ferent. The user must then have EXEC permission on the procedures in both databases. (This same issue arises with views where the ownership chain is broken.)

If you simply do not grant SELECT, INSERT, UPDATE, or DELETE permission to any role and then grant EXEC only to those procedures that users need to use, you are probably in good shape.

For further information on security, refer to Appendix D.

Deferred Name Resolution

The way that a stored procedure gets compiled changed substantially with the arrival of version 7.0. In previous versions, all objects to which the procedure referred had to exist prior to the creation of the procedure itself. You had to create any temporary tables that the procedure used but did not create itself. To go through this exercise just to create the procedure was a major pain. Any industrial-strength system would have more than 100 procedures, and maintaining the build script was a tricky task.

Now, you no longer need to create temporary (or permanent) tables just to allow a procedure to compile. Rather, the compilation process is split. When you create the procedure, it does a rudimentary syntax check and stores the source for your procedure in *syscomments*. It actually checks the objects it uses when you invoke the procedure. It is only at this time that you will realize you have a problem. What this forces you to do is test your code by executing it; a clean compile is not enough. Perish the thought!

> **TIP**   *Even though you can add your procedures in any order, you will get "error" messages that SQL Server was not able to add a row to sysdepends if the called procedure did not already exist. It does, however, successfully create the procedure. This means that you will not get accurate information about dependencies when you run* sp_depends *or check the dependencies in Enterprise Manager. Try to arrange your build scripts in such a way that the called procedures are created ahead of the calling procedures.*

SQL Server versions prior to 7.0 had a system table—*sysprocedures*—in every database, which would store the query tree. Now this table is gone. SQL Server reads the source from *syscomments* when you go to use the procedure, and it creates the tree and query plan in memory. While this little step takes more time than it did in version 6.5, once the plan is in RAM, things go quickly.

To follow this a little further, developers of third-party stored procedures used to delete the entries from *syscomments* to "hide" their code. Since the tokenized form was saved in *sysprocedures*, there was no need for SQL Server to access *syscomments* after creation. When such systems were migrated to 7.0, these procedures were not upgraded, of course. Also, since there's no *sysprocedures* in versions 7.0 or 2000, every time the procedure needs to be compiled, the code is read from *syscomments*, so it must be there. Therefore, in versions 7.0 and 2000, you simply need to use WITH ENCRYPTION to keep your code secret.

> **NOTE**   *Deferred name resolution also applies to triggers and functions.*

Statements Not Permitted Inside a Stored Procedure

There are some statements you cannot have inside a stored procedure, and they are listed below. They are all related to object creation.

    CREATE DEFAULT

    CREATE PROCEDURE

    CREATE RULE

    CREATE TRIGGER

    CREATE VIEW

It makes sense that you cannot create a procedure within a procedure. After all, you need to know when one ends and the other begins.

Transactions and Stored Procedures

In Chapter 7, you dealt with transactions. Now, it's time to revisit the topic in the context of stored procedures. As discussed earlier, stored procedures can call other stored procedures up to 32 levels deep. Transactions can also be nested up to 32 levels deep. Here's the rub—a transaction can be started inside a called stored procedure without any knowledge on the part of the calling procedure. The called procedure does, however, have a way of detecting whether the calling procedure started a transaction. It can use the @@TRANCOUNT function to determine the nesting level of the transactions. If the result is greater than 0, you are already inside a transaction and there is really no need to start another one. Using this knowledge, you can ensure that the transaction nesting level never goes above 1.

The calling procedure could be modified to handle the various situations served up to it by the called procedure, but this can get very complex and confusing. Also, if the called procedure is suddenly modified to increase or decrease its transaction nesting levels, then the calling procedure code could break. This is not the way to write good code. The called and calling procedures should be as independent of each other as possible. If this is not possible, then they should be merged into a single procedure.

Because the called procedure has knowledge of the transactional situation, it also has the responsibility to ensure that it does not break the code of the calling procedure. Most importantly, it has to be careful that BEGIN TRAN, COMMIT TRAN, and ROLLBACK TRAN statements are balanced across all nesting levels. This looks like quite a task, but it can be made simple by proper use of the SAVE TRAN statement.

Inside the calling procedure, check to see if there is already a transaction under way before you begin one yourself. In other words, test to see if @@TRANCOUNT is greater than 0. If it is, you can issue a SAVE TRAN; otherwise, you must issue your own BEGIN TRAN. Remember to give the save point a name—you will need it to roll back to in the event you encounter an error.

You will also need to save the @@TRANCOUNT information as it was when you entered the procedure so you can determine whether you issued your own BEGIN TRAN or you used the existing transaction of the calling procedure (or its calling procedure, or its calling procedure, etcetera). The code fragment in Listing 9-51 shows you how to put it all together.

Listing 9-51: Managing a Transaction Inside a Stored Procedure

```
CREATE PROC usp_MyProc
AS
DECLARE
  @TranCount   int

SET
  @TranCount = @@TRANCOUNT

IF @TranCount > 0
   SAVE TRAN usp_MyProc            -- No existing transaction
ELSE
   BEGIN TRAN usp_MyProc           -- Transaction in progress

-- do work here ...

IF @@ERROR > 0
BEGIN                              -- Failure
  RAISERROR ('usp_MyProc - Bailing out. ', 16, 1)
  ROLLBACK TRAN usp_MyProc
  RETURN
END
ELSE IF @Trancount = 0            -- Started our own transaction
  COMMIT TRAN usp_MyProc          -- Success
GO
```

This code shows you a couple of things related to prudent programming. First, the savepoint is given the name usp_MyProc, which is the same as the procedure itself. Make the savepoint name the same as the name of the procedure so it relates to the procedure in which it occurs. (If you have multiple savepoints, you can append "_1", "_2", etc., to make the name unique.) The second point is that the RAISERROR statement contains the name of the procedure (and transaction) that failed. This, too, will help you when you troubleshoot. Alternatively, you can use RETURN codes or output parameters. Both the RAISERROR and RETURN codes communicate information back to the calling procedure. The calling procedure can then decide whether it wants to roll back its work because of the called procedure's failure or ignore it. The calling procedure does not need to know the inner workings of the called procedure. It just has to know whether it succeeded or failed.

> **TIP** *You can capture the value of* @@ERROR *inside your stored procedures and then use* RETURN *to send the value of* @@ERROR *back to the calling procedure.*

SQL Puzzle 9-1: Creating a Procedure within a Procedure

Earlier in this chapter, you were told of the statements that you cannot execute inside a stored procedure. There is a way to get around this restriction and the method is explained in this chapter. Your assignment is to create a stored procedure that creates another temporary stored procedure that takes the CustomerID for a customer and returns the row from the Customers table for that CustomerID. Use the Northwind database.

SQL Puzzle 9-2: Automatically Creating Stored Procedures

Now that you've had the opportunity to create a stored procedure from another stored procedure, it's time to go to the next level. This time, generalize the stored procedure that you created in the previous puzzle so that the user can feed it a table name and the procedure will generate another procedure, based upon the table you gave it. The generated procedure must have a parameter that receives the primary key of the given table. The procedure should then return the row corresponding to the primary key.

To make things simple, assume that there is only one column that constitutes the primary key and that this column is the first column in the table. In other words, you will not be able to use it for the Order Details table.

The answers to these puzzles can be found on pages 692–695.

CHAPTER 10

Triggers–the Hidden Stored Procedures

TRIGGERS ALLOW YOU TO enforce referential integrity (RI) and domain integrity programmatically, handle physicalization (physical implementation) of logical tables, and implement weird business rules (you've seen those, haven't you?). Alternatively, you can enforce strange business rules through stored procedures—the choice is up to you. Stored procedures are discussed in Chapter 9.

Doing your own RI is necessary when you go across databases; you cannot have foreign key constraints refer to tables outside of their own database. With the introduction of Declarative Referential Integrity (DRI) in SQL Server version 6.5, the need for triggers was greatly reduced, because most triggers were used to enforce RI. It is quite common to see databases that use constraints and have no triggers whatsoever.

Triggers have a look and feel similar to stored procedures, but they are invoked differently. Indeed, you cannot invoke triggers directly. Rather, you have to execute an action on the table or view to which the trigger is attached in order to fire the trigger. This means that triggers are hidden and are not self-evident. One consequence of this is that you cannot feed parameters to the trigger—it only has access to the data modified by the INSERT, UPDATE, or DELETE statement, as appropriate. Another consequence is that troubleshooting can be made difficult because it may not be evident to you that the table or view has a trigger. There are also some issues regarding IDENTITY values, which you will soon see.

Many of the restrictions that you see for stored procedures are also in effect for triggers. However, triggers have their own limitations, too. Just as in a stored procedure, you cannot nest a trigger more than 32 levels deep. Also, you cannot place a trigger on a temporary object. (Temporary tables are discussed in Chapter 12.) Other restrictions are discussed later in this chapter.

Using the CREATE TRIGGER Statement

Just like the CREATE PROCEDURE, CREATE VIEW, and CREATE FUNCTION statements, the CREATE TRIGGER statement must be the first statement in a batch. Take a look at the syntax in Listing 10-1.

Listing 10-1: Syntax for the CREATE TRIGGER Statement

```
CREATE TRIGGER trigger_name
ON { table | view }
[ WITH ENCRYPTION ]
{
  { { FOR | AFTER | INSTEAD OF }
  { [ DELETE ] [ , ] [ INSERT ] [ , ] [ UPDATE ] }
  [ WITH APPEND ]
  [ NOT FOR REPLICATION ]
AS
  sql_statement [ ...n ]
}
|
{ ( FOR | AFTER | INSTEAD OF ) { [ INSERT ] [ , ] [ UPDATE ] }
  [ WITH APPEND ]
  [ NOT FOR REPLICATION ]
AS
{ IF UPDATE ( column )
  [ { AND | OR } UPDATE ( column ) ]
  [ ...n ]
  | IF ( COLUMNS_UPDATED ( ) { bitwise_operator } updated_bitmask )
  { comparison_operator } column_bitmask [ ...n ]
}
  sql_statement [ ...n ]
}
}
```

In the header of the CREATE TRIGGER statement, you provide the name of your trigger, the table or view to which it will be attached, and the action(s) that will cause it to fire. You also have to include the type of trigger—AFTER (or FOR) or INSTEAD OF. (An AFTER trigger fires after all constraints and after the triggering action has taken place. An INSTEAD OF trigger replaces the normal INSERT, UPDATE, or DELETE action on the underlying table or view. Both AFTER and INSTEAD OF triggers are fully discussed later in this chapter, in the "Understanding AFTER Triggers" and "Understanding INSTEAD OF Triggers" sections.) Check out the sample header in Listing 10-2.

Listing 10-2: Sample CREATE TRIGGER Header

```
CREATE TRIGGER tri_Customers ON CUSTOMERS AFTER UPDATE
AS
```

> **TIP** *Use a naming convention that suggests that the object is a trigger, indicates what actions will cause it to fire, and identifies the table to which it is attached. For example, an* UPDATE *and* DELETE *trigger on the Orders table could be named* trud_Orders.

The NOT FOR REPLICATION option indicates that the trigger will not fire if the INSERT, UPDATE, or DELETE action was the result of a replication process modifying the table.

The WITH ENCRYPTION option allows you to encrypt the trigger code so that the entries in *syscomments* for the trigger cannot be read.

The IF UPDATE() and COLUMNS_UPDATED() functions test for an UPDATE action on the given column(s). These functions are discussed in detail later in this chapter, in the "Using the IF UPDATE() and IF COLUMNS_UPDATED() Functions" section.

In the 6.x versions of SQL Server, you could replace a trigger simply by creating another with the same name. However, in versions 7.0 and 2000, you cannot create a trigger with the same name unless you are in 6.5 compatibility mode or earlier. Also in 6.x, you could have only one trigger of each type on a table; for example, you could have only one DELETE trigger on a table. You could, however, have one trigger for multiple actions, such as one trigger for both UPDATE and DELETE; this capability remains in effect for versions 7.0 and 2000.

With the release of 7.0, you could have multiple triggers of the same type, so you could have, say, two UPDATE triggers and three INSERT triggers on the same table. This was handy for modularizing your code because, for example, you could add another INSERT trigger when you added a new table to your schema, leaving the existing triggers intact. Also, you could add a trigger for special temporary handling, such as for monitoring a specific employee's actions on a table. Once the monitoring was complete, you could drop the trigger and not have to update any existing triggers.

To allow multiple triggers of the same type in a database in 6.5 compatibility mode, use the WITH APPEND option.

Finally, the SQL statements that you use in a trigger are much like those in a stored procedure. The differences and restrictions are covered throughout the remainder of this chapter.

The ALTER TRIGGER Statement

Before the introduction of version 7.0, the only way to update a trigger was to drop and re-create it, although you could replace a trigger by doing a CREATE TRIGGER with the same name as the trigger you wanted to replace. This caused problems like those for stored procedures in comparable situations. In the period between the execution of the DROP TRIGGER and CREATE TRIGGER statements, the trigger did not exist and, since triggers are typically used to enforce referential integrity and weird business rules, bad data could enter the database. You might not have found out that the bad data crept in, and troubleshooting it might even have been impossible.

The ALTER TRIGGER statement allows you to change the code of a trigger without actually dropping it. The table is not available while the trigger is being altered, which only makes sense. A Schema-Modify lock is placed on the table during this period; you can't even run sp_help against it. To prove this to yourself, run a BEGIN TRAN as a single batch; then, run the ALTER TRIGGER in the same session. This is shown in Listing 10-3.

Listing 10-3: Modifying a Trigger in a Transaction

```
BEGIN TRAN
ALTER TRIGGER tri_MyTable ON MyTable AFTER INSERT
AS
-- code goes here
GO
```

Finally, try to run sp_help from a separate session. It will wait indefinitely until you either issue a ROLLBACK TRAN or a COMMIT TRAN in the original session. Also, try running sp_lock. You will see the Schema-Modify lock in effect.

The syntax of the ALTER TRIGGER statement is identical to that of the CREATE TRIGGER statement. It, too, must be the first statement in a batch.

Using the DROP TRIGGER Statement

If you want to get rid of a trigger, you use the DROP TRIGGER statement in a manner similar to DROP PROCEDURE, DROP FUNCTION, DROP TABLE, or DROP VIEW. The rules for referencing owners are also the same. However, you cannot specify a database name in the identifier. You must be using the same database in which you wish to drop a trigger. An example is shown in Listing 10-4.

Listing 10-4: Syntax for the DROP TRIGGER Statement

```
DROP TRIGGER tri_MyTable
```

The *deleted* and *inserted* Tables

The *deleted* and *inserted* virtual tables are essentially views of the transaction log. Through them you can see the rows that were inserted, deleted, or modified by the underlying INSERT, UPDATE, or DELETE statement that fired the trigger. The *inserted* table is an "after" image of only the affected rows; the *deleted* table is the "before" image. For a DELETE statement, only the *deleted* table will be populated. For an INSERT, only the *inserted* table will be populated. For an UPDATE, *both* of these tables will be populated. Since a trigger is attached to a single table or view, the *deleted* and *inserted* tables are images of the tables to which the relevant trigger is attached. They have the same columns in name, order, and datatype. The *inserted* and *deleted* tables are available only to triggers, not to stored procedures.

If the compatibility level of the database is 70, you cannot refer to text, ntext, or image columns in the *inserted* or *deleted* tables—those columns cannot be accessed. (These datatypes are covered in Chapter 6.) You can, however, access the updated values in the base table by joining the *inserted* table to the base table; the *inserted* table simply provides you with the keys in this case.

When the compatibility level is 65 or lower, then NULL values are returned for the text, ntext, and image columns in the *deleted* and *inserted* tables, if those columns are nullable. Otherwise, the columns will contain zero-length strings.

If the compatibility level is 80 or higher, you can update the text, ntext, and image columns directly through an INSTEAD OF trigger. INSTEAD OF triggers are presented later in this chapter, in the "Understanding INSTEAD OF Triggers" section.

Firing Triggers

The type of code you write inside a trigger differs from that of stored procedures. In a trigger, you are typically interested in which rows were touched as the result of an INSERT, UPDATE, or DELETE statement. Invariably, you will be relying on the *inserted* or *deleted* tables to determine which rows you wish to manipulate.

As an example, you can use triggers for cascaded deletes (with SQL Server 2000, you can use constraints instead of triggers if the referenced tables are in the same database). Using the Northwind database, try a cascaded delete of rows in the Order Details table corresponding to rows deleted in the Orders table. The trigger script is depicted in Listing 10-5.

Listing 10-5: Cascaded Delete Using a Trigger

```
CREATE TRIGGER trd_Orders ON Orders AFTER DELETE
AS
IF @@ROWCOUNT = 0
  RETURN

DELETE OD
FROM
    deleted         AS D
  JOIN
    [Order Details] AS OD ON OD.OrderID = D.OrderID
GO
```

This example deletes only those rows that correspond to those that were deleted in Orders. It is important to use the *deleted* table and not Orders, since that would delete all rows in Order Details.

If you run this script, the code will execute. However, if you go to delete an order from the Orders table, you will get a foreign key violation because the FOREIGN KEY constraint fires before the trigger. The FOREIGN KEY constraint on the Order Details table that references the Orders table does not use the ON DELETE CASCADE option. To allow this trigger to fire, you either need to drop or disable the constraint.

If you're curious, an example of the syntax for cascaded deletes through DRI is shown in Listing 10-6.

Listing 10-6: Example of Enabling Cascaded Deletes through DRI

```
CREATE TABLE NewOrderDetails
(
  OrderID    int    NOT NULL
                    CONSTRAINT FK1_NewOrderDetails REFERENCES Orders (OrderID)
                      ON DELETE CASCADE,
  ProductID int     NOT NULL
                    CONSTRAINT FK2_NewOrderDetails REFERENCES Products (ProductID)
                      ON DELETE NO ACTION,
 Quantity   smallint NOT NULL,
                    CONSTRAINT PK_NewOrderDetails PRIMARY KEY (OrderID, ProductID),
)
```

Here, the FOREIGN KEY constraint—FK1_NewOrderDetails—uses the ON DELETE CASCADE option. This tells SQL Server that if there are any records deleted from the Orders table, then the corresponding rows in NewOrderDetails must also be deleted. However, since this option is ON DELETE NO ACTION in the second FOREIGN KEY constraint—FK2_NewOrderDetails—then any deletes from the Products table will be rolled back if there are any corresponding rows in NewOrderDetails. Thus, there is no need for a DELETE trigger on Orders to handle the cascaded DELETE. Cascade operations are covered in detail in Chapter 14.

Finally, the WRITETEXT statement, whether logged or unlogged, does not cause a trigger to fire. Similarly, the TRUNCATE TABLE statement does not cause triggers to fire.

First and Last Triggers

In release 7.0, when a table had multiple triggers, there was no way of guaranteeing the order in which they fired. In contrast, SQL Server 2000 allows you *some* latitude in controlling the firing order of AFTER triggers. This is limited to determining the first and last trigger of each type (INSERT, UPDATE, DELETE) per table. Here, you use sp_settriggerorder. Check out the syntax in Listing 10-7.

Listing 10-7: Syntax for sp_settriggerorder

```
sp_settriggerorder [@triggername = ] 'triggername'
    , [@order = ] 'value'
    , [@stmttype = ] 'statement_type'
```

The @triggername parameter is obvious. The @order parameter is either 'first' or 'last'. Finally, the @stmttype parameter is one of 'INSERT', 'UPDATE', or 'DELETE'

Optimizing Trigger Performance

The best trigger is one that is short in duration. You can help keep them short by determining whether there is any work to do. It is good practice to check whether there are any rows affected by the triggering action, because if no rows are affected, it is generally a sign that there is no work for your trigger to do. After passing the rows-affected test, you should then check whether any columns were updated. (This has meaning only in UPDATE triggers.) If columns were updated, then perhaps there is work for the trigger to do. If not, this is another opportunity to bail out.

Keep in mind that you are in a transaction, and locks are kept in place until the transaction is committed or rolled back. Consequently, the longer a trigger runs, the more likely it is that the trigger will block another process. Also, if your triggers are heavily nested, it is possible that it will deadlock with another process. Troubleshooting this type of situation can be very difficult.

The following discussions look at testing to see whether the trigger does any work and at the locks that may block other processes.

Leveraging @@ROWCOUNT

@@ROWCOUNT is a system function that tells you how many rows were affected by the most recent SELECT, INSERT, UPDATE, or DELETE. The first thing you should do inside each trigger is test @@ROWCOUNT to see if any rows were affected by the triggering action—INSERT, UPDATE, or DELETE. If not, there is no work to be done by the trigger, and you should simply return. The piece of code shown in Listing 10-8 should appear at the beginning of every trigger.

Listing 10-8: Testing for Rows Affected in a Trigger

```
IF @@ROWCOUNT = 0
    RETURN
```

Another reason to test @@ROWCOUNT is to check whether the number of rows affected is the number expected. There will always be cases where the trigger is expected to affect only one row, but there were actually more than that being affected. In such instances, you must make sure that your trigger code checks that only the one row was affected. In other words, @@ROWCOUNT = 1.

Using the IF UPDATE() and IF COLUMNS_UPDATED() Functions

If your code got past the @@ROWCOUNT check, it is possible that there is still no work for the trigger to do because your trigger is necessary only if certain columns were touched. This gives you another chance to bail out of the trigger without doing unnecessary work, keeping its duration short.

The IF UPDATE() statement allows you to test a column to see if it was updated through an UPDATE statement. It returns TRUE if there is an UPDATE or INSERT.

It would be useful in the Northwind database to have a trigger that can sense when the UnitsInStock value drops below the ReorderLevel value. This can happen in one of two situations. The most common is when an order has been placed or fulfilled and the UnitsInStock value is decremented by the amount of the order. The less common scenario is when an administrator has reset the ReorderLevel value and you now need to reorder. Your trigger can check either of these two columns and take the appropriate action. This can be done using IF UPDATE(), as shown in Listing 10-9.

Listing 10-9: Using IF UPDATE() in a Trigger

```
CREATE TRIGGER tru_Products ON PRODUCTS FOR UPDATE
AS
IF @@ROWCOUNT = 0
  RETURN

IF UPDATE (UnitsInStock) OR UPDATE (ReorderLevel)
BEGIN
  IF EXISTS (SELECT * FROM inserted WHERE UnitsInStock < ReorderLevel)
  BEGIN
    -- take appropriate action here
  END
END
GO
```

Here, you are interested in whether or not *either* column was updated. If you were interested in checking whether multiple columns were *all* updated, you would use an AND keyword instead of OR in the list of UPDATED() tests.

Using IF UPDATE() is not the only way to determine whether the UnitsInStock column or the ReorderLevel column was touched. The IF COLUMNS_UPDATED() construct allows you to check multiple columns for updates. In this case, you are returned a bit string in a `varbinary`, and each bit corresponds to a column position in the table, starting at bit 0. For example, 2^0 (= 1) represents the first column; 2^1 (= 2) represents the second column; 2^2 (= 4) represents the third column, and so on. All you have to do is use your own bit mask to filter for your columns of interest, and you have your solution. (Bitwise operations are covered in Chapter 4.)

If you use `IF COLUMNS_UPDATED()` and you AND it (using &) with your bit mask, you can compare the result to the same bit mask to determine if all of your columns were touched. This is equivalent to using `IF UPDATE() AND UPDATE()`. However, if you test to see if the result is simply greater than zero, then at least one column was touched. This is equivalent to using `IF UPDATE() OR UPDATE()`.

As an example, suppose you want to know if the second, third, and fifth columns are all updated. Using 2 to the power of (column position − 1) gives you $2^1 + 2^2 + 2^4$, totaling 22. The code fragment in Listing 10-10 shows you how make the comparison.

Listing 10-10: Using IF COLUMNS_UPDATED() to Test for Updates to Columns 2, 3, and 5

```
IF COLUMNS_UPDATED () & 22 = 22
```

From a coding standpoint, there is less to code using this method, particularly if you are interested in a bunch of columns. However, you now have to get out your calculator, calculate 2 to the power of each column number (column position − 1), and sum them up. Furthermore, the number 22 is not self-describing as the column names are. Finally, tables can be altered throughout their lifetime. If, say, the third column is dropped and another one is added, the bit mask must be changed. If the table is dropped and re-created using different column positions, the bit mask must again be recalculated. It is very easy to forget to do this. While the coding may be a bit more involved, the `IF UPDATE ()` construct is safer.

As stated in Chapter 4, you can't AND a `varbinary` with another `varbinary`. You have to cast one to an 8-bit int. So what do you do if you are interested in columns beyond the first 8? In this case, you have to use the `SUBSTRING()` function to pick out one byte at a time and then perform the appropriate logical operation on the byte. It's a little clunky, but it gets you past the restriction.

The code in Listing 10-11 reworks the code in Listing 10-9 to use the `IF COLUMNS_UPDATED()` construct.

Listing 10-11: Using IF COLUMNS_UPDATED() for Testing Updates on Columns 7 and 9

```
CREATE TRIGGER truProducts ON PRODUCTS FOR UPDATE
AS
IF @@ROWCOUNT = 0
```

```
   RETURN

IF SUBSTRING (COLUMNS_UPDATED (), 1, 1) & 64 = 64
  OR SUBSTRING (COLUMNS_UPDATED(), 2, 1) = 1
BEGIN
  IF EXISTS (SELECT * FROM inserted WHERE UnitsInStock < ReorderLevel)
  BEGIN
    -- take appropriate action here
  END
END
GO
```

The UnitsInStock and ReorderLevel columns are columns 7 and 9, respectively. Therefore, the bit mask is 2^6 plus 2^8. You cannot use 2^8, but you can use 2^6. Therefore, you can AND COLUMNS_UPDATED() with 2^6 (which is 64) but you have to use SUBSTRING() to take the second byte from COLUMNS_UPDATED() and then test the lowest bit position, which is 2^0 (or 1). Since you are interested in either column, you OR the two comparisons.

Other Locking Issues

Prudent programming practices do not get tossed out the window just because you are using triggers. Indeed, it is more important to be disciplined in your coding when you are using triggers because locking issues can make or break an application. Although you can use locking hints inside a trigger, you should review why you are using them. Locking hints such as HOLDLOCK and TABLOCKX will increase the likelihood of blocking other processes. However, using locking hints that reduce the amount of locking, such as READPAST and READUNCOMMITTED, can help to reduce the probability of blocking other processes.

Also consider how much work you are doing inside the transaction, since all work done inside your triggers is considered to be part of the overall transaction. If the work truly does not have to be inside a transaction, then narrow down your transaction to just the essentials. For example, if a customer wishes to place an order and change her address, this would cause locks on the Orders, Order Details, and Customers tables, plus any tables that ensuing triggers would modify. Since the customer has changed her address and such a change is not related to her placing an order, the address change should be handled separately.

From the Trenches

A database for managing social assistance contained many tables, most of which had triggers that were 500 lines long. Typically, a BEGIN TRAN statement was issued, followed by INSERTs into many tables. The triggers on these tables then inserted rows into other tables, which also had long triggers. The deadlock rate was about 40 percent.

Disabling Triggers and Constraints

Constraints are attached to tables. So, too, are triggers. INSERT, UPDATE, and DELETE actions on tables cause their constraints to fire. Constraints fire *before* AFTER triggers. Thus, if a constraint is violated, the trigger will not fire, because the statement is considered to be invalid. As of release 7.0, you can turn off this behavior by disabling the constraint, using an ALTER TABLE statement, as demonstrated in Listing 10-12.

Listing 10-12: Sample Code for Disabling a Constraint

```
ALTER TABLE MyTable NOCHECK CONSTRAINT FK1_MyTable
```

In this example, you can assume that the constraint FK1_MyTable is a foreign key to another table. Now, the constraint is temporarily disabled, so it will not fire. However, the trigger will now fire regardless of any RI violations.

In the same vein, just as you can disable a constraint, you can also disable a trigger. To do that, you would use code like that in Listing 10-13.

Listing 10-13: Sample Code to Disable a Trigger

```
ALTER TABLE MyTable DISABLE TRIGGER tri_MyTable
```

Both of these features give you the flexibility to handle certain conditions at particular times. One such example is to use a placeholder, say 0, as a temporary foreign key until a certain condition applies. For example, suppose an item in your inventory has not been assigned to a customer, so the customer ID is 0 until it is assigned. This allows you to avoid NULL values. Check out the code in Listing 10-14 to see how this is implemented.

Listing 10-14: Disabling a Constraint to Permit a FOREIGN KEY Violation

```
CREATE TABLE InventoryItems
(
  ItemID     int NOT NULL
               IDENTITY (1, 1)
               CONSTRAINT PK_InventoryItems  PRIMARY KEY,
  ProductID  int NOT NULL
```

```
                    CONSTRAINT FK1_InventoryItems
                        REFERENCES Product (ProductID),
        CustomerID int NOT NULL
                    CONSTRAINT FK2_InventoryItems
                        REFERENCES Customer (CustomerID)
)
GO


ALTER TABLE InventoryItem NOCHECK CONSTRAINT FK2_InventoryItems
GO


INSERT InventoryItems (ProductID, CustomerID) VALUES (1, 0)
INSERT InventoryItems (ProductID, CustomerID) VALUES (1, 0)
INSERT InventoryItems (ProductID, CustomerID) VALUES (1, 0)
INSERT InventoryItems (ProductID, CustomerID) VALUES (2, 0)
INSERT InventoryItems (ProductID, CustomerID) VALUES (2, 0)
GO


ALTER TABLE InventoryItems CHECK CONSTRAINT FK2_InventoryItems
GO
```

In this example, assume that the Products table has been populated and that the product IDs 1 and 2 exist. After the InventoryItems table is created, the FOREIGN KEY constraint, FK2_InventoryItems, is disabled. This means that there will be no checking on the CustomerID column. The INSERT statements then add rows to the InventoryItems table, using a value of 0 for CustomerID. Finally, the constraint is re-enabled but the existing rows are not checked. Now, if a customer purchases a particular item, the CustomerID can be updated to an existing customer. Otherwise, if the CustomerID is updated to a non-existent CustomerID, the FOREIGN KEY constraint will be violated and the UPDATE will fail.

When you do an ALTER TABLE, a Schema-Modify lock is generated, which makes the table and any metadata for it unavailable, so be careful when you use it.

Using Triggers with ROLLBACK TRANSACTION

When you're inside a trigger, you're inside a transaction, because an individual INSERT, UPDATE, or DELETE statement is an implied transaction. This means that you have to be careful when you issue a ROLLBACK statement inside the trigger. The effect of a ROLLBACK is to roll back all work inside the trigger. Also, if you are inside a transaction and the transaction spans batches, then you can run into an unbalanced ROLLBACK/COMMIT statement, since the ROLLBACK inside the trigger will roll back all work to the "outer" transaction.

Although you can issue a ROLLBACK inside a trigger, the trigger continues to execute, so you can still issue a RAISERROR to communicate back to the batch that caused the trigger to fire that there was a problem. You can also modify data in the remaining trigger code, but the remaining statements in the trigger will not fire any nested triggers. None of the remaining statements in the original batch will be executed after the one that fired the trigger.

Just as in stored procedures, you can issue a SAVE TRAN statement to allow for a partial ROLLBACK in the event that you encounter an error condition inside your trigger. See Chapters 7 and 9 for more details on transactions.

Using @@IDENTITY and SCOPE_IDENTITY() with Triggers

In Chapter 6, you were introduced to the @@IDENTITY and SCOPE_IDENTITY() functions. These functions exist to support the IDENTITY property of columns within tables. Now it's time to review their relevance in the context of triggers.

The @@IDENTITY function is used to retrieve the IDENTITY value of the last inserted row. This can get messy if you are trying to insert a row into a table that has an IDENTITY column. If this table has a trigger that then inserts a row into another table that also has an IDENTITY column, using @@IDENTITY after the original INSERT statement will retrieve the IDENTITY of the *second* INSERT (caused by the trigger)—not of the original. This can be a debugging nightmare for even the most experienced SQL developer.

As discussed in Chapter 6, SQL Server 2000 now has the SCOPE_IDENTITY() function, which allows you to be specific when asking for last-inserted IDENTITY values. You can use the SCOPE_IDENTITY() function to find out the IDENTITY value of the last INSERT within the current scope of the current session. This function takes no parameters. Now, if your code does an INSERT on a table with an IDENTITY column, and it has a trigger that also does an INSERT into another table with an IDENTITY column, your invocation of the SCOPE_IDENTITY() function will retrieve the correct value for your session.

> **NOTE** *One way to work around this type of scenario in versions 6.x and 7.0 is to avoid using a trigger and to do the work entirely inside a stored procedure. This way, you have access to both INSERT statements directly, and you can use @@IDENTITY after either one of them without confusion.*

An example will help to clarify what happens when a trigger is fired and the trigger does an INSERT into tables that have IDENTITY properties. Suppose you have two tables—Raw and Summary—both of which have IDENTITY properties. The Raw table takes the individual entries from INSERT statements into that table. The IDENTITY column generates the keys. The number of rows inserted into the Raw table are contained in @@ROWCOUNT, and this is inserted into the Summary table. Thus, the entries in the Summary table keep track of the number of rows inserted into the Raw table for each individual INSERT.

Execute the script shown in Listing 10-15 while inside the Northwind database. This will make the numbers we present to you shortly make sense.

Listing 10-15: Table Creation Scripts for Raw and Summary Tables

```
CREATE TABLE Raw
(
  ID      int       NOT NULL IDENTITY,
  RawData char (10) NOT NULL
)
GO


CREATE TABLE Summary
(
  ID         int      NOT NULL IDENTITY,
  TotalRows int       NOT NULL
)
GO


CREATE TRIGGER tri_Raw on Raw AFTER INSERT
AS

INSERT Summary (TotalRows) VALUES (@@ROWCOUNT)
GO
```

Now test the trigger with the code in Listing 10-16.

Listing 10-16: Testing a Trigger on a Table with an Identity Property

```
INSERT Raw
(
  RawData
)
SELECT
  'First'
FROM
  sysobjects
WHERE
  type = 'U'

SELECT
  @@IDENTITY                AS 'IDENTITY',
  SCOPE_IDENTITY ()         AS 'SCOPE IDENTITY',
  IDENT_CURRENT ('Summary') AS 'Summary',
  IDENT_CURRENT ('Raw')     AS 'Raw'


INSERT Raw
(
  RawData
)
SELECT
  'Second'
FROM
  sysobjects
WHERE
  type = 'S'

SELECT
  @@IDENTITY                AS 'IDENTITY',
  SCOPE_IDENTITY ()         AS 'SCOPE IDENTITY',
  IDENT_CURRENT ('Summary') AS 'Summary',
  IDENT_CURRENT ('Raw')     AS 'Raw'
```

The first INSERT puts a number of rows into the Raw table, one for every user table in *sysobjects*. The RawData column is populated with the constant 'First'. This causes the tri_Raw trigger to fire and populate one row in the Summary table, and this will cause the @@IDENTITY value to be 1, since the trigger placed one row into the Summary table and did so after the INSERT was carried out on the Raw table. The SCOPE_IDENTITY() value returned is 15, because you have that many user tables in the Northwind database. The two IDENT_CURRENT() calls return the values that correspond to @@IDENTITY and SCOPE_IDENTITY().

> **NOTE** *The sysobjects table is a system table present in every database. It lists metadata information for every object in the database, such as name, type, and so on. Type U designates a user table, while type S represents a system table. See the Books Online for further details on this system table.*

The second INSERT statement in Listing 10-16 is very similar to the first. This time, there is one row for every system table in the database, and the RawData column is populated with the constant 'Second'. Since the last table populated was Summary, and it now has only two rows, @@IDENTITY has a value of 2, while SCOPE_IDENTITY() now has increased by about 19 (if you are working in Northwind).

Understanding AFTER Triggers

Prior to the release of version 2000, the only style of trigger was the FOR trigger. This is a trigger that would fire after all constraints (if any) had been checked. If there was a constraint violation, the constraint would prevent the triggers from firing, and thus a cascaded DELETE was prevented. This is where you use AFTER triggers in SQL Server 2000. Specifying AFTER in SQL Server 2000 is the same as specifying FOR in earlier versions. The name change is more intuitive, and it reflects when the trigger actually fires—after the data modification action on the table.

Unlike INSTEAD OF triggers, you are not allowed to create an AFTER trigger on a view. One welcome difference between versions 7.0 and 2000 is that 2000 supports cascaded DELETEs via DRI. Now, the cascaded DELETEs can occur and also allow the DELETE trigger to fire. The basic rule to remember here is that all constraints in the cascade must succeed before the triggers can fire.

Before DRI was implemented in version 6.5, you used FOR (now AFTER) triggers mostly for enforcing referential integrity. Now, they are used most often for enforcing business rules or handling special situations to help optimize your applications. One such use is for managing datetime columns that are supposed to contain only date information, without a time component. It is quite simple to do this with an AFTER trigger, as seen in Listing 10-17.

Listing 10-17: Using an AFTER Trigger to Remove Time from a datetime Column

```
CREATE TABLE DateTable
(
  ID        int       NOT NULL IDENTITY (1, 1)
                      PRIMARY KEY,
  Txt       char (10) NOT NULL,
  EntryDate datetime  NOT NULL
)
GO

CREATE TRIGGER triu_DateTable ON DateTable AFTER INSERT, UPDATE
AS

IF @@ROWCOUNT = 0
  RETURN

IF UPDATE (EntryDate)
  UPDATE D
  SET
    EntryDate = CONVERT (char (10), I.EntryDate, 112)
  FROM
      inserted  I
    JOIN
      DateTable D ON D.ID = I.ID
GO
```

The DateTable table has a column called EntryDate. For every INSERT or UPDATE action that occurs against the DateTable table, the triu_DateTable trigger fires. If there are no rows touched, it returns immediately. It then goes on to determine whether the EntryDate column was updated. If it was updated or the action that fired the trigger was an INSERT, then the trigger resets EntryDate to chop off the time component, thus resetting the time to midnight.

You can also apply a CHECK constraint on the EntryDate column of the DateTable table. This prevents the EntryDate column from having a time other than midnight, thus precluding the need for the trigger. Think of it as the constraint being proactive while the trigger is reactive. The problem with the constraint is that all client code must be cleansed so that no dates with a time component go across to SQL Server. With the trigger, the client code does not matter, since the data will be scrubbed before you put it into the database.

Chapter 14 goes into detail on cascaded DELETEs. However, in this chapter, you will see the effect of triggers firing on multiple tables through the cascade. Consider the tables Parent, Child, and Grandchild, as shown in Listing 10-18.

Listing 10-18. Table Creation Script for Parent, Child, and Grandchild

```
CREATE TABLE Parent
(
  ID int NOT NULL PRIMARY KEY
)
GO

CREATE TABLE Child
(
  ID int NOT NULL PRIMARY KEY
                REFERENCES Parent (ID)
                ON DELETE CASCADE
)
GO

CREATE TABLE GrandChild
(
  ID int NOT NULL PRIMARY KEY
                REFERENCES Child (ID)
                ON DELETE CASCADE
)
GO

INSERT Parent VALUES (1)
INSERT Parent VALUES (2)
INSERT Parent VALUES (3)
INSERT Parent VALUES (4)
GO

INSERT Child VALUES (1)
INSERT Child VALUES (2)
INSERT Child VALUES (3)
INSERT Child VALUES (4)
GO

INSERT GrandChild VALUES (1)
INSERT GrandChild VALUES (2)
INSERT GrandChild VALUES (3)
INSERT GrandChild VALUES (4)
GO
```

Notice how each table uses the ON DELETE CASCADE option. Next, DELETE triggers are placed on each of the tables. The code for each of these tables in Listing 10-19 just has a PRINT statement to tell you which table's trigger has fired.

Listing 10-19: Trigger Scripts for Cascading DELETEs

```
CREATE TRIGGER trd_Parent ON Parent AFTER DELETE
AS

IF @@ROWCOUNT = 0
  RETURN

PRINT 'Inside Parent trigger.'
GO

CREATE TRIGGER trd_Child ON Child AFTER DELETE
AS
IF @@ROWCOUNT = 0
  RETURN

PRINT 'Inside Child trigger.'
GO

CREATE TRIGGER trd_GrandChild ON GrandChild AFTER DELETE
AS
IF @@ROWCOUNT = 0
  RETURN

PRINT 'Inside GrandChild trigger.'
GO
```

You're ready to go. Just delete rows 2 through 3, using Listing 10-20, and see the results.

Listing 10-20: Firing the Cascaded DELETE

```
DELETE Parent
WHERE
  ID BETWEEN 2 AND 3
```

You get the PRINT messages in reverse order so that the messages originate from tri_GrandChild, then tri_Child, and then tri_Parent. Bear this in mind when you write your own triggers in cascade situations.

Understanding INSTEAD OF Triggers

Wouldn't it be nice if you could replace the standard INSERT, UPDATE, or DELETE functionality with your own? For example, what if someone went to do a physical DELETE and you turned it into a logical DELETE? Well, you can—with INSTEAD OF triggers! These triggers are also new to SQL Server 2000. Unlike AFTER triggers, only one INSTEAD OF trigger per INSERT, UPDATE, or DELETE statement is permitted. INSTEAD OF triggers are permitted on views, except for updateable views WITH CHECK OPTION.

> **TIP** *You can have views of views or views of tables, each with its own* INSTEAD OF *trigger. You can emulate multiple* INSTEAD OF *triggers by creating multiple views on a single table or view that do* SELECT*s of all columns and do not have* WHERE *clauses.*

Recursive triggers were introduced with version 7.0. If you turn on recursive triggers in your database, you can do a data modification on a table, causing a trigger to fire, and then inside that trigger do a modification of that same table causing a trigger on that same table to fire. This can keep going until you hit the nesting limit of 32. With INSTEAD OF triggers, the trigger will fire once and then further modifications to the underlying table will not fire the INSTEAD OF trigger. However, any relevant AFTER triggers will fire recursively.

There are also restrictions with respect to the use of INSTEAD OF triggers where cascaded DELETEs or UPDATEs have been put in place through DRI. You cannot have an INSTEAD OF trigger on a table with the corresponding CASCADE action, so there can be no INSTEAD OF DELETE when ON DELETE CASCADE is in effect. In other words, if you have created a table that has a FOREIGN KEY constraint with ON DELETE CASCADE, then you cannot create an INSTEAD OF DELETE trigger on that same table. The same restriction applies to INSTEAD OF UPDATE triggers and cascaded UPDATEs. If you attempt to create the trigger when the CASCADE option is in effect, the CREATE TRIGGER statement will fail. If you create the trigger first and then alter the table to add the FOREIGN KEY constraint with the CASCADE option, the ALTER TABLE statement will fail.

If you have a table that is referenced by the foreign key of another table, and the referenced table has an INSTEAD OF trigger, the trigger will fire but the FOREIGN KEY constraint will not. An example of this scenario is presented in Listing 10-21.

Listing 10-21. Table Creation Script for Parent and Child with FOREIGN KEY Constraint and INSTEAD OF Trigger

```
CREATE TABLE Parent
(
  ID int NOT NULL PRIMARY KEY
)
GO


CREATE TABLE Child
(
  ID int NOT NULL PRIMARY KEY
                  REFERENCES Parent (ID)
                  ON DELETE CASCADE
)
GO


CREATE TRIGGER trd_Parent ON Parent INSTEAD OF DELETE
AS

IF @@ROWCOUNT = 0
  RETURN

PRINT 'Inside Parent trigger.'
GO


INSERT Parent VALUES (1)
INSERT Parent VALUES (2)
INSERT Parent VALUES (3)
INSERT Parent VALUES (4)
GO


INSERT Child VALUES (1)
INSERT Child VALUES (2)
INSERT Child VALUES (3)
INSERT Child VALUES (4)
GO
```

You will see that the script is similar to the Parent-Child-GrandChild example in Listings 10-18 and 10-19. If you execute the DELETE statement in Listing 10-21, you will find that the rows in the Parent table remain intact, and there is no FOREIGN KEY violation, even though rows were supposed to have been deleted from the Parent table. What happens is that the INSTEAD OF trigger acts in place of the original DELETE, and all it does is print a message, so the rows aren't actually deleted.

Now modify the trigger to do the actual delete of the rows from the Parent table, as shown in Listing 10-22.

Listing 10-22: INSTEAD OF Trigger that Duplicates DELETE Action

```
ALTER TRIGGER trd_Parent ON Parent INSTEAD OF DELETE
AS

IF @@ROWCOUNT = 0
  RETURN

PRINT 'Inside Parent trigger.'

DELETE P
FROM
    Parent P
  JOIN
    deleted D ON D.ID = P.ID
GO
```

Now if you try the DELETE, the INSTEAD OF trigger does the physical DELETE on the Parent table. This causes the corresponding rows in the Child table to be deleted, since there is a FOREIGN KEY constraint with the ON DELETE CASCADE option on the Child table.

Take this just a little further. Add an AFTER trigger to the Child table, as shown in Listing 10-23.

Listing 10-23: AFTER Trigger on Child Table

```
CREATE TRIGGER trd_Child ON Child AFTER DELETE
AS

IF @@ROWCOUNT = 0
  RETURN

PRINT 'Inside Child trigger.'
GO
```

If you delete any rows from the Parent table, the INSTEAD OF trigger fires and does the physical DELETE on the Parent table. This causes the FOREIGN KEY constraint on Child to delete rows in the Child table, which causes the AFTER trigger on the Child table to fire. Consequently, the triggers are fired from top to bottom.

Try out an example of substituting a logical DELETE for a physical one. The sample table for this example has the structure shown in Listing 10-24.

Listing 10-24: Table for INSTEAD OF Trigger for Logical Deletes

```
CREATE TABLE MyTable
(
  ID  int     NOT NULL PRIMARY KEY,
  del char (1) NOT NULL DEFAULT 'N'
)
```

Next, create the INSTEAD OF trigger to join on the *deleted* table, and set the del column to 'Y'. Take a look at the code in Listing 10-25.

Listing 10-25: INSTEAD OF Trigger for Logical Deletes

```
CREATE TRIGGER trd_MyTable ON MyTable INSTEAD OF DELETE
AS

IF @@ROWCOUNT = 0
  RETURN

UPDATE M
SET
  del = 'Y'
FROM
    MyTable AS M
  JOIN
    deleted AS D ON D.ID = M.ID
GO
```

At this point, if you issue a DELETE statement on MyTable, the physical DELETE will not occur. Rather, the del column will be reset. What if you want to have logical DELETEs during the month and then process them as physical DELETEs at the end of the month? Just disable the INSTEAD OF trigger at month end, and proceed as per normal.

Now that triggers are allowed on views, you can also reduce the amount of coding effort you have to do due to physicalization. One such opportunity is where you have implemented vertical partitioning, which is where you split a logical table into two or more physical tables, with the split going between columns. In other words, some columns go into one table and others go into one or more other tables. Each table has a copy of the key, and you reconstitute the logical table through a view that joins the two tables. This makes INSERTs awkward, since you have to create stored procedures to handle splitting up single-row and multi-row INSERTs.

Now these INSERTs can be handled through a single INSTEAD OF trigger. All you have to do is have the trigger do one INSERT for each of the underlying tables, and with that in place you can do all of your INSERTs into the view.

In Listing 10-26, take a look at two tables and a view that reconstitutes them into one logical table.

Listing 10-26: Sample Tables and a View for Vertical Partitioning

```
CREATE TABLE First
(
  ID  int     NOT NULL PRIMARY KEY,
  xyz tinyint NOT NULL
)

CREATE TABLE Second
(
  ID  int     NOT NULL PRIMARY KEY
                       REFERENCES First (id),
  abc int     NOT NULL
)
GO

CREATE VIEW Whole
AS
  SELECT
    F.ID,
    F.xyz,
    S.abc
  FROM
     First  AS F
    JOIN
     Second AS S ON S.ID = F.ID
GO
```

With the INSTEAD OF trigger in Listing 10-27, you do the split at the time of the INSERT, regardless of the number of rows.

Listing 10-27: INSTEAD OF Trigger to Support Vertical Partitioning

```
CREATE TRIGGER tri_Whole ON Whole INSTEAD OF INSERT
AS

IF @@ROWCOUNT = 0
  RETURN
```

```
INSERT First
SELECT
  ID,
  xyz
FROM
    inserted

INSERT Second
SELECT
  ID,
  abc
FROM
    inserted
GO
```

> **NOTE** *Horizontal partitioning is discussed extensively in Chapter 13.*

Some restrictions do apply, and they will be discussed here. When you have an INSTEAD OF trigger on a view, you must supply values for *every* view column that does not allow NULLs (except for those that have defaults), even if they reference columns in the base tables for which values cannot be supplied. These restrictions are as follows:

- Computed columns cannot be used in the base table.

- Identity columns in the base table for which IDENTITY INSERT has not been turned on cannot be used.

- Base table columns with the rowversion datatype cannot be used.

What you have to do to accommodate these restrictions is ensure that the INSERT statement *does* specify a dummy value (or NULL) for the column on the view, and the trigger code *does not* specify a value for the column on the base table.

In the same vein, you must supply values for all of the non-NULL columns of your view when doing an UPDATE statement on a view with an INSTEAD OF UPDATE trigger. This includes those columns mentioned earlier for the INSTEAD OF INSERT trigger. Therefore, INSTEAD OF triggers are not totally transparent to the developer when dealing with views.

In addition to helping out with vertically partitioned tables, the INSTEAD OF trigger can earn its keep in other ways, too. One classic problem is that of a data feed, where the data you are inserting may or may not already exist. Specifically, there may already be an instance of the primary key. Here, you wish to update the non-key information if the key exists and insert the row if the key does not. This can now be handled through the trigger. Check out the sample code in Listing 10-28.

Listing 10-28: Using an INSTEAD OF Trigger to Handle a Data Feed

```
CREATE TABLE FeedTarget
(
  ID    int     NOT NULL PRIMARY KEY,
  Descr char (5) NOT NULL
)
GO


CREATE TRIGGER tri_FeedTarget ON FeedTarget INSTEAD OF INSERT
AS

IF @@ROWCOUNT = 0
  RETURN

UPDATE F              -- rows that already exist
SET
  Descr = I.Descr
FROM
    inserted   AS I
  JOIN
    FeedTarget AS F ON F.ID = I.ID

INSERT FeedTarget    -- new rows
SELECT
  ID,
  Descr
FROM
    inserted AS I
WHERE NOT EXISTS
(
  SELECT
    *
  FROM
      FeedTarget AS F
  WHERE
      F.ID = I.ID
)
GO
```

Try inserting data into the table where there would be duplicate primary keys, using the code in Listing 10-29.

Listing 10-29: Test Script for the FeedTarget Table

```
INSERT FeedTarget (ID, Descr) VALUES (1, 'a')
INSERT FeedTarget (ID, Descr) VALUES (2, 'b')
INSERT FeedTarget (ID, Descr) VALUES (3, 'c')
INSERT FeedTarget (ID, Descr) VALUES (1, 'd')
INSERT FeedTarget (ID, Descr) VALUES (1, 'e')
```

Instead of getting primary key violations, you get the existing data updated. Way cool! The results are presented in Table 10-1.

Table 10-1: Contents of FeedTarget after Running INSERTs

ID	Descr
1	e
2	b
3	c

Even though the INSTEAD OF trigger is overriding the normal INSERT behavior of the underlying table, it is still possible to violate the PRIMARY KEY constraint. In this case, a poorly written trigger could attempt an INSERT into the underlying table, which would cause the PRIMARY KEY constraint to fire.

Using Triggers for Auditing

Triggers are often used in auditing situations. In this situation, you want to keep track of some or all modifications on a table. Typically, you would make a shadow table of the table being audited, and then populate the shadow table with the information you wish to track. You can take two main approaches here: keeping the previous image or keeping all images (both of which are described more fully in the next sections). In either case, you will probably want to add an IDENTITY column in the shadow table to enforce uniqueness. Bear in mind that because "before" and "after" images of the keys can be, and usually are, the same, you cannot have the same keys as you did in the audited table.

Keeping the Previous Image

The simplest method of auditing table data is to maintain a copy of the previous row in the shadow table. If the audited table then is updated, the old shadow record gets overwritten with the before image of the audited table row while the audited table, of course, gets the current version. At most, the shadow table will have the same number of records as the audited table. For managing growth, you have to keep in mind that the shadow table will not grow beyond the size of the audited table, provided you never delete from the audited table. (If you do delete from the audited table, then the shadow table can grow beyond the size of the audited table because the audited table will be shrinking.)

A code example will make this scheme clearer. For example, suppose you wish to audit the Orders table in the Northwind database. You do not need an INSERT trigger, since any new data will be inserted into the Orders table. However, if you UPDATE or DELETE, you will want the old version to go to the Orders_Shadow table. Ignore referential integrity for this exercise. The code to do this is shown in Listing 10-30.

Listing 10-30: UPDATE/DELETE Trigger for Single-Row Audit

```
CREATE TRIGGER trud_AuditOrders ON Orders AFTER UPDATE, DELETE
AS
IF @@ROWCOUNT = 0
  RETURN

-- clear out existing audit data for these OrderIDs
DELETE s
FROM
    deleted       AS D
  JOIN
    Orders_Shadow AS S ON S.OrderID = D.OrderID

-- add before image of rows
INSERT Orders_Shadow
(
  OrderID,
  CustomerID,
  EmployeeID,
  OrderDate,
  RequiredDate,
  ShippedDate,
  ShipVia,
  Freight,
  ShipName,
  ShipAddress,
```

```
      ShipCity,
      ShipRegion,
      ShipPostalCode,
      ShipCountry
)
SELECT
   OrderID,
   CustomerID,
   EmployeeID,
   OrderDate,
   RequiredDate,
   ShippedDate,
   ShipVia,
   Freight,
   ShipName,
   ShipAddress,
   ShipCity,
   ShipRegion,
   ShipPostalCode,
   ShipCountry
FROM
      deleted
GO
```

First, you have to delete the old row(s) from the Orders_Shadow table. Then, you insert the rows from the *deleted* table—the before image of the newly updated or deleted row. Note also that a SELECT * cannot be used in the INSERT SELECT, since you are inserting into a table with an identity column. You must specify all column names.

Keeping All Images

The second approach is scarier. In this scenario, you record every image of every row throughout its lifetime. If a record is updated many times throughout its lifetime, then the shadow table can grow to many times the size of the audited table. You will also need a purge routine to clean out the older records in the shadow table or you could run out of space. Check out the code in Listing 10-31.

Listing 10-31: Update/Delete Trigger for Multi-Row Audit

```
CREATE TRIGGER trud_AuditOrders ON Orders AFTER UPDATE, DELETE
AS
IF @@ROWCOUNT = 0
  RETURN

-- add before image of rows
INSERT Orders_Shadow
(
  OrderID,
  CustomerID,
  EmployeeID,
  OrderDate,
  RequiredDate,
  ShippedDate,
  ShipVia,
  Freight,
  ShipName,
  ShipAddress,
  ShipCity,
  ShipRegion,
  ShipPostalCode,
  ShipCountry
)
SELECT
  OrderID,
  CustomerID,
  EmployeeID,
  OrderDate,
  RequiredDate,
  ShippedDate,
  ShipVia,
  Freight,
  ShipName,
  ShipAddress,
  ShipCity,
  ShipRegion,
  ShipPostalCode,
  ShipCountry
FROM
    deleted
GO
```

Although the code in this example is less complex, since you don't have to clean out the shadow table, you are still faced with the maintenance issue of unlimited growth.

Auditing Last Updated—When and By Whom

Often, you are required to implement an audit scheme where you want to keep track of who last modified a row. This is easily done through a trigger. In this case, your trigger can update the columns identifying who last updated the row and when it was done. You do not necessarily have to keep a shadow table as discussed earlier. You can just keep the auditing information in the row itself. While this type of auditing is simple, it cannot track multiple changes to the same record; you know who last touched the row and when, but you do not know when a particular column was modified.

The table will need a column of datatype sysname and another column of datatype datetime to record the person who made the update and when it was made. The trigger then updates these columns whenever an update occurs. An example is depicted in Listing 10-32.

Listing 10-32: Trigger to Manage Last Update Auditing Information

```
CREATE TRIGGER triu_MyTable ON MyTable AFTER INSERT, UPDATE
AS
IF @@ROWCOUNT = 0
  RETURN

UPDATE m
SET
  LastUpdateDate = GETDATE (),
  LastUpdateUser = SUSER_SNAME ()
FROM
    inserted AS I
  JOIN
    MyTable  AS M ON M.PK_ID = I.PK_ID
GO
```

Note that the trigger also handles INSERTs. One nice feature about this trigger is that any SQL that fires it—either through a stored procedure, INSERT, or UPDATE statement—cannot update the audit columns permanently, since the trigger immediately overwrites them.

Statements Not Permitted Inside a Trigger

There were only a few statements that you could not perform inside a stored procedure. The list for triggers is much larger, as shown next:

ALTER DATABASE	DISK RESIZE
ALTER PROCEDURE	DROP DATABASE
ALTER TABLE	DROP DEFAULT
ALTER TRIGGER	DROP INDEX
ALTER VIEW	DROP PROCEDURE
CREATE DATABASE	DROP RULE
CREATE DEFAULT	DROP TRIGGER
CREATE INDEX	DROP VIEW
CREATE PROCEDURE	LOAD DATABASE
CREATE RULE	LOAD LOG
CREATE SCHEMA	RESTORE DATABASE
CREATE TRIGGER	RESTORE LOG
CREATE VIEW	RECONFIGURE
DISK INIT	UPDATE STATISTICS

This list is shorter than that for SQL Server 7.0, and it does make sense to ban these statements. Triggers are supposed to be fast, and many of these statements can take quite some time to complete. Creating or altering database objects cannot be done in the scope of creating other objects, since there is no way of delineating when one stops and the other begins. Altering the database or altering the schema in any way would potentially make the trigger fail, so these, too, make sense.

SQL Puzzle 10-1: Pending Deletes

Your company has a policy that allows an employee to delete his or her own customers. However, if an employee attempts to delete the customers of other employees, those customers must be moved into a separate table—PendingDeleteCustomers. In the PendingDeleteCustomers table, only the employee who "owns" the customer may delete the customer. Any number of customers may be deleted in a single DELETE. The tables involved are presented here:

```
CREATE TABLE Customers
(
  CustomerID    int         NOT NULL
                            IDENTITY (1, 1)
                            PRIMARY KEY,
  CustomerName varchar (30) NOT NULL,
  Address      varchar (50) NOT NULL,
  Phone        varchar (12) NOT NULL,
  EmployeeID   sysname      NOT NULL
)
GO


CREATE TABLE PendingDeleteCustomers
(
  CustomerID    int         NOT NULL
                            PRIMARY KEY,
  CustomerName varchar (30) NOT NULL,
  Address      varchar (50) NOT NULL,
  Phone        varchar (12) NOT NULL,
  EmployeeID   sysname      NOT NULL
)
GO
```

Create a trigger or triggers to implement these business rules.
The answer to this puzzle can be found on pages 695–696.

User-Defined Functions

STORED PROCEDURES AND VIEWS give you a lot of power and flexibility in terms of programmatic capabilities, security, and performance. There are a few needs, however, that they don't cover. Views cannot be parameterized, and the results of stored procedures cannot be embedded naturally in DML statements, be they scalar return values or rowsets.

User-defined functions (UDFs), introduced with SQL Server 2000, have an answer for those needs; mainly, they can be called from within a query. T-SQL is used to program user-defined functions, so they look similar to stored procedures at first glance. They also get compiled and cached the same way stored procedures do. However, being a different creature, user-defined functions have their own unique features and behavior.

There are three types of UDFs: scalar, inline table-valued, and multistatement table-valued.

Scalar Functions

Scalar functions are functions that return a single value. They can accept zero or more input parameters, which are strongly typed, but they don't support output parameters. Rather, their header contains the return type of the return value. The RETURN clause is used to specify the return value of the function and to abort any further activity.

The function body, hosting the code, is defined in the boundaries of a BEGIN END block. Although the BEGIN END block is not necessary in stored procedures and triggers, it is necessary in user-defined functions.

Listing 11-1 shows the syntax for creating a scalar user-defined function.

Listing 11-1: Syntax for Creating Scalar Functions

```
CREATE FUNCTION [ owner_name. ] function_name
    ( [ { @parameter_name scalar_parameter_data_type [ = default ] } [ ,...n ] ] )
RETURNS scalar_return_data_type
[ WITH { ENCRYPTION | SCHEMABINDING } [,...n] ]
[ AS ]
BEGIN
    function_body
    RETURN scalar_expression
END
```

When referring to a user-defined scalar function, you must supply at least its two-part name, including the function's owner and name, e.g., dbo.f1(). This requirement prevents ambiguity between user-defined and built-in scalar functions with the same name.

It's time to jump right into your first function. The aggregate functions MIN(), MAX(), SUM(), etc., aggregate multiple values from the same column, but there is no equivalent function aggregating values from different columns in the same row. To do this, you can supply the linear_max() function, shown in Listing 11-2, that calculates the maximum value of two given arguments.

Listing 11-2: The linear_max() Scalar Function

```
USE testdb
GO


CREATE FUNCTION dbo.linear_max
(
  @arg1 AS int,
  @arg2 AS int
)
RETURNS int
AS


BEGIN
  RETURN CASE
          WHEN @arg1 >= @arg2 THEN @arg1
          WHEN @arg2 >  @arg1 THEN @arg2
          ELSE NULL
        END
END
GO


GRANT EXECUTE ON dbo.linear_max TO public
GO
```

Notice that EXECUTE permissions are granted on the linear_max() function to the *public* fixed database role using the GRANT Data Control Language (DCL) command. Every user in the database belongs to the public role; in other words, every user in the database will be allowed to invoke the function. You can use this function to calculate the maximum of two arguments as shown in Listing 11-3.

Listing 11-3: Invoking the linear_max() Scalar Function in a Standalone Statement

```
SELECT
  dbo.linear_max(1, 2)
```

You can also incorporate it into a query to calculate the maximum value of two given columns, as the example in Listing 11-4 shows.

Listing 11-4: Incorporating the linear_max Scalar Function in a Query

```
SELECT
  col1,
  col2,
  dbo.linear_max(col1, col2) AS max_col1_col2
FROM
  T1
```

If you want to calculate the maximum value of more than two columns, you can wrap the result of the call to your function with another call. Here, you supply the result of the calculation between two columns as an argument together with the third column. Check out the code in Listing 11-5.

Listing 11-5: Calculating the Maximum of Three Columns

```
SELECT
  col1,
  col2,
  col3,
  dbo.linear_max(dbo.linear_max(col1, col2), col3) AS max_col1_col2_col3
FROM
  T1
```

Similarly, you can create the linear_min() function, depicted in Listing 11-6.

Listing 11-6: The linear_min Scalar Function

```
CREATE FUNCTION dbo.linear_min
(
  @arg1 AS int,
  @arg2 AS int
)
RETURNS int
AS
```

```
BEGIN
  RETURN CASE
            WHEN @arg1 <= @arg2 THEN @arg1
            WHEN @arg2 <  @arg1 THEN @arg2
            ELSE NULL
          END
END
GO


GRANT EXECUTE ON dbo.linear_min TO public
GO
```

Scalar user-defined functions also come in handy when you perform bitwise calculations. (Bitwise calculations are discussed in Chapter 4.) T-SQL supplies bitwise operators: & (bitwise AND), | (bitwise OR), ^ (bitwise XOR), and ~ (bitwise NOT). The operators &, |, and ^ accept two integer values, or at most, one binary value. The operator ~ accepts only one integer value. Many programmers find this very limiting when they want to perform bitwise computations between two binary values, especially if the binary values are larger than 8 bytes, which is the largest integer datatype supplied in T-SQL (`bigint`).

You can create your own bitwise functions that accept two binary values as large as the `binary` or `varbinary` datatypes allow—8,000 bytes. You can achieve this by doing the following:

- Loop through all of the bytes in both variables, extracting one byte at a time from each of the variables.

- Cast one of the extracted bytes to `tinyint`.

- Perform the original bitwise operation between the two bytes and concatenate the result to a variable that will be used as the return value of the function.

For example, the function in Listing 11-7 implements this logic for a bitwise AND operation between two binary values.

Listing 11-7: The bitwise_and() Scalar Function

```
CREATE FUNCTION dbo.bitwise_and
(
  @arg1 varbinary(8000),
  @arg2 varbinary(8000)
) RETURNS varbinary(8000)
AS
BEGIN

  DECLARE
    @result   AS varbinary(8000),
    @numbytes AS int,
    @curpos   AS int

  SET @result   = 0x
  SET @numbytes = dbo.linear_min(DATALENGTH(@arg1), DATALENGTH(@arg2))
  SET @curpos   = 1

  WHILE @curpos <= @numbytes
  BEGIN
    SELECT
      @result = @result + CAST(SUBSTRING(@arg1, @curpos, 1) &
                               CAST(SUBSTRING(@arg2, @curpos, 1) AS tinyint)
                               AS binary(1))
    SET @curpos = @curpos + 1
  END

  RETURN @result
END
GO

GRANT EXECUTE ON dbo.bitwise_and TO public
GO
```

Notice that you use the linear_min() function you created earlier to determine the minimum length of the two input values. This value is used as the number of iterations of your loop. Similarly, you can create functions that implement bitwise OR and bitwise XOR between two binary values. See Listings 11-8 and 11-9.

Listing 11-8: The bitwise_or() Scalar Function

```
CREATE FUNCTION dbo.bitwise_or
(
  @arg1 varbinary(8000),
  @arg2 varbinary(8000)
) RETURNS varbinary(8000)
AS
BEGIN

  DECLARE
    @result   AS varbinary(8000),
    @numbytes AS int,
    @curpos   AS int

  SET @result   = 0x
  SET @numbytes = dbo.linear_min(DATALENGTH(@arg1), DATALENGTH(@arg2))
  SET @curpos   = 1

  WHILE @curpos <= @numbytes
  BEGIN
    SELECT
      @result = @result + CAST(SUBSTRING(@arg1, @curpos, 1) |
                               CAST(SUBSTRING(@arg2, @curpos, 1)
                                 AS tinyint)
                            AS binary(1))
    SET @curpos = @curpos + 1
  END

  RETURN @result
END
GO

GRANT EXECUTE ON dbo.bitwise_or TO public
GO
```

Listing 11-9: The bitwise_xor() Scalar Function

```
CREATE FUNCTION dbo.bitwise_xor
(
  @arg1 varbinary(8000),
  @arg2 varbinary(8000)
) RETURNS varbinary(8000)
AS
BEGIN

  DECLARE
    @result  AS varbinary(8000),
    @numbytes AS int,
    @curpos  AS int

  SET @result  = 0x
  SET @numbytes = dbo.linear_min(DATALENGTH(@arg1), DATALENGTH(@arg2))
  SET @curpos  = 1

  WHILE @curpos <= @numbytes
  BEGIN
    SELECT
      @result = @result + CAST(SUBSTRING(@arg1, @curpos, 1) ^
                                CAST(SUBSTRING(@arg2, @curpos, 1)
                                  AS tinyint)
                            AS binary(1))
    SET @curpos = @curpos + 1
  END

  RETURN @result
END
GO


GRANT EXECUTE ON dbo.bitwise_xor TO public
GO
```

Implementing a bitwise NOT is much simpler. You loop through all bytes, extracting one byte in each iteration of the loop, performing the original bitwise NOT on that byte and concatenating the result to the returned variable. Check out Listing 11-10.

Listing 11-10: The bitwise_not() Scalar Function

```
CREATE FUNCTION dbo.bitwise_not
(
  @arg1 varbinary(8000)
) RETURNS varbinary(8000)
AS
BEGIN

  DECLARE
    @result   AS varbinary(8000),
    @numbytes AS int,
    @curpos   AS int

  SET @result = 0x
  SET @numbytes = DATALENGTH(@arg1)
  SET @curpos = 1

  WHILE @curpos <= @numbytes
  BEGIN
    SELECT
      @result = @result +
                CAST(~CAST(SUBSTRING(@arg1, @curpos, 1)
                AS tinyint)AS binary(1))
    SET @curpos = @curpos + 1
  END

  RETURN @result
END
GO


GRANT EXECUTE ON dbo.bitwise_not TO public
GO
```

To test the bitwise functions you've just created, run the script in Listing 11-11.

Listing 11-11: Testing the Bitwise Scalar Functions

```
SELECT dbo.bitwise_and(0x000000010000000100000001,
                       0xffffffffffffffffffffffffffffffff)
SELECT dbo.bitwise_or (0x000000010000000100000001,
                       0xffffffffffffffffffffffffffffffff)
SELECT dbo.bitwise_xor(0x000000010000000100000001,
                       0xffffffffffffffffffffffffffffffff)
SELECT dbo.bitwise_not(0x000000010000000100000001)
```

Inline Table-Valued Functions

Inline table-valued functions return a rowset as their output. They accept parameters the same way scalar functions do and return the result of a SELECT statement, which can incorporate the parameters supplied to the function. The syntax for creating an inline table-valued user-defined function is shown in Listing 11-12.

Listing 11-12: Syntax for Creating Inline Table-Valued Functions

```
CREATE FUNCTION [ owner_name. ] function_name
    ( [ { @parameter_name scalar_parameter_data_type [ = default ] } [ ,...n ] ] )
RETURNS TABLE
[ WITH { ENCRYPTION | SCHEMABINDING } [ ,...n ] ]
[ AS ]
RETURN [ ( ] select-stmt [ ) ]
```

Allowing the use of the arguments supplied to the function in the SELECT statement makes inline table-valued functions a substitute for *parameterized views*, a feature requested by many programmers. This type of function does not have a body, meaning that there is no BEGIN END block. Rather, a single RETURN clause appears, followed by the SELECT statement. Its return type is a table, but you need not declare this table variable because the function uses the columns and datatypes used in the SELECT statement.

One of the great advantages of the inline table-valued function is that the query's code inside the function is merged internally with the calling query's code in the same way that a SELECT statement in a view is. Thus, you get an efficient, integrated optimization with the calling query.

Using inline table-valued functions is similar to using system-supplied functions that return rowsets. Listing 11-13 gives an example of using the OPENROWSET() function that returns a rowset as a result of a query or a stored procedure issued against a heterogeneous data source.

Listing 11-13: Example of a Built-in Function that Returns a Rowset

```
SELECT
  T1.*
FROM
  OPENROWSET('SQLOLEDB',
              'Server1';'sa';'password',
              'SELECT * FROM pubs.dbo.authors') AS T1
```

Similarly, if you create a function called dbo.f1() that accepts @arg1 as a parameter, you can use it as shown in Listing 11-14.

Listing 11-14: Syntax for Using a User-Defined Function that Returns a Rowset

```
SELECT
  T1.*
FROM
  f1(5) AS T1
```

The nice thing about this type of function is that you can incorporate it any place where you can incorporate a table. For example, you can join the rowset returned by your function to another table, as shown in Listing 11-15.

Listing 11-15: Syntax for Using a User-Defined Function that Returns a Rowset in a Join Query

```
SELECT
  T1.*
FROM
    f1(5)  AS T1
  JOIN
    Table2 AS T2 ON T1.key_col = T2.key_col
```

Here's your chance to create your first inline table-valued function. The function, dbo.custorders(), returns orders for a given customer. Check out the code in Listing 11-16.

Listing 11-16: The custorders() Inline Table-Valued Function

```
USE Northwind
GO

CREATE FUNCTION dbo.custorders (@custid char(5))
RETURNS TABLE
AS

RETURN SELECT
        *
      FROM
        Orders
      WHERE
        CustomerID = @custid
GO
```

Try out your new function to return all orders for the customer 'VINET'. See Listing 11-17.

Listing 11-17: Using the custorders() Inline Table-Valued Function

```
SELECT
  C.*
FROM
  custorders('VINET') AS C
```

Take it one step further now and return order detail information for the customer `'VINET'`. Check out the solution in Listing 11-18.

Listing 11-18: Using the custorders() Inline Table-Valued Function in a Join Query

```
SELECT
  O.OrderID,
  O.OrderDate,
  OD.ProductID,
  OD.Quantity
FROM
    custorders('VINET') AS O
  JOIN
    [Order Details]     AS OD ON O.OrderID = OD.OrderID
```

Looks simple because it is! Not much to it.

Note that the same rules that apply to views regarding the requirement that the result will have only unique column names and that there will be no columns without a name, apply to functions that return rowsets. For example, consider the following function in Listing 11-19, which returns order details for a certain customer.

Listing 11-19: Illegal custorderdetails Inline Table-Valued Function

```
CREATE FUNCTION dbo.custorderdetails
(
  @custid char(5)
)
RETURNS TABLE
AS
```

```
RETURN SELECT
        *,
        UnitPrice * Quantity
     FROM
         Orders          AS O
         JOIN
         [Order Details] AS OD ON O.OrderID = OD.OrderID
     WHERE
         CustomerID = @custid
GO
```

SQL Server does not allow the creation of this function as it has two problems: there are two columns named OrderID, and there is an unnamed column that is the result of a computation. To fix this, you can amend this function as shown in Listing 11-20.

Listing 11-20: Legal custorderdetails Inline Table-Valued Function

```
CREATE FUNCTION dbo.custorderdetails
(
  @custid char(5)
)
RETURNS TABLE
AS

RETURN SELECT
        O.*,
        OD.ProductID,
        OD.UnitPrice,
        OD.Quantity,
        OD.Discount,
        UnitPrice * Quantity AS Value
     FROM
         Orders          AS O
         JOIN
         [Order Details] AS OD ON O.OrderID = OD.OrderID
     WHERE
         CustomerID = @custid
GO
```

Notice that the OrderID column was omitted from the Order Details table, as you already return it from the Orders table. Note, too, that you use a qualifier to supply a column name to the result of the computation.

Multistatement Table-Valued Functions

Multistatement table-valued functions are very similar to inline table-valued functions in the sense that they also return a rowset, and they are invoked the same way. They don't, however, simply return the result of a SELECT statement. Rather, they return a fully declared table variable that is defined after the RETURNS keyword in the function's header.

This type of function has a function body with a BEGIN END block, and in its body, you can use T-SQL code with flow-control elements. The purpose of the code elements inside the function's body is to fill the table variable that will be returned from the function with rows. Listing 11-21 shows the syntax for creating a multistatement table-valued function.

Listing 11-21: Syntax for Creating Multistatement Table-Valued Functions

```
CREATE FUNCTION [ owner_name. ] function_name
    ( [ { @parameter_name scalar_parameter_data_type
        [ = default ] } [ ,...n ] ] )
RETURNS @return_variable TABLE
  ( { column_definition | table_constraint } [ ,...n ] )
[ WITH { ENCRYPTION | SCHEMABINDING } [ ,...n ] ]
[ AS ]
BEGIN
    function_body
    RETURN
END
```

Chapter 16 covers hierarchical structures in depth. Here, you will just create a simple function that returns a certain manager and that manager's subordinates in all levels from the Employees table in the Northwind sample database. Briefly glance over the function in Listing 11-22; it will be explained in full shortly.

Listing 11-22: The get_mgremps() Multistatement Table-Valued Function

```
USE Northwind
GO

CREATE FUNCTION get_mgremps
(
  @mgrid AS int
)
```

```
RETURNS @tree table
(
  EmployeeID      int           NOT NULL,
  LastName        nvarchar(20)  NOT NULL,
  FirstName       nvarchar(10)  NOT NULL,
  Title           nvarchar(30)  NULL,
  TitleOfCourtesy nvarchar(25)  NULL,
  BirthDate       datetime      NULL,
  HireDate        datetime      NULL,
  Address         nvarchar(60)  NULL,
  City            nvarchar(15)  NULL,
  Region          nvarchar(15)  NULL,
  PostalCode      nvarchar(10)  NULL,
  Country         nvarchar(15)  NULL,
  HomePhone       nvarchar(24)  NULL,
  Extension       nvarchar(4)   NULL,
  Photo           image         NULL,
  Notes           ntext         NULL,
  ReportsTo       int           NULL,
  PhotoPath       nvarchar(255) NULL,
  lvl             int           NOT NULL
)
AS

BEGIN

  DECLARE @lvl AS int
  SET @lvl = 0

  INSERT INTO @tree
    SELECT
      *,
      @lvl
    FROM
      Employees
    WHERE
      EmployeeID = @mgrid
```

```
  WHILE @@rowcount > 0
  BEGIN
    SET @lvl = @lvl + 1
    INSERT INTO @tree
      SELECT
        E.*,
        @lvl
      FROM
          Employees AS E
        JOIN
          @tree AS T ON  E.ReportsTo = T.EmployeeID
                    AND T.lvl       = @lvl - 1
  END

  RETURN

END
GO
```

The function `get_mgremps()` accepts the employee ID of a manager and returns a rowset in the form of a `table` variable. Notice that the `table` variable is defined with similar columns to those in the Employees table in the Northwind database. There is also an additional column called lvl, which stores the depth level of the employee, starting with 0 for the top-level manager, and advancing by one for each subordinate level.

You start by setting the `@lvl` variable to 0. Next, you insert into the `table` variable the employee row for the manager, supplied as an argument to the function. All the rest is a loop that inserts the subordinates of the employees from the current level into the `table` variable. Note that you increment the `@lvl` variable in each iteration of the loop. The loop is stopped when `@@ROWCOUNT` equals 0, meaning that there were no rows in the last insert.

Try this function by retrieving the manager with the employee ID of 5 and all of his subordinates in all levels. The solution is shown in Listing 11-23.

Listing 11-23: Using the get_mgremps() Multistatement Table-Valued Function

```
SELECT
  T1.*
FROM
  get_mgremps(5) AS T1
```

User-Defined System Functions

System stored procedures have a very special behavior. They can be invoked from any given database without prefixing their name with the database name, and they refer to system objects in the context of the database from which they are invoked. SQL Server 2000 has similar support for functions.

SQL Server 2000 supplies two kinds of system functions. The first kind includes the functions that are implemented as part of the SQL Server executable program, such as GETDATE(). You can use these functions in your T-SQL statements, but their code is not accessible. The second kind includes the functions that are implemented as user-defined functions and are provided with the SQL Server installation. You can actually see the list of those functions by clicking the User Defined Functions node under the master database in the SQL Server Enterprise Manager. This section covers the latter kind—user-defined system functions—and examines both the functions supplied with SQL Server and ways you can create your own.

Supplied User-Defined System Functions

SQL Server 2000 provides a few user-defined system functions that have the following characteristics:

- They are created in master.

- Their names start with "fn_".

- Their names use only lowercase letters.

- They are owned by the user system_function_schema.

SQL Server also supplies functions that are owned by dbo, but an important benefit of functions that are owned by system_function_schema is that they can be invoked from any database without prefixing the function name with the database name.

To see the list of the user-defined functions in the master database, you can run the query shown in Listing 11-24, which retrieves both scalar functions (type is 'FN') and table-valued functions (type is 'TF') with either system_function_schema or dbo as the owner.

Listing 11-24: Getting Details about User-Defined Functions in master

```
USE master
GO

SELECT
  *
FROM
  sysobjects
WHERE
    type IN('FN', 'TF')
  AND
    uid IN(user_id('system_function_schema'),
           user_id('dbo'))
```

You can review the code that creates those functions. The script files for each function are identified in Table 11-1, and they can be found in SQL Server's install folder.

Table 11-1: Location of Supplied User-Defined System Functions

Function	Script File
fn_chariswhitespace	replsys.sql
fn_generateparameterpattern	replsys.sql
fn_getpersistedservernamecasevariation	replcom.sql
fn_helpcollations	procsyst.sql
fn_listextendedproperty	procsyst.sql
fn_MSFullText	sqldmo.sql
fn_MSgensqescstr	replsys.sql
fn_MSsharedversion	replsys.sql
fn_removeparameterwithargument	replsys.sql
fn_replgetagentcommandlinefromjobid	replcom.sql
fn_replmakestringliteral	replsys.sql
fn_replquotename	replsys.sql
fn_serverid	replsys.sql
fn_servershareddrives	procsyst.sql
fn_skipparameterargument	replsys.sql

Table 11-1: Location of Supplied User-Defined System Functions (Continued)

Function	Script File
fn_sqlvarbasetostr	repltran.sql
fn_trace_geteventinfo	procsyst.sql
fn_trace_getfilterinfo	procsyst.sql
fn_trace_getinfo	procsyst.sql
fn_updateparameterwithargument	replsys.sql
fn_varbintohexstr	replsys.sql
fn_varbintohexsubstring	replsys.sql
fn_virtualfilestats	procsyst.sql
fn_virtualservernodes	procsyst.sql

Invoking a system function owned by system_function_schema is similar to invoking any other system function. You can invoke it from any database without prefixing it with the database name or owner. For example, to check whether a certain character is a whitespace, you can use the fn_chariswhitespace() function. See the example in Listing 11-25.

Listing 11-25: Invoking the fn_chariswhitespace() Scalar System Function

```
SELECT fn_chariswhitespace(' ') -- returns 1
SELECT fn_chariswhitespace('a') -- returns 0
```

On the other hand, invoking a function that is not owned by system_function_ schema, or does not meet all of the system function characteristics mentioned earlier, requires prefixing it with the owner name when invoking it from the same database where it was created, and prefixing it also with the database name when it is invoked from other databases. For example, the function dbo.fn_varbintohexstr() in master converts the hex digits in a binary string to a character string representation. To invoke it from any database, you can use the form shown in Listing 11-26.

Listing 11-26: Invoking the fn_varbintohexstr() Scalar Function

```
SELECT
  master.dbo.fn_varbintohexstr(0x0123456789abcdef)
```

The output is the character string "0x0123456789abcdef". The function dbo.fn_varbintohexsubstring() generates a similar output, but you can also provide it with arguments that specify whether to include the "0x" prefix (first argument), the starting length (third argument), and the number of bytes you want to return as a character string (fourth argument). For example, if you want to return only the two first bytes (four hex digits) of the previous binary string, you can issue the query in Listing 11-27.

Listing 11-27: Invoking the fn_varbintohexsubstring() Scalar Function

```
SELECT
  master.dbo.fn_varbintohexsubstring(1, 0x0123456789abcdef, 1, 2)
```

The output of this query is the character string "0x0123".

Most of the table-valued system functions are documented in the Books Online, but Table 11-2 contains short descriptions of their functionality.

Table 11-2: Table-Valued System Functions

Function	Description
fn_helpcollations()	Returns a list of all collations supported by Microsoft SQL Server 2000.
fn_listextendedproperty()	Returns extended property values of database objects.
fn_servershareddrives()	Returns the names of the shared drives that can be used by the clustered server.
fn_trace_geteventinfo()	Returns information about the events being traced.
fn_trace_getfilterinfo()	Returns information about the filters applied to a specified trace.
fn_trace_getinfo()	Returns information about a specified trace or existing traces.
fn_virtualfilestats()	Returns I/O statistics for database files, including log files.
fn_virtualservernodes	Returns the list of nodes on which the virtual server can run. Such information is useful in failover clustering environments.

Invoking a table-valued system function is slightly different from invoking other table-valued functions. The function name must be prefixed with two colons (::). For example, if you want to return the list of all collations supported by Microsoft SQL Server 2000, you can issue the query shown in Listing 11-28.

Listing 11-28: Invoking the fn_helpcollations() Table-Valued System Function

```
SELECT
  *
FROM
  ::fn_helpcollations()
```

Creating Your Own User-Defined System Functions

SQL Server 2000 was not intended to support users who create their own user-defined system functions. You can create such functions as described in this section, but note that this is an *undocumented* and *unsupported* procedure.

In the previous section, you saw the characteristics of system-supplied user-defined system functions, and by following the same rules, you can create your own. One obstacle that stands in your way is that you cannot create an object with the special owner system_function_schema, as the creation of such an object involves changes in system tables that are not allowed. To overcome this obstacle, you need to turn on the 'allow updates' server configuration option to allow these changes to the system tables.

In this example, the first function you created in this chapter, linear_max(), will be made into a user-defined system function. First, you need to turn on 'allow updates'. This is done in Listing 11-29.

Listing 11-29: Allowing Updates to System Tables

```
EXEC sp_configure 'allow updates', 1
GO
RECONFIGURE WITH OVERRIDE
GO
```

Next, you need to create the function in master, prefix it with "fn_", make sure the name only includes lowercase letters, and create it with the owner system_function_schema. This is shown in Listing 11-30.

Listing 11-30: Creating Your Own User-Defined System Function

```
USE master
GO

CREATE FUNCTION system_function_schema.fn_linear_max
(
  @arg1 AS int,
  @arg2 AS int
)
```

```
RETURNS int
AS

BEGIN
  RETURN CASE
            WHEN @arg1 >= @arg2 THEN @arg1
            WHEN @arg2 >  @arg1 THEN @arg2
            ELSE NULL
          END
END
GO


GRANT EXECUTE ON system_function_schema.fn_linear_max TO public
GO
```

Last, you need to turn off 'allow updates', as shown in Listing 11-31.

Listing 11-31: Disallowing Updates to System Tables

```
EXEC sp_configure 'allow updates', 0
GO
RECONFIGURE WITH OVERRIDE
GO
```

Notice that the 'allow updates' configuration option needs to be set once prior to creating the function and can be turned off later. This is similar to stored procedures—certain server configuration options and environment variables' settings determine the behavior of the stored procedure or function at *create* time and not at *run* time.

Now you can try using your new function from any database as shown in Listing 11-32.

Listing 11-32: Invoking the fn_linear_max() System Function

```
SELECT
  fn_linear_max(1, 2)
```

You can even incorporate the function into a SELECT statement against a particular table. Check out Listing 11-33.

Listing 11-33: Using the fn_linear_max() System Function in a Query

```
SELECT
  col1,
  col2,
  fn_linear_max(col1, col2) AS max_value
FROM
  <table_name>
```

Other Issues Concerning User-Defined Functions

In the previous sections you've seen how to create scalar and table-valued user-defined functions. In this section you'll get acquainted with some more features and issues concerning user-defined functions, such as determinism, deferred name resolution, recursion, and more.

Using Default Values

You can supply default values for the argument of a user-defined function in the same way you supply values for stored procedure parameters—you include an equal sign followed by a default value as part of the argument's definition. For example, if you want to supply 0 as the default value for the second argument of a function called dbo.myudf(), you can use the syntax demonstrated in Listing 11-34.

Listing 11-34: Creating a User-Defined Function with Default Values

```
CREATE FUNCTION dbo.myudf
(
  @arg1 int,
  @arg2 int = 0
)
RETURNS int
AS
BEGIN
  RETURN @arg1 + @arg2
END
GO
```

If you do not want to supply a value at run time for an argument that has a default value, you need to specify the keyword DEFAULT. You cannot simply omit the argument as you can with the last parameters of stored procedures that have default values. For example, to invoke your function with the default value of the second argument, you can issue the query in Listing 11-35.

Listing 11-35: Legal Invocation of a User-Defined Function with Default Values

```
SELECT
  dbo.myudf(1, DEFAULT)
```

Omitting the second argument, as shown in Listing 11-36, will not use its default value. Rather, it will return an error.

Listing 11-36: Illegal Invocation of a User-Defined Function with Default Values

```
SELECT
  dbo.myudf(1)
```

User-Defined Function Limitations

User-defined functions are supposed to be incorporated into SELECT statements, computed columns, and CHECK and DEFAULT constraints. They are not supposed to have any side effects on the database, meaning that they are not supposed to change anything out of their scope. Therefore, you cannot issue any DML modification statements (INSERT, UPDATE, DELETE) that affect an object that was not created by the function. Also, you cannot create a permanent object, such as a table that will remain in the database outside the scope of the function. Nor can you create a temporary table inside the function, but you can create a table variable and modify it, as it is destroyed as soon as you leave the function.

Determinism, Schemabinding, and Participating in Constraints and Indices

You can create an index on a computed column that invokes a user-defined function. Such a computed column can also participate in PRIMARY KEY or UNIQUE constraints, which currently create a unique index under the covers as the constraint's uniqueness enforcement mechanism. You can also create an index on a view that references user-defined functions (indexed views are covered in Chapter 8).

The ability to create an index on a computed column or on a view is dependent on the promise that the referenced functions will always return the same value for the same given input, e.g., that the functions are deterministic. A user-defined function is deterministic if the following conditions are met:

- The function is schema-bound, meaning that you cannot change the schema of the objects referenced by the function.

- All functions called by the user-defined function, including built-in functions or other user-defined functions, are deterministic.

- The body of the function references no database objects outside the scope of the function. For example, a deterministic function cannot reference any tables other than table variables that are local to the function.

Creating a PRIMARY KEY constraint on a computed column that references a user-defined function is not as trivial as one would expect. This section demonstrates how this can be achieved. Furthermore, you will be shown techniques to improve the performance of a function by using a mathematical algorithm.

The deterministic function shown in Listing 11-37 accepts a number and adds a check digit at the end of the number. A check digit is computed by applying a certain algorithm to a value in a source system. The same computation is then performed in a target system to check whether the source value was corrupted on its way to the target system. The check digit shown in the following example is computed with the cast9 algorithm (see the "Cast9" sidebar for details), which recursively adds the digits comprising the number. (This example demonstrates logical recursion using the modulo operator, as explained in the "Cast9" sidebar).

Listing 11-37: Creating the num_with_cast9_checkdigit()
Scalar Deterministic User-Defined Function

```
CREATE FUNCTION dbo.num_with_cast9_checkdigit
(
  @num AS int
)
RETURNS int
WITH SCHEMABINDING

AS
BEGIN
  RETURN @num * 10 + ((@num - 1) % 9 + 1)
END
GO
```

Cast9

The cast9 algorithm calculates a single digit from a given number. It adds the digits that compose the number and continues to add the result recursively until a single digit is left. For example, suppose you want to calculate the cast9 value of the number 13546:

$$1+3+5+4+6=19$$
$$1+9=10$$
$$1+0=1$$

The result of cast9(13546) is 1.

Of course, you can use a loop or recursion to implement the cast9 algorithm, but you can implement it in a much simpler and more efficient way. Hint: How do you know if a number can be divided by 9 with no remainder? Answer: You add all its digits recursively until you are left with a single digit. If you get a 9, it divides by 9 with no remainder; if you get any digit other than 9, it doesn't. Sound familiar?

You can simply use the *modulo* operator (%) of T-SQL to calculate the remainder of your input number divided by 9 to calculate its cast9 value, without the need to actually use recursion or loops, hence the use of the term "logical recursion."

In the example here, (13546 − 1) % 9 + 1 = 1. The reason you need to subtract 1 before performing the modulo and then add it back is that the result of modulo with a base of 9 is in the range 0–8, and the required result digit should be in the range 1–9.

If you need to provide the cast9 algorithm, but instead of implementing it with recursion or loops you want to implement it with the more efficient modulo operation, you need mathematics to prove that both methods will always provide the same result:

$$let\, a = number, a' = cast9(a)$$

The number a can be represented as the sum of its digits multiplied by 10 to the power of the digit's position:

$$a = 10^n a_n + 10^{n-1} a_{n-1} + \ldots + 10^1 a_1 + 10^0 a_0 =$$
$$= 10^n a_n + 10^{n-1} a_{n-1} + \ldots + 10 a_1 + a_0$$

According to the modulo transformation rules, you can write the following equation based on the previous one:

$$\mod_9(a) = \mod_9^n(10) \cdot \mod_9(a_n) + \mod_9^{n-1}(10) \cdot \mod_9(a_{n-1}) + \ldots + \mod_9(10) \cdot \mod_9(a_1) + \mod_9(a_0) =$$
$$= 1^n \cdot \mod_9(a_n) + 1^{n-1} \cdot \mod_9(a_{n-1}) + \ldots + 1 \cdot \mod_9(a_1) + \mod_9(a_0) =$$
$$= \sum_{i=0}^{n} \mod_9(a_i)$$

In addition a' is by definition the sum of a's digits. So you can deduce the following:

$$a' = \sum_{i=0}^{n} a_i$$

$$\Rightarrow$$

$$\mathrm{mod}_9(a') = \mathrm{mod}_9(\sum_{i=0}^{n} a_i) = \sum_{i=0}^{n} \mathrm{mod}_9(a_i)$$

$$\Rightarrow$$

$$\mathrm{mod}_9(a) = \mathrm{mod}_9(a')$$

$$\Rightarrow$$

$$\mathrm{mod}_9(a-1) + 1 = \mathrm{mod}_9(a'-1) + 1$$

Since a' is a single digit in the range of 1–9, the modulo of (a–1) will always be the same as (a–1). Hence you can deduce the following:

$$\mathrm{mod}_9(a-1) + 1 = a' - 1 + 1$$

$$\Rightarrow$$

$$\mathrm{mod}_9(a-1) + 1 = a'$$

Q.E.D.

To demonstrate how to create a constraint on a computed column that references a user-defined function, create the table T1 with one integer column called num and another computed column. The computed column invokes the num_with_cast9_checkdigit() function with the column num as its argument. See Listing 11-38.

Listing 11-38: Using the num_with_cast9_checkdigit() Function in a Computed Column

```
CREATE TABLE T1
(
  num int NOT NULL PRIMARY KEY,
  numwithcheckdigit AS dbo.num_with_cast9_checkdigit(num)
)
GO
```

Since this function is deterministic, you can create an index on the computed column that invokes it. See Listing 11-39.

*Listing 11-39: Creating an Index on a Computed Column
that Invokes a Deterministic Function*

```
CREATE INDEX idx_nci_numwithcheckdigit ON T1(numwithcheckdigit)
GO
```

If you wanted, you could also create a UNIQUE constraint on the computed column. Just drop the index you created first, as it is redundant in this case. See Listing 11-40.

*Listing 11-40: Creating a UNIQUE Constraint on a Computed Column
that Invokes a Deterministic Function*

```
DROP INDEX T1.idx_nci_numwithcheckdigit
GO
ALTER TABLE T1
  ADD CONSTRAINT UNQ_T1_numwithcheckdigit
      UNIQUE(numwithcheckdigit)
GO
```

Suppose you wanted to create a PRIMARY KEY constraint on your computed column numwithcheckdigit instead of on the column num. Try dropping the table first and recreating it, as shown in Listing 11-41.

*Listing 11-41: Illegal Attempt to Create a PRIMARY KEY Constraint on a Computed
Column that Invokes a Deterministic Function*

```
DROP TABLE T1
GO

CREATE TABLE T1
(
  num int NOT NULL,
  numwithcheckdigit AS dbo.num_with_cast9_checkdigit(num) NOT NULL PRIMARY KEY
)
GO
```

The table creation in the preceding code fails because even though the num column is not NULLable, a user-defined function using it as an argument might calculate an expression that overflows, underflows, or is undefined, resulting in either a runtime error or a NULL value. The PRIMARY KEY constraint does not allow NULLs. Hence, the table creation is rejected.

To make sure that a computed column will never result in a NULL value, even if a user-defined function it references might, you can wrap its calculation with the

ISNULL() function and supply an alternative value in case it results in a NULL value. In this case, you can return a 0 as the check digit. See the solution in Listing 11-42.

Listing 11-42: Creating a PRIMARY KEY Constraint on a Computed Column that Invokes a Deterministic Function

```
CREATE TABLE T1
(
  num int NOT NULL,
  numwithcheckdigit AS ISNULL(dbo.num_with_cast9_checkdigit(num), 0) PRIMARY KEY
)
```

Notice that in this case, if you try to insert a row with a value in num that makes the return value of the function overflow, you will get a runtime error, and your insert will be rejected, so you need not worry about having numbers without a check digit in your computed column. Try the following INSERT and verify the error in Listing 11-43.

Listing 11-43: Inserting a Row that Causes an Overflow in a Function Invocation

```
INSERT INTO T1 VALUES(10000000000)
```

```
Server: Msg 8115, Level 16, State 3, Line 1
Arithmetic overflow error converting numeric to data type int.
The statement has been terminated.
```

Now that the PRIMARY KEY issues have been settled, try adding a few legal values, as shown in Listing 11-44.

Listing 11-44: Inserting Rows in a Table with a Computed Column that Invokes a User-Defined Function

```
INSERT INTO T1 VALUES(123)
INSERT INTO T1 VALUES(234)
INSERT INTO T1 VALUES(456)
INSERT INTO T1 VALUES(678)
INSERT INTO T1 VALUES(789)
INSERT INTO T1 VALUES(890)

SELECT * FROM T1
```

You should get the output shown in Table 11-3.

Table 11-3: T1 Values

num	numwithcheckdigit
123	1236
234	2349
456	4566
678	6783
789	7896
890	8908

Understanding Deferred Name Resolution and Recursion

SQL Server supports a process called *deferred name resolution* for procedural units such as stored procedures and user-defined functions. Upon the creation of the object, SQL Server checks only for syntactical errors and not for referenced object existence. It does check for referenced object existence upon first execution.

For example, you can successfully create the function shown in Listing 11-45, even though the table T1 and the function dbo.f2() do not exist in the testdb database.

Listing 11-45: Deferred Name Resolution in User-Defined Functions

```
USE testdb
GO

CREATE FUNCTION dbo.f1
(
  @arg1 AS int
)
RETURNS int
AS
BEGIN
  DECLARE @var1 AS int
```

```
SELECT
   @var1 = col1
FROM
   T1
WHERE
   key_col = @arg1

SET @var1 = dbo.f2(@var1)

RETURN @var1
END
GO
```

You will get an error, however, upon the invocation of this function if these objects do not exist at runtime. Deferred name resolution allows a function to call itself recursively. (There is an example of recursion using stored procedures in Chapter 9.) For example, you can write a function, as shown in Listing 11-46, that calculates a member in a Fibonacci series, where

fibonacci(0) = 0

fibonacci(1) = 1

fibonacci(n+2) = fibonacci(n+1) + fibonacci(n), where n ≥ 0

Listing 11-46: Implementing the fibonacci() User-Defined Function with Recursion

```
CREATE FUNCTION dbo.fibonacci
(
  @n AS int
)
RETURNS int
AS

BEGIN
  RETURN CASE
          WHEN @n > 1 THEN @n + dbo.fibonacci(@n - 1) --recursive invocation
          WHEN @n IN (0, 1) THEN @n
          ELSE NULL
        END
END
GO
```

Just as you have a limit of 32 nesting levels in stored procedures and triggers, you have the same limit in functions. (Stored procedures and triggers are covered in

Chapters 9 and 10, respectively.) In other words, you can successfully invoke the function with 32 as an argument, but not with more than 32. You can verify this with the code in Listing 11-47.

Listing 11-47: Invoking the Recursive fibonacci() User-Defined Function

```
SELECT dbo.fibonacci(32) -- succeeds
SELECT dbo.fibonacci(33) -- fails
```

In many cases, you can rewrite a function to use loops instead of recursive calls. For example, the loop version of the `fibonacci()` function, `fibonacci2()`, is shown in Listing 11-48.

Listing 11-48: Implementing the fibonacci2() User-Defined Function with a Loop

```
CREATE FUNCTION dbo.fibonacci2
(
  @n AS int
)
RETURNS int
AS

BEGIN
  IF @n < 0
    RETURN NULL
  ELSE
    IF @n in (0, 1)
      RETURN @n
  ELSE
  BEGIN
    DECLARE
      @i AS int,
      @f AS int

    SET @i = @n
    SET @f = 0
    WHILE @i > 0
    BEGIN
      SET @f = @f + @i
      SET @i = @i - 1
    END -- loop while @i > 0
  END -- if @n > 0
  RETURN @f
END -- function
GO
```

To invoke the `fibonacci2()` function, use the code in Listing 11-49. Note that since this function uses loops, the 32 nesting levels limitation does not apply to it.

Listing 11-49: Invoking the Loop fibonacci2() User-Defined Function

```
SELECT dbo.fibonacci2(32) -- succeeds
SELECT dbo.fibonacci2(33) -- succeeds
```

Returning Information about User-Defined Functions

The `OBJECTPROPERTY()` function returns information about objects in the current database. This function was extended in SQL Server 2000 to provide information about user-defined functions. The syntax of this function is displayed in Listing 11-50.

Listing 11-50: Syntax for the OBJECTPROPERTY() Function

```
OBJECTPROPERTY ( <object_id> , <property> )
```

The following properties can be checked for a given user-defined function:

```
IsScalarFunction
IsInlineFunction
IsTableFunction
IsDeterministic
IsSchemaBound
```

For example, to check whether the `dbo.fibonacci()` function is a scalar function, you can issue the statement in Listing 11-51.

Listing 11-51: Using the OBJECTPROPERTY() Function

```
SELECT
  OBJECTPROPERTY(OBJECT_ID('dbo.fibonacci'), 'IsScalarFunction')
```

Encrypting the Code of User-Defined Functions

You can encrypt the code for user-defined functions by using the `WITH ENCRYPTION` option in the `CREATE FUNCTION` or `ALTER FUNCTION` statements the same way as with views, stored procedures, and triggers. For details, please refer to Chapter 8.

Using User-Defined Functions
to Manipulate Complex Numbers

User-defined functions, introduced with SQL Server 2000, give you enormous power in providing elegant programmatic solutions to problems that involve data that you need to store in your database. Without user-defined functions, certain problems would be too complicated to solve within SQL Server and would require a solution in the client application incurring round-trip communications between the client and the server, even though all you might need is the results of certain computations on the base data.

One such problem area is the manipulation of *complex numbers*. Speaking of elegant solutions to problems, complex numbers themselves provide elegant mathematical solutions to certain problems that are too complex to solve with real numbers. Sound recursively tricky? Well, it is! Are complex numbers really that complex? Hopefully you will think otherwise as you read along. At any rate, with UDFs encapsulating the complex numbers' algebra, you will not need to worry about that part of the problem.

What Is a Complex Number?

The standard form for representing any complex number is

$z = a + bi$

The complex number z is made of two parts, a real and an imaginary part. a and b are real numbers and i is the square root of -1 ($i = \sqrt{-1}$). a is referred to as the real part of z, and b is referred to as the imaginary part of z.

Complex numbers are also referred to as *imaginary numbers*, and the reason is quite obvious—traditional algebra doesn't supply a solution for the equation $i^2 = -1$. However, if you believe in magic, you can "imagine" that there really is a solution to the equation, hence $i = \sqrt{-1}$.

Why imagine? Why dream? A phrase coined by Alex Giladi (a member of the International Olympic Committee) certainly nails it down: "One may dream, one should dream, and sometimes dreams do come true." Well, it's a fact that imaginary numbers are widely used in many fields and industries nowadays, such as physics, medicine, electronics, graphics, and so on, providing practical solutions to problems that would have been too complex to solve with only real numbers.

Complex numbers can be depicted geometrically in a two-dimensional plane where the x-axis is the *real-axis* and the y-axis is the *imaginary-axis*. Such a plane is referred to as the *complex plane*, or simply the *z-plane*. The complex number itself can be represented in the complex plane as either a point with the coordinates (a, b), or as a vector that starts at the origin and ends in the point with the coordinates (a, b) as Figure 11-1 shows.

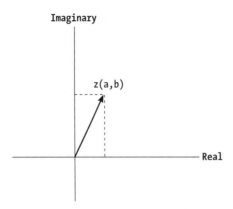

Figure 11-1: Geometrical depiction of a complex number

Why Use Complex Numbers in T-SQL?

You can probably imagine that a complex number requires special handling. It is made of two parts and has a special representation. Also, as you will soon see, the algebra of complex numbers includes unique calculations and arithmetic operations.

T-SQL currently does not support object-oriented capabilities, which means that you cannot create your own classes that represent complex numbers. You can either store the real and imaginary parts as two separate values, or store the whole complex number in a character string, e.g., `'1 + 2i'`. It is much more natural to support complex numbers in an object-oriented environment, such as C++, where you can create a class that represents a complex number and even overload arithmetic operators, such as addition (+), subtraction (–), multiplication (*), division (/), and so on, which can make manipulating complex numbers even more natural. The disadvantage, however, in handling complex numbers in the client application is that all of the base data needs to be brought to the client first. Providing a solution in T-SQL allows you to exploit its power in manipulating sets of data, returning only the results that the client application actually needs.

Although T-SQL does not include object-oriented capabilities, it does allow you to write your own user-defined functions, which can be embedded in your queries, making them the optimal tool in T-SQL for manipulating complex numbers.

Validating, Representing, and Extracting the Parts of Complex Numbers

If you want the values that will be stored and manipulated in the database to have the look and feel of a complex number, you can store them in a variable-length character string (varchar) like this: '1 + 2i'. You can even create a user-defined datatype called *complex* and use it as the datatype in your column and variable definitions. Listing 11-52 shows how to create the complex user-defined datatype.

Listing 11-52: Creating the complex User-Defined Datatype

```
EXEC sp_addtype complex, 'varchar(50)'
```

This, of course, means that you will need to make sure that the value that is supposed to represent a complex number is a legal one. And you will also probably want to be able to extract the real and imaginary parts so you can perform calculations that require only one part of the complex number.

Validating a Complex Number

Now that the background is covered, it's time to start coding! Your first task is to write a function that accepts a varchar representing a complex number as an argument and checks whether it is a legal complex number or not. This function should return 1 if the value is a legal complex number, and 0 if it isn't. The function should perform a series of tests on the input value, @cx, and abort if any of the tests fail.

First, the function trims the input value from any leading and trailing spaces. Note that since the argument supplied to the function is treated as an input parameter, any changes made to the argument inside the function do not affect its value outside the scope of the function. An input parameter is actually a copy of the value supplied to the function and not a pointer to its memory address.

Then, the first test checks whether the rightmost character is the letter *i*. If the string passes this test, the rightmost character is removed from it.

Next, the position of the middle sign (–/+) is stored in the variable @signpos. This is done by using a pattern search: PATINDEX('%_[-+]%', @cx) + 1. This pattern search returns the position of the character that appears prior to the +/- sign that is supposed to exist in the middle of the complex number and adds 1 to the position to indicate the sign's exact position. Note the importance of the underscore, which represents a single character. If the real part of the complex number was entered with a sign (e.g., –3), its sign does not qualify for this pattern search, as the pattern search requires at least one character prior to the sign. If there is no such sign in the middle of the supposed-to-be complex number, PATINDEX returns 0.

Now that the position of the middle sign is stored in a variable, it is simple to extract the real and imaginary parts of the complex number surrounding the middle sign and to use the IsNumeric function to check whether those parts are numeric.

If the string passes all the tests, the dbo.cxValid function returns 1 to indicate that the number is valid; otherwise, it returns 0. Take a look at the script that creates the function, as shown in Listing 11-53.

Listing 11-53: Creation Script for the dbo.cxValid Function

```
----------------------------
-- Complex Validate       --
-- 0 - invalid, 1 - valid --
----------------------------
CREATE FUNCTION dbo.cxValid(
  @cx AS complex)
RETURNS bit
AS

BEGIN
  -- trim leading and trailing blanks
  SET @cx = RTRIM(LTRIM(@cx))

  -- check if last character is 'i'
  IF RIGHT(@cx, 1) <> 'i'
    RETURN 0

  -- remove the character 'i' from the end
  SET @cx = LEFT(@cx, LEN(@cx) - 1)

  -- find the position of the middle -/+ sign
  DECLARE @signpos AS int
  SET @signpos = PATINDEX('%_[-+]%', @cx) + 1
  IF @signpos = 0
    RETURN 0

  -- check if the real part exists and is numeric
  IF IsNumeric(LEFT(@cx, @signpos - 1)) = 0
    RETURN 0

  -- check if the imaginary part exists and is numeric
  IF IsNumeric(RIGHT(@cx, LEN(@cx) - @signpos + 1)) = 0
    RETURN 0
```

```
  -- if not aborted yet, number is a "real" imaginary number. ;-)
  RETURN 1
END
GO
```

If you want to allow only valid complex numbers in columns defined with the complex user-defined datatype, you can create a *rule* that implements the same logic that the dbo.cxValid function implements and bind it to the complex user-defined datatype. Listing 11-54 shows how to create such a rule and bind it to the complex type.

Listing 11-54: Creating the complex_valid rule and Binding It to the complex Type

```
--------------------------------
-- Complex Validate as a rule --
--------------------------------
CREATE rule complex_valid
AS
  -- check if last character is 'i'
  RIGHT(RTRIM(@cx), 1) = 'i' AND

  -- check if the real part exists and is numeric
  IsNumeric(LEFT(LTRIM(@cx),
            PATINDEX('%_[-+]%', LTRIM(@cx)))) = 1 AND

  -- check if the imaginary part exists and is numeric
  IsNumeric(SUBSTRING(LTRIM(@cx),
            PATINDEX('%_[-+]%', LTRIM(@cx)) + 1,
            LEN(RTRIM(LTRIM(@cx))) -
              PATINDEX('%_[-+]%', LTRIM(@cx)) - 1)) = 1
GO

EXEC sp_bindrule 'complex_valid', 'complex'
GO
```

Note that you cannot use the dbo.cxValid function inside the rule because only system functions are allowed inside rules. Also, a rule has to be written as one expression, so you can't break the validating logic into several steps as in the dbo.cxValid function. This, of course, makes the expression less readable, but you can think of it as the single-expression version of the dbo.cxValid function.

Normalizing a Complex Number

Since varchars are used here to store complex numbers, there's a lot of flexibility in storing them. For example, take a look at these legal variations of the same complex number:

```
'1+2i'
'1 + 2i'
'+1 + 2i'
' 1  + 2i'
'1.000 + 2.0i'
```

There's an awkward lack of aesthetics in presenting complex numbers in inconsistent forms. You might prefer to have a consistent representation for your complex numbers. For example, you might choose to present the leading sign of the real part only if it's negative, have the middle sign surrounded with single spaces, trim all leading and trailing spaces, and also trim redundant trailing zeroes from both the real and the imaginary parts. To do so, you can create a normalizing function that accepts a legal complex number as an argument and returns its normalized form: '[-]a {+ | -} bi'.

The dbo.cxNormalize function shown in Listing 11-55 includes embedded comments that describe the steps involved in the normalization process, but in general, it performs the following steps:

1. Removes all spaces using the REPLACE function.

2. Breaks the real and imaginary parts apart and removes all redundant trailing zeroes.

3. Concatenates the real and imaginary parts.

4. Adds single spaces before and after the middle sign.

5. Removes the positive sign before the real part, if one exists.

Listing 11-55: Creation Script for the dbo.cxNormalize Function

```
-----------------------------------------------------------
-- Normalize the complex number to: '[-]a {+ | -} bi' --
-- with no redundant trailing zeros              --
-----------------------------------------------------------
CREATE FUNCTION dbo.cxNormalize(
  @cx AS complex)
RETURNS complex
AS

BEGIN
-- step 1: remove spaces
  SET @cx = REPLACE(@cx, ' ', '')


-- step 2: remove redundant trailing zeros
--          from both the real and imaginary parts

  -- extract the real part
  DECLARE @real AS varchar(25)
  SET @real = LEFT(@cx, PATINDEX('%_[-+]%', @cx))

  -- remove the dot if one exists and only zeros appear after it
  IF CHARINDEX('.', @real) > 0 AND PATINDEX('%.%[1-9]%', @real) = 0
    SET @real = LEFT(@real, CHARINDEX('.', @real) - 1)

  -- remove trailing zeros if there are significant digits after the dot
  IF PATINDEX('%.%0', @real) > 0
    SET @real = LEFT(@real, LEN(@real) - PATINDEX('%[^0]%.%',
                                      REVERSE(@real)) + 1)


  -- extract the imaginary part
  DECLARE @imaginary AS varchar(25)
  SET @imaginary = SUBSTRING(@cx, PATINDEX('%_[-+]%', @cx) + 1,
                    CHARINDEX('i', @cx) - PATINDEX('%_[-+]%',
                                      @cx) - 1)

  -- remove the dot if one exists and only zeros appear after it
  IF CHARINDEX('.', @imaginary) > 0
     AND PATINDEX('%.%[1-9]%', @imaginary) = 0
    SET @imaginary = LEFT(@imaginary, CHARINDEX('.', @imaginary) - 1)
```

```
  -- remove trailing zeros if there are significant digits after the dot
  IF PATINDEX('%.%0', @imaginary) > 0
    SET @imaginary = LEFT(@imaginary,
                        LEN(@imaginary) - PATINDEX('%[^0]%.%',
                                        REVERSE(@imaginary)) + 1)


-- step 3: concatenate the real and imaginary parts
  SET @cx = @real + @imaginary + 'i'


-- step 4: add a space before and after middle sign
  SET @cx = STUFF(@cx, PATINDEX('%_[-+]%', @cx) + 1, 0, ' ')
  SET @cx = STUFF(@cx, PATINDEX('%_[-+]%', @cx) + 2, 0, ' ')


-- step 5: remove positive sign before the real part, if one exists
  IF LEFT(@cx, 1) = '+'
    SET @cx = STUFF(@cx, 1, 1, '')


  RETURN @cx
END
GO
```

Extracting the Real and Imaginary Parts

When you start performing complex arithmetic you will need to extract the real and imaginary parts of a complex number. You can write functions to perform this task for you.

The functions dbo.cxGetReal and dbo.cxGetImaginary are fairly simple. They use the PATINDEX function in the same way it was used in the previous functions to locate the position of the middle sign and return the requested part, either to the left of the sign (the real part) or starting from the middle sign and to the right of it, up to and not including the character *i* (the imaginary part). Listings 11-56 and 11-57 show the creation scripts for the dbo.cxGetReal and the dbo.cxGetImaginary functions.

Listing 11-56: Creation Script for the dbo.cxGetReal Function

```
------------------------------------------------
-- Get Real                                 --
-- Extract real portion of the complex number --
------------------------------------------------
CREATE FUNCTION dbo.cxGetReal(
  @cx AS complex)
RETURNS decimal(19, 9)
AS
```

```
BEGIN
  SET @cx = REPLACE(@cx, ' ', '')
  RETURN CAST(LEFT(@cx, PATINDEX('%_[-+]%', @cx)) AS decimal(19,9))
END
GO
```

Listing 11-57: Creation Script for the dbo.cxGetImaginary Function

```
-----------------------------------------------------
-- Get Imaginary                                    --
-- Extract imaginary portion of the complex number --
-----------------------------------------------------
CREATE FUNCTION dbo.cxGetImaginary(
  @cx AS complex)
RETURNS decimal(19,9)
AS

BEGIN
  SET @cx = REPLACE(@cx, ' ', '')
  RETURN CAST(
          SUBSTRING(
            @cx,
            PATINDEX('%_[-+]%', @cx) + 1,
            CHARINDEX('i', @cx) - PATINDEX('%_[-+]%', @cx) - 1)
          AS decimal(19,9))
END
GO
```

Forming a String Representing a Complex Number out of Its Parts

The same way you would want to break a supplied string representing a complex number into its real and imaginary parts, you would probably also want to do the opposite—form a string representing a complex number from its supplied real and imaginary parts. Now that you have a function that normalizes a complex number, the process is simple. You form a string with the following parts:

- The real part

- The sign of the imaginary part

- The imaginary part

- The character *i*

All you have to do is concatenate the result. Listing 11-58 shows the `dbo.cxStrForm` function.

Listing 11-58: Creation Script for the dbo.cxStrForm Function

```
--------------------------------------------------------
-- Format Complex Number String               --
-- Form a string representing a complex number    --
-- out of its real and imaginary parts        --
--------------------------------------------------------
CREATE FUNCTION dbo.cxStrForm(
  @real      AS decimal(19,9),
  @imaginary AS decimal(19,9))
RETURNS complex
AS

BEGIN
  RETURN dbo.cxNormalize(
    CAST(@real AS varchar(21)) +
    CASE SIGN(@imaginary)
      WHEN -1 THEN '-'
      ELSE '+'
    END +
    CAST(ABS(@imaginary) AS varchar(21)) +
    'i')
END
GO
```

Complex Algebra, Geometry, and Arithmetic Operations

Now that the foundations are all set, you can move on to the implementation of complex arithmetic operations—the reason these foundations were laid. Complex numbers have their own rules for addition, subtraction, multiplication, and division, all of which can be implemented with user-defined functions.

Implementing Complex Addition

To add two complex numbers, you simply add the real and the imaginary parts separately, as shown here:

$$z_3 = z_1 + z_2 =$$
$$(a_1 + b_1 i) + (a_2 + b_2 i) =$$
$$(a_1 + a_2) + (b_1 + b_2)i$$

Geometrical Depiction of Complex Addition

The result of complex addition can be represented as a vector in the complex plane. If you form a parallelogram from the vectors representing the complex numbers being added, the resultant vector is the diagonal of the parallelogram starting at the origin and ending at the counter vertex. The geometrical depiction of complex addition is shown in Figure 11-2.

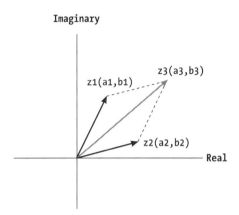

Figure 11-2: Geometrical depiction of complex addition, $z_3 = z_1 + z_2$

Implementing Complex Addition with a User-Defined Function

Implementing the dbo.cxAdd function is an easy task now that all the foundations are laid. The function accepts two arguments representing complex numbers and performs the following steps:

1. Checks whether both arguments are valid, using the dbo.cxValid function, and aborts if either of them is not a valid complex number, returning NULL.

2. Extracts the real and imaginary parts from both arguments using the dbo.cxGetReal and dbo.cxGetImaginary functions and stores them in numeric variables.

3. Calculates the resultant real and imaginary parts following complex addition rules.

4. Returns a normalized string form of the resultant complex number using the dbo.cxStrForm function.

Listing 11-59 shows the script that creates the dbo.cxAdd function.

Listing 11-59: Creation Script for the dbo.cxAdd Function

```
----------------------------------------
-- Complex Add                        --
-- z1 + z2 = (a1 + a2) + (b1 + b2)i --
----------------------------------------
CREATE FUNCTION dbo.cxAdd(
  @cx1 as complex,
  @cx2 as complex)
RETURNS complex
AS

BEGIN

  IF dbo.cxValid(@cx1) = 0 OR dbo.cxValid(@cx2) = 0
    RETURN NULL

  DECLARE
    @a1        AS decimal(19,9),
    @b1        AS decimal(19,9),
    @a2        AS decimal(19,9),
    @b2        AS decimal(19,9)

  DECLARE
    @real      AS decimal(19,9),
    @imaginary AS decimal(19,9)

  SET @a1 = dbo.cxGetReal(@cx1)
  SET @a2 = dbo.cxGetReal(@cx2)
  SET @b1 = dbo.cxGetImaginary(@cx1)
  SET @b2 = dbo.cxGetImaginary(@cx2)

  -- z1 + z2 = (a1 + a2) + (b1 + b2)i
  SET @real =       @a1 + @a2
  SET @imaginary = @b1 + @b2

  RETURN dbo.cxStrForm(@real, @imaginary)

END
GO
```

Implementing Complex Subtraction

Complex subtraction is performed much like complex addition. You perform subtraction between the real and the imaginary parts separately, as follows:

$$z_3 = z_1 - z_2 =$$
$$(a_1 + b_1 i) - (a_2 + b_2 i) =$$
$$(a_1 - a_2) + (b_1 - b_2)i$$

Geometrical Depiction of Complex Subtraction

In geometrical terms, you can think of complex subtraction as a variation on complex addition. You simply negate the second complex number and perform complex addition, as Figure 11-3 shows.

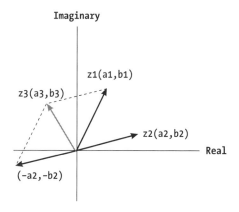

Figure 11-3: Geometrical depiction of complex subtraction, $z_3 = z_1 - z_2 =$

Implementing Complex Subtraction with a User-Defined Function

Implementing the dbo.cxSubtract function is much like implementing the dbo.cxAdd function. The only thing that changes is the formula that calculates the resultant real and imaginary parts.

Listing 11-60 shows the script that creates the dbo.cxSubtract function.

Listing 11-60: Creation Script for the dbo.cxSubtract Function

```
----------------------------------------
-- Complex Subtract                     --
-- z1 - z2 = (a1 - a2) + (b1 - b2)i --
----------------------------------------
CREATE FUNCTION dbo.cxSubtract(
  @cx1 as complex,
  @cx2 as complex)
RETURNS complex
AS

BEGIN

  IF dbo.cxValid(@cx1) = 0 OR dbo.cxValid(@cx2) = 0
    RETURN NULL

  DECLARE
    @a1        AS decimal(19,9),
    @b1        AS decimal(19,9),
    @a2        AS decimal(19,9),
    @b2        AS decimal(19,9)

  DECLARE
    @real      AS decimal(19,9),
    @imaginary AS decimal(19,9)

  SET @a1 = dbo.cxGetReal(@cx1)
  SET @a2 = dbo.cxGetReal(@cx2)
  SET @b1 = dbo.cxGetImaginary(@cx1)
  SET @b2 = dbo.cxGetImaginary(@cx2)

  -- z1 - z2 = (a1 - a2) + (b1 - b2)i
  SET @real =      @a1 - @a2
  SET @imaginary = @b1 - @b2

  RETURN dbo.cxStrForm(@real, @imaginary)

END
GO
```

Implementing Complex Multiplication

The result of complex multiplication relies on the assumption that there is a solution to the equation $i^2 = -1$. The following calculation shows the result of multiplying two complex numbers. Note that at some point in the calculation you get $b_1 b_2 i^2$ and replace it with $-b_1 b_2$.

$$z_3 = z_1 \cdot z_2 =$$

$$(a_1 a_2 - b_1 b_2) + (a_1 b_2 + a_2 b_1)i$$

Explanation:

$$z_1 \cdot z_2 =$$

$$(a_1 + b_1 i) \cdot (a_2 + b_2 i) =$$

$$a_1 a_2 + a_1 b_2 i + a_2 b_1 i + b_1 b_2 i^2 =$$

$$a_1 a_2 + a_1 b_2 i + a_2 b_1 i - b_1 b_2 =$$

$$(a_1 a_2 - b_1 b_2) + (a_1 b_2 + a_2 b_1)i$$

Implementing Complex Multiplication with a User-Defined Function

Again, there is nothing special in implementing the dbo.cxMult function. Only the formulas that calculate the resultant real and imaginary parts change from the earlier functions.

Listing 11-61 shows the script that creates the dbo.cxMult function.

Listing 11-61: Creation Script for the dbo.cxMult Function

```
------------------------------------------------------
-- Complex Multiply                              --
-- z1 * z2 = (a1*a2 - b1*b2) + (a1*b2 + a2*b1)i --
--                                               --
-- Explanation:                                  --
-- z1 * z2 =                                      --
-- (a1 + b1i) * (a2 + b2i) =                      --
-- a1*a2 + a1*b2i + a2*b1i + b1*b2i² =            --
-- a1*a2 + a1*b2i + a2*b1i - b1*b2 =              --
-- (a1*a2 - b1*b2) + (a1*b2 + a2*b1)i             --
------------------------------------------------------
```

```
CREATE FUNCTION dbo.cxMult(
  @cx1 as complex,
  @cx2 as complex)
RETURNS complex
AS

BEGIN

  IF dbo.cxValid(@cx1) = 0 OR dbo.cxValid(@cx2) = 0
    RETURN NULL

  DECLARE
    @a1       AS decimal(19,9),
    @b1       AS decimal(19,9),
    @a2       AS decimal(19,9),
    @b2       AS decimal(19,9)

  DECLARE
    @real      AS decimal(19,9),
    @imaginary AS decimal(19,9)

  SET @a1 = dbo.cxGetReal(@cx1)
  SET @a2 = dbo.cxGetReal(@cx2)
  SET @b1 = dbo.cxGetImaginary(@cx1)
  SET @b2 = dbo.cxGetImaginary(@cx2)

  -- z1 * z2 = (a1*a2 - b1*b2) + (a1*b2 + a2*b1)i
  SET @real =      @a1*@a2 - @b1*@b2
  SET @imaginary = @a1*@b2 + @a2*@b1

  RETURN dbo.cxStrForm(@real, @imaginary)

END
GO
```

Implementing Complex Division

Complex division makes use of complex number *conjugates*. The conjugate of the complex number z is represented as $\bar{z}$, which has the same real part as z, and its imaginary part is the negative of the imaginary part of z. The following calculation shows how to perform complex division.

$$z_3 = \frac{z_1}{z_2} =$$

$$\frac{a_1 a_2 + b_1 b_2}{a_2^2 + b_2^2} + \frac{a_2 b_1 - a_1 b_2}{a_2^2 + b_2^2} i$$

Explanation:

The conjugate of the complex number z is $\bar{z}$:

$$z = a + bi, \bar{z} = a - bi$$

$$z + \bar{z} = 2a, z \cdot \bar{z} = a^2 + b^2$$

$$\frac{a_1 + b_1 i}{a_2 + b_2 i} =$$

$$\frac{a_1 + b_1 i}{a_2 + b_2 i} \cdot \frac{a_2 - b_2 i}{a_2 - b_2 i} =$$

$$\frac{(a_1 a_2 + b_1 b_2) + (a_2 b_1 - a_1 b_2) i}{a_2^2 + b_2^2}$$

$$\frac{a_1 a_2 + b_1 b_2}{a_2^2 + b_2^2} + \frac{a_2 b_1 - a_1 b_2}{a_2^2 + b_2^2} i$$

Implementing Complex Division with a User-Defined Function

Like the previous functions that implement complex arithmetic, you can create the `dbo.cxDivide` function implementing the formulas that calculate the real and imaginary parts of the result complex number. This is shown in Listing 11-62.

Listing 11-62: Creation Script for the dbo.cxDivide Function

```
---------------------------------------------------------------------
-- Complex Divide                                                   --
-- z1 / z2 =                                                        --
-- ((a1*a2 + b1*b2)/(a2² + b2²)) + ((a2*b1 - a1*b2)/(a2² + b2²))i --
--                                                                  --
-- Explanation:                                                     --
--              _                                                   --
-- z = a + bi, z = a - bi                                           --
--                                                                  --
--     _         _                                                  --
-- z + z = 2a, z * z = a² + b²                                      --
-- z1 / z2 =                                                        --
--                                                                  --
--     _       _                                                    --
-- (z1*z2)/(z2*z2) =                                                --
-- ((a1 + b1i)*(a2 - b2i))/(a2² + b2²) =                            --
-- ((a1*a2 + b1*b2) + (a2*b1 - a1*b2)i)/(a2² + b2²) =               --
-- ((a1*a2 + b1*b2)/(a2² + b2²)) + ((a2*b1 - a1*b2)/(a2² + b2²))i --
---------------------------------------------------------------------
CREATE FUNCTION dbo.cxDivide(
  @cx1 as complex,
  @cx2 as complex)
RETURNS complex
AS

BEGIN

  IF dbo.cxValid(@cx1) = 0 OR dbo.cxValid(@cx2) = 0
    RETURN NULL

  DECLARE
    @a1       AS decimal(19,9),
    @b1       AS decimal(19,9),
    @a2       AS decimal(19,9),
    @b2       AS decimal(19,9)

  DECLARE
    @real      AS decimal(19,9),
    @imaginary AS decimal(19,9)

  SET @a1 = dbo.cxGetReal(@cx1)
  SET @a2 = dbo.cxGetReal(@cx2)
  SET @b1 = dbo.cxGetImaginary(@cx1)
  SET @b2 = dbo.cxGetImaginary(@cx2)
```

```
--  ((a1*a2 + b1*b2)/(a2² + b2²)) + ((a2*b1 - a1*b2)/(a2² + b2²))i
SET @real =      (@a1*@a2 + @b1*@b2)/(@a2*@a2 + @b2*@b2)
SET @imaginary = (@a2*@b1 - @a1*@b2)/(@a2*@a2 + @b2*@b2)


RETURN dbo.cxStrForm(@real, @imaginary)


END
GO
```

Polar Forms of Complex Numbers and Calculating Vector Sizes

Complex numbers can be also represented in a polar form (r, θ). The polar form uses the size of the vector (r), which is the distance between the origin and the point (a, b) in the complex plane. The angle (θ) is the angle between the real axis and the vector representing the complex number. Figure 11-4 shows the polar form of a complex number.

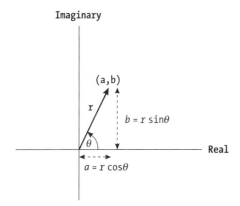

Figure 11-4: Polar form of a complex number

The size (r) of the complex number *z* is also referred to as the magnitude of *z*, or the absolute value of *z*, or the modulus of *z*, and it is the size of the vector representing the complex number. The Pythagorean theorem is used to calculate the vector size. Think of a triangle formed from the points (0, 0), (a, 0), (a, b). According to the Pythagorean theorem, the diagonal's length (r) is the square root of the sum of the triangle's sides, raised by the power of 2:

$$r = |z| = |a + bi| = \sqrt{a^2 + b^2}$$

Figure 11-5 shows the triangle that is formed.

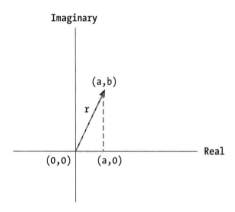

Figure 11-5: Geometrical depiction of a complex number's vector size, $r = |z| = \sqrt{a^2 = b^2}$

Now you can represent a complex number as $z = r\cos\theta + ir\sin\theta$, which supplies the grounds for Euler's equation, which is shown next and is widely used in complex algebra:

$$z = re^{i\theta}$$
$$e^{i\theta} = \cos\theta + i\sin\theta$$

Calculating Vector Size with a User-Defined Function

You can write a user-defined function that calculates the vector size by simply implementing the Pythagorean theorem, as shown in Listing 11-63.

Listing 11-63: Creation Script for the dbo.cxVectorSize Function

```
-----------------------------------------------
-- Complex Vector Length                  --
-- r = |z| = |a + bi| =                   --
-- Pythagoras: SQRT(a² + b²)              --
-----------------------------------------------
CREATE FUNCTION dbo.cxVectorSize(
  @cx as complex)
RETURNS decimal(19,9)
AS

BEGIN

  IF dbo.cxValid(@cx) = 0
    RETURN NULL

  DECLARE
    @real      AS decimal(19,9),
    @imaginary AS decimal(19,9)

  SET @real      = dbo.cxGetReal(@cx)
  SET @imaginary = dbo.cxGetImaginary(@cx)

  -- r = SQRT(a² + b²)
  RETURN SQRT(@real*@real + @imaginary*@imaginary)

END
GO
```

You've now probably got the general idea of how to implement complex algebra with UDFs. You can continue on and implement other complex functions that you might need to use in your implementations, such as finding the nth root of a complex number, and so on.

Implementations of the Complex Functions

All this work with functions that manipulate complex numbers has benefits. It is a good exercise both in writing functions and in complex algebra, and it is also a cool topic in its own right; however, the fact that you can now manipulate complex numbers in the server itself has implications in practical terms, as well.

You can store large amounts of complex numbers in tables and issue queries against them from your client application, and then navigate with record sets on the result of the query. The client application does not need to store such amounts of data locally. Furthermore, some applications work on massive amounts of base complex data but only need aggregate results calculated on the set of base data. This reduces round trips between the client and the server and exploits the database's powerful capabilities in manipulating sets. To give you a sense of what you can do with complex numbers and how you can manipulate them, we will first show you how you can use the complex functions in your queries, and then present an example of their implementation in the sound- and image-processing world.

Using the Complex Functions

To try out the complex functions, you can create a simple table with two columns that will store complex numbers, and then you can issue a few queries against that table. Consider, for example, the table T1 shown in Listing 11-64, which is populated with sample complex numbers.

Listing 11-64: A Table Populated with Sample Complex Numbers

```
CREATE TABLE T1
(
  key_col int NOT NULL PRIMARY KEY,
  cx1 complex NOT NULL,
  cx2 complex NOT NULL
)

INSERT INTO T1 VALUES(1, '5 + 2i', '2 + 4i')
INSERT INTO T1 VALUES(2, '2 + 9i', '4 + 5i')
INSERT INTO T1 VALUES(3, '7 + 4i', '3 + 2i')
INSERT INTO T1 VALUES(4, '3 + 2i', '6 + 3i')
INSERT INTO T1 VALUES(5, '4 + 3i', '7 + 2i')
INSERT INTO T1 VALUES(6, '1 + 4i', '4 + 3i')
INSERT INTO T1 VALUES(7, '7 + 2i', '8 + 1i')
INSERT INTO T1 VALUES(8, '2 + 3i', '3 + 6i')
INSERT INTO T1 VALUES(9, '3 + 6i', '2 + 8i')
INSERT INTO T1 VALUES(10, '2 + 1i', '3 + 2i')
```

To perform addition, subtraction, multiplication, and division between each pair, you simply embed the complex functions in a query, such as the one shown in Listing 11-65.

Listing 11-65: Embedding the Complex Functions in a Query

```
SELECT
  key_col,
  cx1,
  cx2,
  dbo.cxAdd(cx1, cx2)      AS cxAdd,
  dbo.cxSubtract(cx1, cx2) AS cxSubtract,
  dbo.cxMult(cx1, cx2)     AS cxMult,
  dbo.cxDivide(cx1, cx2)   AS cxDivide
FROM
  T1
```

The results are shown in Table 11-4.

Table 11-4: Complex Arithmetic Operations on Pairs of Complex Numbers

key_col	cx1	cx2	cxAdd	cxSubtract	cxMultiply	cxDivide
1	5 + 2i	2 + 4i	7 + 6i	3 – 2i	2 + 24i	0.9 – 0.8i
2	2 + 9i	4 + 5i	6 + 14i	–2 + 4i	–37 + 46i	1.29268292 + 0.63414634i
3	7 + 4i	3 + 2i	10 + 6i	4 + 2i	13 + 26i	2.23076923 – 0.15384615i
4	3 + 2i	6 + 3i	9 + 5i	–3 – 1i	12 + 21i	0.53333333 + 0.06666666i
5	4 + 3i	7 + 2i	11 + 5i	–3 + 1i	22 + 29i	0.64150943 + 0.24528301i
6	1 + 4i	4 + 3i	5 + 7i	–3 + 1i	–8 + 19i	0.64 + 0.52i
7	7 + 2i	8 + 1i	15 + 3i	–1 + 1i	54 + 23i	0.89230769 + 0.13846153i
8	2 + 3i	3 + 6i	5 + 9i	–1 – 3i	–12 + 21i	0.53333333 – 0.06666666i
9	3 + 6i	2 + 8i	5 + 14i	1 – 2i	–42 + 36i	0.79411764 – 0.17647058i
10	2 + 1i	3 + 2i	5 + 3i	–1 – 1i	4 + 7i	0.61538461 – 0.07692307i

Performing aggregate complex arithmetic operations is a bit more difficult, but it is also possible. Suppose you want to calculate the sum of the products of all of the pairs of complex numbers in table T1. Although UDFs are very powerful and provide a lot of functionality, T-SQL does not permit you to develop user-defined aggregate functions that operate on sets of rows and can be embedded in a query like any other system-supplied aggregate functions, such as SUM().

You can, however use a trick. T-SQL allows you to issue an assignment query where you do not return the results of the query to the client application, but rather, assign a value to a variable. You can declare a variable representing a complex number and initialize it with '0 + 0i'. You can use this variable in a query that iterates through all rows in the table and for each row adds the result of the product between each row's pair of complex numbers. Such an example is presented in Listing 11-66.

Listing 11-66: Performing Aggregate Computations with Complex Functions

```
DECLARE @sumproduct AS complex
SET @sumproduct = '0 + 0i'

SELECT
  @sumproduct = dbo.cxAdd(@sumproduct, dbo.cxMult(cx1, cx2))
FROM
  T1

PRINT 'The sum product of the vectors is: ' + @sumproduct

The sum product of the vectors is: 8 + 252i
```

Sound and Image Processing

The purpose of the following example is to start you thinking about possible uses for manipulating complex numbers in your database. It is a theoretical idea and its practical implementations have not been completely tested yet.

The example deals with data representing a sound wave. The data can be stored in a SQL Server table, where each row represents a sample of a sound level at a certain point in time. Listing 11-67 shows how the SoundWave table might look.

Listing 11-67: Original Sound Wave in the Spatial Domain

```
CREATE TABLE SoundWave
(
  time_index  int            NOT NULL
                             PRIMARY KEY,
  sound_level decimal (19, 9) NOT NULL
)
```

Suppose this table holds data for a 5-minute CD-quality track. With a sample rate of 44.1 kHz, the table will hold around 13,230,000 rows (44,100 samples per second for 300 seconds). The purpose of the following process is to produce a filtered sound wave (original sound with certain sound effects and equalizing effects) in the table FilteredSoundWave, based on a filter that exists in a table called Filter. Listing 11-68 shows how the Filter table might look.

Listing 11-68: Filter in the Frequency Domain

```
CREATE TABLE Filter
(
  frequency_index int          NOT NULL
                               PRIMARY KEY,
  filter_vector   complex      NOT NULL
)
```

The problem is that the Filter table holds data in the frequency domain while the SoundWave table holds data in the spatial domain. Before applying the filter to the sound wave, you will first need to transform the sound wave to the frequency domain. This can be done using *Fourier complex transformations*, which involve a mathematical algorithm. We will not discuss Fourier transformations here because it is a whole topic in its own right, but suppose you were supplied with functions that implement Fourier transformations, or even wrote them yourself. You could then apply Fourier transformations on the base data and store the result in the table TransformedSoundWave, which might look like the one shown in Listing 11-69.

Listing 11-69: TransformedSoundWave in the Frequency Domain

```
CREATE TABLE TransformedSoundWave
(
  frequency_index int          NOT NULL
                               PRIMARY KEY,
  signal_vector   complex      NOT NULL
)
```

Each row in the TransformedSoundWave table holds the frequency index and a complex number. The vector size of the complex number represents the magnitude of the signal, and the angle of the vector represents the signal's phase shift. Now, the filter is applied to the sound wave by simply performing a complex multiplication between the filter's vectors and the sound wave's vectors.

Suppose you want to store the filtered sound wave in the frequency domain in the table TransformedFilteredSoundWave, which has the same structure as the table TransformedSoundWave. You could issue the query shown in Listing 11-70.

Listing 11-70: Storing the FilteredSoundWave in the Frequency Domain in a Table

```
INSERT INTO TransformedFilteredSoundWave
  SELECT
    T.frequency_index,
    dbo.cxMult(T.signal_vector, F.filter_vector) AS signal_vector
  FROM
      TransformedSoundWave AS T
    JOIN
      Filter AS F ON T.frequency_index = F.frequency_index
```

Now all that is left to do is apply Fourier's inverse transformation to transform the filtered sound wave in the frequency domain back to a sound wave in the spatial domain. You could store the results in the table FilteredSoundWave, which has the same structure as the table SoundWave. Aside from saving all the round trips between the client and the server, there's also benefit in the fact that you can store and manage your sound data centrally in the database server. A simple process could later download the sound wave to a .wav file.

Note that the purpose of this example was to give you an idea of how you can use the complex functions in your database. It was meant to be as simple as possible. In practice, you might not need the intermediate tables that were presented here, because some calculations can also be performed by using functions embedded in your queries instead of storing intermediate results in tables.

A similar process to the one described here can be applied to image processing, where graphic filters are used to produce image effects.

SQL Puzzle 11-1: Formatting Dates

For a long time now, programmers have struggled when they wanted to convert a datetime value to a character string. You have the CONVERT() function (discussed in Chapter 4), with the third parameter being the style of the converted datetime value, but you must choose a style code from a list of given styles. Your task is to create a function with the following header:

```
CREATE FUNCTION dbo.format_date
(
  @date        AS datetime,
  @formatstring AS varchar(100)
)
RETURNS varchar(100)
AS
...
```

Here, the `@date` parameter is the `datetime` value you need to convert, and the `@formatstring` parameter is a string containing codes, each of which can represent a different date part, to be replaced with the actual date part value from the `@date` parameter. The following table lists the codes for the date parts.

Code	Meaning
yyyy	Four digit year
yy	Two digit year
mm	Month with leading zero
m	Month without leading zero
dd	Day with leading zero
d	Day without leading zero
hh	Hour with leading zero
h	Hour without leading zero
nn	Minutes with leading zero
n	Minutes without leading zero
ss	Seconds with leading zero
s	Seconds without leading zero
ms	Three digit milliseconds with leading zeros

Your function should return the output shown here for the following invocations:

```
SELECT dbo.format_date('2000-09-08 07:06:05.432',
                       'yyyy-mm-dd hh:nn:ss.ms')
```

```
2000-09-08 07:06:05.433
```

```
SELECT dbo.format_date('2000-09-08 07:06:05.432',
                       'yy-m-d h:n:s.ms')
```

```
00-9-8 7:6:5.433
```

```
SELECT dbo.format_date('2000-09-08 07:06:05.432',
                       'dd/mm/yy')
```

```
08/09/00
```

The answer to this puzzle can be found on pages 694–700.

Temporary Tables

IF YOU READ MOST of this book (and we certainly hope you will), then you will be armed to handle most situations without having to resort to using temporary tables. Temporary tables do involve extra overhead, as well as extra programming effort. However, they are useful for doing work that requires multiple passes, to avoid doing repetitive work, or to do work that cannot be done any other way. They also allow you to simplify complex queries. SQL Server has had the capability of creating temporary tables since the Sybase days.

When ANSI-92 support was introduced in version 6.5, the need for temporary tables was reduced but not eliminated. This chapter will show you how to create and use temporary tables so that you can reduce the workload on the server and to provide set-level solutions without resorting to cursors. (Cursors are discussed in Chapter 15.)

Understanding Temporary Objects

Before delving into the nuts and bolts of temporary tables, it's worth taking a look at the role of the tempdb database. As its name implies, tempdb is the repository of temporary objects. When you create temporary tables, as described shortly, they reside in tempdb, just as temporary stored procedures do.

When SQL Server is stopped and then restarted, a brand-new copy of tempdb is built. All traces of anything previously residing in tempdb are removed. In other words, if you create a "permanent" object inside tempdb, it will vanish when SQL Server is next restarted.

If you truly want certain objects to appear inside tempdb every time SQL Server is started, then you will have to create them inside the model database. The model database is the one from which all other databases are "cookie-cut." For example, if you want certain datatypes to exist in tempdb, then run sp_addtype for them in model. Bear in mind that all new databases will have copies of the objects created in model, not just tempdb.

Another alternative for keeping objects permanently in tempdb is to create a stored procedure that creates the required objects on startup. Just use sp_procoption to designate that the procedure be executed at startup. This way, you circumvent having objects in the model database, and consequently, in all new databases.

Creating Temporary Tables

Temporary tables are created in the same way you create a permanent table—with a CREATE TABLE or a SELECT INTO statement. The difference comes in the naming of the table. Permanent table names must conform to the rules for identifiers, and temporary table names begin with either # or ##.

Temporary tables are not created in the current database but instead reside in tempdb. If you are running many queries that use temporary tables, you should consider expanding tempdb. All users are allowed to create temporary tables.

Creating Local Temporary Tables

Tables beginning with # are local to the session in which they are created. They are not visible to any other session, not even to one from the same host or login. This means that a number of sessions can all create a local temporary table with the same name without clobbering each other. How is this possible?

When you create a temporary table, SQL Server takes the name you give it and appends a system-generated suffix. Typically, you will see the name plus a lot of underscores, followed by a 12-digit number with leading zeroes. The suffix, including the underscores, pads the name out to 128 characters, and because of the addition of the suffix, you cannot make your table name the full 128 characters. The name you provide, including the #, cannot be over 116 characters.

If you were to create a local temporary table in one session and then run the system stored procedure sp_help from inside tempdb in another session, you would see a table beginning with the same name as your table but with the underscores and numerical suffix added.

The sample code in Listing 12-1 shows you how to create a local temporary table from a SELECT INTO statement.

Listing 12-1: Creating a Temporary Table with a SELECT INTO

```
SELECT
   CustomerID,
   OrderDate,
   ShippedDate
INTO
   #OrderInfo
FROM
    Orders
```

Temporary tables are automatically destroyed when they go out of scope or the user who created them disconnects from SQL Server. A temporary table goes out of scope when the stored procedure or trigger that created it completes its execution. (Stored procedures and triggers are discussed in Chapters 9 and 10, respectively.) If a stored procedure creates a local temporary table and then calls another stored procedure, the called procedure (and any procedures that it calls) has access to the table. However, the *called* procedure can create a temporary table with the same name as that in the *calling* procedure. In this case, the called procedure references its own table and not the one from the calling procedure.

> **NOTE** *In SQL Server releases prior to 7.0, if a stored procedure referenced a temporary table that did not exist, the* CREATE PROC *statement would fail. This meant that you had to create the temporary table just to create the procedure. Due to deferred name resolution, this problem was eliminated in release 7.0.*

You can also use a DROP TABLE statement to destroy temporary tables in the same way that you destroy a permanent table.

Creating Global Temporary Tables

A global temporary table's name begins with ##. It is visible to any user connection during its lifetime. Unlike local temporary tables, there is only one instance of a global temporary table with any particular name, so you have to be careful that one with the same name does not already exist when you go to create yours. If you build stored procedures that create a global temporary table, you will be responsible for ensuring that there are no collisions when they are executed.

You should be aware that global temporary tables can be accessed by anyone. You do not grant or deny permission. Indeed, if you execute a DENY statement from within tempdb, the statement will execute but all users will still be allowed access.

The sample code in Listing 12-2 shows you how to create a global temporary table with a CREATE TABLE statement.

Listing 12-2: Creating a Global Temporary Table

```
CREATE TABLE ##CustomerSales
(
  CustomerID char (6) NOT NULL,
  Year       smallint NOT NULL,
  Sales      money    NOT NULL
)
```

The lifetime of global temporary tables is somewhat different from that of local temporary tables. The global temporary table will be dropped automatically when the session that created it ends *and when all other processes that reference it have stopped referencing it.* Therefore, even though the process that created the table may have ended, if another process is still using it, then it will still be alive.

If, after you create a global temporary table, you run the system stored procedure sp_help from inside tempdb, you will see the table name appear in the list with no system-generated suffix.

Using Temporary Tables

Although temporary tables are very much like permanent tables, there are some restrictions. Unlike permanent tables, you cannot have foreign keys on a temporary table. If you attempt to create a temporary table with a FOREIGN KEY constraint, the statement will execute and create the table. However, the foreign key will not be created and you will get a warning message.

User-defined functions (UDFs) cannot access temporary tables. (UDFs are discussed in Chapter 11.) If you attempt to create a temporary table inside a function, the CREATE FUNCTION statement will fail. You are, however, allowed to use a table variable inside UDFs. (The table variable is discussed in Chapter 6.)

The table variable has restrictions that do not apply to temporary tables. Once a table variable has been created, you cannot alter the table, which includes adding or removing columns or constraints. You also cannot add any indexes. These restrictions do not apply to temporary tables, with the exception that you may not add FOREIGN KEY constraints, as mentioned previously. Finally, since a table variable is exactly that—a variable—it does not survive beyond the execution of the current batch.

The list of table variable restrictions does not end there. You cannot do a SELECT INTO, BULK INSERT, or INSERT EXEC into a table variable. You also cannot pass a table variable as a parameter to a stored procedure, which means you can only create a temporary table and then let the procedure have a go at it.

However, there are efficiencies to be gained from using table variables instead of temporary tables. There is less recompilation overhead with table variables than with temporary tables. A stored procedure will be recompiled each time a SELECT goes against a temporary table that has been CREATEd or ALTERed within the same procedure in which the SELECT is executed.

In releases prior to SQL Server 2000, it was not possible to create a temporary table within a trigger. This was because the CREATE TABLE statement was not permitted, even for temporary tables. You could, however, use a SELECT INTO to circumvent this restriction. This limitation is now removed.

You can only create a temporary table once inside a stored procedure or trigger—if you create one and then drop it within a stored procedure or trigger, you cannot re-create it within that same stored procedure or trigger. (Stored procedures are discussed in Chapter 9.) You cannot create a trigger on a temporary table. (Triggers are discussed in Chapter 10.)

Avoiding Repetitive Work by Using a Temporary Table

As mentioned at the beginning of the chapter, temporary tables do involve extra overhead and programming effort compared to some other solutions, but they do have their uses. One legitimate use of a temporary table is in situations where you will be doing repetitive querying for the same rows in a table or tables, and then joining onto those rows for several subsequent queries. (Joins are covered in Chapter 1.) This is best explained through an example, and you'll use the Northwind database.

Suppose you need to produce three separate result sets. The first will give a list of all of the client information for those clients in the NAFTA countries—Canada, USA, and Mexico—who did not place orders in 1996 but placed orders in 1997. The second will contain the 1998 orders for those customers found in the first result set, and the third batch will list the order details for those orders. Although the information you are retrieving could be obtained through a single SELECT, much of the information would be repeated—thus the requirement for separate SELECTs.

Temporary tables could be avoided in this scenario, but the code can get to be difficult to read. The code in Listing 12-3 shows the solution for retrieving the first list of customers described in this scenario without using temporary tables.

Listing 12-3: NAFTA Customers with No Orders in 1996 but with Orders in 1997

```
SELECT
  C.*
FROM
    Customers AS C
WHERE NOT EXISTS
(
  SELECT
    *
  FROM
      Orders AS O1
  WHERE
      O1.CustomerID = C.CustomerID
    AND
      O1.OrderDate BETWEEN '19960101' AND '19961231'
)
```

```
AND EXISTS
(
  SELECT
    *
  FROM
      Orders AS O2
  WHERE
      O2.CustomerID = C.CustomerID
    AND
      O2.OrderDate BETWEEN '19970101' AND '19971231'
)
AND
      C.Country IN ('Canada', 'USA', 'Mexico')
```

This code shows two correlated subqueries to determine whether orders were or were not placed during 1996 and 1997, respectively, plus a filter on the country. (Correlated subqueries are discussed in Chapter 2.)

The second and third required results sets take the code in Listing 12-3 and add to it. To get the list of orders placed by these customers, you would join onto the Orders table, as seen in Listing 12-4.

Listing 12-4: Orders in 1998 for NAFTA Customers with No Orders in 1996 but with Orders in 1997

```
SELECT
  O.*
FROM
    Customers AS C
  JOIN
    Orders    AS O  ON O.CustomerID = C.CustomerID
WHERE NOT EXISTS
(
  SELECT
    *
  FROM
      Orders AS O1
  WHERE
      O1.CustomerID = C.CustomerID
    AND
      O1.OrderDate BETWEEN '19960101' AND '19961231'
)
```

```
AND EXISTS
(
  SELECT
    *
  FROM
      Orders AS O2
  WHERE
      O2.CustomerID = C.CustomerID
    AND
      O2.OrderDate BETWEEN '19970101' AND '19971231'
)
AND
    C.Country IN ('Canada', 'USA', 'Mexico')
AND
    O.OrderDate BETWEEN '19980101' AND '19981231'
```

As you can see, the code gets more complicated, and most of it is repeated from the previous query in Listing 12-3. After all that, only six rows are returned. The next step is even worse—you take the code from Listing 12-4 and add to it to get the order details, as seen in Listing 12-5.

Listing 12-5: Order Details in 1998 for NAFTA Customers with No Orders in 1996 but with Orders in 1997

```
SELECT
  OD.*
FROM
    Customers      AS C
  JOIN
    Orders         AS O  ON O.CustomerID = C.CustomerID
  JOIN
    [Order Details] AS OD ON OD.OrderID    = O.OrderID
WHERE NOT EXISTS
(
  SELECT
    *
  FROM
      Orders AS O1
  WHERE
      O1.CustomerID = C.CustomerID
    AND
      O1.OrderDate BETWEEN '19960101' AND '19961231'
)
```

```
AND EXISTS
(
  SELECT
    *
  FROM
      Orders AS O2
  WHERE
      O2.CustomerID = C.CustomerID
    AND
      O2.OrderDate BETWEEN '19970101' AND '19971231'
)
AND
    C.Country IN ('Canada', 'USA', 'Mexico')
AND
    O.OrderDate BETWEEN '19980101' AND '19981231'
```

As you can see, things are getting repetitive and long. Considering that only six customers meet the criteria, it seems a shame to go to all that trouble.

Using a temporary table can simplify things in this example. With or without the temporary table, you still have to pick up the customers, so that part will not get simpler. However, those customers can be saved into a temporary table to be used by subsequent queries. The code to do this is shown in Listing 12-6.

Listing 12-6: Creating a Temporary Table of NAFTA Customers with No Orders in 1996 but with Orders in 1997

```
SELECT
  C.*
INTO
  #NAFTA
FROM
    Customers AS C
WHERE NOT EXISTS
(
  SELECT
    *
  FROM
      Orders AS O1
  WHERE
      O1.CustomerID = C.CustomerID
    AND
      O1.OrderDate BETWEEN '19960101' AND '19961231'
)
```

```
AND EXISTS
(
  SELECT
    *
  FROM
      Orders AS O2
  WHERE
      O2.CustomerID = C.CustomerID
    AND
      O2.OrderDate BETWEEN '19970101' AND '19971231'
)
AND
    C.Country IN ('Canada', 'USA', 'Mexico')

CREATE UNIQUE INDEX #IDX on #NAFTA (CustomerID)
```

All that is different between Listings 12-3 and 12-6 is that the SELECT has been changed to a SELECT INTO. (The SELECT INTO statement is covered in Chapter 3.) The consequence is that no rows are returned to the calling program; they have been saved in the temporary table, #NAFTA. Also, a nonclustered index, #IDX, has been created on CustomerID to help support subsequent queries.

You still need the rows in #NAFTA, so the query in Listing 12-7 retrieves them for you.

Listing 12-7: NAFTA Customers with No Orders in 1996 but with Orders in 1997

```
SELECT
    *
FROM
    #NAFTA
```

So far, what you have done in a single query in Listing 12-3 has now been replaced by two queries in Listings 12-6 and 12-7. Surely, there has to be some payback for your trouble.

Well, here it is. Returning the rows for the orders for these customers is now reduced to the query shown in Listing 12-8.

Listing 12-8: Orders in 1998 for NAFTA Customers with No Orders in 1996 but with Orders in 1997

```
SELECT
  O.*
FROM
    #NAFTA AS C
  JOIN
    Orders AS O ON O.CustomerID = C.CustomerID
WHERE
    O.OrderDate BETWEEN '19980101' AND '19981231'
```

Finally, the order details are returned by the query in Listing 12-9.

Listing 12-9: Orders Details in 1998 for NAFTA Customers with No Orders in 1996 but with Orders in 1997

```
SELECT
  OD.*
FROM
    #NAFTA          AS C
  JOIN
    Orders          AS O ON O.CustomerID = C.CustomerID
  JOIN
    [Order Details] AS OD ON OD.OrderID  = O.OrderID
WHERE
    O.OrderDate BETWEEN '19980101' AND '19981231'
```

To get the orders and details in Listings 12-8 and 12-9, you joined on the #NAFTA table. All you needed from it were the keys. While the query to retrieve the customers was simplified (see Listing 12-7), you probably saved more information than you needed overall. The performance of the above retrievals, as measured by statistics I/O, is summarized later in Table 12-1.

Taking a slightly different approach, you can recast the SELECT INTO to save just the CustomerID column in the temporary table, as shown in Listing 12-10.

*Listing 12-10: Creating a Temporary Table of NAFTA CustomerIDs
with No Orders in 1996 but with Orders in 1997*

```
SELECT
  C.CustomerID
INTO
  #NAFTA
FROM
    Customers AS C
WHERE NOT EXISTS
(
  SELECT
    *
  FROM
      Orders AS O1
  WHERE
      O1.CustomerID = C.CustomerID
    AND
      O1.OrderDate BETWEEN '19960101' AND '19961231'
)
AND EXISTS
(
  SELECT
    *
  FROM
      Orders AS O2
  WHERE
      O2.CustomerID = C.CustomerID
    AND
      O2.OrderDate BETWEEN '19970101' AND '19971231'
)
AND
    C.Country IN ('Canada', 'USA', 'Mexico')

CREATE UNIQUE INDEX #IDX on #NAFTA (CustomerID)
```

Now you can join onto this table for all of the remaining queries. The queries
for retrieving the orders and their details do not change—just the one for returning
the customer information is altered, as seen in Listing 12-11.

Listing 12-11: NAFTA Customers with No Orders in 1996 but with Orders in 1997

```
SELECT
  c.*
FROM
    #NAFTA    AS T
  JOIN
    Customers AS C ON C.CustomerID = T.CustomerID
```

It's worthwhile comparing the relative query cost of each of the three techniques just discussed. Check out Table 12-1 for the numbers.

Table 12-1: Relative Query Costs

Method	Relative Cost (%)
No temporary table	40.81
Temporary table of Customers	29.37
Temporary table of Customer IDs	29.40

As you can see in Table 12-1, either of the two methods that use temporary tables is superior to the situation where no temporary table is used.

The next example you'll see uses a global temporary table and is based upon an actual real-world business problem. In this example, the problem has been recast to use the tables available in the Northwind database, but the idea is the same.

The company wants a list of quarterly sales for each year, for each customer. However, it wants these reports in separate files, one per year. You could create a number of scripts to do this and run each separately through osql or isql, but this looks like a lot of work. You could create a stored procedure or view and then have single osql or isql invocations for each of these. However, this is still a lot of bother, though it is less trouble than the previous solution. You also wouldn't want to have to add scripts as time progresses through the years. Needless to say, you want to have a minimal impact on the system.

The temporary table solution to the problem requires a pivot table with Year and CustomerID as the key and the total sales for the four quarters as the attributes. (Pivot tables are discussed in Chapter 4.) This can be accomplished with the code in Listing 12-12.

Listing 12-12: Pivot Table for Quarterly Sales per Year per Customer

```
SELECT
  YEAR (O.OrderDate) AS Year,
  O.CustomerID,
  SUM (CASE
        WHEN DATEPART(qq, O.OrderDate) = 1
          THEN OD.Quantity * OD.UnitPrice
        ELSE 0
      END) AS Q1,
  SUM (CASE
        WHEN DATEPART(qq, O.OrderDate) = 2
          THEN OD.Quantity * OD.UnitPrice
        ELSE 0
      END) AS Q2,
  SUM (CASE
        WHEN DATEPART(qq, O.OrderDate) = 3
          THEN OD.Quantity * OD.UnitPrice
        ELSE 0
      END) AS Q3,
  SUM (CASE
        WHEN DATEPART(qq, O.OrderDate) = 4
          THEN OD.Quantity * OD.UnitPrice
        ELSE 0
      END) AS Q4
FROM
    Orders        AS O
  JOIN
    [Order Details] AS OD ON OD.OrderID = O.OrderID
GROUP BY
  YEAR (O.OrderDate),
  O.CustomerID
ORDER BY
  Year,
  O.CustomerID
```

The optimizer uses a single scan on each table, resulting in 21 and 10 I/Os for the Orders and Order Details tables, respectively. However, if you want a report for just a single year's sales, the query can be modified by adding a WHERE clause to filter the OrderDate column and removing the year from the SELECT list and GROUP BY and ORDER BY clauses. This is done in Listing 12-13.

Listing 12-13: Quarterly Sales per Customer for a Single Year

```
SELECT
  O.CustomerID,
  SUM (CASE
        WHEN DATEPART(qq, O.OrderDate) = 1
          THEN OD.Quantity * OD.UnitPrice
        ELSE 0
      END) AS Q1,
  SUM (CASE
        WHEN DATEPART(qq, O.OrderDate) = 2
          THEN OD.Quantity * OD.UnitPrice
        ELSE 0
      END) AS Q2,
  SUM (CASE
        WHEN DATEPART(qq, O.OrderDate) = 3
          THEN OD.Quantity * OD.UnitPrice
        ELSE 0
      END) AS Q3,
  SUM (CASE
        WHEN DATEPART(qq, O.OrderDate) = 4
          THEN OD.Quantity * OD.UnitPrice
        ELSE 0
      END) AS Q4
FROM
    Orders          AS O
  JOIN
    [Order Details] AS OD ON OD.OrderID = O.OrderID
WHERE
    O.OrderDate BETWEEN '19960101' AND '19961231'
GROUP BY
  O.CustomerID
ORDER BY
  O.CustomerID
```

This time, the optimizer increases the scan count and logical I/Os on the Order Details table to 152 and 305, respectively, while the numbers for the Orders table have not changed from the solution shown in Listing 12-12. This type of performance hit would have to be taken for each year for which you needed a report. A better solution is to take the I/O hit up front, store the results in a temporary table, and then pull the desired rows from the table. The query in Listing 12-12 is changed to use a SELECT INTO, as seen in Listing 12-14.

Listing 12-14: Creating a Temporary Table for Quarterly Customer Sales for All Years

```
SELECT
  YEAR (O.OrderDate) AS Year,
  O.CustomerID,
  SUM (CASE
        WHEN DATEPART(qq, O.OrderDate) = 1
          THEN OD.Quantity * OD.UnitPrice
        ELSE 0
      END) AS Q1,
  SUM (CASE
        WHEN DATEPART(qq, O.OrderDate) = 2
          THEN OD.Quantity * OD.UnitPrice
        ELSE 0
      END) AS Q2,
  SUM (CASE
        WHEN DATEPART(qq, O.OrderDate) = 3
          THEN OD.Quantity * OD.UnitPrice
        ELSE 0
      END) AS Q3,
  SUM (CASE
        WHEN DATEPART(qq, O.OrderDate) = 4
          THEN OD.Quantity * OD.UnitPrice
        ELSE 0
      END) AS Q4
INTO
  ##Sales
FROM
    Orders        AS O
  JOIN
    [Order Details] AS OD ON OD.OrderID = O.OrderID
GROUP BY
  YEAR (O.OrderDate),
  O.CustomerID

CREATE UNIQUE CLUSTERED INDEX #IDX on ##Sales (Year, CustomerID)
```

Now that you have your temporary table, you can loop through the years to pick up each report. See the solution in Listing 12-15.

Listing 12-15: Creating Annual Sales Reports from the Global Temporary Table

```
DECLARE
  @MaxYear int,
  @CurYear int,
  @ExecStr varchar (8000)

SELECT
  @CurYear = MIN (YEAR (OrderDate)),  -- first year
  @MaxYear = MAX (YEAR (OrderDate))   -- last year
FROM
  Orders

-- loop through all years
WHILE @CurYear <= @MaxYear
BEGIN
  -- build string to send to xp_cmdshell
  SELECT
    @ExecStr = 'osql -E -w2000 -S.\BMCI03_02 '
             + '-Q"SELECT CustomerID, Q1, Q2, Q3, Q4 '
             + 'FROM ##Sales WHERE Year = '
             + STR (@CurYear, 4)
             + '" -oC:\TEMP\'
             + STR (@CurYear, 4)
             + '.txt'

  -- produce report and save to file
  EXEC master..xp_cmdshell @ExecStr

  -- get next year
  SELECT
    @CurYear = @CurYear + 1
END
```

The xp_cmdshell extended system stored procedure allows you to shell out to the operating system to run a command just as if you were at a command prompt. Here, the string to be executed is created on the fly and is based upon the year for which the report is being created. The -E parameter means that a trusted connection should be used; the -w2000 parameter wraps the output at 2,000 characters; the -S parameter specifies which server to use (this one uses the BMCI03_02 instance on the local server); the -Q parameter is used for a single SQL statement; and the -o parameter identifies the output file.

In the real world, you would create a stored procedure for retrieving the rows for a given year and then replace the SELECT in the osql invocation with a stored procedure call.

Using a Temporary Table to Handle Weird Business Rules

Temporary tables can prove useful when you have complex business rules. For example, suppose you have a complicated query that returns rows, but you need a self-join or a correlated subquery between those rows and a duplicate of those rows. Sure, you can use a derived table, but this would involve creating the derived table twice, and in each case, the derived table would contain identical rows. (Derived tables are discussed in Chapter 2.) In this type of situation, you can populate a temporary table once and then use it for your correlated subquery or self-join.

As an example, suppose Northwind Traders has just declared a new discounting scheme. Every fifth order entitles your customer to a discount. The amount of the discount is based upon the total amount of the four orders leading up to the fifth order. The discounting scheme is represented in Table 12-2.

Table 12-2: Discounting Scheme

Amount of Previous Four Orders	Discount (%)
< $10,000	5
$10,000–$15,000	10
> $15,000	20

This is not as difficult as it looks.

First, you need to determine the total amount of the orders for the customer. Next, you need to determine the sequence of the orders so that you can figure out which one is every fifth order. This is straightforward. All you need to do is a SELECT INTO, grouping on OrderID for all of the customer's orders. This is done in Listing 12-16.

Listing 12-16: Creating a Temporary Table of Order Totals for a Customer

```
SELECT
  IDENTITY (int, 1, 1)             AS Sequence,
  O.OrderID,
  SUM (OD.Quantity * OD.UnitPrice) AS Total
INTO
  #Totals
```

```
FROM
    Orders AS O
  JOIN
    [Order Details] AS OD ON OD.Orderid = o.OrderID
WHERE
    O.CustomerID = 'SAVEA'
GROUP BY
  O.OrderID
ORDER BY
  O.OrderID

CREATE UNIQUE CLUSTERED INDEX #Idx on #Totals (Sequence)
```

The ORDER BY is necessary because you need to have the orders in the sequence in which they were placed. The IDENTITY() function is discussed in Chapter 6. Its purpose is to provide consecutive numbers for the orders. The OrderID is not sufficient for this, since there are many customers placing orders and while the OrderIDs may be in ascending order, those for a particular customer are not necessarily consecutive. The IDENTITY() will give you consecutive sequence numbers.

For example, the customer's OrderIDs could be 5, 7, 21, 45, and 67, which are in numerical order but are not consecutive. Adding an identity column to the table would give sequence values that are consecutive, such as 1, 2, 3, 4, 5.

You then calculate the total sales leading up to every fifth order and apply the discounting scheme to it. This is done in two parts. First you calculate the totals leading up to every fifth order by using a correlated subquery. Every fifth order is determined by taking its sequence number, modulo 5, and comparing to zero. The calculation just described is treated as a derived table so that the discounting scheme can then be applied. The solution is presented in Listing 12-17.

Listing 12-17: Calculating the Discount

```
SELECT
  OrderID,
  Total,
  Previous4,
  CASE
    WHEN Previous4 < 10000.00 THEN 5
    WHEN Previous4 BETWEEN 10000.00 AND 15000.00 THEN 10
    ELSE 20
  END  AS Discount
```

```
FROM
(
  SELECT
    T1.OrderID,
    T2.Total,
    (
      SELECT
        SUM (T2.Total) AS Total
      FROM
          #Totals AS T2
      WHERE
          T2.Sequence > T1.Sequence - 4
        AND
          T2.Sequence < T1.Sequence
    )  AS Previous4
  FROM
    #Totals AS T1
  WHERE
      0 = T1.Sequence % 5
)  AS X
```

This is okay if you wish to apply the discounts retroactively. You have all of the customer's orders at your disposal, right from the beginning. In this way, you are able to determine which order is every fifth order. However, if you purge stale orders, then you would have no way of figuring out which order deserves a discount and how much of a discount to give. To support the discounting scheme, allow yourself to apply the discount at the time of the order, and enable the purging of old data, you could add a column to the Customers table to keep the OrderID of the last "fifth" order. Alternatively, you could arrange your purging strategy to chop orders in groups of five.

Using Temporary Tables to Communicate with the EXEC() Statement

The EXEC() statement is covered in Chapter 9. It allows you to execute dynamic SQL. However, despite its power, it does have some limitations. One such restriction is that any variables declared in the calling code are not available inside the scope of the EXEC(), and vice-versa. This is alright if all you want is to send the information from the calling code to the EXEC(), since you can build the string with the value of the variable built right into it, as shown in Listing 12-18.

Listing 12-18: Sending Variable Information to an EXEC() Call

```
DECLARE
  @IntVal int

SET
  @IntVal = 21

EXEC ('usp_MyProc ' + STR (@IntVal))
```

What do you do if you want to get information *back* from inside the EXEC(), as seen in Listing 12-19? Now you're stuck.

Listing 12-19: Illegal Use of Variable in Call to EXEC()

```
DECLARE
  @Variable varchar (25)

EXEC ('SET @Variable = ''my value''')    -- this won't work
```

One solution is to use a temporary table as a buffer to hold variable contents that you wish to pass between the calling code and the EXEC(). Check out the example in Listing 12-20.

Listing 12-20: Using a Temporary Table to Communicate with an EXEC()

```
DECLARE
  @Variable varchar (25)

CREATE TABLE #tmpvar
(
  Variable varchar (25) NOT NULL
)

EXEC ('INSERT INTO #tmpvar VALUES (''my value'')')

SELECT
  @Variable = Variable
FROM
  #tmpvar

DROP TABLE #tmpvar
PRINT @Variable
```

Removing Duplicates with and without Temporary Tables

From time to time, you encounter tables with duplicate keys or duplicate rows and you need to remove the duplicates. This is often done with a temporary table. First, you do a SELECT INTO to create the temporary table with single occurrences of the duplicate rows. Next, you delete all such occurrences from the original table. Finally, you insert the rows from the temporary table back into the original table. An example of a table with duplicate rows is scripted in Listing 12-21.

Listing 12-21: Creating a Table with Duplicate Rows

```
CREATE TABLE Dupes
(
  ID  int       NOT NULL,
  Txt char (10) NOT NULL
)
GO

INSERT Dupes (ID, Txt) VALUES (1, 'x')
INSERT Dupes (ID, Txt) VALUES (1, 'a')
INSERT Dupes (ID, Txt) VALUES (1, 'x')
INSERT Dupes (ID, Txt) VALUES (1, 'x')
INSERT Dupes (ID, Txt) VALUES (2, 'b')
INSERT Dupes (ID, Txt) VALUES (2, 'x')
INSERT Dupes (ID, Txt) VALUES (2, 'b')
INSERT Dupes (ID, Txt) VALUES (3, 'c')
```

To get the temporary table of distinct rows for which there are duplicates to be removed, you do a SELECT INTO, grouping on all of the columns, with a HAVING clause that tests for COUNT(*) > 1. This is done in Listing 12-22.

Listing 12-22: Creating a Temporary Table of Distinct Rows

```
SELECT
  ID,
  Txt
INTO
  #Singles
FROM
   Dupes
GROUP BY
  ID,
  Txt
HAVING
  COUNT (*) > 1
```

The next step is to remove the duplicates from the original table, Dupes, as shown in Listing 12-23.

Listing 12-23: Removing the Duplicates

```
DELETE d
FROM
    Dupes AS D
  JOIN
    #Singles AS S ON  S.ID  = D.ID
                 AND S.Txt = D.Txt
```

The final step is to insert the rows from the temporary table, #Singles, back into the original table, Dupes. This is done in Listing 12-24.

Listing 12-24: Inserting the Former Duplicates

```
INSERT Dupes
SELECT
  *
FROM
  #Singles
```

Just so that no rows fall through the cracks, the work described in Listings 12-21 through 12-24 should be done in a transaction with repeatable reads. This is because you don't want any rows inserted into the Dupes table that may cause duplicates while you're in the process of trying to eliminate duplicates. (Transactions are discussed in Chapter 7.)

What you just saw is a very common way of removing duplicate rows. There is also a way of doing this without involving a temporary table. It involves altering the table and adding an IDENTITY column. This gives you a way of differentiating rows. You then remove the extra rows with a correlated subquery and finish the job by removing the IDENTITY column. For this exercise, use the Dupes table script in Listing 12-21.

You add the IDENTITY column by doing an ALTER TABLE and adding a new column that has the IDENTITY property. Check out the code in Listing 12-25.

Listing 12-25: Altering the Table to Add an Identity Column

```
ALTER TABLE Dupes
ADD
  Ident int NOT NULL IDENTITY (1, 1)
```

Now, all of your rows are unique. You can now delete those rows that were originally duplicated by carrying out the correlated subquery shown in Listing 12-26.

Listing 12-26: Deleting Duplicates with a Correlated Subquery

```
DELETE D1
FROM
    Dupes AS D1
WHERE
    D1.Ident >
(
  SELECT
    MIN (D2.Ident)
  FROM
      Dupes AS D2
  WHERE
      D2.ID  = D1.ID
    AND
      D2.Txt = D1.Txt
)
```

Alternatively, you could also use a join, as seen in Listing 12-27.

Listing 12-27: Deleting Duplicates with a Join

```
DELETE D1
FROM
    Dupes AS D1
  JOIN
    Dupes AS D2 ON  D2.ID    = D1.ID
                AND D2.Txt   = D1.Txt
                AND D1.Ident > D2.Ident
```

The queries in Listings 12-26 and 12-27 delete all duplicates, except for the first such occurrence, using the identity column to discriminate between duplicates. The final task is to remove the identity column, as depicted in Listing 12-28.

Listing 12-28: Removing the Identity Column

```
ALTER TABLE Dupes
DROP COLUMN
  Ident
```

Here, too, you can run into trouble if things are not done as a transaction. Prior to altering the table, all client code expects the table not to have the extra column. Consequently, the client code can fail while you are running your duplicate-removal script. If you do this as a transaction, a Schema-Modify lock will be in place on the table, and no other process will be able to access the table.

One major difference between the two techniques just described is that you have to be the table's owner or a member of the *db_owner* or *sysadmin* roles in order to alter the table. These roles are very powerful, and membership should not be granted to an average user. If a regular user must be allowed to remove duplicates, then you are committed to using a temporary table.

A final note on duplicates—consider adding a PRIMARY KEY or UNIQUE constraint immediately after eliminating the duplicates. This way, you obviate the need to go back and get rid of them in the future. This, too, can be done within the scope of the transaction.

SQL Puzzle 12-1: Creating a Temporary Table and Cursor-Free Solution

This puzzle uses the pubs database. You need to implement a bonus scheme for authors based on relative sales and the quantity sold. The authors in the top quartile are to receive $3,000; those in the second, third, and fourth quartiles are to receive $2,000, $1,000, and $0, respectively. Bear in mind that some authors may not have written a book, and some books may not have sold a single copy.

The answer to this puzzle can be found on pages 700–704.

Horizontally Partitioned Views

EVER HAD TO ORGANIZE your documents in a folder and eventually noticed that it was too messy keeping all of your documents in the same folder? What did you do? Probably split your documents up into several folders with some criteria defining which folders should hold which documents. The same thing happens with our databases. At some point they become so large that looking for a piece of data and maintaining large tables becomes too messy.

This chapter introduces partitioned views, which handle such situations by denormalizing your huge table, splitting it into several smaller partitions. Each of the partitions will hold a slice of the rows from the original table; this way, queries that need only a portion of the data can get it by accessing only the relevant partitions. Although this might result in a more complex configuration, the performance improvement you can achieve is worth it in many cases.

SQL Server 2000 introduced many new capabilities to partitioned views, among them the ability to update data through the views, and also, new optimization techniques. This chapter discusses how to set up and use in local and distributed partitioned views in SQL Server 2000 and in earlier versions.

Partitioning Views Prior to SQL Server 2000

With huge tables, intelligent use of indexes is usually the first approach to take when tuning slow-running queries. Indexes hold a copy of the data in a balanced tree form, allowing fast index traversal while the query looks for the desired data, and using indexes usually results in less I/O than scanning the whole table.

Clustered indexes are very efficient for range queries because the leaf level of the index is the actual data, ordered by the key column(s). The problem with clustered indexes is that there can be only one per table because you can physically organize the table's data in only one way. Furthermore, there might be a lot of historical data in the tables that is not frequently accessed.

With huge tables, maintenance tasks take longer and queries are slowed down. Also, the more recent the data is, the more queries request it, so why not split the data? Well, some queries do request both the recent and the historical data. Such scenarios require a solution that splits the data for maintenance reasons and for fast access to specific parts of the data, yet keeps the data together for the queries that need to access the whole set of data. Partitioned views are the solution for such scenarios.

> **NOTE** *Since this section discusses partitioning techniques in versions prior to SQL Server 2000 the code samples and execution plans you will see were taken from SQL Server 7.0 with Service Pack 2. You should expect different execution plans in SQL Server 2000, but the ideas this section tries to emphasize remain the same.*

Setting Up Local Horizontally Partitioned Views

To set up local horizontally partitioned views, you need to create a few tables with almost the same structure as the original huge table. For our example we will use the Orders table, which we will split into partitions, each of which will hold one year's worth of orders. Suppose our original Orders table had the schema shown in Listing 13-1.

Listing 13-1: Original Orders Table Schema

```
CREATE TABLE Orders
(
OrderID     int      NOT NULL
                     CONSTRAINT PK_Orders_OrderID
                       PRIMARY KEY(OrderID),
CustomerID int       NOT NULL,
OrderDate   datetime NOT NULL
/* ... other columns ... */
)
GO
```

When we split it into partitions by year, we first need to make sure that only rows of the relevant year will be allowed in each partition. We can add a CHECK constraint to take care of that, such as CHECK (YEAR(OrderDate) = 1998). Notice in Listing 13-2 that we add another column with a default value holding only the year part of the order date, which has the same value in all of the rows in each partition. We also add a CHECK constraint on that column that checks that it is really the year we want: CHECK (OrderYear = 1998). This additional column and CHECK constraint might look redundant now, but it will become useful when we start querying our data and examining execution plans.

If we have three years' worth of data in our Orders table, we can split it into three partitions with the schema shown in Listing 13-2.

Listing 13-2: Partitioning the Orders Table

```
CREATE TABLE Orders1998
(
OrderID     int      NOT NULL
                     CONSTRAINT PK_Orders1998_OrderID
                       PRIMARY KEY(OrderID),
CustomerID int       NOT NULL,
OrderDate   datetime NOT NULL
                     CONSTRAINT CHK_Orders1998_OrderDate
                       CHECK (YEAR(OrderDate) = 1998),
OrderYear   int      NOT NULL
                     CONSTRAINT DF_Orders1998_OrderYear
                       DEFAULT 1998
                     CONSTRAINT CHK_Orders1998_OrderYear
                       CHECK (OrderYear = 1998),  -- partitioning column
/* ...  other columns ...  */
)
GO


CREATE TABLE Orders1999
(
OrderID     int      NOT NULL
                     CONSTRAINT PK_Orders1999_OrderID
                       PRIMARY KEY(OrderID),
CustomerID int       NOT NULL,
OrderDate   datetime NOT NULL
                     CONSTRAINT CHK_Orders1999_OrderDate
                       CHECK (YEAR(OrderDate) = 1999),
OrderYear   int      NOT NULL
                     CONSTRAINT DF_Orders1999_OrderYear
                       DEFAULT 1999
                     CONSTRAINT CHK_Orders1999_OrderYear
                       CHECK (OrderYear = 1999),  -- partitioning column
/* ...  other columns ...  */
)
GO
```

```
CREATE TABLE Orders2000
(
OrderID     int       NOT NULL
                      CONSTRAINT PK_Orders2000_OrderID
                        PRIMARY KEY(OrderID),
CustomerID int       NOT NULL,
OrderDate  datetime NOT NULL
                      CONSTRAINT CHK_Orders2000_OrderDate
                        CHECK (YEAR(OrderDate) = 2000),
OrderYear  int       NOT NULL
                      CONSTRAINT DF_Orders2000_OrderYear
                        DEFAULT 2000
                      CONSTRAINT CHK_Orders2000_OrderYear
                        CHECK (OrderYear = 2000),  -- partitioning column
/* ... other columns ... */
)
GO
```

Once we have all our partitioned tables set up, we can create a view that assembles all the pieces by using the UNION ALL operator. This way, the partitioning will be transparent for our users and applications—at least, as far as SELECT queries are concerned. The script shown in Listing 13-3 creates the VOrders view that assembles all the pieces together.

Listing 13-3: A View that Assembles Partitioned Tables

```
CREATE VIEW VOrders
AS

SELECT * FROM Orders1998
UNION ALL
SELECT * FROM Orders1999
UNION ALL
SELECT * FROM Orders2000
GO
```

Modifying Local Horizontally Partitioned Views

There is a price we have to pay with this configuration. Prior to SQL Server 2000, partitioned views were not updateable. We can either update our partitioned tables directly, which will require our applications to be aware of the partitioning configuration, or we must create stored procedures that will route modifications to the relevant partitions.

We can, however, create stored procedures that will perform the modifications in a "smart" way, allowing reuse of execution plans. For example, we can use the sp_executesql stored procedure that accepts a string holding the query in a parameterized form and executes it dynamically. Using the sp_executesql stored procedure allows reuse of execution plans from previous executions of the same query, even if it was run with different parameters. The sp_executesql stored procedure is discussed in Chapter 9.

The script in Listing 13-4 shows a sample stored procedure for inserting a new order. First, the INSERT statement is constructed in a string. Notice that the destination table is determined by concatenating the relevant year to 'Orders'. Once the string is constructed, it is executed using the sp_executesql stored procedure, as Listing 13-4 shows.

Listing 13-4: Stored Procedure that Inserts a New Order in the Right Partition

```
CREATE PROCEDURE InsertOrder
  @OrderID int,
  @CustomerID int,
  @OrderDate datetime
AS

DECLARE @cmd nvarchar(4000)

-- construct the insert statement
SET @cmd =
  'INSERT INTO Orders' +
  CAST(YEAR(@OrderDate) AS nchar(4)) + -- determine destination table
  '(OrderID, CustomerID, OrderDate)' +
  ' VALUES(@OrderID, @CustomerID, @OrderDate)'

-- execute the insert
EXEC sp_executesql @cmd,
  N'@OrderID int, @CustomerID int, @OrderDate datetime',
  @OrderID, @CustomerID, @OrderDate
GO
```

Now, let's insert a new order with the code line in Listing 13-5.

Listing 13-5: Using the InsertOrder Stored Procedure to Insert a New Order

```
EXEC InsertOrder    1, 11111, '19980101'
```

Take a look at the execution plan of this insert, shown in Figure 13-1.

```
Query 1: Query cost (relative to the batch): 100.00%
Query text: INSERT INTO Orders1998(orderid, customerid, orderdate)
                 VALUES(@orderid, @customerid, @orderdate)
```

Figure 13-1: Execution plan of insert into local partitioned table

Notice that only one table was accessed, and, of course, the correct table—Orders1998. Let's insert some more sample orders as shown in Listing 13-6 so we can start querying our view.

Listing 13-6: Using the InsertOrder Stored Procedure to Insert More Sample Orders

```
EXEC InsertOrder    2, 22222, '19980101'
EXEC InsertOrder 1001, 22222, '19990101'
EXEC InsertOrder 1002, 33333, '19990101'
EXEC InsertOrder 2001, 33333, '20000101'
EXEC InsertOrder 2002, 44444, '20000101'

SELECT * FROM VOrders
```

Take a look at the result of the previous SELECT query, shown in Table 13-1.

Table 13-1: Result of SELECT * against the VOrders View

OrderID	CustomerID	OrderDate	OrderYear
1	11111	1998-01-01 00:00:00.000	1998
2	22222	1998-01-01 00:00:00.000	1998
1001	22222	1999-01-01 00:00:00.000	1999
1002	33333	1999-01-01 00:00:00.000	1999
2001	33333	2000-01-01 00:00:00.000	2000
2002	44444	2000-01-01 00:00:00.000	2000

Querying Local Horizontally Partitioned Views

Now that our infrastructure is all set up, we can start querying our view. Consider the query shown in Listing 13-7, which retrieves all orders for a certain customer for a certain year.

Listing 13-7: Inefficient Query against a Local Partitioned View

```
SELECT
    *
FROM
    VOrders
WHERE
    CustomerID = 11111
  AND
    YEAR(OrderDate) = 1998
```

Now take a look at the execution plan, shown in Figure 13-2.

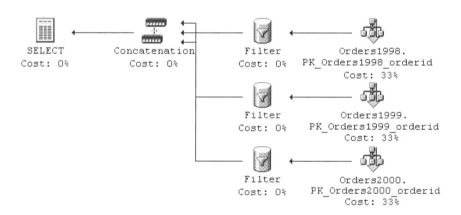

Figure 13-2: Execution plan of inefficient query against local partitioned view

Notice that all of the participating partitioned tables were accessed. The optimizer does not perform partition elimination based on CHECK constraints when a function is used on the partitioning column. It will only perform partition elimination when the partitioning column is used in our search criteria. This explains why we added the OrderYear column and the additional CHECK constraint to our partitioned tables.

Suppose we slightly revise our query to use the partitioning column in our search criteria with no surrounding functions, as in Listing 13-8.

Listing 13-8: Efficient Query against a Local Partitioned View

```
SELECT
    *
FROM
    VOrders
WHERE
    CustomerID = 11111
  AND
    OrderYear = 1998
```

We get the execution plan that is shown in Figure 13-3.

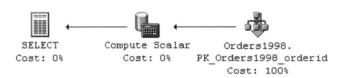

Figure 13-3: Execution plan of efficient query against local partitioned view

We can see that only the relevant table, in this case Orders1998, was accessed. The same applies to more complex queries. Suppose we want to produce a list of all of the customers who placed an order in 1998 or 1999 but not in both years. We can issue the query shown in Listing 13-9 against our view without being concerned about performance, as long as we use the partitioning column in our search criteria.

Listing 13-9: Efficient Complex Query against a Local Partitioned View

```
SELECT
  COALESCE(Cust1998, Cust1999) AS CustomerID,
  CASE
    WHEN Cust1998 IS NULL THEN 'No'
    ELSE 'Yes'
  END AS [Ordered in 1998],
  CASE
    WHEN Cust1999 IS NULL THEN 'No'
    ELSE 'Yes'
  END AS [Ordered in 1999]
```

```
FROM
   (SELECT
      DISTINCT(CustomerID) AS Cust1998
    FROM
      VOrders AS O1998
    WHERE
      OrderYear = 1998) AS O1998
  FULL OUTER JOIN
   (SELECT
      DISTINCT(CustomerID) AS Cust1999
    FROM
      VOrders
    WHERE
      OrderYear = 1999) AS O1999 ON Cust1998 = Cust1999
WHERE
   Cust1998 IS NULL
  OR
   Cust1999 IS NULL
```

Take a look at the execution plan, shown in Figure 13-4, and at the output of the query, shown in Table 13-2.

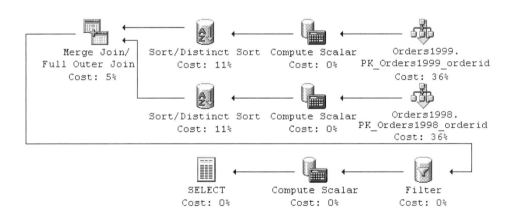

Figure 13-4: Execution plan of efficient join query against local partitioned view

Notice in the execution plan shown in Figure 13-4 that only the relevant tables—Orders1998 and Orders1999—were actually accessed.

Table 13-2: Customers Who Placed an Order Either in 1998 or in 1999 but Not in Both Years

CustomerID	Ordered in 1998	Ordered in 1999
11111	Yes	No
33333	No	Yes

New Partitioning Features in SQL Server 2000

SQL Server 2000 introduced many new features to partitioned views, allowing new ways of improving scalability and providing major performance improvements.

Local partitioned views in SQL Server 2000 have all of the benefits that local partitioned views had prior to SQL Server 2000, and more. SQL Server 2000 introduced new optimization techniques and also enabled views to be fully updateable (with certain limitations), giving them the same look and feel as regular tables.

However, the really major new features have to do with distributed horizontally partitioned views, where the partitions are spread across different servers. We will discuss the new optimization techniques and the ability of views to be updateable in the next section, which discusses distributed horizontally partitioned views. Most of information in the next section applies to local partitioned views as well, apart from the fact that everything is accessed locally.

Distributed (Federated) Horizontally Partitioned Views

Online transaction processing (OLTP) environments and large Web site databases are characterized by a mass of individual queries usually requesting relatively small amounts of data. When the system grows, and more queries are issued against the database, the first thing we try to do in order to improve the response time is to scale up, which means adding more CPUs, replacing the existing CPUs with faster ones, adding more memory, adding more bandwidth, etcetera. At some point we exhaust our options for scaling up, or even if we could scale up, the hardware becomes too expensive. SQL Server 2000 introduces a solution for the growing need for more processing power—*scaling out*.

The idea of scaling out is to split the existing huge tables into smaller partitioned tables, each of which is placed on a separate server. Each of the servers is managed autonomously, but together they form a *federation*. Views with the same names are defined on each of the servers, hiding from the users and the application the fact that it is not a table. These are referred to as *distributed partitioned views.* A user or an application connecting to any of the servers can issue all Data Manipulation Language (DML) statements against the view as if it were the original table. SQL Server 2000 intercepts the statements issued against the view and routes them to the relevant servers. This way, the processing load is spread among all of the members of the federation. Sound like magic? Let's set up such an environment and it will seem like magic.

Setting Up Distributed Partitioned Views

Setting up distributed partitioned views involves three steps:

1. Setting up the linked servers.

2. Creating the partitioned tables.

3. Creating the partitioned views.

Setting Up the Linked Servers

Setting up distributed partitioned views requires a preliminary step, which is not required when setting up local partitioned views. Since our partitioned tables are spread around a few servers, each server needs to point to the other servers that are involved, and we achieve that by configuring the other servers as linked servers. Suppose we want to partition the Customers and Orders tables across three servers called Shire, Hobbiton, and Rivendell. Shire needs to point to Hobbiton and Rivendell; Hobbiton needs to point to Shire and Rivendell, and Rivendell needs to point to Shire and Hobbiton. Figure 13-5 shows the setup for the linked servers. Each arrow in the figure stands for a linked server configuration.

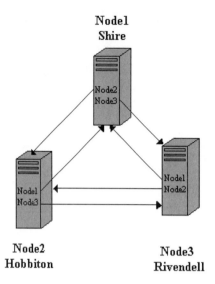

Figure 13-5: Setup for linked servers

To set up the linked servers on Shire (Node1), we need to run the script shown in Listing 13-10.

Listing 13-10: Set Up Linked Servers on Node1

```
-- Run on Node1 - Shire\Shiloh

USE master
GO

-- Connect to Hobbiton\Shiloh, call it Node2
EXEC sp_addlinkedserver
  @server='Node2',
  @srvproduct='',
  @provider='SQLOLEDB',
  @datasrc='Hobbiton\Shiloh'

-- Connect to Rivendell\Shiloh, call it Node3
EXEC sp_addlinkedserver
  @server='Node3',
  @srvproduct='',
  @provider='SQLOLEDB',
  @datasrc='Rivendell\Shiloh'
GO
```

```
-- Postpone requesting metadata until data is actually needed
EXEC sp_serveroption 'Node2', 'lazy schema validation', true
EXEC sp_serveroption 'Node3', 'lazy schema validation', true
GO
```

The `@server` parameter in the `sp_addlinkedserver` stored procedure specifies the name that we will use to refer to the linked server, and the `@datasrc` parameter specifies the actual name of the server we want to point to. Notice that in this script, remote server names are made of two parts separated with a backslash in the form of *server\instance*. SQL Server 2000 supports multiple instances of SQL Server on the same server, so if you want to run these code samples on a single machine, install three instances of SQL Server 2000 on your machine and simply replace the server names used in the scripts with your *server\instance* names. For example, if you have a server called Server1, you can install three instances of SQL Server 2000 called Instance1, Instance2, and Instance3 and refer to them as Server1\Instance1, Server1\Instance2, and Server1\Instance3, respectively.

Notice that we set the lazy schema validation server option for each of the linked servers. This optimizes performance by ensuring that the query processor will not request metadata for any of the linked tables until data is actually needed from the remote member table.

If the views are used for updates, the application can cause deadlocks across partitions. Currently there is no mechanism for distributed deadlock detection. This can hang all connections involved and require DBA intervention. As a workaround you can set the linked server option "query timeout," which will automatically expire deadlocked connections using normal query timeout mechanisms.

When a user executes a distributed query on the linked server, the local server logs on to the linked server on behalf of the user to access that table. If both of the following conditions are met, you don't need to configure linked server security:

- A user is connected to SQL Server using Windows Authentication Mode.

- Security account delegation is available on the client and sending servers; security delegation is available with Windows 2000.

This example meets the requirements. The three servers are member servers in a domain called MIDDLE_EARTH, and the users connecting to the servers connect using the NT Authentication security mode. If your configuration doesn't meet the security requirements, you might need to configure linked server security using the stored procedure `sp_addlinkedsrvlogin`. Please refer to the Books Online for more details on `sp_addlinkedsrvlogin`.

Next, we need to run a script on Hobbiton (Node2) to set up the linked servers. The script is shown in Listing 13-11.

Listing 13-11: Set Up Linked Servers on Node2

```
-- Run on Node2 - Hobbiton\Shiloh

USE master
GO


-- Connect to Shire\Shiloh, call it Node1
EXEC sp_addlinkedserver
  @server='Node1',
  @srvproduct='',
  @provider='SQLOLEDB',
  @datasrc='Shire\Shiloh'

-- Connect to Rivendell\Shiloh, call it Node3
EXEC sp_addlinkedserver
  @server='Node3',
  @srvproduct='',
  @provider='SQLOLEDB',
  @datasrc='Rivendell\Shiloh'
GO


-- Postpone requsting metadata until data is actually needed
EXEC sp_serveroption 'Node1', 'lazy schema validation', true
EXEC sp_serveroption 'Node3', 'lazy schema validation', true
GO
```

And last, we need to run a similar script on Rivendell (Node3). See Listing 13-12.

Listing 13-12: Set Up Linked Servers on Node3

```
-- Run on Node3 - Rivendell\Shiloh

USE master
GO


-- Connect to Shire\Shiloh, call it Node1
EXEC sp_addlinkedserver
  @server='Node1',
  @srvproduct='',
  @provider='SQLOLEDB',
  @datasrc='Shire\Shiloh'
```

```
-- Connect to Hobbiton\Shiloh, call it Node2
EXEC sp_addlinkedserver
  @server='Node2',
  @srvproduct='',
  @provider='SQLOLEDB',
  @datasrc='Hobbiton\Shiloh'
GO


-- Postpone requsting metadata until data is actually needed
EXEC sp_serveroption 'Node1', 'lazy schema validation', true
EXEC sp_serveroption 'Node2', 'lazy schema validation', true
GO
```

Creating the Partitioned Tables

Now that we have configured the linked servers and each server can communicate with the other servers, we can get to the "meat" of distributed partitioned views—creating the partitioned tables. We create a table on each of the servers involved, with almost the same structure as the original table we want to partition. Each table will hold a slice of the original table. The key point in creating the partitioned tables is the partitioning criteria, implemented as a CHECK constraint that defines the rows that each partition will host. The ranges of values in each partition cannot overlap. Later we will see how to create a view that assembles all the pieces together.

SQL Server 2000 introduced an amazing new feature of partitioned views—they are now updateable. You heard right, we can issue all of our DML statements, including SELECT, INSERT, UPDATE, and DELETE directly against the view instead of issuing them against the underlying tables.

If we want to achieve maximum efficiency for our queries, exploit the new optimization capabilities introduced with SQL Server 2000, and allow updates directly to the view, we need to make sure certain conditions are met in our tables:

- The partitioning column must be a part of the primary key of the underlying tables, must not allow NULLs, and cannot be a computed column.

- A CHECK constraint defined on the partitioning column defines the rows that each table will host. The CHECK constraint can use only the following operators: BETWEEN, AND, OR, <, <=, >, >=, and =.

- The tables cannot have identity or timestamp columns, and none of the columns can have a DEFAULT constraint.

The most important decisions we need to make are which column we should use as our partitioning column and which range of values each partition should host. The most efficient partitioning criterion is one that defines a range of values in each partitioned table that is mostly accessed locally and results in as even a spread of rows as possible. This could be a range of customers, parts, or a region. This way, most of the queries will be mainly processed in the local server, and we will minimize the need for distributed processing.

Now that we are aware of all of the requirements that our tables should meet, we can go ahead and create them. We will create tables that are similar in structure to the Customers and Orders tables in the Northwind database. The following code samples are run in a database called testdb, which will be created in each of the servers. Listing 13-13 creates the first partitioned tables in the server Shire\Shiloh (Node1).

Listing 13-13: Create Partitioned Tables on Node1

```
-- Run on Node1 - Shire\Shiloh

-- Create the testdb database
CREATE DATABASE testdb
GO

USE testdb
GO

CREATE TABLE CustomersAF(
    CustomerID   nchar(5)     NOT NULL,
    CompanyName  nvarchar(40) NOT NULL,
    ContactName  nvarchar(30) NULL,
    ContactTitle nvarchar(30) NULL,
    Address      nvarchar(60) NULL,
    City         nvarchar(15) NULL,
    Region       nvarchar(15) NULL,
    PostalCode   nvarchar(10) NULL,
    Country      nvarchar(15) NULL,
    Phone        nvarchar(24) NULL,
    Fax          nvarchar(24) NULL,
    CONSTRAINT PK_CustomersAF PRIMARY KEY CLUSTERED(CustomerID),
    CONSTRAINT CHK_CustomersAF CHECK (CustomerID BETWEEN 'AAAAA' AND 'FZZZZ'))
GO
```

```
CREATE TABLE OrdersAF(
  OrderID        int          NOT NULL,
  CustomerID     nchar(5)     NOT NULL,
  EmployeeID     int          NULL,
  OrderDate      datetime     NULL,
  RequiredDate   datetime     NULL,
  ShippedDate    datetime     NULL,
  ShipVia        int          NULL,
  Freight        money        NULL,
  ShipName       nvarchar(40) NULL,
  ShipAddress    nvarchar(60) NULL,
  ShipCity       nvarchar(15) NULL,
  ShipRegion     nvarchar(15) NULL,
  ShipPostalCode nvarchar(10) NULL,
  ShipCountry    nvarchar(15) NULL,
  CONSTRAINT PK_OrdersAF PRIMARY KEY CLUSTERED(CustomerID, OrderID),
  CONSTRAINT UNQ_OrdersAF_OrderID UNIQUE(OrderID),
  CONSTRAINT FK_OrdersAF_CustomersAF
    FOREIGN KEY (CustomerID)
    REFERENCES CustomersAF(CustomerID),
  CONSTRAINT CHK_OrdersAF CHECK (CustomerID BETWEEN 'AAAAA' AND 'FZZZZ'))
GO
```

Notice a few important points in the script. We have a CHECK constraint on the CustomerID column, which is part of the primary key in both the CustomersAF and the OrdersAF tables. This CHECK constraint makes sure that only customers with customer IDs in the range "AAAAA"–"FZZZZ" are allowed in this table, and as we will later see, the optimizer will use this CHECK constraint in its query optimization and data modification. If we want to partition the Orders table by customer ID, we need to include the customer ID in the primary key, even though it is redundant in this case as far as the primary key is concerned.

Customer ID is quite an obvious partitioning criterion for the original Customers table, but why do we use the same partitioning criterion for the Orders table? This will be explained when we start querying our partitioned view.

Now we create the partitioned tables in the Hobbiton\Shiloh (Node2) server, with customer IDs in the range "GAAAA"–"PZZZZ", as shown in Listing 13-14.

Listing 13-14: Create Partitioned Tables on Node2

```
-- Run on Node2 - Hobbiton\Shiloh

-- Create the testdb database
CREATE DATABASE testdb
GO

USE testdb
GO

CREATE TABLE CustomersGP(
  ... <columns' definition> ...
  CONSTRAINT PK_CustomersGP PRIMARY KEY CLUSTERED(CustomerID),
  CONSTRAINT CHK_CustomersGP CHECK (CustomerID BETWEEN 'GAAAA' AND 'PZZZZ'))
GO

CREATE TABLE OrdersGP(
  ... <columns' definition> ...
  CONSTRAINT PK_OrdersGP PRIMARY KEY CLUSTERED(CustomerID, OrderID),
  CONSTRAINT UNQ_OrdersGP_OrderID UNIQUE(OrderID),
  CONSTRAINT FK_OrdersGP_CustomersGP
    FOREIGN KEY (CustomerID)
    REFERENCES CustomersGP(CustomerID),
  CONSTRAINT CHK_OrdersGP CHECK (CustomerID BETWEEN 'GAAAA' AND 'PZZZZ'))
GO
```

And last, we create the partitioned tables in the Rivendell\Shiloh (Node3) server, with customer IDs in the range "QAAAA"–"ZZZZZ", as shown in Listing 13-15.

Listing 13-15: Create Partitioned Tables on Node3

```
-- Run on Node3 - Rivendell\Shiloh

-- Create the testdb database
CREATE DATABASE testdb
GO

USE testdb
GO
```

```
CREATE TABLE CustomersQZ(
  ... <columns' definition> ...
  CONSTRAINT PK_CustomersQZ PRIMARY KEY CLUSTERED(CustomerID),
  CONSTRAINT CHK_CustomersQZ CHECK (CustomerID BETWEEN 'QAAAA' AND 'ZZZZZ'))
GO

CREATE TABLE OrdersQZ(
  ... <columns' definition> ...
  CONSTRAINT PK_OrdersQZ PRIMARY KEY CLUSTERED(CustomerID, OrderID),
  CONSTRAINT UNQ_OrdersQZ_OrderID UNIQUE(OrderID),
  CONSTRAINT FK_OrdersQZ_CustomersQZ
    FOREIGN KEY (CustomerID)
    REFERENCES CustomersQZ(CustomerID),
  CONSTRAINT CHK_OrdersQZ CHECK (CustomerID BETWEEN 'QAAAA' AND 'ZZZZZ'))
GO
```

Creating the Partitioned Views

Now that our partitioned tables are all set up, we are left with assembling them, which is probably the easiest part of all. We define a view that assembles the rows from each table by using the UNION ALL clause, much as we do with local partitioned views. With local partitioned views we have one view assembling all of the local partitioned tables.

In this federated environment, each server has one local table and two remote tables, so the view looks slightly different in each server. The local table can be referenced by using the table name alone, and the remote tables are referenced by using the full four-part table name. Let's go ahead and create our view in the Shire\Shiloh (Node1) server, as shown in Listing 13-16.

Listing 13-16: Create Partitioned Views on Node1

```
-- Run on Node1 - Shire\Shiloh

CREATE VIEW Customers
AS

SELECT * FROM CustomersAF
UNION ALL
SELECT * FROM Node2.testdb.dbo.CustomersGP
UNION ALL
SELECT * FROM Node3.testdb.dbo.CustomersQZ
GO
```

```
CREATE VIEW Orders
AS

SELECT * FROM OrdersAF
UNION ALL
SELECT * FROM Node2.testdb.dbo.OrdersGP
UNION ALL
SELECT * FROM Node3.testdb.dbo.OrdersQZ
GO
```

At this point, users can start modifying and querying the view, but this requires them to issue their queries while they are connected to Shire\Shiloh (Node1). Creating similar views on the other two servers with the same names, Customers and Orders, will allow the same modifications and queries to be used regardless of the server the users are connected to. This will allow the highest degree of transparency.

Keep in mind, though, that the partitions CustomersAF and OrdersAF, which were local to Node1, are now remote for Node2 and Node3, so you will need to refer to them in your views on those nodes using their full four-part names: Node1.testdb.dbo.CustomersAF and Node1.testdb.dbo.OrdersAF respectively. On the other hand, partitions that are remote for Node1 are local for the other nodes. For example, Node2's partitions, which are remote for Node1 are now local for Node2, so you can refer to them locally as CustomersGP and OrdersGP in the views you create on Node2.

As with our partitioned tables, our views also need to meet a few conditions so that they will be updateable and can exploit the new optimizing capabilities concerning distributed partitioned views:

- No table or column can be referenced more than once.

- Each SELECT list must reference all of the columns participating in the primary key of the underlying tables.

- The columns in the same ordinal position in the SELECT list in all of the SELECT statements must be of the same datatype, precision, scale, and collation. The partitioning columns must also be in the same ordinal position in all of the SELECT statements.

- If a column exists in the base table but is not included in the SELECT list in the view, it must allow NULLs.

Modifying Distributed Partitioned Views

Earlier in the chapter, a few rules were mentioned that tables and views need to meet in order to exploit the new optimizing techniques and in order for views to be updateable. With modifications, INSERT statements run against the views must supply a value to the partitioning column.

We have our entire infrastructure set up, so now it's magic time. We will run the following modifications from our connection to Shire\Shiloh (Node1), but you can actually run them while connected to any of the servers. Make sure the Microsoft Distributed Transactions Coordinator (MSDTC) service is running, because the following modifications will result in a distributed transaction. You must set the XACT_ABORT session setting to ON—it is used to determine whether an entire transaction will be rolled back as a result of any runtime error, but in this case it is required for data modification statements in an implicit or explicit transaction against most OLE DB providers, including SQL Server. Make sure you turn on the Graphical Execution Plan in Query Analyzer to see the detailed execution plan, or SET STATISTICS PROFILE to ON if you prefer to analyze the actual execution plan in a textual mode.

First of all, let's populate the Customers view with all of the rows from the Customers table in the Northwind database, using the script in Listing 13-17.

Listing 13-17: Populating Data through the Customers View

```
-- Run on Node1 - Shire\Shiloh

-- Required for remote modifications
SET XACT_ABORT ON
GO

-- Populate the Customers view
INSERT INTO Customers
  SELECT * FROM Northwind.dbo.Customers
```

Wait a minute; did we see what we thought we saw? The INSERT statement was run against the view. Let's look at the execution plan shown in Figure 13-6 to understand what SQL Server did to implement our INSERT statement.

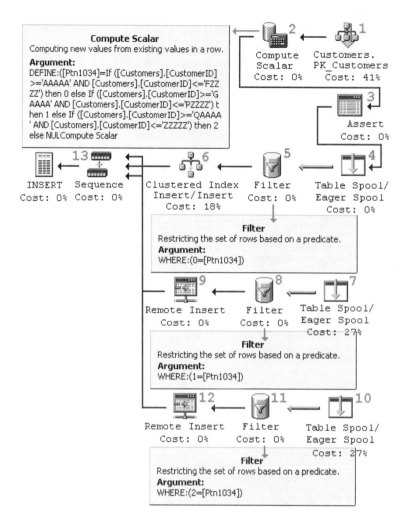

Figure 13-6: Execution plan for INSERT statement against a federated view

Let's analyze the execution plan's important steps:

1. Read all of the rows from the local Customers table in the Northwind database (Clustered Index Scan).

2. For each of the rows read in Step 1, compute a new column called Ptn1034, which will hold a value that will specify to which of the three ranges of rows it belongs. 0 is "AAAAA"–"FZZZZ", 1 is "GAAAA"–"PZZZZ", and 2 is "QAAAA"–"ZZZZZ" (Compute Scalar).

4. Store the rows read in Step 1, including the computed column Ptn1034, which was calculated in Step 2, in a hidden temporary table.

5-6. Read the temporary table and insert only the rows that match the criteria Ptn1034 = 0 into the local CustomersAF table.

7-9. Read the temporary table and insert only the rows that match the criteria Ptn1034 = 1 into the remote Node2.testdb.dbo.CustomersGP table.

10-12. Read the temporary table and insert only the rows that match the criteria Ptn1034 = 2 into the remote Node3.testdb.dbo.CustomersQZ table.

Thus we can issue INSERT, UPDATE, and DELETE statements against our view. Try the modifications shown in Listing 13-18 against the view, and examine and compare their execution plans when they result in modifying a local table and a remote table.

Listing 13-18: Modifying Data through the Customers View

```
-- Modifications resulting in modifying the local table
INSERT INTO Customers(CustomerID, CompanyName, ContactName, ContactTitle, Address,
                      City, Region, PostalCode, Country, Phone, Fax)
  VALUES('AAAAA', 'CompA', 'ContA', 'ContTitleA', 'AddA', 'CityA',
         'RegionA', 'PCA', 'CountryA', 'PhoneA', 'FaxA')

UPDATE Customers
  SET CompanyName = 'CompAA'
WHERE
  CustomerID = 'AAAAA'

DELETE FROM Customers
WHERE
  CustomerID = 'AAAAA'

-- Modifications resulting in modifying a remote table
INSERT INTO Customers(CustomerID, CompanyName, ContactName, ContactTitle, Address,
                      City, Region, PostalCode, Country, Phone, Fax)
VALUES('ZZZZZ', 'CompZ', 'ContZ', 'ContTitleZ', 'AddZ', 'CityZ',
       'RegionZ', 'PCZ', 'CountryZ', 'PhoneZ', 'FaxZ')

UPDATE Customers
  SET CompanyName = 'CompZZ'
WHERE
  CustomerID = 'ZZZZZ'

DELETE FROM Customers
WHERE
  CustomerID = 'ZZZZZ'
```

Before we continue and start querying our view, let's populate the Orders view with all of the rows from the Orders table in the Northwind database, as shown in Listing 13-19.

Listing 13-19: Populating Data through the Orders View

```
-- Populate the Orders view
INSERT INTO Orders
  SELECT * FROM Northwind.dbo.Orders
```

Aside from the points concerning distributed transactions and MSDTC, all of the issues that were discussed here are relevant to local partitioned views, as well.

Querying Distributed Partitioned Views

Now let's start querying our partitioned views. We'll begin with a simple SELECT statement that retrieves all of the rows from our Customers view, as shown in Listing 13-20.

Listing 13-20: Selecting All Rows from the Customers View

```
SELECT
  *
FROM
    Customers
```

Take a look at the execution plan shown in Figure 13-7.

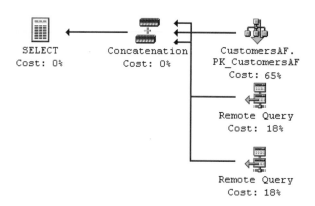

Figure 13-7: Execution plan for a SELECT * statement against a federated view

Notice that the local table CustomersAF is queried locally. A remote query is issued against each of the other remote tables: Node2.testdb.dbo.CustomersGP and Node3.testdb.dbo.CustomersQZ. The result of all the queries is concatenated and returned to the user.

Next, let's perform a query that requests rows only from the local table, as shown in Listing 13-21.

Listing 13-21: Selecting a Local Customer from the Customers View

```
SELECT
    *
FROM
    Customers
WHERE
    CustomerID = 'ALFKI'
```

Take a look at the execution plan shown in Figure 13-8.

SELECT
Cost: 0%   Compute Scalar   CustomersAF.
                   Cost: 0%   PK_CustomersAF
                                        Cost: 100%

*Figure 13-8: Execution plan for a SELECT * WHERE CustomerID = 'ALFKI'
statement against a federated view*

Notice that only the local node, in this case Node1, is accessed in this plan. Nodes 2 and 3 are not accessed at all, as no data are needed from them. The textual output of STATISTICS PROFILE for the same query is shown in Listing 13-22.

Listing 13-22: STATISTICS PROFILE Output for a Query against the Customers View

```
Rows    Executes    StmtText
1       1           SELECT * FROM [Customers] WHERE [customerid]=@1
1       1             |--Compute Scalar
                        (DEFINE:([CustomersAF].[CustomerID]=
                                [CustomersAF].[CustomerID],
                                [CustomersAF].[CompanyName]=
                                [CustomersAF].[CompanyName],
                                [CustomersAF].[ContactName]=
                                [CustomersAF].[ContactName],
                                [CustomersAF].[ContactTitle]=
                                [CustomersAF].[ContactTitle],
```

```
1     1                    |--Clustered Index Seek(OBJECT:
                           ([testdb].[dbo].[CustomersAF].[PK_CustomersAF]),
                           SEEK:([CustomersAF].[CustomerID]='ALFKI')
                           ORDERED FORWARD)
```

Try a similar query to the last one, only replacing the customer ID you are looking for, as in Listing 13-23.

Listing 13-23: Selecting a Remote Customer from the Customers View

```
SELECT
    *
FROM
    Customers
WHERE
    CustomerID = 'OLDWO'
```

The execution plan shown in Figure 13-9 looks similar to the previous one, only now you can see that a remote node is accessed instead of the local node.

*Figure 13-9: Execution plan for a SELECT * WHERE CustomerID = 'OLDWO' statement against a federated view*

The optimizer can perform partition elimination with a complex expression in the WHERE clause. For example, consider the query shown in Listing 13-24.

Listing 13-24: Selecting Local Customers from the Customers View using the OR Operator

```
SELECT
    *
FROM
    Customers
WHERE
    CustomerID = 'ALFKI'
  OR
    CustomerID = 'ANATR'
```

Take a look at the execution plan shown in Figure 13-10—it looks similar to the execution plan shown in Figure 13-8.

Figure 13-10: Execution plan for a SELECT * WHERE CustomerID = 'ALFKI' OR CustomerID = 'ANATR' statement against a federated view

Here also, the only table that is accessed is the local table from Node1. Nodes 2 and 3 are not accessed at all.

Now try the query shown in Listing 13-25. This query is similar to the previous one, only now the required data should be retrieved from a remote node—Node 3.

Listing 13-25: Selecting Remote Customers from the Customers View using the OR Operator

```
SELECT
    *
FROM
    Customers
WHERE
    CustomerID = 'WILMK'
  OR
    CustomerID = 'WOLZA'
```

Take a look at the execution plan shown in Figure 13-11.

Figure 13-11: Execution plan for a SELECT * WHERE CustomerID = 'WILMK' OR CustomerID = 'WOLZA' statement against a federated view

You can see one remote query, which is issued against Node3. Nodes 1 and 2 are not accessed at all.

We are not done yet; let's see some more magic. Consider the GROUP BY query shown in Listing 13-26.

Listing 13-26: Using a GROUP BY Query against the Orders View

```
SELECT
  CustomerID,
  COUNT(*) AS Count_Orders
FROM
  Orders
GROUP BY
  CustomerID
```

Take a look at the execution plan shown in Figure 13-12. Notice that aggregates are calculated in the local node, and a GROUP BY query is issued against each remote node. Later, all of the results are concatenated, and the aggregates from the different nodes are aggregated to form the final result set. This can be much more efficient than bringing all of the base rows from all of the nodes and aggregating them locally, because many fewer rows need to be transferred over the network, and we also exploit the processing power of all servers. This optimization technique is referred to as *local-global aggregation*.

> **NOTE** *You might get a different execution plan for this query. A few tests that we performed on several configurations showed that this plan is used when not much memory is available. This plan is very efficient in spreading the load and exploiting the resources of all of the participating nodes.*

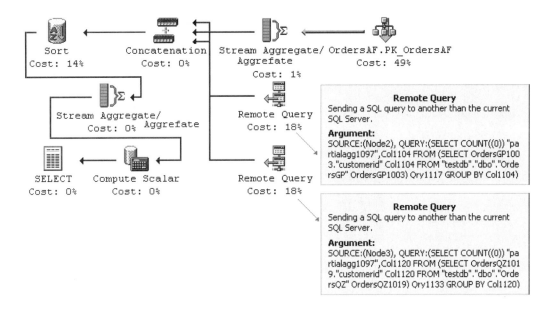

Figure 13-12: Execution plan for a GROUP BY query against a federated view

Similarly, if we have two tables that are partitioned on the same column with the same partitioning criteria, join queries that are run against the views are pushed down through the partitioning. In other words, each server will perform the join locally with the participating local partitioned tables instead of returning all of the rows to the requesting server and performing the join at that server. This splits the join processing to the participating servers and exploits each server's resources to perform its own local join, instead of performing a more intensive join on the local server.

Now let's compare a join query against two views that are partitioned on the same partitioning criteria to a join query against two views that are partitioned on different partitioning criteria—this will demonstrate the efficiency of the former. To do so, we'll partition the Orders table by the OrderID column, as shown in Listing 13-27.

Listing 13-27: Creating Another Partitioned View, with OrderID
as the Partitioning Column

```
-- Run on Node1
-- Create the partitioned table on Node1
CREATE TABLE OrdersA(
  OrderID       int           NOT NULL,
  CustomerID    nchar(5)      NOT NULL,
  EmployeeID    int           NULL,
  OrderDate     datetime      NULL,
  RequiredDate  datetime      NULL,
  ShippedDate   datetime      NULL,
  ShipVia       int           NULL,
  Freight       money         NULL,
  ShipName      nvarchar(40)  NULL,
  ShipAddress   nvarchar(60)  NULL,
  ShipCity      nvarchar(15)  NULL,
  ShipRegion    nvarchar(15)  NULL,
  ShipPostalCode nvarchar(10) NULL,
  ShipCountry   nvarchar(15)  NULL,
  CONSTRAINT PK_Orders1 PRIMARY KEY CLUSTERED(OrderID),
  CONSTRAINT CHK_Orders1 CHECK (OrderID < 10500))
GO

-- Run on Node2
-- Create the partitioned table on Node2
CREATE TABLE OrdersB(
  OrderID       int           NOT NULL,
  CustomerID    nchar(5)      NOT NULL,
  EmployeeID    int           NULL,
  OrderDate     datetime      NULL,
  RequiredDate  datetime      NULL,
  ShippedDate   datetime      NULL,
  ShipVia       int           NULL,
  Freight       money         NULL,
  ShipName      nvarchar(40)  NULL,
  ShipAddress   nvarchar(60)  NULL,
  ShipCity      nvarchar(15)  NULL,
  ShipRegion    nvarchar(15)  NULL,
  ShipPostalCode nvarchar(10) NULL,
  ShipCountry   nvarchar(15)  NULL,
  CONSTRAINT PK_OrdersA PRIMARY KEY CLUSTERED(OrderID),
  CONSTRAINT CHK_OrdersA CHECK (OrderID between 10500 and 10750))
GO
```

```
-- Run on Node3
-- Create the partitioned table on Node3
CREATE TABLE OrdersC(
  OrderID        int         NOT NULL,
  CustomerID     nchar(5)    NOT NULL,
  EmployeeID     int         NULL,
  OrderDate      datetime    NULL,
  RequiredDate   datetime    NULL,
  ShippedDate    datetime    NULL,
  ShipVia        int         NULL,
  Freight        money       NULL,
  ShipName       nvarchar(40) NULL,
  ShipAddress    nvarchar(60) NULL,
  ShipCity       nvarchar(15) NULL,
  ShipRegion     nvarchar(15) NULL,
  ShipPostalCode nvarchar(10) NULL,
  ShipCountry    nvarchar(15) NULL,
  CONSTRAINT PK_OrdersC PRIMARY KEY CLUSTERED(OrderID),
  CONSTRAINT CHK_OrdersC CHECK (OrderID > 10750))
GO


-- Run on Node1
-- Create the partitioned view on Node1
CREATE VIEW Orders2
AS

SELECT * FROM OrdersA
UNION ALL
SELECT * FROM Node2.testdb.dbo.OrdersB
UNION ALL
SELECT * FROM Node3.testdb.dbo.OrdersC
GO


-- Run on Node1
-- Populate the view
SET XACT_ABORT ON
GO
INSERT INTO Orders2
  SELECT * FROM Northwind.dbo.Orders
GO
```

Now run the join query shown in Listing 13-28 against the views Customers and Orders, which are partitioned with the same partitioning criteria.

Listing 13-28: Using a JOIN Query against Two Views that Are Partitioned on the Same Criteria

```
SELECT
    *
FROM
    Customers AS C
  JOIN
    Orders     AS O ON C.CustomerID = O.CustomerID
```

Take a look at the execution plan shown in Figure 13-13.

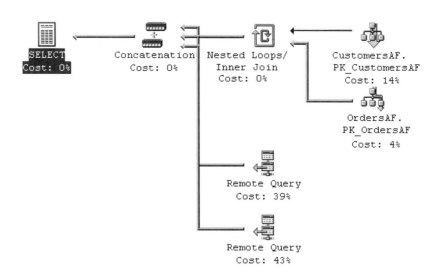

Figure 13-13: Execution plan for a JOIN query against federated views with the same partitioning criteria

Now let's compare that execution plan to the execution plan of the query shown in Listing 13-29, which is run against the views Customers and Orders2, which are partitioned on different partitioning criteria. The execution plan of this query is shown in Figure 13-14.

Listing 13-29: Using a JOIN Query against Two Views which Are Partitioned on Different Criteria

```
SELECT
    *
FROM
    Customers AS C
  JOIN
    Orders2   AS O ON C.CustomerID = O.CustomerID
```

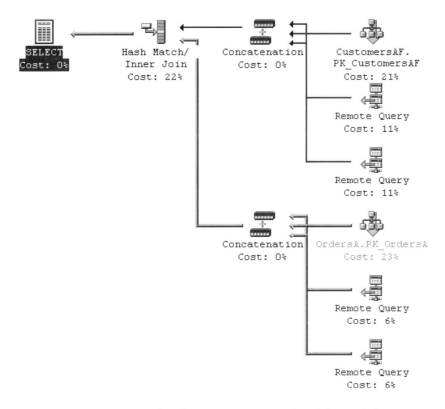

Figure 13-14: Execution plan for a JOIN query against federated views with different partitioning criteria

Notice that in the first query, each node processed the join locally, and later the results were concatenated in the local server. In the second query, the results of the Customer's partitions were all brought to the local server as is, and the results of Orders2's partitions were also brought to the local server as is, and the join was performed entirely locally, without exploiting the resources of the remote servers for the join operation.

The conclusion to be drawn from this comparison is that joins between views based on the same partitioning criteria are much more efficient than joins between views based on different partitioning criteria. You should take this fact into consideration when choosing the partitioning criteria of your distributed partitioned views.

Non-Updateable Distributed Partitioned Views

If for some reason you need to create partitioned views that do not meet the requirements that allow updates to the view, you can create INSTEAD OF triggers

(INSTEAD OF triggers were covered in Chapter 10) that will take care of the modifications against the view. However, the optimizer will probably come up with less efficient plans when querying those views, as some of the new optimizing techniques depend on the rules we discussed.

For example, suppose you don't want to include the CustomerID column in the primary key of the underlying tables of our Orders view. Let's drop and re-create the primary key in all of the partitioned tables participating in the Orders view, as shown in Listing 13-30. You would still probably want an index on CustomerID to improve query performance when searching by the CustomerID column, so Listing 13-30 includes one.

Listing 13-30: Re-create the Primary Key of the Orders' Partitions to Include Only the OrderID Column

```
-- Run on Node1
-- Recreate the primary key only on the OrderID column
ALTER TABLE OrdersAF
  DROP CONSTRAINT PK_OrdersAF
GO


ALTER TABLE OrdersAF
  ADD CONSTRAINT PK_OrdersAF PRIMARY KEY(OrderID)
GO


-- Create an index on CustomerID
CREATE NONCLUSTERED INDEX idx_nci_CustomerID ON OrdersAF(CustomerID)
GO


-- Run on Node2
-- Recreate the primary key only on the OrderID column
ALTER TABLE OrdersGP
  DROP CONSTRAINT PK_OrdersGP
GO


ALTER TABLE OrdersGP
  ADD CONSTRAINT PK_OrdersGP PRIMARY KEY(OrderID)
GO


-- Create an index on CustomerID
CREATE NONCLUSTERED INDEX idx_nci_CustomerID ON OrdersGP(CustomerID)
GO
```

```
-- Run on Node3
-- Recreate the primary key only on the OrderID column
ALTER TABLE OrdersQZ
  DROP CONSTRAINT PK_OrdersQZ
GO


ALTER TABLE OrdersQZ
  ADD CONSTRAINT PK_OrdersQZ PRIMARY KEY(OrderID)
GO


-- Create an index on CustomerID
CREATE NONCLUSTERED INDEX idx_nci_CustomerID ON OrdersQZ(CustomerID)
GO
```

Now try the INSERT statement shown in Listing 13-31.

Listing 13-31: Trying to Insert a Row to a Non-Updateable View

```
-- Run on Node1
-- Try to insert a new row
INSERT INTO Orders(OrderID, CustomerID, EmployeeID, OrderDate, RequiredDate,
                   ShippedDate, ShipVia, Freight, ShipName, ShipAddress, ShipCity,
                   ShipRegion, ShipPostalCode, ShipCountry)
  VALUES(10247, N'VINET', 5, '1996-07-04 00:00:00.000', '1996-08-01 00:00:00.000',
         '1996-07-16 00:00:00.000', 3, 32.3800, N'Vins et alcools Chevalier',
         N'59 rue de l''Abbaye', N'Reims', NULL, N'51100', N'France')
```

You will get the error shown in Listing 13-32.

Listing 13-32: Error for Trying to Insert a Row to a Non-Updateable View

```
Server: Msg 4436, Level 16, State 13, Line 1
UNION ALL view 'Orders' is not updateable
because a partitioning column was not found.
```

Our view is no longer updateable because one of the main requirements, which specifies that the partitioning column must be a part of the primary key, is not met. If we want to allow updates against our view from all of the nodes, we need to create a set of INSTEAD OF triggers on the Orders view on all of the nodes.

So, let's create an INSTEAD OF INSERT trigger. Our trigger will fire instead of the INSERT statement, and while inside the trigger, all of the new rows are available in the *inserted* table.

First, we need to check that all of the new rows are in the boundaries of all of the CHECK constraints we placed on the CustomerID column in all of our partitioned tables. If there are rows that are outside those boundaries, we will need to roll back the INSERT statement.

Next, we perform three INSERT statements, each of which inserts the relevant slice of rows to the relevant table by filtering the rows in the *inserted* table with the same criteria as in the CHECK constraint of the table to which we are inserting the rows.

Before each INSERT, we will perform an existence check to see if we have qualifying rows. This existence check is done locally, and we can avoid performing an unnecessary remote query.

Notice that all of the modifications are performed in a distributed transaction. Also, notice that we refer to the local table with the table name alone and to the remote tables with the full four-part table names. Let's look at the INSTEAD OF INSERT trigger shown in Listing 13-33.

Listing 13-33: INSTEAD OF INSERT Trigger on the Orders View

```
-- Run on Node1
CREATE TRIGGER trg_i_orders ON Orders INSTEAD OF INSERT
AS

-- First, ensure we have rows to process
IF @@ROWCOUNT = 0
  RETURN

-- Next, make sure that all of the data meets the CHECK constraint
IF EXISTS(SELECT *
          FROM inserted
          WHERE CustomerID < 'A'
             OR CustomerID > 'ZZZZZ')
BEGIN
  RAISERROR('Trying to insert illegal customer ids.  Transaction rolled back',
            16, 1)
  ROLLBACK TRANSACTION
END
ELSE
BEGIN

  BEGIN DISTRIBUTED TRANSACTION
```

```
-- insert rows to the OrdersAF table
IF EXISTS(SELECT *
          FROM inserted
          WHERE CustomerID BETWEEN 'AAAAA' AND 'FZZZZ')
  INSERT INTO OrdersAF -- local
    SELECT * FROM inserted
    WHERE CustomerID BETWEEN 'AAAAA' AND 'FZZZZ'


-- insert rows to the OrdersGP table
IF EXISTS(SELECT *
          FROM inserted
          WHERE CustomerID BETWEEN 'GAAAA' AND 'PZZZZ')
  INSERT INTO Node2.testdb.dbo.OrdersGP
    SELECT * FROM inserted
    WHERE CustomerID BETWEEN 'GAAAA' AND 'PZZZZ'


-- insert rows to the OrdersQZ table
IF EXISTS(SELECT *
          FROM inserted
          WHERE CustomerID BETWEEN 'QAAAA' AND 'ZZZZZ')
  INSERT INTO Node3.testdb.dbo.OrdersQZ
    SELECT * FROM inserted
    WHERE CustomerID BETWEEN 'QAAAA' AND 'ZZZZZ'


COMMIT TRANSACTION

END
GO
```

Next we'll create an INSTEAD OF DELETE trigger. It doesn't need to check if our DELETE statement deletes rows in the inclusive range of all of the CHECK constraints placed on the CustomerID column in all of the underlying tables because we are not adding illegal data.

Our DELETE statements perform a join between the underlying tables to the *deleted* table to make sure that only those orders that were deleted from the view will actually be deleted from the underlying tables. The filter we added to the DELETE statements that matches the CHECK constraint of the underlying table is redundant. It is only added here for readability. Let's look at the INSTEAD OF DELETE trigger shown in Listing 13-34.

Listing 13-34: INSTEAD OF DELETE Trigger on the Orders View

```
-- Run on Node1
CREATE TRIGGER trg_d_orders ON Orders INSTEAD OF DELETE
AS

-- ensure we have rows to process
IF @@ROWCOUNT = 0
  RETURN

BEGIN DISTRIBUTED TRANSACTION

-- delete rows from the OrdersAF table
IF EXISTS(SELECT *
          FROM deleted
          WHERE CustomerID BETWEEN 'AAAAA' AND 'FZZZZ')
  DELETE FROM OrdersAF -- local
  FROM OrdersAF AS O JOIN deleted AS D
    ON  O.OrderID = D.OrderID
    AND O.CustomerID BETWEEN 'AAAAA' AND 'FZZZZ'

-- delete rows from the OrdersGP table
IF EXISTS(SELECT *
          FROM deleted
          WHERE CustomerID BETWEEN 'GAAAA' AND 'PZZZZ')
  DELETE FROM Node2.testdb.dbo.OrdersGP
  FROM Node2.testdb.dbo.OrdersGP AS O JOIN deleted AS D
    ON  O.OrderID = D.OrderID
    AND O.CustomerID BETWEEN 'GAAAA' AND 'PZZZZ'

-- delete rows from the OrdersQZ table
IF EXISTS(SELECT *
          FROM deleted
          WHERE CustomerID BETWEEN 'QAAAA' AND 'ZZZZZ')
  DELETE FROM Node3.testdb.dbo.OrdersQZ
  FROM Node3.testdb.dbo.OrdersQZ AS O JOIN deleted AS D
    ON  O.OrderID = D.OrderID
    AND O.CustomerID BETWEEN 'QAAAA' AND 'ZZZZZ'

COMMIT TRANSACTION
GO
```

Now we'll look at the INSTEAD OF UPDATE trigger. It is actually a combination of the previous two triggers. First, we delete all of the old rows by joining the underlying tables to the *deleted* table, the same way we deleted them in the INSTEAD OF DELETE trigger, and then we insert the new image of the rows from the *inserted* table, the same way we inserted them in the INSTEAD OF INSERT trigger.

There are a few limitations with this trigger. An UPDATE statement against our view will fail if there is a foreign key pointing to any of the columns of the underlying tables and we delete rows from the table that have related rows in the referencing table. This limitation has to do with the fact that we split the UPDATE operation to separate DELETEs and INSERTs, and we perform the DELETEs first, which might result in orphaned child rows in the referencing table. We can't perform the INSERTs before the DELETEs, because this will result in a violation of the primary keys in our partitioned tables. We could write a complex INSTEAD OF UPDATE trigger that would support such a scenario, but you might prefer to simply drop or disable the foreign key.

On the other hand, our trigger supports updates to the partitioning column. Rows that have changed their CustomerID and, as a result, belong to another underlying table are simply transferred to the correct table as a result of the delete and insert operations. Let's look at the INSTEAD OF UPDATE trigger shown in Listing 13-35.

Listing 13-35: INSTEAD OF UPDATE Trigger on the Orders View

```
-- Run on Node1
CREATE TRIGGER trg_u_orders ON Orders INSTEAD OF UPDATE
AS

-- ensure we have rows to process
IF @@ROWCOUNT = 0
  RETURN

-- Make sure that all of the data meets the CHECK constraint
IF EXISTS(SELECT *
          FROM inserted
          WHERE CustomerID < 'A'
            OR CustomerID > 'ZZZZZ')
BEGIN
  RAISERROR('Trying to insert illegal customer ids.  Transaction rolled back',
            16, 1)
  ROLLBACK TRANSACTION
END
```

```
    ELSE
    BEGIN

      BEGIN DISTRIBUTED TRANSACTION

      -- delete rows from the OrdersAF table
      IF EXISTS(SELECT *
               FROM deleted
               WHERE CustomerID BETWEEN 'AAAAA' AND 'FZZZZ')
        DELETE FROM OrdersAF -- local
        FROM OrdersAF AS O JOIN deleted AS D
          ON  O.OrderID = D.OrderID
          AND O.CustomerID BETWEEN 'AAAAA' AND 'FZZZZ'

      -- delete rows from the OrdersGP table
      IF EXISTS(SELECT *
               FROM deleted
               WHERE CustomerID BETWEEN 'GAAAA' AND 'PZZZZ')
        DELETE FROM Node2.testdb.dbo.OrdersGP
        FROM Node2.testdb.dbo.OrdersGP AS O JOIN deleted AS D
          ON  O.OrderID = D.OrderID
          AND O.CustomerID BETWEEN 'GAAAA' AND 'PZZZZ'

      -- delete rows from the OrdersQZ table
      IF EXISTS(SELECT *
               FROM deleted
               WHERE CustomerID BETWEEN 'QAAAA' AND 'ZZZZZ')
        DELETE FROM Node3.testdb.dbo.OrdersQZ
        FROM Node3.testdb.dbo.OrdersQZ AS O JOIN deleted AS D
          ON  O.OrderID = D.OrderID
          AND O.CustomerID BETWEEN 'QAAAA' AND 'ZZZZZ'

      -- insert rows to the OrdersAF table
      IF EXISTS(SELECT *
               FROM inserted
               WHERE CustomerID BETWEEN 'AAAAA' AND 'FZZZZ')
        INSERT INTO OrdersAF -- local
          SELECT * FROM inserted
          WHERE CustomerID BETWEEN 'AAAAA' AND 'FZZZZ'
```

```
    -- insert rows to the OrdersGP table
  IF EXISTS(SELECT *
            FROM inserted
            WHERE CustomerID BETWEEN 'GAAAA' AND 'PZZZZ')
    INSERT INTO Node2.testdb.dbo.OrdersGP
      SELECT * FROM inserted
      WHERE CustomerID BETWEEN 'GAAAA' AND 'PZZZZ'

    -- insert rows to the OrdersQZ table
  IF EXISTS(SELECT *
            FROM inserted
            WHERE CustomerID BETWEEN 'QAAAA' AND 'ZZZZZ')
    INSERT INTO Node3.testdb.dbo.OrdersQZ
      SELECT * FROM inserted
      WHERE CustomerID BETWEEN 'QAAAA' AND 'ZZZZZ'

  COMMIT TRANSACTION

END
GO
```

If we want to be able to update our Orders view from all of the nodes, we need to create similar triggers in all of them. The only difference between them and the ones we created on Node1 is that each local table in Node1 is a remote table in the other nodes, and thus needs to be accessed using a four-part name, and vice versa.

Next, try to issue the modifications shown in Listing 13-36 and see the results.

Listing 13-36: Modifying a View with INSTEAD OF Triggers Defined

```
-- Run modifications from any of the nodes to test the triggers,

-- assuming that INSTEAD OF triggers were created on all of them
SET XACT_ABORT ON
GO

SELECT * FROM Orders

DELETE FROM Orders

SELECT * FROM Orders

INSERT INTO Orders
  SELECT * FROM Northwind.dbo.Orders
```

```
SELECT * FROM Orders

UPDATE Orders
  SET OrderID = 21325 - OrderID

SELECT * FROM Orders
```

All of the issues that were discussed in this section are relevant to local partitioned views as well, aside from the following points, which apply only to local partitioned views:

- You only need to create a single set of triggers on one server because, by definition, there is only one server.

- You use regular transactions instead of distributed transactions.

- You reference all of the tables locally instead of using their full four-part names.

When and How to Use Distributed Partitioned Views, Their Limitations, and Their Future

From the queries we ran in this chapter, it should be clearer why the type of systems that can benefit most from distributed partitioned views are OLTP environments or Web site databases where a lot of individual queries retrieve relatively small amounts of data. Each query, if routed to the server that contains most of the data that satisfies the query, can be handled in the most efficient way.

The growing need for processing power in those systems reaches a certain point where trying to scale up by adding more resources to the same server is not possible or is too expensive. Distributed partitioned views offer good performance with regular commodity hardware. We can simply add more and more servers and scale out almost linearly.

Distributed partitioned views are not suitable for data warehouse environments because large amounts of data need to be processed to satisfy most of the queries, and most of the queries will result in accessing most of the nodes involved. The cost of running distributed queries against most of the nodes might be too high to justify such a configuration. On the other hand, local distributed partitioned views are very suitable for data warehouse environments, and much work was done in SQL Server 2000 to enhance them for that use.

If your system must be highly reliable, you can use Microsoft Cluster Services' failover clustering. Each cluster is made of two to four servers that appear to the user or the application as one virtual server. One of the nodes is defined as the primary node, and it is the one that services user requests. Failover clustering does not supply load balancing, but it does supply high availability. If the primary node fails, one of the other nodes in the cluster takes over and starts to service user requests that are sent to the virtual server. This process takes place automatically and is transparent to the users. The recommended configuration for distributed partitioned views where high availability is required is to have each of the members of the federation participate in a failover cluster consisting of at least two servers.

In a multitiered environment, such as Windows DNA, you should incorporate data routing rules into the business services tier so that queries will be routed to the server that stores most of the data that is required by the statement. In the queries we ran, we saw that queries are processed most efficiently when run against the server that holds most, or all, of the data that is required by the query. This can be achieved by storing the keys that each server contains in a routing table, which is checked by a COM+ business component that decides the destination server to which a query should be routed. Applications can call the data routing component when they need to issue a query.

The main current limitations of distributed partitioned views are that there is no support for parallel execution or bulk inserts through the view. We hope that future versions of SQL Server will include support for auto-partitioning where the system will decide on the range for each partition and migrate the data to rebalance the partitions.

> **NOTE**   *The project of distributed partitioned views was code-named Coyote. For many a night with the sunrise, the developers could hear the coyotes' calls, and they sure have come up with something they can be proud of.*

Implementing Referential Integrity and Cascading Actions

CHAPTER 1 DISCUSSED the fact that data is usually spread across several tables, which are related to each other through key columns, and that database normalization is used to avoid duplicates in a database, thus avoiding potential errors. Although it's true that database normalization minimizes the chance for errors, it doesn't eliminate them. There is still the need for a set of data integrity rules that will enforce the relationship between tables and keep the database as consistent as possible. This set of rules is called *referential integrity*, and it is a part of the wider set of rules that enforce *data integrity* in general.

This chapter explores the rules used to maintain referential integrity in various table relationships, with a focus on cascading actions. *Cascading actions* are actions that must be performed on a secondary table to compensate when a primary table is modified.

The Relationship Scenarios

You might face different situations, each of which requires a different approach and different rules that need to be implemented. This chapter focuses on cascading modifications from one table to related tables. It discusses two relationship scenarios:

- **The relationship between a primary and a secondary table.** An example is a one-to-many relationship between a primary table and a secondary table, such as an Orders table and an OrderDetails table, where each order in the Orders table has one or more order parts in the OrderDetails table. Another example is a one-to-one relationship between a primary table and a secondary subtype table, such as a Customers table and a ForeignCustomers table, where each customer in the Customers table can have no more than one row in the ForeignCustomers table. There is no need to discuss other variations of these relationships, because they are treated the same way in terms of cascading. Therefore, only the Orders:OrderDetails scenario will be used in the examples in this chapter.

- **The relationships within one table.** An example of such a scenario is an Employees table, where each employee reports to a manager, who is also an employee.

The Orders and OrderDetails Tables

Listing 14-1 contains the creation script for the Orders and OrderDetails tables. They will be used to illustrate the rules necessary to maintain referential integrity between primary and secondary tables.

Listing 14-1: Schema Creation Script for the Orders and OrderDetails Tables

```
CREATE TABLE Orders(
OrderID    int NOT  NULL,
CustomerID char(5)  NOT NULL,
OrderDate  datetime NOT NULL,
CONSTRAINT PK_Orders_OrderID PRIMARY KEY(Orderid))

CREATE TABLE OrderDetails(
OrderID  int NOT NULL,
PartID   int NOT NULL,
Quantity int NOT NULL,
CONSTRAINT PK_OrderDetails_OrderID_partid PRIMARY KEY(OrderID, PartID))

INSERT INTO Orders VALUES(10001, 'FRODO', '19990417')
INSERT INTO Orders VALUES(10002, 'GNDLF', '19990418')
INSERT INTO Orders VALUES(10003, 'BILBO', '19990419')

INSERT INTO OrderDetails VALUES(10001, 11, 12)
INSERT INTO OrderDetails VALUES(10001, 42, 10)
INSERT INTO OrderDetails VALUES(10001, 72, 5)
INSERT INTO OrderDetails VALUES(10002, 14, 9)
INSERT INTO OrderDetails VALUES(10002, 51, 40)
INSERT INTO OrderDetails VALUES(10003, 41, 10)
INSERT INTO OrderDetails VALUES(10003, 61, 35)
INSERT INTO OrderDetails VALUES(10003, 65, 15)
```

Table 14-1 shows the contents of the Orders table, and Table 14-2 shows the OrderDetails table.

Table 14-1: Content of the Orders Table

OrderID	CustomerID	OrderDate
10001	FRODO	1999-04-17 00:00:00.000
10002	GNDLF	1999-04-18 00:00:00.000
10003	BILBO	1999-04-19 00:00:00.000

Table 14-2: Content of the OrderDetails Table

OrderID	PartID	Quantity
10001	11	12
10001	42	10
10001	72	5
10002	14	9
10002	51	40
10003	41	10
10003	61	35
10003	65	15

Figure 14-1 shows the schema of the Orders and OrderDetails tables.

Figure 14-1: Schema of the Orders and OrderDetails tables

The Employees Table

Listing 14-2 contains the creation script for the Employees table. It will be used to illustrate the rules necessary to maintain referential integrity within a single table.

Listing 14-2: Schema Creation Script for the Employees Table

```
CREATE TABLE Employees
(empid int NOT NULL,
 mgrid int NULL,
 empname varchar(25) NOT NULL,
 salary money NOT NULL,
 CONSTRAINT PK_Employees_empid PRIMARY KEY(empid))

INSERT INTO employees(empid, mgrid, empname, salary)
  VALUES( 1, NULL, 'Nancy',  $10000.00)
INSERT INTO employees(empid, mgrid, empname, salary)
  VALUES( 2,    1, 'Andrew',  $5000.00)
INSERT INTO employees(empid, mgrid, empname, salary)
  VALUES( 3,    1, 'Janet',   $5000.00)
INSERT INTO employees(empid, mgrid, empname, salary)
  VALUES( 4,    1, 'Margaret',$5000.00)
INSERT INTO employees(empid, mgrid, empname, salary)
  VALUES( 5,    2, 'Steven',  $2500.00)
INSERT INTO employees(empid, mgrid, empname, salary)
  VALUES( 6,    2, 'Michael', $2500.00)
INSERT INTO employees(empid, mgrid, empname, salary)
  VALUES( 7,    3, 'Robert',  $2500.00)
INSERT INTO employees(empid, mgrid, empname, salary)
  VALUES( 8,    3, 'Laura',   $2500.00)
INSERT INTO employees(empid, mgrid, empname, salary)
  VALUES( 9,    3, 'Ann',     $2500.00)
INSERT INTO employees(empid, mgrid, empname, salary)
  VALUES(10,    4, 'Ina',     $2500.00)
INSERT INTO employees(empid, mgrid, empname, salary)
  VALUES(11,    7, 'David',   $2000.00)
INSERT INTO employees(empid, mgrid, empname, salary)
  VALUES(12,    7, 'Ron',     $2000.00)
INSERT INTO employees(empid, mgrid, empname, salary)
  VALUES(13,    7, 'Dan',     $2000.00)
INSERT INTO employees(empid, mgrid, empname, salary)
  VALUES(14,   11, 'James',   $1500.00)
```

The content of the Employees table is shown in Table 14-3.

Table 14-3: Content of the Employees Table

empid	mgrid	empname	salary
1	NULL	Nancy	10000.0000
2	1	Andrew	5000.0000
3	1	Janet	5000.0000
4	1	Margaret	5000.0000
5	2	Steven	2500.0000
6	2	Michael	2500.0000
7	3	Robert	2500.0000
8	3	Laura	2500.0000
9	3	Ann	2500.0000
10	4	Ina	2500.0000
11	7	David	2000.0000
12	7	Ron	2000.0000
13	7	Dan	2000.0000
14	11	James	1500.0000

Figure 14-2 shows the schema of the Employees table.

Figure 14-2: Schema of the Employees table

Referential Integrity Enforcement Methods

There are several mechanisms for enforcing referential integrity in general and cascading operations, which is one of the referential integrity actions, specifically. They are divided into two main groups:

- *Declarative Referential Integrity (DRI)*, where rules are declared as part of the table's schema. The main mechanism used to enforce DRI is a FOREIGN KEY constraint.

- *Procedural Referential Integrity*, where rules are checked in procedural code. There are several mechanisms that implement procedural referential integrity—code in the client application, stored procedures, and triggers.

Implementing Cascading Operations Using a FOREIGN KEY

The ANSI SQL-92 standard specifies four referential integrity actions that define the activity that should occur when the tables involved in the relationship are modified: NO ACTION, CASCADE, SET DEFAULT, and SET NULL. In a relationship between two tables, the table that contains the FOREIGN KEY—a.k.a. the *referencing table*—is the secondary or subtype table.

In the first OrderDetails table example, the FOREIGN KEY is placed on the related column in the referencing table, and it references the primary table's (a.k.a. the *referenced table's*) related column, on which a PRIMARY KEY or UNIQUE constraint must be defined. In this example, it is placed on the orderid column in the OrderDetails table, and it references the orderid column in the Orders table.

In the second example—the Employees table—the FOREIGN KEY is placed on the mgrid column, and it references the empid column.

The following sections explore the four referential integrity actions in more detail, using the sample tables to illustrate the way they are implemented in SQL Server.

NO ACTION (restrict)

This type of action was the only one supported by the FOREIGN KEY constraint up until, and including, SQL Server 7.0. It always enforces all of the following integrity rules:

1. You can't delete a row from the primary table if it has related rows in the secondary table. In the Orders and OrderDetails scenario, you can't delete an order that has order details. In the Employees scenario, you can't delete a manager who is in charge of employees.

2. You can't update the primary table's primary key if the row being modified has related rows in the secondary table. In the Orders and OrderDetails scenario, you can't update an order ID if that order has order parts. In the Employees scenario, you can't update a manager ID if that manager is in charge of employees.

3. You can't insert a row into the secondary table if there is no related row in the primary table. For example, you can't insert an order detail for an order that doesn't exist. Also, you can't insert an employee if the entry for the employee's manager doesn't exist.

4. You can't update the secondary table's FOREIGN KEY column if it doesn't have a related row in the primary table. For example, you can't shift an order detail to an order that doesn't exist, and you can't assign an employee to a manager if an entry for the manager doesn't exist.

You can create a FOREIGN KEY as part of the CREATE TABLE statement, or you can add it later by using the ALTER TABLE statement. You'll use the latter method in the examples.

To add a FOREIGN KEY to OrderDetails, run the script shown in Listing 14-3.

Listing 14-3: Adding a FOREIGN KEY to the OrderDetails Table

```
ALTER TABLE OrderDetails ADD CONSTRAINT FK_OrderDetails_Orders
  FOREIGN KEY(orderid)
  REFERENCES Orders(orderid)
```

To add a FOREIGN KEY to the Employees table, run the script shown in Listing 14-4.

Listing 14-4: Adding a FOREIGN KEY to the Employees Table

```
ALTER TABLE Employees ADD CONSTRAINT FK_Employees_Employees
  FOREIGN KEY(mgrid)
  REFERENCES Employees(empid)
```

SQL Server 2000 enables you to specify NO ACTION explicitly with the FOREIGN KEY constraint, because it supports other actions as well, as opposed to a FOREIGN KEY constraint in previous versions. NO ACTION is the default if you don't specify an action. Thus, you could rewrite the previous OrderDetails code as shown in Listing 14-5.

Listing 14-5: Add a FOREIGN KEY with NO ACTION to the OrderDetails Table

```
ALTER TABLE OrderDetails ADD CONSTRAINT FK_OrderDetails_Orders
  FOREIGN KEY(orderid)
  REFERENCES Orders(orderid)
  ON DELETE NO ACTION
  ON UPDATE NO ACTION
```

> **NOTE** *If you are running the code samples and want to create a new* FOREIGN KEY *instead of an existing one, you have to drop the existing one first by including the following code in your script:* ALTER TABLE OrderDetails DROP CONSTRAINT FK_OrderDetails_Orders

You should be aware that using a FOREIGN KEY, even to enforce NO ACTION, incurs a performance penalty. If you review the four integrity rules a FOREIGN KEY enforces, it is clear that for each of them, when you modify one table, SQL Server has to access the related table to see if the rule is going to be broken. On the other hand, those rules are checked before the modification occurs—so if any of the rules are broken, nothing is written to the transaction log, and the operation is canceled. Some implementations prefer to enforce these rules in the client application instead. Just keep in mind that one application might enforce the rules, but another might not, thereby compromising the integrity of your database.

CASCADE

The ANSI SQL-92 standard supports both the DELETE CASCADE and the UPDATE CASCADE actions in the REFERENCES clause of the FOREIGN KEY constraint.

ON DELETE CASCADE means that when a row in the primary table is deleted, you want all the related rows in the secondary table, which has a FOREIGN KEY pointing to the primary table, to be automatically deleted. In our Orders and OrderDetails example, if you delete the order with order ID 10002 from the Orders table, the two order details in the OrderDetails table belonging to that order will be automatically deleted.

ON UPDATE CASCADE means that if you update a column in the primary table, which is pointed at by the FOREIGN KEY in the secondary table, the FOREIGN KEY column in all of the related rows will also be updated with the same values. In the Orders and OrderDetails example, if you change the value of orderid from 10002 to 10004 in the Orders table, the value of the orderid column of the two order parts belonging to that order in the OrderDetails table will automatically be updated to 10004 as well.

> **NOTE** *Declarative cascading actions were not supported prior to SQL Server 2000, and they have been on the wish lists of many programmers and DBAs. At last, they are supported as of SQL Server 2000*

To try out these new concepts, you can run some tests on both examples. First, create a FOREIGN KEY that supports both cascade actions (don't forget to drop the existing foreign key first, if you created one), as shown in Listing 14-6.

Listing 14-6: Adding a FOREIGN KEY with CASCADE to the OrderDetails Table

```
ALTER TABLE OrderDetails ADD CONSTRAINT FK_OrderDetails_Orders
  FOREIGN KEY(orderid)
  REFERENCES Orders(orderid)
  ON DELETE CASCADE
  ON UPDATE CASCADE
```

Each of the following examples expects the tables to contain the same data as initially loaded. Instead of reloading the data each time, you can encapsulate the modification in a transaction and roll it back after you check the result, so the changes will not be committed to the database. You can use the pattern shown in Listing 14-7, and just incorporate your DELETE/UPDATE statement instead of the one in the listing.

Listing 14-7: Template for Modifying Data without Commiting the Changes

```
BEGIN TRAN
  SELECT * FROM Orders
  SELECT * FROM OrderDetails
  DELETE... / UPDATE...
  SELECT * FROM Orders
  SELECT * FROM OrderDetails
ROLLBACK TRAN
```

Next, modify the Orders table and check the results. First, delete the order with the order ID 10002, as shown in Listing 14-8.

Listing 14-8: Testing ON DELETE CASCADE

```
DELETE FROM Orders
WHERE orderid = 10002
```

The result of this DELETE statement is shown in Tables 14-4 and 14-5.

Table 14-4: Testing ON DELETE CASCADE, Orders Table

OrderiD	CustomerID	OrderDate
10001	FRODO	1999-04-17 00:00:00.000
10003	BILBO	1999-04-19 00:00:00.000

Table 14-5: Testing ON DELETE CASCADE, OrderDetails Table

OrderID	PartID	Quantity
10001	11	12
10001	42	10
10001	72	5
10003	41	10
10003	61	35
10003	65	15

You can see that the related order parts in the OrderDetails table were automatically deleted. Examine the execution plan of this DELETE, shown in Figure 14-3. The steps in this execution plan are as follows:

1. Delete the row with order ID 10002 from the Orders table (clustered index delete).

2. Store the deleted order ID 10002 in a temporary table.

3. Read the temporary table created in Step 2.

4. Perform a clustered index seek in the OrderDetails table to find matching order parts.

5. Join the temporary table from Step 3 to the OrderDetails rows found in Step 4 to find the order details that need to be deleted (using a nested-loops join algorithm).

```
Query 1: Query cost (relative to the batch): 100.00%
Query text: DELETE [Orders] WHERE [orderid]=@1
```

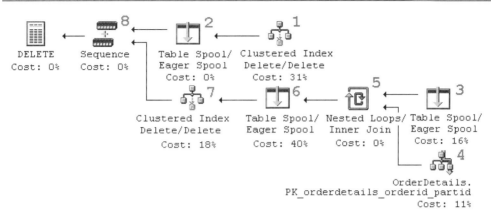

Figure 14-3: Execution plan for ON DELETE CASCADE

6. Store the order details' keys in a temporary table.

7. DELETE order details from the OrderDetails table based on the keys stored in the temporary table from Step 5 (clustered index delete).

8. Perform the modifications in sequence (top to bottom).

Now you can issue an UPDATE against the Orders table that changes order ID 10002 to 10004, as shown in Listing 14-9.

Listing 14-9: Testing ON UPDATE CASCADE

```
UPDATE Orders
  SET orderid = 10004
WHERE orderid = 10002
```

The result of this UPDATE statement is shown in Tables 14-6 and 14-7.

Table 14-6: Testing ON UPDATE CASCADE, Orders Table

OrderID	CustomerID	OrderDate
10001	FRODO	1999-04-17 00:00:00.000
10003	BILBO	1999-04-19 00:00:00.000
10004	GNDLF	1999-04-18 00:00:00.000

Table 14-7: Testing ON UPDATE CASCADE, OrderDetails Table

OrderID	PartID	Quantity
10001	11	12
10001	42	10
10001	72	5
10003	41	10
10003	61	35
10003	65	15
10004	14	9
10004	51	40

Notice that the orderid column of the related order details in the OrderDetails table was updated correctly. Cascade actions also support multirow modifications. Consider the UPDATE statement shown in Listing 14-10.

Listing 14-10: Testing ON UPDATE CASCADE with a Multirow Update

```
UPDATE Orders
  SET orderid = orderid + 1
```

The result of this UPDATE statement is shown in Tables 14-8 and 14-9.

Table 14-8: Testing ON UPDATE CASCADE with a Multirow Update, Orders Table

OrderID	CustomerID	OrderDate
10002	FRODO	1999-04-17 00:00:00.000
10003	GNDLF	1999-04-18 00:00:00.000
10004	BILBO	1999-04-19 00:00:00.000

Table 14-9: Testing ON UPDATE CASCADE with a Multirow Update, OrderDetails Table

OrderID	PartID	Quantity
10002	11	12
10002	42	10
10002	72	5
10003	14	9
10003	51	40
10004	41	10
10004	61	35
10004	65	15

This might seem trivial at first glance, but if you look at the other alternatives to implementing cascading operations, which are mainly stored procedures and triggers (both of which will be explained later in this chapter), you'll see that an UPDATE like this cannot be cascaded with any other mechanism.

Unfortunately, you cannot implement cascading actions in the Employees table the same way. If you try to create a foreign key on the Employees table that supports cascade actions, you will get the error shown in Listing 14-11.

Listing 14-11: Cyclic or Multiple Cascade Paths Error When Trying to Add a Foreign Key

```
Server: Msg 1785, Level 16, State 1, Line 1
Introducing Foreign key Constraint 'FK_Employees_Employees' on table 'Employees'
may cause cycles or multiple cascade paths.  Try using instead option 'On Delete
(Update) No Action' or modifying other Foreign key constraints
Server: Msg 1750, Level 16, State 1, Line 1
Could not create constraint.  See previous errors.
```

As you can see, SQL Server noticed that your cascade operation is cyclic, and it does not allow this type of cascading. This is true not only for a self-referencing table, but also for any chain of relationships between tables in which the cascading operations have a potential to be cyclical. In order to enforce cascading actions in relationships that are potentially cyclic, you'll need to revert to enforcement mechanisms that are used in releases earlier than SQL Server 2000, such as triggers. Such mechanisms are covered later in this chapter.

If you go over the four rules that are enforced by NO ACTION, you should keep in mind that when you use ON DELETE CASCADE, it compensates for a DELETE in the primary table by deleting the related rows in the secondary table instead of enforcing

Rule 1 (which would prevent the DELETE). Similarly, ON UPDATE CASCADE compensates for an UPDATE to the primary table by updating the related rows in the secondary table instead of enforcing Rule 2 (which would prevent the UPDATE). If either of the cascade actions is not used, the related rule will be enforced. Notice that cascade actions compensate only for modifications to the primary table. Rules 3 and 4 concern illegal modifications to the secondary table that result in a row that has no related row in the primary table. These two rules are always enforced by the constraint, even when you define both cascade actions.

When you use declarative constraints, you don't need to worry about Rules 3 and 4 because they are taken care of automatically. However, you should keep them in mind because you will need to be aware of them when you use other mechanisms to enforce cascade actions.

SET NULL and SET DEFAULT

The referential actions SET NULL and SET DEFAULT compensate for modifications to the primary table by setting the related columns in the child rows in the secondary table to NULL or to their default value. These actions are not supported as declarative referential constraints in SQL Server 2000, but you can implement them with triggers, which will be discussed later in this chapter, in the "Implementing Cascading Operations Using Triggers" section.

Implementing Cascading Operations Using Stored Procedures

Using stored procedures to implement cascading actions does not provide a self-maintained solution. It does, however, allow you to keep your FOREIGN KEY enabled, even in SQL Server 7.0, where this is not possible when implementing a trigger-based solution.

To use stored procedures this way, you create a stored procedure that substitutes each type of modification for both the referencing and referenced tables, making sure that the users will modify the data only through the stored procedures so that the cascade actions will take place. You can accomplish this by granting the users permissions to execute the stored procedures, but not allowing them to directly update the underlying tables. Another "gotcha" with this solution is that the stored procedures take care of single-row modifications on the referenced table.

The following examples are run on the Orders and OrderDetails scenario. Before you continue, make sure you have a FOREIGN KEY with no cascade actions enabled, as shown in Listing 14-12.

Listing 14-12: Re-creating the FOREIGN KEY with NO ACTION (Implicitly)

```
ALTER TABLE Employees DROP CONSTRAINT FK_Employees_Employees
GO

ALTER TABLE Employees ADD CONSTRAINT FK_Employees_Employees
  FOREIGN KEY(mgrid)
  REFERENCES Employees(empid)
GO
```

You'll implement a stored procedure for each type of modification on both the Orders and OrderDetails tables.

Deleting a Row in the Primary Table

Taking care of cascade deletes in the Orders table is quite simple. You first delete matching rows from the OrderDetails table, and then delete the row from the Orders table. This way you don't break the FOREIGN KEY. The creation script for the usp_OrdersDelete stored procedure is shown in Listing 14-13.

Listing 14-13: Creation Script for the usp_OrdersDelete Stored Procedure

```
CREATE PROC dbo.usp_OrdersDelete
  @orderid int
AS

BEGIN TRAN

-- delete matching rows from OrderDetails
DELETE FROM OrderDetails
WHERE orderid = @orderid

-- delete row from Orders
DELETE FROM Orders
WHERE orderid = @orderid

COMMIT TRAN
GO
```

Updating a Row in the Primary Table

Updating a row in the Orders table is a bit more complex than deleting a row. First, you need to cascade the UPDATE only if the orderid column is modified. You also need to check whether it is modified to a new value; otherwise, it is the same as not modifying it.

If the orderid value doesn't change, you can perform a regular UPDATE. If it changes, the FOREIGN KEY does not allow a regular UPDATE. To handle this situation, you can break the UPDATE up into a DELETE operation followed by an INSERT operation. After all, you can think of an UPDATE operation as deleting the old value and inserting the new one. First you insert a row with the new order ID and update the matching rows in the OrderDetails table. Then you can DELETE the row with the old order ID.

The creation script for the usp_OrdersUpdate stored procedure is shown in Listing 14-14.

Listing 14-14: Creation Script for the usp_OrdersUpdate Stored Procedure

```
CREATE PROC dbo.usp_OrdersUpdate
  @orderid     int,
  @neworderid int      = NULL,
  @customerid char(5) = NULL,
  @orderdate  datetime = NULL
AS


-- perform cascade update only if the orderid column is modified
--    and also, it is different from the existing order id
-- split the update to insert and then delete so the foreign key will not be broken
IF @neworderid IS NOT NULL AND @orderid <> @neworderid
BEGIN
  BEGIN TRAN

  -- insert a row with the new order id to Orders
  INSERT INTO Orders(orderid, customerid, orderdate)
    SELECT
      @neworderid,
      ISNULL(@customerid, customerid),
      ISNULL(@orderdate, orderdate)
    FROM
      Orders
    WHERE
      orderid = @orderid
```

```
  -- update the orderid column for the matching rows in OrderDetails
  UPDATE OrderDetails
    SET orderid = @neworderid
  WHERE orderid = @orderid

  -- delete the row with the old order id from Orders
  DELETE FROM Orders
  WHERE orderid = @orderid

  COMMIT TRAN
END
-- if the orderid column was not modified, perform a regular update
ELSE
  UPDATE Orders
    SET customerid = ISNULL(@customerid, customerid),
        orderdate  = ISNULL(@orderdate, orderdate)
  WHERE
      orderid = @orderid
GO
```

There are a few issues that this stored procedure deals with. In order to allow the update of only some of the columns in the row, you need to have a signal indicating that certain columns should keep their current values. Because all of the columns in the Orders table do not allow NULLs, this is easy—you can safely use NULLs as your signal. This, however, is not so simple with columns that allow NULLs. If you want to allow a column with a NULL value to be updated, you need another signal indicating that the column should keep its current value. Adding a parameter for each column that allows NULLs can solve this—it can be used as a flag that indicates whether it is a NULL that should be placed in the column, or whether the current column value should be kept.

Also note that this solution is only possible if none of the columns other than the PRIMARY KEY is enforced with a UNIQUE constraint or a UNIQUE index. If there is such a column, your INSERT will fail on a duplicate key. In such a case, you might decide to drop the FOREIGN KEY and handle the UPDATE with an UPDATE statement instead of breaking it into an INSERT followed by a DELETE. Another option that does not require you to drop the FOREIGN KEY is to move all the affected secondary table rows to a temporary table and UPDATE them there. This way you can perform the UPDATE as a DELETE followed by an INSERT and then copy the rows back to the OrderDetails table, and you won't violate the FOREIGN KEY.

Inserting a Row into the Primary Table

Inserting a row into the Orders table is pretty straightforward. The creation script for the usp_OrdersInsert stored procedure is shown in Listing 14-15.

Listing 14-15: Creation Script for the usp_OrdersInsert Stored Procedure

```
CREATE PROC dbo.usp_OrdersInsert
  @orderid    int,
  @customerid char(5),
  @orderdate  datetime
AS

INSERT INTO Orders(orderid, customerid, orderdate)
  VALUES(@orderid, @customerid, @orderdate)
GO
```

Here you don't have the NULLs problem discussed earlier because NULLs are not used as a signal in this script. However, you do have a problem if some of the columns in the table have default values and you want to allow the user to use the defaults for those columns by not specifying a value. If the default values are constants, this could be solved easily by making the default values of the columns also the default values of the parameters in the stored procedure. For example, if the customerid column had the default value "ZZZZZ", you could slightly modify the stored procedure as in Listing 14-16.

Listing 14-16: Creation Script for the usp_OrdersInsert Stored Procedure, with Defaults Included

```
CREATE PROC dbo.usp_OrdersInsert
  @orderid    int,
  @customerid char(5) = 'ZZZZZ',
  @orderdate  datetime
AS

INSERT INTO Orders(orderid, customerid, orderdate)
  VALUES(@orderid, @customerid, @orderdate)
GO
```

If the default values for the columns had been expressions, such as a system function like GETDATE(), this modification wouldn't have been so simple, because a default value for a stored procedure's parameter can only be a constant. In such a situation, you need to add parameters to indicate that a default value is desired for a column and then issue the INSERT using the DEFAULT keyword instead of using a specific value for the column.

Inserting, Updating, and Deleting a Row in the Secondary Table

Inserting, updating, and deleting a row in the OrderDetails table are all straightforward operations, and they have the same issues regarding NULLs and default values as discussed earlier. Listing 14-17 contains the creation script for the usp_OrderDetailsInsert, usp_OrderDetailsUpdate, and usp_OrderDetailsDelete stored procedures.

Listing 14-17: Creation Script for the usp_OrderDetailsInsert, usp_OrderDetailsUpdate, and usp_OrderDetailsDelete Stored Procedures

```
CREATE PROC dbo.usp_OrderDetailsInsert
  @orderid  int,
  @partid   int,
  @quantity int
AS

INSERT INTO OrderDetails(orderid, partid, quantity)
  VALUES(@orderid, @partid, @quantity)
GO

CREATE PROC dbo.usp_OrderDetailsUpdate
  @orderid    int,
  @partid     int,
  @neworderid int = NULL,
  @newpartid  int = NULL,
  @quantity   int = NULL
AS

UPDATE OrderDetails
  SET orderid = ISNULL(@neworderid, orderid),
      partid = ISNULL(@newpartid, partid),
      quantity = ISNULL(@quantity, quantity)
WHERE
    orderid = @orderid
  AND
    partid = @partid
GO

CREATE PROC dbo.usp_OrderDetailsDelete
  @orderid int,
  @partid  int
AS
```

```
DELETE FROM OrderDetails
WHERE
    orderid = @orderid
  AND
    partid = @partid
GO
```

Note that you didn't need to deal with illegal modifications that result in orphaned order details because the FOREIGN KEY takes care of that.

Encapsulating the Logic

Instead of manually creating a set of stored procedures for each table, you can encapsulate the logic in a stored procedure that creates the relevant CREATE PROCEDURE statements and executes them dynamically.

To get an idea of how this can be implemented, visit Dejan Sarka's SQL User's Group Web site—http://sql.reproms.si—and select "English" from the pull-down menu at the bottom of the left pane, "Old presentations" from the Meetings list in the middle of the left pane, and a sample script from the "Procedures that create procedures" offerings in the center pane.

Implementing Cascading Operations Using Triggers

You can use *triggers* to enforce referential integrity and cascading actions when you need a self-maintained solution—you don't need to modify the data through special stored procedures. You can use the same INSERT, UPDATE, and DELETE statements to modify the base tables as you would normally use, and they will cause the triggers to fire and enforce referential integrity and cascade your modifications.

Prior to SQL Server 2000, triggers were the only self-maintained solution you could implement to enforce referential integrity with cascading actions. SQL Server 2000 introduces new features to T-SQL that enable you to approach cascading actions in a variety of new ways, some of which were discussed earlier in this chapter. Others will be discussed in the following sections. Because we approach cascading actions differently in SQL Server 2000 as compared to previous versions, we will discuss the two approaches separately.

Using Triggers Prior to SQL Server 2000

The first thing that you need to keep in mind when you want to provide a solution with AFTER triggers in all versions of SQL Server is that they fire *after* the modification has occurred. This means that you have to drop all existing FOREIGN KEY constraints in order to allow the trigger's code to run after a modification takes place. Otherwise, the constraint will prevent the modification from taking place. In other words, if you keep the constraints and modify a row in the primary table, and related rows in the secondary table exist, the modification will be rejected by the constraint and the trigger will never fire. Furthermore, once you drop the constraint, your trigger solution needs to take care of all referential integrity rules that might be broken, in addition to implementing the cascading actions.

> **TIP** *Instead of dropping the foreign keys, you can just disable them using* ALTER TABLE NOCHECK CONSTRAINT <constraint_name>. *This will enable visual tools such as the Enterprise Manager's database designer to recognize the relationships and display them. Also, when you use the* sp_help *system stored procedure to investigate the tables' schema, it will be easier to recognize the relationships.*

Implementing ON DELETE CASCADE and ON UPDATE CASCADE with Triggers

Before continuing, you need to drop the existing foreign keys, as shown in Listing 14-18.

Listing 14-18: Dropping the Foreign Keys

```
ALTER TABLE OrderDetails DROP CONSTRAINT FK_OrderDetails_Orders
GO
ALTER TABLE Employees DROP CONSTRAINT FK_Employees_Employees
GO
```

Now that you are aware of the implications of using triggers in your solution, take a look at the flow diagram shown in Figure 14-4, which shows the components you should use depending on the types of cascading actions you want to support. Each component is discussed in detail in the following sections.

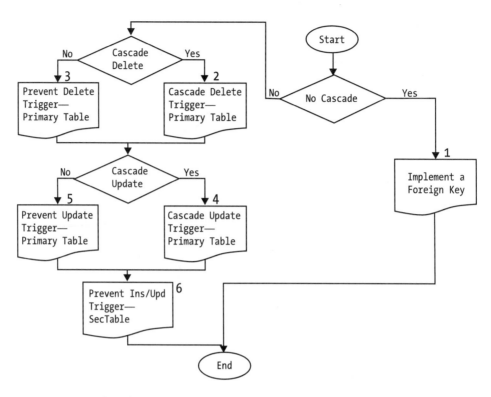

Figure 14-4: Flow diagram of trigger solution to referential integrity enforcement

Cascading Deletes

In the first junction shown in Figure 14-4, you check whether your solution should implement NO ACTION. If this is the case, you simply create a FOREIGN KEY (Component 1 in Figure 14-4), as discussed earlier in the "NO ACTION (restrict)" section of the chapter, and your flow diagram ends.

    If you implement any kind of cascade action, you go to the second junction, where you check whether your solution handles the DELETE CASCADE action. If it does, you implement a DELETE CASCADE trigger (Component 2 in Figure 14-4). You need to implement the cascade trigger a bit differently in a relationship between two tables than in a single-table relationship. In the Orders and OrderDetails example, you can implement the trigger as shown in Listing 14-19.

Listing 14-19: Creation Script for the trg_d_orders_on_delete_cascade Trigger

```
CREATE TRIGGER trg_d_orders_on_delete_cascade ON Orders FOR DELETE
AS
```

```
DELETE FROM OrderDetails
FROM
    OrderDetails AS OD
  JOIN
    deleted       AS D ON OD.orderid = D.orderid
GO
```

> **NOTE** *In order to make the code shorter, most of the triggers displayed in this chapter do not include the* IF @@ROWCOUNT = 0 *check. As discussed in Chapter 10, this check is important to ensure that the code in the trigger will not be invoked if the trigger is fired as a result of a modification that did not affect any rows in the table. In a production environment, you should add these checks.*

To understand how the trigger works, DELETE an order from the Orders table, as shown in Listing 14-20. (Remember, you can wrap the modification in a transaction in the examples so the changes will not commit in the database.)

Listing 14-20: Testing the trg_d_orders_on_delete_cascade Trigger

```
DELETE FROM Orders
WHERE orderid = 10002
```

Take a look at Figure 14-5, which shows what's happening inside the trigger.

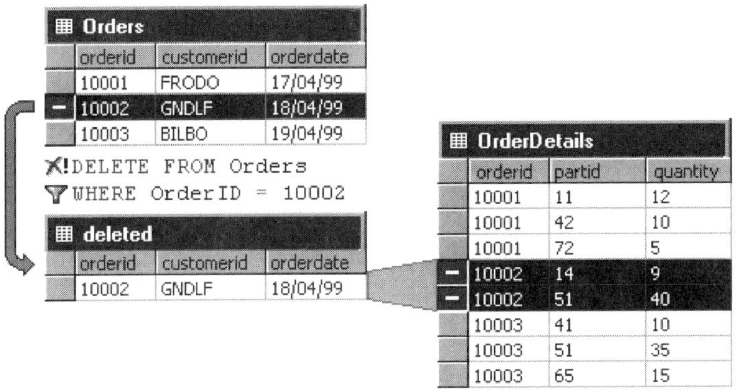

Figure 14-5: Inside the CASCADE DELETE trigger

The DELETE operation in Listing 14-20 starts the following activity:

1. The DELETE operation is written to the transaction log.

2. Order 10002 is deleted from the Orders table.

3. The DELETE trigger is fired. While inside the trigger, order 10002 does not exist in the Orders table. The *deleted* table, which you can think of as a view on the deleted row in the transaction log, contains the row for order 10002.

4. The DELETE trigger deletes all related rows from the OrderDetails table by performing a join between the *deleted* table and the OrderDetails table. The join is used here to filter only the related rows in the OrderDetails table.

Thus you get the required result, as shown in Tables 14-10 and 14-11 .

Table 14-10: Testing the trg_d_orders_on_delete_cascade Trigger, Orders Table

OrderID	CustomerID	OrderDate
10001	FRODO	1999-04-17 00:00:00.000
10003	BILBO	1999-04-19 00:00:00.000

Table 14-11: Testing the trg_d_orders_on_delete_cascade Trigger, OrderDetails Table

OrderID	PartID	Quantity
10001	11	12
10001	42	10
10001	72	5
10003	41	10
10003	61	35
10003	65	15

The trg_d_orders_on_delete_cascade trigger also handles multirow deletes.

On the face of it, it looks like you could implement the same trigger on the Employees table. After all, if you DELETE an employee, you want to DELETE all his or her subordinates, as well. The difference here is that each of the subordinates might have subordinate employees, so your trigger needs to handle recursion; otherwise, it will DELETE the subordinates of the employee you deleted, but will leave their subordinates without a manager.

As discussed in Chapter 10, the ability of triggers to fire recursively is determined in the database level by the setting of the 'recursive triggers' database option, which is disabled by default. If you want to allow recursive triggers, you first need to enable this option, but then you face another problem. Triggers fire as a result of a DELETE operation even if the DELETE operation did not affect any rows. To understand the consequence of the fact that triggers fire even if no rows are affected, suppose you enabled recursive triggers, implemented the DELETE cascade trigger, and deleted Robert's row from the Employees table.

Currently, the Employees table should look like the one shown in Table 14-12.

Table 14-12: Employees Table

empid	mgrid	empname	salary
1	NULL	Nancy	10000.0000
2	1	Andrew	5000.0000
3	1	Janet	5000.0000
4	1	Margaret	5000.0000
5	2	Steven	2500.0000
6	2	Michael	2500.0000
7	3	Robert	2500.0000
8	3	Laura	2500.0000
9	3	Ann	2500.0000
10	4	Ina	2500.0000
11	7	David	2000.0000
12	7	Ron	2000.0000
13	7	Dan	2000.0000
14	11	James	1500.0000

Now try the DELETE statement shown in Listing 14-21.

Listing 14-21: Testing a DELETE CASCADE Trigger on the Employees Table with Recursive Triggers Enabled

```
DELETE FROM Employees
WHERE empid = 7
```

Robert's row is removed from the table, and the trigger fires for the first time. The *deleted* table contains Robert's row. Then the trigger deletes Robert's subordinates (David, Ron, and Dan) by joining the Employees table to the *deleted* table. The result is shown in Table 14-13.

Table 14-13: Testing a DELETE CASCADE Trigger on the Employees Table with Recursive Triggers Enabled the First Time the Trigger Fires

empid	mgrid	empname	salary
1	NULL	Nancy	10000.0000
2	1	Andrew	5000.0000
3	1	Janet	5000.0000
4	1	Margaret	5000.0000
5	2	Steven	2500.0000
6	2	Michael	2500.0000
8	3	Laura	2500.0000
9	3	Ann	2500.0000
10	4	Ina	2500.0000
14	11	James	1500.0000

The trigger is fired again for the second time recursively. The *deleted* table contains the rows of David, Ron, and Dan, and the trigger deletes their subordinates (in this case, only David has a subordinate—James) by joining the Employees table to the *deleted* table. The result is shown in Table 14-14.

Table 14-14: Testing a DELETE CASCADE Trigger on the Employees Table with Recursive Triggers Enabled the Second Time the Trigger Fires

empid	mgrid	empname	salary
1	NULL	Nancy	10000.0000
2	1	Andrew	5000.0000
3	1	Janet	5000.0000
4	1	Margaret	5000.0000
5	2	Steven	2500.0000
6	2	Michael	2500.0000
8	3	Laura	2500.0000
9	3	Ann	2500.0000
10	4	Ina	2500.0000

The trigger is fired again for the third time recursively. The *deleted* table contains James' row. Notice that James doesn't have subordinates, but the trigger is unaware of that because it doesn't perform any existence checks prior to the DELETE, hence the DELETE is issued. The DELETE operation doesn't affect any rows, but it is a DELETE just the same, so another trigger is fired with no rows in the *deleted* table.

This recursive loop would continue endlessly if there were no limitation for the number of nesting levels. However, because there is a nesting level limitation (16 in SQL Server 6.5 and 32 in later versions), all modifications are rolled back once that limitation is reached. To solve the problem of the trigger firing even when the modification affects no rows, you can simply add an existence check to the trigger prior to the DELETE, as shown in Listing 14-22.

Listing 14-22: Creation Script for the trg_d_employees_on_delete_cascade Trigger

```
CREATE TRIGGER trg_d_employees_on_delete_cascade ON Employees FOR DELETE
AS

IF EXISTS(SELECT *
        FROM
            Employees AS E
          JOIN
            deleted   AS D ON E.mgrid = D.empid)
  DELETE FROM Employees
  FROM
     Employees AS E
   JOIN
     deleted   AS D ON E.mgrid = D.empid
GO
```

> **NOTE**   *Be careful when you issue a* DELETE *to the Employees table. Think of what would happen if you removed Nancy's row.*

For another approach to handling deletes in hierarchical structures, see Chapter 16.

Preventing Illegal Deletes from the Referenced Table

Continuing with the flow diagram in Figure 14-4, suppose you don't want to support the DELETE CASCADE action. If you have come this far in the flow diagram, it means that you support the UPDATE CASCADE action; hence, you don't have a foreign key to prevent an illegal DELETE of a row in the primary table that has related rows in the secondary table. Therefore, you need to enforce this rule with a prevent_delete trigger (Component 3 in Figure 14-4). This trigger is implemented the same way in a relationship between two tables as in a single-table relationship.

Using the Orders and OrderDetails relationship as an example, create the trigger shown in Listing 14-23.

Listing 14-23: Creation Script for the trg_d_orders_prevent_delete Trigger

```
CREATE TRIGGER trg_d_orders_prevent_delete ON Orders FOR DELETE
AS

IF EXISTS(SELECT *
          FROM
              OrderDetails AS OD
          JOIN
              deleted     AS D ON OD.orderid = D.orderid)
BEGIN
  RAISERROR('The Orders you are trying to delete have related rows
          in OrderDetails.  TRANSACTION rolled back.', 10, 1)
  ROLLBACK TRANSACTION
END
GO
```

The fact that the activity inside the trigger is part of a transaction started before the modification that fires the trigger enables you to roll back the transaction if you discover an illegal DELETE attempt.

You can use the same kind of trigger in the Employees table, as Listing 14-24 shows.

Listing 14-24: Creation Script for the trg_d_employees_prevent_delete Trigger

```
CREATE TRIGGER trg_d_employees_prevent_delete ON Employees FOR DELETE
AS

IF EXISTS(SELECT *
          FROM
                Employees AS E
            JOIN
              deleted    AS D ON E.mgrid = D.empid)
BEGIN
  RAISERROR('The employees you are trying to delete have subordinates.
            TRANSACTION rolled back.', 10, 1)
  ROLLBACK TRANSACTION
END
GO
```

Cascading Updates

At the next junction in the flow diagram in Figure 14-4, you check whether your solution handles the UPDATE CASCADE action. If it does, you implement an UPDATE CASCADE trigger (Component 4 in the diagram). This trigger is more complex than a DELETE CASCADE trigger. It's not just a matter of locating the related rows in the secondary table—joining the *deleted* table to the secondary table can easily do this. You also need to update the relevant rows in the secondary table with the updated values from the primary table.

For example, if you change the order ID of order 10002 to 10004, you need first to locate all order details belonging to order 10002, and then UPDATE their orderid column to 10004. It is not too complex to handle such an UPDATE as long as only one order ID changes.

In this section, you'll start with single-row updates and then look at the problems (and solutions) involved with multirow updates. Begin by writing a trigger that implements this UPDATE CASCADE operation on the Orders table, as shown in Listing 14-25.

Listing 14-25: Creation Script for the trg_u_orders_on_update_cascade Trigger

```
CREATE TRIGGER trg_u_orders_on_update_cascade ON Orders FOR UPDATE
AS

DECLARE @numrows int
SET @numrows = @@ROWCOUNT
```

```
IF UPDATE(orderid)
  IF @numrows = 1
    UPDATE OrderDetails
      SET orderid = (SELECT orderid FROM inserted)
    FROM
        OrderDetails AS OD
      JOIN
        deleted      AS D ON OD.orderid = D.orderid
  ELSE IF @numrows > 1
  BEGIN
    RAISERROR('Updates to more than one row in Orders are not allowed.
            TRANSACTION rolled back.', 10, 1)
    ROLLBACK TRANSACTION
  END
GO
```

You first save the number of affected rows in a variable so you can later check it. Next you check whether the orderid column was updated. If it wasn't, this UPDATE doesn't involve cascading; hence, it is not your concern. If it was, you continue and check whether more than one row was modified. If this is the case, your trigger cannot handle this situation and it rolls back the modification. If only one row was modified, you perform the CASCADE UPDATE operation. To understand how the CASCADE UPDATE works, UPDATE an order from the Orders table, as shown in Listing 14-26.

Listing 14-26: Testing the trg_u_orders_on_update_cascade Trigger

```
UPDATE Orders
  SET orderid = 10004
WHERE orderid = 10002
```

Take a look at Figure 14-6, which illustrates what's happening inside the trigger. You join the *deleted* table with the OrderDetails table to filter only the related order details, and then update their orderid column to the new value, which is fetched from the *inserted* table by using a subquery. You can issue such a subquery because you know that there is one and only one row in the *inserted* table; otherwise, the subquery would have returned more than one value and the update would have failed. Thus you get the required result, as Tables 14-15 and 14-16 show.

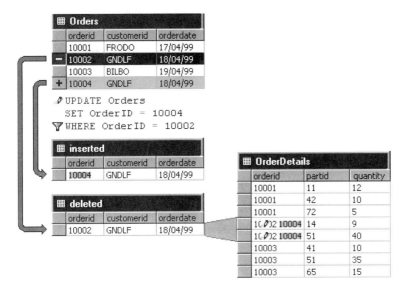

Figure 14-6: Inside the CASCADE UPDATE trigger

Table 14-15: Testing the trg_u_orders_on_update_cascade Trigger, Orders Table

OrderID	CustomerID	OrderDate
10001	FRODO	1999-04-17 00:00:00.000
10003	BILBO	1999-04-19 00:00:00.000
10004	GNDLF	1999-04-18 00:00:00.000

Table 14-16: Testing the trg_u_orders_on_update_cascade Trigger,
OrderDetails Table

OrderID	PartID	Quantity
10001	11	12
10001	42	10
10001	72	5
10003	41	10
10003	61	35
10003	65	15
10004	14	9
10004	51	40

There are no problems with locating the related rows in the OrderDetails table—you simply join it to the *deleted* table, because it still holds the old order ID values. But how do you relate the rows in the *inserted* table to the relevant rows in the OrderDetails table now that they have new order IDs? Your immediate reaction might be to try to access the rows in the *deleted* and *inserted* tables by using cursors, based on the assumption that a record in one cursor is in the same position as the related record in the other cursor. If you could guarantee that, you could loop through both cursors, one record at a time, and update the related rows in the OrderDetails table, as both the old order ID and the new order ID would be related.

The bad news is that this cannot be guaranteed at all. There is no way you can guarantee that the order of the records in the cursor on the *deleted* table will have the same order as the related records in a cursor you place on the *inserted* table. You're pretty much stuck, unless you devise a way to relate the rows prior to the UPDATE to the rows after the UPDATE. One way to handle this is to add a surrogate key to the Orders table, to which UPDATEs will not be allowed. The sole purpose of this key is to be the join column between the *deleted* and the *inserted* tables. You can use the IDENTITY property to automatically generate its values. Also, you will need your UPDATE trigger to make sure that UPDATEs to this column will be rejected.

First, add the surrogate_key column to your Orders table, as shown in Listing 14-27.

Listing 14-27: Adding a Surrogate Key to the Orders Table

```
ALTER TABLE Orders
  ADD surrogate_key int NOT NULL IDENTITY(1,1)
    CONSTRAINT UNQ_orders_surrogate_key UNIQUE
```

The result of this addition is shown in Table 14-17.

Table 14-17: The Orders Table with the Addition of the Surrogate Key

OrderID	CustomerID	OrderDate	surrogate_key
10001	FRODO	1999-04-17 00:00:00.000	1
10002	GNDLF	1999-04-18 00:00:00.000	2
10003	BILBO	1999-04-19 00:00:00.000	3

Now you can modify the trigger to support multirow UPDATEs, as shown in Listing 14-28.

Listing 14-28: Adding Multirow Support
for the trg_u_orders_on_update_cascade Trigger

```
ALTER TRIGGER trg_u_orders_on_update_cascade ON Orders FOR UPDATE
AS

DECLARE @numrows int
SET @numrows = @@ROWCOUNT
IF UPDATE(surrogate_key)
BEGIN
  RAISERROR('Updates to surrogate_key are not allowed.
            TRANSACTION rolled back.', 10, 1)
  ROLLBACK TRANSACTION
END
ELSE
  IF UPDATE(orderid) AND @numrows > 0
    UPDATE OrderDetails
      SET orderid = I.orderid
    FROM
        OrderDetails AS OD
      JOIN
        deleted     AS D ON OD.orderid      = D.orderid
      JOIN
        inserted    AS I ON D.surrogate_key = I.surrogate_key
GO
```

First, you make sure that the UPDATE doesn't affect the surrogate key. Then, you check whether the orderid column was updated and also whether any row was affected by the UPDATE at all. If the orderid column was updated and at least one row was affected by the UPDATE, you perform the cascade UPDATE operation. In all other cases, you don't need to take any action.

To understand how the CASCADE UPDATE works, update all of the orders, as shown in Listing 14-29.

Listing 14-29: Testing the trg_u_orders_on_update_cascade Trigger
with a Multirow Update

```
UPDATE Orders
  SET orderid = 20004 - orderid
```

Take a look at Figure 14-7, which illustrates what's happening inside the trigger.

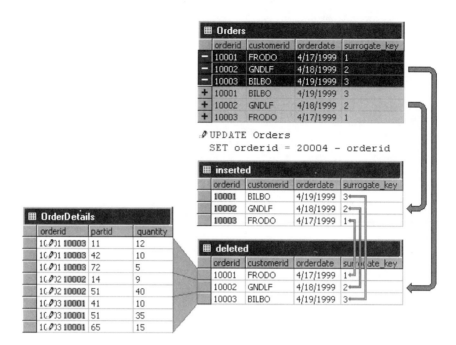

Figure 14-7: Inside the multirow UPDATE CASCADE trigger

As you can see, you join the OrderDetails table with the *deleted* table to filter the relevant rows as you did before. You also join the *deleted* table to the *inserted* table to correlate the rows before and after the UPDATE. You can do this thanks to the surrogate key you added. Now you can use the updated value of the orderid column from the *inserted* table to update the orderid column in the OrderDetails table. Take a look at the results shown in Tables 14-18 and 14-19.

Table 14-18: Testing the trg_u_orders_on_update_cascade Trigger with a Multirow Update, Orders Table

OrderID	CustomerId	OrderDate	surrogate_key
10001	BILBO	1999-04-19 00:00:00.000	3
10002	GNDLF	1999-04-18 00:00:00.000	2
10003	FRODO	1999-04-17 00:00:00.000	1

Table 14-19: Testing the trg_u_orders_on_update_cascade Trigger with a Multirow Update, OrderDetails Table

OrderID	PartID	Quantity
10001	41	10
10001	61	35
10001	65	15
10002	14	9
10002	51	40
10003	11	12
10003	42	10
10003	72	5

You can do basically the same thing in the Employees table, except you don't need recursion because when you update the empid of a certain employee, you only want to update the mgrid of this employee's direct subordinates. You don't need to worry about the fact that you turned on recursion for the database because you first check whether the empid column was updated before you perform the cascade UPDATE.

To see how this works, begin by adding a surrogate key, as shown in Listing 14-30.

Listing 14-30: Adding a Surrogate Key to the Employees Table

```
ALTER TABLE Employees
  ADD surrogate_key int NOT NULL IDENTITY(1,1)
      CONSTRAINT UNQ_employees_surrogate_key UNIQUE
GO
```

Table 14-20 shows the Employees table contents with the surrogate key added. The table shows that the IDENTITY values were generated in order of empid, because the Employees table was scanned in that order, but keep in mind that there is no guarantee of that.

Table 14-20: The Employees Table with the Addition of the Surrogate Key

empid	mgrid	empname	salary	surrogate_key
1	NULL	Nancy	10000.0000	1
2	1	Andrew	5000.0000	2
3	1	Janet	5000.0000	3
4	1	Margaret	5000.0000	4
5	2	Steven	2500.0000	5
6	2	Michael	2500.0000	6
7	3	Robert	2500.0000	7
8	3	Laura	2500.0000	8
9	3	Ann	2500.0000	9
10	4	Ina	2500.0000	10
11	7	David	2000.0000	11
12	7	Ron	2000.0000	12
13	7	Dan	2000.0000	13
14	11	James	1500.0000	14

Now create the cascade UPDATE trigger by running the script shown in Listing 14-31.

Listing 14-31: Creation Script for the trg_u_employees_on_update_cascade Trigger

```
CREATE TRIGGER trg_u_employees_on_update_cascade ON Employees FOR UPDATE
AS

DECLARE @numrows int
SET @numrows = @@ROWCOUNT
IF UPDATE(surrogate_key)
BEGIN
  RAISERROR('Updates to surrogate_key are not allowed.
          TRANSACTION rolled back.', 10, 1)
  ROLLBACK TRANSACTION
END
```

```
ELSE
  IF UPDATE(empid) AND @numrows > 0
    UPDATE Employees
      SET mgrid = I.empid
    FROM
        Employees AS E
      JOIN
        deleted   AS D ON E.mgrid        = D.empid
      JOIN
        inserted AS I ON D.surrogate_key = I.surrogate_key
GO
```

As you can see, the trigger looks the same as the one you used for the Orders table. To see if it works, you can issue the UPDATE shown in Listing 14-32.

Listing 14-32: Testing the trg_u_employees_on_update_cascade Trigger

```
UPDATE Employees
  SET empid = 15 - empid
```

The result in Table 14-21 shows that the trigger did its job.

Table 14-21: Testing the trg_u_employees_on_update_cascade Trigger with a Multirow Update, Employees Table

empid	mgrid	empname	salary	surrogate_key
1	4	James	1500.0000	14
2	8	Dan	2000.0000	13
3	8	Ron	2000.0000	12
4	8	David	2000.0000	11
5	11	Ina	2500.0000	10
6	12	Ann	2500.0000	9
7	12	Laura	2500.0000	8
8	12	Robert	2500.0000	7
9	13	Michael	2500.0000	6
10	13	Steven	2500.0000	5
11	14	Margaret	5000.0000	4
12	14	Janet	5000.0000	3
13	14	Andrew	5000.0000	2
14	NULL	Nancy	10000.0000	1

Preventing Illegal Updates to the Referenced Table

Continuing with the flow diagram in Figure 14-4, suppose you don't want to support the UPDATE cascade action. Instead of creating a cascade UPDATE trigger, you could create a prevent_update trigger (Component 5 in the diagram), which looks like the prevent_delete trigger discussed earlier. All you need to do is find out whether the rows you're trying to update in the primary table have related rows in the secondary table.

Listing 14-33 has the script you need to create the trigger on the Orders table.

Listing 14-33: Creation Script for the trg_u_orders_prevent_update Trigger

```
CREATE TRIGGER trg_u_orders_prevent_update ON Orders FOR UPDATE
AS

IF EXISTS(SELECT *
        FROM
            OrderDetails AS OD
          JOIN
            deleted     AS D ON OD.orderid = D.orderid)
BEGIN
  RAISERROR('The Orders you are trying to update have related rows
        in OrderDetails.  TRANSACTION rolled back.', 10, 1)
  ROLLBACK TRANSACTION
END
GO
```

Listing 14-34 shows the script you need to run to create the trigger on the Employees table.

Listing 14-34: Creation Script for the trg_u_employees_prevent_update Trigger

```
CREATE TRIGGER trg_u_employees_prevent_update ON Employees FOR UPDATE
AS

IF EXISTS(SELECT *
        FROM
            Employees AS E
          JOIN
            deleted   AS D ON E.mgrid = D.empid)
BEGIN
  RAISERROR('The employees you are trying to update have subordinates.
        TRANSACTION rolled back.', 10, 1)
  ROLLBACK TRANSACTION
END
GO
```

Preventing Orphaned Rows in the Referencing Table

You have one more thing to do. If you've gotten this far in the flow diagram (Figure 14-4), it signifies that you chose to use triggers to enforce referential integrity. This means that Rules 3 and 4 discussed in the "NO ACTION (restrict)" section of the chapter need to be enforced with a trigger as well. These rules disallow INSERT and UPDATE operations that result in a row in the secondary table with no related row in the primary table—in other words, operations that create an orphaned row. Because you need to ensure that the result is legal, you can use one trigger that checks the rows in the *inserted* table for both INSERT and UPDATE operations. Unlike all previous triggers, this trigger will be created on the secondary table.

   Run the code shown in Listing 14-35 to create the trg_iu_orderdetails_prevent_insupd trigger.

Listing 14-35: Creation Script for the trg_iu_orderdetails_prevent_insupd Trigger

```
CREATE TRIGGER trg_iu_orderdetails_prevent_insupd
  ON OrderDetails FOR INSERT, UPDATE
AS

DECLARE @numrows int
SET @numrows = @@ROWCOUNT

IF UPDATE(orderid) AND @numrows > 0
  IF @numrows <> (SELECT COUNT(*)
                  FROM Orders AS O JOIN inserted AS I
                    ON O.orderid = I.orderid)
  BEGIN
    RAISERROR('Result rows in OrderDetails are orphaned.
              TRANSACTION rolled back.', 10, 1)
    ROLLBACK TRANSACTION
  END
GO
```

   Notice how the code in the trigger checks whether you have orphaned rows. If you don't have orphaned rows, an inner join between the *inserted* table, which holds the new order details, and the Orders table will result in the same number of rows as in the *inserted* table, because each order detail has a matching order. If at least one of the order details doesn't have a matching order, the number of rows in the *inserted* table will be greater than the number of rows resulting from the inner join. This trigger can also be implemented with an IF NOT EXISTS() to check to see if order detail rows don't have a matching row in the Orders table (the EXISTS() predicate is covered in Chapter 2). You can try to implement this trigger using the NOT EXISTS() predicate as an exercise.

For the Employees table, you need to take a slightly different approach. Keeping in mind that top-level employees have NULLs in the mgrid column, the number of rows affected by an UPDATE to a top-level employee will be different than the number of rows returned by a join between the affected employees and their managers, as NULLs do not match. You can tackle the problem by removing top-level employees from the equation. You compare the number of rows in *inserted*, excluding NULLs, to the number of rows in the result of the join between *inserted* and the primary table, which, in this case, is Employees. Run the script shown in Listing 14-36 to create the trg_iu_employees_prevent_insupd trigger.

Listing 14-36: Creation Script for the trg_iu_employees_prevent_insupd Trigger

```
CREATE TRIGGER trg_iu_employees_prevent_insupd
  ON Employees FOR INSERT, UPDATE
AS

IF @@ROWCOUNT > 0 AND UPDATE(mgrid)
BEGIN
  DECLARE @numrows int

  SELECT
    @numrows = COUNT(*)
  FROM
    inserted
  WHERE
    mgrid IS NOT NULL

  IF @numrows <> (SELECT COUNT(*)
                  FROM Employees AS E JOIN inserted AS I
                    ON E.empid = I.mgrid)
  BEGIN
    RAISERROR('Result rows in Employees are orphaned.
           TRANSACTION rolled back.', 10, 1)
    ROLLBACK TRANSACTION
  END
END
GO
```

Notice that this time you join the Employees table to the inserted table ON E.empid = I.mgrid, as opposed to the previous triggers, where you used the join condition ON E.mgrid = I.empid. Now you are looking for illegal inserts to the secondary table, so you look at the Employees table from the managers' point of view and not from the employees' point of view. The inserted table contains new employees, and you want to check whether their mgrid column represents an existing employee in the Employees table.

Encapsulating the Logic

As you've seen in the previous section, if you want to enforce referential integrity with triggers, there's a pretty straightforward flow diagram (see Figure 14-4) that shows you which triggers to create. You follow the same flow diagram for any pair of tables in a relationship. The only difference between the triggers in each implementation is the names of the tables and the columns.

You can create a stored procedure that encapsulates the logic of the flow diagram and creates the set of triggers for you. It will receive the table and column names as parameters. You would execute the stored procedure as shown in Listing 14-37.

Listing 14-37: Invoking the sp_CreateRelationship Stored Procedure

```
EXEC sp_CreateRelationship
  @prmtbl        = Orders,
  @sectbl        = OrderDetails,
  @prmcol        = orderid,
  @seccol        = orderid,
  @deletecascade = 1,
  @updatecascade = 1

EXEC sp_CreateRelationship
  @prmtbl        = Employees,
  @sectbl        = Employees,
  @prmcol        = empid,
  @seccol        = mgrid,
  @deletecascade = 1,
  @updatecascade = 1
```

Appendix F contains the script that implements the sp_CreateRelationship stored procedure.

Implementing SET NULL and SET DEFAULT with Triggers

ON DELETE SET NULL and ON UPDATE SET NULL are implemented very much the same way as their respective cascade triggers. However, there is a new issue you need to keep in mind. In both a 1:1 (one-to-one) relationship and a 1:M (one-to-many) relationship (such as the one between the Orders table and the OrderDetails table), you cannot keep a PRIMARY KEY or UNIQUE constraint on the secondary table that includes the referencing column as part of the key. In such a case, your cascading operation might result in duplicate keys and would therefore be rolled back. If your primary key contains the referencing column, you can substitute it with an existing alternate key, if one exists in the table, or create a surrogate PRIMARY KEY. Also, if you are implementing SET NULL, the referencing column in the secondary table must allow NULLs, in order to accept them.

If you want to implement ON DELETE SET NULL in your Orders and OrderDetails example, instead of creating a trigger that implements the DELETE cascade logic, as in the previous section, you can create the trigger shown in Listing 14-38 (though first you would need to drop the PRIMARY KEY from the OrderDetails table and alter the orderid column so that it would allow NULLs).

Listing 14-38: Creation Script for the trg_d_orders_on_delete_set_null Trigger

```
CREATE TRIGGER trg_d_orders_on_delete_set_null ON Orders FOR DELETE
AS

UPDATE OrderDetails
  SET orderid = NULL
FROM
    OrderDetails AS OD
  JOIN
    deleted        AS D ON OD.orderid = D.orderid
GO
```

If you want to support the SET DEFAULT action instead, assuming that there is a DEFAULT value defined for the referencing column, you would implement a trigger that looks almost like the trigger that implements the SET NULL action. You just replace the NULL in the SET clause with the keyword DEFAULT, as shown in Listing 14-39.

Listing 14-39: Creation Script for the trg_d_orders_on_delete_set_default Trigger

```
CREATE TRIGGER trg_d_orders_on_delete_set_default ON Orders FOR DELETE
AS

UPDATE OrderDetails
  SET orderid = DEFAULT
FROM
    OrderDetails AS OD
  JOIN
    deleted        AS D ON OD.orderid = D.orderid
GO
```

You can implement the ON UPDATE SET NULL or ON UPDATE SET DEFAULT actions in a similar way by slightly modifying the logic of the respective UPDATE cascade triggers, which were discussed previously in this chapter.

Using Triggers in SQL Server 2000

In SQL Server 2000, there is no compelling reason to use triggers to enforce cascading operations. Declarative referential constraints can take care of this, as discussed in the "Implementing Cascading Operations Using a FOREIGN KEY" section. However, in certain situations, declarative referential constraints can't be implemented. For example, you can't create a FOREIGN KEY that points to a table in another database, but you can still enforce referential integrity with triggers the same way you would in versions prior to SQL Server 2000. In fact, everything covered in the previous section is valid for SQL Server 2000, as well.

As discussed in Chapter 10, the only type of triggers that were supported in previous versions of SQL Server are what are now called AFTER triggers, because SQL Server 2000 supports INSTEAD OF triggers as well. Remember that AFTER triggers fire only after constraints are checked, so if you decide to enforce referential integrity with AFTER triggers, you have to drop or disable all existing foreign keys, just as in previous versions; otherwise, the AFTER triggers will never fire.

With INSTEAD OF triggers, things are slightly different. Because these triggers substitute for the modification that was submitted to the database, they fire before constraints are checked. INSTEAD OF triggers on the primary table can coexist with declarative cascading referential constraints on the secondary table, so you don't need to implement the cascading actions in the trigger if you need to take preliminary actions before the modification actually happens in the primary table.

Before going into details, it's important to review a few issues that were discussed in Chapter 10, as they will come into play here. Now that you have declarative referential constraints that can take care of cascade actions, and also INSTEAD OF triggers and AFTER triggers, a modification to the primary table will be processed in the following order:

1. Modification is issued.

2. If an INSTEAD OF trigger is defined on the relevant type of modification, it substitutes the modification. The INSTEAD OF trigger is responsible for resubmitting the modification.

3. If an INSTEAD OF trigger was not defined, or if the modification was resubmitted by the INSTEAD OF trigger, the constraint performs its safety checks and the cascade operation fires, if one was defined on the relevant type of modification. Note that if the INSTEAD OF trigger modifies the table on which it is placed, it will not be called recursively. However, if it performs modifications that do not result in recursive calls to itself, those modifications will be treated just as any other modification—in other words, they will be processed in the same order described here, starting from Step 1.

4. If the modification was not rejected by a constraint, any defined AFTER triggers fire.

However, if you need an INSTEAD OF trigger on the secondary table, it cannot coexist with a declarative cascading referential constraint of the same type. For example, an INSTEAD OF DELETE trigger cannot coexist with a FOREIGN KEY with ON DELETE CASCADE defined, and an INSTEAD OF INSERT or UPDATE trigger cannot coexist with a FOREIGN KEY with ON UPDATE CASCADE defined. If you need to support both an INSTEAD OF trigger on the secondary table and also cascading actions, you have the following options:

- Drop or disable the FOREIGN KEY, and enforce cascade actions with AFTER triggers.

- Keep the FOREIGN KEY with NO ACTION in the problematic operation, and implement cascade actions for that operation with an INSTEAD OF trigger on the primary table.

You've already learned how to implement the first option. The second option might look appealing at first glance—like getting to have your cake and eat it, too—but don't count your chickens before they're hatched...

First, you need to try and take care of a situation where you have an INSTEAD OF DELETE trigger on the secondary table that has nothing to do with your cascade actions. You'll use the Orders and OrderDetails scenario to run your examples.

> **NOTE**   *Before you start to add triggers, re-create and repopulate the Orders and OrderDetails tables, and add the surrogate key to the OrderDetails table.*

Suppose there's a very important INSTEAD OF DELETE trigger on the OrderDetails table, as shown in Listing 14-40.

Listing 14-40: Creation Script
for the trg_d_orderdetails_on_delete_print_hello Trigger

```
CREATE TRIGGER trg_d_orderdetails_on_delete_print_hello
  ON OrderDetails   INSTEAD OF DELETE
AS

PRINT 'Hello from instead of delete trigger on OrderDetails'
```

```
-- resubmit the delete
DELETE FROM OrderDetails
FROM
    OrderDetails AS OD
  JOIN
    deleted AS D ON  OD.orderid = D.orderid
                AND OD.partid  = D.partid
GO
```

Now you need to add cascade actions for both DELETE and UPDATE. You cannot use the ON DELETE CASCADE option because you have an INSTEAD OF DELETE trigger on the OrderDetails table. Instead, you add the FOREIGN KEY shown in Listing 14-41.

Listing 14-41: Adding a Foreign Key to the OrderDetails Table with ON DELETE NO ACTION

```
ALTER TABLE OrderDetails ADD CONSTRAINT FK_OrderDetails_Orders
  FOREIGN KEY(orderid)
  REFERENCES Orders(orderid)
  ON DELETE NO ACTION
  ON UPDATE CASCADE
GO
```

If you want to support a cascade DELETE action, you have to do it in an INSTEAD OF DELETE trigger on the Orders table; otherwise the constraint will prevent it. The task doesn't look too hard, as Listing 14-42 shows.

Listing 14-42: Creation Script for the trg_d_orders_ON_DELETE_CASCADE Trigger

```
CREATE TRIGGER trg_d_orders_ON_DELETE_CASCADE ON Orders INSTEAD OF DELETE
AS

-- perform the delete cascade action
DELETE FROM OrderDetails
FROM
    OrderDetails AS OD
  JOIN
    deleted       AS D ON OD.orderid = D.orderid

-- resubmit the delete
DELETE FROM Orders
FROM
    Orders  AS O
  JOIN
    deleted AS D ON O.orderid = D.orderid
GO
```

You first delete the rows from the OrderDetails table, and then resubmit the DELETE for the Orders table. This way, at no point do you leave orphaned order details, so you don't break any referential integrity rules enforced by the FOREIGN KEY. The tables should now look the same as they did in the beginning of the chapter (see Tables 14-1 and 14-2), with the addition of the surrogate key to the Orders table.

You can now perform both an UPDATE and a DELETE to see that your solution works (remembering to wrap the modifications in a transaction that you can roll back, so the changes will not persist in the database, of course). First try the update shown in Listing 14-43.

Listing 14-43: Testing an UPDATE to See If the DRI UPDATE CASCADE Works

```
UPDATE Orders
  SET orderid = 10004
WHERE orderid = 10002
```

The result of this UPDATE statement is shown in Tables 14-22 and 14-23.

Table 14-22: Testing an UPDATE to See If the DRI UPDATE CASCADE Works, Orders Table

OrderID	CustomerID	OrderDate
10001	FRODO	1999-04-17 00:00:00.000
10003	BILBO	1999-04-19 00:00:00.000
10004	GNDLF	1999-04-18 00:00:00.000

Table 14-23: Testing an UPDATE to See If the DRI UPDATE CASCADE Works, OrderDetails Table

OrderID	PartID	Quantity
10001	11	12
10001	42	10
10001	72	5
10003	41	10
10003	61	35
10003	65	15
10004	14	9
10004	51	40

Next, you can try the DELETE statement shown in Listing 14-44.

Listing 14-44: Testing the trg_d_orders_ON_DELETE_CASCADE Trigger

```
DELETE FROM Orders
WHERE orderid = 10002
```

```
Hello from instead of delete trigger on OrderDetails
```

Apart from the "Hello" message, you can see the result of this DELETE statement in Tables 14-24 and 14-25.

Table 14-24: Testing the trg_d_orders_ON_DELETE_CASCADE Trigger, Orders Tabl

OrderID	CustomerID	OrderDate
10001	FRODO	1999-04-17 00:00:00.000
10003	BILBO	1999-04-19 00:00:00.000

Table 14-25: Testing the trg_d_orders_ON_DELETE_CASCADE Trigger, OrderDetails Table

OrderID	PartID	Quantity
10001	11	12
10001	42	10
10001	72	5
10003	41	10
10003	61	35
10003	65	15

You can rub your hands with joy as you head on to Chapter 14's puzzle, where you'll take care of a situation where an INSTEAD OF UPDATE trigger exists on the OrderDetails table. This time you'll need to perform some acrobatics to leave the FOREIGN KEY and the INSTEAD OF UPDATE trigger on the OrderDetails table, and implement cascade updates as well.

SQL Puzzle 14-1: Implementing Cascading Operations

This puzzle involves the Orders and OrderDetails tables. You start with the same table structure and content as at the beginning of this chapter, with the addition of the surrogate key to the Orders table. There are three INSTEAD OF triggers on the OrderDetails table that are not related to the cascading actions. Your task is to enforce referential integrity and also to support cascade actions for both DELETE and UPDATE. You cannot use either ON DELETE CASCADE or ON UPDATE CASCADE with the FOREIGN KEY because they cannot coexist with the existing INSTEAD OF triggers on the OrderDetails table.

Here's the script that creates the three INSTEAD OF triggers on the OrderDetails table that are not related to the cascading actions:

```
CREATE TRIGGER trg_d_orderdetails_on_delete_print_hello
  ON OrderDetails  INSTEAD OF DELETE
AS

-- perform the important preliminary tasks
PRINT 'Hello from instead of delete trigger on OrderDetails'

-- resubmit the delete
DELETE FROM OrderDetails
FROM
    OrderDetails AS OD
  JOIN
    deleted AS D ON  OD.orderid = D.orderid
               AND OD.partid  = D.partid
GO

CREATE TRIGGER trg_d_orderdetails_on_insert_print_hello
  ON OrderDetails  INSTEAD OF INSERT
AS

-- perform the important preliminary tasks
PRINT 'Hello from instead of insert trigger on OrderDetails'

-- resubmit the insert
INSERT INTO OrderDetails
  SELECT
    *
  FROM
    inserted
GO
```

```
CREATE TRIGGER trg_d_orderdetails_on_update_print_hello
  ON OrderDetails   INSTEAD OF UPDATE
AS

-- perform the important preliminary tasks
PRINT 'Hello from instead of update trigger on OrderDetails'

-- resubmit the update as delete / insert
DELETE FROM OrderDetails
FROM
    OrderDetails AS OD
  JOIN
    deleted AS D ON  OD.orderid = D.orderid
                AND OD.partid  = D.partid

INSERT INTO OrderDetails
  SELECT
    *
  FROM
    inserted
GO
```

Currently, each of the triggers just prints "Hello" and resubmits the modification, but you should treat this modification as just an example. In practice, the triggers would perform a more complex modification instead of the original one.

Although you cannot use either ON DELETE CASCADE or ON UPDATE CASCADE with the FOREIGN KEY, you can add a FOREIGN KEY with NO ACTION defined for both DELETE and UPDATE:

```
ALTER TABLE OrderDetails ADD CONSTRAINT FK_OrderDetails_Orders
  FOREIGN KEY(orderid)
  REFERENCES Orders(orderid)
  ON DELETE NO ACTION
  ON UPDATE NO ACTION
GO
```

You can then add the following ON_DELETE_CASCADE INSTEAD OF trigger:

```
CREATE TRIGGER trg_d_orders_ON_DELETE_CASCADE ON Orders INSTEAD OF DELETE
AS
```

```
-- perform the delete cascade action
DELETE FROM OrderDetails
FROM
    OrderDetails AS OD
  JOIN
    deleted AS D ON OD.orderid = D.orderid

-- resubmit the delete
DELETE FROM Orders
FROM
    Orders  AS O
  JOIN
    deleted AS D ON O.orderid = D.orderid
GO
```

An additional requirement for your task is to add support for the UPDATE cascade action without dropping the FOREIGN KEY. Keep in mind that your solution should not affect the way the INSTEAD OF triggers on OrderDetails perform. In other words, if you issue an UPDATE to the Orders table, the trigger you develop should cascade the UPDATE to the OrderDetails table, and only the current activity in the INSTEAD OF UPDATE trigger on the OrderDetails should be performed, the same as it would if you had sent that UPDATE manually. You are allowed to modify the INSTEAD OF triggers in order to accomplish the task.

The answer to this puzzle can be found on pages 704–716.

Server-Side Cursors— the SQL of *Last* Resort

IF YOU HAVE SKIPPED through the previous chapters so that you could get to this one right away, stop! Most cases where cursors are being used, they are not really necessary. Cursors are not as clean as using straight SQL, both from a coding and performance standpoint. You should look upon cursors as the SQL of last resort, and it had better be the *last* resort. SQL was designed to be used for set-level (non-cursor) solutions and can handle just about anything you throw at it without the need for a cursor. Sometimes, though, there is no escaping cursors. This chapter will guide you through their proper usage.

The Top 5 Reasons People Use Cursors

Since cursors are the SQL of last resort, let's examine the main reasons why people use them.

1. Bad grasp of SQL.

2. Bad database design.

3. Weird business rules.

4. Need to execute a stored procedure for each row.

5. Need to break up data modifications into manageable chunks.

Obviously, the first reason can be eliminated by experience (yours and others'). Learning SQL is easy; doing it well takes a lot of practice. If you cannot figure out how to do it on your own, find someone who can—a colleague, an author (via his/her books, articles, etc.), or a respondent to a cry for help in the Usenet newsgroups. If you have carefully read the previous chapters and done the SQL Puzzles, you are already well-equipped to avoid using cursors most of the time. If you need more convincing, Joe Celko's books, particularly *SQL Puzzles and Answers* (Morgan Kaufmann Publishers), can change your mind about the need for cursors.

The previous reason dealt primarily with developers. The second reason is aimed at DBAs and data architects. To avoid bad database design, you are going to have to find someone with a good track record to be the DBA. Follow that up with design reviews, and you are most of the way there. The analysis and design part of the show is the most important—screw this up and even the best SQL jockey in the world can't help you. Spend the cash here or you will be spending much more money later.

The most common case of bad design is failure to normalize. Except for such things as star schema in data warehouses, data should be in one and only one place. If data are repeated, then you are looking at having to pick out just the right bit of information and comparing the current row to the previous row to detect a change.

Here's a real-world example. On a conversion at a major retailer, the existing design had employee pay rates for each employee for each day of the year. Now, they weren't giving these people pay hikes every day; it was more like one or two pay increases a year. Migrating the data required using a cursor to go through the data row by row to find the day the pay was increased and what the new rate was. The new table was greatly reduced from the original, but it took a cursor to get there.

From the Trenches

Just because software was written by a vendor does not necessarily mean that it is of high quality. One vendor package had four nested cursors in a stored procedure. A single UPDATE statement could have replaced the stored procedure code.

There is no excuse for the first two reasons. The next three are the real impetus behind cursors. Some application architectures, particularly two-tier architectures, require server-side processing. The consequence of using the front end is sending more data out over the network than is actually necessary. Sure, you can create a Visual Basic or C++ module to do this on the server, but that sounds like work. For example, you may have a discounting scheme that says that every fifth product you buy gets you a discount, based upon the weighted value of the four products leading up to it. SQL Server can handle this quite nicely through a cursor.

It would be nice if the SQL standard allowed for invocation of a stored procedure for every row in a result set, but it does not. Here, you have to loop through the rows and execute the procedure row-by-row.

The name of every database object is kept in the *sysobjects* table. A type of 'U' designates tables in *sysobjects*. DBAs typically use cursors if they want to do something against each table in the database—for example, executing sp_recompile. They loop through every row in *sysobjects* where the type is 'U' and then execute the intended stored procedure once for every table name retrieved by the cursor. You'll see some examples later in this chapter.

The final reason is based on physical constraints of the system. Even though something may be achievable at the set level by a single UPDATE statement, the amount of logging may be prohibitive and may fill up the transaction log or the entire disk. This is usually encountered during conversions, when you are updating millions of rows, and this work can often be broken up into smaller pieces so that the disk I/O is minimized. A simple WHILE loop can often replace a cursor.

The before and after images of your data are written to the transaction log whenever you do any data modification—that is, after INSERTs, UPDATEs, or DELETEs. This is so that SQL Server can restore the database to a consistent state in the event of a server crash. The more rows you touch in a single transaction, the more that gets written to the transaction log. You can imagine what happens if you are hitting hundreds of millions or billions of rows—the transaction log will reach astronomical proportions. You may even reach a point where there is insufficient transaction log space to do the work.

Usually, this type of scenario happens when you are doing a migration from an existing system. Here, too, you may not necessarily need a cursor to do the splitting. A regular WHILE loop may be all you need, but the end result is the same.

Implementing Cursors

To implement a cursor, there is a set of commands you must use. Five of the commands are mandatory and one is optional:

- DECLARE

- OPEN

- FETCH

- UPDATE/DELETE (optional)

- CLOSE

- DEALLOCATE

Using the DECLARE Statement

The DECLARE statement is where you give SQL Server the SELECT statement for which you wish to receive rows. At this time, you tell it the type of cursor and define the type of behavior. There are two basic styles—SQL-92 and Transact-SQL.

SQL-92 Cursors

The most-used cursor is the SQL-92 cursor for a few reasons. First, this is the most common cursor type and it is used on other platforms besides SQL Server. Second, because it is a broadly used standard, it is unlikely to change. Third, it is easier to remember because it has fewer features than do the Transact-SQL extensions. When you get to be Tom's age, "less to remember" is a big plus. ;-)

The DECLARE syntax is shown in Listing 15-1.

Listing 15-1: DECLARE Syntax for SQL-92 Cursor

```
DECLARE cursor_name [INSENSITIVE] [SCROLL] CURSOR
FOR select_statement
[FOR {READ ONLY | UPDATE [OF column_name [,...n]]}]
```

The options are limited but useful and straightforward. The INSENSITIVE option tells SQL Server that you want a snapshot that will not pick up any changes in the underlying rows as you move through the result set. In this case, SQL Server makes a copy of the rows in tempdb before making them available to you, so you might sense a delay before the first row is available to be fetched. Make sure that tempdb is big enough to handle these extra rows. Because this is a copy, and the underlying rows may change, you cannot use the FOR UPDATE option with the INSENSITIVE option.

The SCROLL option is quite useful for those cases where you wish to go back and forth through the rows. Usually you need to do this for some strange business reasons. For example, if the fifth row has a value above a certain level, then you want to look at the third row.

As alluded to previously, the FOR UPDATE option allows you to update each row as it is fetched. The READ ONLY option disallows updates.

Transact-SQL Cursors

The syntax for the DECLARE statement is shown in Listing 15-2.

Listing 15-2: DECLARE Syntax for Transact-SQL Cursor

```
DECLARE cursor_name CURSOR
[LOCAL | GLOBAL]
[FORWARD_ONLY | SCROLL]
[STATIC | KEYSET | DYNAMIC | FAST_FORWARD]
[READ_ONLY | SCROLL_LOCKS | OPTIMISTIC]
[TYPE_WARNING]
FOR select_statement
[FOR UPDATE [OF column_name [,...n]]]
```

Notice that with the Transact-SQL cursor you have many more options than you did with the SQL-92 cursor. Most of the options are stated between the CURSOR and FOR SELECT keywords. Some options have the same effect as an equivalent option in SQL-92 cursors.

The LOCAL and GLOBAL options are mutually exclusive and refer to the scope of the cursor. The LOCAL option means that only the stored procedure that declared the cursor has access to it. The GLOBAL option means that all nest levels of stored procedures can access it. To prevent a real mess, avoid GLOBAL wherever possible.

The FORWARD_ONLY and SCROLL options are also mutually exclusive and determine what FETCH commands you can use. As the name implies, FORWARD_ONLY means that the only FETCH you can use is FETCH NEXT. The SCROLL option allows forward and backward movement as discussed shortly in the "Using the FETCH Statement" section.

The next options deal with the sensitivity of the cursor. The least sensitive is STATIC. SQL Server saves the rows in a worktable in tempdb, and the locks are freed from the original tables. Any modifications made to the base tables will not be reflected in any FETCH—it is effectively a snapshot of your SELECT. This is equivalent to the INSENSITIVE option of the SQL-92 syntax. Needless to say, you cannot update through such a cursor. Since this worktable must be populated before you can use it, there may be a delay before you can retrieve your first row.

The KEYSET option creates a worktable in tempdb of keys based upon your SELECT. The membership and order of the rows remain fixed. Any changes to non-key attributes, either by the cursor owner or by other connections will be reflected in the cursor. Inserts made by other connections are not reflected in the cursor. Any attempt to fetch a row deleted from outside will result in a @@FETCH_STATUS of –2. The effects of updates of key values from outside are very important but can be difficult to troubleshoot because an UPDATE is treated as a DELETE followed by an INSERT. As stated above, any deletion from outside (even if caused by an UPDATE) will cause a @@FETCH_STATUS of –2. However, updates done via the WHERE CURRENT OF clause of the cursor *are* visible.

The DYNAMIC option is more sensitive than the STATIC and KEYSET options. This option will reflect all changes in the underlying tables. The data values, membership, and order of the rows can change on each FETCH. You cannot use a FETCH ABSOLUTE with this option.

The FAST_FORWARD option is a combination of the FORWARD_ONLY and READ_ONLY options, but it is optimized for performance. It cannot be used with the FORWARD_ONLY, SCROLL, or FOR UPDATE options.

The READ_ONLY option acts the same as the READ ONLY option of its SQL-92 counterpart.

The SCROLL_LOCKS option places locks on the rows as they are fetched so that an update made to them through the cursor will be guaranteed to succeed. This option cannot be used with FAST_FORWARD.

The OPTIMISTIC option refers to optimistic locking. If you go to update the table, and the row has changed since you fetched it, you will get error 16934: "Optimistic concurrency check failed. The row was modified outside of this cursor." Although SQL Server supports concurrency via both optimistic with row versioning and optimistic with values, the Books Online claim that Transact-SQL cursors support only row versioning, which would mean that you would need a timestamp column on the underlying table being updated. However, a simple experiment with and without a timestamp showed that both cases worked. This option cannot be used in conjunction with FAST_FORWARD.

For Transact-SQL cursors, if you do not specify the READ_ONLY, OPTIMISTIC, or SCROLL_LOCKS options, then the default behavior is controlled as follows. If the SELECT does not support updates (for example, if it uses aggregates), it becomes READ_ONLY. Both STATIC and FAST_FORWARD default to READ_ONLY, which makes intuitive sense. Finally, DYNAMIC and KEYSET default to OPTIMISTIC. If you want no surprises, declare all of your options explicitly. During development, it's a good idea to use sp_describe_cursor (described later, in the "Ancillary Stored Procedures" section) in your code to determine whether the cursor is behaving as predicted.

The SET Statement

The Transact-SQL (not the SQL-92) cursor allows you to store the cursor in a variable through the SET statement. First, you declare the variable as type CURSOR, as shown in Listing 15-3.

Listing 15-3: DECLARE Syntax for Cursor Variable

```
DECLARE
  @cursor_variable CURSOR
```

Next, you use the SET command to assign a cursor to the variable. This is presented in Listing 15-4.

Listing 15-4: SET Syntax for a Cursor

```
SET
@cursor_variable =
CURSOR
[FORWARD_ONLY | SCROLL]
[STATIC | KEYSET | DYNAMIC | FAST_FORWARD]
[READ_ONLY | SCROLL_LOCKS | OPTIMISTIC]
[TYPE_WARNING]
FOR select_statement
[FOR {READ ONLY
| UPDATE [OF column_name [,...n]] } ]
```

All of the options are the same as for the DECLARE CURSOR command.

You can also use the SET command to set a cursor variable to another cursor variable. Why would you use this approach? You can use a cursor variable as a parameter to a stored procedure. We'll discuss that in the "Using Cursor Variables with Stored Procedures" section.

Using the OPEN Statement

Once you have declared the cursor, you then issue an OPEN command to begin to receive rows. This is the point at which the SELECT defined in the DECLARE statement is executed.

Using the FETCH Statement

To retrieve a row, use the FETCH statement. This retrieves only one row—there is no way of retrieving blocks of rows. Take a look at the syntax in Listing 15-5.

Listing 15-5: FETCH Syntax

```
FETCH
[ [ NEXT | PRIOR | FIRST | LAST
| ABSOLUTE {n | @nvar}
| RELATIVE {n | @nvar}
]
FROM
]
{ { [GLOBAL] cursor_name } | @cursor_variable_name}
[INTO @variable_name[,...n] ]
```

The FETCH options are controlled by the DECLARE CURSOR options. In SQL-92 scroll cursors, all options are supported; otherwise, you can use only NEXT. In Transact-SQL cursors, the rules are bit more arcane. Both FORWARD_ONLY and FAST_FORWARD allow only NEXT, for obvious reasons. If you do not use DYNAMIC, FORWARD_ONLY, or FAST_FORWARD, and you specify KEYSET, STATIC, or SCROLL, then you may use all options. Finally, if you do use DYNAMIC, you may use all but ABSOLUTE. The reason for this is that you really do not know where the end of the result set is until you run out of rows.

Both the ABSOLUTE and RELATIVE options allow you to use variables, as long as they are smallint, tinyint, or int.

If you do not specify an INTO clause, then the entire row will be output, as if you did a SELECT of one row. If you do specify an INTO clause, then you must specify a variable for each column in the SELECT. This is the most common usage.

Keeping Track of Your Cursors

The function @@FETCH_STATUS determines the success or failure of the most recent FETCH. It can assume three values: 0, –1, and –2. These correspond to Success, Failure, and Missing Row. A row would be missing if it was deleted by the time you went to fetch it.

You have to use the @@FETCH_STATUS function to determine when to exit from your FETCH loop. Be careful—@@FETCH_STATUS gives you the status of the last FETCH, regardless of the number of cursors you currently have open.

Another function is very useful when you are using cursors—@@CURSOR_ROWS. SQL Server has the capability of populating large static and keyset cursors asynchronously. This function can tell you whether all of the qualifying rows have been retrieved and how many rows are currently in the cursor. If the number is positive, then the cursor is fully populated. If it is negative, then the cursor is being asynchronously populated and some, but not all, qualifying rows have been retrieved. If the number is zero, then no rows qualify or there is no open cursor. Beware! The variable refers to the last opened cursor, so if you have nested cursors, you can run into trouble.

If you use a stored procedure to create a cursor and then pass the cursor (through a variable) back to a calling procedure, you will find the CURSOR_STATUS() function quite useful. Check out the syntax in Listing 15-6.

Listing 15-6: CURSOR_STATUS() Function Syntax

```
CURSOR_STATUS
(
{'local', 'cursor_name'}
| {'global', 'cursor_name'}
| {'variable', 'cursor_variable'}
)
```

You tell CURSOR_STATUS() the type of cursor and its name (or the name of the variable containing it). It returns a smallint, and the most important return values are 0 and 1. The 0 means there are no rows and the 1 means there are. Well, sort of. A dynamic cursor will not return 0. It will, however, return 1 if it has a result set of zero, one, or many rows.

Using the UPDATE and DELETE Statements

This step is optional and it obviously depends on whether or not you wish to update or delete from the underlying table. You can use the WHERE CURRENT OF clause to tell SQL Server which particular row you wish to update or delete. The update or delete always occurs on the row you last fetched for that particular cursor. The syntax is presented in Listings 15-7 and 15-8.

Listing 15-7: UPDATE Syntax

```
UPDATE <Table Name>
WHERE CURRENT OF <Cursor Name>
```

Listing 15-8: DELETE Syntax

```
DELETE <Table Name>
WHERE CURRENT OF <Cursor Name>
```

From the Trenches

One SQL Server 7.0 data warehouse application experienced performance degradation while it was updating using WHERE CURRENT OF. The initial rows being updated were fetched in a few milliseconds. As the loop progressed, the fetches increased to several seconds. (There were only 1,048 rows.) The cursor was replaced with a FORWARD_ONLY cursor and then used the key information from it to do the UPDATE with a regular WHERE clause. Each subsequent FETCH was about 20 ms. The source of the problem was undetermined.

Using the CLOSE Statement

The CLOSE statement frees up some of the cursor's resources, such as the result set and the lock that it has on the last row you fetched. If you reissue the OPEN statement, you can again have access to the cursor's resources.

The CLOSE statement does not free the cursor itself. This means that you cannot create another cursor with the same name until you use the DEALLOCATE statement. For example, to close the CRS cursor, use the syntax in Listing 15-9.

Listing 15-9: CLOSE Syntax

```
CLOSE CRS
```

Using the DEALLOCATE Statement

Once you have finished with a cursor, you need to free up its resources. This is done through the DEALLOCATE statement. For example, to free up the resources of the CRS cursor, use the code in Listing 15-10.

Listing 15-10: DEALLOCATE Syntax

```
DEALLOCATE CRS
```

At this point, all of the resources for the cursor have been freed, and you may reuse the cursor's name. You can forego the CLOSE statement if you use DEALLOCATE.

Using Cursor Variables with Stored Procedures

As stated in the section on the SET statement, you can use a variable to store your cursor. This allows you to pass a cursor variable between stored procedures. For example, you can DECLARE and OPEN the cursor in one procedure and then FETCH in another. When you DECLARE the parameter list for the stored procedure that creates the cursor, you must DECLARE it as CURSOR VARYING.

As an example, suppose you want to get a list of contact names of your customers. This is implemented in Listing 15-11.

Listing 15-11: Stored Procedure with Cursor Parameter

```
CREATE PROC Contacts
(
  @crsContacts  CURSOR VARYING OUTPUT
)
```

```
AS
SET
  @crsContacts = CURSOR FAST_FORWARD
FOR
SELECT
  ContactName
FROM
    Customers

OPEN @crsContacts
GO
```

All you have to do to use the procedure is to DECLARE a cursor variable, EXECUTE the procedure, and then FETCH. This is done in Listing 15-12.

Listing 15-12: Calling a Stored Procedure with a Cursor Parameter

```
DECLARE
  @crs  CURSOR

EXEC Contacts
  @crs output

FETCH @crs
```

Good programming practice dictates checking the status of the cursor variable returned to you before you use it to FETCH.

Minimizing Locking

Because cursors are much slower than set-level SQL, locking becomes an important issue. The SELECT that you specify in your cursor declaration can use locking hints just as it can when a cursor is not involved. Avoid the use of TABLOCKX, REPEATABLEREAD, and HOLDLOCK, particularly inside a transaction.

Beyond the regular locking issues just mentioned, there are also those related specifically to cursors. The timing of when locks are actually acquired must be considered. Static cursors will retrieve all of their rows when the cursor is opened. Each row of the result set is then locked at that time. A keyset cursor is similar, but just the keys are retrieved from the result set; the rows are locked in the same manner as for static cursors.

DYNAMIC cursors do not retrieve or lock their rows until fetched. The locking behavior of the FORWARD_ONLY cursor varies according to the whims of the optimizer.

If it uses a worktable, then the locks will be acquired when you open the cursor; otherwise, they will be acquired when the rows are fetched.

Scroll locks are kept until the next row is fetched. Use this with caution.

Server Options

System-wide options are set by the system stored procedure sp_configure. One of these—cursor threshold—relates to cursors.

You read earlier about asynchronous population of cursors. This can be tuned at the server level by setting the cursor threshold value. When you use keyset or static cursors, worktables are created in tempdb, and these can be populated asynchronously. SQL Server looks at the estimated number of rows, and if the number exceeds the cursor threshold, it will start a separate thread to populate the worktable. Control is returned to the calling application, which can start fetching rows before all are available. You will have to monitor @@CURSOR_ROWS to ensure that rows are available and that all rows have been populated.

This ruse is efficient only for large numbers of rows, so be careful if you make this number small. Keep in mind, too, that this threshold applies to the entire system. You do not have to stop and restart SQL Server for the new setting to take effect.

Database Options

There are some cursor-specific, database options of which you should be aware. These settings are set by the ALTER DATABASE command in SQL Server 2000. Previously in version 7.0, you used the system stored procedure sp_dboption.

Cursor Close on Commit

This setting, when ON, will close the cursor when a transaction is committed. Otherwise, the cursor is left open. By default, the setting is OFF. You can override the setting for the session by using SET CURSOR_CLOSE_ON_COMMIT ON.

Default to Local Cursor

This setting, when TRUE, will make all cursors local to the stored procedure, trigger, or batch unless explicitly declared GLOBAL. By default, this setting is FALSE, making all cursors global, which matches the behavior of version 6.x.

Setting Database Options

Although Microsoft still supports sp_dboption in SQL Server 2000, you should be using the ALTER DATABASE command. The code in Listing 15-13 shows you how to set the default to local cursor using both methods.

Listing 15-13: Setting Database Option 'Default to Local Cursor'

```
ALTER DATABASE MyDB
SET
  CURSOR_DEFAULT LOCAL

EXEC sp_dboption
  'MyDB',
  'default to local cursor',
  'true'
```

Using Cursors on Stored Procedure Calls

Until version 7.0 came along, you could use a cursor only for a SELECT statement. This is essentially true for 7.0, but with the OPENROWSET and OPENQUERY functions, you can now use a cursor to retrieve rows from a stored procedure call. The OPENROWSET or OPENQUERY call is a means of communicating with an OLE DB data source. In this case, you can have it query the local SQL Server through a stored procedure.

One thing you have to keep in mind is that you have to issue the SET FMTONLY OFF statement inside the OPENROWSET or OPENQUERY call. This is to counteract the SET FMTONLY ON statement issued behind the scenes, used for retrieving column names. Listing 15-14 shows an example.

Listing 15-14: Example of OPENROWSET Call to Stored Procedure

```
DECLARE c CURSOR FOR
SELECT
  *
FROM
    OPENROWSET
    (
      'SQLOLEDB',
      'DRIVER={SQL Server};SERVER=(local);Trusted_Connection=yes',
      'SET FMTONLY OFF EXEC sp_who2'
    )
```

If you wanted to avoid a cursor and do this with a simple WHILE loop, you'd be out of luck.

Putting Cursors to Work—a Practical Example

The median is the value in a group of numbers whereby half occur above and half below that number. Although SQL can give you such statistical functions as MIN(), MAX(), and AVG(), it does not have a median function. This functionality is provided in Analysis Services, however. (There are also some rather cute ways to solve the median problem in straight SQL, which are beyond this discussion.)

Calculation of the median is actually straightforward in SQL when you use a scroll cursor. Scroll cursors let you use FETCH FIRST, FETCH LAST, FETCH RELATIVE, FETCH PRIOR, and FETCH ABSOLUTE to locate particular rows.

If you fetch the last row, then you know that you have populated the result set. This means that @@CURSOR_ROWS will contain the total number of rows. The halfway point is the median. If @@CURSOR_ROWS is odd, add 1 to @@CURSOR_ROWS and then divide by 2. This ensures that you get the actual value that splits the result set in two. Now, pick up the median value by doing a FETCH ABSOLUTE.

If, however, @@CURSOR_ROWS is even, then there is no row corresponding to the median. In this case, you have to calculate the median. This requires two fetches. First, you have to pick up the value corresponding to the row at @@CURSOR_ROWS / 2. Next, you pick up the value for the following row. Average the two and you have the median. Be careful if you are using integers—you can lose accuracy unless you convert to float.

Here's an example. Suppose you want to know the median value of the total quantity of products ordered per order. You set up a scroll cursor that selects the total quantity for each order, and you sort according to quantity. You then make the appropriate fetches to calculate the median. Don't forget that the entire SELECT must be carried out, even though you are making—at most—three fetches. The solution is presented in Listing 15-15.

Listing 15-15: Finding the Median

```
DECLARE
  @Quantity   int,
  @Quantity2  int,
  @Median     float,
  @Row        int

DECLARE c SCROLL CURSOR FOR
SELECT
  SUM (Quantity)
FROM
    [Order Details]
GROUP BY
  OrderID
```

```
ORDER BY
  SUM (Quantity)

OPEN c

FETCH LAST FROM c INTO
  @Quantity

IF @@CURSOR_ROWS % 2 = 1     -- odd number of rows
BEGIN
  PRINT 'Odd'

  SET
    @Row     = CAST (@@CURSOR_ROWS + 1 AS int) / 2

  FETCH ABSOLUTE @row FROM c INTO
    @Quantity

  SET
    @Median     = CAST (@Quantity AS float)
END
ELSE                   -- even number of rows
BEGIN
  PRINT 'Even'

 SET
    @Row     = @@CURSOR_ROWS / 2

 FETCH ABSOLUTE @row FROM c INTO
    @Quantity

 FETCH NEXT FROM c INTO
    @Quantity2

 SET
   @Median     = (@Quantity + @Quantity2) / 2.0
END

CLOSE c
DEALLOCATE c

SELECT
  Median     = @Median
```

If you execute this code, you will find that the median order quantity is 50.0.

SQL Alternatives to Cursors

It is impossible to give you every example of straight SQL that will eliminate cursors. Rather, a few examples will be presented that seem to require a row-by-row solution but don't. The aim here is to get you thinking outside of the cursor box. For all of these examples, you will use the Northwind database.

SQL Server 7.0 brought new enrichments to Transact-SQL, among them the SELECT TOP n statement. (The SELECT TOP n statement is discussed in Chapter 4.) This feature allows you to pick the first *n* rows as determined by the ORDER BY clause. For example, if you want the top ten orders based on total quantity of products, you might think of using a cursor and fetching the first ten rows. Instead, you can use the code in Listing 15-16 to avoid a cursor solution.

Listing 15-16: Selecting the Top Ten Orders by Quantity

```
SELECT TOP 10
  OrderID,
  Quantity    = SUM (Quantity)
FROM
   [Order Details]
GROUP BY
  OrderID
ORDER BY
  Quantity DESC
```

This gets you past having to loop through the rows and counting up to 10. In all versions of SQL Server, you could set the ROWCOUNT to 10 and then do the regular SELECT without the TOP n clause. Doing it that way looks a little clunky.

That last one was too easy, but it sets up this next one. What if you wanted just the eighth, ninth, and tenth top orders based on quantity? For this, you really need a cursor, right? Just use the previous query, but FETCH ABSOLUTE 8, followed by two FETCH NEXTs? Nope! Just take the top ten in a derived table, and then take the bottom three of that. (Derived tables are discussed in Chapter 2.) The solution is presented in Listing 15-17.

Listing 15-17: Finding the Eighth, Ninth, and Tenth Highest Orders by Quantity

```
SELECT TOP 3
  OrderID,
  Quantity
FROM
```

```
(
    SELECT TOP 10
      OrderID,
      Quantity = SUM (Quantity)
    FROM
      [Order Details]
    GROUP BY
      OrderID
    ORDER BY
      Quantity  DESC
)   q
ORDER BY
  Quantity  ASC
```

Pretty sneaky, eh? Notice that the inner ORDER BY is *descending*, while the outer ORDER BY is *ascending*. You can't do that in version 6.x.

Now try another example where you may think you need a cursor but you don't. Say that you are interested in those customers who place orders through one—and only one—employee. You could build a SELECT of CustomerID and EmployeeID for every order in the Orders table. Going through the result set row by row, you could check to see if every EmployeeID for a given CustomerID was the same. Or, you could do it in a single SELECT, *without* a cursor, as shown in Listing 15-18.

Listing 15-18: Finding Customers Who Place Orders through the Same Employee

```
SELECT
  CustomerID
FROM
    Orders
GROUP BY
  CustomerID
HAVING
  MIN (EmployeeID) = MAX (EmployeeID)
```

How does this work? You group the orders by CustomerID. Of all of these, you search for those where the minimum EmployeeID is the same as the maximum EmployeeID. The only possible way this can happen is if they are all the same. Cute, eh? (Thanks to Joe Celko who inspired this one.) For this example, there is only one such CustomerID—'CENTC'.

This next one is based upon an actual query Tom had to conjure up for a client but modified a little so you can use the Northwind database. The approach is the same. This time, you want the order date for the first order in every third month. Obviously, this screams "Cursor!" You just use FETCH RELATIVE 3 and you're there, right?

Try this on for size. See the solution in Listing 15-19.

Listing 15-19: Finding the First Order Date for Every Third Month

```
SELECT
  MIN (OrderDate)
FROM
    Orders
WHERE
    MONTH (OrderDate) % 3 = 0
GROUP BY
  YEAR (OrderDate),
  MONTH (OrderDate)
ORDER BY
  MIN (OrderDate)
```

By using modulo (%) 3, you are getting only March, June, September, and December.

The lesson here is to think your way around having to use a cursor—don't give up so easily. If you want to get your SQL skills sharpened to the point where you rarely need a cursor, check out *SQL Puzzles and Answers* by Joe Celko. These are real-world problems solved without the need for the "SQL of last resort."

WHILE Loops

When row-by-row processing is necessary, the method of choice is usually the WHILE loop. Here, you are looping through a table and updating a variable that you use to pick up the next row. You update the variable by finding the minimum key value in the table that is greater than the current value and continue until you retrieve a NULL. Check out the sample in Listing 15-20.

Listing 15-20: Finding the Next Row

```
SELECT
  @OrderID = MIN (OrderID)
FROM
    Orders
WHERE
    OrderID > @OrderID
```

This example allows you to step through the Orders table. Typically, this is faster than using a cursor. In order for this to work, however, there must be a unique key on the table, and ideally the unique key should be single-column. In the preceding example, OrderID satisfies this requirement. If you execute the scripts in Listings 15-21 and 15-22, you will find that the WHILE loop outperforms the cursor on looping through the Orders table.

Listing 15-21: Cursor on a Single-Column Key

```
DECLARE
  @OrderID    int,
  @Count      int,
  @DateTime   datetime

SELECT                    -- initialize
  @Count    = 0,
  @DateTime = GETDATE ()

DECLARE c CURSOR FOR       -- set up cursor
SELECT
  OrderID
FROM
    Orders

OPEN c

FETCH c INTO              -- get first order
  @OrderID

WHILE @@FETCH_STATUS = 0   -- loop through orders
BEGIN
  SET
    @Count = @Count + 1    -- increment counter

  FETCH c INTO             -- pick up next order
    @OrderID
END

CLOSE c                   -- clean up
DEALLOCATE c

-- show the time difference
SELECT
  @Count,
  DATEDIFF (ms, @DateTime, GETDATE ())
```

Listing 15-22: WHILE Loop on a Single-Column Key

```
DECLARE
   @OrderID    int,
   @Count      int,
   @DateTime   datetime

SELECT                    -- initialize
   @Count    = 0,
   @DateTime = GETDATE ()

SELECT                        -- get first order ID
   @OrderID  = MIN (OrderID)
FROM
    Orders

WHILE @OrderID IS NOT NULL -- loop through orders
BEGIN
   SET                      -- increment counter
     @Count    = @Count + 1

   SELECT                      -- get next order ID
     @OrderID    = MIN (OrderID)
   FROM
       Orders
   WHERE
       OrderID    > @OrderID
END

-- show the time difference
SELECT
  @Count,
  DATEDIFF (ms, @DateTime, GETDATE ())
```

Cursors can outperform WHILE loops in situations where there are multiple columns involved in the key. The WHILE solution then involves nested WHILEs, one for each column in the key. You can avoid this by adding a surrogate or contrived key to the table. This is a single, usually numeric, column. This solution is more of a design issue than an SQL issue.

If you execute the scripts in Listings 15-23 and 15-24, you will find that the cursor usually outperforms the nested loop. Notice also that the cursor solution does not rely on unique keys.

Listing 15-23: Cursor on Multiple-Column Key

```
DECLARE
  @Quantity    float,
  @Count       int,
  @DateTime    datetime

SELECT                    -- initialize
  @Count    = 0,
  @DateTime = GETDATE ()

DECLARE c CURSOR FOR      -- set up cursor
SELECT
  Quantity
FROM
   [Order Details]

OPEN c

FETCH c INTO              -- pick up first order detail
  @Quantity

WHILE @@FETCH_STATUS = 0  -- loop through order details
BEGIN
  SET
    @Count = @Count + 1   -- increment counter

  FETCH c INTO            -- pick up next order detail
    @Quantity
END

CLOSE c                   -- clean up
DEALLOCATE c

-- show the time difference
SELECT
  @Count,
  DATEDIFF (ms, @DateTime, GETDATE ())
```

Listing 15-24: WHILE Loop for Multiple-Column Key

```
DECLARE
  @OrderID    int,
  @ProductID  int,
  @Count      int,
  @DateTime   datetime


SELECT                         -- initialize
  @Count    = 0,
  @DateTime = GETDATE ()


SELECT                         -- get first order ID
  @OrderID  = MIN (OrderID)
FROM
    [Order Details]


WHILE @OrderID IS NOT NULL      -- loop through orders
BEGIN
  SELECT                         -- pick up first product ID for this order ID
    @ProductID = MIN (ProductID)
  FROM
      [Order Details]
  WHERE
      OrderID = @OrderID


  WHILE @ProductID IS NOT NULL  -- loop through product IDs for this order ID
  BEGIN
    SET
      @Count = @Count + 1        -- increment counter


    SELECT                         -- get next product ID for this order ID
      @ProductID    = MIN (ProductID)
    FROM
        [Order Details]
    WHERE
        OrderID       = @OrderID
    AND
        ProductID     > @ProductID
  END
```

```
   SELECT                        -- pick up next order ID
     @OrderID    = MIN (OrderID)
   FROM
       [Order Details]
   WHERE
       OrderID   > @OrderID
END

-- show the time difference
SELECT
  @Count,
  DATEDIFF (ms, @DateTime, GETDATE ())
```

Useful Stored Procedures

Microsoft has provided a number of stored procedures to help make maintenance tasks easier. Some of these are documented; some aren't.

Most experienced DBAs will have lost count of the number of times they have had to create a cursor to step through all of their databases to do the same task, such as for a Database Consistency Check (DBCC) of some sort. Now, you can use an undocumented system stored procedure—sp_MSForEachDB. This will go through all databases and execute whatever you feed it as a parameter. Use a question mark as a placeholder. An example of its usage is shown in Listing 15-25.

Listing 15-25: Example of sp_MSForEachDB

```
sp_MSForEachDB
  "print '?' DBCC CHECKCATALOG (?)"
```

This example steps through each database, printing its name and then executing a DBCC CHECKCATALOG. Behind the scenes, SQL Server is actually using a cursor, but you are spared having to code it yourself. Just feed the procedure whatever you want done, and it takes care of the details.

You have just seen how to process commands across all databases. Can you do this across all tables? Sure! Just use sp_MSForEachTable. This time, you are stepping through all user tables in the current database. The procedure uses a cursor to step through all user tables in *sysobjects*. You can filter the tables by specifying the @whereand parameter. For example, if you wanted to know what space was being used by the Orders and Order Details tables, you could use the code in Listing 15-26.

Listing 15-26: Example of sp_MSForEachTable

```
sp_MSForEachTable
  'print "?" exec sp_spaceused "?"',
  @whereand = 'and name like "Order%"'
```

> **CAUTION**   *The preceding two stored procedures are undocumented and could be altered or replaced at any time.*

One of the most frequent reasons for building a cursor query is to go through all tables and update statistics. There is now a system stored procedure— sp_updatestats—that handles that for you. This, too, uses its own cursor.

Ancillary Stored Procedures

Some system stored procedures exist to help you manage your cursors. We'll make you aware of them here, but you should visit the Books Online to get the full scoop.

To get a list of all active cursors on the current connection, use sp_cursor_list. You can specify whether you want local, global, or both. Although the Books Online say that it gives you a list of all open cursors on that connection, that's not quite true. You will get a row for every cursor you have declared and not deallocated, whether you have actually opened it yet or not. You are to provide a cursor variable as an output parameter because the information you receive back is in the form of a cursor.

You can get more specific and ask for information on just one cursor, instead of a list. For this, you use sp_describe_cursor. The information you get back is the same as for sp_cursor_list.

To find out which tables were being accessed by a cursor, use sp_describe_cursor_tables. You get one row back for every table used in the cursor. Here, too, you feed it a cursor variable and then you pick up the data via FETCH statements.

Similarly, you can get information on the columns used by a cursor through sp_describe_cursor_columns.

Best Practices

Avoid cursors like the plague. If a set-level solution is not readily evident, don't be ashamed to ask for help, whether it be from a colleague or through a posting in the Usenet newsgroups.

Use server-side cursors rather than client-side cursors wherever possible. The former does all its work on the server and then sends the results back to the client. The latter caches all of the rows on the client and then manipulates them there. This puts an unnecessary strain on network resources.

In the same vein, put all of your cursor code into a stored procedure and send only the results back to the client. You should never be issuing FETCH statements across your network.

Use common sense. If you need all of the rows anyway, then use set-level SQL and do all of your fancy manipulation on the client. Using a server-side cursor in this case is wasteful.

Wherever possible, limit the number of rows you will be manipulating via your cursor. The more work your cursor has to do, the longer things will take.

Limit your locks to the minimum that you need to accomplish your task.

When all else fails, use a cursor. Just make sure that *all* else has indeed failed before you do.

SQL Puzzle 15-1: Discounting Scheme

For this puzzle, you want to implement a discounting system based on most-recent sales, using the Northwind database. For a given CustomerID, you want to determine the weighted average based on the three most recent orders for the customer. Total the Quantity * Unit Price for each order. Multiply these totals by 2, 3, and 5, going from oldest to newest, respectively, and then divide by 10. Based on the weighted average, calculate the discount for the customer based on the following schedule:

Table 15-1: Discount Schedule

Average	Discount
< 1,000	0%
>= 1,000 but < 2,000	10%
>= 2,000 but < 4,000	20%
>= 4,000	25%

In the event that the customer has fewer than three orders, the discount is zero. In the spirit of the exercise, please use a cursor, even if you find a set-level solution.

The answer to this puzzle can be found on pages 716–717.

CHAPTER 16

Expanding Hierarchies

HIERARCHICAL STRUCTURES, also referred to as *trees*, are structures that have hierarchical dependencies between their members. A common example of such a structure is an organizational chart describing the relationships between the employees in a company, where a manager is in charge of certain employees, each of whom might be in charge of other employees. Another example is a parts explosion, where parts are made of other parts, which might also be made of other parts.

Hierarchical Structure Representation in a Relational Database

The SQL language does not currently have built-in support for hierarchical structures, nor does the SQL Server product. To understand this, take a look at the organizational chart shown in Figure 16-1, which will be used throughout this chapter.

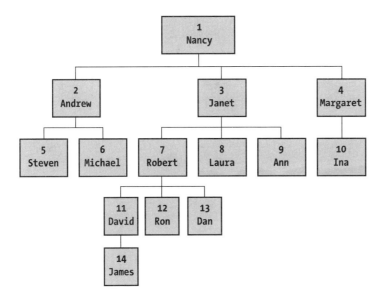

Figure 16-1: Organizational chart

Notice that each employee has a manager except Nancy, who is the top-level manager. The most common way to represent such a structure in a relational database is by means of pairs. One column holds the employee ID and the other holds the ID of his or her manager. In other words, one column holds the children and the other holds their parents.

The problem is that Nancy, the top-level manager, doesn't have a manager, and you still need to store some value in her manager ID column. A common way to handle this problem is to store a NULL in that column, but there are other solutions, as well. For example, you could store Nancy's own employee ID in the manager ID column, making Nancy her own manager. The NULL solution will be used in this chapter.

Creating the Employees Table

Before you go through the examples in this chapter, you need to create a simple table that holds information about the employees presented in the organizational chart. You will track the employee ID and name, the manager's ID, and the employee's salary. The script in Listing 16-1 creates the Employees table and populates it with data.

Listing 16-1: Schema Creation Script for the Employees Table

```
CREATE TABLE Employees
(
  empid   int        NOT NULL,
  mgrid   int        NULL,
  empname varchar(25) NOT NULL,
  salary  money       NOT NULL,
  CONSTRAINT PK_Employees_empid PRIMARY KEY(empid),
  CONSTRAINT FK_Employees_mgrid_empid
    FOREIGN KEY(mgrid)
    REFERENCES Employees(empid))
GO

INSERT INTO employees(empid, mgrid, empname, salary)
  VALUES(1, NULL, 'Nancy', $10000.00)
INSERT INTO employees(empid, mgrid, empname, salary)
  VALUES(2, 1, 'Andrew', $5000.00)
INSERT INTO employees(empid, mgrid, empname, salary)
  VALUES(3, 1, 'Janet', $5000.00)
INSERT INTO employees(empid, mgrid, empname, salary)
  VALUES(4, 1, 'Margaret', $5000.00)
INSERT INTO employees(empid, mgrid, empname, salary)
  VALUES(5, 2, 'Steven', $2500.00)
```

```
INSERT INTO employees(empid, mgrid, empname, salary)
  VALUES(6, 2, 'Michael', $2500.00)
INSERT INTO employees(empid, mgrid, empname, salary)
  VALUES(7, 3, 'Robert', $2500.00)
INSERT INTO employees(empid, mgrid, empname, salary)
  VALUES(8, 3, 'Laura', $2500.00)
INSERT INTO employees(empid, mgrid, empname, salary)
  VALUES(9, 3, 'Ann', $2500.00)
INSERT INTO employees(empid, mgrid, empname, salary)
  VALUES(10, 4, 'Ina', $2500.00)
INSERT INTO employees(empid, mgrid, empname, salary)
  VALUES(11, 7, 'David', $2000.00)
INSERT INTO employees(empid, mgrid, empname, salary)
  VALUES(12, 7, 'Ron', $2000.00)
INSERT INTO employees(empid, mgrid, empname, salary)
  VALUES(13, 7, 'Dan', $2000.00)
INSERT INTO employees(empid, mgrid, empname, salary)
  VALUES(14, 11, 'James', $1500.00)
```

Take a look at the schema of the Employees table shown in Figure 16-2, and at the Employees table's content shown in Table 16-1.

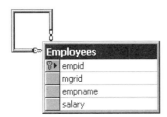

Figure 16-2: Schema of the Employees table

Table 16-1: Employees Table

empid	mgrid	empname	salary
1	NULL	Nancy	10000.0000
2	1	Andrew	5000.0000
3	1	Janet	5000.0000
4	1	Margaret	5000.0000
5	2	Steven	2500.0000

Table 16-1: Employees Table (Continued)

empid	mgrid	empname	salary
6	2	Michael	2500.0000
7	3	Robert	2500.0000
8	3	Laura	2500.0000
9	3	Ann	2500.0000
10	4	Ina	2500.0000
11	7	David	2000.0000
12	7	Ron	2000.0000
13	7	Dan	2000.0000
14	11	James	1500.0000

Querying the Employees Table

Without adding further information of your own to the table, there are a few questions that you can already answer with simple T-SQL statements. For example, "Who is the most senior manager in the organization?" The solution to this lies in Listing 16-2.

Listing 16-2: Senior Manager Query

```
SELECT *
FROM
  Employees
WHERE
  mgrid IS NULL
```

The output of this query is shown in Table 16-2.

Table 16-2: The Most Senior Manager in the Organization

empid	mgrid	empname	salary
1	NULL	Nancy	10000.0000

You can use the query in Listing 16-3 to list the names of all employees and their managers.

Listing 16-3: Employees and Their Managers

```
SELECT
  E.empname AS EmployeeName,
  M.empname AS ManagerName
FROM
    Employees AS E
  LEFT OUTER JOIN
    Employees AS M ON E.mgrid = M.empid
```

The output of this query is shown in Table 16-3.

Table 16-3: The Names of All Employees and Their Managers

EmployeeName	ManagerName
Nancy	NULL
Andrew	Nancy
Janet	Nancy
Margaret	Nancy
Steven	Andrew
Michael	Andrew
Robert	Janet
Laura	Janet
Ann	Janet
Ina	Margaret
David	Robert
Ron	Robert
Dan	Robert
James	David

You use an outer join in this case, because if you had used an inner join, Nancy, who is the most senior manager, wouldn't have been included in the output. The left outer join ensures that all of the rows from the left table—the employees—will be included, whether or not they have matches in the right table—the managers.

A more specific example is the query in Listing 16-4, which asks for the names of the immediate subordinates of Robert (employee ID 7).

Listing 16-4: Subordinates Query

```
SELECT
  *
FROM
  Employees
WHERE
  mgrid = 7
```

The output of this query is shown in Table 16-4.

Table 16-4: The Immediate Subordinates of Robert (Employee ID 7)

empid	mgrid	empname	salary
11	7	David	2000.0000
12	7	Ron	2000.0000
13	7	Dan	2000.0000

The query in Listing 16-5 says, "Show me all the leaf-level employees (employees with no subordinates)." This is a correlated subquery that returns only the employees who are not managers of any other employees. Hence, they are leaf-level employees.

Listing 16-5: Leaf-Level Employees (Employees with No Subordinates), Correlated Subquery Syntax

```
SELECT *
FROM
  Employees AS M
WHERE
  NOT EXISTS
          (
            SELECT
              empid
            FROM
              Employees AS E
            WHERE
              E.mgrid = M.empid
          )
```

The output of this query is shown in Table 16-5.

Table 16-5: Leaf-Level Employees (Employees with No Subordinates)

empid	mgrid	empname	salary
5	2	Steven	2500.0000
6	2	Michael	2500.0000
8	3	Laura	2500.0000
9	3	Ann	2500.0000
10	4	Ina	2500.0000
12	7	Ron	2000.0000
13	7	Dan	2000.0000
14	11	James	1500.0000

Another way to write this query is to use an outer join, which filters only rows containing NULLs. This indicates that a matching row was not found in the unpreserved table. Take a look at Listing 16-6.

Listing 16-6: Leaf-Level Employees (Employees with No Subordinates), Join Syntax

```
SELECT
  M.*
FROM
    Employees AS M
  LEFT OUTER JOIN
    Employees AS E ON M.empid = E.mgrid
WHERE
  E.mgrid IS NULL
```

Problematic Questions

There are a few questions that cannot be answered easily from the existing Employees table structure:

- "Show me all of the employees in a way that it will be easy to see their hierarchical dependencies."

- "Show me details about Robert and all of his subordinates in all levels."

- "Show me details about Robert's subordinates in all levels, excluding Robert."

- "What is the total salary of Robert and all of his subordinates in all levels?"

- "Show me details about all the leaf-level employees under Janet."

- "Show me details about all of the employees who are two levels under Janet."

- "Show me the chain of management leading to James."

Answering such questions with the existing table structure requires using either cursors or temporary tables. This might be handled by a stored procedure or in the client application, which is explained under the topic "Expanding Hierarchies" in the Books Online. Or, you could use a "self-maintained solution" as explained in the next section.

Providing a Solution by Adding Information to the Table

Another way to answer the aforementioned questions is by adding information about the hierarchical structure to the table, which makes it possible to answer those questions with SQL statements. The problem with most of the solutions of this kind is that when the structure is modified—for example, when a new member is added or when an existing member is updated—the additional information gets out of sync and is no longer correct. To avoid such a problem, this kind of solution usually requires that the users modify the data only through stored procedures, or that you run some code that synchronizes the additional information with the data it represents before you issue your queries.

Here's one solution that requires adding information to the table, which you can try now. Re-create the Employees table with the schema shown in Listing 16-7.

Listing 16-7: Schema Creation Script for the New Employees Table

```
IF object_id('Employees', 'U') IS NOT NULL
  DROP TABLE Employees
GO
```

```
CREATE TABLE Employees
(
  empid      int          NOT NULL,
  mgrid      int          NULL,
  empname    varchar(25)  NOT NULL,
  salary     money        NOT NULL,
  lvl        int          NULL,
  hierarchy varchar(900) NULL,
  CONSTRAINT PK_Employees_empid PRIMARY KEY(empid),
  CONSTRAINT FK_Employees_mgrid_empid
    FOREIGN KEY(mgrid)
    REFERENCES Employees(empid)
)
```

Take a look at the schema of the new Employees table, shown in Figure 16-3.

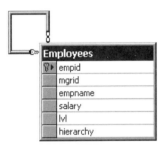

Figure 16-3: Schema of the new Employees table

Note that two columns were added: lvl and hierarchy. The *lvl* column will hold the depth level of the employee in the hierarchy, starting with 0 for the highest level in the hierarchy. The *hierarchy* column will hold the chain of the employee IDs of all managers of the employee, including the employee's own ID, with periods delimiting the employee IDs in the chain. For example, for James, the lvl should be 4 and the hierarchy should be .1.3.7.11.4.. The benefits of adding these two columns will be discussed later. Their maintenance will be discussed first.

> **NOTE**   *One of the most interesting solutions to maintaining hierarchical structures by adding information to the table can be found in Joe Celko's book* SQL for Smarties, *second edition, which also contains a very comprehensive discussion on the subject.*

A Self-Maintained Solution

An important aspect of any solution is its maintenance. Developers usually strive for self-maintained solutions so that they have more time for other tasks (like improving their Minesweeper skills). The solution you will soon see is one that is *self-maintained*, which means that the additional information is automatically updated as the base data is updated. The additional hierarchical information does not need to be updated through special stored procedures.

In order to achieve a self-maintained solution, you need a mechanism that does not have to be invoked explicitly, but is fired automatically as the data in the table changes. Sound familiar? Triggers are used in this solution because they allow programmatic control and they fire automatically after a modification occurs. (Triggers are covered in Chapter 10.)

Supporting Single-Row Inserts

Take a look at the INSERT trigger in Listing 16-8, which calculates values for the lvl and hierarchy columns. Note that after you create the trigger, you need to reinsert the rows into the Employees table to fill it with data.

Listing 16-8: Creation Script for the trg_employees_i_calchierarchy Trigger

```
CREATE TRIGGER trg_employees_i_calchierarchy ON Employees FOR INSERT
AS
DECLARE @numrows AS int
SET @numrows = @@ROWCOUNT
IF @numrows > 1
BEGIN
  RAISERROR('Only single row inserts are supported!', 16, 1)
  ROLLBACK TRAN
END
ELSE
IF @numrows = 1
BEGIN
  UPDATE E
    SET lvl = CASE
                WHEN E.mgrid IS NULL THEN 0
                ELSE M.lvl + 1
              END,
        hierarchy = CASE
                      WHEN E.mgrid IS NULL THEN '.'
                      ELSE M.hierarchy
                    END + CAST(E.empid AS varchar(10)) + '.'
```

```
FROM
    Employees AS E
  JOIN
    inserted  AS I ON I.empid = E.empid
  LEFT OUTER JOIN
    Employees AS M ON E.mgrid = M.empid
END
```

Note that this trigger supports only single-row inserts. It is possible to add logic to support inserts of whole subtrees as well, by using cursors or temporary tables. Multirow inserts will be addressed later.

Now you can refill the Employees table and look at its content. Use the same INSERT statements you used to fill the original Employees table. The results are shown in Table 16-6.

Table 16-6: New Employees Table

empid	mgrid	empname	salary	lvl	hierarchy
1	NULL	Nancy	10000.0000	0	.1.
2	1	Andrew	5000.0000	1	.1.2.
3	1	Janet	5000.0000	1	.1.3.
4	1	Margaret	5000.0000	1	.1.4.
5	2	Steven	2500.0000	2	.1.2.5.
6	2	Michael	2500.0000	2	.1.2.6.
7	3	Robert	2500.0000	2	.1.3.7.
8	3	Laura	2500.0000	2	.1.3.8.
9	3	Ann	2500.0000	2	.1.3.9.
10	4	Ina	2500.0000	2	.1.4.10.
11	7	David	2000.0000	3	.1.3.7.11.
12	7	Ron	2000.0000	3	.1.3.7.12.
13	7	Dan	2000.0000	3	.1.3.7.13.
14	11	James	1500.0000	4	.1.3.7.11.14.

To illustrate what's going on inside the trigger when a new employee is added, suppose you want to add the employee Sean, who reports to Ron. Ron's employee ID is 12. The INSERT statement is depicted in Listing 16-9.

Listing 16-9: Testing the trg_employees_i_calchierarchy Trigger

```
INSERT INTO employees(empid, mgrid, empname, salary)
  VALUES(15, 12, 'Sean', $1500.00)
```

The UPDATE statement inside the trigger updates the Employees table. To accomplish this, it performs a join onto two tables to filter the rows that need to be updated and to obtain the additional information required for the update. Breaking it down into steps, you have the following actions taking place:

1. Join the Employees table and the *inserted* table, which holds only the new row for Sean. This will result in filtering only Sean's row, which is possible because the trigger fires only after the INSERT has already affected the table. This means that Sean already appears in the Employees table, but with NULLs in the lvl and hierarchy columns.

2. Take the result from the first step and left outer join it to the Employees table, which in this case, represents the managers. In other words, the row of Sean's manager is joined to the previous result. The reason a left outer join is used is to allow the addition of an employee who does not have a manager. Such an employee has NULL in the mgrid column, and in such a case, a match for the manager does not exist, causing the row you are trying to modify to disappear from the result of the join.

Figure 16-4 shows what happens logically inside the trigger.

Now that all of the required information is available, you are left with calculating and updating the lvl and hierarchy columns. The code fragment in Listing 16-10 calculates the lvl column.

Listing 16-10: Calculating the lvl Column

```
lvl = CASE
        WHEN E.mgrid IS NULL THEN 0
        ELSE M.lvl + 1
      END
```

If E.mgrid is NULL, it means that you added an employee who has no manager and therefore, his or her level is 0. In all other cases, the employee's level is one level under his or her manager. The code fragment in Listing 16-11 calculates the hierarchy column.

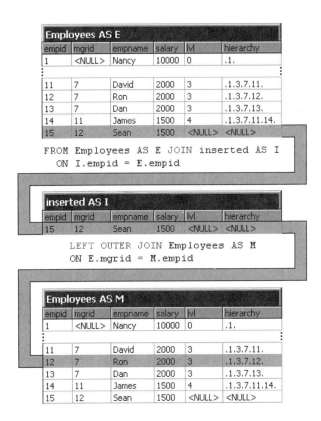

Figure 16-4: Inside the INSERT Trigger on the Employees Table

Listing 16-11: Calculating the hierarchy Column

```
hierarchy = CASE
                WHEN E.mgrid IS NULL THEN '.'
                ELSE M.hierarchy
            END + CAST(E.empid AS varchar(10)) + '.'
```

If the employee has no manager, then the hierarchy column should be .empid.. In all other cases, it should be the employee's manager's hierarchy value concatenated with the employee's ID.

Supporting Multirow Inserts

Supporting multirow inserts in versions prior to SQL Server 2000 requires changing the INSERT trigger you wrote earlier, which handles only single-row inserts. You can implement the same logic that updates the hierarchy and lvl columns in a loop. The loop updates the new employees in steps, starting with the highest-level employees, and advances to the next-level employees in each iteration of the loop. Each level's employees are saved in a temporary table so the update can focus on them. The reason that this solution works is that you control the order of the updates, making sure that when you update employees, their managers' hierarchy and lvl columns are already updated. This is important, because the employees' hierarchy and lvl columns are dependent on their managers' hierarchy and lvl values.

With SQL Server 2000, you can implement a much more elegant solution. It is similar in concept to the one just described, but it does not require changing the current INSERT trigger, other than removing the check for the number of rows inserted, to allow for multirow inserts. You can add an INSTEAD OF INSERT trigger that "catches" the newly inserted employee rows before they enter the Employees table. The trigger simply splits the original INSERT into multiple INSERT statements, starting with the employees at the highest level and continuing to insert employees at lower levels in an ordered fashion in a loop, until there are no more employees left.

The INSTEAD OF INSERT trigger does nothing more than split the original INSERT into multiple INSERTs, each of which contains employees in a lower level. The beauty of this solution is that the original AFTER trigger takes care of the hierarchy and lvl columns the same way it did before, only now it fires a number of times—once for each level. Also, you can use SQL Server 2000's new table datatype, which allows better optimization than temporary tables.

The trigger starts by creating a table variable called @curlvlemps that stores employee IDs and their levels. First, you insert top-level employees into the table variable. Next, you enter a loop that continues while your last insert affected at least one row. Inside the loop, you extract the employees of the current level from the *inserted* table and insert them into the Employees table. This fires the AFTER trigger, which takes care of the hierarchy and lvl columns. Finally, you increment your current level's indicator and insert the next-level employees to your table variable. Take a look at the INSTEAD OF TRIGGER in Listing 16-12.

Listing 16-12: Creation Script for the trg_employees_ioi_splitinsertstolevels Trigger

```
-- add support for multirow inserts by splitting the inserts to levels
CREATE TRIGGER trg_employees_ioi_splitinsertstolevels
  ON Employees INSTEAD OF INSERT
AS

DECLARE @curlvlemps table -- will be filled with employee ids
(
  empid int NOT NULL,
  lvl   int NOT NULL
)
```

```
DECLARE @curlvl AS int -- indicates the level of the employees in the subtree

SET @curlvl = 0

-- insert first top-level employees in the subtree to @curlvlemps
INSERT INTO @curlvlemps
  SELECT
    empid,
    @curlvl
  FROM
    inserted AS I
  WHERE
    NOT EXISTS(
                SELECT
                  *
                FROM
                  inserted AS I2
                WHERE
                  I.mgrid = I2.empid
                )

-- loop while there are employees in the last checked level
WHILE @@ROWCOUNT > 0
BEGIN
  -- insert current level's employees to the Employees table
  -- this will invoke the after trigger that
  -- takes care of the lvl and hierarchy columns
  INSERT INTO Employees
    SELECT
      I.*
    FROM
        inserted    AS I
      JOIN
        @curlvlemps AS C ON  I.empid = C.empid
                         AND C.lvl   = @curlvl

  -- adjust current level
  SET @curlvl = @curlvl + 1
```

```
       -- add next level employees to @curlvlemps
       INSERT INTO @curlvlemps
         SELECT
           I.empid, @curlvl
         FROM
            inserted    AS I
          JOIN
            @curlvlemps AS C ON  I.mgrid = C.empid
                             AND C.lvl   = @curlvl - 1
END
GO
```

Now you need to alter the AFTER trigger so that it will not reject multirow inserts. To do this, you simply remove the single-row safety check, as shown in Listing 16-13.

Listing 16-13: Altering the trg_employees_i_calchierarchy Trigger to Support Multirow Inserts

```
-- alter the insert trigger that maintains the columns lvl and hierarchy
-- to support multirow inserts
ALTER TRIGGER trg_employees_i_calchierarchy ON Employees FOR INSERT
AS
DECLARE @numrows AS int
SET @numrows = @@ROWCOUNT
IF @numrows >= 1
BEGIN
  UPDATE E
  SET lvl =
        CASE
          WHEN E.mgrid IS NULL THEN 0
          ELSE M.lvl + 1
        END,
      hierarchy =
        CASE
          WHEN E.mgrid IS NULL THEN '.'
          ELSE M.hierarchy
        END + CAST(E.empid AS varchar(10)) + '.'
  FROM
      Employees AS E
    JOIN
      inserted  AS I ON I.empid = E.empid
    LEFT OUTER JOIN
      Employees AS M ON E.mgrid = M.empid
END
GO
```

To test this new implementation, you need to clear out the Employees table, fill a temporary table called #Employees with the whole original organizational hierarchy of employees, and perform a multirow insert from the #Employees table into the main Employees table. This is done in Listing 16-14.

Listing 16-14: Testing a Subtree Insert

```
-- test a subtree insert
DELETE FROM Employees
GO

CREATE TABLE #Employees
(
  empid    int        NOT NULL,
  mgrid    int        NULL,
  empname  varchar(25) NOT NULL,
  salary   money      NOT NULL
)
GO

INSERT INTO #Employees(empid, mgrid, empname, salary)
  VALUES(1, NULL, 'Nancy', $10000.00)
INSERT INTO #Employees(empid, mgrid, empname, salary)
  VALUES(2, 1, 'Andrew', $5000.00)
INSERT INTO #Employees(empid, mgrid, empname, salary)
  VALUES(3, 1, 'Janet', $5000.00)
INSERT INTO #Employees(empid, mgrid, empname, salary)
  VALUES(4, 1, 'Margaret', $5000.00)
INSERT INTO #Employees(empid, mgrid, empname, salary)
  VALUES(5, 2, 'Steven', $2500.00)
INSERT INTO #Employees(empid, mgrid, empname, salary)
  VALUES(6, 2, 'Michael', $2500.00)
INSERT INTO #Employees(empid, mgrid, empname, salary)
  VALUES(7, 3, 'Robert', $2500.00)
INSERT INTO #Employees(empid, mgrid, empname, salary)
  VALUES(8, 3, 'Laura', $2500.00)
INSERT INTO #Employees(empid, mgrid, empname, salary)
  VALUES(9, 3, 'Ann', $2500.00)
INSERT INTO #Employees(empid, mgrid, empname, salary)
  VALUES(10, 4, 'Ina', $2500.00)
INSERT INTO #Employees(empid, mgrid, empname, salary)
  VALUES(11, 7, 'David', $2000.00)
INSERT INTO #Employees(empid, mgrid, empname, salary)
  VALUES(12, 7, 'Ron', $2000.00)
```

```
INSERT INTO #Employees(empid, mgrid, empname, salary)
  VALUES(13, 7, 'Dan', $2000.00)
INSERT INTO #Employees(empid, mgrid, empname, salary)
  VALUES(14, 11, 'James', $1500.00)
INSERT INTO #Employees(empid, mgrid, empname, salary)
  VALUES(15, 12, 'Sean', $1500.00)
GO

INSERT INTO Employees(empid, mgrid, empname, salary)
  SELECT
    *
  FROM
    #Employees

SELECT * FROM Employees
```

And it works!

Answering the Problematic Questions

Now that you know that the values of the hierarchy and lvl columns are automatically generated every time a new employee is added, see if you can answer the problematic questions presented earlier. However, before you start answering the problematic questions, take a look at the query in Listing 16-15, which provides an alternative solution to the query shown earlier in Listing 16-2, "Who is the most senior manager in the organization?"

Listing 16-15: Senior Manager Query

```
SELECT *
FROM
  Employees
WHERE
  lvl = 0
```

The output of this query is shown in Table 16-7.

Table 16-7: The Most Senior Manager in the Organization

empid	mgrid	empname	salary	lvl	hierarchy
1	NULL	Nancy	10000.0000	0	.1.

In fact, this type of query can find all the employees in any required level and exploit an index on the lvl column.

Listing 16-16 provides the solution to "Show me all of the employees in a way that it will be easy to see their hierarchical dependencies."

Listing 16-16: Listing the Employees by Their Hierarchical Dependencies

```
SELECT *
FROM
  Employees
ORDER BY
  hierarchy
```

The output of this query is shown in Table 16-8.

Table 16-8: Employees in Their Hierarchical Order

empid	mgrid	empname	salary	lvl	hierarchy
1	NULL	Nancy	10000.0000	0	.1.
2	1	Andrew	5000.0000	1	.1.2.
5	2	Steven	2500.0000	2	.1.2.5.
6	2	Michael	2500.0000	2	.1.2.6.
3	1	Janet	5000.0000	1	.1.3.
7	3	Robert	2500.0000	2	.1.3.7.
11	7	David	2000.0000	3	.1.3.7.11.
14	11	James	1500.0000	4	.1.3.7.11.14.
12	7	Ron	2000.0000	3	.1.3.7.12.
15	12	Sean	1500.0000	4	.1.3.7.12.15.
13	7	Dan	2000.0000	3	.1.3.7.13.
8	3	Laura	2500.0000	2	.1.3.8.
9	3	Ann	2500.0000	2	.1.3.9.
4	1	Margaret	5000.0000	1	.1.4.
10	4	Ina	2500.0000	2	.1.4.10.

This can be modified to make the results easier to read, as you can see in Listing 16-17.

Listing 16-17: Showing Hierarchical Dependencies with Indention

```
SELECT
  REPLICATE(' | ', lvl) + empname AS EmployeeName
FROM
  Employees
ORDER BY
  hierarchy
```

The output of this query is shown in Table 16-9.

Table 16-9: Employees in Their Hierarchical Order, Including Indention

EmployeeName
Nancy
| Andrew
| | Steven
| | Michael
| Janet
| | Robert
| | | David
| | | | James
| | | Ron
| | | | Sean
| | | Dan
| | Laura
| | Ann
| Margaret
| | Ina

Note that with this solution, the order among siblings (in hierarchical terms, that means employees with the same boss) might be surprising. Since you use a character string for the hierarchy column, if you had two siblings with employee IDs 100 and 20, the employee with the ID of 100 would sort before the employee with the ID of 20. Usually the order between siblings is not important as long as the hierarchy is maintained. However, if this is of importance, you can change the format of the hierarchy column slightly. You can hold the employee IDs in the chain in a fixed-length format in the length of the maximum number of digits possible. In the example being used here, you could represent the employee ID of 20 as 0000020 and the employee ID of 100 as 0000100 in the hierarchy column. This, of course, uses a considerable additional amount of space, so as long as you don't care about the order of siblings, you should use the original proposed format.

The next in the series of problematic questions is "Show me details about Robert (employee ID 7) and all of his subordinates in all levels." The solution is shown in Listing 16-18.

Listing 16-18: Details about Robert (Employee ID 7)
and All of His Subordinates in All Levels

```
SELECT
   *
FROM
   Employees
WHERE
   hierarchy LIKE (SELECT
                      hierarchy
                  FROM
                      Employees
                  WHERE
                      empid = 7) + '%'
ORDER BY
   Hierarchy
```

The output of this query is shown in Table 16-10.

Table 16-10: Details about Robert (Employee ID 7)
and All of His Subordinates in All Levels

empid	mgrid	empname	salary	lvl	hierarchy
7	3	Robert	2500.0000	2	.1.3.7.
11	7	David	2000.0000	3	.1.3.7.11.
14	11	James	1500.0000	4	.1.3.7.11.14.
12	7	Ron	2000.0000	3	.1.3.7.12.
15	12	Sean	1500.0000	4	.1.3.7.12.15.
13	7	Dan	2000.0000	3	.1.3.7.13.

The next question is "Show me details about Robert's subordinates in all levels, excluding Robert," which is shown in Listing 16-19.

Listing 16-19: Details about Robert's Subordinates in All Levels, Excluding Robert

```
SELECT
  *
FROM
  Employees
WHERE
  hierarchy LIKE (SELECT
                    hierarchy
                  FROM
                    Employees
                  WHERE
                    empid = 7) + '_%'
ORDER BY
  hierarchy
```

The output of this query is shown in Table 16-11.

Table 16-11: Details about Robert's Subordinates in All Levels, Excluding Robert

empid	mgrid	empname	salary	lvl	hierarchy
11	7	David	2000.0000	3	.1.3.7.11.
14	11	James	1500.0000	4	.1.3.7.11.14.
12	7	Ron	2000.0000	3	.1.3.7.12.
15	12	Sean	1500.0000	4	.1.3.7.12.15.
13	7	Dan	2000.0000	3	.1.3.7.13.

You might have the impression that the previous two queries are identical, but they aren't. A trick is used here. Notice that the second query in Listing 16-19 filters rows that match the pattern emp_hierarchy LIKE mgr_hierarchy + '_%'. The underscore wildcard ('_') replaces a *single* unknown character, whereas the percent sign ('%') replaces *any number* of unknown characters, including 0. Combining them means that at least one additional character must exist in the employee's hierarchy besides the manager's hierarchy. This is why Robert is not included in the result of the second query. In the first query (Listing 16-18), the pattern is slightly different: emp_hierarchy LIKE mgr_hierarchy + '%'. Since the percent sign wildcard can stand for zero or more characters, Robert's hierarchy itself also matches the pattern.

The next question, "What is the total salary of Robert and all of his subordinates in all levels?" is solved in Listing 16-20.

Listing 16-20: The Total Salary of Robert and All of His Subordinates in All Levels

```
SELECT
  SUM(salary) AS total_salary
FROM
  Employees
WHERE
  hierarchy LIKE (SELECT
                    hierarchy
                  FROM
                    Employees
                  WHERE
                    empid = 7) + '%'
```

The output of this query is shown in Table 16-12.

Table 16-12: The Total Salary of Robert and All of His Subordinates in All Levels

total_salary
11500.0000

Listing 16-21 contains the query used to solve "Show me details about all the leaf-level employees under Janet (employee ID 3)."

Listing 16-21: Details of All Leaf-Level Employees under Janet (Employee ID 3)

```
SELECT *
FROM
  Employees AS M
WHERE
    hierarchy LIKE (SELECT
                      hierarchy
                    FROM
                      Employees
                    WHERE
                      empid = 3) + '%'
  AND
    NOT EXISTS(SELECT
                 Mgrid
```

```
FROM
  Employees AS E
WHERE
  M.empid = E.mgrid)
```

The output of this query is shown in Table 16-13.

Table 16-13: Details of All Leaf-Level Employees under Janet (Employee ID 3

empid	mgrid	empname	salary	lvl	hierarchy
8	3	Laura	2500.0000	2	.1.3.8.
9	3	Ann	2500.0000	2	.1.3.9.
12	7	Ron	2000.0000	3	.1.3.7.12.
13	7	Dan	2000.0000	3	.1.3.7.13.
14	11	James	1500.0000	4	.1.3.7.11.14.
15	12	Sean	1500.0000	4	.1.3.7.12.15.

Listing 16-22 is a correlated subquery. It provides the solution for "Show me details about all of the employees who are two levels under Janet."

Listing 16-22: Details of All Employees Who Are Two Levels under Janet, Correlated Subquery Syntax

```
SELECT
  *
FROM
  Employees AS M
WHERE
    hierarchy LIKE (SELECT
                      hierarchy
                    FROM
                      Employees
                    WHERE
                      empid = 3) + '%'
  AND
    lvl - (SELECT
             lvl
           FROM
             Employees
           WHERE
             empid = 3) = 2
```

This can also be done with a join, as shown in Listing 16-23.

Listing 16-23: Details of All Employees Who Are Two Levels under Janet, Join Syntax

```
SELECT
  E.*
FROM
    Employees AS E
  JOIN
    Employees AS M ON E.hierarchy LIKE M.hierarchy + '%'
WHERE
    M.empid = 3
  AND
    E.lvl - M.lvl = 2
```

The output of this query is shown in Table 16-14.

Table 16-14: Details of All Employees Who Are Two Levels under Janet

empid	mgrid	empname	salary	lvl	hierarchy
11	7	David	2000.0000	3	.1.3.7.11.
12	7	Ron	2000.0000	3	.1.3.7.12.
13	7	Dan	2000.0000	3	.1.3.7.13.

The question "Show me the chain of management leading to James (employee ID 14)" is answered with the query shown in Listing 16-24.

Listing 16-24: The Chain of Management Leading to James (Employee ID 14)

```
SELECT
  *
FROM
  Employees
WHERE
  (SELECT
    hierarchy
  FROM
    Employees
  WHERE
    empid = 14) LIKE hierarchy + '%'
ORDER BY
  hierarchy
```

The output of this query is shown in Table 16-15.

Table 16-15: The Chain of Management Leading to James (Employee ID 14)

empid	mgrid	empname	salary	lvl	hierarchy
1	NULL	Nancy	10000.0000	0	.1.
3	1	Janet	5000.0000	1	.1.3.
7	3	Robert	2500.0000	2	.1.3.7.
11	7	David	2000.0000	3	.1.3.7.11.
14	11	James	1500.0000	4	.1.3.7.11.14.

Notice the role reversal that was used here. When looking for the chain of management for a certain employee, you use the opposite approach from looking for a subtree of a certain manager. The manager's hierarchy has a fixed value for each employee row that is checked during a subtree search, so you look for employees that match the pattern `'<emp_hierarchy>' LIKE '<fixed_mgr_hierarchy>%'`. In a search for the chain of management for a certain employee, the employee's hierarchy has a fixed value for each manager's row that is checked; so you look for managers that match the pattern `'<fixed_emp_hierarchy>' LIKE '<mgr_hierarchy>%'`.

Answering Questions with User-Defined Functions

User-defined functions in SQL Server 2000 enable you to answer some of the problematic questions without even needing the additional hierarchy and lvl columns. The process used in Chapter 11 for table-valued multistatement functions can be implemented in this Employees table, as well. Take a look at the script in Listing 16-25. (For a detailed explanation of the function shown in Listing 16-25, please refer to Chapter 11.)

Listing 16-25: Creation Script for the get_mgremps() User-Defined Function

```
CREATE FUNCTION get_mgremps
(
  @mgrid AS int
)
RETURNS @tree table
(
  empid   int         NOT NULL,
  mgrid   int         NULL,
  empname varchar(25) NOT NULL,
  salary  money       NOT NULL,
  lvl     int         NOT NULL
)
```

```
AS

BEGIN

  DECLARE @lvl AS int
  SET @lvl = 0

  INSERT INTO @tree
    SELECT
      empid,
      mgrid,
      empname,
      salary,
      @lvl
    FROM
      Employees
    WHERE
      empid = @mgrid

  WHILE @@ROWCOUNT > 0
  BEGIN
    SET @lvl = @lvl + 1

    INSERT INTO @tree
      SELECT
        E.empid,
        E.mgrid,
        E.empname,
        E.salary,
        @lvl
      FROM
          Employees AS E
        JOIN
          @tree AS T ON  E.mgrid = T.empid
                     AND T.lvl   = @lvl - 1
  END

  RETURN

END
GO
```

Now you can invoke your new function to answer problematic questions. For example, Listing 16-26 provides the answer to "Show me details about Robert and all of his subordinates in all levels."

Listing 16-26: Using the get_mgremps() User-Defined Function for Details about Robert and All of His Subordinates in All Levels

```
SELECT
  *
FROM
  get_mgremps(7)
```

The puzzle at the end of this chapter will give you more practice with user-defined functions.

Maintaining Data Modification

You already took care of maintaining the additional information that you keep in the Employees table when new employees are added with the INSERT trigger. Now you need an UPDATE trigger that will modify that information when employees change their place in the hierarchical structure. Listing 16-27 shows the UPDATE trigger.

Listing 16-27: Creation Script for the trg_employees_u_calchierarchy Trigger

```
CREATE TRIGGER trg_employees_u_calchierarchy ON Employees FOR UPDATE
AS
IF @@ROWCOUNT = 0
  RETURN

IF UPDATE(empid)
BEGIN
  RAISERROR('Updates to empid not allowed!', 16, 1)
  ROLLBACK TRAN
END
ELSE IF UPDATE(mgrid)
BEGIN
  UPDATE E
    SET lvl = E.lvl - I.lvl + CASE
                                WHEN I.mgrid IS NULL THEN 0
                                ELSE M.lvl + 1
                              END,
        hierarchy = ISNULL(M.hierarchy, '.') +
                    CAST(I.empid AS varchar(10)) + '.' +
                    right(E.hierarchy, len(E.hierarchy) - len(I.hierarchy))
```

```
FROM
    Employees AS E
  JOIN
    inserted  AS I ON E.hierarchy LIKE I.hierarchy + '%'
  LEFT OUTER JOIN
    Employees AS M ON I.mgrid = M.empid
END
```

In many cases in production databases, updates to the primary key are not allowed. For this reason, the trigger first checks whether the empid column was modified. If so, the update operation is rolled back and the process is terminated. In addition, you only need to take care of the lvl and hierarchy columns if the employee was moved to another manager, so you check whether the mgrid column was updated. There might be updates that change only the employee's salary, in which case the trigger does not need to change anything. Now that you've performed all the relevant safety checks, you can move to the bulk logic of the trigger, which is performed in the UPDATE statement.

Suppose Andrew needs to report to Janet from now on, instead of reporting to Nancy. This change is depicted in Listing 16-28.

Listing 16-28: Testing the trg_employees_u_calchierarchy Trigger

```
UPDATE employees
  SET mgrid = 3
WHERE empid = 2
```

Andrew's new position did not only affect him, but also affected all of his subordinates in all levels—in this case, Steven and Michael. Their levels in the hierarchy change, and so does their hierarchy chain. Check the results in Table 16-16.

Table 16-16: Result of an Update that Fired
the trg_employees_u_calchierarchy Trigger

Employee	Old Level	New Level	Old Hierarchy	New Hierarchy
Andrew	1	2	.1.2.	.1.3.2.
Steven	2	3	.1.2.5.	.1.3.2.5.
Michael	2	3	.1.2.6.	.1.3.2.6.

You can generalize the effects of an employee's movement on himself or herself and on all of his or her subordinates. The formula that calculates the new value of lvl is this:

```
lvl = lvl - old_emp_lvl + { new_mgr_lvl + 1 | 0 }
```

This formula can be broken down as follows:

- Let old_emp_lvl = the level of the employee who was moved, prior to modifying it.

- Let new_mgr_lvl = the level of the new manager of the employee who was moved.

For example, Michael's new level would be calculated as follows:

```
Michael's current level - Andrew's old level + Janet's level + 1 =
2 - 1 + 1 + 1 = 3
```

Note that if an employee is moved to the highest level, there's no need to retrieve the new manager's level, because he or she will have no manager, and the level is therefore 0.

The formula that calculates the new value of hierarchy is this:

```
hierarchy = { new_mgr_hier | '.' } + mov_empid + '.' + right_hier
```

This formula can be broken down as follows:

- Let new_mgr_hier: This is the hierarchy of the new manager of the employee who was moved.

- Let mov_empid :This is the employee ID of the employee who was moved.

- Let right_hier: This is the right part of the hierarchy of each employee who you need to modify, starting at his or her employee ID.

For example, Michael's new hierarchy would be calculated as follows:

```
Janet's hierarchy + Andrew's employee ID + '.' + Michael's right part of the
hierarchy starting at his employee ID = '.1.3.' + '2' + '.' + '6.' = '.1.3.2.6.'
```

Note that if an employee is moved to the highest level, there's no need to retrieve the new manager's hierarchy, because he or she will have no manager, and the first part simply starts with a dot.

The UPDATE statement inside the trigger updates the Employees table. To do this, it performs a join onto two tables to filter the rows that need to be updated and to obtain the additional information required for the update. Breaking this down into steps, the process begins as follows:

1. First join the Employees table and the *inserted* table, which holds only the new updated row for Andrew. This is a tricky join because it is not based on equality; instead, it is based on the LIKE operator, as shown in Listing 16-29.

   Listing 16-29: Inside the UPDATE Trigger on the Employees Table;
   a Join between Employees and Inserted

   ```
   FROM
       Employees AS E
     JOIN
       inserted  AS I ON E.hierarchy LIKE I.hierarchy + '%'
   ```

   The rows from the Employees table that will be selected are the ones that start with the same hierarchy as the hierarchy in the *inserted* table, which in this case are the rows that start with Andrew's old hierarchy. (Keep in mind that the hierarchy value in the *inserted* table was not modified yet, so it still reflects the old value.) This will result in returning Andrew's row and all his subordinates in all levels.

2. Take the result from the first step and left outer join it to the Employees table, which, in this case, represents the managers. Therefore, the row of Andrew's manager is left outer joined to the previous result. The reason a left outer join is used is the same reason it is used in the insert trigger— you might have updated the employee's manager ID to NULL.

Figure 16-5 shows what happens logically inside the trigger.

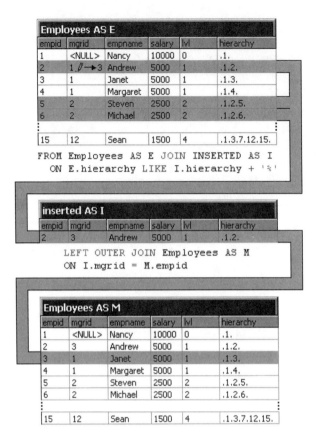

Figure 16-5: Inside the UPDATE trigger on the Employees table

Removing Employees

Member removal is one area you might prefer to handle with stored procedures instead of an automatic mechanism, such as triggers. This is because in different situations you might want to implement different removal logic. You will see a few removal scenarios implemented with stored procedures, but note that if one of them should be applied in all situations, you can implement it as a trigger and thus have a totally self-maintained solution.

The first scenario removes the whole subtree under a certain employee. This stored procedure handles subtree removal. The creation script for the procedure is shown in Listing 16-30.

Listing 16-30: Creation Script for the RemoveSubtree Stored Procedure

```
CREATE PROC RemoveSubtree
(
  @empid int
)
AS

DELETE FROM Employees
WHERE
  hierarchy LIKE (SELECT
                    hierarchy
                  FROM
                    Employees
                  WHERE
                    empid = @empid) + '%'
GO
```

Now use the code in Listing 16-31 to remove Robert and his subtree.

Listing 16-31: Testing the RemoveSubtree Stored Procedure

```
EXEC RemoveSubtree
  @empid = 7
```

Figure 16-6 shows the effects of running this procedure.

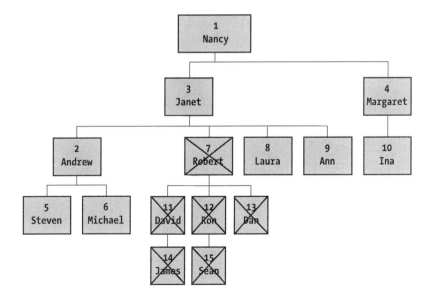

Figure 16-6: Effects of running the RemoveSubtree stored procedure

In the second scenario, you remove the specified employee and have his or her direct subordinates report to the manager of the employee who was removed. Listing 16-32 shows the stored procedure that handles this scenario.

Listing 16-32: Creation Script
for the RemoveEmployeeUpgradeSubs Stored Procedure

```
CREATE PROC RemoveEmployeeUpgradeSubs
(
  @empid int
)
AS

BEGIN TRAN

UPDATE E
  SET mgrid = M.mgrid
FROM
    Employees AS E
  JOIN
    Employees AS M ON E.mgrid = M.empid
WHERE
  M.empid = @empid

DELETE FROM Employees
WHERE
  empid = @empid

COMMIT TRAN
GO
```

Note that you don't need to take any special care of the data in the lvl and hierarchy columns of the employees that moved to the higher level. This is because the UPDATE trigger that was created earlier in Listing 16-27 already takes care of that.

Now remove Andrew from the Employees table. In this case, both Steven and Michael should report to Janet after Andrew is removed. This is implemented in Listing 16-33.

Listing 16-33: Testing the RemoveEmployeeUpgradeSubs Stored Procedure

```
EXEC RemoveEmployeeUpgradeSubs
  @empid = 2
```

Figure 16-7 shows the effects of running this procedure.

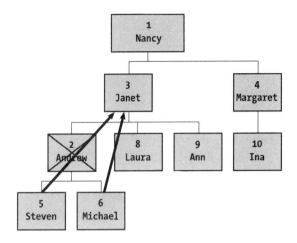

Figure 16-7: Effects of running the RemoveEmployeeUpgradeSubs stored procedure

The third scenario removes the specified employee and has his direct subordinates report to a new specified manager. Listing 16-34 shows the stored procedure that handles this scenario.

Listing 16-34: Creation Script for the RemoveEmployeeMoveSubs Stored Procedure

```
CREATE PROC RemoveEmployeeMoveSubs
(
  @empid  int,
  @newmgr int
)
AS

BEGIN TRAN

UPDATE E
  SET mgrid = @newmgr
FROM
    Employees AS E
  JOIN
    Employees AS M ON E.mgrid = M.empid
WHERE
  M.empid = @empid
```

```
DELETE FROM Employees
WHERE
  empid = @empid

COMMIT TRAN
GO
```

Now remove Janet and have her subordinates report to Margaret, as shown in Listing 16-35.

Listing 16-35: Testing the RemoveEmployeeMoveSubs Stored Procedure

```
EXEC RemoveEmployeeMoveSubs
  @empid  = 3,
  @newmgr = 4
```

Figure 16-8 shows the effects of running this procedure.

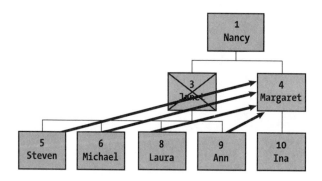

Figure 16-8: Effects of running the RemoveEmployeeMoveSubs stored procedure

Better stop for now, before you lose all the employees in your table.

Practical Implementation

Now that you've seen that the solution that adds the lvl and hierarchy columns is sufficient in the sense that you get the desired results, you can examine the practical implementation of this solution. In the simple example just discussed, all of the rows in the table will fit on a single page and therefore, there would be no considerable performance benefit in using indexes. In the real world, however, the tables would be much larger and, of course, the different queries might benefit considerably from indexing.

Repopulating the Employees Table

To demonstrate the value of indexing, clear the Employees table, and then repopulate the table with 10,000 employees spread in a balanced tree with three levels, as shown in Listing 16-36.

Listing 16-36: Repopulating the Employees Table for Performance Tests

```
-- clear the Employees table
TRUNCATE TABLE Employees

-- fill the table with 10,000 employees:
-- 1000 employees in level 0, each of which has 3 subordinates in level 1,
-- each of which has two subordinates in level 2
-- (there is no president in this case)

SET NOCOUNT ON
DECLARE @emplvl0 AS int, @emplvl1 AS int, @emplvl2 AS int
SET @emplvl0 = 1
WHILE @emplvl0 <= 9991
BEGIN
  -- insert level 0 employees with ids 1, 11, ..., 9991
  INSERT INTO employees(empid, mgrid, empname, salary)
    VALUES(@emplvl0, NULL , 'EmpName' + CAST(@emplvl0 AS varchar), $3000.00)
  SET @emplvl1 = @emplvl0 + 1
  WHILE @emplvl1 <= @emplvl0 + 7
  BEGIN
    -- insert three level 1 employees with ids emplvl0 + 1, + 4, + 7
    INSERT INTO employees(empid, mgrid, empname, salary)
      VALUES(@emplvl1, @emplvl0, 'EmpName' + CAST(@emplvl1 AS varchar), $2000.00)
    SET @emplvl2 = @emplvl1 + 1
    WHILE @emplvl2 <= @emplvl1 + 2
    BEGIN
      -- insert two level 2 employees with ids emplvl1 + 1, + 2
      INSERT INTO employees(empid, mgrid, empname, salary)
        VALUES(@emplvl2, @emplvl1, 'EmpName' + CAST(@emplvl2 AS varchar), $1000.00)
      SET @emplvl2 = @emplvl2 + 1
    END
```

```
      SET @emplvl1 = @emplvl1 + 3
    END
    SET @emplvl0 = @emplvl0 + 10
  END
SET NOCOUNT OFF
```

> **NOTE**   *This would be a good time to grab some coffee, as this loop might run for a minute or two.*

Now look at the first 20 employees using the query in Listing 16-37.

Listing 16-37: Getting the First 20 Employees

```
SELECT TOP 20
  *
FROM
  Employees
ORDER BY
  empid
```

The output of this query is shown in Table 6-17.

Table 16-17: TOP 20 Employees

empid	mgrid	empname	salary	lvl	hierarchy
1	NULL	EmpName1	3000.0000	0	.1.
2	1	EmpName2	2000.0000	1	.1.2.
3	2	EmpName3	1000.0000	2	.1.2.3.
4	2	EmpName4	1000.0000	2	.1.2.4.
5	1	EmpName5	2000.0000	1	.1.5.
6	5	EmpName6	1000.0000	2	.1.5.6.
7	5	EmpName7	1000.0000	2	.1.5.7.
8	1	EmpName8	2000.0000	1	.1.8.
9	8	EmpName9	1000.0000	2	.1.8.9.
10	8	EmpName10	1000.0000	2	.1.8.10.

Table 16-17: TOP 20 Employees (Continued)

empid	mgrid	empname	salary	lvl	hierarchy
11	NULL	EmpName11	3000.0000	0	.11.
12	11	EmpName12	2000.0000	1	.11.12.
13	12	EmpName13	1000.0000	2	.11.12.13.
14	12	EmpName14	1000.0000	2	.11.12.14.
15	11	EmpName15	2000.0000	1	.11.15.
16	15	EmpName16	1000.0000	2	.11.15.16.
17	15	EmpName17	1000.0000	2	.11.15.17.
18	11	EmpName18	2000.0000	1	.11.18.
19	18	EmpName19	1000.0000	2	.11.18.19.
20	18	EmpName20	1000.0000	2	.11.18.20.

This will give you a picture of how the employees are organized in the table. The table has one thousand groups of ten employees. Each group has a top-level manager with three subordinate employees, each of whom has two subordinate employees.

Using Indexes and Running Performance Tests

One of the most important indexes that might improve your queries' performance is a non-clustered index placed on the hierarchy column. The script to do this is in Listing 16-38.

Listing 16-38: Adding an Index on the hierarchy Column

```
CREATE NONCLUSTERED INDEX idx_nc_hierarchy ON Employees(hierarchy)
```

Such an index will make filtering the relevant rows much more efficient when a small portion of the rows are to be returned from the query.

One problem with this is that an index can be placed on a column no larger than 900 bytes, which might limit the maximum number of levels that are supported. Then again, it will still support more than 100 levels, which is rarely reached in implementations of hierarchical structures.

Another problem with this index is that the query processor does not always choose to use it even where you think it should. Usually, you can come up with a few variations for the same query, and in order to choose the one with the best performance, you need to examine execution plans, I/O cost, etc. You will soon see a few performance tests for variations of the same query. Note that the execution plans that are presented here might be different from yours because you might run your tests in a different environment. Furthermore, it is not guaranteed that the query processor will come up with the same execution plan each time. The important thing is to understand the analysis process.

> **NOTE** *Make sure you run* SET STATISTICS IO ON *and turn on the graphical execution plan in Query Analyzer before you run the following queries.*

Conducting Performance Tests with Subqueries

Now run a query that returns employee 5 and all of his subordinates. This query should return only three rows. The code is shown in Listing 16-39.

Listing 16-39: Testing Performance, Query 1

```
SELECT
  *
FROM
  Employees
WHERE
  hierarchy LIKE (SELECT
                    hierarchy
                  FROM
                    Employees
                  WHERE
                    empid = 5) + '%'
ORDER BY
  hierarchy
```

Take a look at the I/O statistics report, graphical execution plan, and textual execution plan of this query shown in Listing 16-40, Figure 16-9, and Listing 16-41, respectively.

Listing 16-40: I/O Statistics Report of a Performance Test Using a Subquery

```
Table 'Employees'.  Scan count 2,     logical reads 90,
                    physical reads 0, read-ahead reads 0.
```

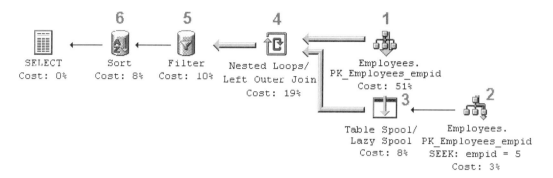

Figure 16-9: Graphical execution plan—testing performance using a subquery

Listing 16-41: Textual Execution Plan—Testing Performance Using a Subquery

```
6 |--Sort(ORDER BY:([Employees].[hierarchy] ASC))
   5 |--Filter(WHERE:(like([Employees].[hierarchy],
       [Employees].[hierarchy]+'%', NULL)))
     4 |--Nested Loops(Left Outer Join)
       1 |--Clustered Index Scan(OBJECT:
             ([testdb].[dbo].[Employees].[PK_Employees_empid]))
       3 |--Table Spool
         2 |--Clustered Index Seek(OBJECT:
               ([testdb].[dbo].[Employees].[PK_Employees_empid]),
               SEEK:([Employees].[empid]=5) ORDERED FORWARD)
```

The execution plan can be broken down to the following steps:

1. A clustered index scan is performed to fetch all of the rows from the Employees table.

2. A clustered index seek is performed to fetch the row for employee ID 5.

3. The result of the previous step is placed in a hidden temporary table.

4. A left outer join is performed between the output from Step 1 (all of the rows from the Employees table) and the temporary table from Step 3 (employee 5's row). This step produces a list of all of the employees, as well as employee 5's details attached to each of the other employees.

5. The output from the previous step is filtered. Only employees containing a hierarchy that matches the pattern '<emp5_hierarchy>%' are returned.

6. The output from the previous step is sorted by hierarchy.

You can see that the index on the hierarchy column was not used at all. The query processor decided on a conservative approach because the value of the hierarchy returned by the subquery is as yet unknown.

Conducting Performance Tests with Constants

The best chance for the index to be used when the LIKE operator is filtering the rows is when you compare a certain column to a constant in the form of 'constant%', as shown in Listing 16-42.

Listing 16-42: Testing Performance, Query 2

```
SELECT
  *
FROM
  Employees
WHERE
  hierarchy LIKE '.1.5.%'
ORDER BY
  Hierarchy
```

Take a look at the I/O statistics report, graphical execution plan, and textual execution plan for this query, shown in Listing 16-43, Figure 16-10, and Listing 16-44, respectively.

Listing 16-43: I/O Statistics Report of a Performance Test Using a Constant

```
Table 'Employees'.  Scan count 1, logical reads 8,
                    physical reads 0, read-ahead reads 0.
```

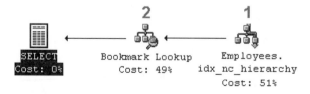

Figure 16-10: Graphical execution plan—testing performance using a constant

Listing 16-44: Textual Execution Plan—Testing Performance Using a Constant

```
2 |--Bookmark Lookup(BOOKMARK:([Bmk1000]),
                    OBJECT:([testdb].[dbo].[Employees]))
  1 |--Index Seek(
      OBJECT:([testdb].[dbo].[Employees].[idx_nc_hierarchy]),
            SEEK:([Employees].[hierarchy] >= '.1.5.' AND
                  [Employees].[hierarchy] < '.1.5/'),
                  WHERE:(like([Employees].[hierarchy],
                            '.1.5.%', NULL)) ORDERED FORWARD)
```

The execution plan can be broken down to the following steps:

1. An index seek is performed on the index placed on the hierarchy column. Notice that the seek operation converted the hierarchy LIKE '.1.5.%' pattern to hierarchy >= '.1.5.' AND hierarchy < '.1.5/'. The slash symbol (/) appears right after the dot symbol (.) in the ASCII table of characters. This might result in returning slightly more rows than you need, so a filter is placed to make sure that only rows matching the 'hierarchy LIKE '.1.5.%' pattern will remain.

2. For each of the remaining index rows from Step 1, the relevant employee rows are looked up from the Employees table.

You can see that the index on the hierarchy column was used efficiently, and you ended up with only eight logical reads. The reason that an index seek is very efficient here is that the query returns a small number of rows. The query processor can estimate the number of rows because a constant is used, and the optimizer does the estimation by checking data distribution statistics. If the query had returned a large number of rows, a logical page read would have been performed for each employee's row lookup, and you might have ended up reading more pages than the total number of pages consumed by the whole table.

The query processor can estimate the number of returned rows—again by checking statistics—and in such a case, it would probably not use the index on the hierarchy column. Thus, the performance of the query is very efficient, but it is not practical to check for the hierarchy value manually each time you want to issue a query.

Conducting Performance Tests with Dynamic Execution

If you encapsulate the previous query inside a stored procedure, you can build the SQL statement inside a character string variable and then execute it dynamically. This will have the same effect of running the query with a constant and will use the index on the hierarchy column where it improves the query performance, the same way the previous query did. Check out the code in Listing 16-45.

Listing 16-45: Testing Performance, Query 3

```
DECLARE @cmd AS varchar(8000)

SET @cmd =
  'SELECT * FROM Employees WHERE hierarchy LIKE ''' +
  (SELECT hierarchy + '%'
   FROM Employees
   WHERE empid = 5) +
  ''' ORDER BY hierarchy'

EXECUTE(@cmd)
```

Take a look at the I/O statistics report, graphical execution plan, and textual execution plan of the first phase of processing this query, as shown in Listing 16-46, Figure 16-11, and Listing 16-47, respectively.

Listing 16-46: I/O Statistics Report
of a Performance Test Building the Query Dynamically

```
Table 'Employees'.  Scan count 1, logical reads 2,
                    physical reads 0, read-ahead reads 0.
```

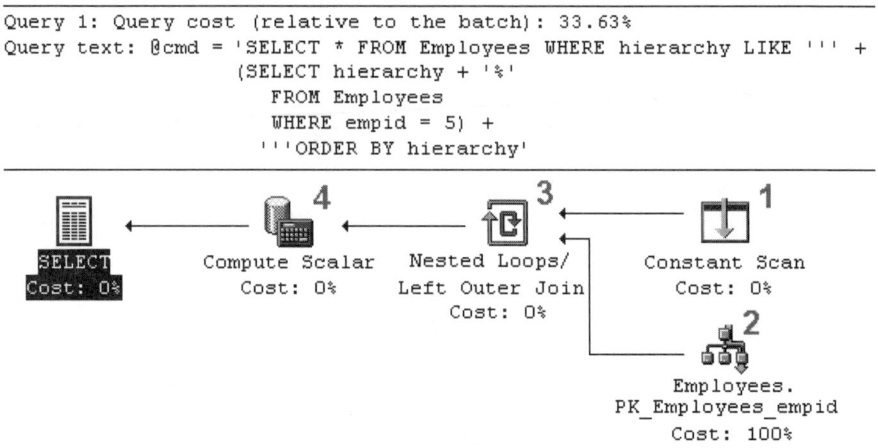

Figure 16-11: Graphical execution plan—building the query dynamically

Listing 16-47: Textual Execution Plan—Building the Query Dynamically

```
4 |--Compute Scalar(DEFINE:([Expr1003]=
     Convert('SELECT * FROM Employees WHERE hierarchy LIKE
     ''+[Employees].[hierarchy]+'%'+''ORDER BY hierarchy')))
  3 |--Nested Loops(Left Outer Join)
    1 |--Constant Scan
    2 |--Clustered Index Seek(OBJECT:
         ([testdb].[dbo].[Employees].[PK_Employees_empid]),
         SEEK:([Employees].[empid]=5) ORDERED FORWARD)
```

The first part of the execution plan is very simple. It is the first phase where the query statement is dynamically built. The value of the hierarchy column for employee ID 5 is retrieved by using a fast clustered index seek, which costs you only two logical reads. This value is concatenated with the other parts of the statement. The clustered index on the empid column was created by the PRIMARY KEY constraint. Note that if there were no empid index on the column, this simple retrieval of the hierarchy value for employee ID 5 would have resulted in a full table scan, making this solution inadequate.

Take a look at the I/O statistics report, graphical execution plan, and textual execution plan of the second phase of processing this query, as shown in Listing 16-48, Figure 16-12, and Listing 16-49, respectively.

Listing 16-48: I/O Statistics Report of a Performance Test Using Dynamic Execution

```
Table 'Employees'.  Scan count 1, logical reads 8,
                    physical reads 0, read-ahead reads 0.
```

```
Query 2: Query cost (relative to the batch): 66.37%
Query text: SELECT * FROM Employees
WHERE hierarchy LIKE '.1.5.%'ORDER BY hierarchy
```

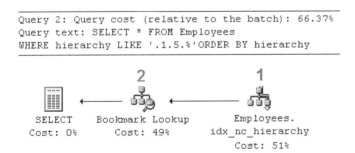

Figure 16-12: Graphical execution plan—dynamic execution

Listing 16-49: Textual Execution Plan—Dynamic Execution

```
2 |--Bookmark Lookup(BOOKMARK:([Bmk1000]),
                     OBJECT:([testdb].[dbo].[Employees]))
  1 |--Index Seek(
       OBJECT:([testdb].[dbo].[Employees].[idx_nc_hierarchy]),
             SEEK:([Employees].[hierarchy] >= '.1.5.' AND
             [Employees].[hierarchy] < '.1.5/'),
             WHERE:(like([Employees].[hierarchy],
                     '.1.5.%', NULL)) ORDERED FORWARD)
```

The query statement that was constructed in the first phase is now executed. You can see that it has the same execution plan as the previous query, where you used a constant.

You probably wonder if it wouldn't be simpler to just write a stored procedure that accepts the employee ID as a parameter, defines a variable, and fetches the hierarchy value into that variable, based on the given employee ID, so that it can later be used in the query. The problem with this solution is that the optimizer optimizes a batch or a stored procedure in one unit. This includes variable declaration and assignment in its body, as well as a query that uses that variable. Thus, the value stored in the variable is unknown when the actual query is optimized. Note that this doesn't apply to a stored-procedure parameter, which is a whole different story. This applies to a variable declaration in the body of a stored procedure or batch.

Conducting Performance Tests with Joins

A join solution provided by SQL Server MVP Umachandar Jayachandran, seems to use the index on the hierarchy column quite efficiently. See Listing 16-50.

Listing 16-50: Testing Performance, Query 4

```
SELECT
  *
FROM
   Employees AS E
  JOIN
   (SELECT
     hierarchy
    FROM
     Employees
    WHERE empid = 5) as M ON E.hierarchy LIKE M.Hierarchy + '%'
```

Take a look at the I/O statistics report, graphical execution plan, and textual execution plan of this query, as shown in Listing 16-51, Figure 16-13, and Listing 16-52, respectively.

Listing 16-51: I/O Statistics Report of a Performance Test Using a Join

```
Table 'Employees'.  Scan count 2, logical reads 10,
                    physical reads 0, read-ahead reads 0.
```

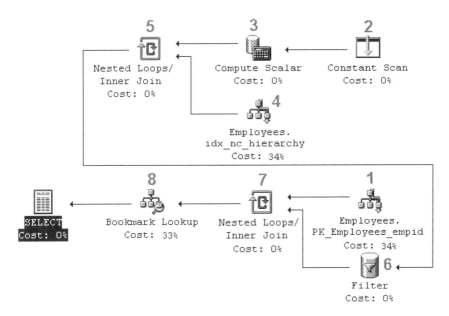

Figure 16-13: Graphical execution plan—testing performance using a join

Listing 16-52: Textual Execution Plan—Testing Performance Using a Join

```
8 |--Bookmark Lookup(BOOKMARK:([Bmk1000]),
    OBJECT:([testdb].[dbo].[Employees] AS [E]))
  7 |--Nested Loops(Inner Join,
      OUTER REFERENCES:([Employees].[hierarchy]))
    1 |--Clustered Index Seek(
        OBJECT:([testdb].[dbo].[Employees].[PK_Employees_empid]),
        SEEK:([Employees].[empid]=5) ORDERED FORWARD)
    6 |--Filter(WHERE:(like([E].[hierarchy],
            [Employees].[hierarchy]+'%', NULL)))
      5 |--Nested Loops(Inner Join, OUTER REFERENCES:([Expr1003],
                  [Expr1004], [Expr1005]))
```

```
3 |--Compute Scalar(
     DEFINE:([Expr1003]=Convert(
     LikeRangeStart([Employees].[hierarchy]+'%', NULL)),
     [Expr1004]=Convert(
     LikeRangeEnd([Employees].[hierarchy]+'%', NULL)),
     [Expr1005]=
     LikeRangeInfo([Employees].[hierarchy]+'%', NULL)))
   | 2 |--Constant Scan
4 |--Index Seek(OBJECT:(
     [testdb].[dbo].[Employees].[idx_nc_hierarchy] AS [E]),
     SEEK:([E].[hierarchy] > [Expr1003] AND
     [E].[hierarchy] < [Expr1004]) ORDERED FORWARD)
```

The execution plan can be broken down to the following steps:

1. Retrieve the row of employee ID 5 by performing a fast clustered index seek. The hierarchy value from this row will be used later.

2. A constant scan introduces a constant row into a query, to be used later.

3. The compute scalar operation calculates start- and end-range values for employee ID 5's hierarchy value, which was retrieved in Step 1. These values, which are calculated here, are similar to what you saw in Step 1 of Query 2 (Listing 16-42). They are placed in the constant row generated in the previous step, to be used later.

4. An index seek on the index placed on the hierarchy column is performed. The seek is performed in a similar way to what you saw in Step 1 of Query 2 (Listing 16-42) using: hierarchy > [Expr1003] AND hierarchy < [Expr1004]. Expr1003 and Expr1004 are the values that were calculated in Step 3.

5. A nested loop join algorithm is used to perform the index seek explained in Step 4 for every matching employee found in Step 3.

6. The previous output is filtered to make sure that only hierarchy values matching the pattern hierarchy LIKE '.1.5.%' will remain.

7. A nested loop join algorithm is performed to repeat Steps 2–6 for every matching row found in Step 1 (which should always be one row).

8. The hierarchy index rows returned in Step 7 are used to look up the matching employees.

You can see that the index is used quite efficiently. The query has an I/O cost of no more than 10 logical reads, and you don't need to use dynamic execution here. (This is also further proof that when you aim for good performance, you should, as always, test, test, and test some more!)

SQL Puzzle 16-1: Hierarchies and User-Defined Functions

In this chapter, you learned how to get hierarchical views of employees by adding the hierarchy and lvl columns. You implemented a self-maintained solution with triggers that automatically update those columns. Your task is to provide an alternative solution by adding the hierarchy and lvl columns as computed columns to the original Employees table created at the beginning of this chapter (which did not include hierarchy or lvl columns). The computed columns call the following user-defined functions, which you will need to create:

```
ALTER TABLE Employees
  ADD lvl AS dbo.NODELEVEL(empid),
      hierarchy AS dbo.NODEPATH(empid)
```

The NODELEVEL() function accepts an employee ID as an argument and returns his or her level in the hierarchy. A top-level employee has level 0, and each subordinate level is incremented by 1.

The NODEPATH() function also accepts an employee ID as an argument and returns his or her hierarchical path in the form '.node0.node1.[...].node(n-1).'.

In this puzzle, you don't need to perform validation checks on the input of the functions because you will only use them in the computed columns and supply them in the empid column as an argument.

The answer to this puzzle can be found on pages 718–721.

Tips and Tricks

THIS CHAPTER IS DEVOTED TO tips and tricks that solve common needs of T-SQL users and programmers. The solutions presented here were collected from our experience and also from the experience of our colleagues, who were kind enough to contribute their unique solutions to problems they encountered.

We would like to express our thanks to all those who contributed their tips.

Unlearning an Old Trick

Before you begin learning new tricks, there is one you should unlearn. Consider the query in Listing 17-1, which determines the first and last order dates in the Northwind database.

Listing 17-1: Query Using MIN() and MAX() on Same Column

```
SELECT
  MIN (OrderDate),
  MAX (OrderDate)
FROM
  Orders
```

Prior to version 7.0, this query would have produced a table scan instead of using the index on OrderDate. The optimizer wasn't bright enough to figure out that it could tap the index twice and come up with the desired information.

The workaround for this problem involved a nested subquery, as shown in Listing 17-2.

Listing 17-2: Using a Nested Subquery to Use an Index

```
SELECT
  MIN (OrderDate),
  (SELECT MAX (OrderDate) FROM Orders)
FROM
  Orders
```

For this query, the optimizer first performed the nested subquery, which was a quick tap on the index. It then did the outer query, which again made a quick tap on the index. If you run these queries in SQL Server 7.0 or 2000, you get identical performance in I/O and speed, as well as identical query plans. What is even more stunning is the fact that the Query Analyzer uses a JOIN. This is because it goes to the index twice and then needs to meld the two pieces of information—the MIN() and the MAX()—to return the results.

At this point, you don't really need to change any existing code because the results and performance are the same. However, if there is no index you can use, and you use the nested subquery trick, you will get two table scans or two clustered index scans. If you eliminate the subquery, you get only one table scan or clustered index scan. Therefore, in versions of SQL Server before version 7.0, the subquery trick would do no harm and would have the same performance as the non-subquery version if there is no index it could use. However, using this trick in SQL Server 7.0 and 2000 gives worse performance.

Keep in mind that indexes can sometimes get dropped, and if this code is not converted, you could be in for a surprise.

Getting NULLs to Sort Last Instead of First

NULLs are special. They are like spoiled children that always need special attention. When you compare them with other values, the result is UNKNOWN even when you compare them with other NULLs. You always need to take special steps, like using the IS NULL operator instead of an equality operator when you look for NULLs. However, in some situations, NULLs are considered to be equal. Those situations include the UNIQUE constraint, GROUP BY, and ORDER BY.

ORDER BY considers NULLs to be equal to each other, but the ANSI committee does not define whether they should have a lower or higher sort value than all other known values, so you might find different implementations in different systems. SQL Server sorts NULLs before all other values.

What do you do if you want to sort them after all other values? For example, suppose you want to return all customers from the Northwind sample database, ordered by Region. If you issue the query shown in Listing 17-3, you will get NULLs first.

Listing 17-3: NULLs Sort First

```
SELECT
  *
FROM
  Customers
ORDER BY
  Region
```

You can use the CASE expression in the ORDER BY clause to return 1 when the region is NULL and 0 when it is not NULL (for similar uses of the CASE expression, please refer to Chapter 4). You can use this result as the first sort value, and the Region as the second. This way, 0s representing known values will sort first, and 1s representing NULLs will sort last. Listing 17-4 shows the query.

Listing 17-4: NULLs Sort Last

```
SELECT
  *
FROM
  Customers
ORDER BY
  CASE
    WHEN Region IS NULL THEN 1
    ELSE 0
  END,
  Region
```

This is all nice and well, but now that the ORDER BY clause uses an expression and not an explicit column, the optimizer will not consider using the index on the region column (which might improve the query performance by not performing an explicit sort operation). Prior to SQL Server 2000, there was not much you could do about it, but with SQL Server 2000, you can create an indexed view with the CASE expression as one of its columns. You can also have the CASE expression as a computed column in the Customers table and create a composite index on the computed column and the original Region column, as Listing 17-5 shows.

Listing 17-5: Adding a Computed Column and an Index on It to the Customers Table

```
ALTER TABLE Customers
  ADD RegionNullOrder AS
    CASE
      WHEN region IS NULL THEN 1
      ELSE 0
    END
GO

CREATE INDEX idx_nci_RegionNullOrder_Region ON
  Customers (RegionNullOrder, Region)
GO
```

Now you can rewrite your query as Listing 17-6 shows, and if you turn SHOWPLAN on to display the execution plan, you will see that it makes use of the new index, as shown in Listing 17-7. The SHOWPLAN option is covered in Appendix C.

Listing 17-6: NULLs Sort Last and an Index Is Used

```
SET SHOWPLAN_TEXT ON
GO

SELECT
  *
FROM
  Customers
ORDER BY
  RegionNullOrder,
  Region
GO
```

Listing 17-7: SHOWPLAN's Output, the Index on the Computed Column Is Used

```
|--Bookmark Lookup(BOOKMARK:([Bmk1000]),
     OBJECT:([Northwind].[dbo].[Customers]))
   |--Index Scan(OBJECT:(
     [Northwind].[dbo].[Customers].[idx_nci_RegionNullOrder_Region]),
       ORDERED FORWARD)
```

Using a Parameter for the Column in the ORDER BY Clause (by Bruce P. Margolin)

The ORDER BY clause accepts only explicit column names or expressions; it won't accept a column name stored in a variable. Suppose you want to write a stored procedure that returns an ordered output of the authors in the Authors table in the pubs sample database, but you want to pass it a parameter that tells it which column to ORDER BY. There are a few ways to approach this problem. You can use either the column number or name as a parameter and use a CASE expression to determine the column, or you can use the column number or name with dynamic execution.

Using the Column Number as Parameter and CASE to Determine the Column

You can pass the column number as a parameter to a stored procedure and use a CASE expression in the ORDER BY clause to pick the relevant column, as Listing 17-8 shows.

Listing 17-8: Passing the ORDER BY Column as a Parameter,
Using a Column Number, First Try

```
CREATE PROC GetAuthors1
  @colnum AS int
AS

SELECT
  *
FROM
  authors
ORDER BY
  CASE @colnum
    WHEN 1 THEN au_id
    WHEN 2 THEN au_lname
    WHEN 3 THEN au_fname
    WHEN 4 THEN phone
    WHEN 5 THEN address
    WHEN 6 THEN city
    WHEN 7 THEN state
    WHEN 8 THEN zip
    WHEN 9 THEN contract
    ELSE NULL
  END
GO
```

Notice, however, what happens when you try to execute the `GetAuthors1` stored procedure, providing 1 as an argument to indicate that you want the output to be sorted by au_id, as shown in Listing 17-9.

Listing 17-9: Error When Trying to Invoke the GetAuthors1 Stored Procedure

```
EXEC GetAuthors1
  @colnum = 1

Server: Msg 245, Level 16, State 1, Procedure GetAuthors1, Line 5
Syntax error converting the varchar value '172-32-1176'
to a column of data type bit.
```

The reason for this error is that the `CASE` expression's return value's datatype is determined by the highest datatype, according to the datatypes precedence rules (see the Books Online for details). In this case, the `bit` datatype of the contract column has the highest precedence, so it determines the datatype of the result of the `CASE` expression. Error 245 indicates that the author ID `'172-32-1176'`, which is of the datatype varchar, cannot be converted to bit, of course.

You can get around this problem by casting the problematic contract column to a char datatype, as Listing 17-10 shows.

Listing 17-10: Passing the ORDER BY Column as a Parameter,
Using a Column Number, Second Try

```
ALTER PROC GetAuthors1
  @colnum AS int
AS

SELECT
  *
FROM
  authors
ORDER BY
  CASE @colnum
    WHEN 1 THEN au_id
    WHEN 2 THEN au_lname
    WHEN 3 THEN au_fname
    WHEN 4 THEN phone
    WHEN 5 THEN address
    WHEN 6 THEN city
    WHEN 7 THEN state
    WHEN 8 THEN zip
    WHEN 9 THEN CAST(contract AS CHAR(1))
    ELSE NULL
  END
GO
```

Note that you will have the same problem with numeric columns, but simply casting a numeric column to a character datatype won't be sufficient. You will also need to prefix the cast values with the proper number of zeros so that they will sort properly. For example, suppose you have a qty column holding the value 10 in one row and 2 in another row. Simply casting those values to the character strings `'10'` and `'2'`, respectively, will result in 2 being sorted after `'10'`, because a character sort will be performed here instead of a numeric sort.

To avoid this problem, you can prefix the qty column with the proper number of zeros, causing all of the cast values to have the same length as the maximum possible length of the qty column, say ten digits in our example. Listing 17-11 shows how this can be achieved.

Listing 17-11: Prefixing a Numeric Value with Zeros

```
RIGHT (REPLICATE ('0', 10) + CAST (qty AS varchar (10)), 10)
```

Using Dynamic Execution

Another option using the column number is to construct the SELECT statement in a variable, and execute it dynamically with the EXEC command, as Listing 17-12 shows.

Listing 17-12: Passing the ORDER BY Column as a Parameter,
Using Dynamic Execution

```
CREATE PROC GetAuthors2
  @colnum AS int
AS

DECLARE
  @cmd AS varchar (8000)

SET @cmd =
  'SELECT *'      + CHAR (13) + CHAR(10) +
  'FROM authors' + CHAR (13) + CHAR(10) +
  'ORDER BY '     + CAST (@colnum AS varchar (4))

EXEC(@cmd)
GO
```

Using the Column Name as Parameter
and CASE to Determine the Column

Finally, you can pass the column name as a sysname (nvarchar(128)), which is used for identifiers, and check it using a CASE expression similar to the first example, but now it checks for column names rather than column numbers, as Listing 17-13 shows.

Listing 17-13: Passing the ORDER BY Column as a Parameter,
Using a Column Name

```
CREATE PROC GetAuthors3
  @colname AS sysname
AS
```

```
SELECT
  *
FROM
  authors
ORDER BY
  CASE @colname
    WHEN 'au_id' THEN au_id
    WHEN 'au_lname' THEN au_lname
    WHEN ...
    WHEN 'contract' THEN CAST (contract AS CHAR (1))
    ELSE NULL
  END
GO
```

Formatting Output that May Be Null (by Robert Skoglund)

Sometimes you need a SQL trick because of the requirements of the front end. For example, suppose your client-side GUI uses a multiline edit box for displaying the customer's address. Some of your customers have region information, such as state or province, and for others this is NULL. Concatenating NULL with anything will give you a NULL. What is needed is a way to provide the formatted address information while handling NULL information.

Using the Northwind database, Robert creates a view of the form as shown in Listing 17-14.

Listing 17-14: A View to Build a String and Handle NULLs

```
CREATE VIEW MailingList
AS
SELECT
  CustomerID,
  CompanyName + CHAR (13) + CHAR (10) +
  Address    + CHAR (13) + CHAR (10) +
  City       + CHAR (13) + CHAR (10) +
  CASE WHEN Region IS NOT NULL THEN Region + CHAR (13) + CHAR (10)
       ELSE ''
  END +  Country AS ContactAddress
FROM
  Customers
```

The carriage returns and line feeds—CHAR(13) + CHAR(10)—are provided to format the text for the multiline edit box. When Region is not NULL, then Region plus the carriage return and line feed are added to the address. Otherwise, an empty string is added. Robert's original design involved the use of the SUBSTRING() function, which has been replaced here with a CASE construct.

Embedding Stored Procedure Rowsets in SELECT and SELECT INTO Statements

Chapter 11 covers user-defined functions and shows you how to build table-valued functions that return a rowset. You can embed a call to such a function in a SELECT query that performs a join, for example, or even in a SELECT INTO statement to create a target table and populate it with the result of the function. User-defined functions (UDFs) are not available in SQL Server 7.0. You can create a stored procedure that accepts parameters and returns a rowset as a result, but you can't embed it naturally in SELECT or SELECT INTO statements. However, you insist! Of course, you refuse to be left empty handed.

Suppose you wanted to embed the result of the stored procedure shown in Listing 17-15, which returns authors from the pubs sample database for a given state, into your SELECT or SELECT INTO statements.

Listing 17-15: Creation Script for Stored Procedure AuthorsInState

```
USE pubs

GO

CREATE PROC AuthorsInState
  @state char(2)
AS

SELECT
  *
FROM
  authors
WHERE
  state = @state
GO
```

You have three options: using the INSERT EXEC statement, the OPENROWSET() function, or the OPENQUERY() function. These options are presented in the next three sections. Later, in the section "Using OPENROWSET() in a View," you will build on your skill with OPENROWSET. Finally, in the section "Choosing between SQL and OPENQUERY()," you will see how to make the decision to use OPENQUERY().

Using the INSERT EXEC Statement

You can create a temporary table with the same structure as the rowset returned from the stored procedure, as Listing 17-16 shows.

Listing 17-16: Schema Creation Script for the #TmpAuthors Table

```
CREATE TABLE #TmpAuthors
(
  au_id     varchar(11) NOT NULL,
  au_lname  varchar(40) NOT NULL,
  au_fname  varchar(20) NOT NULL,
  phone     char(12)    NOT NULL,
  address   varchar(40) NULL,
  city      varchar(20) NULL,
  state     char(2)     NULL,
  zip       char(5)     NULL,
  contract  bit         NOT NULL
)
```

You can then use the INSERT EXEC statement to populate it, as Listing 17-17 shows.

Listing 17-17: Using the INSERT EXEC Statement

```
INSERT INTO #TmpAuthors
  EXEC AuthorsInState 'CA'
```

Now you can use the temporary table in SELECT or SELECT INTO statements just like any other table, as Listings 17-18 and 17-19 show.

Listing 17-18: Embedding the Result of the INSERT EXEC Statement in a SELECT Statement

```
SELECT
  *
FROM
  #TmpAuthors
GO
```

*Listing 17-19: Embedding the Result of the INSERT EXEC Statement
in a SELECT INTO Statement*

```
SELECT
  *
INTO
  #TmpAuthors2
FROM
  #TmpAuthors
GO
```

Using the OPENROWSET() Function

The OPENROWSET() function is used to issue ad hoc queries against heterogeneous
data sources. You can also use it to invoke remote stored procedures. As a result,
you can use it to invoke the AuthorsInState stored procedure as if the local server
were a remote one. Listing 17-20 shows how to embed the OPENROWSET() function in
a SELECT statement.

*Listing 17-20: Embedding the Result of the OPENROWSET Function
in a SELECT Statement*

```
SELECT
  T1.*
FROM
  OPENROWSET('SQLOLEDB','<server>';'<user>';'<pass>',
             'EXEC pubs..AuthorsInState ''CA''') AS T1
```

Listing 17-21 shows you how to embed the OPENROWSET() function in a SELECT
INTO statement.

*Listing 17-21: Embedding the Result of the OPENROWSET Function
in a SELECT INTO Statement*

```
SELECT
  *
INTO
  #TmpAuthors
FROM
  OPENROWSET('SQLOLEDB', <server>';'<user>';'<pass>,
             'EXEC pubs..AuthorsInState ''CA''') AS T1
```

Using the OPENQUERY() Function

The OPENQUERY() function is used to issue pass-through queries against a linked server. You can also use it to invoke a remote stored procedure from the linked server. You can refer to your own local server as a linked server by turning on the 'Data Access' server option as Listing 17-22 shows.

Listing 17-22: Turning On the 'Data Access' Server Option

```
EXEC sp_serveroption '<server>', 'Data Access', 'true'
```

Now you can embed the OPENQUERY() function in a SELECT statement as Listing 17-23 shows.

Listing 17-23: Embedding the Result of the OPENQUERY Function in a SELECT Statement

```
SELECT
  T1.*
FROM
  OPENQUERY([<server>],
          'EXEC pubs..AuthorsInState ''CA''') AS T1
```

You can also embed the OPENQUERY() function in a SELECT INTO statement, as Listing 17-24 shows.

Listing 17-24: Embedding the Result of the OPENQUERY Function in a SELECT INTO Statement

```
SELECT
  *
INTO
  #TmpAuthors
FROM OPENQUERY([<server>],
          'EXEC pubs..AuthorsInState ''CA''')
```

Using OPENROWSET() in a View

From time to time, you have to use vendor products that do not support stored procedures. Rather, they can do SELECTs on tables and views. This is no problem; with the OPENROWSET() function, you can create a view that acts as a wrapper for the stored procedure call. Check out Listing 17-25.

Listing 17-25: Creating a View on a Stored Procedure Call

```
CREATE VIEW StoredProcWrapper
AS
SELECT
  *
FROM
   OPENROWSET
   (
     'SQLOLEDB',
     'SERVER=.;Trusted_Connection=yes',
     'SET FMTONLY OFF EXEC sp_who2'
   )
```

Here, the SERVER=. piece refers to the default instance of SQL Server on a machine on which SQL Server 2000 is running. You will have to specify the correct instance if you are not using the default, e.g., SERVER=BMCI03\BMCI03_02.

Choosing between SQL and OPENQUERY()

The server closest to the data is the one that should work with that data. Consider the following scenario, using the Northwind database. You have a Customers table on your local server, but you want to know the quantity of product ID 17 purchased by your local Canadian customers on the remote server, and you want it broken down by customer ID. The code in Listing 17-26 shows you how to do this with an SQL statement that uses the four-part naming convention to reference the tables.

Listing 17-26: Using Remote Tables with the Four-Part Naming Convention

```
SELECT
  C.CustomerID,
  SUM (OD.Quantity) AS Quantity
FROM
   Customers                         C
  JOIN
   Remote.Northwind.dbo.Orders        O  ON O.CustomerID = C.CustomerID
  JOIN
   Remote.Northwind.dbo.[Order Details] OD ON OD.OrderID   = O.OrderID
WHERE
   C.Country    = 'Canada'
  AND
   OD.ProductID = 17
GROUP BY
  C.CustomerID
```

This query did all of the work on the local server, even though the remote server had most of the data. Now compare this to using the OPENQUERY() function, as shown in Listing 17-27.

Listing 17-27: Using OPENQUERY() to Do the Majority of the Work on the Remote Server

```
SELECT
  C.CustomerID,
  O.Quantity
FROM
    Customers                   C
  JOIN
    OPENQUERY
    (
      Remote,
      'SELECT
        O.CustomerID,
        SUM (OD.Quantity) AS Quantity
      FROM
          Northwind..Orders         O
        JOIN
          Northwind..[Order Details] OD ON OD.OrderID = O.OrderID
      WHERE
          OD.ProductID = 17
      GROUP BY
        O.CustomerID'
    )                             O ON O.CustomerID = C.CustomerID
WHERE
    C.Country = 'Canada'
```

Here, the heavy work was done on the remote server where you had most of the data. Even the aggregation could be done there. Also, consider where you want the query to execute. In this case, the local server had the least amount of the data but it was the one managing the query.

You can also execute the query on the "remote" server and reference the Customers table from the "local" server, as shown in Listing 17-28.

Listing 17-28: Running the Query on the Remote Server

```
SELECT
  C.CustomerID,
  SUM (OD.Quantity) AS Quantity
FROM
    Local.Northwind.dbo.Customers C
  JOIN
    Orders                     O  ON O.CustomerID = C.CustomerID
  JOIN
    [Order Details]            OD ON OD.OrderID   = O.OrderID
WHERE
    C.Country    = 'Canada'
  AND
    OD.ProductID = 17
GROUP BY
  C.CustomerID
```

The trick here is to experiment with where you run the query and whether you directly access the remote table (via four-part naming) or use the OPENQUERY() function.

Using CASE in a JOIN (by Robert Vieira)

Suppose that you have a "Provider" institution that may have multiple children that are all "Company" institutions. Companies have Regions and Sites. Also, a Provider has both restricted and unrestricted users. The problem is to figure out the algorithm.

If a Provider user is unrestricted, then they will only have the Provider institution in their institution list. If they are a restricted user, then they will have the Provider plus all the companies to which they have rights. Therefore, the query needed is a bit different depending on whether they have just the provider or a list of companies.

The code shown in Listing 17-29 gets the institution list that the user can see (all institutions under the provider if it only finds the Provider row; just the list of company rows if it finds more than the provider). It works quite well. It does the query without a stored procedure, and all in a single round trip to the server.

Listing 17-29: Using CASE in a JOIN

```
USE RiskNet

-- GET INSTITUTION CHILDREN
SELECT
  v.InstitutionID,
  v.Name,
  v.HierarchyLevelID,
  v.HierarchyLevelName,
  v.Disabled,
  v.CompanyID,
  v.ParentInstitutionID
FROM
    vInstitution v
  JOIN
    Security.dbo.AccountInstSecurityRole s
  ON s.InstitutionID =
      CASE -- If count is 1 or less, then is unrestricted,
          -- otherwise, different join
        WHEN (SELECT
                COUNT(*)
              FROM
                  vInstitution v
                JOIN
                  Security.dbo.AccountInstSecurityRole s
                ON (v.InstitutionID = s.InstitutionID)
              WHERE
                  v.ParentInstitutionID = @ProviderInstitution
                AND
                  s.AccountID = @LoginID
                AND
                  v.HierarchyLevelID > 1
                AND
                  v.Disabled = 0
            ) <= 1
        THEN v.ParentInstitutionID
      ELSE v.InstitutionID
    END
```

```
WHERE
    v.ParentInstitutionID = @ProviderInstitution
  AND
    s.AccountID = @LoginID
  AND
    v.HierarchyLevelID > 1
  AND
    v.Disabled = 0
ORDER BY
  v.Name
```

Using COALESCE() with a LEFT JOIN

Consider the following scenario. You have a table of customers and another table containing their phone numbers. They can have a home and/or a business phone number. You wish to produce a phone list consisting of the customer's name and either the business number or home number, but not both. You also prefer to see the business number in the event that the customer has both a business and a home number. The list must show whether the number is a business or home phone number. Finally, you do not wish to see any customers who have no phones—after all, this is a phone list. The tables and some sample data are presented in Listing 17-30.

Listing 17-30: Tables and Sample Data for the Phone List

```
CREATE TABLE Customers
(
  CustomerNo int          NOT NULL
                          PRIMARY KEY,
  LastName    varchar (10) NOT NULL,
  FirstName  varchar (10) NOT NULL
)
GO


INSERT Customers VALUES (1, 'Smith', 'John')
INSERT Customers VALUES (2, 'Jones', 'Jim')
INSERT Customers VALUES (3, 'Stockwell', 'Mary')
INSERT Customers VALUES (4, 'Harris', 'Mike')
GO
```

```
CREATE TABLE Telephones
(
  CustomerNo   int       NOT NULL
                         REFERENCES Customers (CustomerNo),
  TelType      char (1) NOT NULL
                         CHECK (TelType IN ('H', 'B')),
  TelephoneNo int       NOT NULL,
                         PRIMARY KEY (CustomerNo, TelType)
)
GO

INSERT Telephones VALUES (1, 'H', 5550000)
INSERT Telephones VALUES (1, 'B', 5550001)
INSERT Telephones VALUES (2, 'H', 5550002)
INSERT Telephones VALUES (3, 'H', 5550003)
INSERT Telephones VALUES (3, 'B', 5550004)
GO
```

The solution requires two LEFT JOINs—both from the Customers table to the Telephones table. One LEFT JOIN will pick out the business numbers while the other will pick out the home numbers. The traps associated with LEFT JOINs are outlined in Chapter 1. The filter criteria for the unpreserved table, Telephones, are placed with the ON clauses to ensure that only those rows conforming to the filter criteria are chosen.

The trick is to determine which customers have phones. This is where the COALESCE() function comes to the rescue. This function takes a comma-delimited list of values and returns the first non-NULL value in the list. If all of the values are NULL, it returns a NULL. For this problem, you can list one column from each of the unpreserved tables. If COALESCE() returns a non-NULL value, then you have found a customer with a phone.

You also need to present the correct number according to the selection criteria— business numbers are preferred over home numbers. Here, too, you use the COALESCE() function and place the columns from the Telephones table in the order (business, home). The final solution is presented in Listing 17-31.

Listing 17-31: Generating the Phone List

```
SELECT
  C.CustomerNo,
  C.LastName,
  C.FirstName,
  COALESCE (TB.TelephoneNo, TH.TelephoneNo) AS TelephoneNo,
  COALESCE (TB.TelType, TH.TelType)         AS TelType
```

```
FROM
    Customers  C
  LEFT JOIN
    Telephones TB ON  C.CustomerNo = TB.CustomerNo
                 AND TB.TelType   = 'B'
  LEFT JOIN
    Telephones TH ON  C.CustomerNo = TH.CustomerNo
                 AND TH.TelType   = 'H'
WHERE
    COALESCE (TB.TelephoneNo, TH.TelephoneNo) IS NOT NULL
```

This example can be extended to add cell phone numbers.

Case-Sensitive Searches (by Umachandar Jayachandran)

If you have a case-insensitive installation but you still want to issue a few case-sensitive queries, then the following trick is for you. Consider the case-insensitive query shown in Listing 17-32, which retrieves authors with the last name "green" from the pubs sample database.

Listing 17-32: Authors with the Last Name "green", Case-Insensitive Search

```
SELECT
  *
FROM
  Authors
WHERE
  au_lname = 'green'
```

In a case-insensitive installation, this query returns one row, although the actual last name stored in the row is "Green" and not "green". This is, by definition, how case-insensitivity should work. To run a case-sensitive search, you can cast both the searched value and the au_lname column to a binary datatype. Since the letter *G* has a different binary value than the letter *g*, "Green" will not be equal to "green", and so the query shown in Listing 17-33 will find no match.

Listing 17-33: Authors with the Last Name "green", Case-Sensitive Search

```
SELECT
  *
FROM
  Authors
WHERE
  CAST (au_lname AS varbinary (40)) = CAST ('green' AS varbinary(40))
```

The problem is that using the CONVERT and CAST functions preclude the use of an index because the searched column is now inside a function. However, by adding a redundant equality comparison between the au_lname column and the searched value as is, as shown in Listing 17-34, the optimizer can use an index on the au_lname column, and *then* check for the case.

Listing 17-34: Authors with the Last Name "green", Case-Sensitive Search Using an Index

```
SELECT
  *
FROM
  Authors
WHERE
    au_lname = 'green'
  AND
    CAST (au_lname AS varbinary (40)) = CAST ('green' AS varbinary (40))
```

Getting Correct Values from @@ Functions

System functions starting with @@ supply very useful information. For example, @@IDENTITY holds the last identity value inserted by the session (see Chapter 6 for details), @@ROWCOUNT holds the number of rows affected by the last statement, and @@ERROR holds an integer number representing the way the last statement that was run finished (see Chapter 7 for details).

The problem with system functions is that most of them are very volatile—almost every statement can change their values, and thus you lose the previous value that was stored in them. For this reason, it is a good practice to store their values in local variables for safekeeping, and later inspect the local variables.

This will be better explained with an example. The script shown in Listing 17-37 creates the T1 table which will be used to generate some errors that you will try to trap.

Listing 17-37: Schema Creation Script for the T1 Table

```
CREATE TABLE T1
(
  pk_col    int NOT NULL PRIMARY KEY CHECK (pk_col > 0),
  ident_col int NOT NULL IDENTITY (1,1)
)
```

Now run the code shown in Listing 17-38, which inserts new rows and checks whether there was a duplicate key violation (error 2627) or a CHECK constraint violation (error 547).

Listing 17-38: Unsuccessful Attempt to Trap Both Primary Key and CHECK Constraint Violations

```
INSERT INTO T1 VALUES(0) -- violate the check constraint

IF @@ERROR = 2627
  PRINT 'PRIMARY KEY constraint violation'
ELSE IF @@ERROR = 547
  PRINT 'CHECK constraint violation'
GO
```

The first IF that checks for a PRIMARY KEY violation is a statement in its own right. It runs successfully, and thus @@ERROR will return 0 when the second IF that checks for a CHECK constraint violation is run. This code will never trap a CHECK constraint violation.

To avoid this problem, you can save the value of @@ERROR in a variable, as Listing 17-39 shows.

Listing 17-39: Successful Attempt to Trap Both Primary Key and CHECK Constraint Violations

```
DECLARE
  @myerror    AS int

INSERT INTO T1 VALUES(0) -- violate the check constraint

SET @myerror = @@ERROR

IF @myerror = 2627
  PRINT 'PRIMARY KEY constraint violation'
ELSE IF @myerror = 547
  PRINT 'CHECK constraint violation'
GO
```

Now, suppose you want to capture the number of rows affected by the statement, and the last identity value inserted, by storing @@ROWCOUNT and @@IDENTITY in your own local variables. You could run the code shown in Listing 17-40.

Listing 17-40: Unsuccessful Attempt to Capture @@IDENTITY, @@ROWCOUNT, and @@ERROR

```
DECLARE
  @myerror    AS int,
  @myrowcount AS int,
  @myidentity AS int

INSERT INTO T1 VALUES(10) -- used to make the next statement cause a PK violation
INSERT INTO T1 VALUES(10) -- PK violation

SET @myidentity = @@IDENTITY
SET @myrowcount = @@ROWCOUNT
SET @myerror    = @@ERROR

PRINT '@myidentity: ' + CAST(@myidentity AS varchar)
PRINT '@myrowcount: ' + CAST(@myrowcount AS varchar)
PRINT '@myerror   : ' + CAST(@myerror AS varchar)
GO
```

The output, shown in Listing 17-41, shows that @myerror stores 0 instead of 2627 (primary key violation), and @myrowcount mistakenly stores 1 instead of 0. The variable assignment prior to assigning @@ERROR to @myerror was successful, and thus the original value of @@ERROR was lost, and the number of rows affected is 1.

Listing 17-41: Output of Unsuccessful Attempt to Capture @@IDENTITY, @@ROWCOUNT, and @@ERROR

```
@myidentity: 3
@myrowcount: 1
@myerror   : 0
```

To make sure none of the environment variables are lost, you can assign values to all of them in one statement using a SELECT statement instead of multiple SET statements, as shown in Listing 17-42.

Listing 17-42: Successful Attempt to Capture @@IDENTITY, @@ROWCOUNT, and @@ERROR

```
DECLARE
  @myerror    AS int,
  @myrowcount AS int,
  @myidentity AS int
```

```
INSERT INTO T1 VALUES(10) -- PK violation

SELECT @myidentity = @@IDENTITY,
       @myrowcount = @@ROWCOUNT,
       @myerror    = @@ERROR

PRINT '@myidentity: ' + CAST(@myidentity AS varchar)
PRINT '@myrowcount: ' + CAST(@myrowcount AS varchar)
PRINT '@myerror   : ' + CAST(@myerror AS varchar)
GO
```

The output in Listing 17-43 shows that all of the environment variables were successfully captured.

Listing 17-43: Output of Successful Attempt to Capture @@IDENTITY, @@ROWCOUNT, and @@ERROR

```
@myidentity: 3
@myrowcount: 0
@myerror   : 2627
```

Using PWDCOMPARE() and PWDENCRYPT() in SQL Server 6.5 and 7.0 (by Brian Moran)

This tip demonstrates how to use the undocumented PWDCOMPARE() and PWDENCRYPT() functions when moving between SQL Server 6.5 and SQL Server 7.0, but the same techniques can be used to build your own password encryption tools in SQL Server 2000. The problem at hand has to do with the fact that SQL Server 6.5's versions of PWDENCRYPT() and PWDCOMPARE() are not supported in SQL 7.0. Passwords created in 6.5 can't be decrypted in SQL Server 7.0 using PWDCOMPARE.

PWDENCRYPT() and PWDCOMPARE() are internal, undocumented features used by SQL Server to manage passwords. PWDENCRYPT() is a one-way hash that takes a clear string and returns an encrypted version of the string. PWDCOMPARE() is used to compare an unencrypted string to its encrypted representation to see if it matches. Microsoft cautions people against using internal undocumented features, but sometimes you just can't help yourself. With that said, yes there is a secret, undocumented, relatively unknown way to make "strings" encrypted with the SQL Server 6.5 version of PWDENCRYPT() work with the SQL Server 7.0 version of PWDCOMPARE().

Let's assume you've built an application that stores a four-character PIN number that is used within the application for a simple password check. You could have spent a bunch of time writing your own encryption algorithms, or you could have used the Microsoft Cryptography API, but you're a rebel so you decided to use the undocumented and unsupported PWDENCRYPT() and PWDCOMPARE() functions. You use

PWDENCRYPT() to encrypt the PIN and then use PWDCOMPARE() to check a clear text version of the PIN against the encrypted version to see if they match. Everything worked perfectly until you tried to upgrade to SQL Server 7.0, at which time the PWDCOMPARE() function started returning FALSE even when the clear text and encrypted versions of the PIN string did match. How do you make the old encrypted PIN numbers work with PWDCOMPARE() when you upgrade to a newer version of SQL Server?

> **NOTE**   *Listing 17-47 at the end of this section includes a code sample for using these functions in a SQL Server 7.0 or 2000 environment.*

SQL Server 7.0 must have a way to compare the old SQL Server 6.5 passwords encrypted with PWDENCRYPT() since the passwords from an upgraded SQL Server 6.5 database work fine. Doing a little detective work with the T-SQL source code behind sp_addlogin and sp_password can give you all the answers you are looking for. (Reading system procedures is always a great way to learn new tricks!) These two stored procedures both make internal use of the SQL Server encryption functions, and they both need to deal with SQL Server 6.5 versions of passwords.

Reading the sp_addlogin T-SQL code and supporting Books Online documentation shows a possible value of 'skip_encryption_old' for the @PWDENCRYPT() parameter, and the Books Online tell us this value means, "The password is not encrypted. The supplied password was encrypted by an earlier version of SQL Server. This option is provided for upgrade purposes only."

Reading further through the T-SQL code for sp_addlogin clearly shows that the SQL Server 7.0 version of PWDENCRYPT() is not applied to the @passwd string if @encryptopt = 'skip_encryption_old'. But SQL Server 7.0 does apply some CONVERT() gymnastics to the @passwd parameter to store the string in the "new" SQL Server 7.0 datatype format for passwords. The relevant snippet of T-SQL code from sp_addlogin is shown in Listing 17-44.

Listing 17-44: Excerpt from sp_addlogin

```
ELSE IF @encryptopt = 'skip_encryption_old'
BEGIN
    SELECT @xstatus = @xstatus | 0x800,    -- old-style encryption
    @passwd = CONVERT(sysname,CONVERT(varbinary(30),
                      CONVERT(varchar(30), @passwd)))
```

Pay close attention to the three-step CONVERT() process that SQL Server makes the @passwd parameter jump through. You'll be reusing it shortly.

Now take a look at the T-SQL code for sp_password. One of the checks is to see if the old password matches. You'll see the snippet of code shown in Listing 17-45.

Listing 17-45: Excerpt from sp_password

```
PWDCOMPARE(@old, password,
          (CASE WHEN xstatus & 2048 = 2048 THEN 1 ELSE 0 END))
```

This shows that the SQL Server 7.0 version of PWDCOMPARE() now takes three parameters rather than two parameters like the SQL Sever 6.5 version used. Some experimentation helped me understand that the third parameter is optional and defaults to 0. When set to 0, PWDCOMPARE() uses the "new" SQL Server 7.0 algorithm, but setting this parameter to 1 tells SQL Server 7.0 to use the "old" SQL Server 6.5 version of the PWDCOMPARE() algorithm.

Listing 17-46 has a stored procedure sample that shows how you can leverage these tricks to use effectively "old" SQL Server 6.5 encrypted strings with the SQL Server 7.0 version of PWDCOMPARE(). This stored procedure assumes your application asks a user to provide their Social Security Number (SSN) and "secret" PIN, which were stored in a table called MyTable. The value of the PIN had previously been encrypted using the SQL Server 6.5 version of PWDENCRYPT().

Listing 17-46: Creation Script for the CompareSQL65EncryptedString Stored Procedure

```
CREATE PROCEDURE CompareSQL65EncryptedString
(
  @SSN char(9),
  @pin  char(4),
  @return int OUTPUT)
AS
IF EXISTS
(
SELECT
  *
FROM MyTable (NOLOCK)
WHERE
    SSN = @ssn
  AND
    PWDCOMPARE(@pin,
      CONVERT(sysname,
        CONVERT(varbinary(30),CONVERT(varchar(30),pin))),
      1) = 1
)
  SELECT @return = 1
```

```
ELSE
  SELECT @return = 0
GO
```

For those of you running SQL Server 7.0 or 2000, the code snippet in Listing 17-47 shows how to use the current versions of PWDENCRYPT() and PWDCOMPARE() to create your own one-way hash password-management algorithms.

Listing 17-47: Using the PWDENCRYPT() and PWDCOMPARE() Functions

```
DECLARE
  @ClearPIN     varchar (255),
  @EncryptedPin varbinary(255)

SELECT
  @ClearPin = 'test'

SELECT
  @EncryptedPin = CONVERT (varbinary(255), PWDENCRYPT (@ClearPin))

SELECT
  PWDCOMPARE (@ClearPin, @EncryptedPin, 0)
```

The final SELECT statement will return 1, indicating TRUE. In other words, @ClearPin is put through a one-way encryption hash, and SQL Server tells you the unencrypted string matches the encrypted version.

Creating Sorted Views

You cannot sort a view, right? Not until SQL Server 7.0! You can now use the TOP n PERCENT feature of the SELECT statement to take all of the rows. How? Just take TOP 100 PERCENT. Check out the code in Listing 17-48.

Listing 17-48: Creating a Sorted View

```
CREATE VIEW SortedView
AS
SELECT TOP 100 PERCENT
  C.CompanyName,
  O.OrderDate
```

```
FROM
    Customers C
  JOIN
    Orders    O ON O.CustomerID = C.CustomerID
ORDER BY
  O.OrderDate
GO
```

See Chapter 8 for more details on the effects of this technique.

Getting Rows in Order

In the relational model, table rows don't have any specific order. According to the ANSI standards, a query that uses the ORDER BY clause doesn't return a table; rather, it returns a cursor. This is why an ORDER BY clause is not allowed in a view, and why the TOP clause is not ANSI compliant. Both deal with rows in a specific order.

The TOP T-SQL extension and the special needs it can answer are covered in Chapter 4. There are still other needs, though, dealing with rows with a specific order, that simple TOP queries cannot answer. The following sections deal with examples of such needs.

Getting Rows m to n

If you order the authors in the pubs sample database by author ID, you can use a simple TOP query to ask for the first five authors. However, if you want the second group of five authors—authors six to ten—things become a little bit more complex.

You can use the ANSI-compliant query shown in Listing 17-49. For each author, this query performs a correlated subquery that calculates the number of authors with author IDs that are smaller than or equal to the current author ID.

Listing 17-49: Getting Rows m to n in One Query

```
SELECT
    *
FROM
  Authors AS A1
```

```
WHERE
  (
    SELECT
      COUNT(*)
    FROM
      Authors AS A2
    WHERE
      A2.au_id <= A1.au_id
  ) BETWEEN 6 AND 10
ORDER BY
  au_id
```

Note that this query has poor performance, as it needs to scan the Authors table as many times as there are authors in the table. This query also requires the column that you order by, in this case the au_id column, to be unique. We can improve our query's performance by splitting our solution into two steps. First we can place the authors' rows in a temporary table, along with their ordinal position according to the author ID column. We can achieve this by using the IDENTITY() function (the IDENTITY() function is discussed in detail in Chapter 6), as Listing 17-50 shows.

Listing 17-50: Placing the Authors in a Temporary Table Along with Their Ordinal Positions

```
SELECT
  IDENTITY (int, 1, 1) AS rownum,
  *
INTO
  #TmpAuthors
FROM
  Authors
ORDER BY
  au_id
```

You can now issue a simple query to retrieve authors six to ten, as Listing 17-51 shows.

Listing 17-51: Retrieving Authors Six to Ten from the Temporary Table

```
SELECT
  *
FROM
  #TmpAuthors
WHERE
  rownum BETWEEN 6 AND 10
```

Note that this technique did not always work prior to SQL Server 2000 (tested on SQL Server 7.0, Service Pack 2). When using the SELECT INTO statement, sometimes the Identity values were calculated prior to the sort, making this solution improper for the problem at hand. SQL Server 2000 solved this problem, and if you examine the execution plan of the SELECT INTO statement, you can actually see that a sort is performed prior to calculating the IDENTITY value. In both versions, however, if you create the temporary table manually with an additional IDENTITY column and use an INSERT SELECT statement to populate it, the execution plans show that a sort is performed prior to calculating the IDENTITY values, making this solution valid for both versions. Hopefully this bug will be resolved in SQL Server 7.0 in one of the next service packs.

If you want to do everything in a single statement, you can use the TOP feature of the SELECT statement. First, you need to determine the first ten authors, which you do with a TOP 10, and you ORDER BY au_id ASC. This SELECT then acts as a derived table from which you can do a TOP 5, this time with ORDER BY au_id DESC. This gives you the second group of five; however, it is sorted in reverse order to what is desired. This result is then used as a derived table, where you do a regular SELECT and just sort the rows with au_id ASC. The solution is presented in Listing 17-52.

Listing 17-52: Retrieving Authors Six through Ten

```
SELECT
  *
FROM
(
  SELECT TOP 5
    *
  FROM
  (
    SELECT TOP 10
      *
    FROM
      Authors
    ORDER BY
      au_id ASC
  ) X
  ORDER BY
    au_id DESC
) Y
ORDER BY
  au_id ASC
```

Getting the First *n* Rows for Each Occurrence of...

Things can get even more complex than the previous example. Suppose you want to provide the first three orders for each customer for all orders shipped to the U.S. (order data appears in the Orders table in the Northwind sample database). You can use a query similar to, but slightly more complex than, the one used in the previous section to supply a solution using a single query. The solution is shown in Listing 17-53.

Listing 17-53: Getting the First Three Orders for Each U.S. Customer in One Query

```
SELECT
  *
FROM
  Orders AS O1
WHERE
    ShipCountry = 'USA'
  AND
  (
    SELECT
      COUNT(*)
    FROM
      Orders AS O2
    WHERE
      ShipCountry   = 'USA'
    AND
      O2.CustomerID = O1.CustomerID
    AND
      O2.OrderID    <= O1.OrderID
  ) <= 3
ORDER BY
  CustomerID,
  OrderID
```

This query suffers from the same problems as the one in the previous section, mainly from poor performance. It incurred a scan count of 123 and had 2,329 logical reads against the Orders table.

However, the problem can be approached in a totally different way. For example, if you have the exact list of customer IDs, you can perform a UNION ALL between a number of queries, each of which retrieves the first three orders for a certain customer. Listing 17-54 shows a template for such a query.

Listing 17-54: Getting the First Three Orders for Each Customer, for a Known List of Customers

```
SELECT
  *
FROM
  (
    SELECT TOP 3
      *
    FROM
      Orders
    WHERE
      ShipCountry = 'USA'
      AND
      CustomerID = <first_cust>
    ORDER BY
      CustomerID,
      OrderID
  ) AS T1

UNION ALL

SELECT
  *
FROM
  (
    SELECT TOP 3
      *
    FROM
      Customers
    WHERE
      ShipCountry = 'USA'
      AND
      CustomerID = <second_cust>
    ORDER BY
      CustomerID,
      OrderID
  ) AS T2

UNION ALL
...
UNION ALL
```

```
SELECT
  *
FROM
  (
    SELECT TOP 3
      *
    FROM
      Customers
    WHERE
      ShipCountry = 'USA'
    AND
      CustomerID = <last_cust>
    ORDER BY
      CustomerID,
      OrderID
  ) AS Tn
```

To make this query dynamic so that it will run for an unknown list of customers simply as they appear in the Orders table, you can use this template to build the query in a variable, and execute it dynamically, as shown in Listing 17-55. This script iterates through all customers in a loop, retrieves a customer with a higher customer ID in each iteration, and adds another SELECT statement to the UNION ALL query.

Listing 17-55: Getting the First Three Orders for Each Customer,
for an Unknown List of Customers

```
DECLARE
  @lastindid AS char (5),
  @i         AS int,
  @cmd       AS varchar (8000)

SET @cmd = ''
SET @i = 1

SELECT
  @lastindid = MIN (CustomerID)
FROM
  Orders
WHERE
  ShipCountry = 'USA'
```

```
WHILE @lastindid IS NOT NULL
BEGIN
  SET @cmd = @cmd +
  'SELECT * FROM ' +
    '(SELECT TOP 3 * FROM Orders ' +
    'WHERE ShipCountry = ''USA'' AND CustomerID = ''' + @lastindid + ''' ' +
    'ORDER BY CustomerID,OrderID) AS T' +
    CAST(@i AS varchar) + CHAR (13) + CHAR(10)

  SELECT
    @lastindid = MIN (CustomerID),
    @i         = @i + 1
  FROM
    Orders
  WHERE
      ShipCountry = 'USA'
    AND
      CustomerID  > @lastindid

  IF @lastindid IS NOT NULL
    SET @cmd = @cmd + 'UNION ALL' + CHAR (13) + CHAR(10)

END

PRINT @cmd -- just for debug
EXEC (@cmd)
```

You might think that I/O performance is improved significantly as the I/O statistics for the dynamically constructed UNION ALL query show a scan count of 13 and 99 logical reads, but you need to take into account the I/O generated as a result of the loop that dynamically constructs the UNION ALL statement. The total logical reads are very high due to the loop. This solution might not render better performance, but it may give you some ideas about constructing statements dynamically.

Now, for the pièce de résistance. Have a go at the query in Listing 17-56.

Listing 17-56: Getting the First Three Orders for Each Customer
for an Unknown List of Customers, Using a Correlated Subquery

```
SELECT
  O1.*
FROM
  Orders O1
WHERE
    O1.ShipCountry = 'USA'
  AND
    O1.OrderID IN
(
  SELECT TOP 3
    O2.OrderID
  FROM
    Orders    O2
  WHERE
      O2.ShipCountry = 'USA'
    AND
      O2.CustomerID  = O1.CustomerID
  ORDER BY
    O2.OrderID
)
ORDER BY
  O1.CustomerID,
  O1.OrderID
```

The scan count is 123 while the logical reads are 927. This query uses the TOP feature inside a correlated subquery with an IN predicate. The outer query needs to find those OrderIDs that correspond to the first three OrderIDs for each CustomerID. The correlation is on CustomerID. This solution gives you the rows you want for the lowest query cost.

Top Countries per Employee

You have seen, in Chapter 2, the use of correlated subqueries, including those on the HAVING predicate of a GROUP BY clause. This problem requires you to find the country for which each employee has the most orders shipped. You will use the Orders table of the Northwind database. You can use a correlated subquery on the HAVING predicate of the GROUP BY clause, as shown in Listing 17-57.

Listing 17-57: Determining the Country that Keeps Each Employee the Busiest

```
SELECT
  O1.EmployeeID,
  O1.ShipCountry,
  COUNT (*) AS Orders
FROM
    Orders O1
GROUP BY
    O1.EmployeeID,
    O1.ShipCountry
  HAVING
    COUNT (*) =
(
  SELECT TOP 1
    COUNT (*) AS Orders
  FROM
    Orders O2
  WHERE
    O2.EmployeeID = O1.EmployeeID
  GROUP BY
    O2.EmployeeID,
    O2.ShipCountry
  ORDER BY
    Orders DESC
)
ORDER BY
  O1.EmployeeID
```

The COUNT(*) in the SELECT list of the outer query is there just to provide supporting information. The problem simply required finding out who served which country the most.

Are You Being Served?

This next problem is a variation on the previous one. It requires you to find the employee who processes the most shipments for each country. Again, you will use the Orders table in the Northwind database. The first try solves the problem in a single SELECT, with a correlated subquery on the GROUP BY clause. This is shown in Listing 17-58.

Listing 17-58: Employee Who Serves Each Country the Most, First Try

```
SELECT
  O1.ShipCountry,
  O1.EmployeeID,
  COUNT (*) AS Orders
FROM
    Orders O1
GROUP BY
    O1.ShipCountry,
    O1.EmployeeID
  HAVING
    COUNT (*) =
(
  SELECT TOP 1
    COUNT (*) AS Orders
  FROM
    Orders O2
  WHERE
    O2.ShipCountry = O1.ShipCountry
  GROUP BY
    O2.ShipCountry,
    O2.EmployeeID
  ORDER BY
    Orders DESC
)
ORDER BY
  O1.ShipCountry
```

The inner query has to calculate the count for every occurrence of ShipCountry and EmployeeID. The outer query is also calculating the counts. This gives a scan count of 22 and 36,042 logical reads. It solves the problem, but perhaps there is a way to reduce the I/O.

Since the counts have to be used twice, you can do the calculation once and store the results in a temporary table. This is done in Listing 17-59.

Listing 17-59: Employee Who Serves Each Country the Most, Second Try

```
SELECT
  O1.ShipCountry,
  O1.EmployeeID,
  COUNT (*) AS Orders
INTO
  #Temp
FROM
    Orders O1
GROUP BY
    O1.ShipCountry,
    O1.EmployeeID

SELECT
  T1.*
FROM
  #Temp T1
WHERE
  T1.Orders =
(
  SELECT
    MAX (T2.Orders)
  FROM
    #Temp T2
  WHERE
      T2.ShipCountry = T1.ShipCountry
)
ORDER BY
  T1.ShipCountry
```

The correlated subquery no longer involves the GROUP BY clause. The total scan count is 2, while the logical reads are just 24. The relative query cost for this version is 23.04 percent versus 76.96 percent for the previous version. Now you're cookin'!

Can't improve on perfection? You can dispense with the temporary table by casting its query as a derived table. The same derived table appears twice in the statement. However, there is only one scan and 21 counts. Looks like the optimizer is smart enough not to consider it twice. See the code in Listing 17-60.

Listing 17-60: Employee Who Serves Each Country the Most, Third Try

```
SELECT
  T1.*
FROM
  (SELECT
     O1.ShipCountry,
     O1.EmployeeID,
     COUNT (*) AS Orders
   FROM
     Orders O1
   GROUP BY
     O1.ShipCountry,
     O1.EmployeeID) T1
WHERE
  T1.Orders =
(
  SELECT
    MAX (T2.Orders)
  FROM
    (SELECT
       O1.ShipCountry,
       O1.EmployeeID,
       COUNT (*) AS Orders
     FROM
       Orders O1
     GROUP BY
       O1.ShipCountry,
       O1.EmployeeID) T2
  WHERE
       T2.ShipCountry = T1.ShipCountry
)
ORDER BY
  T1.ShipCountry
```

SQL Puzzle 17-1: Top Gun: The Best of the Best

Congratulations! You have reached the final puzzles of this book. By now, you are ready to take on anything. Resist the urge to go to the Answers section, even though it is only a few pages away. It will be worth it.

In the two previous problem scenarios, you saw which country kept each employee the busiest and who the best employee was, broken down by the country served. This puzzle requires you to find the standings of the top sellers. In other words, you are interested only in those employees who were the number one sellers in a country. The employee who appears as numero uno the most is the top employee.

SQL Puzzle 17-2: Filling a Table with Magic Square Data in T-SQL

This puzzle encapsulates various T-SQL elements and requires creativity. It deals with magic squares, a subject that is the source for many mathematical puzzles. The solution to the magic squares problem will be found in the T-SQL world.

What Is a Magic Square?

A magic square is a square matrix—a matrix with the same number of rows and columns for which if you sum up the values in each row, column, and diagonal you always get the same number. For example, a 3 × 3 magic square might look like this:

8	1	6
3	5	7
4	9	2

Notice that if you sum up the values in each row, column, and diagonal, you always get 15. There is a simple method for filling an odd-sized magic square on paper, and you can use that method to fill the magic square's data in a table with T-SQL. Filling an even-sized magic square is too complex to handle with T-SQL, so we will not consider even-sized magic squares in this puzzle.

The rules for filling an odd-sized magic square are very simple:

1. Write the first number (1) in the middle cell of the first row.

2. Write the next consecutive number in the cell that is one cell to the right, and one cell above the current cell. If this cell is occupied, go to the cell beneath the current cell. When you bump to an edge of the magic square, you go all the way around. Think of the square as a ball where all of the edges of the rows, columns, and diagonals are connected to each other.

3. Repeat the second step until the magic square is full.

Figure 17-1 shows the steps involved in filling the magic square presented earlier.

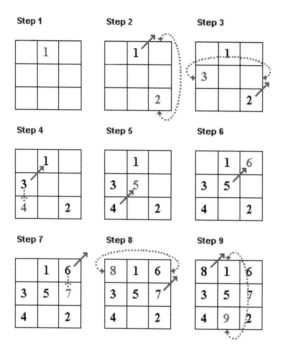

Figure 17-1: Filling the magic square

Representing a Magic Square in a Table

A normalized table will represent the magic square, with each row in the table representing a cell in the square. Each row in the table records the cell's row and column coordinates in the square, as well as its value. This table structure allows you to represent a magic square of any given size.

```
CREATE TABLE MagicSquare
(
  row   int NOT NULL,
  col   int NOT NULL,
  value int NOT NULL,
  CONSTRAINT PK_magicsquare_row_col PRIMARY KEY (row, col),
  CONSTRAINT UNQ_magicsquare_value  UNIQUE     (value)
)
```

SQL Puzzle 17-2-1: Filling a Table with a Magic Square's Data in T-SQL

Your first task is to write a stored procedure that accepts the magic square's size as a parameter and fills your table with its data. First, you need to clear all existing rows in the table. Second, you will insert the first number in the middle cell of the first row. Third and last, you will insert the rest of the numbers in a WHILE loop. To make it a real challenge, you will limit yourself to using a nonblocked WHILE loop with a single INSERT statement.

The template of the FillMagicSquare stored procedure looks like this:

```
CREATE PROC FillMagicSquare
  @size AS int
AS

DELETE MagicSquare

-- Insert the first number in the middle cell in the first row
INSERT INTO MagicSquare
  (row, col, value)
VALUES
  (...) -- ?

-- Insert the rest of the numbers in a while loop
WHILE ... -- ?
  INSERT INTO MagicSquare(row, col, value)
    ... -- ?
GO
```

SQL Puzzle 17-2-2: Displaying the Magic Square as a Cross-Tab Table

Your second task is to display the magic square in a more meaningful cross-tab format. For example, if the size of your magic square is 3, the output should look like this:

ol1	Col2	Col3
8	1	6
3	5	7
4	9	2

It shouldn't be too hard to generate a cross-tab query that provides such an output for a known magic square size, but your solution should produce such an output without a prior knowledge of the size of the magic square stored in the table.

SQL Puzzle 17-2-3: Checking whether the Table Represents a Magic Square Correctly

Your last task is to write a single IF statement that checks whether the table represents a magic square correctly or not. You are not allowed to use a complex condition, such as ORs or ANDs. The template for your IF statement looks like this:

```
IF ... -- ?
  PRINT 'This is a Magic Square. :-)'
ELSE
  PRINT 'This is not a Magic Square. :-('
```

You can assume that the table consists of a complete square—that is, that all cell coordinates exist in the table.

The answers to these puzzles can be found on pages 721–733.

SQL Puzzle Solutions

WE HOPE YOU DIDN'T "fast-forward" to the puzzle answers without giving the solutions a try on your own.

SQL Puzzle 1: Joins

To solve this puzzle, you might have tried to implement both of the limitations in the WHERE clause like this:

```
SELECT
  *
FROM
    Departments AS D
  LEFT OUTER JOIN
    Employees   AS E ON  D.deptno = E.deptno
WHERE
    D.deptno IN(300, 400)
  AND
    E.salary > 2500.00
```

However, the output doesn't seem to include the Sanitation department:

deptno	deptname	empid	empname	deptno	jobid	salary
400	Management	1	Leo	400	30	10000.00
400	Management	4	Rob	400	30	3000.00
400	Management	5	Laura	400	30	3000.00

By specifying both filters in the WHERE clause, the following logical order of execution is determined (notice, this is not necessarily the internal order of execution that the optimizer uses):

Step 1. Perform D LEFT JOIN E ON D.deptno = E.deptno.

The output of this step is as follows:

deptno	deptname	empid	empname	deptno	jobid	salary
100	Engineering	3	Chris	100	10	2000.00
200	Production	2	George	200	20	1000.00
300	Sanitation	NULL	NULL	NULL	NULL	NULL
400	Management	1	Leo	400	30	10000.00
400	Management	4	Rob	400	30	3000.00
400	Management	5	Laura	400	30	3000.00

Step 2. Filter the result by `D.deptno IN(300, 400) AND E.salary > 2500.00`.
The output of this step is as follows:

deptno	deptname	empid	empname	deptno	jobid	salary
400	Management	1	Leo	400	30	10000.00
400	Management	4	Rob	400	30	3000.00
400	Management	5	Laura	400	30	3000.00

You can change the order of the execution by moving the criteria for the salary to the ON clause:

```
SELECT
  *
FROM
    Departments AS D
  LEFT OUTER JOIN
    Employees   AS E ON  D.deptno = E.deptno
                    AND E.salary > 2500.00
WHERE
  D.deptno IN(300, 400)
```

In this case, the order of execution is as follows:
Step 1. Perform `D LEFT JOIN E ON D.deptno = E.deptno AND E.salary > 2500.00`.

Because this is a left outer join with the Departments table as the preserved table, non-matches from the Employees table are replaced with NULLs:

deptno	deptname	empid	empname	deptno	jobid	salary
100	Engineering	NULL	NULL	NULL	NULL	NULL
200	Production	NULL	NULL	NULL	NULL	NULL
300	Sanitation	NULL	NULL	NULL	NULL	NULL
400	Management	1	Leo	400	30	10000.00
400	Management	4	Rob	400	30	3000.00
400	Management	5	Laura	400	30	3000.00

Step 2. Filter the result by D.deptno IN(300, 400).
And the output will be as follows:

deptno	deptname	empid	empname	deptno	jobid	salary
300	Sanitation	NULL	NULL	NULL	NULL	NULL
400	Management	1	Leo	400	30	10000.00
400	Management	4	Rob	400	30	3000.00
400	Management	5	Laura	400	30	3000.00

SQL Puzzle 2-1: Bank Interest

To solve this puzzle, you first need to know which interest group was in effect on the balance date. To obtain this information, you take the maximum interest date that is less than or equal to the balance date. Once you have this date, you also have the interest group.

The interest group is the group of stepped interest rates, with each step's threshold being based upon the balance in an account. The next thing you need to know is which threshold (step) within the interest rate group to use. To obtain this information, you find the maximum rate where the step is less than or equal to the balance on that date.

Once you have the rate and the balance, you can calculate the interest for the period. The solution is as follows:

```
SELECT
  R.AccountID,
  CONVERT (money,
    SUM (r.Rate * r.Balance) / 36500.00) AS Interest
FROM
(
  SELECT
    B.AccountID,
    B.Balance,
    MAX (i.Rate) AS Rate               -- Highest rate
  FROM
      Interest AS I
    JOIN
      Balance  AS B ON I.Step <= B.Balance  -- at or below balance
  WHERE
      I.Date =
  (
    SELECT                             -- Most recent interest date
      MAX (II.Date)
    FROM
        Interest AS II
    WHERE                              -- in effect on balance date
        II.Date <= B.Date
  )
  GROUP BY
    B.AccountID,
    B.Date,
    B.Balance
) AS R
GROUP BY
  R.AccountID
```

You use the correlated subquery to find the most recent date within the Interest table on or before a balance date in the Balance table. This date is the one you use to choose the group of stepped interest rates for the interest calculation.

Next, you join the Interest table to the Balance table, but it is not an equi-join. The join criterion is to use the interest steps in the Interest table at or below the balance in the Balance table. You want only the highest step in the interest rate group, and so you can use the MAX() function. Since you need this broken down by account and you need the balance as well as the interest rate, you GROUP BY AccountID and Balance. You use the rows from this result in a derived table for the next part of the calculation—the summation.

Now that you have the balance and the interest rate appropriate for that balance, you need to sum up the rate times the balance for each account. You divide by 365, because the interest rate is an annual rate, and divide by 100, because the rate is a percent. Thus, you divide the sum by 36,500 and GROUP BY AccountID to get the interest amounts by account.

The interest results are as follows:

AccountID	Interest
1	1.77
2	2.51

SQL Puzzle 2-2: Managing Orders and Their Payments

You might have been tempted simply to join the three tables and group the results by the relevant columns, like this:

```
SELECT
  O.orderid,
  custid,
  odate,
  SUM(qty)   AS sum_of_qty,
  SUM(value) AS sum_of_value
FROM
    Orders       AS O
  LEFT OUTER JOIN
    OrderDetails  AS OD ON O.orderid = OD.orderid
  LEFT OUTER JOIN
    OrderPayments AS OP ON O.orderid = OP.orderid
GROUP BY
  O.orderid,
  custid,
  odate
```

However, notice that the quantities and the values are greater than what they are supposed to be:

Orderid	custid	odate	sum_of_qty	sum_of_value
1	1001	2001-01-18 00:00:00.000	30	300
2	1002	2001-02-12 00:00:00.000	20	200

To understand the unexpected results, first perform the join without the GROUP BY:

```
SELECT
  O.orderid,
  partno,
  qty,
  paymentno,
  value
FROM
    Orders       AS O
  LEFT OUTER JOIN
    OrderDetails  AS OD ON O.orderid = OD.orderid
  LEFT OUTER JOIN
    OrderPayments AS OP ON O.orderid = OP.orderid
```

You get the following result:

rderid	partno	qty	paymentno	value
1	101	5	1	75
1	102	10	1	75
1	101	5	2	75
1	102	10	2	75
2	101	8	1	50
2	102	2	1	50
2	101	8	2	50
2	102	2	2	50

Notice that for each order, all possible combinations of order parts and order payments are returned, instead of returning each order part and each order payment only once. But this is how the join is supposed to work—the request is wrong.

There are several ways to approach this problem. The following query shows the first approach:

```
SELECT
  O.orderid,
  custid,
  odate,
  sum_of_qty,
  sum_of_value
FROM
    Orders AS O
  JOIN
    (SELECT
        orderid,
        SUM(qty) AS sum_of_qty
     FROM
        OrderDetails
     GROUP BY
        orderid) AS OD ON O.orderid = OD.orderid
  JOIN
    (SELECT
        orderid,
        SUM(value) AS sum_of_value
     FROM
        OrderPayments
     GROUP BY
        orderid) AS OP ON O.orderid = OP.orderid
```

You use derived tables to generate one table with the sum of quantity for each order in the OrderDetails table and a second table with the sum of payment values for each order in the OrderPayments table. Then, you join the Orders table with the derived tables. No need to worry that rows in the result of the join will be repeated more than once, because the relationship between the Orders table and each of the derived tables is 1:1/0 (one-to-one or one-to-zero).

The following query shows a second approach for handling the problem:

```
SELECT
  OOD.orderid,
  custid,
  odate,
  sum_of_qty,
  sum_of_value
```

```
FROM
    (SELECT
        O.orderid,
        custid,
        odate,
        SUM(qty) AS sum_of_qty
      FROM
          Orders       AS O
        LEFT OUTER JOIN
          OrderDetails AS OD ON O.orderid = OD.orderid
      GROUP BY
        O.orderid,
        custid,
        odate) AS OOD
  JOIN
    (SELECT
        O.orderid,
        SUM(value) AS sum_of_value
      FROM
          Orders       AS O
        LEFT OUTER JOIN
          OrderPayments AS OP ON O.orderid = OP.orderid
      GROUP BY O.orderid) AS OOP ON OOD.orderid = OOP.orderid
```

You generate two derived tables: one joining the Orders and the OrderDetails tables, grouping the result by order ID, so you get a row for each order with the sum of the quantity of its order parts, and the other joining the Orders and the OrderPayments tables, grouping the result by order ID, so you get a row for each order with the sum of the value of its payments. Now you join the two derived tables based on order ID.

The following query shows a third approach for handling the problem:

```
SELECT
  O.orderid,
  custid,
  odate,
  (SELECT
     SUM(qty)
   FROM
     OrderDetails AS OD
   WHERE
     O.orderid = OD.orderid) AS sum_of_qty,
```

```
(SELECT
    SUM(value)
  FROM
    OrderPayments AS OP
  WHERE
    O.orderid = OP.orderid) AS sum_of_value
FROM
  Orders AS O
```

This approach uses correlated subqueries. You get order information from the Orders table, and for each order, you calculate the sum of the quantity of its order parts and the sum of the value of its order payments in a separate subquery.

SQL Puzzle 2-3: Finding Unread Messages

To approach this problem, you can first produce the list of all possible combinations of users and messages, as with the following query:

```
SELECT *
FROM
    Users    AS U
  CROSS JOIN
    Messages AS M
```

Here's the result of this query:

msgid	userid
1	1
1	2
1	3
2	1
2	2
2	3
3	1
3	2
3	3

Next, you left join the previous output to the Messagesread table as in the following query:

```
SELECT *
FROM
    (SELECT *
     FROM
         Users     AS U
        CROSS JOIN
         Messages AS M) AS UM
   LEFT OUTER JOIN
     Messagesread AS MR ON  UM.userid = MR.userid
                    AND UM.msgid  = MR.msgid
```

The result contains NULLs for non-matches:

UM.msgid	UM.userid	MR.msgid	MR.userid
1	1	1	1
2	1	NULL	1
3	1	3	1
1	2	1	2
2	2	2	2
3	2	NULL	2
1	3	NULL	3
2	3	2	3
3	3	3	3

Now all that's left is to filter the non-matches. Use the following query:

```
SELECT
   UM.username,
   UM.msg
FROM
    (SELECT *
     FROM
         Users     AS U
        CROSS JOIN
         Messages AS M) AS UM
```

```
      LEFT OUTER JOIN
         Messagesread AS MR ON  UM.userid = MR.userid
                          AND UM.msgid  = MR.msgid
WHERE
   MR.userid IS NULL
```

The results are shown in the following table:

username	msg
BPMargolin	Your Floppy disk experienced a crash
Darren	Someone sprayed instant glue on all keyboards. Don't touuuccchhh
Umachandar	Someone called and said that you made her heart double-click

SQL Puzzle 3-1: Populating the Customers Table

To solve this puzzle, you first need to create tables for FirstName, LastName, Street, and City. The Province is an attribute of the City. The Number column is generated through a calculation, as you will soon see.

Typically, there is more variability in last names than there is in first names, so you should have more rows in the LastName table than you do in the FirstName table. Here's the code to create the FirstName and LastName tables and to populate them with data:

```
CREATE TABLE FirstName
(
   FirstNameID int       NOT NULL
                         IDENTITY (1, 1)
                         PRIMARY KEY,
   FirstName    char (25) NOT NULL
)
GO

INSERT FirstName (FirstName) VALUES ('Tom')
INSERT FirstName (FirstName) VALUES ('Dick')
INSERT FirstName (FirstName) VALUES ('Harry')
GO
```

```
CREATE TABLE LastName
(
  LastNameID int        NOT NULL
                        IDENTITY (1, 1)
                        PRIMARY KEY,
  LastName    char (30) NOT NULL
)
GO

INSERT LastName (LastName) VALUES ('Smith')
INSERT LastName (LastName) VALUES ('Jones')
INSERT LastName (LastName) VALUES ('Goldman')
INSERT LastName (LastName) VALUES ('Wong')
INSERT LastName (LastName) VALUES ('Martinez')
INSERT LastName (LastName) VALUES ('Yeung')
INSERT LastName (LastName) VALUES ('Gates')
INSERT LastName (LastName) VALUES ('Croft')
INSERT LastName (LastName) VALUES ('Bush')
INSERT LastName (LastName) VALUES ('Van Halen')
INSERT LastName (LastName) VALUES ('Santana')
GO
```

The Street table can have any number of rows, but it's best to keep the number down to a few at this point, unless you're looking for a very large number of customers. Bear in mind that when you use CROSS JOINs, you are multiplying the number of rows from one table by the number of rows in the other. Here's the code to create the Street table and populate some typical rows:

```
CREATE TABLE Street
(
  StreetID int        NOT NULL
                      IDENTITY (1, 1)
                      PRIMARY KEY,
  Street    char (50) NOT NULL
)
GO

INSERT Street (Street) VALUES ('Main St.')
INSERT Street (Street) VALUES ('Colorado Blvd.')
INSERT Street (Street) VALUES ('Pine Ave.')
INSERT Street (Street) VALUES ('Elm St.')
GO
```

It doesn't matter that every city you create has the same street names. For example, you can have an Elm St. in Toronto and another Elm St. in Vancouver. Here's code to create the City table and populate it with some typical data:

```
CREATE TABLE City
(
  CityID      int        NOT NULL
                         IDENTITY (1, 1)
                         PRIMARY KEY,
  City       char (30) NOT NULL,
  Province   char (2)  NOT NULL
)
GO


INSERT City (City, Province) VALUES ('Toronto', 'ON')
INSERT City (City, Province) VALUES ('Vancouver', 'BC')
INSERT City (City, Province) VALUES ('Calgary', 'AB')
INSERT City (City, Province) VALUES ('Montreal', 'QC')
GO
```

The grand finale is to do the CROSS JOINs and create a street number that does not put all customers on that street at the same address. You can use the ID values on each of the tables, together with multipliers, to conjure up a street number. Check out the INSERT SELECT statement, which utilizes a CROSS JOIN:

```
INSERT Customers
(
  FirstName,
  LastName,
  Number,
  Street,
  City,
  Province
)
SELECT
  F.FirstName,
  L.LastName,
  S.StreetID     *  1000 +
    L.LastNameID  *   100 +
    F.FirstNameID *    10 +
    C.CityID,
  S.Street,
  C.City,
  C.Province
```

```
FROM
    FirstName F
  CROSS JOIN
    LastName  L
  CROSS JOIN
    Street    S
  CROSS JOIN
    City      C
GO
```

Based on the number of rows in each base table, you will have $3 \times 11 \times 4 \times 4 =$ 528 customers.

SQL Puzzle 4-1: Euro 2000 Theme

One approach to solving this puzzle is to join the Teams table with the Results table. The question is, what is the join condition? You want to match each team with its game results, but in the Results table they appear in one set of columns for one team, and in another set of columns for the other team. To overcome this, instead of using the base Results table, you can perform a union between the base Results table and a query that flips the columns for team1 and team2:

```
SELECT
  *
FROM
  Results
UNION ALL
SELECT
  matchid,
  team2     AS team1,
  team1     AS team2,
  team2goals AS team1goals,
  team1goals AS team2goals
FROM
  Results
```

You can wrap this query with a derived table, and join it to the Teams table, comparing the teamid column in the Teams table to the team1 column in the derived table. You should use `Teams LEFT JOIN <derived_table>` to make sure that teams that did not participate in matches will still appear in the table. Now you can group your result by country and calculate the different columns.

- Calculation for total matches (P):

```
COUNT(*) AS P
```

- Calculation for matches won (W):

```
SUM(CASE SIGN(team1goals - team2goals)
        WHEN 1 THEN 1
        ELSE 0
    END) AS W
```

- Calculation for matches with a draw (D):

```
SUM(CASE SIGN(team1goals - team2goals)
        WHEN 0 THEN 1
        ELSE 0
    END) AS D
```

- Calculation for matches lost (L):

```
SUM(CASE SIGN(team1goals - team2goals)
        WHEN -1 THEN 1
        ELSE 0
    END) AS L,
```

- Calculation for goals in opponent's net (F):

```
SUM(team1goals) AS F
```

- Calculation for goals in team's own net (A):

```
SUM(team2goals) AS A
```

- Calculation for points (Win=3, Draw=1, Lose=0):

```
SUM(CASE SIGN(team1goals - team2goals)
        WHEN 1 THEN 3
        WHEN 0 THEN 1
        ELSE 0
    END) AS Points
```

Putting it all together, you get the following:

```
SELECT
  country,
  COUNT(*) AS P,
  SUM(CASE SIGN(team1goals - team2goals)
        WHEN 1 THEN 1
        ELSE 0
      END) AS W,
  SUM(CASE SIGN(team1goals - team2goals)
        WHEN 0 THEN 1
        ELSE 0
      END) AS D,
  SUM(CASE SIGN(team1goals - team2goals)
        WHEN -1 THEN 1
        ELSE 0
      END) AS L,
  SUM(team1goals) AS F,
  SUM(team2goals) AS A,
  SUM(CASE SIGN(team1goals - team2goals)
        WHEN 1 THEN 3
        WHEN 0 THEN 1
        ELSE 0
      END) AS Points
FROM
    Teams AS T
  LEFT OUTER JOIN
    (SELECT *
     FROM Results
     UNION ALL
     SELECT
       matchid,
       team2     AS team1,
       team1     AS team2,
       team2goals AS team1goals,
       team1goals AS team2goals
     FROM Results) AS R
  ON T.teamid = R.team1
GROUP BY
  country
ORDER BY
  Points DESC
```

The results look like this:

Country	P	W	D	L	F	A	Points
Portugal	1	1	0	0	3	2	3
Romania	1	0	1	0	1	1	1
Germany	1	0	1	0	1	1	1
England	1	0	0	1	2	3	0

SQL Puzzle 5-1: Management Levels

To solve this puzzle, you first need to calculate the number of customers in each area. You can use the ROLLUP option, since you need to calculate the total for each combination of country, region, city, and also grand totals from left to right. You don't need to use the CUBE option because there is no meaning in calculating the total number of customers the other way around—from right to left. For example, you don't need to calculate grand totals for each unique combination all countries, all regions, and cities. Even if there were a city with the same name in more than one region, it would be meaningless to count the number of customers in all cities with the same name. Also, remember that a region can be NULL for certain customers, so you need to identify a NULL that means <ALL>, and a NULL that means <N/A>.

Here's the first part of the query:

```
SELECT
  ISNULL(Country, '<ALL>') AS Country,
  ISNULL(Region, CASE GROUPING(Region)
                  WHEN 1 THEN '<ALL>'
                  ELSE '<N/A>'
                END) AS Region,
  ISNULL(City, '<ALL>') AS City,
  COUNT(*) AS Custs
FROM
  Customers
GROUP BY
  Country,
  Region,
  City
WITH ROLLUP
```

Now you need to join the result to the Mgrlevels table, matching the Custs column from the result to the relevant range in the Mgrlevels table. If all management levels had a minimum and a maximum, you could have used the following join criteria:

```
ON Custs BETWEEN MinCusts AND MaxCusts
```

However, these criteria fail for management level 4 because it has a NULL in the MaxCusts column. So, you can use the following trick:

```
ON Custs >= MinCusts AND Custs <= ISNULL(MaxCusts, Custs)
```

These criteria work the same as the previous ones with all management levels that have values in both the MinCusts and MaxCusts columns. However, it actually tests only the first part of the condition (Custs >= MinCusts) for management level 4, because the other part of the condition will always be true (Custs <= Custs).

You have two options for writing the full query. The first option is to use the result of the ROLLUP operation as a derived table, as follows:

```
SELECT
  C.*,
  M.MgrLvl
FROM
    (<rollup_query>) AS C
  JOIN
    Mgrlevels        AS M ON  Custs >= MinCusts
                     AND Custs <= ISNULL(MaxCusts, Custs)
GO
```

Or, you can wrap it in a view, as follows:

```
CREATE VIEW VCusts
AS

SELECT
  ISNULL(Country, '<ALL>') AS Country,
  ISNULL(Region, CASE GROUPING(Region)
                   WHEN 1 THEN '<ALL>'
                   ELSE '<N/A>'
                 END)  AS Region,
  ISNULL(City, '<ALL>') AS City,
  COUNT(*)              AS Custs
FROM
  Customers
```

```
GROUP BY
  Country,
  Region,
  City
WITH ROLLUP
GO


SELECT
  C.*,
  M.MgrLvl
FROM
    VCusts     AS C
  JOIN
    Mgrlevels AS M ON  Custs >= MinCusts
                 AND Custs <= ISNULL(MaxCusts, Custs)
```

You can use a CASE statement to specify the type of area each row represents:

```
SELECT
  CASE
    WHEN City <> '<ALL>' THEN 'City'
    WHEN Region <> '<ALL>' AND Region <> '<N/A>' THEN 'Region'
    WHEN Country <> '<ALL>' THEN 'Country'
    ELSE 'The whole world'
  END AS AreaType,
  C.*,
  M.MgrLvl
FROM
    VCusts     AS C
  JOIN
    Mgrlevels AS M ON  Custs >= MinCusts
                 AND Custs <= ISNULL(MaxCusts, Custs)
```

SQL Puzzle 6-1: Customers with and without Sales

The following solution leverages the sql_variant datatype to meet the requirement of having the word 'None' appear in the same column as primarily numeric data:

```
SELECT
  C.Country,
  C.CustomerID,
  CASE
    WHEN ISNULL (SUM (OD.Quantity * OD.UnitPrice), 0) = 0
      THEN 'None'
    ELSE CAST (SUM (OD.Quantity * OD.UnitPrice) AS sql_variant)
  END AS TotalSales
FROM
  Customers       AS C
  LEFT
  JOIN
  Orders          AS O  ON O.CustomerID = C.CustomerID
  LEFT
  JOIN
  [Order Details] AS OD ON OD.OrderID    = O.OrderID
WHERE
  C.Country IN ('Spain', 'France')
GROUP BY
  C.Country,
  C.CustomerID
ORDER BY
  C.Country,
  C.CustomerID
```

Left joins are used because there are two customers who have never placed orders. The trick comes in handling the TotalSales column. The SUM() will produce nonzero numbers for customers with sales and NULL for those who have never placed an order. Casting the result of SUM() to an sql_variant then enables you to use whatever you like.

SQL Puzzle 7-1: Eliminating an Explicit Transaction

You can sometimes save yourself the need for explicit BEGIN TRAN and COMMIT TRAN statements. The trick is limited to multiple updates to the *same* table. Instead of making two passes at the table, you can use the WHERE clause to filter all the rows that would be touched in either pass and then fine-tune the update with a CASE statement. In this puzzle, you are looking only at the title ID of 'BU1032'. You also want the author IDs of '213-46-8915' and '409-567008'. To get both authors, you list the author IDs in an IN predicate. Now you have enough to build the WHERE clause.

The author ID of '213-46-8915' is to be assigned a royaltyper of 60, while the author ID of '409-567008' is to be assigned a royaltyper of 40. This can be done with a CASE construct that tests the value of au_id and assigns royaltyper accordingly.

Here's the solution:

```
UPDATE titleauthor
SET
  royaltyper = CASE au_id
                  WHEN '213-46-8915' THEN 60
                  WHEN '409-56-7008' THEN 40
                  ELSE royaltyper
               END
WHERE
  au_id    IN ('213-46-8915', '409-56-7008')
  AND
  title_id = 'BU1032'
```

SQL Puzzle 8-1: Updateable Ordered View

The answer to this puzzle is very tricky. You connect to your local server as if it were a linked server by turning on the 'data access' server option, as the following code shows:

```
EXEC sp_serveroption <server_name>, 'data access', true
```

Now you use the OPENQUERY() function inside the view to retrieve an ordered result from your local table, as if it were a remote table:

```
CREATE VIEW V1
AS

SELECT
  *
FROM
  OPENQUERY(
    <server_name>,
    'SELECT * FROM <db_name>..T1 ORDER BY data_col') AS T1
```

This view, as surprising as you might find it to be, is updateable!

SQL Puzzle 9-1: Creating a Procedure within a Procedure

Since the optimizer does not validate the SQL string invoked by the EXEC() command, you can put your "illegal" commands inside the command string and let the EXEC() command do your dirty work for you. Here's how:

```
CREATE PROC usp_Generate_Customer_Proc
AS

DECLARE
  @str  varchar (8000)

-- create proc script
SELECT
  @str = 'CREATE PROC usp_Customer_Proc
          (
              @CustomerID char (5)
          )
          AS
          SET NOCOUNT ON

          SELECT
            *
          FROM
            Northwind..Customers
          WHERE
            CustomerID = @CustomerID'

-- create the proc
EXEC (@str)
GO

EXEC usp_Generate_Customer_Proc
GO

EXEC usp_Customer_Proc
  'VINET'
GO

DROP PROC usp_Customer_Proc
GO

DROP PROC usp_Generate_Customer_Proc
GO
```

The `usp_Generate_Customer_Proc` stored procedure builds the code for the `usp_Customer_Proc` stored procedure and stores it in the `@str` string variable. The procedure is then created via the call to `EXEC()`. The `usp_Customer_Proc` stored procedure is then tested using the customer ID `'VINET'`. Finally, both of the procedures are dropped.

SQL Puzzle 9-2: Automatically Creating Stored Procedures

Since release 7.0, SQL maintains SQL-92 views on the system catalogs. These views are independent of the system tables and allow applications to work, even though significant changes have taken place in the system tables.

Among these views is the `INFORMATION_SCHEMA.COLUMNS` view. This view maintains a list of all columns in all tables and views. It includes (among other things) the table name (`TABLE_NAME`), column name (`COLUMN_NAME`), datatype (`DATA_TYPE`), and ordinal position (`ORDINAL_POSITION`) of each column. You can search this view for a given table name and an ordinal position of 1, and pick up the column name and its datatype. You then incorporate the column name into the `EXEC()` string.

The syntax for doing all this is as follows:

```
CREATE PROC usp_Generate_Table_Proc
(
  @Table sysname
)
AS

DECLARE
  @Str      varchar (8000),
  @Column   sysname,
  @DataType sysname

-- pick up column name and datatype of primary key
SELECT
  @Column   = COLUMN_NAME,
  @DataType = CASE
              WHEN DATA_TYPE IN
                ('char', 'nchar', 'varchar', 'nvarchar')
                THEN DATA_TYPE
                  + '('
                  + LTRIM (STR (CHARACTER_MAXIMUM_LENGTH))
                  + ')'
              ELSE
                DATA_TYPE
              END
```

```
                 FROM
                   INFORMATION_SCHEMA.COLUMNS
                 WHERE
                     TABLE_NAME        = @Table
                   AND
                     ORDINAL_POSITION = 1

-- create proc script
SELECT
  @Str = 'CREATE PROC usp_' + @Table + '_Proc
          (
              @' + @Column + ' ' + @DataType + '
          )
          AS
          SET NOCOUNT ON

          SELECT
            *
          FROM
            Northwind..' + @Table + '
          WHERE
            ' + @Column + ' = @' + @Column

print @str
-- create the proc
EXEC (@Str)
GO


EXEC usp_Generate_Table_Proc
  'Customers'
GO


EXEC usp_Customers_Proc
  'VINET'
GO

DROP PROC usp_Customers_Proc
GO

DROP PROC usp_Generate_Table_Proc
GO
```

There is a potential bug in this solution. It does not handle numeric (p, s) or decimal (p, s) datatypes for the primary key. To do this, you need to add another WHEN/THEN to the CASE construct and build the datatype string, using the NUMERIC_PRECISION and NUMERIC_SCALE columns.

Finally, you can put the usp_Generate_Table_Proc procedure inside a loop, iterating once for every user table in your database to generate procedures to do single-row retrievals for all of your tables.

SQL Puzzle 10-1: Pending Deletes

The first part of this problem can be solved with an AFTER trigger on the Customers table to handle the business rule that an employee can delete his or her own customers. It must also be able to handle the movement of rows to the PendingDeleteCustomers table for those customers who do not belong to the employee. Here's the code:

```
CREATE TRIGGER trd_Customers ON Customers AFTER DELETE
AS

-- check if there is anything to do
IF @@ROWCOUNT = 0
  RETURN

-- move all rows not belonging to employee
-- to PendingDeleteCustomers
INSERT PendingDeleteCustomers
(
  CustomerID,
  CustomerName,
  Address,
  Phone,
  EmployeeID
)
SELECT
  CustomerID,
  CustomerName,
  Address,
  Phone,
  EmployeeID
FROM
  deleted
WHERE
  EmployeeID <> USER_NAME ()
GO
```

At first glance, it appears that this solution is not correct. However, the fact remains that all customers can be deleted from the Customers table by any employee. Only those customers who don't belong to the employee have their records inserted into the PendingDeleteCustomers table. The trigger is needed only to place copies of the rows deleted from the Customers table into the PendingDeleteCustomers table.

The trigger uses the USER_NAME() function, which gives you the name of the user within the database. This is compared with the employee ID. If the employee ID is different from the value returned from USER_NAME(), then rows are copied.

An INSTEAD OF trigger on the PendingDeleteCustomers table is then required to prevent employees from removing customers other than their own. Here's the code:

```
CREATE TRIGGER trd_PendingDeleteCustomers
  ON PendingDeleteCustomers INSTEAD OF DELETE
AS

IF @@ROWCOUNT = 0
  RETURN

DELETE P
FROM
    PendingDeleteCustomers P
  JOIN
    deleted                 D ON D.CustomerID = P.CustomerID
WHERE
    D.EmployeeID = USER_NAME ()
GO
```

This trigger looks similar to the one on the Customers table. This time, it allows a DELETE only if the EmployeeID is the same as the value returned from the USER_NAME() function. None of the other rows will be deleted.

SQL Puzzle 11-1: Formatting Dates

The dbo.format_date function accepts two parameters: @date is a value of a datetime datatype, and @formatstring is a value of a varchar datatype. The function formats the value supplied in the @date parameter according to the codes supplied in the @formatstring parameter. The function contains embedded comments that explain the code.

```
/* function dbo.format_date

    input:

      @date AS datetime -
        any given date

      @formatstring AS varchar(100) -
        a formatted string with codes
        to be replaced by datetime values:

        yyyy - year four digits
        yy   - year two digits
        mm   - month with leading zero
        m    - month without leading zero
        dd   - day with leading zero
        d    - day without leading zero
        hh   - hour with leading zero
        h    - hour without leading zero
        nn   - minutes with leading zero
        n    - minutes without leading zero
        ss   - seconds with leading zero
        s    - seconds without leading zero
        ms   - milliseconds three digits with leading zeros

    process:

      The function is a series of calls to the
      replace(@s1, @s2, @s3) function, which accepts three
      strings as parameters, and replaces each occurrence of
      @s2 in @s1 with @s3.
      You use it to replace a code representing a certain
      date part with the actual date part extracted from
      the @date parameter.
      Notice that there is an importance to the order of
      date parts manipulation.  For example, if you replaced
      each occurrence of the code m (month without leading zeros)
      with the month before replacing the code ms (milliseconds)
      you would get a wrong output.
      Similarly, you need to replace the seconds without leading
      zeros (s) after you replace milliseconds.
```

```
    output:

        SELECT dbo.format_date('2000-09-08 07:06:05.432',
                               'yyyy-mm-dd hh:nn:ss.ms')

        2000-09-08 07:06:05.433

        SELECT dbo.format_date('2000-09-08 07:06:05.432',
                               'yy-m-d h:n:s.ms')

        00-9-8 7:6:5.433

        SELECT dbo.format_date('2000-09-08 07:06:05.432',
                               'dd/mm/yy')

        08/09/00
*/

CREATE FUNCTION dbo.format_date
(
  @date AS datetime,
  @formatstring AS varchar(100)
)
RETURNS varchar(100)
AS

BEGIN
  DECLARE @datestring AS varchar(100)

  SET @datestring = @formatstring

  -- handle year - yyyy
  SET @datestring =
    replace(
      @datestring,
      'yyyy',
      cast(year(@date) AS char(4)))

  -- handle year - yy
  SET @datestring =
    replace(
      @datestring,
      'yy',
      right(cast(year(@date) AS char(4)), 2))
```

```
-- handle milliseconds - ms
-- handle before months and seconds not to confuse a single m or s
SET @datestring =
  replace(
    @datestring,
    'ms',
    replicate('0', 3 - len(cast(datepart(ms, @date) AS varchar(3)))) +
                cast(datepart(ms, @date) AS varchar(3)))

-- handle month - mm - leading zero, m - no leading zero
SET @datestring =
  replace(
    @datestring,
    'mm',
    replicate('0', 2 - len(cast(month(@date) AS varchar(2)))) +
                cast(month(@date) AS varchar(2)))

SET @datestring =
  replace(@datestring,
          'm',
          cast(month(@date) AS varchar(2)))

-- handle day - dd - leading zero, d - no leading zero
SET @datestring =
  replace(
    @datestring,
    'dd',
    replicate('0', 2 - len(cast(day(@date) AS varchar(2)))) +
                cast(day(@date) AS varchar(2)))

SET @datestring =
  replace(@datestring,
          'd',
          cast(day(@date) AS varchar(2)))

-- handle hour - hh - leading zero, h - no leading zero
SET @datestring =
  replace(
    @datestring,
    'hh',
    replicate('0', 2 - len(cast(datepart(hh, @date) AS varchar(2)))) +
                cast(datepart(hh, @date) AS varchar(2)))
```

```
SET @datestring =
  replace(@datestring,
          'h',
          cast(datepart(hh, @date) AS varchar(2)))

-- handle minute - nn - leading zero, n - no leading zero
SET @datestring =
  replace(
    @datestring,
    'nn',
    replicate('0', 2 - len(cast(datepart(n, @date) AS varchar(2)))) +
                  cast(datepart(n, @date) AS varchar(2)))

SET @datestring =
  replace(@datestring,
          'n',
          cast(datepart(n, @date) AS varchar(2)))

-- handle second - ss - leading zero, s - no leading zero
SET @datestring =
  replace(
    @datestring,
    'ss',
    replicate('0', 2 - len(cast(datepart(ss, @date) AS varchar(2)))) +
                  cast(datepart(ss, @date) AS varchar(2)))

SET @datestring =
  replace(@datestring,
          's',
          cast(datepart(ss, @date) AS varchar(2)))

  RETURN @datestring
END
GO
```

SQL Puzzle 12-1: Creating a Temporary Table and Cursor-Free Solution

To solve this puzzle, you first need to determine the number of books sold by author—you will have to save this in a temporary table for later work, which will involve the bonus scheme. You do this by selecting from the authors table and using a LEFT JOIN onto the titleauthor table, because not every "author" necessarily wrote a book. (They could have been entered into the system prior to writing a book.) Next, you use a LEFT JOIN onto the sales table, because not every book necessarily sold a copy. You take the sum of the qty column from sales and use a GROUP BY on au_id. You use a SELECT INTO to store the results in a temporary table.

Here's the code to create the temporary table:

```
SELECT
  A.au_id,
  ISNULL (SUM (qty), 0) AS Sales,
  3 AS Quartile
INTO
  #Sales
FROM
    authors     AS A
  LEFT JOIN
    titleauthor AS TA ON TA.au_id   = A.au_id
  LEFT JOIN
    sales       AS S  ON S.title_id = TA.title_id
GROUP BY
  A.au_id
```

The Quartile column was created to determine in which quartile each author's sales fell. It is initialized to 3. The reason for this will be clarified later.

Now that you have the sales results, it's time to implement the bonus scheme. You need to divide the table into quarters and apply the bonus. The natural impulse is to use a cursor, but this can be avoided by taking advantage of the TOP n PERCENT feature of the SELECT statement in the context of a nested scalar subquery using an IN clause.

You need to update the Quartile column in order to implement the bonus scheme. First, update the Quartile column to 1 for all those in the top quartile, as follows:

```
UPDATE #Sales
SET
  Quartile = 1
WHERE
  au_id IN
(
  SELECT TOP 25 PERCENT WITH TIES
    au_id
  FROM
    #Sales
  ORDER BY
    Sales DESC
)
```

The nested scalar subquery gives you the author IDs of those authors in the top quartile. This feeds the IN clause, which allows you to update the Quartile column only for those authors.

The next step is to update the Quartile column for those authors in the second quartile. This is a little trickier and takes the previous UPDATE and extends it as follows:

```
UPDATE #Sales
SET
  Quartile = 2
WHERE
  au_id IN
(
  SELECT TOP 25 PERCENT WITH TIES
    au_id
  FROM
    #Sales
  WHERE
    Au_id NOT IN
  (
    SELECT TOP 25 PERCENT WITH TIES
      Au_id
    FROM
      #Sales
    ORDER BY
      Sales DESC
  )
  ORDER BY
    Sales DESC
)
```

The NOT IN is used to eliminate those rows already in the top quartile. Thus, you get the top 25 percent of the remaining rows in the table—in other words, the second quartile.

The next step is to update the Quartile column for the authors in the bottom quartile. You use the same technique as for those in the top quartile, except that you eliminate the DESC keyword from the ORDER BY clause, like this:

```
UPDATE #Sales
SET
  Quartile = 4
WHERE
  au_id IN
```

```
(
  SELECT TOP 25 PERCENT WITH TIES
    au_id
  FROM
    #Sales
  ORDER BY
    Sales
)
```

Since the default value for the Quartile column was 3, you do not need to update the #Sales table for the third quartile.

All that remains is to return the results:

```
SELECT
  *,
  (4 - Quartile) * 1000 As Bonus
FROM
  #Sales
ORDER BY
  Sales DESC
```

Here are the results:

au_id	Sales	Quartile	Bonus
899-46-2035	148	1	3000
998-72-3567	133	1	3000
846-92-7186	50	1	3000
213-46-8915	50	1	3000
427-17-2319	50	1	3000
267-41-2394	45	1	3000
724-80-9391	45	1	3000
807-91-6654	40	2	2000
722-51-5454	40	2	2000
238-95-7766	30	2	2000
486-29-1786	25	2	2000
472-27-2349	20	3	1000
648-92-1872	20	3	1000

au_id	Sales	Quartile	Bonus
672-71-3249	20	3	1000
756-30-7391	20	3	1000
172-32-1176	15	4	0
409-56-7008	15	4	0
274-80-9391	15	4	0
712-45-1867	10	4	0
724-08-9931	0	4	0
527-72-3246	0	4	0
341-22-1782	0	4	0
893-72-1158	0	4	0

SQL Puzzle 14-1: Implementing Cascading Operations

If you've already attempted to solve this puzzle, you've probably noticed that this is no simple business. Try to build your solution a step at a time. First, there's no doubt you will need to create an INSTEAD OF UPDATE trigger to accomplish the task. You can't use an AFTER trigger because the foreign key will reject the update, and the AFTER trigger will never fire.

Here's the first try:

```
CREATE TRIGGER trg_u_orders_ON_UPDATE_CASCADE ON Orders INSTEAD OF UPDATE
AS

DECLARE @numrows int
SET @numrows = @@ROWCOUNT

-- updates to surrogate_key are not allowed
IF UPDATE(surrogate_key)
BEGIN
  RAISERROR('Updates to surrogate_key are not allowed.
          TRANSACTION rolled back.', 10, 1)
  ROLLBACK TRAN
END
ELSE
```

```
BEGIN

  -- if orderid was updated, perform cascade
  IF UPDATE(orderid) AND @numrows > 0
  BEGIN
    UPDATE OrderDetails
      SET orderid = I.orderid
    FROM
        OrderDetails AS OD
      JOIN
        deleted      AS D ON OD.orderid      = D.orderid
      JOIN
        inserted     AS I ON D.surrogate_key = I.surrogate_key
  END

  -- resubmit the update only if at least one row was updated
  -- perform it as a delete / insert operation
  IF @numrows > 0
  BEGIN
    DELETE FROM Orders
    FROM
        Orders  AS O
      JOIN
        deleted AS D ON O.orderid = D.orderid

    INSERT INTO Orders(orderid, customerid, orderdate)
      SELECT
        orderid,
        customerid,
        orderdate
      FROM
        inserted
  END

END
GO
```

First, make sure that the surrogate key is not updated. Next, perform the cascade operation, and last, resubmit the UPDATE as separate DELETE and INSERT statements. Now try to issue the following update:

```
UPDATE Orders
  SET orderid = orderid + 1
```

```
Hello from instead of update trigger on OrderDetails
```

```
Server: Msg 547, Level 16, State 1, Procedure
trg_d_orderdetails_on_update_print_hello, Line 13
INSERT statement conflicted with COLUMN FOREIGN KEY constraint
'FK_OrderDetails_Orders'.  The conflict occurred in database 'testdb', table
'Orders', column 'orderid'.
The statement has been terminated.
```

The update fails. The UPDATE statement that performs the cascade operation fires the INSTEAD OF UPDATE trigger on the OrderDetails table. The INSTEAD OF trigger prints "Hello" and then resubmits the UPDATE as a DELETE and an INSERT. The DELETE succeeds, but the INSERT fails because it tries to insert order parts with order IDs that do not yet exist in the Orders table, which the foreign key does not allow. If you try to change your trigger so that it will first resubmit the modification and then perform the cascade, it will fail the foreign key as soon as it tries to delete the old orders from the Orders table. Also, even if this had succeeded, the surrogate key with the IDENTITY property would have been all messed up because you substitute the original update with a DELETE and an INSERT.

To take care of the foreign key problem, you can save the order details that should be affected in a temporary table, modify them there, and delete them from the OrderDetails table. You can then resubmit the modification to the Orders table and copy the modified order parts from the temporary table back to the OrderDetails table. To take care of the surrogate key problem, you can resubmit the modification to the Orders table as an UPDATE, instead of using separate DELETE and INSERT statements. You can use the surrogate key to correlate the old orders with the new orders. This is safe because you don't allow changes to the surrogate key. Here's the second try:

```
ALTER TRIGGER trg_u_orders_ON_UPDATE_CASCADE ON Orders INSTEAD OF UPDATE
AS

DECLARE @numrows int
SET @numrows = @@ROWCOUNT
-- updates to surrogate_key are not allowed
IF UPDATE(surrogate_key)
BEGIN
  RAISERROR('Updates to surrogate_key are not allowed.
            TRANSACTION rolled back.', 10, 1)
  ROLLBACK TRAN
END
```

```
ELSE
BEGIN

  -- if orderid was updated, perform cascade in a temporary table
  IF UPDATE(orderid) AND @numrows > 0
  BEGIN
    -- copy the affected order parts to a temp table
    SELECT
      OD.*
    INTO
      #OrderDetails
    FROM
        OrderDetails AS OD
      JOIN
        deleted       AS D ON OD.orderid = D.orderid

    -- delete the affected rows from OrderDetails
    DELETE FROM OrderDetails
    FROM
        OrderDetails AS OD
      JOIN
        deleted       AS D ON OD.orderid = D.orderid

    -- perform the update to the order parts in the temp table
    UPDATE #OrderDetails
      SET orderid = I.orderid
    FROM
        #OrderDetails AS OD
      JOIN
        deleted       AS D ON OD.orderid        = D.orderid
      JOIN
        inserted      AS I ON D.surrogate_key = I.surrogate_key
  END

  -- resubmit the update only if at least one row was updated
  IF @numrows > 0
  BEGIN
    UPDATE Orders
      SET orderid    = I.orderid,
          customerid = I.customerid,
          orderdate  = I.orderdate
    FROM
        Orders   AS O
      JOIN
        inserted AS I ON O.surrogate_key = I.surrogate_key
  END
```

```
    -- copy modified order parts back to the Orders table
  IF UPDATE(orderid) AND @numrows > 0
    INSERT INTO OrderDetails
      SELECT
        *
      FROM
        #OrderDetails

END
GO
```

Here is the update again:

```
BEGIN TRAN

SELECT
  *
FROM
  Orders

SELECT
  *
FROM
  OrderDetails

UPDATE Orders
  SET orderid = orderid + 1

SELECT
  *
FROM
  Orders

SELECT
  *
FROM
  OrderDetails

ROLLBACK TRAN
```

Here's the Orders table before the UPDATE:

orderid	customerid	orderdate	surrogate_key
10001	FRODO	1999-04-17 00:00:00.000	1
10002	GNDLF	1999-04-18 00:00:00.000	2
10003	BILBO	1999-04-19 00:00:00.000	3

Here's the OrderDetails table before the UPDATE:

orderid	partid	quantity
10001	11	12
10001	42	10
10001	72	5
10002	14	9
10002	51	40
10003	41	10
10003	61	35
10003	65	15

Notice that the INSTEAD OF DELETE trigger and INSTEAD OF INSERT trigger printed the following messages:

```
Hello from instead of delete trigger on OrderDetails
```

```
Hello from instead of insert trigger on OrderDetails
```

Here's the Orders table after the UPDATE:

orderid	customerid	orderdate	surrogate_key
10002	FRODO	1999-04-17 00:00:00.000	1
10003	GNDLF	1999-04-18 00:00:00.000	2
10004	BILBO	1999-04-19 00:00:00.000	3

Here's the OrderDetails table after the UPDATE:

orderid	partid	quantity
10002	11	12
10002	42	10
10002	72	5
10003	14	9
10003	51	40
10004	41	10
10004	61	35
10004	65	15

As you can see, the update cascade does its job all right, but the wrong INSTEAD OF triggers fire. This is the result of the DELETE and INSERT operations performed on the OrderDetails table. Notice that the INSTEAD OF UPDATE trigger doesn't fire at all, because the cascade operation doesn't explicitly perform an update. And here you thought you were finally done with your solution. Well, don't give up yet…

Try to think of a way to signal to the INSTEAD OF triggers that they shouldn't perform their usual activity if the UPDATE was sent from the update cascade trigger, but instead, simply resubmit the modification. Also, you can perform a dummy update to the OrderDetails table once you are done. This will cause the INSTEAD OF UPDATE trigger on the OrderDetails table to fire. To take care of the signal, the cascade trigger can create a temporary table, and the INSTEAD OF triggers on the OrderDetails table can check if it exists. Here's another try:

```
ALTER TRIGGER trg_u_orders_ON_UPDATE_CASCADE ON Orders INSTEAD OF UPDATE
AS

DECLARE @numrows int
SET @numrows = @@ROWCOUNT
-- updates to surrogate_key are not allowed
IF UPDATE(surrogate_key)
BEGIN
  RAISERROR('Updates to surrogate_key are not allowed.
          TRANSACTION rolled back.', 10, 1)
  ROLLBACK TRAN
END
ELSE
```

```
BEGIN

  -- if orderid was updated, perform cascade in a temporary table
IF UPDATE(orderid) AND @numrows > 0
  BEGIN

    -- copy the affected order parts to a temp table
    SELECT
      OD.*
    INTO
      #OrderDetails
    FROM
        OrderDetails AS OD
      JOIN
        deleted      AS D ON OD.orderid = D.orderid

    -- create the signal for the false delete
    SELECT 1 AS col1 INTO #falsedelete

    -- delete the affected rows from OrderDetails
    DELETE FROM OrderDetails
    FROM
        OrderDetails AS OD
      JOIN
        deleted      AS D ON OD.orderid = D.orderid

    -- perform the update to the rows in the temp table
    UPDATE #OrderDetails
      SET orderid = I.orderid
    FROM
        #OrderDetails AS OD
      JOIN
        deleted       AS D ON OD.orderid       = D.orderid
      JOIN
        inserted      AS I ON D.surrogate_key = I.surrogate_key
  END

  -- resubmit the update only if at least one row was updated
  IF @numrows > 0
  BEGIN
    UPDATE Orders
      SET orderid    = I.orderid,
          customerid = I.customerid,
          orderdate  = I.orderdate
```

```
        FROM
            Orders    AS O
          JOIN
            inserted AS I ON O.surrogate_key = I.surrogate_key
      END


      IF UPDATE(orderid) AND @numrows > 0
      BEGIN
        -- create the signal for a false insert
        SELECT 1 AS col1 INTO #falseinsert

        -- copy modified rows back to the order details table
        INSERT INTO OrderDetails
          SELECT
            *
          FROM
            #OrderDetails

        -- perform a dummy update to fire the instead of update trigger on OrderDetails
        UPDATE OrderDetails
          SET orderid = I.orderid
        FROM
            OrderDetails AS OD
          JOIN
            inserted      AS I ON OD.orderid = I.orderid
      END

    END
    GO
```

Now you need to modify the relevant INSTEAD OF triggers on OrderDetails:

```
ALTER TRIGGER trg_d_orderdetails_on_delete_print_hello
  ON OrderDetails  INSTEAD OF DELETE
AS

-- check if a signal exists that tells us not to perform the usual activity
IF OBJECT_ID('tempdb..#falsedelete') IS NOT NULL
  DELETE FROM OrderDetails
  FROM
      OrderDetails AS OD
    JOIN
      deleted      AS D  ON  OD.orderid = D.orderid
                        AND OD.partid  = D.partid
```

```
ELSE -- perform the usual activity
BEGIN
  PRINT 'Hello from instead of delete trigger on OrderDetails'

  DELETE FROM OrderDetails
  FROM
      OrderDetails AS OD
    JOIN
      deleted      AS D ON  OD.orderid = D.orderid
                       AND OD.partid  = D.partid
END
GO

ALTER TRIGGER trg_d_orderdetails_on_insert_print_hello
  ON OrderDetails  INSTEAD OF INSERT
AS

-- check if a signal exists that tells us not to perform the usual activity
IF OBJECT_ID('tempdb..#falsedelete') IS NOT NULL
  INSERT INTO OrderDetails
    SELECT
      *
    FROM
      inserted
ELSE -- perform the usual activity
BEGIN
  PRINT 'Hello from instead of insert trigger on OrderDetails'

  INSERT INTO OrderDetails
    SELECT
      *
    FROM
      inserted
END
GO
```

Now test an UPDATE again:

```
BEGIN TRAN

SELECT
  *
FROM
  Orders

SELECT
  *
FROM
  OrderDetails

UPDATE Orders
  SET orderid = orderid + 1

SELECT
  *
FROM
  Orders

SELECT
  *
FROM
  OrderDetails

ROLLBACK TRAN
```

Here's the Orders table before the UPDATE:

orderid	customerid	orderdate	surrogate_key
10001	FRODO	1999-04-17 00:00:00.000	1
10002	GNDLF	1999-04-18 00:00:00.000	2
10003	BILBO	1999-04-19 00:00:00.000	3

Here's the OrderDetails table before the UPDATE:

orderid	partid	quantity
10001	11	12
10001	42	10
10001	72	5
10002	14	9
10002	51	40
10003	41	10
10003	61	35
10003	65	15

Notice that the INSTEAD OF UPDATE trigger printed the following message:

```
Hello from instead of update trigger on OrderDetails
```

Here's the Orders table after the UPDATE:

orderid	customerid	orderdate	surrogate_key
10002	FRODO	1999-04-17 00:00:00.000	1
10003	GNDLF	1999-04-18 00:00:00.000	2
10004	BILBO	1999-04-19 00:00:00.000	3

Here's the OrderDetails table after the UPDATE:

orderid	partid	quantity
10002	11	12
10002	42	10
10002	72	5
10003	14	9
10003	51	40

(*Continued*)

orderid	partid	quantity
10004	41	10
10004	61	35
10004	65	15

:-)

You have seen that some real acrobatics were needed to support both a foreign key and update cascade when INSTEAD OF triggers exist on the OrderDetails table. This might be nice as an exercise, but there are negative performance implications to this solution, as you create temporary tables and also perform extra modifications in order not to break your foreign key constraint. In such a situation, you should consider dropping or disabling the foreign key, and enforcing referential integrity and cascade actions with AFTER triggers, as discussed in Chapter 14.

SQL Puzzle 15-1: Discounting Scheme

This solution uses 'FRANK' as the given customer ID. You do a FETCH LAST to pick up the first order and test to see whether there are three rows. You bail out if there are fewer than three rows. If there are three rows, then you FETCH the next two, applying the weights in turn. Next, you take the weighted average. Finally, you calculate the discount, based on the weighted average and discounting scheme. Here's the code:

```
DECLARE
    @Sum     money,
    @Total   money

-- set up cursor for 3 most-recent orders
DECLARE c INSENSITIVE SCROLL CURSOR FOR
SELECT TOP 3
    sum (od.Quantity * od.UnitPrice) AS Total
FROM
        Orders          O
JOIN    [Order Details] OD    ON O.OrderID = OD.OrderID
WHERE
    O.CustomerID = 'FRANK'
GROUP BY
    OD.OrderID,
    O.OrderDate
ORDER BY
    O.OrderDate     DESC
```

```
OPEN c

FETCH LAST FROM c INTO            -- earliest order
    @Total

IF @@CURSOR_ROWS < 3             -- fewer than 3 orders
  SELECT
    0.00 AS Discount
ELSE
BEGIN
  SET
      @Sum = @Total * 2.0

  FETCH PRIOR FROM c INTO
      @Total

  SET
      @Sum = @Sum + @Total * 3.0      -- 2nd most-recent order

  FETCH PRIOR FROM c INTO
      @Total

  SET
      @Sum = @Sum + @Total * 5.0      -- most-recent order

  SET
      @Sum = ISNULL (@Sum, 0) / 10.0  -- calculate weighted average

  SELECT                             -- display discount
      CASE
          WHEN @Sum < 1000 THEN 0.00
          WHEN @Sum >= 1000 AND @Sum < 2000.00 THEN 0.10
          WHEN @Sum >= 2000 AND @Sum < 4000.00 THEN 0.20
                                          ELSE 0.25
      END  AS Discount
END

-- clean up
CLOSE c
DEALLOCATE c
```

SQL Puzzle 16-1: Hierarchies
and User-Defined Functions

The algorithm for the function in this puzzle is fairly simple. You form a loop that iterates through the path of employees starting from the employee ID you got as a parameter. In the next iteration, you go up to that employee's manager, then to the manager's manager, and so on, until you've reached the top. In each iteration, you increment the @nodelevel variable, which was initialized with –1. You start with –1 because your loop will iterate an additional time when it reaches the top-level employee, in order to find out that that employee doesn't have a manager. This way, a top-level employee will have a node level of 0, the first subordinate will have 1, the second-level subordinate will have 2, and so on. Here's the solution:

```
-- UDF that finds the level of the node in the tree
-- root is 0, increments by 1 for each subordinate level
CREATE FUNCTION dbo.NODELEVEL(@empid int) RETURNS int
AS
BEGIN
  DECLARE @nodelevel AS int
  SET @nodelevel = -1

  -- go up one level and increment @nodelevel each iteration
  WHILE @empid IS NOT NULL
    SELECT
      @empid     = mgrid,
      @nodelevel = @nodelevel + 1
    FROM
      Employees
    WHERE
      empid = @empid

  RETURN @nodelevel
END
GO
```

Notice that the @empid parameter that was an argument to the function is used as the variable that stores the current employee ID of the loop. You update the value of @empid to that employee's manager and increment the @nodelevel variable in the same SELECT statement. This makes your loop very efficient. If you want to support calls to the function that might supply an employee ID that doesn't exist in the table, you can add the following existence check in the beginning of the function:

```
            -- if node does not exist return NULL
        IF NOT EXISTS (SELECT *
                        FROM
                          Employees
                        WHERE
                          empid = @empid)
          RETURN NULL
```

The NODEPATH() function is implemented in a similar way. The only difference here is that instead of incrementing a variable representing the level in the hierarchy, you gradually build the path of the employee in a variable by concatenating the variable to a dot followed by the current employee ID in the loop. Here's how:

```
-- UDF that finds the path of the node in the tree
-- in the form of '.node0.node1.[...].node(n-1).'
CREATE FUNCTION dbo.NODEPATH(@empid int) RETURNS varchar(900)
AS
BEGIN
  DECLARE @nodepath AS varchar(900)
  SET @nodepath = '.' + CAST(@empid AS varchar(10)) + '.'

  -- go up one level and increment @nodelevel each iteration
  WHILE @empid IS NOT NULL
    SELECT
      @empid    = mgrid,
      @nodepath = CASE
                    WHEN mgrid IS NULL THEN ''
                    ELSE '.' + CAST(mgrid AS varchar(10))
                  END + @nodepath
    FROM
      Employees
    WHERE
      empid = @empid

  RETURN @nodepath
END
GO
```

Now you can use your new functions in queries:

```
SELECT
  *,
  dbo.NODELEVEL(empid) AS lvl,
  dbo.NODEPATH(empid)  AS hierarchy
FROM
  Employees
```

Note that the output of this query includes the lvl and hierarchy columns, which hold the results of the functions NODELVL() and NODEPATH(), respectively:

empid	mgrid	empname	salary	lvl	hierarchy
1	NULL	Nancy	10000.0000	0	.1.
2	1	Andrew	5000.0000	1	.1.2.
3	1	Janet	5000.0000	1	.1.3.
4	1	Margaret	5000.0000	2	1.1.4.
5	2	Steven	2500.0000	2	.1.2.5.
6	2	Michael	2500.0000	2	.1.2.6.
7	3	Robert	2500.0000	2	.1.3.7.
8	3	Laura	2500.0000	2	.1.3.8.
9	3	Ann	2500.0000	2	.1.3.9.
10	4	Ina	2500.0000	2	.1.4.10.
11	7	David	2000.0000	3	.1.3.7.11.
12	7	Ron	2000.0000	3	.1.3.7.12.
13	7	Dan	2000.0000	3	.1.3.7.13.
14	11	James	1500.0000	4	.1.3.7.11.14.

You can even use the NODELEVEL() and NODEPATH() functions in computed columns:

```
ALTER TABLE Employees
  ADD lvl       AS dbo.NODELEVEL(empid),
      hierarchy AS dbo.NODEPATH(empid)
GO

SELECT
  *
FROM
  Employees
```

Using the NODELEVEL() and NODEPATH() functions in computed columns provides an alternative to adding regular columns that contain hierarchical information to the Employees table and maintaining them with triggers as discussed in Chapter 16. This solution looks much easier than the one you implemented in Chapter 16, so why did you go through all that trouble? There are two main reasons:

- User-defined functions were not available prior to SQL Server 2000.

- You can't place an index on either of the two computed columns you've just created because you access a table in both of the functions. One of the limitations of user-defined functions that access tables, other than ones created by the function in a table variable, is that you can't create an index on them.

SQL Puzzle 17-1: Top Gun: The Best of the Best

This solution will look familiar because it is based on the solution shown in the "Are You Being Served?" section in Chapter 17. That solution produced a rowset that gave you the top employee for each country served. This can be used as a derived table to give the count of the number of such occurrences per employee. Sort it by the count and you're there. Here's the code:

```
SELECT
  O1.ShipCountry,
  O1.EmployeeID,
  COUNT (*) AS Orders
INTO
  #Temp
FROM
    Orders O1
GROUP BY
    O1.ShipCountry,
    O1.EmployeeID

SELECT
  EmployeeID,
  COUNT (*) AS Countries
FROM
(
  SELECT
    T1.*
  FROM
    #Temp T1
```

```
WHERE
  T1.Orders =
(
  SELECT
    MAX (T2.Orders)
  FROM
    #Temp T2
  WHERE
      T2.ShipCountry = T1.ShipCountry
)
) X
GROUP BY
  EmployeeID
ORDER BY
  Countries DESC
```

The temp table stores the distribution of orders by country by employee. The derived table gives you the best employees for each country. You then summarize the contents of the derived table by counting the number of rows per employee and sort in descending order by the count.

SQL Puzzle 17-2-1: Filling a Table with a Magic Square's Data in T-SQL

Here's a possible solution to the puzzle. You can go over it briefly, and then return to it while you read the explanations following the stored procedure.

```
CREATE PROC FillMagicSquare
  @size AS int
AS

DELETE MagicSquare

-- Insert the first number to the middle cell in the first row
INSERT INTO MagicSquare
  (row, col, value)
VALUES
  (1, @size / 2 + 1, 1)

-- Insert the rest of the numbers while
-- the last number does not exist in the table
WHILE NOT EXISTS (SELECT * FROM MagicSquare WHERE value = SQUARE(@size))
```

```
INSERT INTO MagicSquare(row, col, value)
  -- decide which coordinates to use (above / right cell or cell beneath)
  -- based on the NULLs returned from the ROJ
  SELECT
    CASE
      WHEN MS.row IS NULL THEN O1.row
      ELSE O2.row
    END AS row,
    CASE
      WHEN MS.col IS NULL THEN O1.col
      ELSE O2.col
    END AS col,
    O1.value
  FROM
    -- Input 1: base table
    MagicSquare AS MS
    -- Join 1: existing_cell ROJ above / right cell
    -- NULLs indicate cell is not occupied
    RIGHT OUTER JOIN
    -- Input 2: above / right cell info
      (SELECT
        CASE
          WHEN row - 1 = 0 THEN @size
          ELSE row - 1
        END AS row,
        CASE
          WHEN col + 1 > @size THEN 1
          ELSE col + 1
        END AS col,
        value + 1 AS value
      FROM MagicSquare
      WHERE
        value = (SELECT
                   MAX(value)
                 FROM
                   MagicSquare)) AS O1 ON  MS.row = O1.row
                                       AND MS.col = O1.col
    -- Join 2: existing_cell ROJ above / right cell CJ cell beneath
```

```
        CROSS JOIN
     -- Input 3: cell beneath info.
       (SELECT
           CASE
             WHEN row + 1 > @size THEN 1
             ELSE row + 1
           END AS row,
           col,
           value + 1 AS value
         FROM MagicSquare
         WHERE
           value = (SELECT
                       MAX(value)
                     FROM
                       MagicSquare)) AS O2
GO
```

Calculating the column number of the middle cell in the first row is no big deal. You simply perform integer division of @size by 2 and add 1. The real tough problem is to calculate the coordinates of the rest of the cells. Your loop doesn't use a counter because you were limited to one statement inside the loop. To overcome this, your loop condition checks whether a row with a value of SQUARE(@size) exists in the table. SQUARE(@size) is the largest number in your magic square. If it exists in your table, this means that you have inserted all rows.

To understand how the coordinates of the destination cell are calculated, start with the result of the query marked as Input 2 in the comments. This query generates one row with the coordinates of the cell that is above and to the right of the last inserted cell. Join 1 performs a RIGHT OUTER JOIN between the base table (Input 1) and Input 2. A matching row will be found in the base table only if these coordinates are already occupied in the magic square. Look again at Figure 17-1 in Chapter 17, which shows how to fill the magic square. Each step in the figure is numbered. This join will produce the following result for Step 2, because the destination cell is not occupied:

MS.row	MS.col	MS.value	O1.row	O1.col	O1.value
NULL	NULL	NULL	3	3	2

On the other hand, in Step 4, the destination cell is occupied:

MS.row	MS.col	MS.value	O1.row	O1.col	O1.value
1	2	1	1	2	4

Next, examine the result of the query marked as Input 3 in the comments. This query generates one row with the coordinates of the cell that is beneath the last inserted cell. Join 2 simply concatenates it with the result of Join 1. Check the result of this join for Step 2:

MS.row	MS.col	MS.value	O1.row	O1.col	O1.value	O2.row	O2.col	O2.value
NULL	NULL	NULL	3	3	2	2	2	2

The result of this join for Step 4 is the following:

MS.row	MS.col	MS.value	O1.row	O1.col	O1.value	O2.row	O2.col	O2.value
1	2	1	1	2	4	3	1	4

Now it is easy to decide which are the correct coordinates of the destination cell. If you have NULLs in the base table, you use the coordinates from O1, because this means that the right cell above is not occupied. If you don't have NULLs in the base table, this means that it is occupied, and you use the coordinates of the cell beneath, which are represented by O2. To try this stored procedure, execute it with a given size of your choice; for example:

```
EXEC FillMagicSquare 3
```

Now, see if the table was populated with the correct values:

```
SELECT * FROM MagicSquare ORDER BY row, col
```

The result of the query is shown in the following table:

row	col	value
1	1	8
1	2	1
1	3	6
2	1	3
2	2	5
2	3	7
3	1	4
3	2	9
3	3	2

SQL Puzzle 17-2-2: Displaying the Magic Square as a Cross-Tab Table

If you want to display a magic square with a known size, say 3, in a more meaningful way, you can use the following cross-tab query:

```
SELECT
  SUM(CASE col
        WHEN 1 THEN value
        ELSE 0
      END) AS col1,
  SUM(CASE col
        WHEN 2 THEN value
        ELSE 0
      END) AS col2,
  SUM(CASE col
        WHEN 3 THEN value
        ELSE 0
      END) AS col3
FROM
  MagicSquare
GROUP BY
  row
ORDER BY
  row
```

You get the following magic square:

col1	col2	col3
8	1	6
3	5	7
4	9	2

This query does generate the result you wanted, but the problem with it is that you have to know the magic square's size. What if you don't know the size ahead of time, and you want your query to handle any given size? You can write a stored procedure that finds the magic square's size by calculating the square root of the largest number in the magic square, dynamically constructs a query similar to the previous one, and executes it. The following stored procedure implements this logic:

```
CREATE PROC ShowMagicSquare
AS

DECLARE
  @size  AS int,
  @cmd   AS varchar(8000),
  @col   AS int,
  @ENTER AS char(1)

SET @ENTER = CHAR(13) + CHAR(10)

SELECT @size = SQRT(COUNT(*)) FROM MagicSquare

SET @cmd = 'SELECT' + @ENTER

SET @col = 1
WHILE @col < = @size
BEGIN
  SET @cmd = @cmd +
    '  SUM(CASE col' + @ENTER +
    '    WHEN ' + CAST(@col AS varchar) + ' THEN value' + @ENTER +
    '    ELSE 0' + @ENTER +
    '  END) AS col' + CAST(@col AS varchar) +
```

```
      CASE
        WHEN @col < @size THEN ','
        ELSE ''
      END +
      @ENTER

   SET @col = @col + 1
END

SET @cmd = @cmd +
    'FROM' + @ENTER +
    '  MagicSquare' + @ENTER +
    'GROUP BY'  + @ENTER +
    '  row' + @ENTER +
    'ORDER BY'  + @ENTER +
    '  row' + @ENTER

EXEC (@cmd)
GO
```

Test this stored procedure by repopulating the table with a 5 × 5 magic square:

```
EXEC FillMagicSquare 5
EXEC ShowMagicSquare
```

SQL Puzzle 17-2-3: Checking whether the Table Represents a Magic Square Correctly

One approach to solving this puzzle is to calculate the sum of each row, column, and diagonal first. You can calculate the sum of all the rows, columns, and each diagonal separately, and UNION the results:

```
SELECT
   'row'      AS line,
   row        AS ordinal,
   SUM(value) AS sum_line
FROM
   MagicSquare
GROUP BY
   row

UNION ALL
```

```
SELECT
  'col'      AS line,
   col       AS ordinal,
  SUM(value) AS sum_line
  FROM
    MagicSquare
  GROUP BY
    col

UNION ALL

SELECT
  'diagonal' AS line,
  1          AS ordinal,
  SUM(value) AS sum_line
FROM
  MagicSquare
WHERE
  row = col

UNION ALL

SELECT
  'diagonal' AS line,
  2          AS ordinal,
  SUM(value) AS sum_line
FROM
  MagicSquare
WHERE
  col - 1 = (SELECT
                SQRT(COUNT(*))
             FROM
               MagicSquare) - row
```

The following is the output of this query for a magic square with a size of 5:

line	ordinal	sum_line
row	1	65
row	2	65
row	3	65
row	4	65
row	5	65
col	1	65
col	2	65
col	3	65
col	4	65
col	5	65
diagonal	1	65
diagonal	2	65

Now you can wrap this query as a derived table, making it easy to check if your table represents a magic square. You have two options, depending on the way you ask the question.

Option 1: Is the line with the maximum value equal to the line with the minimum value?

```
IF EXISTS(SELECT
             MIN(sum_line) AS min_line,
             MAX(sum_line) AS max_line
          FROM
           (SELECT
              'row'       AS line,
              row         AS ordinal,
             SUM(value) AS sum_line
           FROM
             MagicSquare
          GROUP BY
             row
```

```
        UNION ALL

        SELECT
          'col'      AS line,
           col       AS ordinal,
          SUM(value) AS sum_line
          FROM
            MagicSquare
          GROUP BY
            col

        UNION ALL

        SELECT
          'diagonal' AS line,
           1         AS ordinal,
          SUM(value) AS sum_line
        FROM
          MagicSquare
        WHERE
          row = col

        UNION ALL

        SELECT
          'diagonal' AS line,
           2         AS ordinal,
          SUM(value) AS sum_line
        FROM
          MagicSquare
        WHERE
          col - 1 = (SELECT
                        SQRT(COUNT(*))
                      FROM
                        MagicSquare) - row)
        HAVING
          MIN(sum_line) = MAX(sum_line))
    PRINT 'This is a Magic Square. :-)'
ELSE
    PRINT 'This is not a Magic Square. :-('
```

Option 2: Is the value of the first line equal to all of the values in all of the lines?

```
IF (SELECT
    SUM(value)
   FROM
    MagicSquare
   WHERE
    row = 1) = ALL(SELECT
                      SUM(value) AS sum_line
                   FROM
                     MagicSquare
                   GROUP BY
                     row

                   UNION ALL

                   SELECT
                     SUM(value) AS sum_line
                   FROM
                     MagicSquare
                   GROUP BY
                     col

                   UNION ALL

                   SELECT
                     SUM(value) AS sum_line
                   FROM
                     MagicSquare
                   WHERE
                     row = col

                   UNION ALL

                   SELECT
                     SUM(value) AS sum_line
                   FROM
                     MagicSquare
```

```
                WHERE
                  col - 1 = (SELECT
                                 SQRT(COUNT(*))
                             FROM
                              MagicSquare) - row)
  PRINT 'This is a Magic Square. :-)'
ELSE
  PRINT 'This is not a Magic Square. :-('
```

APPENDIX A
DML Basics

ALTHOUGH THIS IS AN advanced Transact-SQL book, we will provide you with some of the basics of the Data Manipulation Language (DML). DML includes the SELECT, INSERT, UPDATE, and DELETE statements. Each of them is summarized here.

Using the SELECT Statement

The SELECT statement is the one you will use most often. Its purpose is to retrieve rows from SQL Server tables. The syntax is summarized in Listing A-1.

Listing A-1: Syntax for the SELECT Statement

```
SELECT [ ALL | DISTINCT ]
[ { TOP integer | TOP integer PERCENT } [ WITH TIES ] ]
< select_list >
[ INTO new_table ]
[ FROM { < table_source > } [ ,...n ] ]
[ WHERE < search_condition > ]
[ GROUP BY [ ALL ] group_by_expression [ ,...n ]
[ WITH { CUBE | ROLLUP } ]
]
[ HAVING < search_condition > ]
[ ORDER BY < sort_criteria> ]
```

The SELECT Clause

The SELECT keyword is mandatory. The ALL keyword means that you want all rows that match the search criteria—this is the default. Explicitly specifying the ALL keyword is typically not done. The DISTINCT keyword means that you want no duplicate rows.

The TOP clause is fully explained in Chapter 4. Its purpose is to limit the number of rows returned to an integer between 0 and 4,294,967,295 that you specify. Alternatively, you can add the PERCENT keyword to specify a percentage of the rows to be returned. You typically use the TOP clause with an ORDER BY clause, which sorts the rows in the result set. The ORDER BY clause is discussed later in this appendix.

If you do use the TOP clause with an ORDER BY, you have the option of including the WITH TIES keyword. This specifies that additional rows be returned from the base result set if they have the same value in the ORDER BY columns as the last of the TOP n (PERCENT) rows.

The SELECT list specifies the column names or expressions—separated by commas—that you want to retrieve. These will be displayed as columns in your result set. You can specify columns from particular tables by prefixing the column name with the table name, separated by a period. For example, to specify the OrderID column from the Orders table, use Orders.OrderID.

If you want all columns, you can use * in your SELECT list instead of specifying every column name. If you want all columns from a particular table, you can prefix * with the table name, separated by a period. For example, if you want all columns from the Orders table, use Orders.*.

Aliases are used to rename the columns and expressions that appear in your SELECT list. Columns and expressions in the SELECT list can be aliased in one of three ways. First, you can use the alias name, followed by an equal sign (=), followed by the expression or column name. For example, to use Order as an alias for the OrderID column, use Order = OrderID.

The second way to alias is to use the AS keyword. In this case, you specify the column or expression to be aliased, followed by AS, followed by the alias name. For example, to use Order as an alias for the OrderID column, use OrderID AS Order.

The final way is a variation on the previous method. In this case, you proceed in the same manner as with the AS keyword, but just omit the AS keyword. Thus, you can use OrderID Order.

The INTO Clause

The INTO clause is not a pure DML statement, it is actually a hybrid of DML and DDL (Data Definition Language), since it not only manipulates data but it also creates an object—a table. The INTO clause tells SQL Server not to return the results back to the calling program. Rather, it indicates that the results are to be placed into a new table, which it creates at the same time it carries out the SELECT statement. The INTO clause is covered in detail in Chapter 3.

The FROM Clause

The FROM clause is where you specify the table(s) and view(s) from which you want to retrieve data. The simplest case is where you are using only one table or view. If you are using more than one table or view, you use JOINs to link together your tables and views. Joins are treated fully in Chapter 1.

Just as you can use an alias for a column name, you can also use an alias for a table name. This makes specifying which table you are referring to inside your SELECT list or WHERE clause much easier, since you can alias a long table name to just one or two letters. This will be made clearer in a moment.

You alias your table inside the FROM clause. You specify the table name, followed by the AS keyword, followed by the alias. You can also omit the AS keyword if you prefer. For example, you can alias the Orders table to O by using `Orders AS O` or `Orders O`.

Once you have aliased a table, you can use the alias instead of the full table name when you are referencing columns in the SELECT list. For example, using the alias of O for the Orders table, you can now refer to the OrderID column from the Orders table as `O.OrderID`, instead of `Orders.OrderID`.

The WHERE Clause

The WHERE clause is used to filter the rows you intend to receive. You can specify a condition or conditions inside the WHERE clause to determine which rows you want to receive. For example, if you only want rows where the ShipCountry column is 'Germany', then use `WHERE ShipCountry = 'Germany'`. Each condition is called a *predicate* and evaluates to TRUE, FALSE, or UNKNOWN. If the condition is TRUE, then the row qualifies to be included in the result set.

You can have multiple predicates in your WHERE clause. These are separated by AND or OR keywords. For example, if you want the ShipCountry to be either 'France' or 'Germany', then use `WHERE ShipCountry = 'France' OR ShipCountry = 'Germany'`.

The IN predicate allows you to simplify a number of OR predicates. It simply compares one expression against a number of values. If the expression equates to any of the values inside the list of values, then the IN predicate is TRUE. The syntax for the OR predicate is given in Listing A-2.

Listing A-2: Syntax for the IN Predicate

```
expression [NOT] IN ( expression [ ,...n ] )
```

Thus, you can recast `WHERE ShipCountry = 'France' OR ShipCountry = 'Germany'` to `WHERE ShipCountry IN ('France', 'Germany')`.

You can use the NOT keyword to negate the result of a Boolean expression. In other words, if an expression returns TRUE, using NOT will make it return FALSE, and vice-versa. For example, if you are interested in rows in which the ShipCountry column is neither 'France' nor 'Germany', you can use `WHERE ShipCountry NOT IN ('France', 'Germany')`.

You can use the BETWEEN predicate to specify an inclusive range of values. For example, if you want the OrderID values from 11,000 to 11,100, use `OrderID BETWEEN 11000 and 11100`.

The LIKE predicate can be used for pattern matching of character columns. It tests a match expression against a pattern and returns TRUE is there is a match. The syntax is given in Listing A-3.

Listing A-3: Syntax for the LIKE Predicate

```
match_expression [ NOT ] LIKE pattern
```

The pattern can contain wildcards. The percent sign (%) means any string of zero or more characters. The underscore sign (_) means any single character. Square brackets ([]) mean any single character in a list or range of values. For example, '[a-d]' or '[abcd]' means 'a', 'b', 'c', or 'd'. You can also use the caret (^) to designate a character that is not within the specified range. For example, '[^a-d]' would mean any character not in the range 'a' through 'd'.

You can determine whether an expression is NULL by using IS NULL or IS NOT NULL. For example, to test if ContactName is NULL, use ContactName IS NULL.

The GROUP BY Clause

You can summarize your result set with a GROUP BY clause. The GROUP BY clause specifies how you want the result set grouped. Each criterion is separated with a comma. The GROUP BY criteria act as keys in the result set. In other words, there will be no duplicates of these keys in the result set.

The syntax for the GROUP BY clause is shown in Listing A-4.

Listing A-4: Syntax for the GROUP BY Clause

```
[ GROUP BY [ ALL ] group_by_expression [ ,...n ]
      [ WITH { CUBE | ROLLUP } ]
]
```

For example, if you want to summarize your result set according to ShipCountry, use GROUP BY ShipCountry. The GROUP BY clause is fully discussed in Chapter 5.

The HAVING Clause

The HAVING clause is used in conjunction with the GROUP BY clause. It lets you filter the grouped result set in the same manner as the WHERE clause filters the ungrouped data. You can refer only to the columns used in the GROUP BY as well as any aggregated columns, which must appear inside aggregate functions, such as SUM(), COUNT(), MAX(), and MIN().

The ORDER BY Clause

The ORDER BY clause is used to sort your result set. Check out the syntax in Listing A-5.

Listing A-5: Syntax for the ORDER BY Clause

```
[ ORDER BY { order_by_expression [ ASC | DESC ] }    [ ,...n] ]
```

The order_by_expression specifies the column on which to sort. You can use a column name or an alias, an expression, or a non-negative integer that determines the position of the name, alias, or expression in the SELECT list. The ASC and DESC keywords specify that the column should be sorted in ascending or descending order, respectively. There is no limit to the number of items in the ORDER BY clause.

For example, if you want to sort by OrderID with the highest one first, use ORDER BY OrderID DESC.

Using the INSERT Statement

The INSERT statement is used to add rows to a table or view. Without it, you would have no data in your database. The INSERT statement is covered fully in Chapter 3. The simplified syntax is summarized in Listing A-6:

Listing A-6: Syntax for the INSERT Statement

```
INSERT [ INTO]
  { table_name  | view_name  }
  {    [ ( column_list ) ]
    { VALUES
      ( { DEFAULT | NULL | expression } [ ,...n] )
      | derived_table
      | execute_statement
    }
  }
  | DEFAULT VALUES
```

The INSERT Clause

The INSERT clause is used to specify into which table or view you want your data to go. The INTO keyword is optional. If you are inserting into a view, the view must be updateable and cannot affect more than one of the base tables referenced in the FROM clause of the view. The rules for INSERTs and UPDATEs to views are explained further in the "The UPDATE Clause" section in this appendix.

The Column List

The column list is optional in most cases. It specifies the columns of the target table or view for which you will be providing data through your INSERT statement. If you omit the column list, SQL Server will assume that you want all of the columns of the target table or view, and the data you provide will be in the same order as the positions of the columns of the target table or view. If you do specify a column list, the columns can appear in any order you want.

The column list is surrounded by parentheses, and each column is delineated with commas. If a column in the target table or view is an IDENTITY or rowversion column, it must not appear in the column list. IDENTITY and rowversion columns generate their own values and are explained fully in Chapter 6.

If you do not specify all columns of the destination table or view, defaults or NULLs will be used if the missing columns support defaults or NULLs. Otherwise, the INSERT will fail. The INSERT can also fail if there is a violation of any PRIMARY KEY, UNIQUE, FOREIGN KEY, or CHECK constraint.

The VALUES Clause

The VALUES clause is used when you want to INSERT a single row. The values to be specified are delineated with parentheses, following the VALUES keyword. The values are separated with commas. The position of a data value in the VALUES list corresponds to the position of the column in the column list. In other words, the third data value is for the third column specified in the column list.

You can specify a constant, a variable, a function, or the DEFAULT or NULL keywords for a data value. The DEFAULT keyword indicates that the actual data value will be generated by a DEFAULT constraint on the table. The NULL keyword is used to insert a NULL value for the column; the target column must, of course, be NULLable or the INSERT will fail.

The code in Listing A-7 shows you how to use the INSERT VALUES statement.

Listing A-7: Using the INSERT VALUES Statement

```
INSERT MyTable
(
  PK_ID,
  Quantity,
  EntryDate
)
VALUES
(
  1107,
  2010,
  GETDATE ()
)
```

The Derived Table Clause

Instead of the VALUES clause, you can instead use a derived table. This is essentially a SELECT statement and is most often referred to as an INSERT SELECT statement. Because a SELECT can return many rows, using a derived table allows you to insert multiple rows into your table or view with a single INSERT statement.

The columns that you specify in the SELECT clause will correspond to the columns in the column list, if you have one, or the columns of the target table or view if you don't have a column list.

The code in Listing A-8 shows you how to use an INSERT SELECT.

Listing A-8: Using an INSERT SELECT

```
INSERT MyTable
(
  PK_ID,
  Quantity,
  EntryDate
)
SELECT
  PK_ID,
  Quantity,
  EntryDate
FROM
  HerTable
WHERE
  PK_ID BETWEEN 2000 AND 2999
```

The Execute Clause

Besides using an INSERT SELECT to insert multiple rows, you can use an execute clause. This is commonly known as an INSERT EXEC statement. In this case, you use the execution of a stored procedure to provide the rows, instead of a native SELECT statement—a SELECT statement inside the stored procedure provides the rows. Stored procedures are discussed fully in Chapter 9. A sample INSERT EXEC is shown in Listing A-9.

Listing A-9: Using the INSERT EXEC Statement

```
INSERT MyTable
(
  PK_ID,
  Quantity,
  EntryDate
)
EXEC
  sp_MyProc
```

The DEFAULT VALUES Clause

The DEFAULT VALUES clause allows you to INSERT only the default values for all columns in a table. An example is shown in Listing A-10.

Listing A-10: Using the INSERT DEFAULT VALUES Statement

```
INSERT MyTable
(
  PK_ID,
  Quantity,
  EntryDate
)
DEFAULT VALUES
```

Using the UPDATE Statement

The UPDATE statement is used to update data in a table or view. The simplified syntax is summarized in Listing A-11.

Listing A-11: Syntax for the UPDATE Statement

```
UPDATE
{
 table_name | view_name
}
SET
 { column_name = { expression | DEFAULT | NULL }
 | @variable = expression
 | @variable = column = expression } [ ,...n ]
{ [ FROM { < table_source > } [ ,...n ] ]
[ WHERE
    < search_condition > ]
}
```

The UPDATE Clause

The UPDATE clause is used to specify which table or view you are trying to update. If you are using a view, it must be updateable. To be updateable, a view cannot have a TOP, GROUP BY, DISTINCT, or UNION clause. (See Chapters 8 and 13 for exceptions to this rule.) In addition to this restriction, for a view to be updateable, the columns in the view's SELECT list must not be derived. Derived columns are result set columns formed by anything other than a simple column expression, such as using functions or addition or subtraction operators.

Another requirement for a view to be updateable is that there must be at least one table in the FROM clause inside the view. A SELECT that is based upon nontabular expressions—expressions not based upon a table—cannot be used.

The modifications made to the view cannot affect more than one underlying base table.

The SET Clause

The SET clause is used to designate which columns or variables are to be updated.

Whether you are updating a table or a view, you can update columns from only one of the tables or views you are using.

To update a column, you can set the column equal to an expression, to the default (if there is a DEFAULT constraint on the column), or to NULL.

You can use the UPDATE statement to update a variable. This is handy if you want to get a "before" image of a column at the same time as you are updating it. This is best explained with an example. Check out the code in Listing A-12.

Listing A-12: Using the UPDATE Statement to Update a Variable

```
UPDATE MyTable
SET
  @Before  = MyColumn,
  MyColumn = 'After Value'
```

You can simultaneously update a variable and a column, as shown in Listing A-13.

Listing A-13: Simultaneous Update of a Column and a Variable

```
UPDATE MyTable
SET
  @Value  = MyColumn = 3
```

In this case, both the @Value variable and the MyColumn column are set to 3.

The FROM Clause

The FROM clause is optional. If you are doing an UPDATE and do not need to correlate the table being updated with another table, then you do not need a FROM clause. In the event that you use table aliases, you can use the alias in the UPDATE clause for the table or view to be updated.

The rules for the FROM clause for an UPDATE are the same as those for a SELECT statement.

The WHERE Clause

The WHERE clause for an UPDATE is the same as for a SELECT. Here, you specify the criteria to determine which rows are to be updated. If you fail to include a WHERE clause, all rows in the table will be updated.

Using the DELETE Statement

The DELETE statement is used to delete rows from a table or view. The syntax is shown in Listing A-14.

Listing A-14: Syntax for the DELETE Statement

```
DELETE
[ FROM ]
  { table_name | view_name }
[ FROM { < table_source > } [ ,...n ] ]
[ WHERE
  { < search_condition > }
]
```

The DELETE Clause

The DELETE clause is fairly simple. Here, you name the table or view from which you want to delete rows. The FROM keyword in this clause is optional. You can specify one—and only one—table or view. The FROM keyword is used in two portions of the DELETE statement. This is the first FROM clause.

The FROM Clause

The FROM clause is optional. If you are doing a DELETE and do not need to correlate the table being deleted with another table, then you do not need a FROM clause. In the event that you use table aliases, you may use the alias in the DELETE clause for the table or view to be deleted.

The rules for the FROM clause for a DELETE are the same as those for a SELECT statement.

The WHERE Clause

The WHERE clause for a DELETE is the same as for a SELECT. Here, you specify the criteria to determine which rows are to be deleted. If you fail to include a WHERE clause, all rows in the table will be deleted.

Checking for ANSI Compatibility with SET FIPS_FLAGGER

IF YOU WANT TO WRITE SQL code that will be portable between different relational database management systems (RDBMSs), with a smooth and painless migration, your code should be ANSI (American National Standards Institute) compliant, because most of the major RDBMSs are ANSI compliant to some extent. The ANSI committee releases standards for SQL once every few years, and the major releases have been SQL-89, SQL-92, and SQL-99.

The Federal Information Processing Standards (FIPS) apply to computer systems purchased by the U.S. government. Each FIPS standard is defined by the National Institute of Standards and Technology (NIST). The current standard for SQL products is FIPS 127-2, which is based on the ANSI SQL-92 standard.

T-SQL provides the SET FIPS_FLAGGER command, which enables you to check whether your code complies with the FIPS 127-2 standard. The syntax for using this command is shown in Listing B-1.

Listing B-1: Using the SET FIPS_FLAGGER Command

```
SET FIPS_FLAGGER level
```

You can choose the level of compliance you want to check. Available levels are ENTRY, FULL, INTERMEDIATE, and OFF. As of this writing, SQL Server 2000 complies with the SQL-92 entry-level standard. T-SQL also supports many non-ANSI compliant extensions, such as the TOP extension, which expands the ANSI-compliant SQL and makes SQL programmers' lives much easier in many cases. However, you should be aware that not all of the extensions work on all systems. To test whether your T-SQL statements are fully ANSI SQL-92 compliant, you can issue the command shown in Listing B-2.

Listing B-2: Checking for Full ANSI SQL-92 Compliance

```
SET FIPS_FLAGGER 'FULL'
```

Listing B-3 shows the output of running this command.

Listing B-3: Checking for Full ANSI SQL-92 Compliance

```
FIPS Warning: Line 1 has the non-ANSI statement 'SET'.
```

Notice that SQL Server already warns you that the SET statement is not ANSI compliant. Now you can run the query shown in Listing B-4 to check whether the code is ANSI SQL-92 compliant. Make sure you are connected to the pubs sample database when you run this query.

Listing B-4: ANSI SQL-92 Compliant Query

```
SELECT
  *
FROM
  Authors
```

You get no warning message when you run this query, meaning that it is ANSI compliant. Now try the query shown in Listing B-5.

Listing B-5: Non-ANSI SQL-92 Compliant Query

```
SELECT
  TOP 5 *
FROM
  Authors
ORDER BY
  au_id
```

You should get the warning shown in Listing B-6, because the TOP clause is not ANSI compliant.

Listing B-6: Warning for Non-ANSI SQL-92 Compliant Query

```
FIPS Warning: Line 2 has the non-ANSI clause 'TOP'.
```

To turn ANSI-compliance checking off, issue the command shown in Listing B-7.

Listing B-7: Turning Off ANSI-Compliance Checking

```
SET FIPS_FLAGGER OFF
```

Analyzing Query Performance

YOU HAVE PROBABLY ENCOUNTERED queries that seemed to take an eternity to complete. Without a set of tools and a methodology with which to use them, you are shooting in the dark. This appendix aims to equip you for battle against those queries that irk your users and sully your reputation.

Tools

You can't troubleshoot without a good set of tools. SQL Server provides most of them and one (System Monitor) comes with Windows NT/2000.

> **NOTE** *In Windows NT, System Monitor was known as Performance Monitor. This appendix will use the term System Monitor to refer to either tool.*

In the next few sections, you will see what's available.

System Monitor (Performance Monitor)

If you have been using Windows NT/2000 at all, you are probably familiar with the System Monitor. This tool allows you to depict graphically the activity on machines within your enterprise. Every NT/2000 machine generates counters that can be polled by System Monitor. In Windows 2000, System Monitor is now a snap-in for the Microsoft Management Console (MMC).

For SQL Server 7.0, the submenu from the Start menu had an entry for System Monitor. This was not a different form of the executable; rather, it invoked System Monitor using a stored chart settings file, SQLCTRS.pmc. Here, certain counters were preselected for you and these were the ones that were the most relevant. This feature has been discontinued in SQL Server 2000.

There are five major areas to monitor when searching for bottlenecks:

- Memory usage

- CPU utilization

- Disk I/O

- User connections

- Blocking locks

When investigating memory usage, pay close attention to Page Reads/sec. If this number is consistently high, then the page is not being found in cache and has to be retrieved from disk. If you run a query and see this number spike up, run the query again. If you see the number spike up again, this means that you likely have insufficient memory for the SQL Server cache. If the number stays low, however, the data are being read from cache and you likely have sufficient memory.

Still in the same vein, the Buffer Cache Hit Ratio is an important number. In the ideal world, this number is 100, meaning that 100 percent of the pages needed to satisfy a query are found in cache, obviating the need for I/O. If it drops below the high 90s, you could be looking at a lack of sufficient RAM. Total Server Memory will tell you how much memory is actually being used. Under load, this should go up to meet demand and then fall off when things are quiet.

Another useful counter is the Memory object's Pages/sec. This tells you the number of pages being swapped into or out of memory. It can give you a feel for how much disk thrashing is going on due to insufficient RAM.

While the memory usage counters are useful, the CPU utilization counters are equally important. You should display the % Processor Time for *each* CPU on each machine you are monitoring. This gives you a feel for which machines are the busiest but can also alert you to some brewing trouble. If, for example, you see all CPUs on a server being maxed out, then this can lead you to conduct further investigation using other tools to sniff out the offending queries.

From the Trenches

Believe it or not, *low* CPU activity is sometimes indicative of a slow query. A data warehouse load once had a query showing 70 percent CPU for a long time and then periodically dropped to zero. One would expect the query to be finished, but it wasn't. It turned out that tempdb was filling up and had to expand itself to handle the query, a `SELECT DISTINCT`. During this period of high I/O, the CPU had nothing to do but wait, which it did.

Even though a server's CPU may be busy, it is not always clear whether it is SQL Server that is responsible. That's why it is a good idea to monitor the SQL Server instance of the Process object. If CPU usage is high and SQL Server is most of it, then you know it's time to put on your DBA hat and get to work.

Although you don't often need to look at the Logical Disk or Physical Disk objects, Disk I/O counters can be used to determine whether the disk subsystem is the bottleneck. To use these objects, you must turn them on by issuing the `DISKPERF -Y` command at a command prompt and then reboot your server.

By default, the chart counters are sampled once per second, although this can be changed. You can go to a finer resolution by sampling more frequently, but this makes the CPU busier, artificially pumping up the % Processor Time counter.

The User Connections counters give you a feel for the load on a server because the greater the number of connections, then the greater the number of queries that the server has to handle. Also, there is extra overhead for the server when opening a connection.

Blocking Locks tells you if one query is blocking another. This type of activity is normal in order to allow concurrency. However, if the amount of blocking goes up, it suggests that the overall throughput of the system is slow, due to blocking.

One subtle change occurred when SQL Server 7.0 was released. In version 6.5, you were able to look at a counter for total locks. Now, although you see break-downs by lock type (a good thing), you are looking at lock requests per second, not total locks in effect. Now if only you could roll your own counters…

Actually, you can create your own counters—up to ten of them. They have to be integers, but it is up to you what you want to track. It is also up to you when and how to update the counter. The user-defined counters are updated through system stored procedures `sp_user_counter1` through `sp_user_counter10`. You will have to update these counters whenever there is a change in your counter value. Each of these procedures takes the value that you wish to set the counter to as the input parameter. The Books Online suggests that you can use a trigger to do the update of a counter; however, you cannot put a trigger on a system table such as *syslocks*. What you can do in this case is create a `WHILE` loop to update the counter every second. That should be sufficient to keep your counter current while you are troubleshooting.

One very useful feature of System Monitor is its ability to store a session to a log file. This is great if you want to let it run overnight; it saves you from having to sit there and watch it in its graphical chart mode. (Think of all of the coffee this will save!) Bear in mind that the log will record all counters for a particular object. The interval is 15 seconds by default, but you can change this, too.

Once you have recorded your session, you can play it back, slicing off the time portion in which you are interested. At this point, you can choose which particular counter you wish to observe.

One very good reason to use the log-file feature is to get a baseline against which you can compare when you do system or application upgrades.

> **TIP**   *Use Ctrl+H (or the Backspace key in Windows NT 4 only) to highlight a particular counter in your System Monitor display. It will show up as a broad white line.*

You can also use SQL Profiler to audit the activity of your server. SQL Server 2000 provides C2 security auditing capabilities by using SQL Profiler.

Profiler

SQL Trace was introduced with version 6.5 of SQL Server, and it is now known as the Profiler in versions 7.0 and 2000. When you are trying to troubleshoot problems in a production client/server environment, this one tool is worth its weight in gold. In a nutshell, what this tool allows you to do is to spy on the SQL being thrown at SQL Server. You can apply filters so that you can monitor a specific user, application, etcetera.

Some History

There's an important difference between the trace architecture in version 6.5 and in versions 7.0 and 2000. In version 6.5, SQL Trace was more like a network sniffer (more accurately, an ODS sniffer). It could sniff the traffic to/from the server but it couldn't tell what was going on inside it. This made it hard to troubleshoot statements within a stored procedure, analyze the cause of deadlocks, and so on.

As of version 7.0, the whole concept of tracing changed. You can now trace events generated by various components, some of which are server-internal, allowing you to troubleshoot the stuff that you were unable to before.

General

You can save the trace data to a file or to a table to be analyzed later. Tracing to a file is more advisable as it consumes fewer resources than tracing to a table. When you trace to a table, the events go through some form of events consumer and back to the server. You would usually want to trace to a table when you need to analyze dynamically the trace data. You can use Microsoft Excel or Microsoft Analysis Services to pivot the traced events. You have to set a maximum size for your trace file, but you can enable the file rollover capability, which will open up a new trace file each time the current trace file reaches the maximum defined size and will start appending events to the new trace file. This way, you can start analyzing the trace output of the inactive files.

By default, the client side processes the trace data. In this mode, when the server is under stress, some events might not be traced because the server may be unable to send the information. You cannot guarantee full auditing this way.

Alternatively, you can request that the server will process the trace data. This is an important feature that guarantees that all events will be traced, but you should keep in mind that the performance of your server might be affected, especially if you capture a lot of events.

When you trace to a table, you can limit the number of rows that will be written to the table. You can also set the trace to stop automatically at a certain time.

Events

You can trace a wide variety of events, including cursor activity, data and log files' auto shrink and auto growth, locks and deadlocks, parallelism events, execution plans, security audit events, statements within batches and stored procedures, and even your own raised events. The important thing to remember concerning events is that you need to be selective. You don't pay for events you don't collect. The fewer events you collect, the less overhead your trace incurs.

Data Columns

Data columns are the pieces of information that will be supplied with your events. These include the text data of the event; CPU and I/O performance statistics, such as CPU time, duration, reads, and writes; environmental details, such as the NT user name, host name, application name, and so on.

You can group the events by certain data columns, but you might prefer not to group the events when you define the trace, so you can get a chronological view of the events as they occur. You can always reopen a saved trace file or table and define your grouping later.

Filters

You can define powerful server-side event filters. These include threshold and equality filters (e.g., `CPU >= 200`, `SPID = 10;=12;=15`), include and exclude filters ("Not like SQL Profiler"), and many others. You can also exclude system IDs.

You can use predefined trace templates or define your own trace templates for later reuse.

You can also define server-side traces with a supplied set of stored procedures and return information on your traces using a set of table-valued functions. You can create your own stored procedures that instantiate server-side traces. This way, you can invoke a trace as a response to an error event in your system by using SQL Server Agent jobs and alerts. You can also set such a trace to auto-start whenever your server starts. You can define a trace graphically and let Profiler generate a script with the required set of stored procedures that will generate such a server-side trace. Profiler allows you to script a trace in either SQL Server 2000 or SQL Server 7.0 format. You can later amend the script to fit your needs.

You can use a saved trace file or table from a production server to replay the events that were saved in order to regenerate a problematic scenario and analyze it on a test server. The replay capabilities allow a multiuser replay. If the trace includes multiple connections, SQL Profiler will replay them all. SQL Profiler will consider concurrency and synchronization issues as accurately as possible.

Some tracing capabilities are also embedded into SQL Query Analyzer in SQL Server 2000. From the Query menu, you can turn on the Show Server Trace option (Ctrl+Shift+T). This option will open a new pane displaying statistics on CPU, duration, reads, and writes for your SQL statements. You can also turn on the Show Client Statistics option (Ctrl+Shift+S). This option will open a new pane displaying application profile statistics, network statistics, and time statistics.

Searching for Trouble

For the most part, you will not want to record every little thing that is coming across the wire. For example, many APIs use client-side cursors. You do not need to see every `sp_cursorfetch` statement; all you need to see is the one query that caused all of the fetches. Also, if you have one specific user who is complaining about slow performance, then filter out everyone else. This will make your search a lot easier.

If you are still getting way more information than you need, you can filter on query duration by specifying the minimum and maximum duration for which you are searching. More often than not, you will not want to set a maximum, since you want to catch all of the bad ones.

What if you are interested in finding the worst-performing queries? SQL Server 7.0 had a Create Trace Wizard. If you clicked the Wizard icon and selected "Find the worst performing queries" from the drop-down menu, this created a trace that would show you a breakdown of queries with a duration greater than one second, grouped by duration. The worst ones fell to the bottom of the display. There were also other canned traces that you could generate for specific problems. The bad news is that SQL Server 2000 does not have this wizard. Pity. The good news is that it has an assortment of templates from which you can cookie-cut your own traces. You can even make your own trace templates.

You can choose to keep the results from the Profiler in a trace file or a table for further analysis. This is also helpful if you wish to use the Index Analyzer and need a representative load script. You can also play back the trace, which is helpful for regression testing.

One very nice feature of SQL Server 2000 is that the Query Analyzer has been enhanced to allow you to profile your own session so that you don't have to jump out of Query Analyzer to obtain a trace.

From the Trenches

On a very long project, the development team started with SQL Server version 4.21a and then 6.0 and 6.5 were released. The DBA group was small, compared to the large pool of PowerBuilder developers, and thus they did both development and production support. Usually, the support calls would come after the Power-Builder guys went home, leaving the DBAs to try and figure out what was happening. Since there was no mapping document that would state which screen was using which stored procedure, the DBAs were essentially flying blind until SQL Trace came about with version 6.5. To add insult to injury, the manager in charge of the PowerBuilder group tried to stop the project from going to version 6.5 and instead wanted to stay with version 6.0. Fortunately, he was moved aside.

SQL Enterprise Manager

Let's assume that you are already used to using SQL Enterprise Manager. From a performance-monitoring point of view, the part of this tool that you will use the most is the Current Activity option under the Management menu. Here, you can see who is logged on, which processes are active, what locks are being used by which processes, etcetera. One annoying feature is that you have to keep refreshing this display on your own. Unfortunately, it can't update itself like the Replication Monitor.

Essentially, this portion of Enterprise Manager is just a glitzy version of the system stored procedures `sp_who2` and `sp_lock`, both of which are described in the "System Stored Procedures" section, later in this appendix.

Query Analyzer

The tool you will probably use the most is the Query Analyzer. It's not solely for troubleshooting—indeed, for the most part, you will use it just to submit queries. However, as its name implies, you can also use it to analyze queries. Specifically, you can use it to determine what the optimizer is using to solve your query, be it a clustered index seek, table scan, etcetera.

There are two ways of looking at the graphical output. First, you can ask it just to show the plan without executing the query. You can do this by choosing Display Estimated Execution Plan from the Query menu or pressing Ctrl+L. This gives you an estimate of how many rows will be touched in each step. Alternatively, you can ask SQL Server to execute the query *and* show the *actual* plan. You do this by choosing Show Execution Plan from the Query menu or pressing Ctrl+K. This will show you the correct numbers for each step. This is how you should use it most often.

The graphics themselves are very useful. Each icon can tell you what is going on—the type of join, which type of index is being used, whether or not parallelism is being employed. The arrows connecting the icons show direction of flow, and their thickness tells you roughly the number of rows being used.

The graphical execution plan in Figure C-1 was produced for two queries that return the same values but are written slightly differently.

Relative Costs

If you want to compare the relative costs of several queries, you can write them all in the Query Analyzer and either leave the whole text unselected or highlight the queries you are interested in analyzing. The first line of text that is presented for each query contains the cost (in percent) of the query, relative to the whole batch. This way, you can compare the costs of several queries that return the same values but are written differently, such as comparing a join version to a subquery version of the same query. The cost (in percent) of each operator, relative to the whole query, appears underneath the icon representing it. This information is helpful in focusing on the operators that incur larger costs as you analyze and tune your queries.

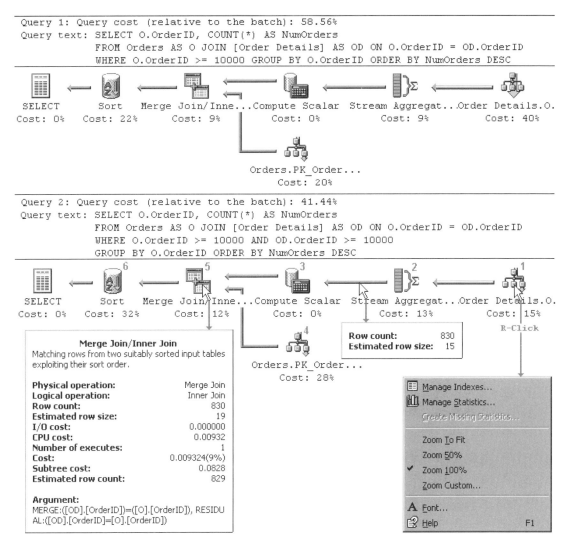

Figure C-1: Sample graphical execution plan

Steps, Nodes, and Sequence of Steps

Steps are the units of work used to process a query, and the *sequence of steps* is the order in which they are processed. Each step can include several *nodes* or *operations*, each of which is displayed as an icon in the graphical execution plan.

Each node is related to a parent node that appears to the left of it (and optionally also to the top of it). If you place the mouse pointer over an arrow that connects a node to its parent node, you get the number of rows that are transferred between the nodes and the estimated row size. You should "read" the graphical execution plan from right to left and from top to bottom.

If you right-click a node, a pop-up window appears, allowing you to manage your indexes and statistics and to create missing statistics. If the optimizer detects that statistics are missing, the operator will be colored in red and a message indicating that statistics are missing will appear as you place the mouse pointer over the operator.

Information Window

If you place the mouse pointer over one of the nodes in the graphical execution plan, a yellow information window appears with the logical and physical operations and performance information.

Logical and Physical Operations

The caption contains the logical and physical operations represented by the icon.

The *logical operators* describe the relational algebraic operation used to process a statement, such as performing an inner join. Not all steps used to process a query or update involve logical operations.

The *physical operators* describe the physical implementation algorithm used to process a statement, such as a NESTED LOOP JOIN. Each step in the execution of a query or UPDATE statement involves a physical operator. Physical operators are explained shortly in the "Physical Operators Explained" section.

Performance Information

The middle section of the Information window contains the following performance information:

- **Row count**: The number of rows output by the operator.

- **Estimated row size:** The estimated size of the row output by the operator.

- **I/O cost**: The estimated cost of all I/O activity for the operation. This value should be as low as possible.

- **CPU cost**: The estimated cost for all CPU activity for the operation.

- **Number of executes**: The number of times the operation was executed during the query.

- **Cost**: The cost to the query optimizer in executing this operation, including the cost of this operation as a percentage of the total cost of the query.

Because the query engine selects the most efficient operation to perform the query or execute the statement, this value should be as low as possible.

- **Subtree cost**: The total cost to the query optimizer in executing this operation and all operations preceding it in the same subtree.

- **Argument**: In the lower part of the window you can find the Argument column, which indicates the predicates and parameters used by the operation.

Physical Operators Explained

This section explains some of the commonly used physical operators in the graphical execution plan. These are grouped here into access methods, join strategies, and miscellaneous operators.

Access Methods

 The *table scan* retrieves all rows from the table specified in the Argument column. If a WHERE:() predicate appears in the Argument column, only those rows that satisfy the predicate are returned.

 The *index seek* or *clustered index seek* uses the seeking ability of indexes to retrieve rows from a nonclustered index. The Argument column contains the name of the index being used. If the Argument column contains the ORDERED clause, the query processor has determined that the rows must be returned in the order in which the index has sorted them—it will vertically traverse the index's balanced tree starting at the root and ending at the leaf level, and continue by following the linked list forming the index's leaf level if a range of keys is required. If the ORDERED clause is not present, the storage engine searches the index in the optimal way, optionally using the Index Allocation Map (IAM) pages (which does not guarantee that the output will be sorted). Allowing the output to retain its ordering may be less efficient than producing unsorted output.

 The *bookmark lookup* uses a bookmark (row ID or clustering key) to look up the corresponding row in the table or clustered index.

 The *index scan* or *clustered index scan* retrieves all rows from the index specified in the Argument column. If the Argument column contains the ORDERED clause, the query processor has determined that the rows will be returned in the order in which the index has sorted them—it will horizontally traverse the index's leaf level following the linked list. If the ORDERED clause is not present, the storage engine will search the index in the optimal way, optionally using IAM pages (which does not guarantee that the output will be sorted).

Join Strategies

SQL Server 2000 supports three kinds of join algorithms: nested loops, merges, and hashes.

 Nested loops perform a search on the inner table for each row of the outer table, typically using an index on the inner table. SQL Server decides, based on anticipated costs, whether to sort the input from the outer table in order to improve efficiency of the searches on the index over the input from the inner table. The inner input is usually the smaller table.

 Merge performs a merge join between the two inputs. The merge join operator requires two inputs sorted on their respective columns, possibly by inserting explicit sort operations into the query plan. A merge join is particularly effective if explicit sorting is not required, such as when both inputs have a clustered index on the join column or when a previous operation in the plan already performed a sort.

 The *hash match* physical operator builds a hash table by computing a hash value for each row from its build input, which is usually the smaller input. Then, for each probe row (as applicable), it computes a hash value using the same hash function and looks in the hash table for matches.

The hash algorithm is usually used for joins when no useful indexes exist on the inputs. If multiple joins use the same join column, these operations are grouped into a hash team. The hash algorithm can also be used for the DISTINCT or aggregate operators; it uses the input to build the hash table (removing duplicates and computing any aggregate expressions). When the hash table is built, the table is scanned, and all entries are output. The hash algorithm can be also used for the UNION operator. It uses the first input to build the hash table (removing duplicates) and the second input (which must have no duplicates) to probe the hash table, returning all rows that have no matches, then scan the hash table and return all entries to produce the final result set to the calling program.

Miscellaneous

 Filter scans the input, returning only those rows that satisfy the filter expression that appears in the Argument column.

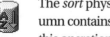 The *sort* physical operator sorts all incoming rows. The Argument column contains a DISTINCT ORDER BY:() predicate if duplicates are removed by this operation, or an ORDER BY:() predicate with a comma-separated list of the columns being sorted. The columns are prefixed with the value "ASC" if the columns are sorted in ascending order, or the value "DESC" if the columns are sorted in descending order.

 Compute scalar evaluates an expression to produce a computed scalar value, which may be returned to the user or referenced elsewhere in the query, such as in a filter predicate or join predicate.

Stream aggregate optionally groups rows by a set of columns and calculates one or more aggregate expressions returned by the query or referenced elsewhere within the query. This operator requires an input that is ordered by the columns within its groups. If the stream aggregate operator groups by columns, a GROUP BY:() predicate and the list of columns appear in the Argument column. If the stream aggregate operator computes any aggregate expressions, a list of them will appear in the Defined Values column of the output from the SHOWPLAN_ALL statement, or the Argument column of the graphical execution plan.

 Table spool scans the input and places a copy of each row in a hidden spool table (stored in the tempdb database and existing only for the lifetime of the query).

DBCC

The Database Consistency Check (DBCC) commands have been around since early versions of SQL Server. However, various specific commands, such as DBCC SHOWCONTIG and DBCC OPENTRAN showed themselves only with the 6.x releases.

DBCC SHOWCONTIG is one of the most useful of the DBCC commands when you are troubleshooting performance issues. Indeed, you are expected to know this command for the MCDBA exams. Over time, a table can get seriously fragmented due to large numbers of inserts and deletes. In a worst-case scenario, you could have only one row taking up an entire eight-page extent. DBCC SHOWCONTIG is the diagnostic tool that you can use to determine how badly fragmented a table is.

One DBCC command that can solve a major problem for you is DBCC OPENTRAN. This command tells you which spid (system process ID) has the longest-running open transaction. If you run it several times and the same spid keeps showing up, then you probably have a long-running transaction.

From the Trenches

During load testing, the transaction log was filling up. As well, a number of users were being blocked. By running DBCC OPENTRAN in a continuous loop every five seconds, the spid that was causing the problem was revealed. Then, sp_who was used to figure out who was causing it, and the problem was narrowed down quickly.

System Stored Procedures

Most DBAs appreciate GUI tools, but some still like to get down to the bare metal and send queries off to SQL Server to determine the source of performance problems. You have already seen examples of bare-metal troubleshooting in the discussion of DBCC. System stored procedures are in the same vein.

You can begin by using sp_who or sp_who2 to determine who is logged onto the system and what applications they are using to connect to SQL Server. Since sp_who2 looks better than sp_who because it presents the information in a nicer format and can identify who is blocking whom. However, it does create a temporary table that can give you some locking problems in tempdb in versions of SQL Server prior to 7.0. Similar problems have been observed with the GUI in Enterprise Manager.

After you know who is on the system, you can drill down to find out which locks they have by using sp_lock. This procedure will give you only the object IDs—not the names. You'll have to use the built-in function OBJECT_NAME() to get the name of the object. These locks are fleeting in normal circumstances, but if the same locks are staying up for extended periods of time, you have just identified a target.

One of the many reasons that a query may be slow is because it has a lot of data to read. What you are interested in is how much space and how many rows a table has. You can get the number of rows by selecting COUNT(*), which can take a while to come back. Alternatively, you can execute sp_spaceused, which will give you not only the row count but also the amount of space the table is taking on disk. This information is kept in *sysindexes* and is automatically updated.

> **NOTE** *The sysindexes information is not always fully synchronized with the exact current data in the table, so it is good to use it when a rough estimate is needed. However, the* @updateusage *parameter of* sp_spaceused *forces synchronization as does* DBCC UPDATEUSAGE.

If you want to know how much data is in each table, you can use sp_MSForEachTable to execute sp_spaceused for every user table in your database. (The sp_MSForEachTable system stored procedure is discussed in Chapter 17.) See Listing C-1.

Listing C-1: Using sp_MSForEachTable

```
sp_MSForEachTable 'exec sp_spaceused "?"'
```

The question mark in Listing C-1 is a placeholder for the table name.

SET Options

The most useful of the SET options, with respect to performance troubleshooting, are the following:

- STATISTICS IO

- STATISTICS TIME

- SHOWPLAN_TEXT or SHOWPLAN_ALL

- STATISTICS PROFILE

You can turn them on as shown in Listing C-2.

Listing C-2: Using the SET Option

```
SET <option> ON
```

You can also turn on or off the options SHOWPLAN_TEXT, STATISTICS IO, and STATISTICS TIME in Query Analyzer's Current Connection Properties dialog, which is accessible from the Query menu.

Turn on STATISTICS IO while you are developing stored procedures as a means of quality control. You can see, at the end of each SELECT, how many scans you generated and how many pages were hit. *Scans* are the number of passes the optimizer had to make through the table or index. If you run STATISTICS IO with the before and after versions of your code, you can compare to see how much of an improvement you were able to make to the query.

Use STATISTICS TIME in much the same way. It will tell you the duration of each individual step in the procedure.

SHOWPLAN_TEXT and SHOWPLAN_ALL provide a textual execution plan. The SHOWPLAN_ALL option provides more detailed information than SHOWPLAN_TEXT. If any of these options is turned on, you get an estimated execution plan; the query itself is *not* executed.

STATISTICS PROFILE provides detailed information of the actual execution plan that was used to execute the query, unlike SHOWPLAN_ALL. The query itself is executed and the execution plan is provided when the query finishes.

Methodology

To analyze performance issues, be prepared to ask a lot of questions. Here is a list of questions to which you should get definitive answers:

- Is it a SQL Server problem?

- Which query is slow?

- Is the query blocked or deadlocked?

- What objects does the query use?

- Are all objects actually being used?

- How does the optimizer access the objects?

- How much data is being accessed?

- Will an index help or hinder?

- Are loops and cursors necessary?

To help in your troubleshooting quest, you should also perform load and volume testing. This will help reveal problems that may otherwise go undetected. This topic will be discussed at the end of this section.

Is It a SQL Server Problem?

Quite often, the performance problem is not related to SQL Server at all, but rather, the issue is the network. On one project, the LAN was a 16 Mbps token ring, which was adequate for the task. However, there was a remote site where the link was a mere 128 Kbps. Trying to synchronize large, replicated tables through that line was a major hassle. System Monitor can be used to show you the throughput.

At the very least, you need to know that the server is on speaking terms with the rest of the world. Use the `ping` utility to determine whether TCP/IP communication is possible between your workstation and the server. If it is, check the transit time. If this number is over 100 ms, then it appears that the network may be slow. You can then follow up with `tracert` to find out where the bottleneck is. At that point, you can pass it off to the network group, unless, of course, you're also the network group.

If you cannot communicate at all with the server, then there is a network problem. Rebooting, checking connections, etcetera, may seem trite, but they are essential. Try accessing the server from another machine; if it is okay, the problem is your machine or the line connecting it to the network. (One DBA moved his foot, only to disconnect his token-ring cable. He didn't feel a thing.)

Not all communication problems are directly network-related. Sometimes, the problem is due to configuration of the client machine. For example, your machine may be using the wrong TCP/IP port number, default gateway, or subnet mask.

The preceding discussion is not so much related to slow query performance but, rather, to *no* query performance.

From the Trenches

Performance Monitor has helped to prove that a problem was not due to SQL Server but to a vendor package that was talking to SQL Server. The vendor tried to blame the network, so the network guys were brought in, and they proved there was nothing wrong with the network. The vendor then tried to blame SQL Server. Performance Monitor was fired up, and it recorded various counters throughout the night. In the morning, it was shown that the Working Set for their application shot up and stayed up. The vendor reluctantly fixed the problem.

More from the Trenches

Here's another war story that proves the usefulness of System Monitor but also suggests how it should be used. The system administrator was getting complaints about a slow server. He looked around, and nothing stood out as the culprit. He started Performance Monitor at the server, and all was well and stayed well while he was there. He then tried monitoring it from an adjacent machine. After about 15 minutes, the CPU usage went to 100 percent. He looked across and saw the newfangled screen saver kick into gear. Moving the mouse on the server stopped the screen saver, and the CPU usage went back down. Needless to say, the screen saver was removed. This does show, however, that remote—not local—monitoring of a server can be the only way to determine the source a performance issue.

System Monitor can, of course, be used to determine whether the problem *is* SQL Server–related.

Which Query Is Slow?

You can take either the shotgun or the stiletto approach to determining which is the slow query. Which approach you take depends upon the situation. If you are interested in overall throughput and want to sniff out the slow queries of all that are being fired at SQL Server, then the shotgun is your weapon of choice. If, however, a user has called you with a specific response-time problem—"It's slow when I click on this."—then the stiletto is your best bet. Now, please don't go using these weapons on your users; this is only a metaphor!

In both cases, you are using the Profiler to look at each piece of SQL coming down the (named) pipe. The shotgun vs. stiletto approach comes down to how you customize your filter.

In the shotgun approach, you are not filtering out much in the way of specific users. What you may choose to do is filter just on a specific application. You want to look at all users and all of the SQL they send you. You also want to flag long-running queries. To cut down on the amount of data you record, you may wish to filter on Duration, searching only for those queries that take more than a few seconds to run.

In the stiletto approach, you have just the one user who is having trouble. You filter on user ID and maybe even host name. To narrow down your search even more, don't turn on the trace until the user is ready to click on that one button that causes the problem. Now turn on the trace and capture the little bit of relevant SQL. You can still study what the Profiler has to say about it, paying close attention to Duration.

Is the Query Blocked or Deadlocked?

The problem could very well be that your query is fine but that another query is blocking yours, forcing yours to spin its wheels until the other one completes. For this reason, the stiletto approach may not necessarily give you sufficient clues as to who is the real villain. Running your query in a quiescent (don't you just love that word?) system can prove that the query runs fine on its own but that it does not run well when others are running concurrently.

At this point, you need to determine what else is running and whether your query is being blocked. For those of you who are not mouse-challenged, SQL Enterprise Manager can show you what's going on at a glance if you go to Management ➤ Current Activity ➤ Process Info. This will tell you who is blocking whom. If you don't mind the keystrokes, use sp_who2.

You can also use a modified shotgun approach with the Profiler by narrowing your window—when you turn the Profiler on and off. Hopefully, you will have captured a list of all possible suspects.

Now go to Management ➤ Current Activity ➤ Locks / Process ID in Enterprise Manager to find out what objects are being locked. You can also use `sp_lock` to get object IDs of locked objects.

> **NOTE**   *In SQL Server 7.0 only, to detect deadlocks, use System Monitor and select all instances for the Number of Deadlocks/sec counter of the SQL Server:Locks object. If this goes greater than zero, you have a problem. The Profiler also allows you to diagnose deadlocks, and here, too, the wizard earns its keep. This time, select "Identify the cause of a deadlock" from the drop-down menu. The Books Online give you the details on how to diagnose deadlocks using this tool.*

What Objects Does the Query Use?

If you are troubleshooting stored procedures, you should have the source code available to you. Failing that, you can have SQL Enterprise Manager generate the script from *syscomments*, provided that the procedure was not created with the `WITH ENCRYPTION` option. Once you have the code, you can browse through it to find out what objects are being used.

A more streamlined means of getting the same information is through the use of the system stored procedure `sp_depends`. It reports on which objects the procedure uses and which objects use the procedure. The same thing can be done through Enterprise Manager by right-clicking on the procedure and selecting All Tasks ➤ Display Dependencies.

Are All Objects Actually Being Used?

Don't laugh. Sometimes people start building queries with the intention of bringing back all kinds of data. In the end, they only need a subset of what they thought they needed, but they leave the query as is. After all, they have deadlines to meet. Meanwhile, the database accumulates more data and the query gradually slows down.

From the Trenches

This one comes from a large international investment bank. The month-to-date profit and loss report took an hour and fifteen minutes to run by the end of the month. SQL Server 4.2B was being used on an OS/2 platform. One of the big features was a nine-table join, many of which were left joins. Picking through the query, you could see that many of the tables were not even being used in the query. The query was whittled down to just a few tables, the indexing was adjusted slightly, and it ran in two minutes. The night operator was shocked that it ran in so little time.

Don't limit your search to just tables or views. Check to see that every column and every row you are sending back to the client is actually needed. This will cut down on needless network traffic as well as unnecessary client processing. In a high-volume OLTP environment, this will make a difference. Such things as SELECT * are obvious suspects.

Another thing to be alert for is the "one proc does it all" mentality. Although several users require different columns, the lazy coder makes just one procedure, and a number of users call it and throw away any columns or rows they don't need.

How Does the Optimizer Access the Objects?

The Query Analyzer is the tool to use here. It gives you a graphical depiction of the indexes, together with the join strategies it is using for each part of the query. Obviously, table scans are the big resource-wasters. If you let the mouse hover over each icon, you can see the number of rows used by each step. Even though a table scan is not being used, you can still see large numbers of rows being accessed in some cases.

How Much Data Is Being Accessed?

You can use the Profiler to look at total number of reads and writes for each line of SQL. It does not, however, tell you how much I/O took place on any specific table. For this, you will need to turn on STATISTICS IO or use the Query Analyzer to look at the rows touched in each step. The thickness of the arrow determines where the greater amount of data is being accessed.

Will an Index Help or Hinder?

Once you have determined that you are accessing a lot of data, you can look at indexing as a potential solution. First, you have to see if your query is using an index. If it is not, you have to determine whether adding an index will help or hinder your application. Notice we said "application," not "query." Adding an index may make one query work well but insert and update procedures may begin to slow.

Perhaps how you have a table indexed is the problem. Sometimes, changing the order of the columns in a multicolumn, clustered index can take a query from many minutes down to a few seconds. Before you make the indexing decision, you have to find out how the table is to be used. Gut feel is not sufficient, although for experienced DBAs it often leads in the right direction.

There are times when indexing is more art than science. Also, trying to keep the big picture in your head can often be impossibly challenging. Enter, the Index Tuning Wizard (ITW). As stated previously, you have to know how the table is to be accessed before you can make an informed decision about indexing. The most complete way of doing this is to look at all of the SQL your server is going to receive, and then analyze that to come up with a strategy. Don't forget that every stored procedure called would have to be dissected as well. Sound intimidating?

The Index Tuning Wizard can take a script file or a trace file and analyze it to determine the most frequently used queries and assess each stored procedure call. In the end, it makes a recommendation based on the load you gave it and can even build the indexes for you at that time or schedule that for later.

The ITW examines the workload and can recommend dropping existing indexes and creating new ones. It can also recommend creating indexed views, and the views themselves. The analysis process is purely cost-based. In fact, it uses the query optimizer's cost-based analysis. It is important to provide the ITW with a workload that includes a set of queries that adequately represent the activity in your database. If the workload is not representative, the index recommendations may not be adequate for your database.

You can specify whether you want the ITW to perform a fast, medium, or thorough analysis. A thorough analysis takes longer and may stress your server harder, but it can come up with a more efficient combination of indexes than the faster options will provide.

You can limit the number of queries that will be sampled from the workload file, the total size that the recommended indexes will consume, and also the number of maximum columns in composite indexes.

If certain tables currently do not contain the anticipated number of rows, but other tables do, you can manually specify the projected number of rows for each table. This feature is useful when you build a small sample database and you want to tune it before you implement your larger-scale production database. Keep in mind that the tables in the sample database should have a reasonable size (several percent of the production database—usually thousands of rows per table), otherwise the scaled data-distribution histograms may be inaccurate, and the set of recommended indexes for the sample database may be inefficient for the production database.

The ITW provides several cost analysis reports both on the current configuration of indexes and on the recommended configuration of indexes. You can choose to apply the changes immediately, schedule them for later creation, or save them as an SQL script file, which you can later modify and run manually.

Use common sense when you index. Analyze the need for the index together with the distribution of the data that you have. Putting an index on gender, where the only values could be *M* or *F*, gives you no payback and could hinder your update performance. Also, putting an index on just about every column will slow down updates.

From the Trenches

One DBA encountered slow insert performance on a table and discovered that someone had put 26 indexes on the table!

Are Loops and Cursors Necessary?

Do everything in your power to avoid cursor usage. Have someone prove to you that there is absolutely no way to do it at set level, or that by using cursors you can somehow get better performance over a standard SQL solution. There are many Usenet newsgroups where you can post a plea for help and somebody will assist you. The bulk of this book has shown you set-level solutions to avoid cursor usage. Also, check out Kalen Delaney's book to understand the inner workings of SQL Server and Joe Celko's books to maximize the power of set-level SQL. These are listed in Appendix G.

Volume and Load Testing

The query is not finished unless it has been tested with a representative volume of data. All tables must have a sufficient number of rows to represent what will happen in production. This type of testing is known as *volume testing*. Having just a few rows in each table does not give you any idea of how things will run in production. A table scan may be okay in development, but that same table scan in a billion-row table can be a showstopper.

Just because you have lots of data in your test database, it does not necessarily mean that they have real "business meaning." For example, if the last names you have put into the Customers table are only Smith or Jones, you can imagine how a query will run on a last name search. This will make you troubleshoot a query that is not necessarily bad. Similarly, putting in only one order per customer is not necessarily realistic; your query to bring up all of the pending orders for a customer may be unusually fast in test, but slow in production. In other words, the *distribution* of the data is just as important as the *amount* of data.

Load testing tests how the application will behave when you have a representative number of users firing off transactions at the database. This is where you are likely to detect any deadlocks. Also, the locks thrown up by one query may influence another query that normally runs well on its own. Load testing will expose this type of problem.

APPENDIX D

Ownership Chains

THE DISCUSSION ABOUT ownership chains is separated into an appendix of its own for two main reasons. First, this book is not focused on security issues, and second, the discussion about ownership chains is relevant to all of the following object types, each of which is discussed separately in this book: views, stored procedures, triggers, and user-defined functions. The term *object* will be used to refer to each of these object types. The term *action* will be used to replace the type of action, which could be any SELECT, INSERT, UPDATE, DELETE, or EXECUTE (of stored procedures).

Granting Permissions

Views and stored procedures are often used as security mechanisms. You can grant action permissions on an object to a database user or a role without granting explicit permissions on the underlying objects that are referenced by that object. This way, the calling user is allowed to issue the action on the top-level object he or she was granted permissions for without having permissions to issue actions against the underlying objects directly.

This can be better explained with an example. Suppose you have a stored procedure called dbo.Proc1, which performs an INSERT operation into a table called dbo.Table1 and a SELECT operation from a view called dbo.View1. View1 in turn, performs a JOIN operation between the tables dbo.Table2 and dbo.Table3. The user—user1—is granted EXECUTE permissions on Proc1 and can execute the stored procedure even though user1 wasn't granted explicit permissions on the underlying objects. Figure D-1 shows a graphical representation of the participating objects.

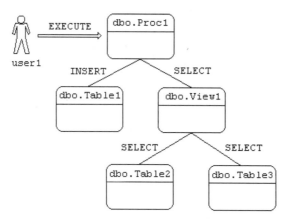

Figure D-1: Unbroken ownership chain

Guidelines for Granting Permissions

The calling user does not need explicit permissions on the underlying objects if all of the following conditions are met:

- The objects in the chain are owned by the same owner.

- Only DML statements are used or other stored procedures are called.

- Dynamic execution is not used.

- The calling database user's login is mapped to a user in another database if objects in that other database are referenced.

Each of these points are discussed in the following sections.

Ownership of Objects in the Chain

In Figure D-1, all of the objects in the chain are owned by the same owner, dbo, (which stands for the *database owner*), meaning that it is an *unbroken ownership chain*, and so you do not need to grant the user explicit permissions on the under-lying objects. However, if there are objects in the chain that are owned by a different owner than the owner of the top-level object, you have a *broken ownership chain*, and the calling user needs to be granted explicit permissions on those objects to successfully perform the desired action.

For example, suppose user2 is the owner of Table1 and user3 is the owner of Table2. user1 would need to be granted explicit INSERT permissions on user2.Table1 and SELECT permissions on user3.Table2 in order to successfully execute the stored procedure dbo.Proc1. Figure D-2 reflects the new chain.

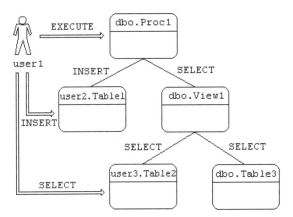

Figure D-2: Broken ownership chain

It will make your life a lot easier if you make sure the same owner owns all of the objects in the chain, and the most natural owner would be, of course, dbo.

Use of Statements in Stored Procedures

The calling user does not need explicit permissions on the underlying objects if only DML statements are used (SELECT, INSERT, UPDATE, or DELETE), or if another stored procedure is called using the EXECUTE statement. In the case of the latter, this applies only to using the EXECUTE statement to call another stored procedure, and not for dynamic execution.

If other types of statements are issued within any of the objects in the chain, the calling user needs to be granted explicit permissions to issue those statements. For example, if your stored procedure, Proc1, issues a CREATE TABLE statement, user1 needs to be granted CREATE TABLE permissions, because this is a DDL (not DML) statement.

Dynamic Execution

If dynamic execution is used in any of the objects in the chain, the calling user needs to be granted explicit permissions for the action performed dynamically with the EXECUTE statement. This limitation applies to the use of the EXECUTE statement for dynamic execution and not for calling a stored procedure.

For example, suppose one of the objects in the chain, be it a stored procedure or a trigger, issues the statements shown in Listing D-1:

Listing D-1: Using Dynamic Execution

```
DECLARE @cmd AS varchar(100)
SET @cmd = 'DELETE FROM T1'
EXECUTE (@cmd)
```

In such a case, the calling user needs to be granted explicit DELETE permissions on T1.

Object References

If one of the objects in the chain references an object in another database, the login that is mapped to the calling database user has to be mapped to a user in the other database. For example, suppose you have a stored procedure called dbo.Proc1 in a database called db1. Proc1 calls a stored procedure called dbo.Proc2, which is stored in a database called db2. You have a login called user1, which is mapped to the database user user1 in the db1 database. Granting the db1 database user— user1—EXECUTE permissions on Proc1 is not sufficient. You also have to map user1 to a database user in the db2 database.

Figure D-3 shows the ownership chain and the permissions and mappings that need to be set in order for user1 to execute Proc1 successfully.

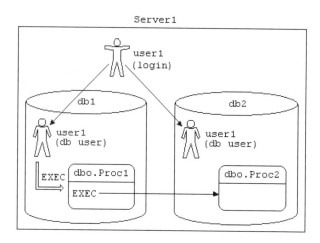

Figure D-3: Referencing objects in other databases

pubs and Northwind Database Schemas

NORTHWIND AND PUBS ARE sample databases that come with the SQL Server installation. Northwind contains the sales data for a fictitious company called Northwind Traders, which imports and exports specialty food from around the world, and pubs contains data for a book publishing company. Northwind and pubs are used in the examples presented in the online documentation content and in many examples in this book.

The schema for the pubs database is presented in Figure E-1, and the schema for the Northwind database is presented in Figure E-2. You can consult them when you want to write queries or to understand better those queries that refer to these databases.

If you've made any changes in the sample databases and want to re-create them from scratch, their creation and population scripts are available in the Install directory of your SQL Server installation. The instpubs.sql and instnwnd.sql scripts create and populate the pubs and the Northwind databases, respectively.

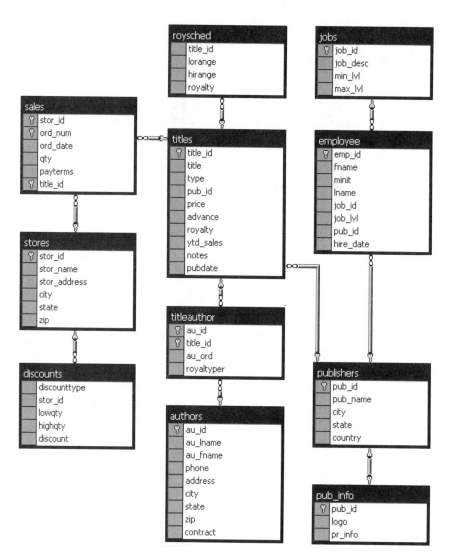

Figure E-1: pubs sample database schema

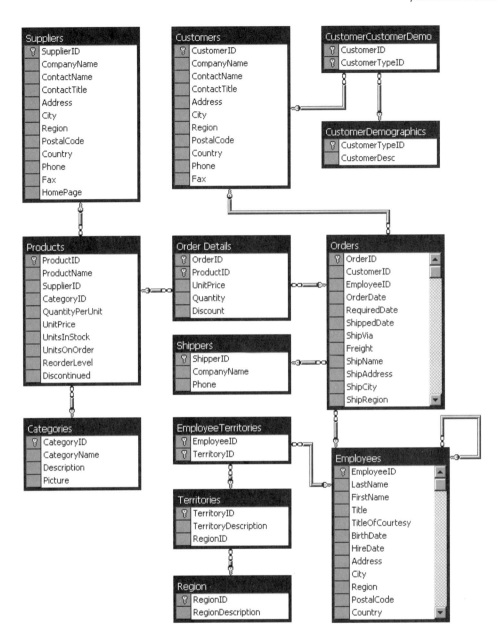

Figure E-2: Northwind sample database schema

Dynamically Creating Triggers for Cascade Actions

IN CHAPTER 14, YOU LEARNED how to maintain cascade actions with various mechanisms. You've seen a flow diagram that shows which triggers you need to create in order to maintain referential integrity and how to cascade actions with triggers. (Triggers are covered in Chapter 10.) You also learned how to implement those triggers. In this appendix, you will learn how to encapsulate the logic of the flow diagram in stored procedures that create the relevant set of triggers for you. (Stored procedures are covered in Chapter 9.)

Each stored procedure creates a different trigger, and there is one stored procedure that encapsulates the logic and decides which stored procedures to call. The idea should sound familiar:

One ring to rule them all... (J.R.R. Tolkien, *The Lord of the Rings*)

The four stored procedures that actually create the triggers accept the names of the tables and columns involved as parameters. The encapsulating stored procedure also accepts the tables' column names, together with an indication of whether to support DELETE CASCADE and/or UPDATE CASCADE. According to the values of the last two parameters, the stored procedure decides which of the other four stored procedures to call. The stored procedures construct the CREATE TRIGGER statement in a varchar variable and execute it using the EXECUTE command dynamically. (Dynamic execution was covered in Chapter 9.) These procedures are implemented as system stored procedures in the master database, which enables you to use them from any user database.

Creating a Delete Cascade Trigger on the Primary (Referenced) Table

The sp_RICascadeDelete stored procedure creates one type of trigger for a relationship between two tables and another type for a single-table relationship. It distinguishes between the two by comparing the parameter @prmtbl to the parameter @sectbl.

Also, in a single-table relationship, the trigger will not work properly if recursive triggers are not enabled in the database. In this case, the stored procedure will print a warning and will also print the sp_dboption statement that needs to be run in order to enable recursive triggers in the database. The script shown in Listing F-1 creates the sp_RICascadeDelete stored procedure.

Listing F-1: Creation Script for the sp_RICascadeDelete Stored Procedure

```
CREATE PROC sp_RICascadeDelete
  @prmtbl sysname, -- Primary (referenced) table
  @sectbl sysname, -- Secondary (referencing) table
  @prmcol sysname, -- Primary (referenced) column
  @seccol sysname  -- Secondary (referencing) column
AS

DECLARE @ENTER AS char(1)
DECLARE @cmd   AS varchar(8000)

SET @ENTER = CHAR(13) + CHAR(10)

IF @prmtbl != @sectbl
BEGIN
  SET @cmd =
  'CREATE TRIGGER trg_d_' + @prmtbl + '_on_delete_cascade ON ' +
    @prmtbl + ' FOR DELETE' + @ENTER +
  'AS' + @ENTER +
  @ENTER +
  'IF @@ROWCOUNT = 0' + @ENTER +
  '  RETURN' + @ENTER +
  @ENTER +
  'DELETE FROM ' + @sectbl + @ENTER +
  'FROM ' + @ENTER +
  '    ' + @sectbl + ' AS S' + @ENTER +
  '  JOIN' + @ENTER +
  '    deleted AS D ON S.' + @seccol + ' = D.' + @prmcol + @ENTER
END
```

```
ELSE
BEGIN
  SET @cmd =
  'CREATE TRIGGER trg_d_' + @prmtbl + '_on_delete_cascade ON ' +
    @prmtbl + ' FOR DELETE' + @ENTER +
  'AS' + @ENTER +
  @ENTER +
  'IF EXISTS(SELECT *' + @ENTER +
  '          FROM ' + @ENTER +
  '              ' + @prmtbl + ' AS S' + @ENTER +
  '          JOIN' + @ENTER +
  '              deleted AS D ON S.' + @seccol + ' = D.' + @prmcol +')' + @ENTER +
  '  DELETE FROM ' + @sectbl + @ENTER +
  '  FROM' + @ENTER +
  '      ' + @sectbl + ' AS S' + @ENTER +
  '    JOIN' + @ENTER +
  '      deleted AS D ON S.' + @seccol + ' = D.' + @prmcol + @ENTER

  PRINT 'Recursive triggers should be turned on.' + @ENTER +
        'Use EXEC sp_dboption ' + DB_NAME() +
        ', ''recursive triggers'', ''true'''+ @ENTER
END

EXECUTE(@cmd)
GO
```

Creating a Prevent Delete Trigger on the Primary (Referenced) Table

The sp_RIPreventDelete stored procedure creates the trigger that prevents illegal DELETEs from the primary table. The script shown in Listing F-2 creates the sp_RIPreventDelete stored procedure.

Listing F-2: Creation Script for the sp_RIPreventDelete Stored Procedure

```
CREATE PROC sp_RIPreventDelete
  @prmtbl sysname, -- Primary (referenced) table
  @sectbl sysname, -- Secondary (referencing) table
  @prmcol sysname, -- Primary (referenced) column
  @seccol sysname  -- Secondary (referencing) column
```

```
AS

DECLARE @ENTER AS char(1)
DECLARE @cmd   AS varchar(8000)

SET @ENTER = CHAR(13) + CHAR(10)

SET @cmd =
'CREATE TRIGGER trg_d_' + @prmtbl + '_prevent_delete ON ' +
   @prmtbl + ' FOR DELETE' + @ENTER +
'AS' + @ENTER +
@ENTER +
'IF @@ROWCOUNT = 0' + @ENTER +
'   RETURN' + @ENTER +
@ENTER +
'IF EXISTS(SELECT *' + @ENTER +
'          FROM ' + @ENTER +
'             ' + @sectbl + ' AS S' + @ENTER +
'          JOIN' + @ENTER +
'             deleted AS D ON S.' + @seccol + ' = D.' + @prmcol + ')' + @ENTER +
'BEGIN' + @ENTER +
'   RAISERROR(''You are trying to delete rows from ' + @prmtbl +
'             ' that have related rows in ' + @sectbl +
'             '.TRANSACTION rolled back.'', 10, 1)' + @ENTER +
'   ROLLBACK TRANSACTION' + @ENTER +
'END'

EXECUTE(@cmd)
GO
```

Creating an Update Cascade Trigger on the Primary (Referenced) Table

As you learned in Chapter 14, without adding a non-changing surrogate key, the trigger can only support single-row updates to the primary table. The sp_RICascadeUpdate stored procedure not only creates such a trigger, but it also prints the commands to add a surrogate key and alter the trigger so that it will support multirow actions. The script shown in Listing F-3 creates the sp_RICascadeUpdate stored procedure.

Listing F-3: Creation Script for the sp_RICascadeUpdate Stored Procedure

```
CREATE PROC sp_RICascadeUpdate
  @prmtbl sysname, -- Primary (referenced) table
  @sectbl sysname, -- Secondary (referencing) table
  @prmcol sysname, -- Primary (referenced) column
  @seccol sysname  -- Secondary (referencing) column
AS

DECLARE @ENTER AS char(1)
DECLARE @cmd   AS varchar(8000)

SET @ENTER = CHAR(13) + CHAR(10)

SET @cmd =
'CREATE TRIGGER trg_u_' + @prmtbl + '_on_update_cascade ON ' +
  @prmtbl + ' FOR UPDATE' + @ENTER +
'AS' + @ENTER +
@ENTER +
'DECLARE @numrows AS int' + @ENTER +
'SET @numrows = @@ROWCOUNT' + @ENTER +
'IF UPDATE(' + @prmcol + ')' + @ENTER +
'  IF @numrows = 1' + @ENTER +
'    UPDATE ' + @sectbl + @ENTER +
'      SET ' + @seccol + ' = (SELECT ' + @prmcol + ' FROM inserted)' + @ENTER +
'    FROM ' + @ENTER +
'        ' + @sectbl + ' AS S' + @ENTER +
'      JOIN' + @ENTER +
'        deleted AS D ON S.' + @seccol + ' = D.' + @prmcol + @ENTER +
'  ELSE IF @numrows > 1' + @ENTER +
'  BEGIN' + @ENTER +
'    RAISERROR(''Updates to more than one row in ' + @prmtbl +
              ' are not allowed. TRANSACTION rolled back.'', 10, 1)' + @ENTER +
'    ROLLBACK TRANSACTION' + @ENTER +
'  END' + @ENTER

EXEC(@cmd)

PRINT 'Only single row updates are allowed to ' + @prmtbl + '.' + @ENTER +
      'To support multi-row updates add a surrogate key and alter the trigger:' +
@ENTER
```

```
PRINT 'ALTER TABLE ' + @prmtbl + @ENTER +
    '  ADD surrogate_key int NOT NULL IDENTITY(1,1)' + @ENTER +
    '      CONSTRAINT UNQ_' + @prmtbl + '_surrogate_key UNIQUE' + @ENTER +
    'GO' + @ENTER

PRINT 'ALTER TRIGGER trg_u_' + @prmtbl + '_on_update_cascade ON ' +
    @prmtbl + ' FOR UPDATE' + @ENTER +
    'AS' + @ENTER +
    @ENTER +
    'DECLARE @numrows AS int' + @ENTER +
    'SET @numrows = @@ROWCOUNT' + @ENTER +
    'IF UPDATE(surrogate_key)' + @ENTER +
    'BEGIN' + @ENTER +
    '  RAISERROR(''Updates to surrogate_key are not allowed. TRANSACTION rolled
back.'', 10, 1)' + @ENTER +
    '  ROLLBACK TRANSACTION' + @ENTER +
    'END' + @ENTER +
    'ELSE' + @ENTER +
    '  IF UPDATE(' + @prmcol + ') AND @numrows > 0' + @ENTER +
    '    UPDATE ' + @sectbl + @ENTER +
    '      SET ' + @seccol + ' = I.' + @prmcol + @ENTER +
    '    FROM ' + @ENTER +
    '        ' + @sectbl + ' AS S' + @ENTER +
    '      JOIN' + @ENTER +
    '        deleted AS D ON S.' + @seccol + ' = D.' + @prmcol + @ENTER +
    '      JOIN' + @ENTER +
    '        inserted AS I ON D.surrogate_key = I.surrogate_key' + @ENTER +
    'GO' + @ENTER
GO
```

Creating a Prevent Update Trigger
on the Primary (Referenced) Table

The sp_RIPreventUpdate stored procedure creates the trigger that prevents
illegal UPDATEs from the primary table. The script shown in Listing F-4 creates
the sp_RIPreventUpdate stored procedure.

Listing F-4: Creation Script for the sp_RIPreventUpdate Stored Procedure

```
CREATE PROC sp_RIPreventUpdate
   @prmtbl sysname, -- Primary (referenced) table
   @sectbl sysname, -- Secondary (referencing) table
   @prmcol sysname, -- Primary (referenced) column
   @seccol sysname  -- Secondary (referencing) column
AS

DECLARE @ENTER AS char(1)
DECLARE @cmd    AS varchar(8000)

SET @ENTER = CHAR(13) + CHAR(10)

SET @cmd =
'CREATE TRIGGER trg_d_' + @prmtbl + '_prevent_update ON ' +
   @prmtbl + ' FOR UPDATE' + @ENTER +
'AS' + @ENTER +
@ENTER +
'IF @@ROWCOUNT = 0' + @ENTER +
'  RETURN' + @ENTER +
@ENTER +
'IF EXISTS(SELECT *' + @ENTER +
'          FROM' + @ENTER +
'               ' + @sectbl + ' AS S' + @ENTER +
'            JOIN' + @ENTER +
'               deleted AS D ON S.' + @seccol + ' = D.' + @prmcol + ')' + @ENTER +
'BEGIN' + @ENTER +
'  RAISERROR(''You are trying to update rows in ' + @prmtbl +
'            ' that have related rows in ' + @sectbl +
'            '.TRANSACTION rolled back.'', 10, 1)' + @ENTER +
'  ROLLBACK TRANSACTION' + @ENTER +
'END'

EXECUTE(@cmd)
GO
```

Creating a Prevent Insert or Update Trigger on the Secondary (Referencing) Table

As with the `sp_RICascadeDelete` stored procedure, the `sp_RIPreventInsUpd` stored procedure should create a different trigger for a relationship between two tables and for a single-table relationship. It determines whether to create a trigger that handles a relationship between two tables or for a single-table relationship by comparing the parameter @prmtbl to the parameter @sectbl. The script shown in Listing F-5 creates the sp_RIPreventInsUpd stored procedure.

Listing F-5: Creation Script for the sp_RIPreventInsUpd Stored Procedure

```
CREATE PROC sp_RIPreventInsUpd
    @prmtbl sysname, -- Primary (referenced) table
    @sectbl sysname, -- Secondary (referencing) table
    @prmcol sysname, -- Primary (referenced) column
    @seccol sysname  -- Secondary (referencing) column
AS

DECLARE @ENTER AS char(1)
DECLARE @cmd    AS varchar(8000)

SET @ENTER = CHAR(13) + CHAR(10)

IF @prmtbl != @sectbl
BEGIN
SET @cmd =
    'CREATE TRIGGER trg_iu_' + @sectbl + '_prevent_insupd ON ' +
      @sectbl + ' FOR INSERT, UPDATE' + @ENTER +
    'AS' + @ENTER +
    @ENTER +
    'DECLARE @numrows int' + @ENTER +
    'SET @numrows = @@ROWCOUNT' + @ENTER +
    @ENTER +
'IF UPDATE(' + @seccol + ') AND @numrows > 0' + @ENTER +
    '  IF @numrows <> (SELECT' + @ENTER +
    '                        COUNT(*)' + @ENTER +
    '                      FROM' + @ENTER +
    '                        ' + @prmtbl + ' AS P' + @ENTER +
    '                      JOIN' + @ENTER +
    '                        inserted AS I ON P.' + @prmcol + ' = I.' + @seccol + ')' +
@ENTER +
    '  BEGIN' + @ENTER +
    '    RAISERROR(''Result rows in ' + @sectbl + ' are orphaned.
                TRANSACTION rolled back.'', 10, 1)' + @ENTER +
    '    ROLLBACK TRANSACTION' + @ENTER +
    '  END' + @ENTER
END
```

```
ELSE
BEGIN
SET @cmd =
  'CREATE TRIGGER trg_iu_' + @sectbl + '_prevent_insupd ON ' +
    @sectbl + ' FOR INSERT, UPDATE' + @ENTER +
  'AS' + @ENTER +
  @ENTER +
  'IF @@ROWCOUNT > 0 AND UPDATE(' + @seccol + ')' + @ENTER +
  'BEGIN' + @ENTER +
  '  DECLARE @numrows int'  + @ENTER +
  @ENTER +
  '  SELECT' + @ENTER +
  '    @numrows = COUNT(*)' + @ENTER +
  '  FROM' + @ENTER +
  '    inserted' + @ENTER +
  '  WHERE' + @ENTER +
  '    ' + @seccol + ' IS NOT NULL' + @ENTER +
  @ENTER +
  '  IF @numrows <> (SELECT' + @ENTER +
  '                    COUNT(*)' + @ENTER +
  '                  FROM' + @ENTER +
  '                    ' + @prmtbl + ' AS P' + @ENTER +
  '                  JOIN' + @ENTER +
  '                    inserted AS I ON P.' + @prmcol + ' = I.' + @seccol + ')' +
@ENTER +
  '  BEGIN' + @ENTER +
  '    RAISERROR(''Result rows in ' + @sectbl + ' are orphaned.
              TRANSACTION rolled back.'', 10, 1)' + @ENTER +
  '    ROLLBACK TRANSACTION' + @ENTER +
  '  END' + @ENTER +
  'END' + @ENTER
END

EXECUTE(@cmd)
GO
```

Encapsulating the Logic

The sp_CreateRelationship stored procedure encapsulates the logic and decides which of the previous stored procedures to call in order to create the right triggers based on the user's input. The script shown in Listing F-6 creates the sp_CreateRelationship stored procedure.

Listing F-6: Creation Script for the sp_CreateRelationship Stored Procedure

```
CREATE PROC sp_CreateRelationship
   @prmtbl sysname,          -- Primary (referenced) table
   @sectbl sysname,          -- Secondary (referencing) table
   @prmcol sysname,          -- Primary (referenced) column
   @seccol sysname,          -- Secondary (referencing) column,
   @deletecascade bit = 1, -- determines whether to support cascade delete
   @updatecascade bit = 1  -- determines whether to support cascade update
AS

DECLARE @ENTER AS char(1)
DECLARE @cmd   AS varchar(8000)

SET @ENTER = CHAR(13) + CHAR(10)

IF @deletecascade = 1
BEGIN
  PRINT 'Creating delete cascade trigger on ' + @prmtbl + '...' + @ENTER
  EXEC sp_RICascadeDelete
    @prmtbl = @prmtbl,
    @sectbl = @sectbl,
    @prmcol = @prmcol,
    @seccol = @seccol
END
ELSE
BEGIN
  PRINT 'Creating prevent delete trigger on ' + @prmtbl + '...' + @ENTER
  EXEC sp_RIPreventDelete
    @prmtbl = @prmtbl,
    @sectbl = @sectbl,
    @prmcol = @prmcol,
    @seccol = @seccol
END

IF @updatecascade = 1
BEGIN
  PRINT 'Creating update cascade trigger on ' + @prmtbl + '...' + @ENTER
  EXEC sp_RICascadeUpdate
    @prmtbl = @prmtbl,
    @sectbl = @sectbl,
    @prmcol = @prmcol,
    @seccol = @seccol
END
```

```
ELSE
BEGIN
  PRINT 'Creating prevent update trigger on ' + @prmtbl + '...' + @ENTER
  EXEC sp_RIPreventUpdate
    @prmtbl = @prmtbl,
    @sectbl = @sectbl,
    @prmcol = @prmcol,
    @seccol = @seccol
END

PRINT 'Creating prevent insert / update trigger on ' + @sectbl + '...' + @ENTER
EXEC sp_RIPreventInsUpd
  @prmtbl = @prmtbl,
  @sectbl = @sectbl,
  @prmcol = @prmcol,
  @seccol = @seccol
GO
```

Testing the sp_CreateRelationship Stored Procedure

To see how to test the sp_CreateRelationship stored procedure, run a test on the tables you worked with in Chapter 14. First, re-create and repopulate the Orders, OrderDetails, and Employees tables. Do not create foreign keys or triggers.

To create the set of triggers on the Orders and OrderDetails scenario, execute the script shown in Listing F-7.

Listing F-7: Using the sp_CreateRelationship Stored Procedure
to Create Cascading Triggers in a Two-Table Relationship Scenario

```
EXEC sp_CreateRelationship
  @prmtbl = Orders,
  @sectbl = OrderDetails,
  @prmcol = orderid,
  @seccol = orderid,
  @deletecascade = 1,
  @updatecascade = 1
```

The output should look like Listing F-8.

Listing F-8: Output from the sp_CreateRelationship Stored Procedure in a Two-Table Relationship Scenario

```
Creating delete cascade trigger on Orders...


Creating update cascade trigger on Orders...


Only single row updates are allowed to Orders.
To support multi-row updates add a surrogate key and alter the trigger:


ALTER TABLE Orders
  ADD surrogate_key int NOT NULL IDENTITY(1,1)
      CONSTRAINT UNQ_Orders_surrogate_key UNIQUE
GO


ALTER TRIGGER trg_u_Orders_on_update_cascade ON Orders FOR UPDATE
AS


DECLARE @numrows AS int
SET @numrows = @@ROWCOUNT
IF UPDATE(surrogate_key)
BEGIN
  RAISERROR('Updates to surrogate_key are not allowed.
            TRANSACTION rolled back.', 10, 1)
  ROLLBACK TRANSACTION
END
ELSE
  IF UPDATE(orderid) AND @numrows > 0
    UPDATE OrderDetails
      SET orderid = I.orderid
    FROM
       OrderDetails AS S
    JOIN
       deleted AS D ON S.orderid = D.orderid
    JOIN
       inserted AS I ON D.surrogate_key = I.surrogate_key
GO


Creating prevent insert / update trigger on OrderDetails...
```

To create the set of triggers on the Employees scenario, execute the script shown in Listing F-9.

Listing F-9: Using the sp_CreateRelationship Stored Procedure to Create Cascading Triggers in a Single-Table Relationship Scenario

```
EXEC sp_CreateRelationship
  @prmtbl = Employees,
  @sectbl = Employees,
  @prmcol = empid,
  @seccol = mgrid,
  @deletecascade = 1,
  @updatecascade = 1
```

The output should look like Listing F-10.

Listing F-10: Output From the sp_CreateRelationship Stored Procedure in a Single-Table Relationship Scenario

```
Creating delete cascade trigger on Employees...

Recursive triggers should be turned on.
Use EXEC sp_dboption testdb, 'recursive triggers', 'true'

Creating update cascade trigger on Employees...

Only single row updates are allowed to Employees.
To support multi-row updates add a surrogate key and alter the trigger:

ALTER TABLE Employees
  ADD surrogate_key int NOT NULL IDENTITY(1,1)
      CONSTRAINT UNQ_Employees_surrogate_key UNIQUE
GO

ALTER TRIGGER trg_u_Employees_on_update_cascade ON Employees FOR UPDATE
AS

DECLARE @numrows AS int
SET @numrows = @@ROWCOUNT
IF UPDATE(surrogate_key)
BEGIN
  RAISERROR('Updates to surrogate_key are not allowed.
            TRANSACTION rolled back.', 10, 1)
  ROLLBACK TRANSACTION
END
```

```
ELSE
  IF UPDATE(empid) AND @numrows > 0
    UPDATE Employees
      SET mgrid = I.empid
    FROM
       Employees AS S
     JOIN
       deleted   AS D ON S.mgrid = D.empid
     JOIN
       inserted  AS I ON D.surrogate_key = I.surrogate_key
GO
```

Creating prevent insert / update trigger on Employees...

References

Articles

SQL Server Magazine (http://www.sqlmag.com)

You can search *SQL Server Magazine*'s site by topic, author, or issue.
For T-SQL articles you can visit the following URL:
`http://www.sqlmag.com/Articles/Index.cfm?TopicID=796`

You can find Itzik's articles at the following URL:
`http://www.sqlmag.com/Articles/Index.cfm?AuthorID=679`

In this list you can find the following articles (current as of November 2000):

- "Dynamic Crosstab Queries" (November 2000)

- "Modifying Views with INSTEAD OF Triggers" (October 2000, co-authored with Kalen Delaney)

- "Finding the Lost Identity" (October 2000)

- "Short Circuit" (September 2000)

- "Querying Distributed Partitioned Views" (September 2000, co-authored with Kalen Delaney)

- "Distributed Partitioned Views" (August 2000, co-authored with Kalen Delaney)

- "Using T-SQL with Magic Squares" (August 2000)

- "Maintaining Hierarchies" (July 2000)

- "Using Joins to Modify Data" (July 2000)

- "SQL Server's Black Box" (April 2000)

- "Boost Performance with the Index Tuning Wizard" (April 2000)

- "Problem-Solving with SQL Profiler" (April 2000)

- "Trace that Event with SQL Server Profiler" (April 2000)

- "Advanced JOIN Techniques" (December 1999, co-authored with Kalen Delaney)

- "Maintaining Referential Integrity" (August 1999)

Kalen Delaney's articles are a *must* read! You can find them at the following URL: `http://www.sqlmag.com/Articles/Index.cfm?AuthorID=431`

SQL Server Professional (http://www.pinnaclepublishing.com/SQ)

You can search *SQL Server Professional's* site by topic, author, or issue.

For T-SQL articles, you can visit the following URL:
`http://www.pinnaclepublishing.com/SQ/SQMag.nsf/index/$searchForm!SearchView`

You can find Tom's articles at the following URL:
`http://www.pinnaclepublishing.com/SQ`

Click "World's Best Authors" and page through to Tom Moreau. Click Tom, and you'll get the current list of articles. In this list you can find the following articles (current as of September 2000):

- "Troubleshooting, Part 3: The Solutions" (November 2000)

- "Troubleshooting, Part 2: The Methodology" (October 2000)

- "Changing Attitudes" (September 2000)

- "Calling DTS Packages from SQL" (August 2000)

- "Troubleshooting, Part 1: The Tools" (July 2000)

- "Multi-threading in SQL" (July 2000)

- "How a SELECT Can Affect Your Transaction Log" (May 2000)

- "The Power of Derived Tables" (April 2000)

- "Tip: Multilingual Date Handling" (March 2000)

- "Pulling Out the Stops" (March 2000)

- "Tip: Scheduling Distribution in SQL Server 7.0" (March 2000)

- "Tip: Intuitive Sorting Using ROLLUP" (December 1999)

- "Tip: Database Owner Problem in SQL Server 7.0" (November 1999)

- "A Dialog on Moving Database Files in SQL Server 7.0" (October 1999)

- "Much Ado About Nothing" (July 1999)

- "Moving Database Files in SQL Server 7" (June 1999)

- "Transaction Logs" (May 1999)

- "Backup and Recovery in SQL Server 7.0" (April 1999)

- "Tip: What's a Month?" (November 1998)

- "Loading Dumps from One Database to Another" (September 1998)

- "Tip: Starting and Stopping the Server" (June 1998)

- "The Pleasures and Pitfalls of Left Joins" (December 1997)

White Papers

"Microsoft SQL Server Query Processor Internals and Architecture" by Hal Berenson and Kalen Delaney can be found at
`http://msdn.microsoft.com/library/backgrnd/html/sqlquerproc.htm`

SQL Server white papers can be found at the following URL:
`http://www.microsoft.com/sql/index.htm#W`
This Web site includes the following white papers and more:

- "Distributed Queries: OLE DB Connectivity"

- "Index Tuning Wizard"

- "Performance Tuning Guide"

- "Query Processor"

- "Storage Engine"

- "Storage Engine Capacity Planning Tips"

Books

Inside Microsoft SQL Server 2000 by Kalen Delaney (ISBN: 0735609985)
http://www.insidesqlserver.com

Instant SQL Programming by Joe Celko (ISBN: 1-874416-50-8)
http://www.celko.com

SQL for Smarties, second edition, by Joe Celko (ISBN: 1-55860-576-2)

Joe Celko's SQL Puzzles and Answers by Joe Celko (ISBN: 1-55860-453-7)

Data and Databases: Concepts in Practice by Joe Celko (ISBN: 1-55860-432-4)

The Art of Computer Programming: Fundamental Algorithms, vol. 1,
third edition, by Donald Ervin Knuth (ISBN: 0-20189-683-4)

The Art of Computer Programming: Seminumerical Algorithms, vol. 2,
third edition, by Donald Ervin Knuth (ISBN: 0-20189-684-2)

The Art of Computer Programming: Sorting and Searching, vol. 3,
second edition, by Donald Ervin Knuth (ISBN: 0-20189-685-0)

SQL Server : Common Problems, Tested Solutions by Neil Pike
(ISBN: 1-893115-81-X) You can find Neil's FAQ articles at
http://www.mssqlserver.com/faq

Index

The Story Behind Apress

APRESS IS AN INNOVATIVE PUBLISHING COMPANY devoted to meeting the needs of existing and potential programming professionals. Simply put, the "A" in Apress stands for the "author's press™." Our unique author-centric approach to publishing grew from conversations between Dan Appleman and Gary Cornell, authors of best-selling, highly regarded computer books. They wanted to create a publishing company that emphasized quality above all—a company whose books would be considered the best in their market.

To accomplish this goal, they knew it was necessary to attract the very best authors—established authors whose work is already highly regarded, and new authors who have real-world practical experience that professional software developers want in the books they buy. Dan and Gary's vision of an author-centric press has already attracted many leading software professionals—just look at the list of Apress titles on the following pages.

Would You Like
to Write for Apress?

APRESS IS RAPIDLY EXPANDING its publishing program. If you can write and refuse to compromise on the quality of your work, if you believe in doing more then rehashing existing documentation, and if you are looking for opportunities and rewards that go far beyond those offered by traditional publishing houses, we want to hear from you!

Consider these innovations that we offer every one of our authors:

- Top royalties with *no* hidden switch statements. For example, authors typically only receive half of their normal royalty rate on foreign sales. In contrast, Apress' royalty rate remains the same for both foreign and domestic sales.

- A mechanism for authors to obtain equity in Apress. Unlike the software industry, where stock options are essential to motivate and retain software professionals, the publishing industry has stuck to an outdated compensation model based on royalties alone. In the spirit of most software companies, Apress reserves a significant portion of its equity for authors.

- Serious treatment of the technical review process. Each Apress book has a technical reviewing team whose remuneration depends in part on the success of the book since they, too, receive a royalty.

Moreover, through a partnership with Springer-Verlag, one of the world's major publishing houses, Apress has significant venture capital behind it. Thus, Apress has the resources both to produce the highest quality books *and* to market them aggressively.

If you fit the model of the Apress author who can write a book that gives the "professional what he or she needs to know™," then please contact any one of our editorial directors, Gary Cornell (gary_cornell@apress.com), Dan Appleman (dan_appleman@apress.com), or Karen Watterson (karen_watterson@apress.com), for more information on how to become an Apress author.

Apress Titles

ISBN	LIST PRICE	AVAILABLE	AUTHOR	TITLE
1-893115-01-1	$39.95	Now	Appleman	Dan Appleman's Win32 API Puzzle Book and Tutorial for Visual Basic Programmers
1-893115-23-2	$29.95	Now	Appleman	How Computer Programming Works
1-893115-09-7	$24.95	Now	Baum	Dave Baum's Definitive Guide to LEGO MINDSTORMS
1-893115-84-4	$29.95	Now	Baum, Gasperi, Hempel, Villa	Extreme MINDSTORMS
1-893115-82-8	$59.95	Now	Ben-Gan/Moreau	Advanced Transact-SQL for SQL Server 2000
1-893115-14-3	$39.95	Winter 2000	Cornell/Jezak	Visual Basic Add-Ins and Wizards: Increasing Software Productivity
1-893115-85-2	$34.95	Winter 2000	Gilmore	A Programmer's Introduction to PHP 4.0
1-893115-17-8	$59.95	Now	Gross	A Programmer's Introduction to Windows DNA
1-893115-86-0	$34.95	Now	Gunnerson	A Programmer's Introduction to C#
1-893115-10-0	$34.95	Now	Holub	Taming Java Threads
1-893115-04-6	$34.95	Now	Hyman/Vaddadi	Mike and Phani's Essential C++ Techniques
1-893115-79-8	$49.95	Now	Kofler	Definitive Guide to Excel VBA
1-893115-75-5	$44.95	Now	Kurniawan	Internet Programming with VB
1-893115-19-4	$49.95	Now	Macdonald	Serious ADO: Universal Data Access with Visual Basic
1-893115-06-2	$39.95	Now	Marquis/Smith	A Visual Basic 6.0 Programmer's Toolkit
1-893115-22-4	$27.95	Now	McCarter	David McCarter's VB Tips and Techniques
1-893115-76-3	$49.95	Now	Morrison	C++ For VB Programmers
1-893115-80-1	$39.95	Now	Newmarch	A Programmer's Guide to Jini Technology
1-893115-81-X	$39.95	Now	Pike	SQL Server: Common Problems, Tested Solutions
1-893115-20-8	$34.95	Now	Rischpater	Wireless Web Development
1-893115-24-0	$49.95	Now	Sinclair	From Access to SQL Server
1-893115-16-X	$49.95	Now	Vaughn	ADO Examples and Best Practices

	LIST PRICE	AVAILABLE	AUTHOR	TITLE
	$44.95	Winter 2000	Wells	Code Centric: T-SQL Programming with Stored Procedures and Triggers
1-893115-05-4	$39.95	Winter 2000	Williamson	Writing Cross-Browser Dynamic HTML
1-893115-02-X	$49.95	Now	Zukowski	John Zukowski's Definitive Guide to Swing for Java 2
1-893115-78-X	$49.95	Now	Zukowski	Definitive Guide to Swing for Java 2, Second Edition

To order, call (800) 777-4643 or email sales@apress.com.